THE WEST EUROPEAN CITY

INTERNATIONAL LIBRARY OF SOCIOLOGY

AND SOCIAL RECONSTRUCTION

Founded by Karl Mannheim

Editor W. J. H. Sprott

A catalogue of books available in the INTERNATIONAL LIBRARY OF
SOCIOLOGY AND SOCIAL RECONSTRUCTION and new books in
preparation for the Library will be found at the end of this volume

THE
WEST EUROPEAN CITY

A GEOGRAPHICAL INTERPRETATION

by

ROBERT E. DICKINSON, M.A., Ph.D

PROFESSOR OF GEOGRAPHY,
UNIVERSITY OF LEEDS

AUTHOR OF *Regions of Germany* and
City, Region and Regionalism

LONDON
ROUTLEDGE & KEGAN PAUL LIMITED
BROADWAY HOUSE: 68-74 CARTER LANE, E.C.4

First Published 1951
Second edition revised 1961
Reprinted 1963
Reprinted 1968

© *Robert E. Dickinson 1961*

Printed in Great Britain by Butler & Tanner Ltd., Frome and London

CONTENTS

PART ONE

PART TWO

LIST OF MAPS

PART I

PART II

LIST OF PLATES
(between pages 238–9)

ACKNOWLEDGMENTS

Plates 4, 15, 16, and 17 are Crown Copyright and reproduced by permission of the Royal Air Force.

Plates 1, 19, and 20 are reproduced from Gantner, *Die Schweize Stadt* and *Grundformen der Europäischen Stadt*.

Plates 2, 3, 5, 6, 7, 8, 9, 10, 21, 22, 23, 24, and 26 are reproduced from E. Diesel, *Das Land der Deutschen*.

Plate 11 is reproduced from A. Demangeon, *France Économique et Humaine* (*Géographie Universelle*), by permission of Armand Colin.

Plate 18 is reproduced from E. de Martonne, *Europe Centrale*, Tome II (*Géographie Universelle*), by permission of Armand Colin.

Plates 27 and 28 are reproduced from W. Geisler, *Die Deutsche Stadt*.

Plate 29 is reproduced from Doyon and Habrecht.

Figures 1, 2, 3, and 107 are reproduced from works by John B. Leighley by permission of the author and the University of California Publications in Geography.

Figures 98, 99, 100, 101, and 102 are reproduced from an article by the author in the *Geographical Review*, by permission of the American Geographical Society.

The remainder of the maps are either redrawn from sources which are indicated, or have been specially drawn under the direction of the author.

PREFACE

The purpose of this book is to examine the physical structure of the urban habitat in western Europe, north of the Alps and Pyrenees, but excluding specific treatment of the British Isles. It is a morphological study, in which the form of the habitat is interpreted in the light of its functions and historical development.

Physical structure is taken to mean the character and grouping of the individual component structures of the habitat. Character implies the function and form of the structures. Grouping implies the spatial arrangement of the structures in terms of terrain, streets, dominant buildings, public spaces, and monuments, and the ideas of planning prevalent in different epochs. The character and development of civilization in western Europe as defined in this book have common features that distinguish this area from eastern and southern Europe. Any generalizations thus refer to this area only and are not necessarily applicable to other areas. It is urged, however, that such studies should be undertaken of comparable culture areas.

Within this single culture area of occidental civilization, there are marked similarities and differences in the nature of the urban habitat from place to place and from area to area that reflect differences in the origins and growth of urban life. The family likenesses of town types and the regional groupings of towns are clearly apparent in the numerous small towns that cover the countryside, since these bear the predominant imprint of their medieval origins and of their subsequent development during the period down to the middle of the 19th century. While modern urbanism in the western world has everywhere similar traits, it is markedly concentrated in the larger centres, and the small towns have been little affected by the rapid metabolism of modern urban growth. Moreover, there are marked differences in urban structures and planning from State to State that reflect differences in conditions, traditions, and policies.

The work is based on material drawn from a great variety of sources and on visits to numerous towns during the 'thirties. It has also involved the collection of hundreds of plans and town studies. Though the material was ready in 1939, the writing of the book was delayed until after the end of the war. Urban buildings and their modes of grouping in particular towns and in all towns in particular areas have been classified by inductive methods in terms of their origins and functions. This is the essence of the morphological approach that is the basis of the study. Attention is also directed to possible remedial measures, for the analysis of what is should help to understand what should be. The study should thus help to elucidate principles of urban planning in the light of the past.

The book is divided into two parts. Part I begins with a chapter on the scope and method of urban geography. Then follow two comparative studies of groups of towns, ten in central Sweden, and about a hundred in Switzerland. More detailed studies of several small towns in France indicate the processes and character of urban growth in the historic town. A study of Basel, a medium-sized city, serves to portray in some detail the main features of the growth and structure of the historic city and its modern growth and transformation. Then follows a series of eight chapters on individual large cities. These studies vary somewhat in treatment, for different aspects receive special attention in different cases according to the availability of good illustrative material. The common theme and basis of these studies, however, are provided by the series of maps of the functional zones of each city. These maps are selected from about a hundred prepared on the same basis and on the same scale.

Part II is a broad comparative study of the urban habitat in western Europe. It is based on the illustrative material in Part I and upon much additional material of a similar kind. It deals with the general functions and organization of the urban habitat and the way in which these functions determine the character and grouping of the component units of the habitat. It portrays the physical structure of the medieval town in the light of its social and economic history. There then follows a study of various types of town and their regional groupings in western Europe. Next, the changing social and economic needs in the period from the end of the Middle Ages to the dawn of the modern age are examined in their effects on the changing build of the urban complex. Finally, in the last chapters, the growth of modern urbanism is outlined, and the plan, build, and demographic structure of the modern urban area are considered.

I wish to acknowledge my indebtedness to Mr. John C. Duvall of Syracuse for carefully editing the proofs.

ROBERT E. DICKINSON.

SYRACUSE,
   February 22nd, 1949.

PREFACE TO THE SECOND EDITION

The present work remains in its second edition as it was first intended and the reader will find little reference to war-time destruction or post-war developments. It is a study of the physical structure of the urban habitat in its historico-geographic aspects down to the late thirties. A new book would be required to deal with the growth and planning of post-war cities.

The book has been favourably received by some who skimmed it, and criticized by others who read it carefully. In particular I have to thank Professor O. H. K. Spate for trenchant criticisms, but many useful suggestions, which in general have been observed in this second edition. It is pointed out that the book is too long and contains too much topographic detail. Part I and Part II were, in fact, written as two separate books, and it would be best to regard them as such. The reader may follow one of two courses. Read Part II first, and regard Part I as a source from which particular chapters may be selected according to one's purpose and interest. Alternatively, work straight through the book, but read only the following chapters in Part I— Chapter 1, Scope and Method of Urban Geography ; Chapter 2, Towns of Central Sweden ; Chapter 3, (1) Poitiers ; Chapter 5, Basel ; Chapter 6, (1) Cologne ; Chapter 7, (1) Toulouse and (2) Limoges ; Chapter 8, Brussels ; Chapter 9, Amsterdam, Rotterdam and The Hague ; and Chapter 12, Paris.

R. E. D.

Leeds,
May 15th, 1960.

PART ONE

CHAPTER 1

THE SCOPE AND METHOD OF URBAN GEOGRAPHY

In social surveys and regional town-planning schemes it is invariably assumed that the geographer is primarily concerned with the physical ground-plan on which the city rests. This is the only field to which he is given undisputed claim by his colleagues. It is sometimes further conceded that the " human " geographer follows up such appraisal by tracing the effects of this physical ground-plan on the growth and character of the city, but as a rule the investigation of these particular aspects is handled by the economist, sociologist, historian or architect. There are, however, numerous thorough studies of cities by foreign geographers, which indicate clearly that urban geography has a well-established scope and techniques. It seems necessary, therefore, to assess the contribution of geography to the examination of the city as revealed in such studies in order to indicate to the geographer and to specialists in the cognate fields the status of the subject and to suggest lines of future investigation. Such a review will also demonstrate to the student of urban problems, that the trained geographer has an equipment and technique which can be applied to the examination of particular problems of social and physical planning.

Modern geography is concerned with the areal differences and associations of the facts and phenomena of the earth's surface. The raw materials of such study, writes Hettner, are " the facts of the earth's surface which are locally different and whose local differences are significant for other kinds of phenomena, or, as it has been put, are geographically efficacious ". This conception gives a standard of relevance to those facts and phenomena with which the geographer is definitely concerned, and we would emphasize this point at the outset as a guide to the scope and limits of the geographical study of the city. It means that in the countryside the land itself, but in the urban area, which is an exclusively man-made habitat, the buildings in which the people live and work, are the most important facts in terrestrial differentiation. It should be carefully noted that this conception of geography differs in emphasis from that which proclaims geography to be the study of human adjustments to the physical environment. The same conception also makes it clear that a homogeneous terrestrial unit exists when certain areal facts have a coincident distribution and are causally interrelated. Regions, in the popular sense, are more or less arbitrary units used for particular purposes. Geography, as the study of areal or regional associations, is concerned in its human aspect with the areal differences of human activity and their imprint upon the earth's surface.

The geographical interpretation of the urban settlement is concerned, according to Raoul Blanchard, in his essay on method in urban geography, with four main problems ; first, the physical and cultural conditions involved in the origin of the nucleus of settlement ; second, the reactions of this nucleus, in its functional and topographic or areal formation, to the impact of historical events ; third, the life and organization of the contemporary settlement, viewed areally, both as a whole and with respect to the differentiation of its parts ; fourth, the interrelations between the settlement and the surrounding territory. These four problems are concerned with the study of the individual urban settlement. There is a further, a comparative, aspect of study. The size, function and form of settlements vary regionally with the development and present social and economic structure of the human groups which they represent and serve. It is for the geographer to investigate those features of the urban habitat that are areally repetitive and significant, just as he studies the rural habitat.

In other words, as in the field of geomorphology, the geographical study of urban, as of rural, settlements has three aspects. There is the physical *structure* of the settlement—the mode of grouping of its buildings and streets ; there is the *process* which determines this structure—the social and economic character of the community ; and third, there is the *stage* in the historical development of the settlement. This historical or developmental treatment may lay equal emphasis on the settlement at each phase of its development, but the final aspect of study, and that to which all else should be subordinated, is the depiction and interpretation of the settlement of to-day, both as a whole and as to the areal differentiations, by building, street, and district, within it.

Economist, historian, sociologist, and geographer study the

urban settlement from different angles, and we must define the geographer's conception of such a settlement as distinct from a rural settlement, since this conditions his particular approach. Size and administrative status are not essential criteria of true urban character. Function and form are the essentials of the matter. The word urban, as opposed to rural, implies an activity divorced from the cultivation of the soil and carried out in close association with kindred activities at fixed places. These activities, in the broadest sense, are cultural (especially religious), commercial, industrial, administrative, and residential. The last include non-producers who are dependent on the urban workers and the countryside for their wants. Farming, however, is not excluded from the occupations of the urban community. A farming element is particularly characteristic of the towns of the Mediterranean lands and of east central Europe ; it was important in the origin of the early medieval towns of western Europe, though it dwindled as trade and industry grew, and it is still not unimportant in many semi-urban settlements on the Continent.

The specifically urban activities are all located either in relation to a surrounding territory, or so as to carry out activities that are tied down to certain resources or where such resources can be conveniently assembled. Such activities may be carried out separately at different places. This occurs in the beginnings of permanent settlement in an area and also in thinly peopled or backward areas, where the settlement may assume a semipermanent character. In the forested lands of north Sweden there are churches around which cluster timber buildings that are only occupied during the seasonal fairs. The tribal markets of Morocco are temporary settlements. Urban activities occur as a marked feature in the lands of Western civilization owing to the development of transport facilities. They take the form of an isolated factory, a group of workers' houses in the open country, a mining camp, or a seaside or inland resort. All these may be described as urban settlements. When, however, these activities occur in some kind of combination, in a permanent and compact settlement with some measure of community organization, the place assumes the character of a town. A city is simply a king among towns, enjoying leadership over its neighbours. A fundamental trait of both town and city, in all ages, has been that they serve as institutional centres (commercial, cultural and administrative) for a surrounding territory. It is only in recent times that industry has become a primary cause of urban growth.

Upon the basis of regional service and industry there grows up a pyramidal structure of secondary occupations, catering for the needs of these specialist occupations and for the personal requirements of the inhabitants.

Since the urban settlement has distinct activities, its lay-out and build are likewise distinct from those of the rural settlement. The urban activities are accommodated in shop, workshop, office, warehouse, and public building, and find their mutual and outside contacts by street, road, river and, latterly, rail. The houses of the workers and their dependants normally occupy most of the built-up area. They have distinctive features in structure and style according to the economy and needs of the occupants and the architectural ideas prevalent at the time they were built. All these are the form-elements of the settlement group. The problem of the geographer is to determine not only the distinctive functions of an urban settlement, but also how these form-elements are arranged in relation to each other and to the streets and places, and to interpret these groupings in relation to historical development and physical conditions. The way in which these form-elements are grouped will be referred to as the process of topographic formation.

Generalization cannot safely be applied to all climes and times, and we confine our comments to western Europe, where numerous towns have been thoroughly studied, though even here comparative studies, upon which to base valid generalizations, are often lacking. Thus, in England, the simplest urban functions may appear in the occasional village that stands out from its neighbours, since, scattered among the houses along the village street, are a number of buildings that are devoted to urban functions. Even the small English village, which is primarily a cluster of workers' cottages, is above all a service centre for the dispersed farmsteads around it, and itself contains very few farmsteads. More of these urban functions are concentrated in the small town, which normally has its nucleus in a market-place of medieval origin or a wide main street, on which the urban buildings now form a continuous frontage. The larger the town the more the institutions. These spread from the nucleus along the main streets, and special functions seek special sites. The railway station has invariably become the nucleus of a new urban segregation. In the large town, the urban functions are so numerous and varied that they compete for space as close as possible to the nucleus so as to form a central district which throbs with activity in the day and is a " dead heart " at night. Around this central district there are sub-centres, while still other functions are more widely distributed without segregation so as to be in immediate contact with the groups they serve. The core, to-day popularly called the " town " or " city ", together with the factory clusters, are areas of work separate from the areas of residence in which the workers live. The existence of the core and the marked separation of work and residence are the most distinctive features of the build of the large city as opposed to the smaller town.

Finally, these characteristics of urban settlements, their size, spacing, lay-out, and build, vary regionally with the physical environment, with the density of population, and with the character of human economies and cultures. There are vast differences in urban character between the English Lowland, the Ganges Plain and the Australian Riverina. There are also important differences in urban character between the different sectors of western Europe. Most of these features of settlement are obvious to any careful observer. Their scientific examination, classification, and the elucidation of their regional variations, both over wide areas and within the urban complex itself, are essential problems of urban geography.

The first task of a geographical study of a town is to determine the characteristics of its *site* and *situation*. The situation embraces the general conditions, both physical and human, throughout a wide area around the town that affect its origin, development, and character. The site embraces the precise physical features of the ground on which the town began and over which it has spread. This study demands thorough examination of the initial physical setting of the medieval town, and the ways in which it has been modified by human action. The term nodality is used to express the significance of the town as a node or focus of routes. Hitherto, the geographer has been too prone to assess the position, size, and function of a town in terms of the natural routes centred on it. The nodality of a town is to be measured not in terms of the physical setting nor simply by the number of man-made routes that radiate from or pass through it, but, ultimately, by the traffic of all kinds which uses these routes. In other words, nodality should be measured on the basis of the functions of the town as a focus. We need a measure of such centralized or nodal functions in terms of the relations of the town with the countryside and towns around it.

No human settlement can be understood as to its place and its function on the earth's surface unless it is considered in relation to the land on which it is situated and which surrounds it. The French geographer, Vidal de la Blache, wrote many years ago (1911) that " Nature prepares the site, and man organizes it in such a way that it meets his needs and wants ". This view needs modification, for there are numerous sites and situations apparently favourable to urban growth which have in fact never had towns upon them, and on the other hand there are many towns, large and small, which have the most unfavourable sites and poor natural situations. Neither site nor situation as pure physical facts has any compelling force on human choice. The town is a most complicated human organization, and its destiny depends in the first place on its effectiveness as a going concern and on its power of adjustment to new human conditions and to the physical conditions of its site and situation. Moreover, the way in which a town grows into shape is by no means conditioned by the site. At all periods of history we find particular cases of street plans not adjusted to the lie of the land, but actually imposed upon it. The streets of Priene were hewn out of the solid rock. Many medieval planned towns were imposed on hill sites. Street patterns in the American city cut right across hill and dale. Skyscrapers were first erected on the sandy foundations of Chicago and later developed on the granites of Manhattan. Many large cities occupy low-lying unhealthy sites, which present permanent problems of a special nature in matters of water supply, sewage disposal, building and communications, both above and below the surface. " Man chooses the site as prepared by Nature and then organizes it in such a way that it meets his desires and wants " should be the rewording of this dictum, as a critic has suggested. The functional development, topographic formation and areal organization of any urban settlement are to be examined as an historical process of adjustment to the physical conditions of the site and the situation. " Geographical determinism " is as dead as the dodo.

The varied aspects of situation and site are seldom all favourable to the growth of a particular city. There are towns with excellent situations on most unfavourable sites. On the other hand, an excellent site may have no urban settlement at all because of its unfavourable situation. A site may be good for the original siting of a town, but present serious problems in the topographical extension of its built-up area. Other towns have such favourable sites that the difficulties of an isolated situation have been overcome. Such unfavourable conditions retard the development and topographical extension of the city, and in order to overcome them some decisive historic event is needed as an incentive. In all cases Nature presents certain latent possibilities, but these are not realized until time and circumstance are ripe and Man makes the choice.

Thus, having once determined precisely the physical conditions of situation and site which affected the beginnings of the town, the geographer examines how, with the passage of time, the settlement utilizes, adapts itself to, and transforms, these conditions in the process of its topographic formation and expansion. History must be made subsidiary to this main object. This point is important. British studies have usually traced the historical character of the adjustments of the town to the physical conditions of its site and situation. They fail thereby to give a clear picture of the present physiognomic and functional structure of the settlement as an entity in space, which, as stated above, should be the central object of the study.

In the fullest sense this aspect of study portrays the development of the city as a functioning entity in space and its development in time. Since the growth of the town proceeds by fits and starts, it is often convenient to treat its growth at significant phases of stability and to trace the changes from one phase to the next. This should lead to the depiction of the geographical structure of the modern city and the processes that determine it. Most cities of western Europe and North America have existed continuously on the sites of their origin. Elsewhere, however, there are sites upon which several cities have been successively built and destroyed, as old cultures died and newer cultures replaced them.

The modern city, then, is the culminating and the central aim of urban geography. *Après l'étude dans le temps, l'étude dans l'espace*, writes (and practises) Raoul Blanchard. In this study there are two viewpoints : first, the functional and the demographic structure, and second, the plan and the build of the city. These are intimately interrelated and permit the recognition of homogeneous functional regions.

This approach demands careful mapping of the city as a preliminary to depiction and interpretation. This aspect is neglected in French, but figures prominently in German and American, studies. It is essential, however, to remember that the city is not merely an assembly of patterns and empty buildings. It is a habitat, and the arrangement of its parts must be examined in the light of the processes that determine their function. Functional differentiation within the urban complex involves the classification and mapping of land uses, of building types, of industry and commerce, of the density and occupations of the population, and of traffic density on roads and at nodal points. Here too must be included the distribution of such vital services as gas, electricity, water, sewage disposal, telegraph and telephone lines, for the reticulation of pipes and wires above and below ground are closely related to the distribution of the built-up land and the pattern of streets, and to the conditions of surface relief and underlying geology. For this latter field, the services of the engineer will obviously have to be drawn upon. Classification, field methods and cartographic techniques are essential to all aspects of such study. It is an approach that hitherto has been the peculiar concern of the geographer, but is becoming a matter of particular interest to-day to all those who deal with the structure of the city. We would emphasize that this is not merely a matter of drawing maps as a cartographer. It involves the careful analysis and classification of a given set of data in relation to a particular problem before the question of the facts to be mapped is decided upon.

It is now being increasingly realized that this geographical method is essential to the understanding of the anatomy of the urban community before its reconstruction can be planned. Where such investigations have been undertaken on a large scale in the last twenty years (as in the city inventories of Chicago and New York in the United States) the results are apparent in large publications, which, in the case of New York, for example, have been summarized by J. K. Wright in an admirable geographical essay on that city. Similar, though less elaborate, studies have appeared in Britain in recent years.

The study of the morphology of the urban habitat has received virtually no serious attention from English-speaking geographers. It is concerned with the plan and build of the habitat, viewed and interpreted in terms of its origin, growth and function. Much work of inferior quality has appeared in this field, with regard to both rural and urban settlements, because the approach is so often empirical rather than genetic. The latter is the only approach that permits real understanding and the recognition of the significant elements. The genetic approach was first undertaken about fifty years ago by German scholars. The method involves a consideration of the lay-out of the streets and blocks in relation to the site, the public buildings and the relative importance of unplanned growth and human design. The precise site and lay-out of the initial settlement and the mode of its extension are analysed in close conjunction with the conditions of its historical development. The building structures are mapped and interpreted in their areal arrangement from the standpoint of their age, grouping, architectural style and use. German scholars have undertaken many such studies of individual towns as well as of groups of towns in selected areas. But the only geographers in the English-speaking world who gave the matter serious attention between the wars were H. J. Fleure, formerly Professor of Geography at the University of Manchester, and J. B. Leighly, Professor of Geography at the University of California.

The city cannot be interpreted adequately as a mass of materials or in terms of dead patterns. It must be interpreted as a part of a social group, in terms of its four functions—dwelling, work, recreation and transport. In each of these respects every city forms part of a geographic, economic, social and cultural unit, upon which its development depends. This was the theme of our former book *City Region and Regionalism*, but the main argument may be summarized here.

Viewed from this aspect every urban centre has a two-way relation with its surroundings that extends beyond its political boundary. First, the countryside calls into being settlements which we call urban to carry out functions in its service. Second, the urban settlement, by the very fact of its existence, influences its surroundings, in varying degree, by the spread of its network of functional relations and the expansion of its settlement area. This regional factor varies greatly. In some cities, such as historical regional capitals, and in market and country towns it is highly significant. In others, especially in specialized urban communities, which owe little directly to servicing the countryside, such as industrial settlements and health resorts, the regional component is at a minimum.

Two problems arise in this connection : first, the assessment of the ways in which the urban centre acts as a focus and how these activities are reflected in its functional structure and build ; and second, the range and potency of the functional relations of the city with its environs. These relations are concerned with the housing of city workers outside the urban limits ; with the

factories located on the outskirts of the city ; with the inward
movement of food supplies, raw materials and manufactured goods
for collection, consumption and redistribution ; and with the outward movement of goods, both consumers' and producers' goods,
and of services—commercial, educational (schools, newspapers,
cultural organization), and administrative ; and with the range
of distribution of public utility supplies, which frequently extends
beyond the urban limits over a wide area.   The geographer is not
so much concerned with the precise analysis of urban distributions
and of particular urban service areas ; this is ultimately a study
for which the economist or engineer is better qualified.   He is
more interested in the totality of these relationships as they are
reflected in the aspect and functions of the urban centre.

With the ever-growing interest in the problems of the modern
city—the problems of its physical growth and reconstruction, its
sociological and economic structure, and its art and architecture,
as well as its historical development—it is not surprising that there
is a great deal of overlap between the approaches from slightly
different angles of different specialists in the same field.   This is
as it should and must be.   It will be obvious, however, that the
trained historian is best fitted to handle the documentary evidence
relevant to the topographic formation of cities, and that the art
historian can best deal with individual and comparative studies
of urban architecture.   The geographer has introduced new fields
of study in the structure of cities, and it is likely that these will be
taken up by other specialists.   Indeed, for many years various
specialists have shown an interest, from their particular points of
view, in the same phenomena.

This consideration is of very great importance in relation to
the field of social study.   The social ecologist is concerned with
Man in Society.   He thinks in terms of social phenomena and
social interactions in their distribution in time and space.   Such
interactions, by a process of competition and selection, are
expressed in the physical and social mobility of persons, that is,
write Gist and Halbert, in " change of residence, change of
employment, or change of location of any utility or service ".
The processes accounting for these distributions in urban growth
are referred to by R. D. McKenzie, the American sociologist, as
concentration, centralization, decentralization, segregation, invasion, and succession.   Immigrants tend to segregate in areas
populated by persons with a similar background of culture and
economic status—birds of a feather flock together.   In conse-

quence of this process, the city tends to become a kind of mosaic of " cultural and racial islands ". Such islands are called by the ecologists " natural areas ", since they grow up by natural (uncontrolled) processes, and each area tends to select certain population types, this selection being based on economic status, racial characteristics, religious beliefs, moral codes, and the like. Thus to the social ecologist " the natural area as a form of ecological patterning is primarily a social rather than a geographic phenomenon ". In the American city at present language and customs are especially potent in the formation of natural areas, but, as the immigrant is absorbed and his own language and customs disappear, " social differentiation will manifest itself in other ways—through differences in religion, occupation, education and income ".

The geographer, on the other hand, is concerned with the differentiation of the whole of every urban settlement into functional areas and social groupings as expressed in the areal structure of the urban habitat.   He does not limit his study to the measure of relationships of the city to its site and situation.   His primary emphasis is on the city area as a habitat, that is, as a homogeneous area of human occupance, as a " whole ".   He is concerned with geographic distributions in the city in so far as they represent areal differences in function that are significant for other kinds of phenomena in the same area and for the same population group. The geographer has not an established terminology for these component functional units in the city.   It is unfortunate that Blanchard refers to them as " natural " regions, but he is using the word exactly as it would be interpreted by the sociologist, the planner and the economist, that is, as a unit in the city that has emerged through the operation of uncontrolled processes of growth and differentiation.

Many sociological studies of the " natural areas " of American cities have appeared, but what is of most interest to the sociologist is the distribution of social maladjustment in disorganized areas— delinquency (adult and juvenile), vice, suicide, mental disorders, alcoholism, divorce and desertion, poverty, mortality, and disease. The areal interrelationships of such phenomena have also been studied, and indexes of social disorganization calculated.   In a study of Cleveland, Ohio, for example, a map of cultural areas was prepared, by H. W. Green, based on the monthly rental figures as indicating the economic status of the residents, and correlations of social phenomena were made with districts in low and high income categories. The sociologists are also more concerned with, and equipped for, the investigation of social groups in the city, such as " neighbourhoods " and the larger " community areas ".

This whole field of study, geographical and ecological, has now become of great importance in western Europe in view of the need for reconstruction. Significant advances in concept and techniques have been made in recent years. We may mention the work in Britain sponsored by the Association for Planning and Regional Reconstruction, the West Midland Group on Post-War Reconstruction and Planning, and the Nuffield Reconstruction Survey. More directly connected with town planning are the surveys of Hull and Middlesbrough organized by Max Lock, and those of Durham and Exeter by Thomas Sharp, and the survey of Birmingham and the Black Country by the West Midland Group. There is need, however, for more research workers with adequate training, for the development of techniques of recording, classifying and mapping data. There is also need for the standardization of concept and terminology. There is no clear-cut division between one discipline and another, and the emergence of disciplines in the common pursuit of particular problems is a characteristic of the development of science in our time. In the field of the study of Man, there is a real need for institutes of research as the common ground of the social sciences. For without diagnosis of all aspects of the problem, the planner cannot provide for the optimum use of the land, and the architect cannot build to suit the needs of Man, either as an individual or as a member of the community.

CHAPTER 2

THE TOWNS OF CENTRAL SWEDEN

We have already defined the scope of comparative urban study, and it is now appropriate to submit one such study to the reader. For this purpose we shall summarize the monograph of the American geographer, Professor J. B. Leighly, on the towns of Mälardalen in central Sweden, a fascinating pioneer study among English-speaking geographers. This study will draw attention to the great amount of first-class pioneer work in urban geography that has been carried out by the Swedish geographers since the days of Sten de Geer. It also serves to illustrate the form-elements of the urban habitat and the relations they bear to each other and to the site in the formation of the whole habitat, and the changes that the habitat has experienced in the historic phases of its development.

(1) LOCATION AND DEVELOPMENT OF THE TOWNS

Mälardalen is the area around the lake that stretches west-wards from Stockholm and at the eastern end of which the capital city is situated. Ten towns in this area were selected by Leighley for study. Their location is shown on Fig. 1. The plains on the shores of this lake formed the nucleus of the Swedish State, for they afforded easy communication eastwards beyond Stockholm with the old culture lands of Europe and westwards with the uplands of Bergslagen. Iron and copper were exploited in abundance in the latter area during the Middle Ages, and attracted many German settlers. Situated in the midst of predominantly forested uplands, the lake plains, being free of stones, were easily tilled, while prominent gravel ridges up to 30 metres high, known as eskers, laid down at the base of river beds during the Ice Age, facilitated communication to north and south through the densely forested uplands.

Not all the towns in this area are studied. Stockholm, in particular, and the mining towns of the Bergslagen are excluded. Three of the ten towns selected had about 30,000 inhabitants, the remainder below 6,000. The selected towns are related to the lake shore and its streams and the cultivated smooth plains.

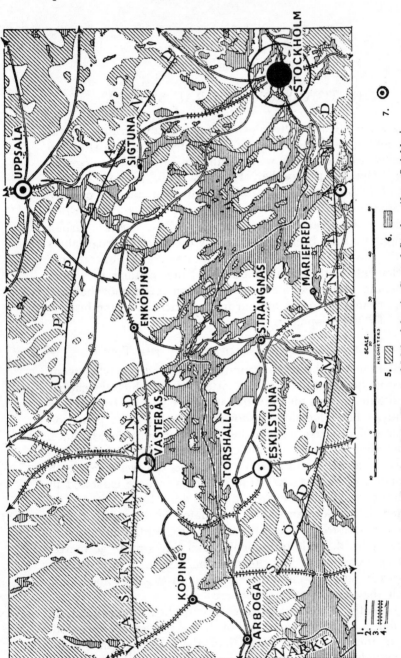

FIG. 1.—The Location of the Towns of Mälardalen in Central Sweden (from Leighley).
1. Boundary of historic province (*Landskap*). 2. Main road of the 18th century. 3. Section of a main road which follows an esker.
4. Route of the medieval Eriksgatan. 5. Scattered cultivation. 6. Water. 7. Town with 2,500 inhabitants in 1800 and 10,000 in
1925. The inner (full) circle and the outer have areas proportional to the town's population on these dates, respectively. The
unshaded areas are mainly under cultivation.

Uppsala and Enköping are at the intersection of eskers at the head of navigation of southward-flowing streams. An esker carries the most famous route from Bergslagen to the shores of Mälar lake not far east of Västerås, where the route leaves the esker to join the town on open water. Between Västerås and Köping there is an ideal site for the growth of a town, that is characteristic of many Swedish towns, situated at the intersection of an esker and a stream, with easy access to lake Mälar and a central location in a fertile agricultural area. But, though archæological remains are abundant, no historic town developed here, because the two towns mentioned above adequately served the urban needs of the country. In recent times, however, the advent of the railway has facilitated the growth of a town, Kolbäck, that is comparable in size to the smaller historic towns (3,000–4,000). The town of Arboga lies at the first rapids which hinder navigation upstream from lake Mälar.

On the northern side of the lake, towns are situated in the fertile plain where routes from the north strike the lake shore. The distance between Uppsala and Enköping and between the latter town and Västerås is such that each of the towns served its surroundings as a trade centre, whereas in the western end of the basin the towns are more widely spaced, since they are backed by the highland and thus have a less extensive and less productive " hinterland ". Stockholm at the eastern end of the lake has limited the modern growth of the towns, except as its satellites. On the southern side of the basin, plains are less extensive, and only one historic route leads south, though this has been used since the Bronze Age. Three places in turn have commanded this route, Skogstorp, Eskilstuna and Torshälla, the last appearing as a town in 1317 as a rival to Eskilstuna, which dates from early times as a seat of settlement. The latter, outrivalled by Torshälla, regained its activity through the establishment of iron works, through the grant of royal privileges in the 17th century. Strängnäs was an historic episcopal seat, and Mariefred clustered around its castle, but neither became flourishing economic centres.

The first settlement of urban character in central Sweden was at Birka on the island of Björkö. This place was visited by German missionaries in the 9th century, when it was described as " the port of their (the Swedes') realm ", serving as an intermediary for trade between the Orient and western Europe. The kings of Sweden accepted Christianity about A.D. 1000, but the

B

faith spread slowly among the pagan Swedes. In the 11th century the seat of urban culture shifted to Sigtuna, but Visby on Gothland island eventually became the great emporium of the northern lands. Sigtuna was founded as a Christian seat in the 11th century and became an unfortified bishop's town, although its religio-commercial guilds early added to its economic importance. Christianity spread slowly. Bishoprics appeared before the middle of the 12th century at the seats of heathen cults at Strängnäs (shifted from Eskilstuna) and Västerås, and the bishop's seat was moved from Sigtuna to (Gamla) Uppsala in 1130. The main seats of trade at this time lay at the eastern end of the lake. Evidence of a mint at Västerås speaks of its growth as an economic centre for trade and indicates the exploitation of silver and iron deposits, and it had already been a bishop's residence for nearly a century.

The 13th century witnessed the growth of the towns as economic centres. This was encouraged by the establishment of religious houses (Dominican and Franciscan) in six of the towns, by the increasing wealth of the Church, and by the immigration of Germans from the Hansa towns to mine the ores of Bergslagen. Chief exports from these towns in the early Middle Ages were furs and skins. In the 13th century began the exploitation of the minerals of Bergslagen, and this affected in particular the prosperity of the towns in the west and north of Mälardalen which collected the produce from the highlands to the north-west by way of the great valleys and their accompanying eskers. Köping and Arboga appear as privileged towns in the early 14th century ; Torshälla received full town rights in 1317. Germans from the Hansa towns appeared in large numbers and became dominant in the municipal government. Stockholm grew as the chief Swedish terminus of the trans-Baltic trade with the Hanseatic port of Lübeck.

Internal strife marred urban prosperity in the 15th and 16th centuries. Gustav I and his successors fostered the development of industry in the kingdom, particularly by transferring commerce from the hands of the Germans to those of the Swedes. Iron and textile industries were encouraged in the towns of Mälardalen during the following two centuries. The towns were affected adversely, however, by the increasing concentration of trade in Stockholm and by the foundation of new towns in the mining areas in the north-west. The steamboat appeared on the lake in the second decade of the 19th century and the railway came in the period from 1857 to 1890, during which time modern large-scale industrial plants grew up in some of the towns. Examples of this are the iron plants at Västerås and Köping and the electrical engineering plant at Västerås.

The privileges of the towns were increased during the 17th century, but the privileges of the town guilds were gradually broken down by individual enterprise. In the latter half of the 18th century guild restrictions were relaxed and factories were established outside the historic towns. Chief of these changes was the founding of iron works in a " free town " at Eskilstuna in 1771, without guild restrictions. This was founded by a merchant from Riga at the instigation of Karl Gustav X. The State purchased the old iron works there and attracted new settlers.

(2) SITE AND PLAN OF THE TOWNS

We may now turn to the morphological structure of the towns, which, in its main features, is closely conditioned by these circumstances of historical development as well as by the effects of the terrain of the town sites. Provision must be made in the compact urban settlement for the market-place, the public buildings, the harbour, as well as for the houses and the streets, which, in effect, make up the greater part of the urban habitat. Moreover, the mode of grouping of these form-elements is affected by the presence of an existing, often pre-urban nucleus of settlement, by the pattern of the streets that extend outwards from it through the surrounding country to adjacent towns, and by the configuration of the site. In uncontrolled, spontaneous growth, buildings and streets avoid steep slopes and follow level ground as far as practicable. Market-place and streets are the main centres of activity and attract building. But the arrangement of the buildings is dependent on the current ideas of urbanism and by the degree of regulation that enters into the growth of the town. Irregularity means that the town develops spontaneously. Regularity indicates a uniform growth according to certain conceptions of planning. The former here marks the development of the medieval town. The latter characterizes many of the towns of Sweden that were entirely rebuilt in the 17th century and after.

The plan and build of the towns of Mälardalen have been markedly affected by their location on the shores of the lake or river. Probably all lay originally on the shores of the lake, although uplift has shifted the lake shore from some of them.

The courses of streams have oriented the main axes of the growth of others. The older growth in the riverside towns was alined with the stream, with a street parallel to the stream, with narrow passageways leading down to it, and with a main route forming a second axis at right angles to that along the stream. Many narrow passageways (called *Vattergränder*) often separate a single row of lots between the stream and the street parallel to it, so as to permit all occupants to draw water from the river. In such cases, domestic life is centred on the stream, just as public life is centred on the market-place. Back from the stream, the plan depends on the relationship of route and the public buildings, that dominate the site. These conditions are clearly shown in the cases of Sigtuna, Strängnäs, Uppsala and Enköping (Fig. 2).

Sigtuna. The main street curves along the shore line with many narrow passageways running from the shore to the street. Behind this are hilly slopes on which lie the ruins of many churches founded in the early Middle Ages, of which only one remains, now the parish church, and this dominates the town. There is no railway, and the town has experienced little growth or structural change. Its houses are separate, with large gardens.

Strängnäs. The route across the water is the line of the esker followed by the historic highway of ancient Sweden, the Eriksgatan. The promontory on which the town stands is mostly esker material with a rock nucleus. On the latter stands the cathedral, dominating the settlement. The land is lowest in the centre of the promontory where the roads from south and west meet and lead to the ferry wharf. Between the wharf and the cathedral is the market-place. Shores are steep, and there is no street development parallel to them. Fires have ravaged the town at different dates and few of the old houses and streets remain. Modern growth has been on the flatter land to the west.

Uppsala and its predecessor, Gamla (old) Uppsala, were the seats of the national religious cult of the Swedes since the dawn of history. Gamla Uppsala was the seat of the pre-Christian cult and of its chief temple. It became a bishop's see in 1130 and was raised to an archbishopric in 1164. This see was transferred in 1270 to the settlement, ultimately known also as Uppsala, which began as the port of old Uppsala. This town was regularized in 1643–4, so that little remains of its medieval plan, which is shown on Fig. 2, as it was just before this date. The town lies on a stream with a cathedral-castle nucleus on the raised land of the esker on the west bank and the port and commercial settlement on the flatter valley floor on the east side. The cathedral early attracted ecclesiastical dependants, and around it grew a concentric building arrangement with roads running radially to the country. The castle complex south of the cathedral was begun in 1550 by the Vasa kings. The University was also added to this complex, so that the whole western district, sited on raised land, forms a distinct politico-cultural complex. The first settlement was undoubtedly around the old market-place, which probably lay in the area of long blocks stretching at right angles to the stream. South of this

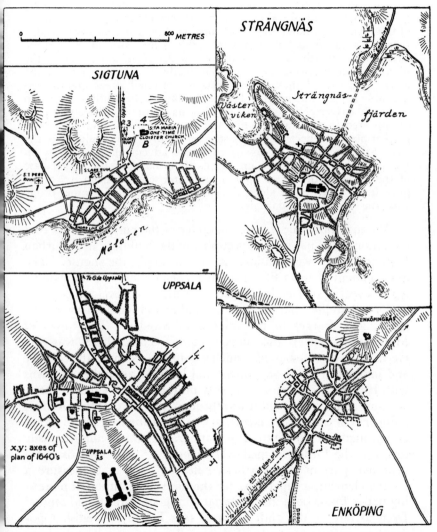

FIG. 2.—The Plans of Four Towns of Mälardalen in Central Sweden (from Leighley)
(Scale, 1 : 20,000.)

built-up area lay the royal estate ; north of it there is the usual riverside development of a street parallel to the stream with a row of " block-lots " facing street and stream. The new plan of the 1640s has a rectilinear lay-out with the two axes at right angles and the market-place at their intersection, but the cathedral-castle complex retains its historic plan.

Enköping lies at the point where an esker, a raised ridge, is cut by a stream—an extremely common site in middle Sweden. Main routes from Uppsala and Stockholm enter together along the eastern bases of the high, steep-sided esker that runs north-east to south-west and is thence continued to the south-west ; this is the route of the historic Eriksgatan. North-east to south-west is the main alinement of the plan, and cross-streets curve concentrically around the foot of the esker. On one of these cross-streets the original street market was probably held. The town ends at the stream to the south-west, which was both a river crossing and a head of navigation. This street plan disappeared in 1799 after a fire and a new one was laid out. The market-place " reflects the weak striving towards rectangularity of the later Middle Ages ". Growth since the advent of the railway in the 1870s has taken place on the flat land north of the higher part of the esker north-east of the old town and separate from it. Some growth has taken place along the stream as a result of steamer traffic with the towns of Mälardalen.

We may now turn to the character of the cultural forces that conditioned the nature and grouping of the buildings in the urban habitat. First we consider its main item, the house. The development of town life in southern Scandinavia in the Middle Ages reveals two trends. There was first the development of a native urban life, that grew up around church, monastery, castle, route, and market in the interior of Sweden. The towns of Mälardalen reflect this development. Then there was the German mode of urban life which was introduced into the country and influenced the development and build of a number of towns with Hanseatic affinities, especially on the coast. Chief of these, of course, was Visby, and it was through this city that the German influences of trader and missionary reached the east Baltic shores and brought into being the Hanseatic trading towns and the castle towns of the Order in medieval Livonia. " The town is not a primitive part of the Northern culture ; it is in a measure a foreign element, a superfluity for the native life, although possessing native forms both in a material and in an institutional sense." Even as late as the 18th century, says Leighly, Swedish topographers write repeatedly of the small towns that " agriculture is the calling which supports most of the inhabitants ". But while the urban idea was an imported one, the material elements in urban building were native, the house forms emerging gradually from rural prototypes.

(3) BUILD OF THE HISTORIC TOWNS : THE FORM-ELEMENTS

The leading feature in the development of the house forms is the gradual adaptation of the rural farmstead to urban requirements. The most primitive house type in Sweden was a rectangular structure with a forehall or porch formed by projecting roof and side timbers. This single building was not sufficient for a farmstead, which required a number of separate buildings, each serving a single function. These buildings were grouped around two enclosed courtyards, one on the house-yard, the other on the stable-yard, on rectangular building lots. In the country towns this same grouping was used, for many of the people continued as farmers (it was only during the 19th century that cattle and swine disappeared from these towns), though some modifications were introduced because lots were smaller than in the country and were not always rectangular. Thus, the town house consists of a group of buildings set around a central yard. If the lot is large enough separate buildings may lie on its sides, or they may be grouped near the street with the vegetable garden behind. Cellar and brewhouse and bakehouse frequently stood apart in the middle of the lot. At the opening of the 19th century the town houses which had grown on the basis of this native tradition had a well-defined character. The dwelling-houses are oriented towards the street and are in many cases two storeys in height. Entrance to the enclosure is by one or two gates. Buildings are one room in width (with no longitudinal partitions) and there are several buildings with liberal space for livestock. Buildings are all of timber except for the cellars, which are built of stone. This was characteristic of houses of the " mercantile class " in the small towns in the first half of the 19th century. (Fig. 3.)

The 19th century, after the 'thirties, brought the main changes in these building styles. A single large house facing the street was developed to perform the functions of the scattered buildings it replaced. These changes had started earlier with the importation of French and Italian building ideas in the 17th century, when the great magnates built their palaces in Stockholm and on their country estates. Other new features introduced at this time were the pilastered façade and the mansard roof with dormer windows ; and these occur also in the remodelling of the old houses. Thus, the house at the front of the lot gradually emerged as the dominant member of the group of buildings, and this is the character of the buildings in those parts of the towns of to-day

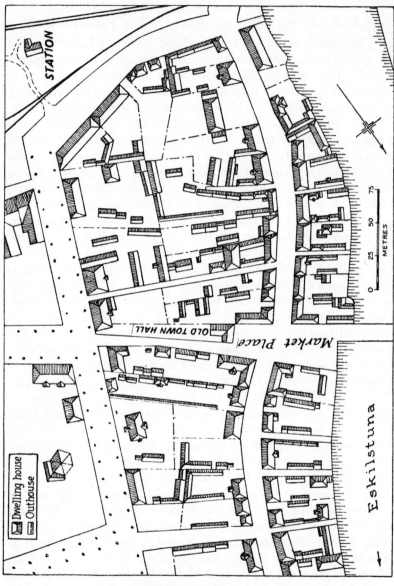

Fig. 3.—The Towns of Mälardalen in Central Sweden.

Distribution of buildings in the older part of Eskilstuna at the present time. The wide, tree-bordered streets at the top of the figure were laid out in the later 19th century (from Leighley).

that have not been burned down during the last 150 years, and where new buildings have not replaced the old. The main house in each lot is built lengthwise on the street front, but these adjacent buildings are not contiguous. In modern brick buildings the lots have been more fully built up, the street front is closed up, since the buildings are contiguous, and the houses are built up to several storeys.

Building in brick was introduced into Mälardalen by the monks at the end of the 12th century. But though brick was used in the cathedrals of Uppsala, Västerås and Strängnäs in the 14th and 15th centuries, it was only slowly that the material came into more common use, and burgesses and noblemen lived in " humble, turf-roofed, wooden houses " as late as the 16th century, after which the monarchs endeavoured to prescribe building in brick as a safety measure against fire. This, while applying specially to Stockholm, was probably true for the majority of the houses in the country towns too. In the country towns houses are still built of timber. Foreign influences again began to penetrâte to the provincial towns through Stockholm in the 17th century. Attention was given primarily to plans rather than to house forms, but the timbered house began to be coated with red ochre and vitriol (rather than painting the timbers with tar, which was very inflammable), and this finish is still in general use to-day. In the 18th century the sides of the house began to be sheathed with boards, or, in more pretentious houses, with a plaster coating, This served to give the required effect in the classical motives through enhancing the long eaves line and the rhythmic spacing of doors and windows. The timber building painted red with ochre is thus the commonest house type in the smaller towns, and a good number of them date from the 17th century.

The ravages of fire have affected every town time and time again, so that the night-watchman, responsible for keeping the peace and for watching for fires, became a traditional figure. Building regulations have been concerned above all else with protection from fire. By 1600 the building of wooden houses in central Stockholm was checked, but though similar provisions were made in the provincial towns they were generally ignored. Fire has occasioned the replanning of many towns, but as a rule even repeated conflagrations have failed to change either street plans or building styles. The influence of the State in the 17th century caused a good deal of replanning, but local interests tried to retain as much of the old lay-out as possible, in order to prevent the reallocation of land that was associated with the planning of new lots. Some street plans were regularized, as at Uppsala in the 1640s, and street lines were straightened, though the irregular lots behind them were retained. Parts of a town not destroyed by conflagration retain their irregular arrangement of lots and houses as opposed to the regularity of the rest of the plan. The rectangular pattern introduced during the 17th century, which in fact fitted in well with the type of grouping of buildings in the Swedish town houses, held sway until the end of the 19th century.

While the house was the main unit in the structure of the pre-industrial town, there were also extra-domestic elements. The communal elements were the market-place, church, town hall and other public buildings. Streets and, especially in these lake-side towns, the harbour, and old industrial establishments, were the other principal form-elements of these historic towns.

The market-place was originally a street market before the appearance of the rectangular place or *torg*. This street market is the equivalent of the street market of northern Germany that characterized the earliest mercantile settlements (see page 369). Earlier market-places have a street form or an elongated, wedge-shaped, widening of the main street, but though the original market-places have retained their identity and position, they have been expanded to form a rectangle (*torg*), and, as the towns grew, new market-places were laid out. Thus, the replanning of Uppsala in the 1640s included a new market-place which replaced the old one. But the greatest change in the market-place has been in its function. Fairs and markets were equipped with temporary booths on the place, but these were often replaced by fixed buildings. The historic market-place thus became smaller and less important. Business was gradually shifted from the open market to the merchant's premises, and to covered halls, shops and inns. Thus the *torg* gradually acquired its current function as a space to set off public buildings, and is occasionally used for retail vendors on market days. This æsthetic motif was a primary consideration in the replanning of the 17th century.

Streets had to have a minimum width of 4 to 8 metres in the 14th century. Almost all the main streets exceeded this minimum, but many minor " living streets " (German, *Wohnstrassen*) were much narrower. The streets were made wider after the Middle Ages, but did not increase steadily with time, for the greatest widths are found in the streets of the early 19th century. A marked feature of the medieval street is the lack of parallelism between its two sides ; it grew house by house and not as planned thoroughfare. Adjacent houses are not only irregularly placed next to each other, but are often arranged en échelon, and the streets, curved and narrow, follow the line of least resistance. From 1600 to 1900 the rectangular street plan was adopted without exception. The plan of Göteborg in 1620 (Fig. 121, p. 441), as quoted from a Swedish source by Leighly, has been characterized as " the North European militarized echo of the more luxurious and more subtle planning of the south, which thereby took root in our land and was followed by the plans of, for example, Jönköping, Uppsala, and Stockholm ". The two main axes of Uppsala have widths of 12 metres with a large torg at their intersection. This plan was carried out by the governor in Stockholm, who was also responsible for the plans for Norrmalm and Södermalm in the capital. The empty schematism of the town-planning in the middle of the 17th century was improved upon by the æsthetic concepts of the later decades, with the finest example of this era in Karlskrona. This town was planned by the older Tessin, a French architect, and his son. It has a great enclosed square and three monumental buildings on an acropolis that dominates the town. Tessin also drew up a magnificent plan for the area around the castle in Stockholm, but this came to nought owing to the degeneration in planning that set in during the 18th century, when there was a return to rectilinear formalism. Enköping was replanned in 1799, with main streets 18 metres and minor streets 12 metres wide with a rectilinear pattern. A late 19th-century addition to Uppsala has a street width of 20 metres ; here the process of street widening reached its peak.

The harbour was an important form-element of the pre-industrial town. Its importance in the lay-out is most clearly evident in Sigtuna, with a parallel street growth along the lake front, and Strängnäs, with a radial street growth from the landing-places on its steep shores. While the town was fixed (except when totally burnt out), the water often receded and landing-places had to be shifted away from their initial sites, that lay as near as possible to the town, so as to keep pace with the decreasing depth of water and the increasing size of vessels. Dredging also has been necessary to keep navigable water within reach of the town. Modern wharf and railway lie along the old harbour fronts. New basins, as at Västerås, have been built to accommodate steamer traffic.

Craftsmen in the pre-industrial complex plied their trades in their homes. This was also in large measure true of the merchants, whose warehouses were attached to their homes on the same building lot, if not in the upper storey or cellar of the same building. Swedish industry, however, was never strictly limited to the towns, for iron working had to be located at the point of production of the ore. The iron works of Bergslagen were built in the country near the ore, water power, and timber (for charcoal), though some of the settlements associated with these industries ultimately became towns. The first big separate establishment in any town was the iron works founded near old Eskilstuna. The works were equipped in a series of single-storey smithies with gables fronting the street and buildings behind them along the stream to use the power of the running water. But even in the 18th century, tanner, weaver or dyer found room like the other craftsmen for the pursuit of their trade inside their dwellings or in outlying buildings. Such concentration, of course, meant an increase in the density of building and of inhabitants per unit of area.

(4) Plan and Build of the Modern Town

The pre-industrial complex was a compact closed settlement unit. Industrialization and the railway added outer areas of more open settlement on the periphery of this central compact unit. In the outer areas there is a relatively low density of buildings per unit of ground, while in the old central area building has expanded laterally over most of each building lot and vertically by an increase in the number of storeys. Heavy industry and new dwellings share in the peripheral growth. One-family houses are the rule, and they have been built for the most part by private enterprise. Only in Uppsala have close-built tenements been erected. Such buildings occur in unplanned and planned units. Estates have been erected at the discretion of the builders. Houses have been built by individuals. Building lots have been sold separately so that houses are irregularly spaced, reflecting both the pattern of the farm buildings, and the locations of the streets, on which the houses have a frontage. Complete dissemination of houses on rural land may be the result of such trends, as in many villa quarters on the urban outskirts.

Houses erected as groups do not necessarily show adjustment to either site or community needs. The old houses have not fared too badly in the towns with under 30,000 inhabitants, where there is not a great demand for space, and where old houses remain or are converted to new uses. There is scarcely any change in towns with under 6,000 people. This is generally true of the small town on the Continent. In England, however, as on the outskirts of all large modern urban complexes, the impact of urban activities is reflected in the change in function of old buildings and their replacement by modern commercial premises. The old market-place of St. Albans, for example, retains its medieval plan, but it is overlooked by the 19th-century Corn Hall and the more recent frontages of multiple shops like Woolworth's, Marks and Spencer's, Timothy White's and Boots, as well as by other older buildings converted to modern office uses. This change has gone far in England, whereas in the small town on the Continent, over large areas that are remote from the influence of big cities, the historic buildings still remain more or less intact.

Modern growth has brought marked functional differentiation in the space-structure of the urban complex. A main feature of the pre-industrial urban settlement was that most of its buildings were interchangeable and were used as dwellings as well as for warehouses and workshops. Thus, the complex was compact. In the modern urban complex, the keynote of the space-structure is specialization by function in large units. Consequently there is specialization of building and building site, and functional districts emerge through the segregation of similar functional units, all of which are interrelated with each other and grouped around the central business core. The core is the most specialized functional district, and usually lies on the site of the old town at the centre of affairs.

Urban land uses are classified and mapped in numerous ways for different purposes. They may be grouped, in geographical study, as the *closed forms* of the compactly built-up central areas and the *open forms* of the peripheral areas, which are mainly industrial and residential areas. The distinction between the two types is difficult to define quantitatively but it appears remarkably clear on the map or air photo, and one has usually no difficulty in mapping the two broad types. The open areas have not merely a relatively low density of building per unit of area, though this is the essential feature of the housing areas ; they are also interspersed with much open, unbuilt-on land. Moreover, they do not form an integral part of the historic built-up core, although frequently closed forms of settlement develop around nuclei on the periphery.

The problem of functional differentiation within the closed and open areas varies with the size and social structure of the community. In the small towns of Mälardalen it is relatively simple. In the closed settlement areas Leighley recognizes two types of land use, the retail commercial sections, that are on the main street frontages rather than covering entire blocks, and light industrial sections, which include all but the smallest handicraft workshops. Industrial establishments in the closed built-up area are often numerous. There they may be described as " mixed areas ", as at Eskilstuna. Heavy industrial plants with large areal lay-out, on the other hand, are characteristic of Västerås, and such plants lie in the open areas outside the central nucleus. It is clear that as fuller urban character is evident, more complicated urban forms appear ; Leighley differentiates in one town between " close built " and " half open " apartment houses. The rest of the closed built-up area is undifferentiated and is mainly residential with an irregular intermixture of other uses.

The open areas in these towns are classified throughout, since these areas have complete specialization of function, including zones of heavy industry on rail and river, and open-built one-family residential areas. The better dwellings are found on the higher land. The poorer grade houses are found on the " less specialized sites ". The rest of Leighly's classification includes " poorer " and " better " residential areas, warehouses, public institutions, parks, cemeteries and athletic fields.

This study is an attempt to classify broadly all the categories of urban land use that enter into the composition of a group of small towns from the strict geographical point of view. It illustrates both the techniques and the problems of such investigation.

CHAPTER 3

THE SMALL HISTORIC TOWN IN FRANCE

The mode of approach we have just discussed can be best exemplified by examining several quite small towns. Moreover, the small town exhibits, in miniature, all the essential characteristics of urban growth. The functions of the urban community call for appropriate sites in the urban habitat. The application of ideas of æsthetic and practical planning, each appropriate to its age, extend and transform the habitat in each successive historical phase of its development. Such changes are accomplished by the erection of new structures, the demolition of old buildings, their conversion to new uses, and by the addition of new means of communication. Thus, while the historic town is closely adapted to its site, its lay-out and build also clearly reflect its functional character as an economic, cultural and administrative focus for the surrounding countryside. These and the new functions that it acquires, or with which it is endowed by high authority, demand space and appropriate sites within the urban complex.

All these traits may be illustrated by reference to several small towns of France, each of which exemplifies a mode of growth and a type of town characteristic of that country.

In France the cathedral was placed either in a Roman *castrum* or on a new site. In the early Middle Ages it was protected by a wall and the enclosure is known to this day as the *cité*. This nucleus remained the heart of the community and dominated the life of the urban settlement that clustered around it. This is in marked distinction to the English cathedral town, where the cathedral appeared much later and was associated with monasticism, so that cathedral and cloister sought a secluded area walled off from the life of the town, in a " close " away from the market centre. Monasteries and churches clustered around the cathedral in considerable numbers. The castle sprang up everywhere during the feudal era of the 9th to 12th centuries, and counts and dukes sought seats in the existing towns from which to rule their territories. In the Midi some towns were sought by many lesser nobles who lived in fortified mansions, as at Carcassonne and

Montpellier—a marked difference from northern France, where the feudal lord more often lived in a castle in the country. Thus, secular buildings of the feudal nobility appeared in the towns, while small urban communities were encouraged to grow up under the aegis of the country castle. During the latter half of the 12th century the craftsmen and traders acquired their independence of cleric and lord and became self-governing communities. Henceforth the lay-out and organization of the town was the responsibility of the town council, and the market-place and its numerous offshoots became the centre of town life, grouped around the cathedral at the focus of roads. But the cathedral dominates the profile and plan of the town to this day. It is very remarkable that there are few early public buildings, the symbols of the townsmen, in the *cités* of France. A medieval *hôtel de ville* is a rarity, outside of northern France, where in Picardy and Flanders the *hôtel de ville* and the guild houses, grouped around the market-place, dominate the town. On the other hand, as we go eastwards, beyond the Meuse towards the Rhine, towns are fewer and in general were more tardy in their development. Notable exceptions were the towns of Champagne, which became famous for their medieval fairs, and those of the north–south Moselle valley. These towns in particular, both in the Middle Ages and in the days of the expansion of France's frontiers eastward, owed much of their growth to the medieval castle and then to the bastioned fortress of the Renaissance and Baroque eras. Special attention should be drawn to the numerous small towns that were founded during the Hundred Years War in southern France, especially to the *bastides* in the south-west. The rectangular plan of the *bastide*, which was usually situated on a hill-top, and is often to-day virtually a farming community, though with all the external aspects of a medieval planned town, give to this area a quite special character.

(1) POITIERS (Figs. 4 and 5)

The city of Poitiers lies on a promontory between the confluence of the Clain, the main river, and a small tributary, the Boivre, flowing in a valley far too wide for it, that was converted into a chain of ponds by the monks of the Middle Ages. The flat-topped promontory narrows to form an isthmus at the south where these two valleys approach to within 500 metres of each other (La Tranchée). The peninsula, 115 to 120 metres high, is about 2 kilometres long and 1 kilometre wide, and falls steeply by

25 metres to the west, and more gradually to the north and east. The rocks of this promontory are horizontal limestones and frequently outcrop as cliffs, with caves and quarries, on the steep undercut sides of the wide flat valleys, that face more gradual slopes on the convex bends of the opposite banks. The good natural defences offered by this site, rather than its position at the confluence of two valley routes, probably accounted for the initial significance of the site as a seat of Gallic settlement. It was an *oppidum* of the Gallic *Pictones*, but was of little importance, owing in part to the fact that, though a good place of refuge, it lacked commanding views of the surrounding country. This, together with the large area of the plateau top, nullified the advantages of its natural defences, which were too long to be effectively manned. In addition to the natural defences of its site, stone was available for building, and water could be obtained from well and spring. The peninsula, while too large for effective settlement and defence, was on the other hand a natural store-house, since its soil was cultivable, and the presence of cultivated land and orchards within its walls remained a characteristic feature until the 19th century.

It is probable that in Celtic times trackways led to the surrounding capitals and that the main axis of settlement ran along the top of the plateau from north-east to south-west on the route from the Loire to the Gironde. The Roman lieutenant Crassus became master of the Gallic settlement and established it as *Limonum* in 56 B.C. as an administrative and military capital. Remains of this period as shown on Fig. 4 are concentrated along the north-east to south-west axis and on the more gentle slopes eastwards to the Clain. The amphitheatre, with a seating capacity of 40,000, suggests the importance of the place at this heyday of Roman power. On the main north-east to south-west axis, that became the main highway of the medieval town, clustered public monuments and the Roman market (to-day the Place d'Armes) and the Roman prætorium ; the capitol probably lay on the site of the medieval palace of the dukes of Poitou. Another road ran parallel to this on its western side, and three streets ran at right angles to the main axis eastwards down the steepest slopes to the river Clain. Shorter streets ran roughly along the contours of the land. Water was conducted by aqueducts from the south and south-west of the town.

The invasions of the 3rd century A.D. caused the construction of a new settlement as a *castrum* or stronghold on a smaller area

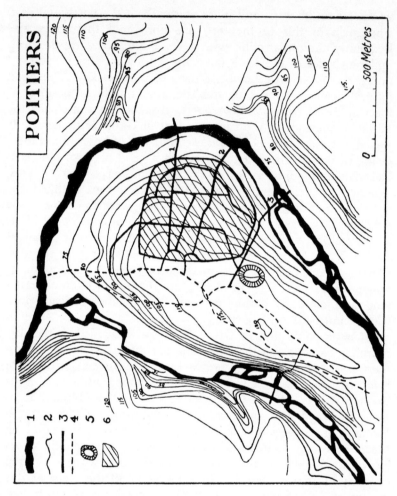

FIG. 4.—The Site of Poitiers (adapted from Clozier). (Scale, about 1 : 20,000.)

1. Water. 2. Contours at intervals of 5 metres. 3. Probable course of Roman roads down the steep eastern slopes of the promontory and along the contours. 4. Main north–south roads. 5. Roman amphitheatre. 6. Roman walled settlement in the 3rd century. The medieval roads of probable Roman origin are Grande Rue (1), Rue de la Cathédrale (2), and Rue St. Cyprien (3).

within a massive wall. This wall, shown on Fig. 4, had a peri-
meter of 2,600 metres and was quadrangular in shape, enclosing
an area of 43 hectares (about 100 acres). It lay on the eastern
side of the promontory where the land gently slopes down to the
river Clain, and the lower wall actually followed the edge of the
valley floor. The amphitheatre was left outside and the upper
wall ran across the level top of the plateau. Outside the south-
west corner of this upper wall lay the amphitheatre and the main
axis of the earlier settlement, together with the market-place next
to it. The walls were 6 metres thick, and reliance was placed
on these rather than on the careful exploitation of the site's
defences, and no attempt was made to adjust this new Roman
settlement to the existing one. The policy was evidently a
defeatist one, for there is a remarkable break between the old
Roman settlement and the new castrum which is clearly reflected
in the history of the decline of Roman civilization. Temples,
cemeteries, and buildings were demolished and their materials
used in the construction of the walls, a change that reveals the
decadence of Roman urbanism and the introduction of Christianity.
It is usually asserted that the new strongholds were hastily constructed, but the massiveness of these walls indicates that they
were not built in a day. The change from the days of culture
and safety to the new era of decadence and insecurity spread over
many years, and, as illustrated by Poitiers, was slow and deliberate.

The settlement in the early Middle Ages was moulded by the
new ideas of a Christian and feudal society (Fig. 5). Cathedral
and baptistery lie near the foot of the eastern slope near the eastern
wall. One of the three west–east streets linked the *Palais des
Comtes* and the seat of the bishopric : this was the Rue de la
Cathédrale. A second of these streets became the Grande Rue.
The third led to the site of the St. Cyprien bridge. At an early
date satellite sanctuaries appeared around the cathedral. New
religious foundations also grew up outside the walls and their
churches and chapels became centres of *bourgs*. On the great
route westwards to Bordeaux and Saintes on the Boivre slope
Saint-Hilaire-le-Grand church and its satellites were founded
after the end of the 4th century on territory that was covered
with pagan burials. In the mid 6th century the abbey of Sainte
Croix and its annex, Sainte-Marie-hors-des-Murs, later called
Sainte-Radegonde, were built east of the cathedral near the Clain
river, and here also a new *bourg* grew up. Meanwhile, many
new churches were built within the walls, especially along the

Grande Rue and the Rue de la Paille (the old Roman Via Palea).
Others were added outside the walls between the 9th and the

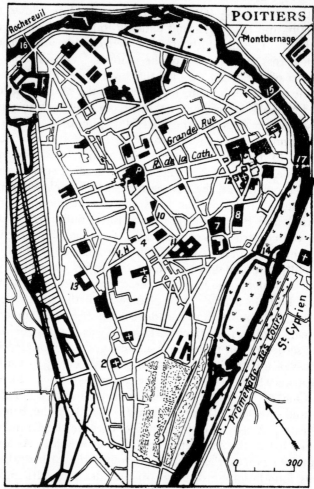

FIG. 5.—The Modern Plan of Poitiers. (Scale, 1 : 20,000).

1. Ste. Radegonde. 2. St. Hilaire le Grand. 3. St. Porchaire. 4. Place
d'Armes (Marché Vieux or Old Market). 5. Place du Palais (Corn Market).
6. Halles. 7. Carmelites. 8. Filles Notre Dame. 9. Visitation. 10. Hôtel de
Ville. 11. Lycée. 12. St. Jean and Ste. Croix. 13. Prefecture. 14. St. Cyprien
Bridge. 15. Engelbert Bridge. 16. Rochereuil Bridge. 17. New Bridge. C =
Cathedral and P = Palais de Justice at E. and W. ends of Rue de la Cathédrale.
V.H. = Rue Victor Hugo. Hatched area shows railways and factory area. Site
of Castle in extreme top-right, on S. side of river and W. of bridge.

12th centuries, the most active era of Christian and feudal
civilization in Poitiers. Hospices of various kinds appeared on

the roads outside the town, especially to the north and south. Thus, church, monastery, and cemetery took up a large area of Poitiers and vied with houses, buildings and streets in their demands on space. Poitiers was thus one of the most conspicuous seats of Romanesque architecture.

Poitiers, however, was not only a town of clerics and monks. It was also the headquarters of the Dukes of Poitou. The *Palais des Comtes* and its donjon appeared on the top of the plateau, its tower having an extensive field of vision. A great outlook tower was built in the late 11th century at the northern entrance to the town at the confluence of the valleys as a protection against the Counts of Anjou. In the following century the Counts, with the aid of the townsfolk, built round the whole of the promontory a wall over 6 km. long, which is evidence of the flourishing condition of the city during this epoch. The wall enclosed all the satellites of the old nuclei, both commercial faubourgs and monastic *bourgs*. This wall was closely adjusted to the site ; in much of its course it was reinforced by the rivers Clain and the Boivre (the mills on the former and the ponds on the latter were made by the monks in the 11th century and served to regularize the flow). The wall was also built across the isthmus between the rivers and was parallelled by a ditch across the *Tranchée*, as the narrowing was called. Bridges were early built across the rivers at St. Cyprien (Rue de Paille), Engelberti, recorded in 1083 (Grande Rue), and Rochereuil, recorded in 1077. Along the main route, on the backbone of the promontory, commercial installations appear : the Marché-Vieux (now the Place d'Armes and the site of the early Roman forum), the *Halles*, recorded in 1188, where the fairs of Mi-Carême were held, the corn market (Place St.-Didier, to-day the Place Alphonse-le-Petit or du Palais), the hucksters' market, the butchers' shambles (Rue des Vieilles-Boucheries), and the Marché-Neuf (Place de la Liberté). This main commercial centre of the medieval town lay west of and outside the Roman walls of the *cité*, and it became the geographical focus of the new town within its new walls. There were tanneries as well as corn mills and fulling mills along the rivers, and most of these mills were in the hands of the abbeys. On the plateau, within the walls, were large stretches of land devoted to farming.

The later Middle Ages accentuated the older elements of the build and did not effect any further radical transformation. More churches were erected in the centre and east of the town by Dominicans in 1218, Franciscans in 1267, Augustinians in 1345,

Carmelites in 1367. Intellectual life originally centred in the annex of the cathedral, but in 1431–2 the University was founded and in 1445–64 the building of the Grandes Écoles came as a modest contribution to the architecture of the town. The University quarter clustered between the churches of St. Porchaire and St. Opportune. The wall was rebuilt in the 14th and 15th centuries, and at the end of the 14th century the castle was built at the confluence of the two river valleys. The *Palais des Comtes* and the *Tour Maubergeon* were sumptuously decorated, and the *Tour d'Horloge* erected.

The self-governing *commune* was established in 1199, but it was the beginning of the 14th century before the Hôtel de Ville appeared on the north-east to south-west axis near the priory of St. Porchaire. The Halles were rebuilt on their original site and a mint established near them in the middle of the 14th century. Some fine burgesses' houses remain to-day which date from the 15th and 16th centuries, some of them built in the Flamboyant Gothic and Renaissance styles by wealthy families of that time.

During the 17th and 18th centuries two forces profoundly affected the town. The re-establishment of the Catholic Church had effects on Poitiers, which had espoused the Calvinist cause, and led to the introduction of new Catholic churches and monasteries. Since there was no room in the old *cité* or along the main thoroughfare of the town, these were established on peripheral sites on the north and east slopes, and even on the west towards the Boivre. These new districts included the convents of the Ursulines, Visitation, Filles de Notre Dame, Carmelites, and Frères de la Charité. These are often bounded by solid walls that enclose large sheltered gardens, and together they cover a wide area. Intendants and governors as the servants of absolutism also wrought significant changes, which are of interest as indicative of changes that were taking place in many French towns during this period. Since Poitiers had now lost its military significance the ramparts were abandoned ; the castle at the confluence of the valleys was in ruins and was abolished in 1726. In 1686 the Intendant Foucault began the building of the promenades or *Cours* on the right bank of the Clain on territory acquired from the abbey of St. Cyprien. In 1687, with the enthusiasm following on the revocation of the Edict of Nantes, Poitiers received, like many other French cities, its statue of Louis XIV on the Place Marché-Vieux. Another Intendant had the promenade of Poñt-Guillon built on the site of the demolished castle. The Intendant Bourdonnais de Blossac, the most distinguished of them, had a park, which remains one of the charms of Poitiers to this day, laid out on the eastern flank of the isthmus of the Tranchée on territory acquired from the canons of St. Hilaire and the Capucine monks. He also had the Pont Neuf built in 1778, to connect the Faubourg St.-Saturnin with the route to Limoges. But the old town still lacked adequate wide, direct routes through its centre, and Blossac's plans for providing them were not carried out. Boulevards gradually replaced the old ramparts at the base of the promontory at the line of contact with the valley floors. This epoch, however, left few civil buildings of architectural worth, so that, as compared with Bordeaux (Ch. 7), Poitiers is in its modern aspect pre-eminently a medieval city.

Poitiers was, indeed, relatively stable during this period. It suffered setbacks through the Wars of Religion and, like other cities in the west of France, from the revocation of the Edict of Nantes. But it also suffered from the economic competition of the growing ports of the lower Loire and the Gironde, for it had no navigable waterway to the sea and was the centre of an exclusively agricultural countryside. Even the encouragements of the Intendants could not effect an economic revival, and the town remains to this day an administrative, judicial, university, religious and military centre. These facts have markedly affected the aspect of the present town. The Prefecture, which in other regional capitals is usually found in the old building of the Intendants, here occupies a substantial edifice erected in 1864–8 overlooking the Boivre. The Hôtel de Ville, in pseudo-Renaissance style, was built about the same time on the Place du Marché-Vieux, and a fine new street (Rue Victor Hugo) was cut. The judicial functions have their home in the ancient *Palais des Comtes*. The educational functions have been slowly provided with accommodation and for long have been carried on in various old historic buildings. The military function is reflected in the school of artillery and the barracks on the city outskirts, both east of the Clain and west of the Boivre, situated near to the *champs de manœuvre*, the *champ de tir*, and the airfield.

Economic activity has had relatively little effect on the growth of the modern city. Factories are few and small, and are concerned with light industries that produce little smoke. They are found mainly on the edge of the promontory, and use the water of the river and the transport facilities offered by the boulevards and the railway, which runs north–south along the Boivre valley.

Some of these industries such as grain mills, creameries, and leather dressing, arise from the agricultural character of the countryside. Other industries are printing and coffee roasting, but none are of special importance. Early schemes for canalizing the Clain and for the construction of a canal south to the Gironde were stopped by the opening of the railway to Paris in 1851, to Angoulême in 1853, and to La Rochelle in 1856. The railway was built through the valley of the Boivre. The old ponds had to be drained and the stream diverted to a new fixed channel and the tracks carried through a tunnel under the head of the peninsula. Roads with steep gradients climb from the station in the valley to the town on the plateau. Eight main roads radiate from the city's outskirts. Traffic is mainly concentrated on the north–south Paris–Bayonne route which skirts the western side of the town alongside the railways in the Boivre valley. Here, in consequence, are garages, warehouses, shops for the sale of farm machinery and fertilizers, agricultural co-operatives, and cafés, adjacent to the station and the factories. In this way, road traffic avoids the old town on the plateau.

The mid 19th century witnessed changes in the old town. The Roman amphitheatre was wantonly destroyed and its place taken in part by narrow streets, a covered market, and a number of new straight thoroughfares. The Rue Jean Jaurés was cut in 1831 to join directly the Pont Neuf and the town centre. On the north side of Notre-Dame-la-Grande a large market has been built, and on the western side of the promontory an old convent has been displaced by the railway hotel, while around it are modern apartment blocks. The last is a unique feature in Poitiers, for in general apartments are formed by the conversion of old burgesses' houses, and the dwellings on the outskirts are mainly single-family houses.

Expansion outside the historic core has been rapid between the wars. This fact is due, of course, not to the growth of population, but to the provision of new dwellings for a population living in congested and unhealthy quarters in the centre. The undercut slopes of the right bank of the Clain to the north-east cause houses to cling to the foot of the slopes near the river and to spread up the narrow valley to the plateau top in Montbernage. Many houses here, dating from the 17th century, have an outside staircase and flattish roof, and are surrounded by fields and vineyards. A larger area of expansion lies to the east and south-east, where ancient faubourgs, such as that of St. Cyprien, have been transformed by the addition of barracks, military establishments, prison, cemetery, sports fields and new houses. To the south-west, expansion is along the main Paris–Bayonne road. Here are a sports stadium, tramway and bus depots, a cemetery, and cheap dwellings. To the west, there has been expansion beyond the river, the railway and the road, all of which are crossed by two bridges 1,500 km. apart, so that this quarter is cut off from the old town. The steep valley sides and the plateau beyond have been occupied by houses grouped in *cités ouvrières*, such as the Quartier de la Roche. The population of this last district includes military personnel and railway workers and required the building of a school and a church, the latter being transferred brick by brick from the centre of the town. Expansion to the north has been confined to the valley by the rocky and steep slopes of its sides.

The population of the city in 1801 was 18,000, and by 1936 it had increased to 44,000. Of this total, about 22,000 live in the promontory in the old town, the remainder in the suburbs beyond the river valleys. The town with its rural banlieue probably has a population of about 50,000.

On a miniature scale these features of the growth and character of Poitiers are characteristic of the historic regional capitals of France in general.

(2) BLOIS

Blois (Figs. 6, 7 and 8) is an example of a castle-town. It lies on steep slopes on the north bank of the Loire, facing flat floodable lands on the south bank. Steep slopes rise from the river bank by some 10–20 metres to the edge of the plateau of horizontal limestone, and this is cut by the steep-sided valley of a small stream, the Arrou, that here enters the Loire. The latter is at this point about 300 metres wide. Blois is a purely medieval growth with urban beginnings in the 10th to 11th centuries, when the castle and many religious foundations appeared as separate nuclei of settlement. The castle was built in the 10th century on the promontory between the Arrou and the Loire, protected by steep slopes and a ditch across the plateau at its western end. Within the walls of the castle there were religious buildings in its *basse-cour*. A small *bourg*, with its beginnings in a 10th-century abbey, grew at the foot of the promontory. It lay at the mouth of the Arrou on the flat land that commanded the Loire crossing, where a bridge was built in 1080. This was the Bourg Moyen,

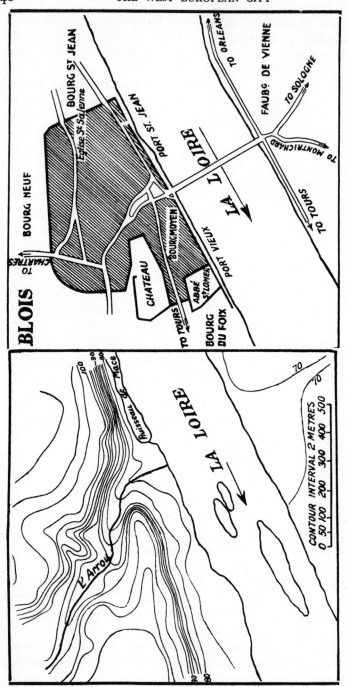

Fig. 7.—Medieval Blois (from Crozet).
(Scale, approx. 1 : 12,000.)

Fig. 6.—The Site of Blois (from Crozet).
(Scale, 1 : 12,000.)

the nucleus of the medieval town. Another *bourg*, later to be absorbed within the town wall, lay along the Loire around the Abbey of St. Lomer (873). Bourg Neuf lay on the edge of the plateau, and, east of the Arrou, the cathedral had its predecessor in a church founded in the 10th century. The Bourg St. Jean

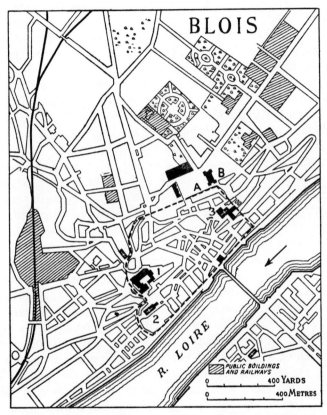

FIG. 8.—The Modern Plan of Blois. (Scale, 1 : 20,000.)

1. Château. 2. Abbey. 3. Cathedral. A = Place de la Republique B = Champ de Foire. Public buildings are hatched. Dashed line shows the medieval wall.

lay along the Loire to the east. A *faubourg* lay on the flat south bank at the approach to the bridge. The Bourg Moyen was walled in the 11th century and was controlled by the counts of Blois, who occupied the castle that dominated it. Slight extensions were made later to enclose religious buildings, notably the abbey of St. Lomer. The wall is shown on Fig. 8. This nucleus has narrow winding streets with steep gradients, negotiated by

flights of steps up the hill slopes.   Two street directions dominated
the plan, one along the Loire and the other at right angles to it,
going up the Arrou valley—the only outlet available for wheeled
traffic.   At their convergence lay the heart of the medieval town,
and here clustered trades and crafts around the market-place
(present Place Louis XII).   Many new monasteries were added
in the later Middle Ages (as at Poitiers) with enclosures, cemeteries,
buildings and churches.   As far back as 1188 mills and houses
were built on the bridge.   The town did not receive the right
of self-government from the counts of Blois, however, until 1196.

In the 16th and 17th centuries changing functions brought a
change of aspect.   The counts were displaced by the kings, and
Blois became a court city, in which resided nobles, ecclesiastics
and their retainers.   Buildings were reconstructed in Gothic and,
after the reign of Francis I, in the Italian style.   Many *hôtels*
appeared, clustering on the higher ground outside the town on
the hill slopes beneath the castle and on the steeper slopes east
of the Arrou.   This was the *ville haute*.   The *ville basse* remained
the centre of trade and crafts.   Roads began to be paved.   The
river was embanked.   Houses were built against the wall, which
was no longer needed for defence.   Francis II had gardens and a
great avenue laid out west of the castle.   This avenue was 18
metres wide and 2 km. long, and led from the castle to the forest.
The castle was gradually transformed to a palatial residence.
Glove- and clock-makers catered for the nobility.   Then in the
17th century came another big change.   The Catholic revival
was marked by the establishment of many new religious foundations.   These had their own enclosures with much space and were
located on the outskirts of the town beyond the walls.   Their
names, which recur in most historic towns of France, should be
noted—Minims, Capuchins, Ursulines, Visitation, Jesuits.   A
hospital was also founded.   Thus, the walled town was surrounded
by the big enclosures of monasteries and the royal gardens to the
west.   In 1697, for the first time, Blois was made a bishopric.
The new cathedral was built on the hill slopes east of the Arrou
in the aristocratic quarter, where buildings and the ramparts were
demolished and garden terraces laid out on their site.   This work
was carried out by Gabriel, the French architect, and reflected
the new ideas of urbanism at that time.   Other changes were
made in the 18th century in accordance with these new ideas.
The bridge was rebuilt, a little above the site of the old one that
was destroyed by floods in 1716.   The river embankment and

quays were improved. The old ramparts were demolished, and replaced by boulevards which were lined in part with trees. New road approaches were built to the bridge through the old town, and the Arrou was gradually covered over. The city ceased to be a court residence in 1668.

The changes just noted affected the periphery rather than the centre of the old town. After the Revolution new street cuts were designed to relieve congestion in the centre. These were often effected at the expense of the religious bodies which were deprived of their properties after the Revolution—another very important change that greatly affected the morphology of the town. The castle became a barracks and its gardens disappeared. One monastery became a college, others a theatre, a hospital, a prison, a covered market, and yet others were demolished to make room for open spaces. Administrative changes had their effects. Blois became the capital of one of the new Departments created in 1789. The city had lost its bishopric, but this was revived in 1833. The Prefecture (which had been temporarily housed in the old bishop's palace) was installed in a building on the site of a convent around what is now called the Place de la République; here too appeared the Palais de Justice. Many other public buildings have since been built in this north-eastern sector of the town.

The railway attracted building to the north-western sector. This was built in the 'forties and a wide new avenue (Victor Hugo) was built from the town westwards to the station. The navigation on the Loire, that had enlivened the quays of Blois for centuries, had a short spell of steam navigation after 1828, but when the railway came river traffic was killed and the quays were quickly deserted. New industries clustered along the railway in the north-west, but these are of very little importance, except for the essential gas-works, for Blois is in no sense an industrial town. Here, too, in the north and north-west, along the railway and at the approaches to the grain-land of the Beauce, for which Blois is a market centre, are the fair grounds, granaries and warehouses. The markets of the old town deal with retail produce. A major problem within the old town was that of communications between the plateau and the basse ville, and many changes were effected between 1850 and 1870, the railway station being entirely rebuilt in the 'nineties. The modern town has spread on the plateau and even on to the low-lying south bank, in spite of the dangers of flood.

Blois is to-day, as it always has been, a small town. It had 16,500 inhabitants in 1600 and 14,000 in 1801. In 1891 it had 23,500, and since then its total population has not changed. In spite of this, however, it has served as a real centre of regional affairs, as a cultural, economic, and administrative focus. Moreover, in spite of its smallness, it contains very distinct quarters arising in part from the adaptation of its functional growth to the diversity of its site.

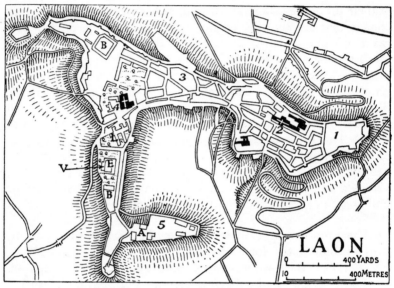

Fig. 9.—The Site and Plan of Laon. (Scale, approx. 1 : 20,000.)

1. St. Georges or Chevresson, the first merchants' and artisans' quarter with a large market-place, destroyed in 1595 and replaced by citadel. 2. The Gallic *oppidum*, Roman settlement and medieval *cité* with cathedral. 3. Bourg. 4. Abbey St. Martin. 5. Abbey St. Vincent. A = Arsenal. B = Barracks. L = Lycée. E = École Normale. V = Quarters of Ville et Villette St. Vincent.

(3) Laon

Laon (Fig. 9) owed its medieval growth in the first place to its cathedral. It is situated on a very steep-sided, narrow, flat-topped ridge composed of horizontal limestone, which completely dominates the surrounding plains, which were originally marshy and forested. This hill site offered early man a refuge and an observation post. It was the site of a Gallic *oppidum* that sheltered a temple and a market. This lay at the extreme eastern end of the plateau. A Roman settlement was established on the Gallic site, which extended west to the narrowing of the ridge, and afforded a good natural defence (here is the Roman Porte de Mars and its medieval successor, the Porte Martelle). The first Christian church appeared in the 3rd century as a dependency of the bishopric of Rheims, but in the 6th century the church of Ste. Marie became an independent bishopric and the cathedral became the dominant factor in the development of the town. The cathedral lay within the walls of the Roman settlement. Beyond it monastic institutions were established, the chief of which was the Abbey of St. Vincent, sited at the south-western end of the ridge. Under the Carolingians the place was also selected as a royal residence, owing probably to its excellent natural defences. Authority was divided among king, bishop and abbot, but during the 11th century the town emerged as a self-governing community.

At the end of that century there were four parts on the east end of the hill site—St. Georges, *Cité*, Cloître, and Ste. Geneviève. St. Georges (or Chevresson), at the eastern end of the ridge, was the merchants' and artisans' quarter, and its market-place was on the site of the Roman forum and remained until 1595. The *Cité* included all the chief monuments of the feudal age. The Cloître was an enclave in the *Cité*, the domain of the bishop and his chapter, and offered rights of asylum. Here were the cathedral, cloister, canons' houses and the episcopal palace. Ste. Geneviève was grouped around a church that was probably founded in the 9th century on the Rue des Bouchers.

During the 11th century the *Bourg* developed as a cluster of hovels that offered refuge from the Northmen, along the route running west from the *Cité* at the neck of the ridge. House lots were laid out on the street, churches were founded for new parishes and Jews settled here, since they were excluded from the *Cité*. Craftsmen and merchants rose against the bishop and wrested from him the rights of a self-governing *commune*. In this century, Laon acquired one of the first universities in the Western world. The *Hospice* for lepers was erected also at this time, as well as the abbey of St. Martin on the main westward extension of the axis of the town. The citizens rebuilt the cathedral, and the abbeys of St. Vincent and St. Martin were also rebuilt. The *Bourg* was surrounded by ditch and ramparts adjoining the *Cité*, churches were built for new parishes, and the Place du Bourg became the centre of town life. The position of this new market centre, which had displaced that of St. Georges at the east end of the ridge, is worthy of note. It lay at the junction of the *Cité* and the *Bourg*, just outside the western gate of the latter, at the narrow neck in the centre of the ridge. From it the main street ran west and forked to the two abbeys on the extensions of the ridge.

The surrounding lowlands were cultivated for wheat, and vineyards and orchards covered the hill-slopes on the southern slopes of the ridge. Spinning, weaving and cooperage were important crafts. Tanneries were numerous along the streams at the foot of the hill, and here too wool was washed. In the 13th century there were 880 dwellings in the *Cité*, 750 in the *Bourg* and 50 in the Villette St. Vincent at the western end of the ridge. There was thus a population of about 7,000, which together with the religious establishments made a total of about 9,000 inhabitants. The town served as a focal point, a capital, for the surrounding district traditionally called the Laonnais. Its weavers were renowned.

The Renaissance brought decline, accounted for by the competition of English cloths, and the ravages of war and epidemics. Many houses were abandoned and the quarter of the west end of the ridge disappeared. The town was unable to maintain its walls and public buildings and roads. Henry IV, to hold the citizens of Laon in check, destroyed the old quarter of St. Georges (Chevresson), the cradle of the *Cité*. He erected a citadel on its site, and the primary function of the town now was to guard the entrances to the Île de France and to Paris in those troublous times.

In the 17th century came a slight revival. The centre of affairs in the town remained the Place du Bourg. But the town remains to this day predominantly a seat of clerics and officials. The ground plan remained the same, but new buildings were erected in the classical style for royal officials, magistrates, and notable merchants. Houses of timber and *torchis* were replaced by *hôtels*, and old gables by mansard roofs on rectangular foundations. The ditch before the Porte Martelle (Porte de Mars) was filled in, so that the *Bourg* and the *Cité* became one. As the town lost its significance as a fortress, the walls were removed and replaced by boulevards. The abbeys lost their importance during the 18th century, and at the time of the Revolution the abbey of St. Vincent had only 12 monks compared with an earlier total of 300.

Then came the modern era. After the Revolution, old buildings were put to new uses, were demolished or allowed to go to ruin. Thus, the convent of Minims became the Lycée, another became a prison and police headquarters, and still another the theatre. The remains of St. Vincent became the arsenal and St. Martin, the Hôtel Dieu. The Place du Bourg was widened by the demolition of two historic buildings, and the new Hôtel de Ville was erected there in 1832.

To-day, Laon is a local market and administrative centre. Its only industry is sugar refining for the beet-sugar-growing district around it. The railway lies on the plain on the northern side of the town whither building has spread. But the chief part of the town remains on the hilltop centred on the Place de Bourg at the narrow neck in the centre of the ridge.

These brief town studies reveal characters that typify, in varying degree, every historic town in western Europe. Each has been, and still is to-day, primarily a seat of economic, cultural and administrative functions for its environs. Each reflects the stages in the general historical and cultural development of France as a whole. Each emerged in the Middle Ages as a distinctive regional focus, and in the 17th century and after we can see the effects upon the urban structures of the new functions bestowed upon them as part of the nation-wide policy of development and of the effects of the current ideas of urbanism that appeared throughout France. Each had a definite nucleus of crystalliza-tion that in its initial placement and its expansion was closely adjusted to the relief of the site. Each has been affected by the advent of the railway, and especially by new administrative and military functions and industrial activities in the 19th century. A further fact to be strongly emphasized is that even in these small towns there is a marked specialization as between one quarter and another. This is also evident in a town such as Bar-le-duc, where there were several distinct and self-governing sectors each surrounded with its own wall (Fig. 10). In the ecclesiastical cities, the *Cité* nucleus was dominant and extension took place outside its limits. In the modern growth we find distinct districts growing around the medieval core. An aristocratic quarter grew up in Blois on the raised slopes around castle and church. The same attraction was exercised by the *Cité* in Poitiers. But the new activities of the 19th century resulted in the development of separate administrative, military and industrial sectors, and beyond these in the last twenty years the new housing districts have emerged. These towns to-day have well under 50,000

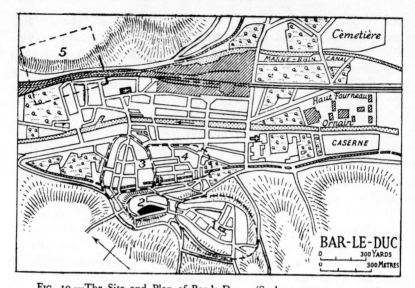

FIG. 10.—The Site and Plan of Bar-le-Duc. (Scale, approx. 1 : 20,000.)
1. Ville Haute. 2. Château. 3. Bourg. 4. Ville Neuve. 5. Site of Roman
camp. Hatched area shows railway tracks and factories.

inhabitants. The selection of special sites for special uses is a
matter both of necessity and choice, and its effects on the urban
plan are clearly evident in these towns, which are small replicas
of the larger cities.

CHAPTER 4

THE TOWNS OF SWITZERLAND

The character and conditions of urban development in Switzerland serve as a useful illustration of urban development throughout western and central Europe. The one main difference is that in Switzerland there has been no great urban increase as a result of the development of the coal and iron and other heavy industries. Down to our own day the primary factor in urban growth has been commerce, and the modern growth of commerce and industry has crystallized around the already existing historic centres. The distribution of the towns is shown on Fig. 11.

(1) LOCATION AND GROWTH OF THE HISTORIC TOWNS.

In the Roman era, in Switzerland as a whole, there were 19 towns, 5 in the Jura, 9 in the Central Plateau and 5 in the Alps. Only 8 of these again became towns in the Middle Ages, each beginning as a bishopric. Nine other towns were added in the 10th and 11th centuries, 16 in the 12th, 97 in the 13th, 12 in the 14th, and 2 in the 18th century. Of these, however, 23 never developed and to-day are either small villages or have entirely disappeared. Others have lost their urban functions and retain only the features of their medieval build. Traffic increased towards the end of the 18th century with the improvement of roads, and increased further with the advent of the railway in 1844. The domestic industries of clock-making and linen-weaving became more localized in factories on rivers and roads. Thus may be explained the growth of the towns as industrial centres in the latter half of the 19th century. To-day there are 30 places with over 10,000 inhabitants, housing (with their suburbs) one and a half million people, or three-eighths of the total population of the country. If all towns, both old and new, with over 2,000 inhabitants are considered, there are 347 in the State, which gives a density of 5·9 towns per 1,000 square kilometres. This density reaches 12·8 in the Jura and 10·6 in the Central Plateau. The Central Plateau (*Mittelland*), in which all the main routes converge, is the most densely settled area. Three of its towns have over 100,000 inhabitants and four over 50,000. In the Jura

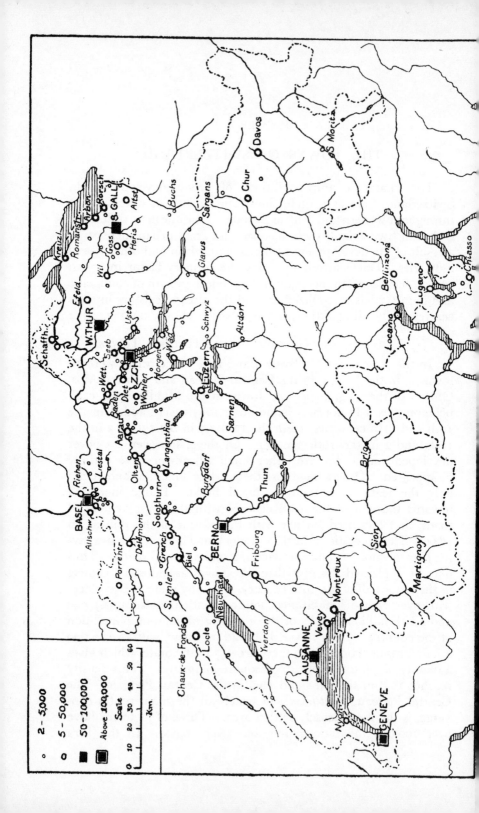

through-traffic is more important and towns lie along the main routeways, although the exploitation of thermal waters and recent industrialization (especially clock-making) have added to urban growth.

Routeways, closely adjusted to physical features, have been predominant in determining the position and relative importance of these towns. The network of routes has remained essentially the same in Roman, medieval, and modern times. The Central Plateau contains the majority of the towns and routeways converge on it from all directions. One series runs east to west in the direction of the trough between the Jura and the Alps, and the other runs roughly north to south after crossing the passes in the Jura and the Alps, which link Italy with western Europe. Across the Alps there are three groups of passes of importance, the Great St. Bernard and Simplon in the west, the Bündner Passes in the east, and the St. Gotthard Pass in the centre. On the northern border of the Alps the routes from the passes converged at points where towns developed early, Chur and Martigny in Roman times, Lucerne and Bellinzona in the Middle Ages. The command of these passes was a primary function of the Society of the Oath (*Eidgenossenschaft*) and the extension of the Swiss State served to protect their southern approaches. Routeways, industry, and the tourist trade account for the towns of the Jura.

We may narrow down our attention to German Switzerland, which roughly embraces the drainage area of the Rhine inside that country (Fig. 12). It had 88 medieval towns, characterized by their law, market and wall, although not every town had all three. This means that there was one town for about every 300 sq. km. as compared with one to every 137 sq. km. in Württemberg, 124 sq. km. in Hesse and about the same in Alsace. But this crude figure includes all the thinly-peopled Alps and Jura, whereas almost all the towns were on the Central Plateau, so that the canton of Aargau, for example, had a density of one town to every 100 sq. km., which compares with maximum densities in certain other areas of central Europe. Towns of Roman origin were Basel, Constance, and Chur. Each was named as a *civitas* in the 9th century, and each had Roman fortifications. Urban life developed during the 12th century, but had its roots in the 10th. *Cives* or burgesses are first mentioned at Constance in 1150, at Basel in 1118, and at Chur in 1227. In Zurich, clustered around its abbey, *cives* are first mentioned in 1149. Several other centres developed in this early period. Burgesses appear in

Schaffhausen in 1190, in Solothurn in 1182 and in St. Gallen in 1170. Lucerne grew up around its monastery and was already of some importance when the Leutkirche was established in 1178, but burgesses are not recorded there until 1244.

At the same time planned towns were already being established in the last decades of the 12th century. The best known are Freiburg (1175) and Bern (1191), both of which were established by the Zähringen as fortresses. They also founded Rheinfelden, adjacent to the castle on an island in the Rhine, in the second half of the 12th century, and burgesses are recorded here in 1212.

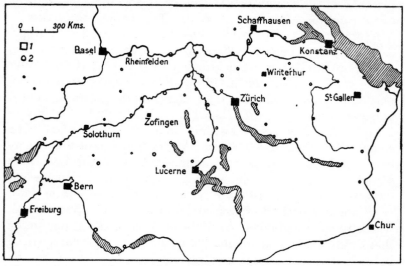

Fig. 12.—The Distribution and Size of the Medieval Towns of German Switzerland (redrawn from Ammann).

1. Towns in 1200. 2. Towns after 1200. The size of the symbols varies according to the importance of the towns.

Zofingen was founded by the Frohburgen, after an ecclesiastical establishment was already in existence there. The Kyburgs founded Winterthur, where merchants (*mercatores*) are recorded in 1180 and burgesses are first mentioned in 1230. In 1178 Diesenhofen received town law from the Kyburgs, though burgesses are not recorded until 1246. Thus by the end of the 12th century there were already in existence the beginnings of fourteen towns. Sixty-four towns appeared during the 13th century, three-quarters of the historic towns of Switzerland. Thereafter town foundation slowed down. Only ten appeared in the 14th and one in the 15th century.

An outstanding feature of the geographical distribution of these towns is that there are none in the Alps except in the deep valleys that cross the mountains, as at Thun, Chur and Lucerne. The overwhelming majority are on the Central Plateau which was the main area of settlement, where towns could derive advantage from the trade and administration of their surroundings as well as from the long-distance traffic along the main through routes. The location of the towns on navigable rivers and lakes is also remarkable. The Rhine, Aar, Limmat and Reuss are each accompanied by a regularly spaced series of towns, sited at points where roads cross the rivers. Moreover, the towns cluster at the foci of natural valley routeways, especially where east–west and north–south routeways cross.

Many of the smaller towns, however, are situated with no relation to routeways. These are usually fortress towns situated on isolated hilltops, their sites having been selected for reasons of defence rather than trade. Freiburg and Bern are themselves examples of such sites. Economic and political factors played varying parts in the location and development of towns, and these find expression, in almost every town, in its market-place and its wall, while the legal status served both needs. The beginnings of town life were associated with the growth of trade on the main routes adjacent to existing secular and ecclesiastical seats. Thus the oldest towns grew up. Once the concept of the town was developed and trade flourished, the territorial lords sought to gain advantage from their privilege of controlling the establishment of towns for their own political or economic profit, and they vied with each other in the process.

Ten towns achieved something more than purely local significance. These were Basel, Zurich, Schaffhausen, Winterthur, Solothurn, Chur, Lucerne (which grew to importance with the opening of the St. Gotthard Pass in the 13th century), Bern, Freiburg, and St. Gallen. Basel in particular flourished in the 15th century, when it occupied a leading place in the economy of the south German lands. Constance and St. Gallen were outstanding centres of linen textile working, and the others had more modest woollen industries. Zurich was the only city north of the Alps to have a silk industry. These towns not only grew in economic importance ; they were also politically independent.

(2) The Distribution, Functions and Size of the Historic Towns in the Aargau

Compared with these ten cities the remaining 78 were very small, and their character and the reasons for their small size may be illustrated from the case of the towns of the Aargau (Fig. 13). The density here is one town to every 100 sq. km. and they are all small towns to-day. They originated in the 14th and 15th centuries and all were deliberately sited and established by their founders. They all lie on main trade routes, the majority on

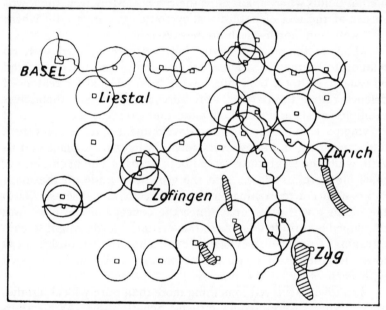

Fig. 13.—The Distribution of the Medieval Towns of Aargau in Switzerland. Each town is given a market radius of 5 km. (after Ammann).

rivers and some at bridge points. A deterrent to their growth was the fact that there were too many of them for the service of the area. This is revealed by their interlocking trade areas when these are theoretically defined as having a radius of 5 km. The area is crossed by some of the chief medieval routeways and the various dynasties sought to profit from the towns, but there were far too many to share even the long-distance trade, let alone the local market trade. Another disadvantage was their tardy origin, which made it far more difficult for them to acquire trade and services that were already handled by other towns.

Moreover, with one exception, they were all subject to a lord and were not politically independent, so that they could not pursue policies of their own. Handicrafts also were of very little importance. Commerce was very feebly developed and was concerned almost exclusively with the local market trade. The country had few products for export and needed such luxury goods as wines (from Alsace) metal wares and textiles. The medium of selling and buying in the towns was the weekly market, but the fairs of the surrounding big cities were also visited by the merchants of the small towns of the Aargau, none of which had an important fair, with the exception of Zurzach. The burgesses of the Aargau towns, especially the cloth merchants, regularly visited the Frankfurt fairs in the later Middle Ages, as well as the fairs at Geneva and its successor (after 1470) at Lyons. But there were no large merchants in any of the Aargau towns.

The population of these towns in the 18th century was in most cases below 1,000 ; the biggest, Aarau and Zofingen, had just over that number. Their populations were largest and they were therefore most active before 1400 ; in the 15th century their numbers fell, but increased again very slowly during the following two centuries. The area was thinly peopled and many villages had under 100 inhabitants at the end of the Middle Ages, though from 1500 to 1800 their numbers increased fourfold. The rural population at the end of the Middle Ages was about twice the urban, and subsequently the rural increase was far greater than the urban, the ratio in 1764 being seven to one. The town population at the end of the Middle Ages was a third or even a quarter of the total population, and a hundred years earlier in 1400 it was certainly much less. The towns were in fact too numerous and contained too many people for the modest service of a thinly peopled countryside, and a considerable number of the townsfolk must have lived directly by farming or by trade.

How far can these characteristics of the small towns of the Aargau be extended to those of Switzerland in general ? Usually the small town had a good nodal position and an adequate market area to support it, though there were exceptions, such as the hilltop towns and towns that were too close to each other. They were, however, mostly not politically independent and therefore could not pursue their own economic policies. Agriculture was an occupation of importance in the towns, especially in the vine-growing areas as along the Rhine valley. Industry was of very little significance as a special occupation seeking outside markets, save for the small towns around St. Gallen which developed linen handicrafts in the 14th and 15th centuries—Wil, Bischofszell, and Appenzell. On the main routes, small towns played a part in long-distance traffic, for they had hostelries, saddlers and folk engaged in coaching and sailing. The retail trades were concerned with supplying the local market area and for this purpose some towns had their special buildings—*Kaufhäuser*. Merchants visited neighbouring larger towns for the sale of the special products of the town or of its market area. This was true of the small towns in vine-growing areas, though their products were not marketed over very long distances. Fairs were visited but rarely and by few merchants.

The size of the Aargau towns is representative of the country as a whole and of the small towns of central and western Europe in general. The great majority had under 1,000 inhabitants and there were not a few with less than 100. The size of these smaller towns should be compared with that of towns of greater importance. Chur had a population of 1,500 in 1481, Solothurn 2,000 ; Lucerne in 1350, Schaffhausen in 1390 and St. Gallen in 1400 had each about 3,000 inhabitants ; in 1500 St. Gallen had 4,000. Freiburg in 1444 had 5,000, compared with 3,000 in 1379. Constance had about 5,000 in the 15th century, and Bern had between 5,000 and 6,000 in the middle of that century. Zurich had 6,500 in 1350, falling to 4,000 in 1450. Basel had no less than 9,000 in the first half of the 15th century. Thus, none of the towns had over 10,000 inhabitants, and the majority had between 3,000 and 5,000. These figures may be compared with 20,000 for Strasbourg, Nuremberg and Lübeck in the 15th century. The Swiss towns were therefore small. While the larger ones took part in specialized trade and industry, the small towns were pre-eminently concerned with the service of their market areas, receiving supplies for consumption and marketing their products elsewhere, finding their special commodity requirements elsewhere, and marketing them through the medium of the retailer and the small merchant.

(3) Site, Plan and Build of the Historic Town

We may now turn to consider briefly the sites and plans of these towns. The early medieval towns grew around pre-urban nuclei, sometimes on Roman sites, but the sites of the smaller towns were often selected primarily in the interests of defence. All of them are walled—the unwalled market settlement is a rare exception—and the majority have planned forms and character-istic architectural and architectonic features which exhibit marked regional variations.

While the route position (*Verkehrslage*) or nodality is the primary determinant of the growth of these towns, the site (*Ortslage*) has been decisive in their plan and build. Towns that have developed as route centres and as centres for a surrounding market area, have lowland sites (*Tiefenlage*) on important roads and at crossways or at the crossings of rivers or on lake shores. In valley constrictions and defiles along a lake shore, the town, as well as being a local market centre, could cut off a route and thereby acquire strategic importance (Bellinzona, St. Maurice, Rheineck). The edge of a terrace (Zofingen), an alluvial fan in the Alps (Chur), a lake delta (Steckbon) or lake embayment (Morges), are sites that determine the lay-out of the town. Some towns clustered around the nucleus of crystallization of a Roman settlement (Geneva and Basel). Others grew, as a *Vorburg* or *Faubourg*, a parasitic settlement, around a castle on a hilltop (Lenzburg), around a church foundation or bishop's see (Lausanne, Chur), an abbey (St. Gallen), or a church (Bischofszell).

Aerial views of selected small towns are shown on Plate 1. The plans of the towns are usually rectilinear with the exception of the older ones, where an irregular rounded nucleus is apparent, clustered around the ecclesiastical core. This type, in its simplest form, is apparent in Bischofszell, where a line of buildings forms a circle around the church. Frequently among the small founded towns there is the grouping of a double row of buildings facing a widened street, sometimes situated on a hilltop. Examples are Aarburg and Avenches. A series of parallel streets, with narrow connecting streets like the rungs of a ladder, is found in Bern and Freiburg, Neunkirch and Waldenburg. All of these illustrate carefully designed planned forms, the first two being closely adjusted to the site, while the third has a regular plan on flat land enclosed by a rectangular wall. Cross streets produce a grid-like pattern as at Aarau and Brügg, though the planned grid with a central market does not appear in a single Swiss town. Planned forms are often closely adjusted to the relief of the site, as at Thun, Stein and Locarno.

The expansion of the historic town has followed the direction of the routes and traffic towards the station, and along roads leading into the country, as at Basel, where suburbs developed outside the walls. The larger cities have a circle of satellites. Hindrances to traffic and expansion are overcome and rail and railyards are relegated to the outskirts, again as at Basel. Distinctive districts appear as the complex grows. Such trends, though especially characteristic of modern growth, appeared in the historic town. Some grew in concentric fashion through the construction of new walls, as at St. Gallen ; others grew along a main route through the annexation of suburbs, as at Basel, or through the annexation of new towns, like Basel–Kleinbasel and Winterthur. Complicated forms appear, where the old town is on a hill and the new urban centre is on the lowland next to it, as at Basel and Chur, or where a monastery, as a separate nucleus, was absorbed into the growing town, as at Lausanne. In small towns the hilltop settlement is often decadent, while the present active centre lies on the plain adjacent to the road and railway.

The build of the Swiss town is determined above all by the *Bürgerhaus*, the home of the burgess. This is closely related in origin and structure to the farmsteads of the countryside, and has been transformed in its development by the changing functions of urban economy, by lack of building space, and by the introduction of new building styles. Architectural styles of particular epochs affect not only the public monument but also the house, and thereby the aspect of the whole town. It should be emphasized, however, that whereas the plan of the town normally dates back to its origins in the early Middle Ages, except where great devastation by fire has destroyed the town and it has been entirely replanned and rebuilt, the buildings were crudely built and often burned down or demolished. Thus the earliest buildings seldom antedate the 15th century, and the majority, except for the public buildings, date from the 17th and 18th centuries. In the west of Switzerland and in the Jura the *Traufhaus* is dominant, and is similar to the Alemannic and Burgundian farmsteads in the surrounding country. The eaves of the house lie parallel to the street ; hence the name.

The historic town house was built on a small lot, with only one room in depth and often had four to five storeys. Around Lake Constance is the domain of the Swabian half-timbered house which has gables facing the street and is comparable with the Frankish farmstead. In the Alps the town house is related to the *Länderhaus* with a flattish roof. In the southern Alps the stone-built house appears in the Italian areas ; this type that reached its fullest development during the Renaissance period. It has a flattish roof, high façades with evenly spaced windows, arcades and loggias and faces on a narrow street. Examples of this type of architecture are found at Locarno and Lugano. Late Gothic styles are rare in Switzerland and reflect the economic decline of urban activity in the 16th and 17th centuries. Renaissance and Baroque buildings give a distinct character to Freiburg and Bern, where they have arcades, evenly spaced windows of a

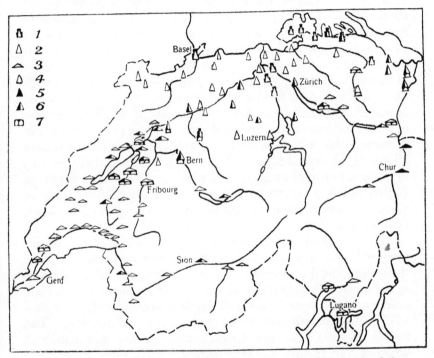

Fig. 14.—The Distribution of House Types in Switzerland (from Vosseler).

Note the broad contrast between the areas with flat and steep gables. 1. Stepped gable (*Treppengabel*). 2. Steep roof (*Steildach*). 3. Flat roof. 4. Eaves house. 5. Gable house. 6. Ziergabel. 7. Arcades (*Laubengänge*).

uniform design, and stone mouldings. Tenements and workers' estates characterize the modern growth, with stone buildings dominating in the north and west, and smaller timber houses in the east.

The building material affects the aspect of the town. Red sandstone appears in the areas adjacent to south-western Germany, as at Basel, limestone in the Jura, sandstone (*Molasse*), grey-green in colour, in the towns from Lausanne to St. Gallen, and granite

and gneiss along the shores of Lake Geneva, the Rhône valley
and the Ticino. The distribution of certain architectural features
of the town houses is shown on Fig. 14.

(4) URBAN SETTLEMENTS OF TO-DAY.

We may now turn our attention to the urban settlements of
to-day. In order to map the urban areas of Switzerland on a
scale of 1 : 250,000, Hans Carol [1] of Zurich worked on the
standard scale of 1 : 25,000. He used a grid of quarter-kilometre
squares, and when such a square contained 30 or more separate
buildings he described this as urban land, on the assumption that
this density was too high for a farming community (i.e. a minimum
of 30 buildings for 25 hectares or about 62·5 acres), and that such
an area would then form part of the urban fringe. In the case
of ribbon building he decided to demarcate as urban any groups
of roadside houses that numbered more than 15 per 500 metres of
frontage. An area so defined, that covers more than one square
kilometre, he described as a *Grosssiedlung*, of which there are 113
in the country, embracing 214 *Gemeinden*. The largest is that of
Zurich, which covers 51 sq. km. with an average density of about
7,000 persons per square kilometre, and this is followed by Basel,
Geneva and Bern.

The character and extent of the urban areas of to-day are
discussed by Carol, and his specific remarks serve to crystallize
the geographical approach. Having defined the urban areas as
in the previous paragraph, Carol classifies them according to their
dominant functions. Two main kinds are recognized, the industrial centres and the centres of trade and administration. The
former in particular are characterized by the dominance of
factories and factory workers' homes. They often draw their
labour from the surrounding areas and find markets for their
products far and wide, within and beyond the boundaries of the
State. The centre of trade and administration is closely linked
with its environs, for which it functions as a *chef-lieu*, the seat of
what have been described as centralized services. Many specialized industries are attracted to such centres and are located,
according to their needs, in small installations in the centre or
in large plants on the periphery. A third type of compact
settlement is that which is pre-eminently a seat of agriculture.
This is the village, and it may range from a few farmsteads to a

---

[1] H. Carol, " Begleittext zur Wirtschaftsgeographischen Karte der Schweiz ",
Geographica Helvetica, 1. Jahrgang, 1946, Heft 3, pp. 185-245.

large agglomeration of 1,000 to 5,000 or more inhabitants. All nucleated settlements owe their functional character to varying permutations and combinations of these functions. Though the agricultural element is of least importance and is negligible in fully fledged towns, it is significant in the small country towns and townlets with a few hundred to a thousand inhabitants.

Three main functional types of compact settlement were recognized for Switzerland : agricultural districts (*Gemeinden*) with over half of the occupied persons engaged in agriculture ; agricultural-urban districts with 10 to 50 per cent. engaged in agriculture ; and urban districts with less than a tenth of the occupied persons so engaged. This classification was arrived at through a consideration of the external aspect of the settlement. The agricultural settlements include just over 40 per cent. of all *Gemeinden* and the urban settlements numbered nearly 9 per cent. of the total, while the intermediate types included just under a half of the whole. The urban settlements are divided into seats of industry, in which over half the occupied persons are engaged in industry and crafts, and seats of trade and administration in which less than half the occupied persons are engaged in industry and crafts. A similar sub-division has been used by many other writers.

The separation of work-place and dwelling-place gives a particular character to the function and aspect of the modern settlement. On the basis of the detailed data for *Gemeinden* of the separation of work-place and dwelling-place, three types of urban settlement were recognized—working districts (*Arbeitsgemeinden*), working-dwelling districts (*Arbeits-Wohngemeinden*) and dwelling districts (*Wohngemeinden*). A *Gemeinde* with all its workers 110 per cent. in excess of the resident workers falls into the first category, with corresponding percentages between 75 and 100 per cent. or below 75 per cent. in the second and third categories respectively. All *Gemeinde* with over 2,000 inhabitants are so classified.[1]

A hundred years ago urban and rural settlements were sharply differentiated from each other in respect of function and aspect. Between the two was the *Flecken*, or market town, that had the build of a village, centred often on church or market-place, but the functions of a town. Such is the typical country town in England, where it is more in evidence than in any other country.

---

[1] Swiss workers are indeed fortunate (as in some of the German States) in having so much detail regarding *Pendelverkehr*—the daily movement of workers from home to factory. Details of railway traffic (*Abonnementkarten*) are also available. This is a glaring and serious deficiency in British demographic statistics.

But such historic settlements in Switzerland were rare. To-day the urban functions are more widely scattered and there are many settlements that are transitional in both function and aspect. Moreover, some villages have become urban and small settlements have become rural villages in function though retaining their aspect as medieval towns. Carol shows on his map the old town of the modern settlement in black, so that settlements without a black core either grew around an old village or are entirely new. On this map 99 *Gemeinden* are designated as medieval towns, of which a half are to-day larger settlements (*Grossiedlungen*), and 32 of these are the nuclei of urban agglomerations of several *Gemeinden*, while 18 are *Grossgemeinden* with over 2,000 inhabitants. The 18 largest urban settlements (*Grosssiedlungen*) have 1,363,000 inhabitants, or a third of the total population of Switzerland. Modern urban population has thus grown preeminently around the historic towns, the chief exceptions being the industrial agglomerations of the Jura and the resorts of the Alps.

CHAPTER 5

BASEL : A STUDY IN URBAN GEOGRAPHY

(1) SITUATION

On a relief map, Basel would seem to be destined to be a really great city. It lies at the head of the Rhine plain on the great right-angle bend of the river where the natural lowland routeways converge. The Burgundian Gate lies to the south-west, the Rhine plain to the north, and the upper Rhine valley to the east. To the south there are short valleys which are now used by railways, and tunnels cut through the narrow belt of the Jura to Zurich, Leizen-Gotthard and Bern. Basel is often referred to as the " golden gate to Switzerland ". The Vosges, the Black Forest, and the Swiss Jura frame the lowland around the city. The Sundgau lies between the Vosges and the outliers of the Jura. The river Birs which flows through the gorges of the Jura, joins the Rhine above Basel. The Wiese, a stream flowing from the Black Forest, empties into the Rhine on the right bank below the city. The dying ends of the Black Forest approach the Rhine as low hill country in the vicinity of Basel.

However, in spite of all of these natural advantages, Basel, though of great historic and cultural importance, is only a medium-sized city. In 1941 the population was only 162,000, and *Kanton* Basel had but 170,000 inhabitants that year. Also, the administrative area of the city covers only 37·0 sq. km. The reasons for the apparent retardation in the growth of the city are, in general, physical and political. The Rhine is not regularly navigable above Strasbourg, and this has had serious economic consequences, as commerce and industry have been curtailed. But political conditions have had an even greater effect. Since the Middle Ages, Basel has been on the frontiers of three States : Switzerland, France and Germany. Political frictions and result-ant wars have obviously restricted the normal growth of the city. Tariff barriers among the three nations are other obvious factors which have adversely affected normal development. As a con-sequence of such political and economic artifices, Basel has never achieved the size and importance which favourable location and site would seem to have assured it.

(2) HISTORICAL DEVELOPMENT

The left bank of the Rhine is undercut at the bend of the river to a height of 25 metres. The land on which Basel was built rises by low terraces inland to the steep edge of the hills of the Sundgau (Fig. 15). The valley of the Birs to the east sets a limit to this country. Most important in the site and growth of the medieval city is the valley of the little river Birsig, which has a narrow valley 20 metres deep in the town, and, between it and the mouth of the Rhine, there is a long narrow hill that overlooks the Rhine. This hill is the nucleus of the *Altstadt* which contains the Cathedral, Bishop's Palace, part of the University, and St. Martin's Church. An easy route led down the Birsig valley to its mouth where firm land offered a practicable river crossing and, at a later date, a site for the first bridge across the Rhine.

The right bank of the Rhine rises very gradually from the river front. Kleinbasel lies on the delta of the Wiese, which was diverted to the north in 1770. In the 13th century a channel was made to the ditch around the town of Kleinbasel to drive mills for bleaching and dyeing cloths, and later for the silk, leather and timber industries. The first bridge across the river dates from the early 13th century ; the other two, on either side of it, from the end of the 19th century. At the same time a market-place was established on the covered-in course of the Birsig, so that the town was able to thrive in the Middle Ages both as a centre for through-traffic and a market centre for the districts on both sides of the river. The foundation of Kleinbasel coincided with the building of the bridge.

The medieval town had its beginning in a Celtic settlement,

FIG. 15.—The Growth of Basel (after Hassinger). (Scale, 1 : 25,000.)

1. Site of Celtic, Roman, and Celto-Roman settlement. 2. Walled town in 1280. 3. Walled town in the early 15th century. 4. Built-up area about 1870. 5. Areas built-up 1870–1905. 6. Areas built-up 1905–26. 7. Main streets of the old town leading to the town gates.

Churches : I. Munster. II. St. Martin. III. St. Leonard. IV. St. Peter. V. St. Theodor. VI. St. Alban. VII. (1), (2), and (3) Gates through the walls. (4) The old Rhine bridge. (5) Säu Platz (to-day Barfüsser Platz). (6) Kornmarkt (Corn Market), to-day Markt Platz (Market-place). (7) Old Badischer Bahnhof (Baden Station), to-day Muster Messe (Exhibition Hall). (8) New Badischer Bahnhof. 9. Bundesbahnhof (Swiss Station).

Hachures indicate steep slopes of over 5 metres north of Basel, over 10 metres in the Birsig valley, and over 20 metres in the south. There is a fairly steep rise of 3 metres on the north side of the river within the walled town. There are two minor, parallel breaks of slope of 3 to 5 metres running north-west to south-east across the area, that are crossed in the south by the outer wall ; town gate (1) corresponds with the inner of these two breaks.

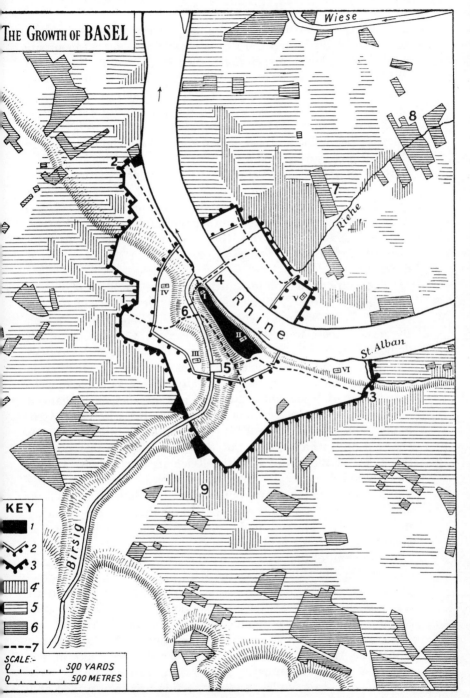

THE GROWTH OF BASEL

Wiese

Rhine

Riehe

St. Alban

Birsig

2
8
7
4
I
III
IV
II
V
1
6
VI
5
III
3
9

KEY

1
2
3
4
5
6
7

SCALE:-
0   500 YARDS
0   500 METRES

65

established in the middle of the 1st century B.C. on the spur between the Birsig and the Rhine. On this same acropolis site was established a Roman *castellum* called Basilia, on the important route from Augusta Rauracorum (Augst) via Cambete (Kembs) to Argentoratum (Strasbourg). On the acropolis were the castell and the temple, which probably in the 4th century A.D. became a Christian church. This settlement housed soldiers, officials and priests. Below in the Birsig valley and on the Rhine bank were the craftsmen, traders and ferry folk. There was thus a complete contrast of hilltop and valley settlement, which persists to this day. While the Roman fortifications of the *limes* far to the east protected the Roman-occupied lands, Basilia had little association with the Rhine ; but when the Alemanni broke through the *limes* and threatened to cross the Rhine, the settlement was strongly fortified and a new *castrum* was erected, the site of which is disputed.

The settlement continued through the ensuing centuries. Absorbed into the Frankish kingdom in the middle of the 6th century, Basel became one of a series of Rhine towns, and on the terrace there was established a Frankish *Königshof*, a church dedicated to St. Martin, and a cathedral on the site of the Roman temple. Already the nuclei of States appeared in the fertile storehouse around Basel, so that the city itself was unable to weld together an independent State unit, and its allegiance changed after the 9th century from one State to another—Lorraine, Germany, and Upper Burgundy. Its frontier location was not changed until its absorption into the German Reich in 1006, and the union of Burgundy with the Reich in 1033. Now at last, Basel was able to exploit fully its position on the great north–south route and the route southwest to the State of Burgundy, and to take its share in the east–west traffic that developed during the Crusades. The southward pass across the St. Gotthard was opened in the 13th century.

At the end of the 11th century the growing urban settlement, clustered in the valley along· the road and around the market-place, was walled—although this has left no mark on the modern aspect of the town. Settlement also took place outside the wall. St. Alban's church was founded in 1083 by the Cluniac monks, who diverted the Birs river to drive their mills. An Augustinian monastery and the church of St. Leonard were built in the middle of the 12th century. The town also spread up the west slopes of the Birsig Valley, and this section was soon walled and became a parish with St. Peter's Church, situated on the terrace edge overlooking the valley. These outlying settlements were all enclosed at the beginning of the 13th century by a new wall, which embraced both the hill and valley towns. It was so designed as to protect the settlement on the road and to reach to the edge of the plateau terrace which commanded views of the town below it. The chief axis of the town was the Roman route at the foot of the upper town along the Birsig valley. On the right bank of the river the small town of Kleinbasel was regularly laid out to command the new bridge. The two previously existing villages disappeared, presumably because their people moved into the town. More craftsmen and monastic settlements appeared outside the walls, and new walls were erected about 1400, and these remained until the middle of the 19th century. The two towns were combined in 1372. Bastions were added in the 16th and 17th centuries. The area between the walls was mainly open in Sebastian Munster's time and was not built on until the 19th century.

The territorial disintegration of Upper Germany had its repercussions on the fate of Basel. The Hapsburg territories were split up in the 13th century, in the Rhine plain and the upper Rhine valley and in the Sundgau and Breisgau, so that these territories impinged on the tributary area of Basel. The towns-men, whose closest relations had hitherto been with the plains people, therefore turned south to the Swiss Confederation, and in the 15th century obtained control of the passes across the Jura.

But the political importance of Basel was modest in comparison with its economic and cultural position. With an area of 13 sq. km. and a population of 20,000, it was one of the greatest cities in Germany in the 15th century. It exceeded Frankfurt and Strasbourg in size and population, and was not far behind Nuremberg. In 1460 its University was founded. It became a centre of printing and paper working (in the St. Alban district), and reached its greatest prosperity in the Humanist and Renais-sance periods. In 1501 the city finally threw in its lot with Switzerland, and thus relinquished its association with the Reich and its claims to political power in exchange for a more modest status as a city state in the Swiss Confederation. It adhered not to Lutheranism, but to the Reformed Church and ultimately to Calvinism. This marked the end of the monasteries, and the town also ceased to be the seat of a bishopric. Trade suffered from the wars in its surroundings, and from the decline in traffic after the discovery of the New World and from the advance of the Turks into south-eastern Europe. Nevertheless, Basel remained a trade and financial centre of considerable importance. Religious refugees came to the city in the 16th and 17th centuries, and they added to its industries—silk, velvet, and woollen weaving —and became the patrician class of the town.

(3) TOPOGRAPHIC FORMATION (Fig. 15)

This historical development is clearly reflected in the topographic formation and build of the old town. Many of the medieval buildings are preserved to this day (Fig. 16), especially in the narrow steep streets which lie on the slopes of the Birsig valley—even though the town was largely destroyed by fire on several occasions, in 1294, 1327, 1417, and above all by the earthquake and fire of 1356. Red sandstone and limestone are the general building materials, in common with the towns of south-western Germany. Rows of narrow-fronted craftsmen's houses of two or three storeys, with a good deal of half-timbered work, are still to be found in the old quarter of Spalenberg on the Birsig and along the Rheinweg of Kleinbasel. Larger burgesses' houses have two to four windows and two or three storeys. The mansions (Höfe) of the nobility and city patricians have large gate entrances leading to courts both back and front. Common to these three main types of old house is the tiled span-roof (Satteldach) with its eaves parallel to the street front as in south-western Germany. Until the 16th century the town was rich in colourful house paintings, gold-coloured exterior decorations, ornamental figures on fountains in public places and on streets, which are characteristic of the Renaissance period. But this was brought to an end by the advent of Puritanism. Buildings erected after the 16th century are simpler in design and more austere. The Baroque era left its mark on the city. The Margraves of Baden, whose lands lay outside the town gates, built a new palatial mansion in French style as their town residence in 1698, and frequently resided there until 1807. This structure had its influence on the buildings of the patricians of Basel, who imitated French ways. Their new town mansions were built on the Rhine front, and country mansions in gardens were built between the town and its walls or in nearby villages (especially in the village of Riehen) in the styles of Louis XV and Louis XVI. The mansard roof is characteristic of these mansions.. Their walls are plastered and painted in grey and white, and the windows have grey shutters ;

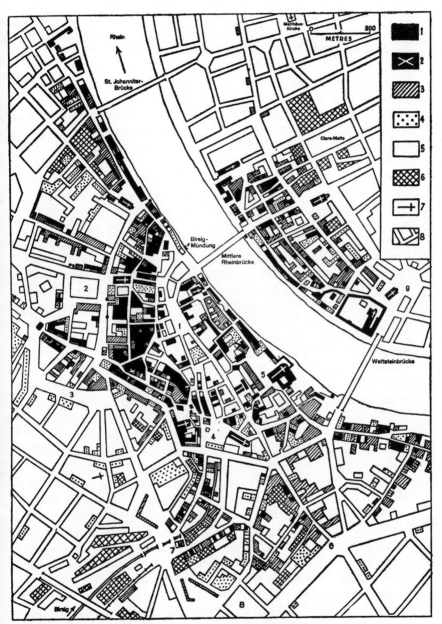

FIG. 16.—Architectural Periods in Basel (from Schaefer). (Scale, 1 : 12,500.)

1. Medieval (Gothic) up to 1500. 2. Renaissance, 16th century. 3. Baroque and Classical, 1600–1800. 4. Neo-Romanesque, Neo-Gothic, and Neo-Classical, 1800–50. 5. Modern, since 1850. 6. Technical and Industrial. 7. Churches. 8. Open Spaces and Parks.

the same roofing has been used in the houses and flats of modern Basel.

The fact that Basel grew from the combination of a hilltop settlement and a valley settlement and was walled three times resulted in the formation of an irregular ground-plan, and this was further accentuated by the spread of building on the land between the town and its walls (Fig. 15). Factories were now built on these outskirts among the country houses and gardens, especially in the St. Johannvorstadt next to the first railway station (Basel–Strasbourg) in Switzerland, that was built inside the town wall in 1844. At the time of the destruction of the town wall in 1859 Basel still had sharply defined limits, for there were no suburbs outside it ; only a few small factories along the mill streams and scattered country houses and farms. But the mobility of persons after the building of the railway changed the picture. Surrounding villages absorbed workers from the new factories in the environs, and houses spread along the roads between these villages. Riehen became even more the suburban seat of the burgesses of Basel. During the second half of the 19th century groups of country and suburban houses, small factories, sand pits and brickworks and gardens grew up between the villages and the roads. This forms what Hassinger calls the town *Weichbild*, that is, the urban-rural zone around the town.

In 1897 there was a further significant change, for the advent of the tramway system made possible the separation of work-place and living-place for the workers as well as for the well-to-do. The nucleus of an industrial area was formed to the north of the town by the establishment of the gas works in 1860 on the left bank of the Rhine, next to the river, and near the Alsace railway. Here also clustered the slaughter-house and dyeing works and factories on the Kleinbasel side, which had been shifted from Alsace. To-day, chemical works lie on both banks of the river. Electricity works and briquette works have since been added to this cluster. All of these industries are closely dependent on the Rhine as a source of water and a means of transport. Industrial development was favoured on the Kleinbasel bank by the opening of the Baden railway (Badischer Bahnhof) in 1855, and later by the opening of a new Rhine port to the north. Working-class quarters have grown up nearby at St. Johann, between the old suburb of that name and the Alsace station, and between the old town of Kleinbasel and the new station.

To the east of the town the Swiss station was opened in 1854, but it was soon shifted to the south (Bundesbahnhof), to the area between the Birsig and Birs behind which rise the steep slopes of the high terrace. The railway runs east–west, but north–south streets cross over the tracks and expansion was not restricted. Here there grew up a modern nucleus with a hotel quarter on the town side, while beyond, between the railway and the terrace, there arose in the 'seventies a working-class quarter for railway and customs employees, along with scattered factories. A belt railway was built in 1860 to link the Baden, Swiss, and Alsace stations on the east, south, and west of the town. Thus Basel was equipped to be a great transit centre for the traffic of Switzerland. The western tracks, built over the Birsig at street level, hindered the free flow of town traffic westward and the expansion of the town. The tracks were demolished and replaced by a wide boulevard, called the Ring (which might be taken for the site of old fortifications) and the new lines were built farther out and partly underground in 1902. Working-class and middle-class quarters have since expanded in the north-west of the town, and good residential quarters to the south-west. By the end of the 19th century the Baden station and tracks were both too small and were also a hindrance to the expansion of the town. They were demolished (1913), and their place was taken by the exhibition buildings (Mustermesse) in 1920 and a wide thoroughfare (Riehenring) as in the west. At the same time, the new station and track for the Darmstadt and Karlsruhe lines were shifted farther out and modernized with large goods yards. The industrial quarter has spread out to the railway, and beyond are good-class residential areas and open country leading to the village of Riehen.

The best residential quarters of Basel lie to the south-east of the town in the St. Alban quarter. It enjoyed in part the advantages of an unrestricted outlook over the Rhine, plenty of parks and open spaces, and, outside the walls, it was long favoured as a residential quarter grouped around a park, which was the former summer Casino. A newer first-class residential quarter has developed in the south-west between a former military shooting ground and the meadows of the Birsig, where the Zoological Gardens are situated. Tradition and the mutual attraction of people of the same class, as well as site conditions, have favoured the growth of these select residential quarters. Cemeteries have also been shifted farther out with the expansion of the town. Earlier cemeteries that were at first just outside the town walls are to-day the sites of the Botanical Gardens, the Elizabeth Gardens near the Bundesbahnhof, and the *Rosentalanlage* in Kleinbasel. The new cemeteries opened on the outskirts of the urban area have already been reached by the expanding town, and a central cemetery is to be established on the heights east of Kleinbasel.

The surrounding suburban belt has been steadily filled up, its inner boundary retreating before the advance of the compact urban area of the town, so that the scattered islands of this transition zone became peninsulas of the central town area, and gradually lost this character once more as the built-up area extended between them.

(4) FUNCTIONAL ZONES OF THE MODERN CITY (Fig. 17)

The whole urban area falls into four zones : the town nucleus or *Stadtkern* ; the more open built-up zone around it ; then the outer transition zone or *Weichbild* ; and, finally, the suburban zone or *Zone der Vororte*. The resident population of the nucleus has steadily decreased in numbers since 1870. The population of the *Altstadt* has decreased as follows :—1870–88, 4·2 per cent ; 1888–1910, 19·6 per cent., and 1910–20, 11·2 per cent.

The town nucleus consists of the Valley Town and the Hill Town (*Talstadt* and *Bergstadt*). The Hill Town is an administrative and educational centre, with the seats of public administration, the University, educational museums, schools, and the cathedral. The Valley Town is the business centre, with banks, insurance offices, Exchange, Post Office, newspaper offices, and

---

FIG. 17.—Land Uses in Basel (after Hassinger). (Scale, 1 : 25,000.)

Settlement.

1. *The City*, including administrative, cultural, and commercial sections.

2. *The Inner Residential Area.* Fully built-up and densely populated, houses mainly 4 to 5 storeys.

3. Medium density of building and population, houses 2 to 3 storeys, with private gardens.

4. Open built-up areas, houses 1 to 3 storeys, with large private gardens.

5. *The Outer Residential Area or Urban Fringe (Weichbild).* Open, low groups of buildings.

Economy.

6. Transport facilities—stations and yards, garages, wharves, storage yards (more open stipple shows these areas in the urban fringe, closer stipple in the compact urban area).

7. Vineyards.　8. Woods.　9. Public Gardens.

10. Market Gardens and Orchards.

11. Cemeteries (Christian and Jewish).　　　12. Industrial Plants.

13. High buildings connected with industry and commerce (towers, elevators, etc.).

14. Gasometers.　15. Ferries.　16. Wharves.

17. Main shopping thoroughfares.

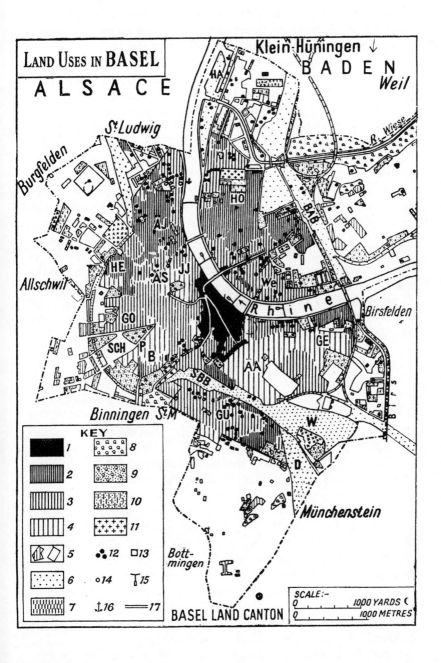

LAND USES IN BASEL

ALSACE

BADEN

Klein-Hüningen ↓
Weil

St Ludwig

Burgfelden

Allschwil

HA

HO

AJ

HE MU JJ
AS

Wei

R. Wiese

BAB

Rhine

Birsfelden

GO

SCH P
B

GE

AA

SBB

Binningen S.M

GU

W

D

Münchenstein

Bott-
mingen

KEY

■	1	▦	8
▥	2	▨	9
▥	3	▥	10
▥	4	+ + +	11
◇	5	•• 12	□ 13
∴	6	∘ 14	⊤ 15
▦	7	⊥ 16	═══ 17

BASEL LAND CANTON

SCALE:–
0 — 1000 YARDS
0 — 1000 METRES

shops with great window displays on the main street and their upper storeys let off as offices ; there are also a few warehouses. This commercial centre has spread beyond the limits of the old town, to the south and east towards the railway station, along the road on the bottom of the Birsig valley and up the steep valley slopes on its western side. The " city " has many new buildings of three to five or more storeys. Old burgesses' houses on the western slopes of the Birsig are gradually being invaded by offices and business concerns, though there is still a considerable number of old houses let off at low rentals. The steep slopes of its narrow streets discourage heavy traffic and have helped to preserve the old character of this section. The main concentration of traffic is at the bottom of the valley along the main historic road, which is to-day the city's principal thoroughfare.

To the north-west the palace of the Margraves of Baden, transformed into a hospital, and the old monastery garden of Petersplatz, formed the nucleus of the modern cluster of clinics and University buildings. Steinenvorstadt in the south of the Birsig valley preserves its old industrial character and its chief street is a mixture of shopping premises and houses. Around the Bundesbahnhof cluster hotels, travel bureaux, and forwarding agents, housed mainly in five-storey buildings converted to these uses. This district, and likewise the inner part of the old St. Alban Vorstadt, have been invaded by the " city " ; below the terrace edge lies the old factory quarter, along the St. Alban mill-stream where there are to-day paper, string, and tobacco factories. The workers live in the district immediately adjacent to the east on the flat land next to the river (Breite). Farther afield, along the St. Alban mill-stream, are various factories, and beyond is the exclusive residential quarter of outer St. Alban, which, as we have seen, has moved out in stages from inside the old town walls. Large factories and warehouses lie to the south alongside the railways, and the working-class district extends to the south of the railway belt to the foot of the steep terrace slope. Beyond the latter, on the plateau, is open country, but some scattered residential development has taken place there. The western outer quarters are good-class residential districts fronting partly on the Ring, partly on the radial routes. Here single-family houses and some flats are found. The northern district of St. Johann, lying next the riverside industrial quarter, is in marked contrast, for here there are large blocks of four- to five-storey flats for factory workers, some of them of recent construction.

On the Kleinbasel side, the salient features are the nucleus of Kleinbasel itself, and the great belt of railway tracks, which is almost linked with the new harbour quarter of Klein-Hüningen. Between these two are extensive workers' and industrial quarters. Beyond the railway belt is open country, notably along the Wiese valley, though new buildings are going up along the main road to the village of Riehen which for long has been a favourite residential spot for Basel people ; it is now a villa quarter and has all but lost its real village character.

A marked feature of Basel is the dominance of the small house. Cellar and attic each count as one storey in official records, but even so the average number of storeys is only 3·59—even in the city it is only 3·89—and there is a corresponding low density of persons per house—11·92 persons in 1920 (10 in 1930) per building as compared with Bremen 7·96 (one of the lowest in Germany), Berlin 77, Vienna 60, and Stettin 48. The three-room house is dominant, making up one-third of the total. Densities of population are correspondingly low. Densities in the inner town in 1920 were 186·8 per hectare (a decrease from 218·9 in 1910), with Auf Burg (the Hill Town) 46, the Gellert district (part of the St. Alban quarter) 20·7, and Bläsi, a working-class quarter in Kleinbasel, 50·1.

The population of the town has increased as follows :—21,660 in 1835, 61,000 in 1880, 112,000 in 1900, 139,000 in 1926, 148,000 in 1930 and 163,000 in 1941. In the last century the population has increased sevenfold, and the area fivefold—from 160 to 800 hectares—and the number of houses has grown from 2,208 in 1835 to 12,300 in 1925 and to 16,757 in 1937. The number of single-family houses has increased twofold since 1910, and in 1920 they made up 22 per cent. of the total. The overall density of population was 175 persons per hectare in 1925.

(5) INDUSTRY AND COMMERCE

Basel has a little under a half of its people dependent on industry, a fourth on trade and a little more than a tenth on transport. There were nearly 410 factories occupying nearly 24,000 persons in 1929. As a seat of industry Basel exhibits the tendency to decentralization. Many small factories lie in the old quarters along the mill-streams, along the Birsig and inside the walls. But some have migrated and new ones have been established outside the city boundaries. The chief industries in order are textiles, chemicals and machinery. Wool and silk weaving have long since disappeared, and to-day silk ribbon-making, with dyeing and finishing, are the chief industries, employing 5,500 persons in 1925 (1,200 in 1938), and exporting large quantities to Britain and Germany. The chemical industry was introduced in the 'sixties from Mühlhausen, and serves the textile industries of Basel and Mühlhausen and the export market (U.S.A. and Britain) ; 5,000 people were employed in this group in 1925. Metal working, machinery and electrical products also began in order to supply the textile industries.

Transport plays an important part in the life of Basel. Railways and warehouses cover 247 hectares (about 600 acres) in the city, and new marshalling yards and an airfield lie outside its boundaries. The airfield, established in 1946, lies in Alsace, so as to serve both Basel and Mühlhausen. Basel is the greatest transit centre in Switzerland and accounts for a third of the country's customs dues. Wholesaling, banking, and collection and distribution rank high among the city's functions.

The Rhine traffic has played a small part in the recent growth of Basel and in the sum-total of its traffic as compared with the railways. Passenger traffic on the river ceased in 1843. At the beginning of this century attempts were made to develop goods traffic between Basel and Mannheim. A harbour was opened on the left bank at St. Johann in 1907–11, and in 1919–26 a new harbour was built on the right bank at Klein-Hüningen with silos, warehouses, and oil tanks, and connections with the Reichsbahn. Both harbours had a traffic in the middle 'twenties of about 1·5 million tons (3·0 million in 1937), but this is a modest total and varies from year to year according to the conditions of navigation on the river—depending mainly on the vagaries of the rainfall.[1] The shallows below Basel at Istein could not be crossed at low water, and at high water only with tugs.[2] Upstream paddle steamers draw one or two barges of 300 to 1,400 tons with an average load of 500 tons in 25 to 30 hours from Strasbourg to Basel. Downstream traffic, a quarter of the upstream traffic, takes 4 to 5 hours. There is a canal link at Hüningen with the

---

[1] Compare this with the goods traffic of the railways in 1925 :—

		1925	(1938)
Schweizer Bundesbahn	. .	4·7 million tons	(4·6)
Deutsche Reichsbahn	. .	2·9 ,,	—
Elsässer Bahn	. .	3·8 ,,	—
Rheinhafen (1925)	. .	0·9 ,,	—
Rheinhafen (1926)	. .	0·3 ,,	(2·7)

[2] This barrier is to-day avoided by a side-canal from Kembs (Grand Canal d'Alsace), with barrage and locks.

Rhine–Rhône canal for 300-ton barges, though navigation is uncertain ; it is used for bringing coal up from Strasbourg. The projects for the improvement of this canal, as of the side-canal through Alsace, and for improving the Rhine upstream to Lake Constance,[1] are of peculiar concern to Basel.

(6) General Features of Urban Growth.

All the principal traits and trends in the development of the modern city are illustrated by Basel on a sufficiently small scale to be clearly grasped in their essentials. Thus, we note the formation of the pre-modern town with its medieval nucleus at a focus of natural and man-made routes, compact in area as defined by the river front and by its walls, and clearly marked in the modern plan by the lay-out of its streets and the congestion of its buildings. From this nucleus, and mainly outside the walls, the built-up areas have extended along the principal roads of approach to the city. This form of linear growth, known in our age as ribbon development, is a fundamental natural mode of urban topographic expansion. A main focus of attraction in all 19th century growth was the railway centre, and towards it the principal business centre of the city tended to shift from the medieval core, often to open land along the site of the ancient walls or to more open land outside them. In addition to uncontrolled linear development, there occurred, as in the 17th and 18th centuries, instances of planned lay-outs with a rectangular arrangement, designed as good residential quarters. With rapid territorial expansion there came specialization of function by districts, the industrial areas in particular seeking the open land alongside the railways, which was also the low-lying land, normally along or near the river. The walls set barriers to expansion until their destruction towards the end of the last or the early years of this century. The growth during the modern period, which we may take as beginning with the advent of cheap and rapid transport and the general improvement in urban amenities, began towards the end of the 19th century. It is marked above all else by the wide expansion of the urban areas outwards along the routes and to old villages and towns on the margins, such areas being mainly residential, though they have also attracted non-residential functions, especially industries. The counterpart to this expansion is the growth of business in the centre, resulting in the formation

[1] There are barrages with locks and power plants at Augst-Wyhlen, Rheinfelden and Nieder-Schwörstadt.

of the central business district. This is concentrated in part in the old medieval town. The latter, however, normally has narrow streets and its buildings are old, derelict, and ill-adapted to new uses. Consequently, it has often become a slum, and the same conditions spread from the centre outwards, affecting buildings usually according to their age. There is a tendency, well marked in big cities, for new immigrants to settle in makeshift cheap quarters in these slum areas or on their margins, and for the old settled native inhabitants, seeking better living conditions, to shift outwards to newer houses. The business district needs new buildings—shops, offices and public buildings. Space for these is assured by the demolition of old property. But often these new buildings find sites on the line of the demolished town walls, which are frequently followed by fine boulevards. There is also a tendency for the new business district to shift in two directions : on the one hand towards the railway station, taking up a place between it and the old town ; and on the other hand, towards the areas of most prosperous residential settlement with the greatest buying power and demanding the best shops. A further trait of urban development, especially in the last fifty years, is the emergence of sub-commercial centres in the newly developed residential districts. This has come about with the spread of commercial and social services, the bank, the multiple shop, the cinema, and so on. For centuries the principal binding force in community life in the town was the church, and the church dominated the lay-out of numerous urban districts as the original centre of the newly established parishes. The modern substitute for this is the commercial sub-centre which, through the accretion of shops and offices, etc., serves essentially the same district and often assumes real neighbourhood significance. Places of worship are to-day more sporadically distributed and do not exhibit such marked nucleation around these centres, except when the latter have themselves grown around an old nucleus. Lastly, the expansion of the city in the last twenty-five years has been marked particularly by the deterioration of the centre, and by the spread outwards of both residence and industry and by the increasing grip of the city on the life of the surrounding towns and countryside.

CHAPTER 6

THE STRUCTURE OF THE GERMAN CITY

The first chapters have been concerned with the character and processes of urban growth and areal differentiation within the urban habitat. Groups of small towns in Sweden, Switzerland and France have been studied as illustrations of how urban communities develop. The brief study of Basel has served to show the distinctive processes which characterize the growth of a larger city. The analysis of Basel is also designed to demonstrate the geographic methods employed in the study of the urban habitat.

The study of some of the larger urban agglomerations is the concern of the next chapters. There are many aspects to such study, and a detailed analysis of some of them requires a selection of particular phases in different cities which have been especially studied by other investigators. The study is also based on a standardized classification and zonal grouping of the main types of urban structures. The basic instruments employed are the maps of the urban areas, and these are likewise fundamental to the general conclusions in the second part of the book.

These maps are selected from a series prepared for all the cities of western Europe with over 100,000 inhabitants on a scale of 1 : 25,000 from the standard maps of the countries concerned. The facts shown, drawn from these sources, are mapped with standard symbols. The whole urban area of each city is divided into zones that are uniform in their build. These zones are illustrated from Cologne on Plate 4. Their features may be summarized as follows. The historic town within its late medieval walls is fully built-up with buildings and streets. It is marked by a quite distinctive pattern from the rest of the city, and has usually become the central business district of the modern city. A second type of area surrounds this, and was built-up in the latter half of the 19th century. It is a zone of tenements built on a rectilinear grid of streets. The building blocks are completely built-up, owing to the absence at that time of municipal building restrictions, and there are many small factories and workshops mixed up with the tenements. The tenements are obsolescent, there is practically no enclosed open space in the blocks behind them, there are no private gardens and no public open spaces. This zone merges into one of similar general character but with a smaller proportion built-up in the blocks ; the tenement is dominant, although there are also better-class houses that have now deteriorated ; here too there are usually fewer factories, and it is more exclusively a living quarter. Finally, on the outskirts are the sub-urban areas in which rows of newer tenements or country houses of the more wealthy or, more rarely on the Continent, single-family houses for the working people, are interspersed with open rural areas ; these have been built almost entirely since 1918. These four categories cover the residential areas, the mixed areas and the central old town that is now the business district.

Next, the industrial areas are shown. These are areas in which factories and yards cover the whole ground space and are sufficiently large to be blocked out on the scale of 1 : 25,000. They are located almost entirely on the outskirts of the city. In some cases such factories are located in residential areas, and they are then shown by the industrial shading overlapping the appropriate built-up shading. Railways, goods and marshalling yards, and river wharves are also shown, in solid black. Public buildings are shown by a distinct shading. The representation of these is difficult when the base map has to be reduced to 1 : 50,000 or even 1 : 75,000. In general, we have blocked out main areas, that are clearly recognizable on this scale, in which public buildings are dominant. Such areas form distinct quarters or zones. They include administrative buildings, hospitals, clinics, university buildings, and barracks (the latter often a very conspicuous feature in large garrison cities). The old town centre contains nearly all the ancient monuments and buildings, which often lie alongside modern structures, so that they are not shown separately. Open spaces, main squares and boulevards and principal roads are also shown. Brick works on the outskirts of a city are often so conspicuous as to merit a special symbol. Inside the old town we have also shown the stages of growth of the medieval nucleus, so that one can see at a glance how the historic city has grown into shape.

Thus, each city falls into clearly defined zones, each distinct in its predominant combination of land uses and consequently as to its economic and demographic character. These zones, in their location, extent and character, depend on both physical and historical conditions, and have their hub in the central core. The latter formerly contained within its walls all the city's activities, but during the last hundred years or less has become, with an increasing tempo of change, the specialized focus for the activities of the whole expanded urban complex.

The foregoing statement of procedure is, in effect, a summary of the structure of the modern urban complex and, in particular, of the complex that had its nucleus in a historic city. It is a general interpretation based on detailed studies of many cities before the method of representation used on the maps was decided upon. The following case studies of German, French and other continental cities will reveal the validity of these conclusions and bring out any deviations from them.

(1) COLOGNE [1] (Figs. 18, 19 and Plates 3 and 4)

(a) Location, Site and Development

Cologne is situated on the left bank of the Rhine in the centre of a bay of fertile lowland that juts south into the great block of the Rhine Plateau. It lies at a focus of routes the chief of which run northwards along the Rhine valley and from east to west along the northern edge of the plateau. The city is framed in its nearer surroundings by the low ridge known as the Ville to the west of it, stretching from south-east to north-west, and the low, wooded country to the east of the Rhine that borders the edge of the Rhine Plateau.

It was with their usual keen appreciation of terrain that the Romans chose this site for their camp—the Colonia Claudia Agrippensis—for here is the last point at which firm rising ground reaches the river bank before the flood plain widens northwards and makes approaches to the river difficult. It should be emphasized, however, at the outset that Cologne was not a bridge-town. The river was far too wide for bridging until the 19th century, and has always played the rôle of a frontier in the political divisions of the lowland. In fact the early significance of Cologne was as an outpost against the non-Roman lands to the east. Also the main north–south Roman road, which continued in the Middle Ages and to this day to be a great trade artery,

---

[1] Cologne is now in ruins and its normal relations to its environs completely disrupted. These will, however, be re-established, and the following study, though based on statistics twenty years old, affords a good average picture of the structure of this great inland metropolis.

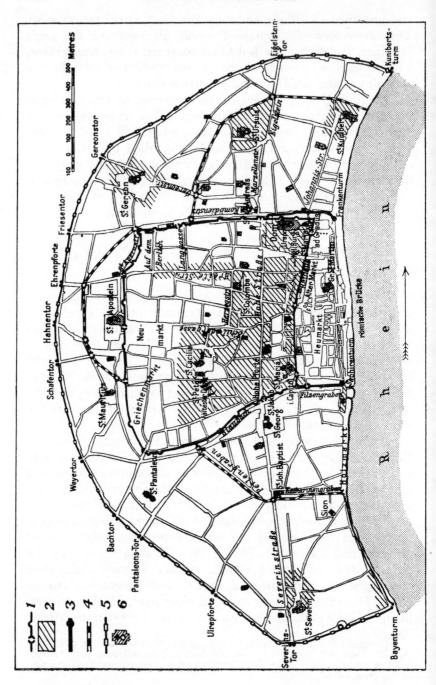

formed the axis of the old town along what is locally called the Hohe Strasse.

Thus established as a Roman centre, Cologne early became the seat of a bishopric, and grew to be one of the greatest commercial centres in the Europe of the Middle Ages. It lay at the junction of the great east–west highway from Flanders to eastern Germany and of the north–south route from the towns of north Italy and south Germany along the Rhine valley to Flanders and the northern ports. Like many other cities of less importance in the Rhinelands the political disintegration of the lands around it after the 16th century hampered the free flow of goods and restricted relations with its region. Cologne was an Imperial Free City, but immediately beyond its boundaries lay the territory of the archbishop of Cologne, extending as a long belt on the west side of the Rhine from near Bonn to Krefeld, while to the west and east, stretching on to the edges of the Rhine plateau, were the extensive territories of the dukes of Jülich and Berg respectively. At the beginning of the 19th century the city fell to the Prussians and was then developed as a frontier fortress against France and passed through a period of relative decline. The chief administrative centres of the newly established Rhineland province were located at Koblenz and Düsseldorf. The old University, which dated from the 14th century, was closed down (to the profit of Bonn), and the Technical High School founded in later years to serve west Germany was placed at Aachen. The new University in Cologne was established in the present century. Cologne's administrative status has been confined to its function as the centre of a *Regierungsbezirk*. It is thus pre-eminently an economic metropolis, a seat of the skilled industries of its past, producing high-quality finished goods, as well as of the heavy engineering and other industries that have developed in the last two generations. It is also a pre-eminent seat of commerce, serving the daily needs of its inhabitants and industries, as well as taking a large share of the goods and of the organization of the Rhineland province and neighbouring lands in north-west Germany.

The city is sited on flat land on the left bank of the Rhine and has a marked spider-web plan. (Fig. 19.) This is due to the normal

---

Fig. 18.—The Historic City of Cologne (from Aubin & Niessen). (Scale, 1 : 22,500.)

1. Roman walls. 2. Settled area about A.D. 900. 3. First extension of the Rheinvorstadt in the 10th century. 4. Extension in 1106. 5. Extension in 1180 (the final medieval wall). 6. Churches.

tendency for routes to radiate from a town centre, coupled with the concentric semi-circular belt of its ancient town walls and its series of 19th-century fortifications. Four zones may be recognized in the build of the city area on the left bank—the inner old town (*Altstadt, Ring,* and *Neustadt*), the inner suburbs (*Vorstädte*), the outer suburbs (*Vororte*), and the outer industrial-agricultural areas that are allied, socially and economically, in varying degree with the city.

(*b*) *Inner Town (Altstadt–Ring–Neustadt).*[1]

Cologne has grown from its nucleus in the rectangular Roman *castrum* of Colonia (Figs. 18 and 19). The *Rheinvorstadt,* a narrow strip between the reoccupied Christian settlement in the *castrum* and the Rhine front, was incorporated in the 10th century (992) as a new trading centre (*mercatus coloniae*). At the end of the 12th century the buildings that had grown on the roads just outside the Roman walls were enclosed by a new wall, semi-circular in shape, which is still easily traceable in the town by the lay-out of its streets and by its remains. Against this wall the new Prussian fortifications were built in the 1820s, the whole of which in turn were destroyed in the 1880s and replaced by the *Ring*— a wide semi-circular ring of boulevards—and the streets on the Rhine front. The medieval town (the *Altstadt*) had an area of 400 hectares or 1,000 acres and a total circumference of 8 km. and a Rhine frontage of about 2,500 metres. After the demolitions of the 'eighties a new semi-circular system of fortifications was built about 600 metres from the medieval walls, and between the two the semi-circular belt of the *Neustadt* was developed. In the *Altstadt* there were some open spaces to the north and south (gardens, orchards, and vineyards) where new factories and streets were built. Congestion, through the addition of railway tracks and stations, barracks, and public buildings, as well as of commercial premises, was already apparent in the 'forties. Industry in the *Altstadt* was necessarily confined to numerous small concerns demanding little space, in office, warehouse, and home ; and larger factories had to be built outside it. The *Altstadt* became increasingly the centre of city affairs. The districts between it and the fortifications were being rapidly built-up as working-class quarters, though some old burgesses' families retain their old houses in the city. The *Neustadt,* which grew with extraordinary

---

[1] Bruno Kuske, *Die Grossstadt Köln als Wirtschaftlicher und Sozialer Körper,* 1928, pp. 1–24.

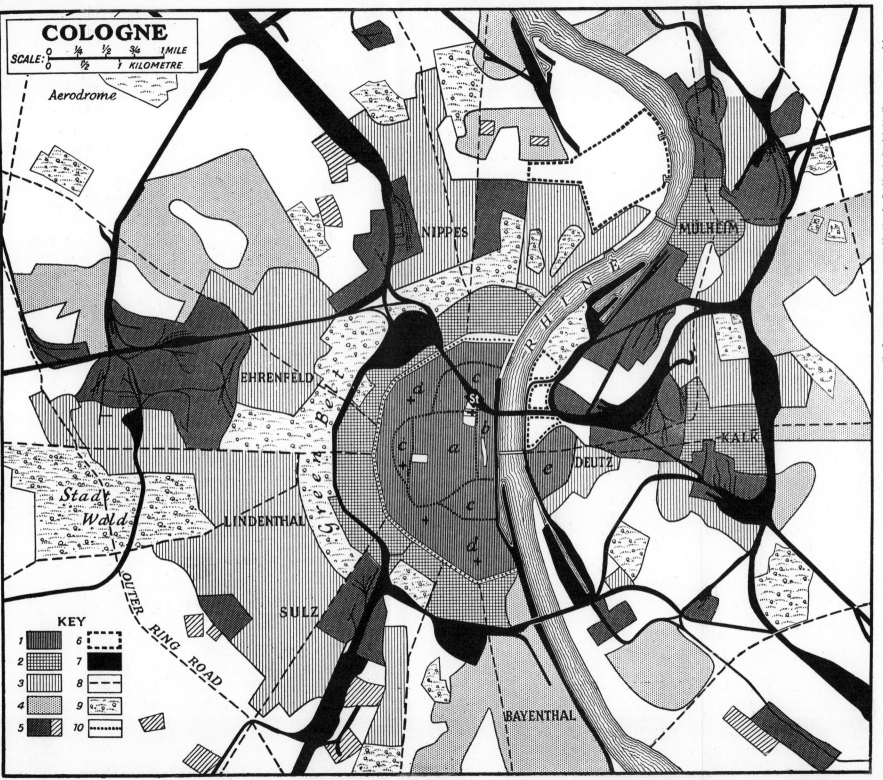

COLOGNE

SCALE: 0 1/4 1/2 3/4 1 MILE
0 1/2 1 KILOMETRE

Aerodrome

NIPPES

MÜLHEIM

RHINE

EHRENFELD

Green Belt

St

c a c

KALK

DEUTZ

Stadt Wald

LINDENTHAL

c

d

e

OUTER RING ROAD

SULZ

BAYENTHAL

KEY

1   6
2   7
3   8
4   9
5   10

FIG. 19.—The Functional Zones of Cologne. (Scale, 1 : 50,000.)

1. Central or Inner Zone. 2. Middle Fully Built-up Zone. 3. Middle Partly Built-up Zone. 4. Outer or Sub-urban Zone. 5. Industrial Zones, with separate indication of brickworks. 6. Public buildings. 7. Railways, goods and marshalling yards. 8. Main roads from the inner town. 9. Parks and public spaces. 10. Medieval walls dividing the sectors of the old town. The old town falls into the following parts : (a) earliest town on site of the Roman castrum, (b) the Rheinvorstadt (992), (c) areas enclosed by walls in 1106, (d) areas enclosed by walls in 1180.

rapidity in the last decades of the 19th century, served as an over-flow from the *Altstadt* for housing, as well as for offices, public buildings and factories that needed more space. The railway goods station was built between the fortifications and the inner town, and the main passenger station was located in the heart of the city next to the cathedral. The whole city suffered from congestion owing to the barrier of the fortifications. This was aggravated by the fact that along the new wall (1880s) encircling railway tracks were built, and on their outer side a belt 500–600 metres wide (called the *Innerer Rayonbezirk*) was closed to permanent building, as in Paris and other big continental cities, and was used for all sorts of undesirable temporary, makeshift purposes. This inner system of fortifications became, in effect, obsolete almost as soon as complete, and was completely demilitarized between 1906 and 1914. In 1897 plans were already being discussed for shifting the fortified belt outwards to the circle of detached forts that had been erected between 1873 and 1881 beyond the *Vororte*, so as to form an outer fortified zone (*äusserer Rayonbezirk*). This was begun in 1906. The building on the inner belt was, however, rigidly controlled by the city authorities, unlike *Neustadt*, where building on the rectangular pattern of blocks proceeded without restriction. Open spaces were fixed at 60 per cent. of the area and buildings were limited to two and three storeys except on certain specified streets. It was intended to use the outermost area on the edge of the built-up *Vororte* and as far as the outer fortifications for peripheral uses such as cemeteries, an airfield, municipal public utility services, railway tracks, and factories. Then after 1918 came the problem of uniting the inner town—*Altstadt* and *Neustadt*—with the suburbs (or *Vorstädte*) that had grown around and outside this wide "fortified" belt. The city administrative limits ended at the inner fortifications. Beyond, for centuries, it was ringed in by the independent bishop's State of Kurköln, so that the suburbs were independent of the city.

(c) Inner and Outer Suburbs (Vorstädte and Vororte).

In 1888 these districts were finally annexed by the city. The suburbs outside the fortified zone grew up in the first half of the 19th century as independent administrative units—both towns and villages—two or three kilometres from the centre of the city. They rapidly assumed full urban character, as sites for villa residential quarters, but, above all, for new industries. Thus developed Nippes, Ehrenfeld, Bayenthal, and Lindenthal, each a separate built-up area, with its axis on a main radial route from the city, and each occupying a sector of a great semi-circle round the city of Cologne. These districts were not annexed to the city until 1888, the first and most essential expansion of its area.

At last the right bank was drawn into the orbit of urban development. Here the only settlement hitherto had been the small fortified bridgehead settlement of Deutz, designed to protect the approach to Cologne across the Rhine. But Deutz was founded by the State of Kurköln and was an independent town and neglected by its bishop-rulers. The wide river Rhine, which was without fixed bridges until late in the 19th century, though not a national or political boundary, was for centuries a frontier between the German States and communes on its banks, and the right bank had no important towns until the development of modern industry in the late 19th century. The lack of bridges presented a problem that was common to the Rhine cities, all of which lay on the west bank of the Rhine. The annexation of Deutz by Cologne was not effected until 1888. The Prussian fortifications around Deutz, built as part of the city's defences, were even more confined than the latter. This affected the building of railways that were laid out as an independent rail terminal opposite Cologne before the first fixed iron bridge across the Rhine was built in 1859. Here, in contrast to the finished and skilled industries handled by small concerns in Cologne, heavy engineering and chemical industries, with extensive plant layouts, grew up together with working-class quarters on the open land near the railways and the river at Mülheim and Kalk.

Since 1900 the open spaces between these inner suburbs (*Vorstädte*) have been steadily filled in by new goods stations, new industrial plants, and workers' dwelling quarters, which spread especially along the right bank in the district of Poll. But in Cologne itself building along the Rhine was forbidden by the old military regulations. Thus the city could not take advantage of its favourable situation next to the Rhine for the transport of heavy raw materials like other Rhine cities.

The *Vorstädte*, though politically independent until 1888, were so near to the city that they were both economically and culturally a part of it. This resulted in the great concentration of urban centralized services in the *Altstadt*, such as shops, hotels, restaurants, places of amusement, and the offices of industrial concerns with their plants in the suburbs. This is particularly true of the big concerns on the right bank. Here there was no business centre, although after the war of 1914–18 the city government sought to raise the tone of the east side by building the Fair and Exhibition Buildings there. Routes ran radially from the inner town and the building of interconnecting ring roads in the fortified zone was forbidden. The net result was a great concentration of traffic in the *Altstadt* which, coupled with the extreme narrowness of its streets, caused it to be one of the most congested city centres in Germany.

(d) Post-1918 Extensions of the Administrative Area.

The conditions of the peace settlement at the end of the First World War resulted in the complete demilitarization of the outer circle of forts. This facilitated the expansion of the great city complex, notably the establishment of industrial sites on the Rhine. Improved diagonal and circular roads, and the great expansion of the housing area were other beneficial results. This expansion, which had begun during the 19th century, was reflected in the periodic extension of the administrative limits of the city. The first big expansion in 1888 added the inner suburbs of Deutz, Nippes, Ehrenfeld, and Bayenthal, the city area being thus increased by about 10,000 hectares or 25,000 acres, to reach 27,500 acres. With the absorption of the places on the right bank (Cologne was the first city in Germany to effect such a change), bridges had to be built to serve local traffic, for the existing bridges served primarily for long-distance railway traffic. The pontoon bridge to Deutz was replaced by a great suspension bridge. Further, new harbours and stations were needed in symmetrical arrangement to balance the industrial needs of the right bank and handle the in and out traffic in all directions. More right bank annexations were made in 1910 and 1914, bringing the city to its present eastern limits which are bounded by a belt of woodland. Cologne now had a symmetrical shape on both banks, its frontiers to north and south lying opposite to each other on the Rhine. The Rhine frontage measured 14 km. on each bank and the city stretched about 21 km. at its widest from east to west.

But expansion had not ceased. With a view to acquiring land for industrial sites and a harbour on the Rhine front, extensive open areas were acquired to the north along the Rhine in 1922. These had hitherto been a part of the old fortified zone with training grounds, shooting ranges and forts. This latest accession forms an isolated prong jutting northwards from the compact administrative area. ˙ Opposite the northern prong are the great chemical works of Leverkusen and Wiesdorf. The total administrative area amounts to 251 sq. km. (about 100 sq. miles) with a circumference of 120 km. It is second in area of the German cities after Berlin. The area on the left bank of the Rhine covers 152 sq. km. and that on the right bank 99 sq. km., whereas the *Altstadt* and *Neustadt* together make up 1,000 hectares or only 4 per cent. of the whole area.

This great city area is now a suitable political unit for long-term physical planning. Only a quarter of it is in urban use. Planning problems await the city, but these, as compared with English conditions, are eased by the facts that, first, the greater part of the actual and potential city settlement area can take place within its boundaries ; and second, the city owns a third of the land, the use of which it is thus in a position to control.

(e) Outer Settlement Area.

The settlement area of Cologne is not limited to the administrative area, extensive as this is. The areas around the city boundaries that are closely allied—socially and economically—with the city centre had 300,000 inhabitants in 1939, so that the population of the total Cologne city complex was about one million, and this area, through the absence of close competing cities, is relatively clearly defined.

The division between the left and right bank sectors is fundamental. The right bank districts do not extend so far as the left bank districts, and the neighbouring places not absorbed into the city, though closely allied with it, are more populous on the right than on the left bank. On the right bank there is an alternation of small agricultural and industrial settlements. On the left bank lies the extensive brown coal field in the Ville district that runs as a strip from north-west to south-east. This field produces 30 per cent. of Germany's enormous output of brown coal. It has great electricity plants, which supply power to Cologne, the Ruhr and throughout north-west Germany, as well as briquette, brick, and other works. Here there is a north–south series of small industrial centres 10 to 15 km. apart, all of them old agricultural villages that have been industrialized. To the north-west, the brown coalfield extends beyond the sphere of Cologne's influence, although economic organization is controlled from it. In the south, especially around Bruhl and Rondorf, are the chief industrial plants—power plants, metals, chemicals, sugar, margarine, and brewing industries. On the Rhine front at Wesseling is the big brown coal harbour. South of the city, towards Bonn, there is a concentration of market gardening, grouped about the villages at the edge of the Ville and adjoining the brown coalfield.

The whole of this outer zone is a transition belt from the city area to the open country, in which industries are based in large measure on local resources—sugar, brown coal, and stones and earths. Established within it are those industries which sell their products in the Cologne market, and take advantage of local labour and cheap land. In 1925, of the 133,000 persons employed throughout this zone, 14,000 (10·5 per cent.) worked in Cologne. There was then a larger proportion of these city workers on the left than on the right bank, where local industry is more widely scattered. Further, a larger proportion of city workers was drawn from the agricultural parishes, except for the market-gardening districts where the cityward movement is small. There is also a considerable daily movement of workers from the city to the brown coal quarries. Women city workers come less frequently from the farming districts where they are indispensable on the farms, than from the industrial districts (as in the brown coal area), where there is little employment for them in industry. Families in outer residential districts, however, send a larger proportion of their daughters to work in the city.

The character and intensity of this movement depend on local transport facilities. The environs of Cologne were served about 1930 by 12 electric railways and 23 longer omnibus lines, with terminals averaging 30 to 40 km. from the city centre, though some reached distances of over 70 km. The longest of these 35 lines have branch routes 10 to 20 km. long, especially on the right bank as far as the edge of the hills towards the Solingen area. Here the belt of woodland serves as a main attraction for outings and recreation. The main railways parallel to the river keep well away from its banks, so that villages on the Rhine are somewhat isolated and unaffected by urban trends. Until the advent of the electric railway these were connected with Cologne by steamboat.

(f) *Distribution of Population.*

The population of Cologne was about 700,000 in 1925, 756,500 in 1933, and 768,000 in 1939—it was thus the third city in the

Reich, next after Berlin and Hamburg. The population of the whole area increased by 17 per cent. from 1910 to 1925, and by 9·7 per cent. from 1925 to 1939. The *Altstadt* has been declining since 1900 and the *Neustadt*, after an insignificant increase of 11 per cent. in the 1910–25 period, decreased by 14 per cent. from 1925 to 1939. In 1939 the *Altstadt* and *Neustadt* together had 260,000 inhabitants, with a density of 290 persons per hectare of total area. Below the average increase in this period (1910–39) were also the old inner suburbs (*Vorstädte*). But large increases are recorded in the south-west, and in the north-east and south-east districts on the right bank of the river Rhine, which together had 196,000 people on a third of the total area in 1939. In aggregate, the outer suburbs (*Vororte*) increased by 40 per cent. as compared with the *Altstadt* and *Neustadt*, which decreased by only 6 per cent.

It is of interest to compare these population data with the main types of land use. In the *Altstadt* and *Neustadt* combined one-half of the total area was occupied by buildings, yards and private gardens, a third by streets, places, railways and public open spaces, and 3 per cent. by public buildings. In other words, nearly 90 per cent. of the whole area was built-up. There are no cemeteries or fortifications, and water and rural land covered a small fraction of the total (60 and 67 hectares respectively). Of the circle of suburbs on the left bank, just under twenty per cent. was built-up (buildings, streets, railways and public open spaces), whereas nearly three-quarters were classified as in rural uses. In the industrial and railway sectors on the right bank, about 20 per cent. was built-up and three-quarters was in rural uses.

(2) BRESLAU (Fig. 20 and Plate 6)

(a) Location, Site and Development

Breslau is a compact and densely populated city, which in 1925 had 552,000 people living on an administrative area of 12,500 acres. In 1928 the area was greatly extended, adding 50 square miles and 70,000 people, so that by 1933 Greater Breslau had an area of nearly 70 square miles and a population of 620,000 inhabitants.

Let us first consider the origin and topographic formation of old Breslau (Fig. 20). Several distinct sectors are recognizable in its ground-plan. The cathedral quarter and the adjacent group of churches stand out to the north of the old town, situated on the islands called the *Dominsel* and the *Sandinsel*. On the south bank of the Oder is the town proper. Along the river there is an irregular group of blocks ending in the irregularly shaped Ritterplatz. Next comes the regular rectangular plan of the core of the modern city with its square market-place, the *Ring*, and a regular disposition of rectangular blocks around it. A second market—the *Neumarkt*—lies on the eastern margin of this plan. Then there is a more irregular group of blocks east of the *Neumarkt* without a market-place. This is called the *Neustadt*. Between the *Altstadt* and the *Neustadt* a main street runs from south to north, skirting the Ritterplatz and then crossing the Sand island. This is the oldest highway in Breslau ; it was the main route from Bohemia to Poland, and used the easiest crossing of the Oder. Finally, there is the semicircular belt around the old town. This is composed of two, or in places three, parallel curved streets, beyond which there is a wider, open zone on the site of the 16th-century fortifications that were demolished in the first years of the 19th century.

The initial Slav settlement lay along the Bohemian highway that crossed the river by the Sand island, with its centre in the Ritterplatz as its market, and with the Adalbert church to the south (adjacent to the Dominikaner Platz) at a convergence of routes. German settlers were clustered around the latter. The bishopric was established in A.D. 1000, and the cathedral lay on what was then an island east of the Sand island and off the main route. Here was a cluster of churches before the eve of the Mongol destruction, which occurred in 1241, when the town was burnt to the ground. The Herzog Boleslaw then founded a new town which was laid out as a German settlement on the grid plan of the *Kolonialstadt*. This was provided with a vast central market-place—the *Ring*. A second market, the *Neumarkt*, was opened a few years later on the eastern side of the town adjacent to the ancient south–north highway. There were also two parish churches, one for the merchants (Elisabeth Church) and one for the craftsmen (Maria Magdalen, which was founded before 1241). Merchants' houses lined the west and south sides of the *Ring*, and their buildings extended behind, as is evidenced by such street names as Herrenstrasse and Junkernstrasse. The crafts-men's houses lined the north and east sides and spread back from them, as is proved by such street names as Kupferstrasse and Schmiederstrasse. The Herzog had his residence and held the land on the north side of the town bordering the river. There were two lines of defences around the town, an inner palisade

(*Wall*) and a dry ditch, with a second ditch 300 metres outside. The area inside the first ditch must have been quickly built up, for in 1261, with the consent of the Herzog, the town was extended to the limits of the outer ditch. Two streets emerged parallel with the inner ditch, one outside, the other inside it. The inner *Wall* and *Graben* were replaced by a stone wall (*Mauer*) in 1272, and in 1291 Henry V diverted the Ohle river along the outer ditch that had hitherto been dry (*Stadtohle*). This was not filled in till 1866, and since then has formed a middle street, or, where there are only two, the inner of the ring streets. This town covered 150 acres.

The foundation of the *Neustadt* took place in 1263. Founded by Henry III as a competitor to the *Altstadt*, it was sited to the east of it, adjacent to the east side of the main south–north highway. But as it lay between the two arms of the river Ohle and the Oder there was no room for expansion ; it also had no marketplace. In 1327 it was absorbed by the *Altstadt*, though retaining some of its independence until the 16th century, when it was embraced by the new town walls and became an integral part of the town.

Owing to the spread of buildings to the zone between the inner and outer ditches, a new wall was begun in 1330 to embrace the territory annexed in 1261. Outside this new wall was the great ditch called the *Stadtgraben*. Thus the town had a double girdle of water, the Ohle and the Stadtgraben, and was bounded northwards by the Oder. In the 17th century the town defences were strengthened. Breslau was a fortress. Fortifications were built on the Vauban system with eleven bastions, and the Stadtgraben was much widened. These defences were removed in the first years of the 19th century.

The massive defences of the 17th century cut off the town from its environs, and there was little change in its extent until the 19th century. The *Vorstädte* were legally independent of the *Stadt* and their chief landowners were the bishop and the monasteries with lands to the north along the river and on the islands. It was not until 1808 that the *Vorstädte* were finally brought into the full jurisdiction of the town. Thus at this time the town was enlarged in area by 5,000 acres and in population by 14,000 inhabitants, and in 1888 the total population of the whole town, including its garrison, was about 65,000.

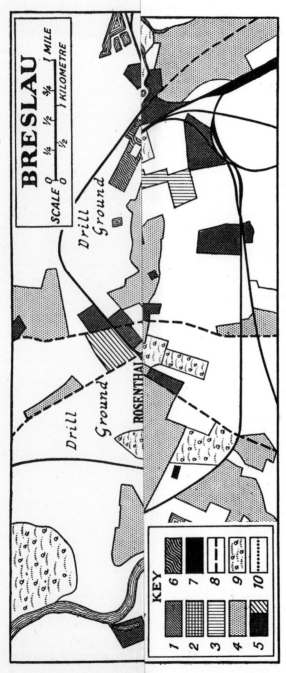

Fig. 20.—The Functional Zones of Breslau. (Scale, 1 : 50,000.)

1. Central or Inner Zone. 2. Middle Fully Built-up Zone. 3. Middle Partly Built-up Zone. 4. Outer Sub-urban Zone. 5. Industrial Zones, with separate indication of brickworks (none shown). 6. Public buildings. 7. Railways, goods and marshalling yards. 8. Main roads from the inner town. 9. Parks and public spaces. 10. Medieval walls in the inner town. There are three sectors in the historic town : (a) the cathedral quarter, north of the Oder (not numbered), (b) the Altstadt, (c) the Neustadt and extensions to the limits of the last medieval wall. Names indicate districts (Vierteln), as listed in the table on p. 95.

(b) *Functional Zones* (Fig. 20)

During the 19th century the advent of the railway tracks, coupled with the division made by the Oder and the girdle of defences round the old town, split up the town as a whole into distinct sectors. In the west, the railway divided the Nikolaivorstadt, which became a thickly populated tenement district for industrial workers, from the south-west, which extended, like the former, along a main radial highway. To the south there developed the most exclusive residential sector, since it was relatively isolated from both rail and radial road ; to-day building here extends south to the belt line. To the south-east is a large marshalling yard alongside which has developed a new settlement planned on garden city lines with 9,000 inhabitants. South of the Oder Breslau thus falls into four clearly defined outside sectors.

North of the Oder the pattern is more complicated. Two districts stand out clearly. The Bürgerwerder was chosen by Frederick the Great as the barracks and training quarters for the army. The cathedral quarter, with the cathedral and other churches and public buildings, lies on both the islands and includes the strip of land on the south side of the river adjacent to the old town. Extension to the east along the Oder and to the north was slow and uncontrolled. But a big expansion has taken place in more recent years, and this is now one of the best quarters of Breslau. It embraces the Scheitniger Park, containing the Jahrhunderthalle (Exhibition Hall), an enormous sports stadium, the zoological gardens, and the new exclusive residential settlements of Zimpel and Bishofswalde. To the north-east, the ship canal between Bartheln and Karlowitz and a main railway route to Upper Silesia provides the only place in the region where large industrial plants may be sited. These are found north of Karlowitz and Rosenthal.

An urban–rural fringe surrounds the city. To the west and south this lies inside the new city boundaries. To the north and east, factories and marshalling yards and villages are all allied with the life of the city, but actually lie outside its boundaries.

The map of the present structure of the city (Fig. 20) reveals the main zones into which it falls. The old town is the chief business area, with a great concentration of commercial and administrative activities in multi-storeyed buildings of various dates, public buildings, and old buildings of brick adapted to modern uses. The southern and central portions of the old town are almost exclusively commercial and administrative, but in the northern portion (north of the Ring) there are thickly populated tenement blocks.

An open belt on the site of the old fortifications surrounds the old town. Beyond this belt there are compact fully built-up residential areas interspersed with non-residential districts. The inner residential areas are almost entirely made up of tenement blocks. According to the density of population per acre of building, Breslau ranks with Berlin and Hamburg as one of the three most densely populated cities in Germany.[1] These inner districts thus fall into clearly defined sectors. Outlying recent " suburban areas " are not characteristic, since most of the population lives in old or new tenements in the town itself. An exception is found to the east of the town beyond the Oder. Here are parks, exhibition grounds, the Zoological Gardens, and an extensive area of high-class houses and modern flats (the Zimpel district). To the north of the city is the so-called Garden City of Karlowitz. These outlying areas are designed primarily for the more wealthy classes, not for the lower-paid workers, who are still housed in the urban area proper.

Industrial areas are particularly extensive. There is a great concentration of small firms in shops, warehouses and workshops in the central districts, that do not appear on the map. These are concerned particularly with the textile industries. There are three outstanding districts exclusively devoted to industry in large plant lay-outs. These lie on the outskirts of the urban complex adjacent to the railway tracks to the west (engineering), and to the south-east, around the goods yards (including the gas works). To the north there are separate plants along the railways and the canal ; these include the town harbour and several factories and wharves along the Oder, and, north of the canal, Rosenthal and Karlowitz. There are two main railway stations, known as Breslau-West and Breslau-Ost, near to which there are extensive goods yards and sidings, and adjacent to the latter are large railway workshops. To the south-east of the city is one of the largest marshalling yards in Germany, situated on the main route to Upper Silesia.

---

[1] In the city as a whole there were over 700 tenements housing more than 100 persons each and 15 housing over 200 persons ; see E. Müller, *Die Altstadt von Breslau, Citybildung und Physiognomie : Ein Beitrag zur Stadtgeographie, Schlesische Ges. z. Erdkunde,* 1931.

(c) *Distribution of Population*

Figures for the density of population reveal interesting features. Below are the figures by districts for the city administrative area in 1925. It will be seen that two-thirds of the total population lived in a roughly circular area of about six square miles in extent. The greatest concentrations of tenement blocks with over 100 inhabitants per block are in the Oder, Schweidnitz South, Sand, and Nikolai districts. The distribution of population is shown on Fig. 21.

DENSITY OF POPULATION IN BRESLAU IN 1925
(from E. Müller, *op. cit.*, Table 10, p. 106)

District	Total Area (acres)	% Built-up	Population (000s)	Density per acre Total Area	Density per acre Built-up Area
1. Inner Town . . .	375	77	41	100	140
2. Schweidnitz North .	375	71	45	120	160
3. Oder.	1,250	38	72	56	150
4. Sand	2,500	38	97	36	100
5. Ohlauer	1,100	42	58	53	130
6. Strehlener	1,500	37	45	30	80
7. Schweidnitz South .	3,000	47	103	34	70
8. Nikolai	2,200	46	88	44	90
Breslau (1925) . . .	12,500	45	550	45	100
Greater Breslau . . .	44,000	13	620	13·5	100

The distribution of population shown in the above table may be expressed in another way, by using figures for smaller districts, and arranging them in concentric belts. The figures are old, but nevertheless illustrate important features.

DENSITY OF POPULATION IN BRESLAU BY CONCENTRIC RINGS (1910)
(from Müller)

Km.	Area (hectares)	Population Thousands	% of Total	Density per hectare (acre)
0–1	314	79·3	13	253 (100)
1–2	912	323	53	343 (137)
2–3	1,571	90	14·5	57·2 (23)
3–4	2,199	26·7	4·5	12·2 (5)
4–5	2,827	8·3	1·5	2·9 (1·2)
5–6	3,456	8·5	1·5	2·4 (1·0)
6–7	4,085	16·8	2·6	4·1 (1·6)
7–8	4,712	6	1·0	1·3 (0·5)
8–9	5,341	6·2	1·0	1·2 (0·5)
9–10	5,970	5·2	9·7	0·9 (0·4)
10–·5	39,265	41·8	6·7	1·1 (0·5)
	70,652	611·8	100·0	8·6 (3·4)

DENSITY OF POPULATION IN BRESLAU BY BELTS (1925)
(approximate only)

Belt	Area (acres)	Population (1925)
Central City	750	86,000
Inner Residential Belt . . .	3,000	338,000
Outer Residential Belt . . .	8,750	128,000
Suburban Belt	31,500	68,000
Total Greater Breslau . . .	44,000	620,000

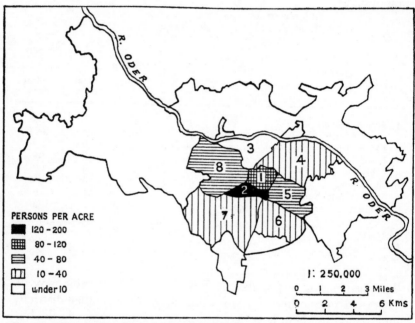

FIG. 21.—The density of population in Greater Breslau. The districts are as listed in the Table on p. 95. (Scale, 1 : 250,000.)

The Inner Town or *Altstadt* has become in increasing measure the central business and commercial district, and, in fact, its centralized functions are spreading beyond the limits of the inner town. The population here in 1800 was 44,000 out of a total for the whole city of about 59,000. By 1860 it reached its maximum of about 70,000. Then came a period of about thirty years in which the population remained fairly steady at about 65,000. In 1890 there were 327,700 people in the whole city and 61,500, or about one-fifth, in the inner town. After 1890 a steady decrease set in, and the population of the *Altstadt* fell to 54,500 in 1900, to 42,800 in 1910, and to 39,600 in 1930. In this last year,

555,600 inhabitants lived in the city as a whole, so that the inner town then contained only about 7 per cent. of the total, as compared with 20 per cent. forty years before. Since 1900, the northern Schweidnitz district and the inner districts of the other *Vorstädte* immediately outside the belt of open land around the old town have shown a decreasing population. This process of *Citybildung* is most marked in the two southern districts of the *Altstadt*, and less advanced in the two northern sectors as noted above. The inner district of the *Vorstädte* which shows the biggest decrease is the northern Schweidnitz district.

(3) HANOVER (Fig. 22)

(a) Location, Site, and Development

At the junction of the central uplands and the northern plain in the valley of the Leine river and its tributary the Ihme, lies the city of Hanover, at the convergence of historic and modern routes from north to south and east to west. The Leine is an historic routeway through the central uplands to Frankfurt, Nuremberg and beyond. The old east–west routes crossed the Leine at Hanover and are now supplemented by the trunk railway from Cologne to Berlin, and the new Mittelland Canal and the Autobahn, both of which lie a few miles to the north of the city.

To the west of the city is the slight but prominent hill known as the Lindener Berg, with a height of 87 metres. The plan of the medieval town is shown on Fig. 98 (p. 378). A slight swell of the chalk rocks affords a relatively easy crossing-place over the river by a low island between the Ihme and the Leine. To north and south the marshy floor of the river bed widens out ; it is to-day an area of low-lying meadow liable to flood. The original Carolingian settlement, a *curia regis*, was situated on the right bank of the river so as to command the crossing. This formed the nucleus of the medieval town that was founded as a market settlement attached to the south side of the *curia*, with two streets parallel to the river and a central market-place and market church. Oval in shape, this settlement received town law in 1241 and was walled in the latter half of the century. The *Neustadt*, first recorded in 1283, lies on the left bank of the river adjacent to the medieval *burg* of Lauenrode which was destroyed in 1371. *Altstadt* and *Neustadt* were enclosed in a single wall in the 17th century but remained legally separate until the 19th century.

In 1636 Hanover became a royal residence and in 1837 the

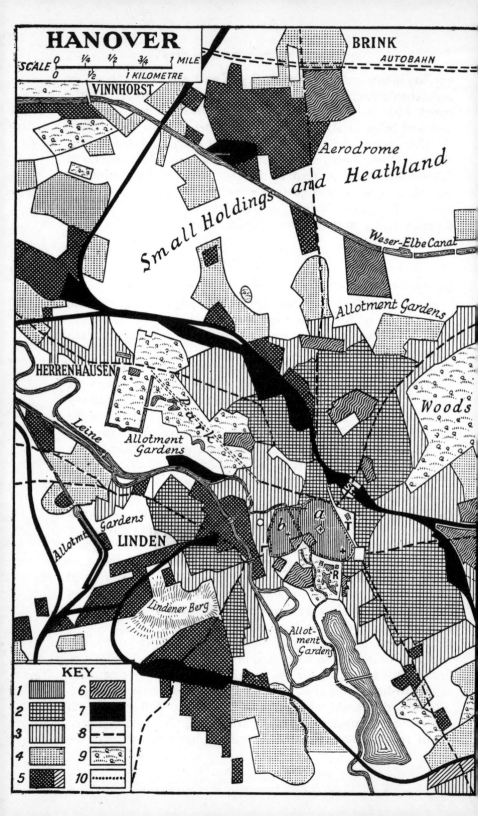

HANOVER

BRINK

AUTOBAHN

SCALE 0 ¼ ½ ¾ 1 MILE
0 ½ 1 KILOMETRE

VINNHORST

Aerodrome

Small Holdings and Heathland

Weser-Elbe Canal

Allotment Gardens

HERRENHAUSEN

Woods

Park

Leine

Allotment Gardens

Allotmt. Gardens

LINDEN

Lindener Berg

Allot-
ment
Gardens

KEY

1		6	
2		7	
3		8	
4		9	
5		10	

capital of the kings of Hanover. It is for this reason that the city owes much of its development and architectural character to the Baroque period. The Royal Palace was built in the 17th century and the Royal Theatre in 1845–52. The Schloss Herrenhausen, situated in the country to the north-west of the city, was a favourite residence of the Georges. It was built in 1698, and the great tree-lined avenue leading to it from the city was laid out in 1726. Finally, its excellent nodal position and its proximity to the Mittelland canal to the north have occasioned the development of large-scale modern industry in recent years, including heavy engineering, rubber, and oil refining.

(b) Functional Zones

The city had about 444,000 inhabitants on 33,000 acres in 1933. The map (Fig. 22) shows that it has a well-defined zonal arrangement. The fully built-up heart of the complex is the old town, in which there were many half-timbered buildings dating from the 15th to the 17th centuries. Around this nucleus were added the extensions of the 17th and 18th centuries. The royal buildings were added on the meadows on the south side of the town. Here are the palace, the new town hall, and barracks, all situated in parkland that leads down to the river. On the eastern side of the town the fortifications were replaced by the Georg Strasse. This is the main modern thoroughfare, on which there are many modern buildings, including the Royal Theatre. There is also a distinct quarter between the Georg Strasse and the railway station, which, as in most other cities, was built-up on the edge of the town towards the station in the latter half of last century. This quarter contains many offices, warehouses, shops and hotels, as well as public buildings. Public buildings are to be found east of the railway grouped around the Law Courts, and also around the Aegidien Platz.

The fully built-up residential areas are very compact except in the south and north-west, where the building is more open and there are public buildings. The average density of population

FIG. 22.—The Functional Zones of Hanover. (Scale, 1 : 50,000.)

1. Central or Inner Zone. 2. Middle Fully Built-up Zone. 3. Middle Partly Built-up Zone. 4. Outer or Sub-urban Zone. 5. Industrial Zones, with separate indication of brickworks. 6. Public buildings. 7. Railways, goods and marshalling yards. 8. Main roads from the inner town. 9. Parks and public spaces. 10. Site of walls surrounding the old town : (a) Altstadt, (b) Neustadt. St. = Station. T = Theatre. R = Rathaus or Town Hall.

in these districts is 100 to 150 persons to the acre of total area and 60 to 75 per cent. of all buildings have four to five storeys. The tenement areas are dovetailed with inner industrial districts, which include relatively small plants in areas that are small and closely built-up. This feature is generally characteristic of the older industrial districts that developed in the latter half of the 19th century. Goods yards and open spaces also help to split up the residential belt into segments. Two inner tenement areas are to be found in Linden west of the Ihme ; one in the north, crossed by railways and factories ; the other in the south-east in a district that was built-up mainly between 1900 and 1914. On the outer side of these tenement areas, and between them and the city centre in the south and north-west, there are less closely built-up districts with densities of 60 to 70 persons per acre. These relatively low densities are to be associated with the better-class single-family residences that were built during the court period of Hanover's history.

Industrial areas fall into two groups, those embedded in the urban complex and those on its periphery. There are two congested industrial sectors in the main urban area, one along the Ihme river, the other in the north along the north side of the railway goods yards. A third and important industrial area lies on the south-western outskirts of the complex and is identified in particular with engineering industries. Miscellaneous industries in small plants are associated with the ribbon extensions to the north-east and south-east of the city. A large new industrial area with heavy industries in extensive plant lay-outs lies along the Mittelland canal.

(c) Distribution of Population

The density and growth of population in Hanover has been studied with some thoroughness by H. Knibbe. Unfortunately the distribution has not been mapped with accuracy ; but figures are given by concentric belts of equal distance from the city centre, as for Breslau. The results are summarized on p. 101.

It will be observed that two-thirds of the total population live within 3 km. (about 2 miles) of the heart of the city, and that the density of resident population is highest, approaching 100 persons per acre, in the central circle of 1 km. ($\frac{5}{8}$ mile) radius. Moreover, the number of people in each concentric belt decreases with increased distance from the centre. This is substantially the same pattern of distribution as in Breslau, except that in

Hanover the densities in the main central urban area are considerably lower than in the same areas of Breslau.

DENSITY OF POPULATION IN HANOVER BY CONCENTRIC RINGS (1931)
(from H. Knibbe)

Km.	Population	% of Total	Density per acre
0–1	74,700	14·4 ⎫	95
1–2	165,700	32·0 ⎬ 66·3	70·5
2–3	103,300	19·9 ⎭	26·5
3–4	39,000	7·5	7·1
4–5	34,700	6·7	4·9
5–6	19,900	3·9	2·3
6–7	11,600	2·3	1·2
7–8	15,100	2·9	1·3
8–9	13,300	2·6	1·0
9–10	5,200	1·0	0·35
10–15	35,500	6·8	0·34
Total	518,000	100	

(4) FRANKFURT-AM-MAIN (Fig. 24 and Plate 5)

(a) Location, Site and Development

This city, situated on the northern bank of the river Main, is the major partner in an urban complex that includes Sachsenhausen and Offenbach on the opposite bank of the river. Downstream are the settlements of Höchst and Griesheim, each attached to an independent industrial complex, but both parts of the social and economic complex of Frankfurt. Frankfurt had about 556,000 inhabitants in 1939, and Offenbach had 81,000.

The original nucleus of settlement was a *curia regis*, which was also an imperial residence in the Carolingian era. First mentioned about A.D. 800, and recorded as a *castellum* in A.D. 994, this site was later chosen for the cathedral. This initial settlement forms an oval nucleus and was the beginning of the *Altstadt*, with its centre on the east–west street-market called the *Alter Markt*. It is usually supposed that the first wall ran along the north side of this nucleus parallel to the river, so that the town formed a strip alongside the river front. There is, however, no evidence of a wall west of the Römerberg. Thus, the *Altstadt* proper grew westwards from the royal stronghold nucleus, and on the western border of the latter there was the open space of the Römerberg. This extended settlement had an area of 100 acres as compared with 12 acres for the stronghold. It consists of two streets parallel to the river front. The next extension to the *Altstadt* proper took place to the north in the latter half of the 12th century. This

area was built during the 13th century, and included several
monasteries in the more open land near the walls. The chief
streets were the Fahrgasse and Schnurgasse. In the middle of
the 15th century two-thirds of the population of the town (total
8,000) lived in the *Altstadt*. The bastioned wall system was built
in the middle of the 17th century just beyond the wall. In the

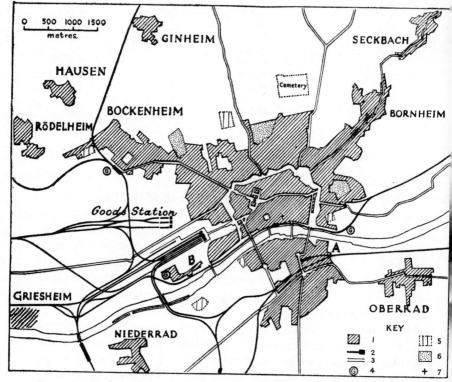

FIG. 23.—Frankfurt-am-Main in 1890 (drawn from a map reproduced by Gley).
(Scale, 1 : 75,000.)

1. Built-up area. 2. Railway station. 3. Main roads. 4. Gas works. 5.
Public buildings. 6. Parks. 7. Cathedral. A = Abattoirs. B = Barracks.

first decade of the 19th century these fortifications were demolished
(unlike Strasbourg, for example, where the walls remained until
the 'seventies), so that the urban area could freely expand.
Gardens and public buildings were laid out on the site of the
fortified belt. At this time only a little over 2 per cent. of the
population lived outside the walls. A map for 1890 (Fig. 23)
shows that there was then a sprinkling of houses with gardens.

right round the outskirts of the town.   The principal station, railway tracks and yards lay to the west, and another station lay to the east of the town.   One railway ran along the river front and a second crossed the river from the western station so as to encircle the south side of Sachsenhausen.   The river port lay on the eastern side of the town.

(b) Functional Zones

Fig. 24 shows the functional zones of the city and its contiguous urban areas.   The nucleus of the *Altstadt*, clustered around the cathedral and the Römerberg, has narrow and irregular streets and congested half-timbered buildings, that are densely populated. On its north side is the wide thoroughfare of the Zeil and its continuation in the Schiller Platz and the Rossmarkt which lie on the site of the first northern limit of the old town.   The Zeil is the main commercial thoroughfare of the city.   North of it occur predominantly modern buildings devoted to business and administration.   The whole of this area is the *Altstadt* which is enclosed by a wide belt of boulevards, gardens and public build- ings, on the site of the demolished fortifications.   Beyond this core are the inner built-up areas.   These are fully built-up and contain a considerable variety of small factories.   The main districts lie just outside the old town and in Sachsenhausen. Open built-up areas with wide thoroughfares and some tenements, but usually with large two- or four-family houses with gardens back and front are typical of Frankfurt.

The suburban areas have a low density of housing and include both single-family houses and rows of three- or four-storey apart- ment blocks.   Outlying villages have been partly absorbed and bear urban traits in both their aspect and function.   The Industrial Zone is located west of the city next to the main railways, although Sachsenhausen has many brewing industries and Offenbach has clothing, machine tool, and chemical industries. The greatest plants lie west of the city ; these are the chemical plants at Höchst and Griesheim, and the Opel automobile works at Rüsselsheim.   Port areas have developed since the improve- ment of the Rhine and Main rivers.   The main port area lies to the east of the city and contains extensive wharves and gas and electricity works.   A smaller area lies on the west side of the city, but both port zones are on the north side of the river.

Within this whole urban framework, rich farm land stretches to the north and a continuous belt of woodland on the sand-

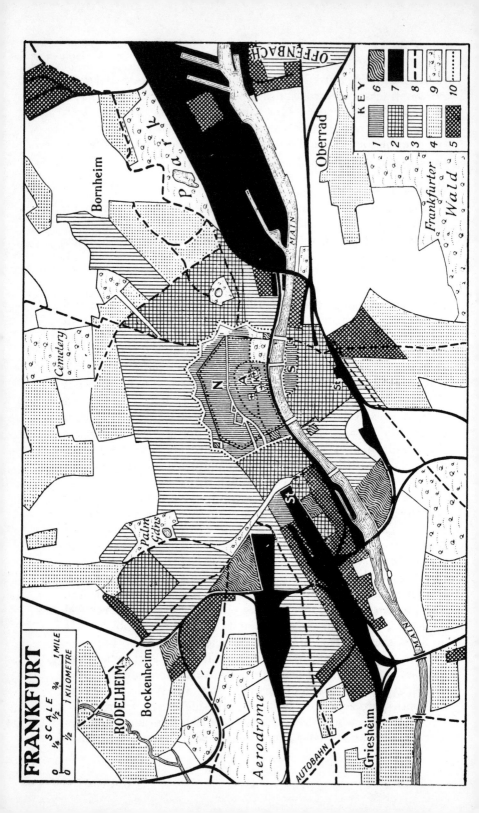

covered plain to the south. Workers travel daily from many communities to Frankfurt and other industrial sites. The chief centres of attraction for such movements, and the main seats of general activities, are the towns that extend from Mainz–Wiesbaden to Hanau, but Frankfurt is the dominant centre of this complex.

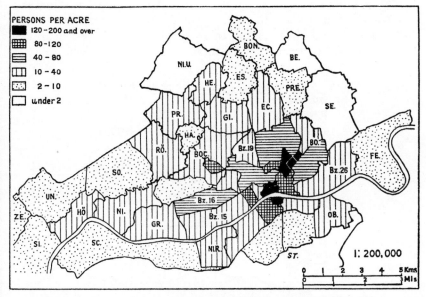

FIG. 25.—The Density of Population in Frankfurt-am-Main (from Gley). (Scale, 1 : 200,000.)

(c) The Distribution of Population (Fig. 25)

The number of people living outside the town was 13 per cent. in 1858 and 19·6 per cent. in 1864. The population of the inner town, as we may now call it, was 48,855, and of Sachsenhausen 7,793, giving a total of 56,648 in the inner town and 19,270 outside it. Since 1895 the city has made many accessions to its administrative area and its 71 districts now embrace 26 independent *Gemeinde*. Before these extensions, the city covered 28 square miles, but to-day the area has reached nearly 80 square miles.

FIG. 24.—The Functional Zones of Frankfurt-am-Main. (Scale, 1 : 50,000.)

1. Central or Inner Zone. 2. Middle Fully Built-up Zone. 3. Middle Partly Built-up Zone. 4. Outer Sub-urban Zone. 5. Industrial Zones. 6. Public buildings. 7. Railways, yards and wharves. 8. Main roads from the inner town. 9. Parks. 10. Site of medieval walls. Districts in the old town are the Altstadt (A), Neustadt (N), and Sachsenhausen (S). St. = Station. K = *curia* and cathedral.

The beginnings of *Citybildung* are to be found in the *Altstadt* in the 'seventies, but the steady decrease of population did not begin till after 1890. The rates of decline are shown in the diagram (Fig. 26). The *Altstadt* and the *Neustadt* and *Sachsenhausen*—the town lying immediately on the south side of the Main opposite Frankfurt—housed 66,000 people or 72 per cent. of the total population of the city in 1871. An absolute maximum was reached in 1900 with 72,000 people, exactly a quarter of the total population of the city.   In 1933 there were 53,000 people, or just under 10 per cent. of the total population of the whole city.

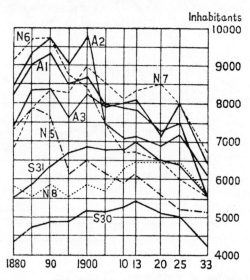

Fig. 26.—Population Changes in the central city of Frankfurt-am-Main, 1880–1930.

A 1–3 is Bezirk Altstadt.
N 5–8 is Bezirk Neustadt.
S 30–1 is Bezirk Sachsenhausen (from Gley, p. 81).

The population of the outer districts has increased rapidly, for in 1871 they included 27·7 per cent. of the total, in 1885 46·8 per cent., and in 1925 they had five times as many people as the inner town.

We may note here particularly the planning work of the Oberbürgermeister Franz Adicke, who not only built the new Town Hall (1900–5), but issued a new building ordinance (*Bauordnung*) in 1891 which preserved the Innenstadt and reserved districts for residence, mixed uses and industry. He also had

DENSITY OF POPULATION IN FRANKFURT-AM-MAIN BY CONCENTRIC RINGS
(from W. Gley)

Km.	Population	Density per acre
0–1	65,500	98
1–2	160,000	68
2–3	95,500	24·4
3–4	68,500	12·4
4–5	48,000	6·8
5–6	86,500	10·0
6–7	54,000	5·2
7–8	25,000	2·1
8–12	98,000	1·2

built the Promenadenring, and new thoroughfares in the north-east and in the south-west of the town.

The more recent expansion of Frankfurt may be traced from its population trends. It early acquired dormitory towns or *Trabantenstädte*. Bornheim, Oberrad and Niederrad were entirely rural in 1823, but by 1866 they were already urbanized and regarded as parts of Frankfurt. This is also true of Bockenheim. These may now be described as *Vorstädte*, so closely are they allied with Frankfurt. Fourteen *Vororte* were annexed to Frankfurt in 1914. Since 1910 they have grown faster than the city itself (1910–25, by 26 per cent. as against 10·5 per cent., 1925–33 29·5 per cent. as against 0·3 per cent.). In 1928 nine more *Vororte* were added to the city, with an area of 15,000 acres and a population of 80,000. The biggest of these is Höchst. To-day nearly a third of this enormous city area lies in these annexed outer districts. Their close ties with the city are clearly shown by the fact that sixteen railways and two electric lines radiate in all directions to transport workers daily into the city. In 1900 out of 15,000 gainfully employed workers in Frankfurt who were drawn from outside the city, 6,500 were drawn from a 7-km. radius and 12,300 from a 15-km. radius. In 1927 there were 19,000 workers coming from the 15-km. radius and 13,700 from beyond it. Thus, in 1900 the 15-km. radius sent 78 per cent. and in 1927 58 per cent. of the outside workers. In 1927 these outside workers represented 17·5 per cent. of all workers in Frankfurt. These figures show the process of decentralization in action, and since 1925 it has been planned. At tremendous cost the Frankfurt authorities have established dormitory towns, especially in the 6-km. ring beyond the Nidda river.

The general distribution of population in the city by administrative districts is shown on Fig. 25. The arrangement of the population in terms of concentric zones from the heart of the city is shown on the Table above. Within one kilometre of the Römerberg there were 98 persons per acre of total area and 68 persons per acre in the belt with a radius of one to two kilometres. On the basis of administrative districts, however, the old town had overall densities of 80 to 120 persons per acre and well over this figure in its most densely peopled sectors.

POSTSCRIPT—1949

We have described these cities as they were in 1939, before their devastation by war-time bombing. Three of them were revisited in 1949. The old cores of Cologne, Hanover and Frankfurt were in ruins, scarcely a building standing intact. The surrounding closely built-up residential areas were laid flat over large areas or the buildings severely damaged. Statistics of population and housing were as under.

	Population 1939	1946	Decrease 1939–46	% of Houses Destroyed
Cologne . . .	768,000	491,000	− 36·0	56
Frankfurt . . .	548,000	424,000	− 22·5	35
Hanover . . .	464,000	355,000	− 23·5	48

From *Berichte zur Deutschen Landeskunde*, Band 6, 1949, pp. 112–17.

Very few houses had been built or rehabilitated since 1945. In 1948–9 building activity was concerned mainly with commercial and public buildings. Over large areas not even the rubble had been removed. The planning and rebuilding of these German cities is a task that will cover several decades.

In point of fact, in 1960, the task in West Germany is well on the way to completion. The city centres are for the most part reconstructed and dwellings are being built at the rate of 500,000–600,000 per year—twice the rate of Britain. At this rate West Germany will solve its housing problem in a few more years.

CHAPTER 7

THE STRUCTURE OF THE FRENCH CITY

The characteristics of the urban development of the towns of France have been illustrated in Chapter 4 by a somewhat detailed study of three examples, Poitiers, Blois and Laon. The purpose in this chapter is to select five larger French cities and to examine more broadly their present physical and demographic structure in the light of their historical development. Toulouse, Bordeaux, Limoges, Lille and Strasbourg have been selected for this purpose, and the maps upon which the interpretations are based have been prepared in the same way as the preceding maps of the German cities.

(1) Toulouse (Fig. 27 and Plate 11)

(a) As a Capital

Toulouse had modest beginnings.[1] The Gallic *oppidum* was situated to the south of the present city on the edge of the Lauraguais plateau, in a dominant position overlooking the river. The Roman settlement was placed on the east bank of the river, at a sharp bend where there was also a ford. At this point there enters from the south-east a " dry " valley which leads to the wide valley of the Hers. This is roughly parallel to the Garonne and leads to the gap commanded by Carcassonne and thence to Narbonne. Toulouse was the outpost, against the west, of the Roman province of Narbonne on the Mediterranean shores. It became, however, in 419, a focal political capital as the seat of the Visigothic kingdom that lay between the Pyrenees, the ocean and the Garonne, with an extension north to Poitiers. Toulouse was also a frontier outpost for the Germans against the Mediterranean lands, when the kingdom of Alaric II (484–509) reached to the Mediterranean, the Rhône and the Alps.

A castle (Château-Narbonnais) was built on the south side of the site of the Roman *cité* at the end of the Mediterranean

---

[1] The site of the Gallic *oppidum* lay on the promontory to the south. North of it, St. Roch, near the river, was the seat of boatmen and traders in the Iron Age, to which succeeded the *oppidum* ; then the Roman settlement was sited north again, at the bend of the river on its right bank at a ford crossing. See a useful chapter on Toulouse in P. Arqué, *Géographie due Midi Aquitain*, Paris, Editions Rieder, 1939.

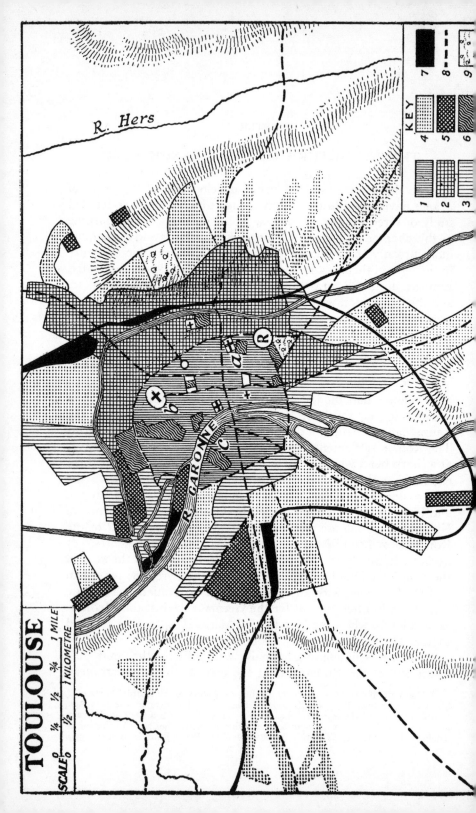

route. Around it a *salvetat* was built by the Counts. The basilica of St. Saturnin or Sernin (1096) and the *faubourg* around it were located at the north side of the Roman *cité* at the junction of the routes from Aquitaine. The *faubourg* of St. Cyprien grew on the opposite bank of the Garonne, where it commanded the crossing, and thus the approach, to the city. Thus, land routes radiated from the Garonne crossing. The river itself and the Pyrenean streams were too rapid and capricious for boats, and have never been used for anything but the floating of timber to the town. But the river was navigable downstream and a harbour was cut at Daurade in the Middle Ages. Industry rather than commerce sought the river front at Toulouse. Flour mills, bleaching, tanning, fullers, dyers, were clustered along the river in the town and gave to it an industrial character. The river, however, has not played a significant part in the growth of Toulouse, or in its functions as a regional capital, although its great width, dominating the whole of the city and its environs, has obviously been an important factor in the development of its plan. The fact that Toulouse in the 11th and 12th centuries was a centre of trade speaks of its economic rôle as a market centre, and in 1152 it was endowed with full municipal institutions.

Toulouse was above all a political and cultural capital in the early phase of its development. The French kings made it the key of their policy of centralization of authority in the south-west. It was the capital of Languedoc, and the kings gave to the seigneurs of high rank the powers of viceroys. The *États* of Languedoc had its scope reduced, but from this assembly, as later from the Parlement (founded 1443), Toulouse drew much of its importance. It also attained pre-eminence through the foundation of its University in 1229 by Count Raymond VIII, with the aim of strengthening royal control over the lands of the *langue d'oc*, and of ousting the Albigensian heretics and of supporting Catholic doctrine. The University became a cultural focus for all southern France and even northern Spain. Arising from this stimulus, together with the pilgrimage to St. Sernin, Toulouse became a great seat of religious thought and the chief stronghold

---

Fig. 27.—The Functional Zones of Toulouse. (Scale, 1 : 50,000.)
1. Central or Inner Zone (the old town). 2. Middle or Fully Built-up Zone. 3. Middle or Partly Built-up Zone. 4. Outer or Sub-urban Zone. 5. Industrial Zones. 6. Public buildings. 7. Railways, yards and wharves. 8. Main roads. 9. Parks and public spaces. Sectors of the old town are : (a) *Cité*, (b) *Bourg*, St. Sernin, (c) *Faubourg* St. Cyprien. R = Grand Rond. Hachures show sharp breaks of slope.

of Catholicism in southern France. After the Albigensian wars, the religious orders, formerly sited outside the city walls, moved into the city itself, which in the 16th and 17th centuries had many religious houses. Colleges were built for poor students around St. Sernin, which became a veritable *quartier latin*. Toulouse was, thus, the administrative and cultural capital of the province of Languedoc, its influence extending from the Pyrenees to the Central Plateau and east to the Mediterranean shores and the lower Rhône.

Its emergence as a great city, however, depended above all upon its economic development. The first extended commercial relations of the city came about in the 15th and 16th centuries, with its partial monopoly of trade in woad or *pastel*, which was cultivated in Lauraguais, prepared in Toulouse, and sold to distant markets. In the 16th century Toulouse was one of the five great cities of France. Its activities were reflected in many private mansions (*hôtels*), the sumptuous buildings of the Parlement and the residences of its representatives, the merchants' residences, specialized commercial streets, and old stone houses wherein was transacted much of the regional commerce in *pastel*, grain, leather, etc. This prosperity was founded on commerce. Improved transport facilities caused changes in the 17th and 18th centuries. In 1622 Toulouse acquired one of the first five post offices for letters and was connected by road with Paris. In 1623 a *courrier ordinaire* was established to Bordeaux, in 1629 to Marseilles, and via Montpellier and Nîmes to Lyons. Then between 1667 and 1681 the Canal du Languedoc, later called the Canal du Midi, was built, and Toulouse, situated at the juncture of this canal from the Mediterranean with the Garonne downstream to the Atlantic, became the chief of all the towns on this route. Finally, the *États* of Languedoc had the roads radiating from Toulouse and the bridges repaired, or new ones built, so that in 1723 the Intendant averred that the roads of Languedoc were the best in the kingdom. Hitherto, Toulouse had been a crossing of long-distance east–west and north–south routes. Now it became a focus of radiating routes which added to its importance as a focus of regional exchange. Thus in the 18th century it was one of the chief commercial centres in the Midi. Its industries at this time included flour milling, and the making of starch, woollen, silk and cotton cloths, and bricks.

Growth in the 19th century emphasized this predominance and in some measure changed the physiognomy of the town. In

1821 it had 52,000 inhabitants—a scarcely perceptible change in size since the Revolution. But thenceforth its growth was rapid— 83,000 in 1846, 127,000 in 1866, 140,000 in 1881, 150,000 in 1906, 213,000 in 1936. The advent of the railway strengthened its regional functions. It became a centre of supply for the surrounding country and for those small towns which had hitherto been independent centres. It became a centre of wholesale trade and now has great department stores on the Paris model, which have branches in other towns. The Eighth Economic Region, with Toulouse as capital, roughly coincides with its trade area.

Industry has grown in the city. It has its traditional flour mills (though these employ relatively few workers) on the river front (Ramier de Bazacle and Ramier du Château) and alongside the canal. It also has engineering industries. The making of boots and shoes, formerly dispersed in small workshops, has been concentrated in forty factories in the town, specializing in the production of women's and children's wear. Its female labour surplus has been absorbed in various clothing industries—ready-made clothing, underwear and hats. It also has plants making tobacco, cartridges, nitrogen, aeroplane parts, and agricultural implements. The development of hydro-electricity in the Pyrenees, with which the city is closely associated, is likely to have unpredictable effects on its future industrial development. A large factory producing nitrogenous manures lies on the island of Ramier ; it covers 125 acres and employs 3,000 workers.

(b) Plan and Build

The site of Toulouse [1] lies on the east side of a bend of the Garonne on a terrace a few metres above river level. The river near Toulouse has on its left bank a large expanse of flat land, locally known as *la plaine*. On its right bank the valley floor is narrow, and only one terrace of 8 or 9 metres above river level is preserved. The centre of Toulouse is on this right-bank terrace. The borders of two plateaux approach the town, from the east and south respectively. These plateaux are 190 to 255 metres high and are separated by a broad dry valley, the former course of the Hers in its northward issue to the Garonne. The built-up area stops abruptly at the foot of the hills to the south, but has spread over the plateau fragment to the east. The broad flat valley floor between the two plateau remnants is the natural field

---

[1] Wanda Rewienska, " Quelques remarques sur la physiognomie de la Ville de Toulouse ", *Rev. Géog. des Pyrenées et du Sud-ouest*, Tome VIII, 1937, pp. 73–88.

of urban expansion, along the great route eastwards to Narbonne. The second line of expansion is down the valley of the Garonne. Here the plain between the Garonne and the Hers is admirably suited for urban use, and new suburbs extend for several kilo-metres, reaching beyond the administrative limits of the city. On the left bank, inside the meander, the urban area has extended uniformly in all directions along the routes. Beyond it, to the west, rises the steep edge of the valley plain to a height of 100–150 metres, and this effectively limits the extent of the urban area.

The plan of the town shows that the old city is separated from the new by a circle of boulevards on the site of the old fortifica-tions. Within the old city the plan reveals its three original component parts, namely, the *bourg* and the *cité* on the right bank, and the *faubourg* St. Cyprien on the left. The ground-plan shows the close relation of the town to the bridgehead and the routes radiating from it.

The *cité* dates from the Roman era. The *bourg* is later, originating from the 5th-century basilica of St. Sernin. The two settlements originally had separate walls. During the feudal age the *bourg* was a royal stronghold and the *cité* was the strong-hold of the Counts of Toulouse. It was not until the 16th century that both were enclosed in a common wall that was begun in the 14th century. The *faubourg* St. Cyprien served as a bastion to guard the river crossing.

The axis of the old town is the north–south route, that runs due south from the church of St. Sernin, following the Rue du Taur and the Rue St. Rome. Other streets ran parallel to it, especially in the *cité*, and probably served as alternative through routes. The east–west streets, on the other hand, are more complicated, with many narrow winding connections and culs-de-sac, with the exception of the street that leads to the bridge. These streets served mainly for residence and for local traffic. The principal determinant of this plan is clearly the main north–south route. The river Garonne has been of little significance as a navigable highway. It is liable to sudden changes of flow, and it was not till 1838–56 that a side-canal was built. The river itself above Toulouse served for the floating of timber. Toulouse has always been essentially a route centre, and none of its east–west streets runs direct to the river except the one to the bridge. The Intendants of the 18th century effected the construction of the Capitol, the Esplanade (to-day the Grand-

Rond), and the Allées that radiate from it. St. Cyprien was protected from floods by the building of a dyke on the west bank of the river. Then, too, the Canal du Midi was cut. In the early 19th century the Prefects had the walls replaced by boulevards and the districts between them and the outer line of the Canal grew rapidly. The 19th century added two main new features. In 1869 the great north–south route was opened, east of and parallel to the Rue du Taur and in 1871 it was named the Rue Alsace-Lorraine. In 1890 the Rue de Metz was cut perpendicular to the first, as shown on Fig. 27. These new routes are the main avenues of commerce in the modern city and correspond to the radial routes to its hinterland.

The new town dates from the second half of the 19th century. It extended along the roads that radiated from the old town, while the construction of the railway caused the growth of a new quarter between the old town and the station to the east. Since 1918 large areas of new cheap houses have been built. The new town presents two main features: first, the extension of the built-up area, especially along the roads ; second, the emergence of distinct quarters, each with its own ground-plan. Radial expansion along roads has been accentuated to the south-east towards the dry valley of the Hers beyond the semicircular belt of the Canal du Midi and the railway. These prevented expansion until bridges over the canal and the railways were built. The wall, which was built in the 19th century for purposes of collecting the *octroi*, was another deterrent to expansion. This wall encircled the town and St. Cyprien, although the built-up area spread beyond it. It still remains a barrier to urban circulation except along the main radial routes. There is still much open land between the roads on both sides of the walls. The whole urban area is divided into about ten quarters. Some are separate colonies, as to the north of the town, but to the east they are contiguous and compact, although their separate origin is revealed by their independent ground-plans.

Industrial plants lie on the outskirts. The chief are the *Office National Industriel de l'Azote* on the island of Ramier (in the river south of the town), the tobacco factory, and gas works. There is also a cluster of flour mills at Bazacle and Château-Narbonnais. On the other hand, numerous boot, shoe and clothing works are located in the mass of houses in the outer town. Owing to electrification there are few industrial chimneys and the factories are recognizable by their special build (such as the gas works), or

large size, as those on the banks of the Garonne and near the
Canal du Midi.

The administrative area of Toulouse embraces about 30,000
acres. It is covered partly by buildings, partly by cultivated
fields and market gardens. It also includes villages and isolated
farms, although some of these are almost submerged by urban
building, so that only those buildings remain which are used as
warehouses, garages and stores. Farms remain in the districts
which are especially adapted to farming. Thus there are many on
the border of the terrace, only 3 or 4 km. west of Toulouse.
Several types of soils make up these farm-holdings, and they are
able to produce cereals and the vine and meadowland. Other
farms are found on the humid floor of the Hers valley near the
canal and along the Garonne. The large tenement blocks
(*maisons locatives*) occur as islands in the outer town, especially
on the route to the north and along the Narbonne route, thus
accentuating the main north–south axis of the city. But urban
and rural house types and land uses are greatly intermixed on
the outskirts.

(c) Types of Building (Fig. 28)

The centre is fully built-up with *grandes maisons locatives* or
tenements, which have no open spaces except for a few private
gardens and market-places. The buildings have long frontages
and are closely built-up in their back courts. Red brick and
tiles are the traditional building materials, and give to the city
the name of *ville rose*. But there are many multi-storeyed, densely
populated tenements of 19th-century origin. There still remains
a scattering of the old houses of the bourgeoisie and nobility
dating mainly from the 16th and 17th centuries.

New building types appear in the new outer areas. These
buildings are smaller than those of the inner town, lower in height,
with a basement and one storey at most and they have narrower
frontages. Such buildings indicate the first stage of urbanization
in many villages. They house the artisan class, and small traders
and their shops. In Toulouse they appear along the main routes
and the streets branching immediately from them. These
" urban " and " sub-urban " types are intermixed on the outskirts, the latter being a kind of transitional building between
the urban and rural ways of living. They are best represented
in St. Cyprien.

More varied types of single-family house are found in the

FIG. 28.—Types of Building in Toulouse (from Rewienska, " Quelques remarques sur la physiognomie de la ville de Toulouse ", *Rev. Géog. des Pyrenées et du Sud-ouest*, Tome VIII, 1937). Centre illustration is a bird's-eye view of the central city, looking north ; note the flattish roofs and multi-storeyed buildings in foreground. Upper illustration shows the " sub-urban " building, single-family houses along the roads (*faubourg* St. Cyprien). Lower illustration shows the small house (*échoppe*) that is very characteristic of the worker's home (Saint-Roch district on the outskirts of the city).

quiet residential streets away from the main roads.   These have mansard roofs, annexes and galleries.   They are occupied by the *employés* and *petite bourgeoisie*.   In working-class quarters, as at St. Roch, there are monotonous arrays of small single-family houses. A distinct feature is found in the houses of market (flower and vegetable) gardeners who make up a large proportion of the suburban population.   Their buildings are like cottages with extensions for tools and storage.   They are dominant on the left bank of the river and especially on the right bank along the 9-metre terrace north of the inner town.   They are spaced at 20 or 30 metres apart along the roads.

Villas are a fourth and widespread type of house.   These are found near the outskirts of the city and in the better-class residential districts of the *riche bourgeoisie* in the town.   They are segregated in particular in the higher districts, thus avoiding the dense fogs to which Toulouse is subject, especially in winter.

(d) Demography of the Districts round Toulouse [1]

Rural depopulation in the whole of this area within a radius of 15 km. of the city set in after 1851, and 60 per cent. of its inhabitants were lost between 1851 and 1931.   The only communes with an increase are those contiguous with the city boundaries, especially in the north, and this fact is undoubtedly to be related to the growth and attraction of Toulouse.   What is just as noteworthy is that the communes with a declining population reach right up to the boundaries of Toulouse in certain districts to the east and south.   The main causes of this are threefold. First, the great plain of the Garonne is well adapted to intensive farming, whereas the plateaux to the east have heavy clay soil which is not nearly so fertile.   These plateaux also rise abruptly from the plains around them to heights of 300 metres (1,000 ft.). They are also deeply dissected, and remain isolated and remote from the routes and traffic of Toulouse.   The steep edges of the two plateaux set limits to the expansion of the compact urban area.

There are 13 communes contiguous with Toulouse that record increases of population.   These may be referred to as the " sub-urban zone ".   There are thoroughly urban communes on the left bank of the Garonne, with most of their people dependent on urban occupations—artisans, labourers and employees.   In effect these form part of the town and share its démographie

---

[1] Wanda Rewienska, " Études sur la Démographie des Alentours de Toulouse ", *Rev. Géog. d. Pyrénées et du Sud-ouest*, Tome VII, Fasc. 4, 1936, pp. 325–39.

characteristics. Special reference should be made to two communes on the right bank of the Garonne. These lie in the plain and are mostly intensive market-gardening areas with 70 per cent. of their workers classed as horticulturists. With closely spaced houses separated by market gardens, these two communes have densities of about 300 and 250 persons per square kilometre, almost the same as the densities in industrial areas. It is quite impossible to draw a dividing line between this district and Toulouse on the grounds of aspect or demography : it is in reality a part of the city. The communes of the eastern border have been more recently urbanized since 1918.

(2) Limoges (Fig. 29) [1]

(a) Military Function

Limoges, the capital of Limousin, the westernmost sector of the Central Massif, is situated at the convergence of old routeways on the north bank of the river Vienne at a point where the river could be crossed, first by a ford and later by a bridge. The walled Gallo-Roman settlement lay on the north bank of the river at a ford above the present town at the convergence of routes from Bordeaux to Bourges and Lyons to Saintes. The Roman bridge stood on the site of the St. Martial bridge and the Roman wall embraced the settlement around the bridgehead. Outside the wall were an amphitheatre, and a temple that lay on the site of the cathedral. St. Martial died at Limoges in the 5th century and near his tomb a small church, St. Pierre-du-Sépulcre, was erected, from which grew the abbey of St. Martial on the site of the present theatre.

During the Germanic invasions the inhabitants shifted from the Gallo-Roman settlement to a low hill, which was relatively easy to defend. On the summit of this rise they erected a Christian basilica on the site of the Roman temple. The bishop was the defender of the town—*defensor civitatis*—which became the *cité*, as street names still suggest. It was walled by Roman decree about 396 by a circular defence work that is to-day reflected in the circular streets that surround it. The settlement was repeatedly attacked during the next five hundred years ; then the wall was reconstructed in the 11th century and a new bridge built in the 12th (Pont St. Étienne). The city was besieged for the last time in 1589, and the walls were abolished shortly after.

[1] A. Perrier, " Limoges, Étude de géographie urbaine ", *Rev. de Géog. des Pyrénées et du Sud-ouest*, Tome IX, 1938, Fasc. 4, pp. 317–86.

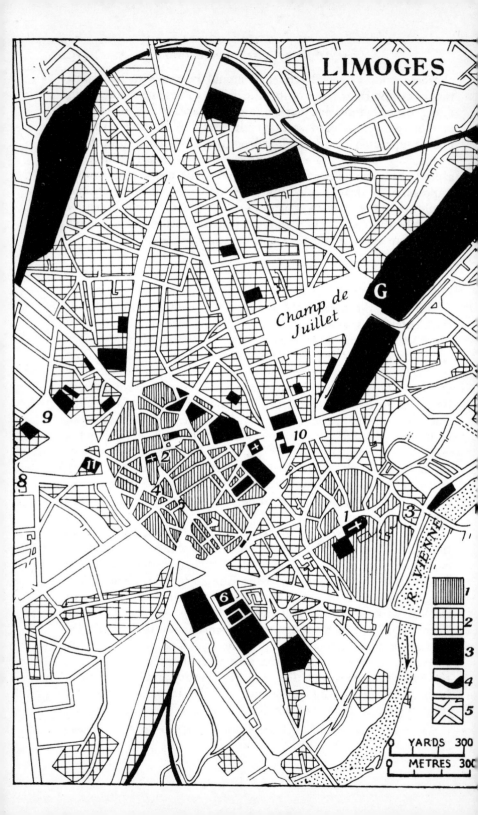

In the 6th century a new settlement clustered around the tomb of St. Martial and the church of St. Pierre-du-Sépulcre. The former became an abbey in the 9th century. It lay on the main Lyon–Saintes route. The abbots had houses built and during the Norman invasions invited the populace of the surroundings to construct defences around the settlement. The first of these defences around the *bourg* St. Martial dates from the 10th century. A market was held outside the abbey and the population grew through its fame as a pilgrimage centre. The inhabitants struggled for rights of self-government with the abbots, who called in the help of the *vicomte* of Limoges. In 1157 the *vicomte* built a castle at the highest point of the town on the site of the Place de la Motte. Thenceforth the settlement took the name of *château*, within which there were now two rival powers, the *vicomte* and the *abbé*. The townsfolk formed a *commune* at the end of the 12th century, and thenceforward it was known as a *ville*. Conflicts continued between these three authorities. The walls were entirely rebuilt, though not on the former site, in 1182, on the site of the boulevards that were constructed in their place at the end of the 18th century. These walls embraced industrial and commercial quarters that had grown outside the old nucleus : Puy-Vielle-Monnaie and Manigne (metal working) ; Queyroix and Vieux-Marché (markets) ; Lansecot (small traders). A small lake at the Place de la Motte, that supplied water to the 10th-century moat, was made into a reservoir. During the 17th century the wall was a hindrance. It was demolished at the end of the 18th, and gradually transformed during the first decades of the 19th century.

(b) Commercial Function

Until the Revolution, the *cité* and the *château* were two separate topographic and legal units. Each was an individual town. The old Gallo-Roman settlement farther upstream was an inactive cluster of houses of vintners and weavers. The *cité* was a religious community, containing the bishop's residence, the basilica of St.

FIG. 29.—The Functional Zones of Limoges. (Scale, approx. 1 : 15,000.)

1. The inner old town, containing the *cité* and the *château*. 2. Compactly Built-up areas. 3. Public buildings. 4. Railways and yards. 5. Street pattern of Outer Sub-urban Zones. (1) Cathedral (*cité*). (2) Town (*ville*) (*château*), grouped around the church of St. Martial. (3) Medieval bridge (St. Étienne). (4) Place de la Motte. (5) Place des Bancs. (6) Hôtel de Ville. (7) Place Manigne. (8) Place des Carmes. (9) Champ de Foire. (10) Place Jourdan. (11) Palais de Justice. G = Gare des Bénédictins.

Étienne, a monastery, and several churches and convents. Vine growers and peasants lived here also. The *château* or *ville* was the commercial and industrial community. The grain market was held in front of the abbey of St. Martial till the 18th century (*le marché de la claustre cloître*). Beyond the 10th-century wall there were originally various food markets outside the gates—Queyroix (vegetables, fish, and meat) ; Poulaillère (fowl) ; Vieux-Marché (bread, later meat) ; and to the west what is to-day called the Marché des Bancs Charniers. Craftsmen working in metals clustered on the route to Périgord (Rue des Claceliers). The church of St. Michael dates from the 14th century. The new wall in 1182 embraced all these extensions. The Place de la Motte remained the seat of the *vicomte*, then of the *sénéchal*, and finally of the *intendants*.

Outside the 1182 wall there again grew new *faubourgs* or suburbs, mainly around the ancient churches that were built outside the walls on the main routes. The *faubourg* of Entre deux Villes grew up between the *cité* and the *château*. It was separated from the latter by a lake on which were tanneries and dyeing mills. Peasants were its principal occupants. With the improvement of the roads in the middle of the 18th century the *faubourgs* extended along roads with open spaces between. As the town grew the whole area inside the walls was closely built-up by 1765. The old markets in the centre of the town disappeared, since they were too far from the points where the routes entered the town. Larger markets were held on the outskirts at the Place Manigne (wines), Place des Carmes (wheat, wine and cattle, the last still being held). In 1805 on the site of the old cemetery of the Arènes a fair was established (*champ de foire*). These markets were held till the advent of the railway.

The *cité* and the *château* were still legally separate until 1792, but they were joined by the streets and houses of Entre deux Villes. At this time, commerce and administration were concentrated in the *château* inside the area of the *first* wall, around the abbey of St. Martial and the church of St. Michael. Commerce in food-stuffs, instead of being carried on in several small markets in the centre, was grouped in large market-places—the Place des Bancs and its prolongation in the Vieux-Marché. Here was the produce market and the site of the first butchery established in 1218. Here, too, the first central market was built in the 18th century. The ponds of La Motte were filled in in 1819 and on their site appeared the Halles Centrales. Wholesale trade was concentrated on the market-places of Carmes and Manigne at the gates of the town. In the early 19th century the expansion of the town took place along the radial routes, especially to the west and north. The railway came in 1856 and the first station (Gare des Bénédictins) brought growth to the north and east sectors. A road bordered by cafés and hotels joined the station to the town. In 1874 the second station was opened in the north-west of the town. This was mainly a goods station, and around it an industrial quarter developed.

(c) *Industrial Function*

Industry began to play a significant part in the land uses of the city after 1800. Tanneries and dyeing mills were located alongside the lakes and on the banks of the Vienne. Craftsmen's workshops were to be found in the heart of the city. With the development of weaving at the end of the 18th century factories were established on the outskirts of the town, one on the site of the present Bank of France, another on the Cours Tourny, a third on the Place Manigne. The first porcelain factory was on the Paris road. From 1800 to 1850 textiles were the chief group of industries ; there were 25 factories in 1837. Porcelain factories appeared on the main roads in large open spaces. The town plan of 1883 showed the chief extensions of the built-up area to the north-east and west ; this was mainly due to the opening of porcelain factories. Peripheral position along the routes is still the dominant factor in the location of these plants. Older plants in similar sites nearer the town have disappeared. Boot and shoe manufacture has grown greatly in recent decades, but the factories are widely distributed.

(d) *Urbanism : Planning*

Until the end of the 18th century, Limoges, like other French towns, was a dirty, badly constructed, insanitary place, with narrow, congested streets. The Intendants sought to widen the roads. New roads were cut through the walls during the 18th century. After a great fire in 1790 in the quarter of Manigne the Intendants laid out three wide parallel roads (Banc-Leger, Haute-Vienne and de la Loi). In 1772 all the cemeteries inside the old town near the churches were eliminated and removed first to the Arènes and shortly afterwards to the cemetery of Louyat, outside the town.

The 19th century witnessed a great expansion of the city. Some quarters owed their growth to private initiative, others to public authority. The municipal authorities built new avenues and bridges during the century. The Champ-de-Juillet was laid out in 1830. Private bodies erected new quarters on the site of the ancient abbey of St. Martial, the new quarter of the Arènes, and others. These extensions permitted slum clearances by the municipal authorities in 1900 and 1915. In 1930 the Gare des Bénédictins was reconstructed and houses for working people have been built on the outskirts. Many public monuments were built in the 19th and 20th centuries. The Hôtel de Ville and Palais de Justice have been erected along the boulevards outside the old town. Public buildings were put up on the site of the clearance area in Viraclaud and Verdurier. The theatre is on the site of the abbey of St. Martial which was demolished in 1792. The covered market (Halles) was built on the site of the Place de la Motte in 1886. On the other hand, the slaughter-house was shifted to the outskirts of the town in 1832. The centre thus retains its essentially administrative character. In 1870 the city became a regional military headquarters. In addition to the conversion of old religious houses to military uses, new barracks had to be built between 1875 and 1885.

The expansion of the built-up area and the concentration of functions in the centre were accompanied by a specialization of functions between the quarters. Commerce is mainly localized in the ancient *château*, and expands beyond it from the Place St. Martial to the Place Jourdan, and along the Rue Centrale to the Boulevard Louis Blanc. The centre of commerce and business is the Carrefour Tourny and the Place Jourdan. Hotels and cafés are situated around the Carrefour Tourny, the Place Jourdan, and the Avenue de la Gare. Administrative services are concentrated around the Place de la Motte. During the 19th century new buildings were erected along the boulevard and in the slum areas that were cleared in the Veraclaud and Verdurier quarters, in the heart of the town. The *cité* remains the secluded ecclesiastical and residential quarter. Industrial establishments lie in the suburbs along the main routes. The factories along the line of the old walls, where industry was first localized, are to-day of little importance. New housing estates have been established on the outskirts of Limoges and are connected with the city centre by tramway.

(3) BORDEAUX (Fig. 30)

(a) Site and Medieval Development

The plan of the historic town and the transformations effected in the mid 18th century are shown on Fig. 31. The functional zones of the modern city and the historical phases of its expansion are shown on Fig. 30. These two maps should be compared. The city of Bordeaux was sited at the point where the Garonne impinges for the last time on firm ground on its left bank. On this site converged the routes from the Rhineland to the Pyrenees and from the Garonne to the Mediterranean shores. The first site of settlement was formed by two low hills (St. André and Puy-Paulin) on either side of the west–east valley of the Devèze and the adjacent low plateaus to the south and to the north-west. The open Roman city of the first three centuries of this era spread over all this area, around which lay low-lying marshland. The main road axes of this settlement are roughly marked to-day by the north–south route of the Rue Ste. Catherine and the east–west St. Remi-Porte-Dijeaux and the north-west route that passed by the amphitheatre, Rue du Palais-Gallien. Other main streets can be traced. The first Germanic invasions in A.D. 276 caused a confinement of the settlement to a strongly fortified *castrum* around the *porte de la Devèze* on the hills of St. André and Puy-Paulin (Fig. 76, p. 342). The square *castrum*, crossed in its centre from west to east by the Devèze stream, was built about A.D. 300 and was the nucleus of subsequent growth. The present street pattern reflects the rectangular network of the Roman *castrum*, with the cathedral in the south-west sector (marked 1 on Fig. 30 ; see also Fig. 31). In contrast, the irregular pattern of the St. Pierre quarter in the eastern half developed in the Middle Ages on the silted port of the Devèze, although here two streets recall the direction of the Roman quays. To the south of the *castrum* a new settlement (marked 2 on Fig. 30), the *bourg* of St. Eloi, developed during the middle of the 12th century, following on the revival of trade after the annexation by England (*Bourg anglais*). This old town has been largely effaced by street cuts in the 19th century but the line of its wall is clearly marked on the ground to the south by the *Fossés* of the Cours Victor Hugo, Cours Pasteur and the Duffour-Dubergier that mark the site of the old ditch (marked 2 on Fig. 31). This nuclear area is clearly defined by the concentric arrangement of streets around it, the oval area lying half in the area of the *castrum* (south-east area)

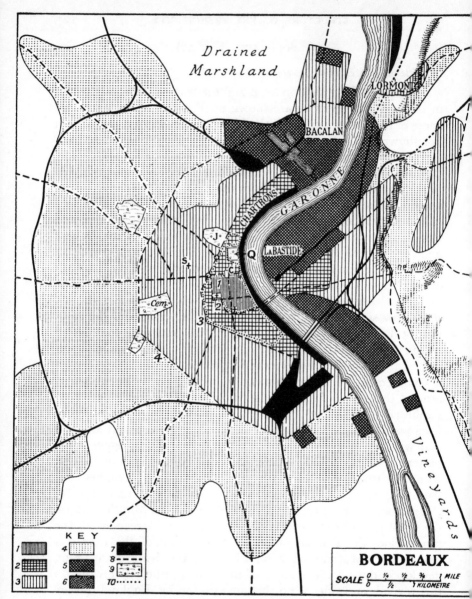

Drained
Marshland

LORMON

BACALAN

GARONNE

CHARTRONS

LABASTIDE

J

Q

C

S

Cem

2

3

4

Vineyards

KEY

1   4   7
2   5   8
3   6   9
         10

BORDEAUX

SCALE 0   ¼   ½   ¾   1 MILE
      0   ½   1 KILOMETRE

FIG. 30.—The Functional Zones of Bordeaux. (Scale, 1 : 50,000.)
1. Central or Inner Zone (the old town). 2. Middle or Fully Built-up Zone.
3. Middle or Partly Built-up Zone. 4. Outer or Sub-urban Zone. 5. Industrial
Zones. 6. Public buildings. 7. Railways, yards and wharves. 8. Main roads.
9. Parks and public spaces. 10. Medieval walls of the old town. Stages in the
expansion of the town are shown by : (1) limits of the *cité* on site of the Roman
castrum. (2) *Fossé* on south side of the *castrum* to enclose the *bourg* St. Eloi.
(3) Early 14th-century wall followed by *cours* or inner boulevards built in the 18th century.
(4) Outer boulevards built in the 19th century. Q = the Place de Quinconces.
S = St. Seurin Church. J = Botanical Gardens. C = Place de la Comédie.
Cem. = the La Chartreuse cemetery. Hachures indicate sharp breaks of slope.

and half outside the *castrum*, south to the Cours Victor Hugo. The third enclosing wall (marked 3 in Fig. 30), which dates from the early 14th century, was built so as to embrace all the settlement, including the numerous convents with their extensive gardens, which had been established outside the existing walls during the 13th century, and the three populous *faubourgs* of St. Michel, St. Croix to the south, and de Trompette to the north along the banks of the Garonne. The district of St. Pierre was also formed at this time at the mouth of the Devèze, east of the *castrum*. The walled area long remained larger than the built-up area.

To the north-west of the *cité* the religious *faubourg* of St. Seurin was outside the walls. This basilica was established in the 4th century, and the settlement was a distinct and autonomous town. A second *faubourg* was Chartrons, which grew up on drained marsh because of the needs of the port to the north of the town alongside the Garonne. This drainage had been started in the 6th century by the monks of St. Croix. Now a new district emerged.

(b) Development in the 17th century and after

It was during the 18th century that Bordeaux, like many other French cities, was greatly transformed by the good work of the Intendants of Guienne, notably Claude Boucher. He took up his position in 1720 and in 1729 called in the advice of an expert architect named Jacques Gabriel. Aubert de Tourny, who held the post of Intendant of the province from 1743 to 1757, continued this work. The plan of Bordeaux at this time is shown on Fig. 31.

The architect Gabriel prepared a project for a " place " in the new port area. He designed the Place Royale (now Place de la Bourse) and also put forward projects for promenades around the royal fortress of the Château-Trompette built by Louis XIV ; for the Place de la Comédie ; the realinement of the Rue Ste. Catherine ; and for the improvement of the *faubourg* Paludate behind the port of Bordeaux. Most of these schemes were subsequently carried out, largely during Tourny's period of office. Tourny also widened the façade on the river. He built *Allées* on the *glacis* of the Château-Trompette. The medieval ramparts were filled up and avenues or *cours* built on them. These interconnected large oval and rectangular " places ", that were surrounded by uniform building lines, and on the sites of the old town gates. The Jardin Public was also laid out in

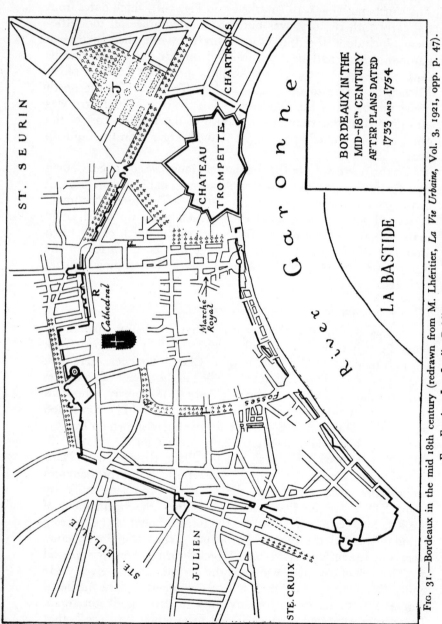

FIG. 31.—Bordeaux in the mid 18th century (redrawn from M. Lhéritier, *La Vie Urbaine*, Vol. 3, 1921, opp. p. 47). F = Fossés. J = Jardin Public. R = Rue des Remparts.

accordance with a plan by Tourny and around it grew a new quarter between St. Seurin and Chartrons.

Under Louis XVI the old *castrum* suffered further changes by the building of a new episcopal palace (to-day the Hôtel de Ville). The erection of the Grand Théâtre entailed the creation of the Place de la Comédie, henceforth the heart of Bordeaux, and the building of houses between these and the river on the south side of the *glacis* of Château-Trompette. On the site of the latter, the great esplanade of the Quinconces, with its surrounding buildings, was erected after the Restoration. Dupré de St. Maur, the last of the Intendants, effected the demolition of the Château-. Trompette and planned the extension of the city well beyond the *cours* laid out by Tourny. He also planned a canal to follow the boulevards and drain the marshes. A bridge across the river to La Bastide was later built by Napoleon.

During the 19th century, the town spread beyond Tourny's *cours*. The general growth was conditioned by the roads that had existed from medieval times, and new roads concentric with the *cours* were built to connect them. The result is a spider-web plan. Growth was rapid after 1850. The new quarters in the west include low single-storey houses (*échoppes*) with gardens, and present an aspect that is half urban and half rural. The municipalities of the Second Empire and the Third Republic erected a second belt of boulevards, as conceived in 1782 by the Intendant, Dupré de St. Maur. To the north, the drainage of the marshes was continued by the cutting of two new wet docks (*bassins à flot*) in 1869–82 and 1906–12 which have transformed Bas-Bacalan into a commercial and industrial district. On the right bank of the river, a new port was built during the 1914–18 war at Bassens. So the port spread downstream, culminating in the formation of an oil plant at Bec d'Ambès and an outport at Verdun in 1933. Big extensions of the residential area have taken place to the west and a large park has been formed at Caudéran. The time is ripe for the absorption of communes contiguous with the city.

In 1841 Bordeaux had 100,000 inhabitants, 20,000 more than in the days of Louis XVI. At that time it did not extend beyond the *cours* created by the Intendants. But in 1891 it had 252,000 inhabitants. This large increase was due in part to the annexation of adjoining communes, which numbered 10,000 persons in 1864. But immigrants to the city accounted for most of this growth. Thus in 1891, out of 252,000 inhabitants, 40 per cent.

were born in Bordeaux and 60 per cent. out of the city. This
immigration reached its maximum from 1860 to 1865. To-day,
out of every 100 inhabitants, 30 are born outside the city. The
population in 1936 was 258,000. The whole agglomeration of
13 communes has 400,000 people.

The growth of the built-up area has taken the form of a great
crescent outside the old town, partly on the territory of the old
city, and partly on that of adjacent communes, from which 2,500
acres were annexed in 1864. This outer city impinges on two
old *faubourgs* to the north and south, where it meets the river
and is bounded inwards by the *cours* of the 18th century and
outwards by the *grands boulevards* (marked 4 on Fig. 30). This
crescent-shaped area lies on the site of the ancient *banlieue* of the
historic city and retains many of its original features. The main
streets are sometimes winding and irregular, while others, which
are extensions from the old town, are straight and wide. There
are remnants of arable land, remains of a stream in which the
women still do their washing, and remnants of the high walls,
which enclosed trees and gardens of the religious houses. The
great cemetery of La Chartreuse breaks the crescent in two parts.
The actual built-up areas of this crescent are arranged in long
streets with narrow pavements, with low houses of one storey
(*échoppes*), and there is a lack of shopping facilities. There are
also many large, bare, open spaces, bordered by lines of trees.
Changes are taking place, however, as people shift from the old
town to its periphery. Roads are being widened, and squares
transformed by planting plantains and acacias. Urban ways
spread and the single-storey houses are often built up to two
storeys. Open land is being built on and shops and cinemas are
opening up. But the contrasts between the old centre and the
new periphery remain.

(c) The Port

The development of the port resembles that of many other
port-cities that are situated at the head of long river estuaries.
The original, small wharves lay adjacent to the city. Modern
growth has proceeded on the opposite bank and downstream
on areas of flatter land with water facilities. The port of
Bordeaux falls into three sectors, an arc of three kilometres on the
left bank extending from the stone bridge to the Bacalan quarter ;
then the two wet docks (*bassins à flot*) at the extremity of these
quays and connected with the Garonne by locks ; and, third,

the quays on the right bank that serve the industrial quarter of La Bastide.

The quays on the left bank that reach to the heart of the old town have excellent equipment for cargo and passenger traffic and receive over a third of the vessels coming into Bordeaux. All passengers and over one million tons of varied merchandise, a fifth of the total traffic of the port, are normally handled on these quays. The two wet docks are situated in the heart of the industrial quarter of Bacalan, where there are naval shipyards, constructional engineering works, timber mills, oil mills and sugar refineries. The docks handle coal, timber and the export of pit-props from the Landes. On the opposite, right, bank the quays receive bulk commodities for heavy industry. These include coal, phosphates, minerals, cement and cereals. Behind is the quarter of La Bastide with large industrial plants treating these raw materials—shipyards, chemicals, saw-mills, oil and grain mills.

Beyond the hills of Lormont there is a western extension of the port at Bassens (north of Lormont). This was created during the 1914 war, and was later rebuilt and reorganized. It is primarily a port for storage and transit. Vast spaces are available for the storage of heavy goods such as coal, pyrites, scrap iron and colonial timbers. There are also special facilities for the storage and transit of cereals. Industries have also been attracted —heavy chemicals, foodstuffs and saw-mills.

Farther downstream, at the confluence of the Garonne and Dordogne (Bec d'Ambès) there is a petrol port, opened in 1930, which had a traffic of 325,000 tons of petrol in 1933. Still farther downstream on the right bank of the Gironde, Furt and Blaye import hydrocarbons, and export pit-props and road-making materials. Pauillac, on the left bank, is a large petrol port with a vast refinery. The outport of Verdun was opened in 1933. It is situated at the mouth of the Gironde on its left bank and is accessible at all times by the largest vessels afloat. Passengers disembark here from incoming vessels and so avoid possible delays in navigating the channel to Bordeaux.

The dominance of the single-family house and the large number of private gardens and open spaces explain why Bordeaux has an area of nearly 10,000 acres, nearly a half of the area of Paris, with a twelfth of its population. The minor roads on the periphery are often the successors of country tracks and are narrow and winding. Hence there are problems of street cleaning, lighting, and paving. Drainage is a difficulty too, owing to the small gradient and the rise of the tides that hinder the out-flow of the waters. There is also a particular problem of com-munications, not only to the distant western suburbs but also across the river to the industrial areas of the Bastide. There is only one bridge, and another cannot be built below its site since this would interfere with the navigation of the river.

(4) LILLE (Fig. 32)

(a) Site and Medieval Development

Situated at the junction of the chalk land of Picardy—open, arable, wheat land, with marshy valley floors—to the south, and the flat clay lands of Flanders—hedged meadow land—to the north of it, and at the junction of the Flemish- and French-speaking lands, Lille grew up at the head of navigation of the river Lys on its tributary, the Deule. South of Lille the river Deule flows through a broad marshy valley in the chalk. North of Lille it cuts into the clay to form a clearly defined, single, navigable channel. On the site of Lille, in the midst of marshes, the branches of the river enclosed islands that could be defended. On one of these islands Lille had its origin. It had adequate local natural defences, and commanded a land route to the south and a water route to the north. Site and situation helped Lille to develop as a strategic point, and as a seat of commerce and industry.

The beginnings of the town date from the first half of the 11th century. It had three nuclei : a *castrum*, dating probably from the 11th century (the parish of St. Pierre) ; beyond it, to the south-east, a *forum*, a commercial settlement focused on the site of the Grande Place; and a *suburbium* around the bridge of Fives (*fines* ?), towards the church of St. Maurice. The settlement was thus elongated from north-west to south-east, a feature that it retained till the middle of the 19th century. The *castrum* over-looked the extensive marshes of the Deule to the west, where there was no room for expansion. But the *forum* and *suburbium* lay to the south-east on higher and better-drained land, on an old route that crossed the Deule at the *Pont de Fins* where it was joined by the routes from Bovines and from Picardy. Here took place the chief expansion of the town. An ancient route ran from the site of Valenciennes to that of Ypres, crossing the valley of the Marque at the bridge of Bovines, and where that route

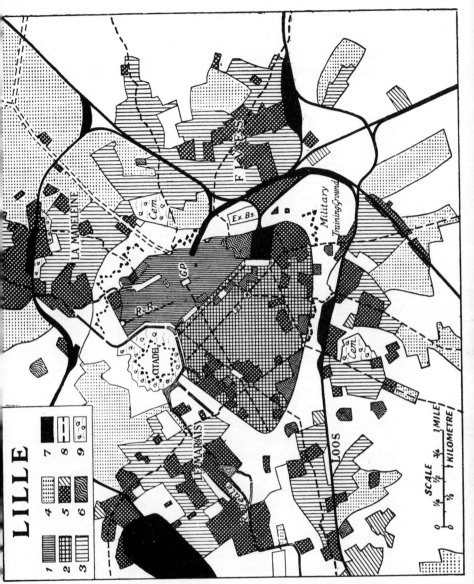

LILLE

Legend:
1
2
3
4
5
6
7
8
9

SCALE

0   ¼   ½   ¾   1 MILE

0   ½   1 KILOMETRE

Fig. 32.—The Functional Zones of Lille.

(Scale, 1 : 75,000)

1. The Old Town.
2. Middle Fully Built-up Zone. 3. Middle Partly Built-up Zone. 4. Outer or Sub-urban Zone.
5. Industrial Zones, with separate indication of brick-works. 6. Public buildings.
7. Railways and yards.
8. Main roads. 9. Parks.
GP = the Grande Place or central market-place.
RR = the Rue Royale.
Ex Bs = old brickworks.
Note the orientation, with west at the top of the map.

133

skirts the valley of the Deule, which describes a meander to the north-east, there clustered the first inhabitants of Lille.

Commerce contributed mainly to the early growth of the town. The lower Deule was canalized in 1237 and the upper Deule in 1271 (above La Bassée). Cloth weaving from the wools of Artois and England early became a speciality, and continued till the 18th century. In 1144 the *suburbium* expanded to absorb a new parish, St. Sauveur, which was incorporated in the town at the end of the 12th century. In the 13th century the town had four parishes and three large *faubourgs*, two along the Deule (St. André and Weppes), and another to the east, Courtrai. It had grown to be a rival of Bruges and Ghent. But its strategic situation in the following centuries impaired its economic prosperity.

(b) Development in the 17th century and after

After the 14th century Lille became a shuttlecock between France and Flanders. Woollen cloth-making declined during the French occupation, but was revived in the 15th century with some changes under the Dukes of Burgundy. To the fine cloths made by fulling there were added serge stuffs and cloths made from a mixture of wool with flax. But at this period domestic spinning and weaving in the countryside developed to the detriment of the towns throughout Flanders. The shortest period of peace was reflected in a speedy revival of the town's economy, at a time when the urban economy of Flanders was indeed in a decline. Lille was prosperous, for example, during the 17th century after the Treaty of the Pyrenees and even at the end of the 16th century it probably had about 40,000 inhabitants. It was one of the chief towns of the Low Countries. But such periods of prosperity were rare and chequered. In 1617, after the civil wars, it had only 32,000 people. It became a citadel and its topographic expansion in this period was dictated by military needs. In 1603–5 the *faubourg* of Weppes was added to the town to strengthen the fortifications, and for similar reasons (to smooth out re-entrants) the *faubourg* of Courtrai was absorbed. But the main change came when it fell permanently to France and was then fortified by Vauban as a frontier fortress. He erected the main defensive citadel to the north-west of the town, where it would be surrounded by marshes, " un pays tout entrecoupé de water-gands (water ditches) et fossés pleins d'eau en tout temps ", as it is described in Vauban's own words. This was the best site in the town from which the walls could be defended, the northern sector bearing the brunt of attacks in 1667, 1708 and 1792. This isolated citadel was connected to the town in a quarter where building had never hitherto extended because of its flat, marshy character. Here grew up the quarter of St. André, built by Vauban from 1670 to 1672 with the Rue Royale as its axis. But this extension, occasioned exclusively by military necessity, never flourished like the districts to the south-east, and it remained a residential district for the *bourgeoisie*. It is to-day the aristocratic quarter of Lille, with squat houses and *hôtels* in the old style. This general form the town retained till 1860, when it extended over two kilometres from the Ypres gate along the Rue Royale, in the direction of the old causeway across the marshes on which it had its origin.

For a century and a half these extensions, prompted by military necessity, sufficed for the town. Under the security of French control, the city throve again and the French market was ready to absorb its products. From 32,000 people in 1617, it reached 45,000 in 1677 and 55,000 in 1699. But the increase was slowed in the next century, for the countryside was a formidable economic competitor. Domestic industry was flourishing in the middle of this century. It was then that Roubaix appeared as a rival. Lille then had 65,000 people and, after the wars of the Revolution, in 1804 it had 59,000 inhabitants. There was still plenty of room to spare inside the massive brick ramparts and bastions.

Growth and congestion came in the 19th century. In this modern period Lille became the leading industrial city of France, outside Paris. Textiles, above all, and chemicals and engineering, account for its industrial growth. The first steam spinning mill in France was installed at Lille in 1801. In 1913 25,000 people worked in cotton textile industries, 15,000 in flax and linen spinning, and 8,000 in linen working. The making of ready-made clothing in small workshops (not factories) occupied 3,000 people. Coal, transport facilities, local enterprise, and a labour supply from Flanders and from Belgium across the frontier contributed to this growth. The population reached the 100,000 mark in 1850—twice the population of the mid 18th century, but all concentrated inside the walls. Congestion reached fantastic proportions. Houses increased in height. People lived in cellars. Through building up the blocks, the densities reached appalling figures. Add to this the marshy character of the land, the foulness of the water in the river and its distributaries, and it will be appreciated

that living conditions were dreadful. Population began to over-
flow beyond the walls. Under the Second Empire new fortifications were built to enclose the chief of these suburbs. These
enclosed Fives, which lay beyond the railway tracks that now
entered Lille from the east. The new extension was to the south,
on the chalk platform, and south-west, across the valley of the
Deule. The area inside the new fortifications was tripled in
extent, but it was soon filled up. The last area to be built over
was the sector in the extreme south-west, a marshy tract along
a branch of the Deule. New suburbs extend beyond the walls
to the south on the chalk platform.

Within the fortifications there are now three sectors, distinct
in physiognomy and function (Plate 16). To the north-east, the
old town has narrow winding streets, and multi-storeyed houses
with steep gables and many windows. A few new streets cut
through it. There are no factories, owing to lack of space : but
here are concentrated both retail and wholesale commerce.
Here, too, are the few ancient buildings of Lille—the Exchange
(Bourse) of the 17th century with its old belfry, the old churches
and the Grande Place. At the point where the old ramparts
lay there begins a new world—a modern city, " regular and
banal ", with a rectilinear street plan and a few radial boulevards,
lined with modern public buildings, and houses of the *bourgeoisie*.
To the south, just as abruptly, one enters the workers' quarters,
where the old *faubourgs* have been annexed and gradually welded
into one area. Here are numerous one-storey houses, built of
brick, massive cube-shaped factories with chimneys, and textile
mills.

New factories have been built beyond the borders and new
housing estates established. Lille itself is not growing within its
walls. It had a population of 216,000 in 1896, 217,500 in 1911,
210,000 in 1901 and 200,000 in 1936. But growth has gone on
apace on the outskirts. The 15 communes around the city passed
from 95,000 in 1901 to 120,000 in 1911—an increase of 25,000
as compared with 7,500 for the city. This trend has continued
since. The city is expanding towards Roubaix and Tourcoing,
which have a combined population of about 300,000, so that the
whole agglomeration has a total population of nearly 750,000
people.

(5) STRASBOURG (Fig. 33)

(a) Location, Site, Plan, Population

Strasbourg lies in the Rhine valley on the western edge of the river flood plain, where it is bordered by a slightly raised terrace (145 metres) covered with loess deposits. This terrace rises westwards over smooth, well-drained country, to 180–190 metres, that

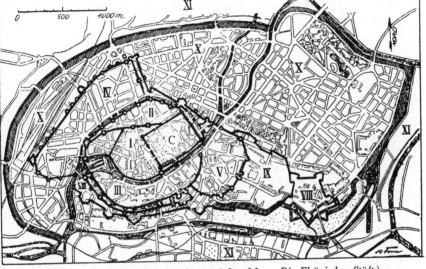

FIG. 33.—The Growth of Strasbourg (after Metz, *Die Elsässischen Städte*). (Scale, 1 : 40,000.)

C = the *Cité*, on the site of the Roman *castrum*. I. *Nova urbs*, walled at the end of the 9th century, with its axis on the Langestrasse and extended to include the small Alt St. Peter parish in the 10th century. II. Jung St. Peter parish, walled 1202–20. III. St. Nicholas parish, walled 13th–14th centuries. IV. St. Johann parish, walled 1374–90. V. St. Wilhelm parish, walled 1387–1441. This frame existed for over 400 years, though walls were strengthened. VI. and VII. Minor extensions. VIII. Citadel erected by Vauban. IX. Intervening military section. X. Great extension of area 1875–79. XI. Extensions beyond the Prussian fortifications. The zone of Prussian fortifications lay just inside the Ill to the south and the water to the north (Orangerie) and occupied the site of the railway tracks in the west, as shown by the hatched border.

leads direct to the Saverne Pass through the Vosges and thence to Lorraine and so to Paris. The town thus lies between two types of country, the open, arable, well-drained, loess platform to the west of it, and the flood plain of the Rhine and its tributary the Ill. The settlement had its beginnings in the many islands formed by the distributaries of the Ill and the Rhine. The Ill crosses through the heart of the town. On one of these original islands is the cathedral, which lies at the heart of the ancient town. The island has a height of 144 metres, and has been raised by long occupation to some 7 metres above the surrounding plains.

The site and extent of the ancient Roman *castrum* is indicated in the street plan. This *castrum*, with walls 3·5 metres wide and 13 metres high, was called *Argentoratum*. It was devastated by the Germanic invasions, but reappears in the 6th century as *Stratisburg*, and shortly after it was selected as a bishop's see. The nuclei of settlement were situated inside the Roman walls : the abbey of St. Stephan in the south-east corner, the bishop's demesne (*Fronhof*) in the south-west corner, where later the cathedral was built, and a *Königshof*. The settlement was refortified at the end of the 9th and early 10th century. This nucleus has retained something of the original Roman plan, but its lay-out is to be attributed to the adaptation of the new street pattern to the four gates, and to the dominance of the new cathedral, and to the continued general alinement of the *decumanus* and *cardo*, the right-angled crossways of the Roman plan.

A settlement with more of an urban character developed on the western side of this nucleus in the 9th century and was called the *nova urbs*. It had its axis on the Langestrasse (earlier called the Oberstrasse) with narrow side streets branching from it. The Gutenberg Platz was its market, on which later stood the Rathaus and St. Thomas' church. This new settlement was embraced by a wall in the late 9th and early 10th century, so that the area of the place was increased from 18 hectares (the *castrum*) to 45 hectares. About A.D. 1000 the whole settlement was brought under the control of the bishop. The building of the cathedral was begun in 1015. Wine trade and shipping brought growth to the place and in 1129 it was given the full legal privileges of a town (*civitas*). In 1150 it had about 4,000–5,000 inhabitants. A small district to the north-west, centred on its church of Alt St. Peter, was added towards the end of the 12th century.

With the growth of population another extension of the wall was made between 1202 and 1220, so that the whole of the island enclosed by the Ill and the Falschwallgrabenkanal was walled, enclosing an area of 71 hectares. This now embraced the parish to the north with its church in Jung St. Peter. After 1228 the strip south of the Ill was gradually built on during the next hundred years till 1344—a period of relatively slow territorial expansion. This parish was centred on St. Nicholas church. At the end of the century a new wall was built right round the town, which now included this last parish beyond the Ill, the wall running roughly parallel to the river. The whole area of the walled town was now 99 hectares. During this period the town gradually released itself from the control of the bishop, and it became a *Reichsstadt* in 1205. Its growth was steady with the increase of its commerce and crafts. Two *faubourgs* or *Vorstädte* were walled at the end of the 14th century, one to the north-west, centred on the church of St. Johann (1374–90), the other to the south-east, the Krutenau district, centred on the church of St. Wilhelm (1387–1441). At this time it was decided to keep an open belt around the outer side of the walls as an added means of defence after a siege in 1392. The demands for adequate defences grew stronger. The town was repeatedly besieged. In preparation for a siege in 1473–7, some 680 buildings in the *Vorstädte* were demolished and the town's walls were strengthened. A dreadful flood due to an abnormally high river level in 1480 also called for the strengthening of the walls. But the fortifications, apart from the small extension to the south, remained the same for 430 years, embracing an area of 202 hectares, and the population remained steady, reaching its maximum of about 32,000 in the first decades of the 17th century. The picture of the town at this time is revealed by contemporary views. The high towers of the cathedral dominated the town and the many towers of its parish churches. The sea of streets and alleys was dominated by the multi-storeyed houses. These usually had four storeys, with gables parallel to, seldom facing the street. The houses had steep gables, narrow façades and small courts. Congestion was marked in contrast to the usual character of the medieval town.

The main change in this period was the reconstruction of the defences to meet the new and revolutionized conditions of siege warfare. In 1681 Strasbourg fell to the French, and at once a citadel was constructed. Strasbourg, like Lille, was now a city on the new frontier of France. The citadel was, as at Lille, built on the outskirts of the town, south-east of it, in the midst of marshes. Like Lille, it was joined to the town walls, which were fortified in their entirety by Vauban with forts, bastions and redoubts (1720–26). At this time the citadel had a garrison of 10,000 to 12,000 soldiers. Moreover, not only was the already overcrowded city enclosed within this strait-jacket; its architecture was changed, for Baroque façades in the French style were added to the German Gothic buildings (Fig. 123). Under the

French occupation the town prospered in security and the population again increased, although the Thirty Years War had greatly
depleted its numbers, so that in 1680 the population was reduced
to 22,000. But in 1709 it reached 32,500, in 1789 50,000 and
in 1812, 54,500. Of this last total, only 4,900 lived in the
Vorstädte. The population of the walled town increased from
49,600 to 61,000 at the end of the French occupation. It was
greatly overcrowded, and the suburbs had only 17,100 inhabitants
in 1871 with another 10,200 in three suburbs to the north. In
this way, together with the garrison, Strasbourg had 95,700
inhabitants in 1871, of whom 68,400 lived inside the walls.

Strasbourg came under Prussian control as a result of the
Franco-German War. The massive fortifications were a serious
impediment to the expansion of the built-up area, and in 1875–9
entirely new fortifications were erected by the Prussian Government which involved a great expansion of the town area in which
residential districts were laid out on a geometrical plan to the
east and north. These new defences, as in other modern fortified
cities, were accompanied by an open, unbuilt-on zone on their
outer side. Expansion was left mainly to private builders, except
for the public buildings. The area has not yet been fully built-
up, for there are large open areas especially to the north-east.
But the population inside the walls increased to 118,600.
Even greater, however, was the increase of the suburbs, and the
whole area increased from 95,700 in 1871 to 208,000 about 1920.
Like all other big cities, it is thus surrounded by a group of
residential and industrial satellites. It is distinctive, however, in
the large area of its late 19th-century fortifications, which are
adequate to contain the bulk of its population.

(b) Modern Growth (X and XI on Fig. 33).

It will be well to indicate briefly the circumstances of the
modern growth of Strasbourg and the way in which these are
reflected in its urban expansion. Here, the two main facts are
the period of German occupation from 1871 to 1919 and the
modern period of French occupation since 1919. Outstanding
events during the 19th century were the advent of the canals at
the beginning of the century, the opening of the Strasbourg–
Basel railway in 1841 and of the Strasbourg–Saarburg railway
in 1851. The main railway station was built to the west of the
town between 1878 and 1882, whereas the original station lay
farther in the town on the site of the Markthalle on the north

bank of the Ill. This exterior location has tended to pull the main axis of the town from north to south as compared with its traditional direction from east to west. The Langestrasse, the most ancient trade thoroughfare, is thus avoided by heavy traffic, whereas the Kleber Platz and Broglie Platz are the focal points of the city, since they are focal to the new areas, built since 1871, to the east and north. The most important extension within the new fortifications is the spacious lay-out of avenues and places, parks and the new University buildings to the east. The south-eastern sector, embraced in the Vauban fortifications as far as the citadel, is an almost exclusively military area with barracks, arsenal, citadel, and military hospital. To the south, just beyond the fortifications, are also public buildings, such as the hospital and clinics which cover a large area.

Beyond the fortifications new areas have grown up in the last fifty years. A residential and industrial area lies to the north and to the north-east between the Ill and the Rhine, while the new Rhine harbour on the Sporen island to the south stands as a counterpart to the still greater area on the opposite (German) side of the Rhine frontier. A belt railway runs round the south side of the town joining up with the new port area. The Rhine–Rhône canal enters the Ill on the south-east of the city, the Rhine–Marne canal on the north side.

In the middle of last century, the port was confined and congested within the walls of the town on the banks of the Ill, and had no more than local importance. In 1843 was first suggested the idea of the construction of a new port alongside the Rhine. In 1882 the junction canal was made to the Rhine–Rhône canal and the Rhine–Marne canal. In 1892 the first stage in the development of the port was inaugurated by the opening of the port of Austerlitz. Then came the Rhine port, and since 1919 more extensions have been effected. As a result of improvements of the Rhine between 1907 and 1915 Strasbourg became accessible to Rhine barges throughout the year. In 1882 the traffic of the port reached 11,500 tons, and in 1901, 570,000 tons, and almost 2 million tons in 1913 (with canal traffic, $2\frac{3}{4}$ million tons). In 1930 the traffic reached 5·7 million tons, while that of the canals in 1931 reached 2·1 million tons. This development is due to the fact that before 1918 Strasbourg was a regional port, with its hinterland limited by the Franco-German frontier. But after 1918 it was reannexed by France with Alsace, and its function assumed a national importance.

CHAPTER 8

BRUSSELS

The process of urban growth involves the transformation of the historic city, within its ancient walls, in order to meet the modern needs of urban living, while the growth in numbers and movement of people out from the centre to the periphery involve the growth of areas around the historic core. In this study of Brussels we shall pay special attention to this transformation of the historic city since the end of the 18th century.

(1) Site and Situation (Fig. 34)

The site of the medieval town was on the eastern banks of the northward-flowing river Senne at a point where wooded hills on the right (east) bank drop steeply down to the flat marshy plain of the river. The old town lay on the steep valley slopes and extended to the plain on the west and the level plateau on the east. The ancient east–west highway from Cologne to Bruges crossed, as at Louvain, the northward-flowing river at a convenient point. This road traversed the hills and then went down the steep hill slope to the river crossing in the centre of what became the medieval town. The river was navigable to the north along the route now followed by the modern ship canal. Developing in the Middle Ages as a small town with textile industries, considerably less important than its neighbours, such as Louvain, Brussels owed its later growth to its choice as a royal residence. In the 11th century the Counts of Louvain, who later became the Dukes of Brabant, established a castle on the edge of the wooded plateau on the hill of Coudenberg overlooking the town and the bridgehead. The Dukes of Burgundy, and, finally, at the end of the 15th century, the Hapsburgs, established their court residence on the hill. With the separation of the United Provinces from the Spanish Netherlands, Brussels became the capital of the latter, and from that time it has always been a capital city, the residence of sovereigns, the seat of government and administration. On its hill are intermingled the buildings and monuments of the Dukes of Brabant, of the Hapsburgs and of the modern kingdom.

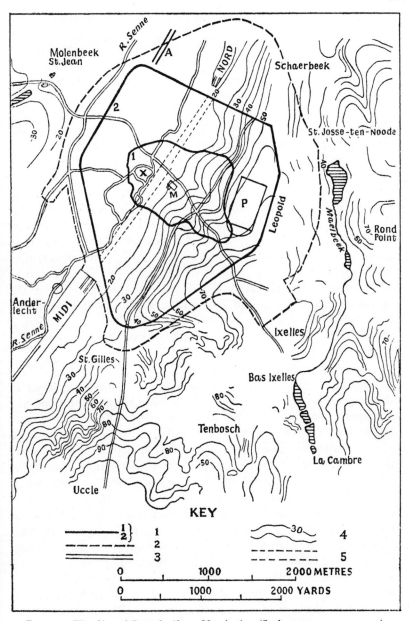

FIG. 34.—The Site of Brussels (from Verniers). (Scale, approx. 1 : 40,000.)

1. The first and second town walls (1 and 2). 2. Approximate limit of the built-up area in 1862. 3. Main routes. 4. Contours at intervals of 5 metres. 5. Rue Neuve and Rue du Midi. A = Allée Verte. P = Le Parc. M = Grande Place. X = Site of the 9th-century *castrum*.

F

Like Paris, it has emerged as a great administrative and cultural city.

The east–west routeway dominated the topographic development of the town, but in the 19th century the north–south valley of the Senne has governed its development in respect of both canal and rail communications.

The first stronghold (*castellum*) was founded in the 9th century, on the island of Gery. This island, lying on the west side of the river and protected by a channel diverted from the river Senne, also lay just south of the main east–west routeway where it crossed the river. A trading colony or a *portus* appeared in the 11th century at the northern end of the stronghold. On the island was the residence of the duke and his retainers (*ministeriales*) and the garrison. Then during the 12th century a new settlement appears, the *forum*, centred on the Grande Place. Full constitutional rights were obtained at the end of the 12th century when the first wall was built around the town. At the end of the 13th century Henry I, Duke of Brabant, abandoned the *castrum* on the river island and built a castle on the heights of Coudenberg to the east. In the middle of the 14th century a second wall was built around the town, which was still in existence at the end of the 18th century.[1]

Thus, at the dawn of the modern era, the town had two clearly defined parts, the *basse ville* or lower town on the valley floor of the Senne, the seat of commerce and industry, and the *haute ville* or upper town, the seat of palaces, administration and aristocratic residences. This dual character is preserved with ever-increasing distinction to this day, although the whole city, and particularly the *basse ville*, was radically transformed during the 19th century. The *basse ville* is centred on the Grande Place, around which cluster the Town Hall, the old houses of the guilds, the Exchange, the Halles and a number of small market-places, the stations, the harbour, industry, and working-class quarters. The *haute ville*, on the higher ground, has the palaces, the ministries, the museums, the law courts, academies, and the residences of the aristocracy and the wealthy. We shall trace the stages in the transformation of the city from its condition at the end of the 18th century to the present day.

---

[1] G. des Marez, " Le développement territorial de Bruxelles au Moyen age ", *Congrès International de Géographie Historique*, Tome III, 1935. See also a review by P. L. Michotte on Brussels and Louvain in *Bulletin de la Société Belge d'Études Géographiques*, December, 1935.

(2) BRUSSELS IN 1790

At the end of the 18th century Brussels was still enclosed by the 14th-century wall, although the destruction of its gates began in 1782. Inside the town there were important remnants of the first stone walls of the nucleus of the town erected in the 13th century, although houses were built right up against them. This central nucleus, the oldest part of the town, was fully built up in the 16th century, as is revealed by the map of Jacques de Deventer. But between its limits and those of the second wall there was still a good deal of open space in 1800. Since the 16th century, houses had been built along the first wall and along the main roads radiating to the gates through the second wall, and the land between had already been partly built on, especially nearer the centre of the town. Open land lay along the low, flat banks of the Senne and on the slopes of the hills on the right bank. To the highly irregular net of crooked narrow streets of the medieval centre, more regularly laid-out sectors were added in the latter half of the 18th century in the quarters of the Parc and of the Place Royale, and around the Place St. Michel (to-day the Place des Martyrs).

This medieval town was the result of natural, unplanned growth, except for the areas just mentioned. Streets from east to west ran steeply down the hill slopes to the centre of the town. The chief of these was the main Cologne–Bruges route (Montagne de la Cour, Rue de la Madeleine, Rue du Marché aux Herbes, Rue Ste. Catherine, Rue de Flandre). Some of these streets were too steep for traffic and were usable only by pedestrians. From north to south there was not a single direct route from one gate to another. The only route was winding, and was the ancient Roman track along the slopes of the hills of the right bank, that is to-day known as the Rue Haute. The Senne and the Petite Senne were open to the sky, flowing northwards across the marshes. They were liable to flood and their banks were dotted with tanneries, breweries, and workshops. The axis of the settlement was thus the east–west *Steenweg* from Coudenberg to the Flanders Gate which passed just to the north of the Grande Place, the focus of the town.

Outside the walls were fields and meadows, crossed by routes from the gates to the surrounding villages and the towns farther afield. All these villages were sited on the banks of or near to the Senne or one of its tributaries, and were surrounded by market gardens, wheat fields, orchards and woods.   The villages were usually strung along the main roads.   The surrounding countryside was dotted with the country mansions of wealthy citizens, and a few cotton mills and tanneries had already appeared at Molenbeek and Anderlecht.   The intimate association of the town with its surrounding countryside is clearly demonstrated by the organization of the *Cuve* of Brussels.   From early times this consisted of the surrounding villages together with the town *intra muros*, which, together, formed an administrative unit.   This area was subjected to the magistrature of Brussels, and the villagers enjoyed the liberties and rights of the city. These relations grew up in the 13th and 14th centuries.

(3) Topographic Growth from 1795 to 1860

The topographic growth of the city in the 19th century may be divided into two periods, from 1795 to 1860 and from 1860 to the present day.   The location of buildings and streets will be found in Fig. 35.   The zones are shown on Fig. 36 and an aerial photograph of the centre is shown on Plate 17.

The period from 1795 to 1860 was one of important topographic changes in the city.   The monastic orders were suppressed in 1783 by Joseph II.   Here a barracks, there a prison or a market-place, took the place of a convent in the old town, while the gardens in the more open areas along the Senne were crossed by new streets.   In 1842 about a tenth of the total area of Brussels was under gardens, but in twenty years these had almost entirely disappeared, since they were used for the location of new streets, shops and workshops.   Many old houses, formerly containing one family, housed several in 1860.   Meadows along the Senne were built on.   Cemeteries were forbidden in the city area by Joseph II (1784) and new ones were formed on the outskirts, the old ones being used for streets and " places."   As the land was built on, new cemeteries were opened on the outskirts.

The destruction of the walls was decreed in 1810 by Napoleon I, who had boulevards laid out on their site.   This work, completed by 1840, gave the city a circle of wide avenues 8 km. long, lined with double or quadruple rows of trees.   The salubrity of the boulevards as promenades was vitiated by the foul water of the Senne and by the appalling tenements alongside it.   Outside the boulevards there still remained the *fossé de l'octroi* as a barrier between town and country, and one could only enter or leave the city by the gates which led through the barrier formed by

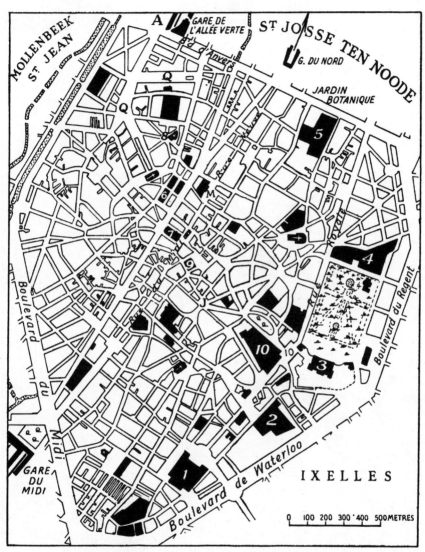

Fig. 35.—The Plan of Central Brussels. The street plan and chief buildings in the old town. (Scale, 1 : 20,000.)

1. Palais de Justice. 2. Barracks. 3. Palais du Roi. 4. State buildings. 5. Hôpital St. Jean. 6. Halles Centrales (Markets). 7. Bourse (Exchange). 8. Place and Church of the Béguinage. 9. Hôtel de Ville. 10. Museum. A = Allée Verte. Q = Old quays. North of the Museum are the University and the Palais des Arts, and at their feet, to the west, the cleared area. The open space between the Royal Palace and the State buildings is the Park (Parc).

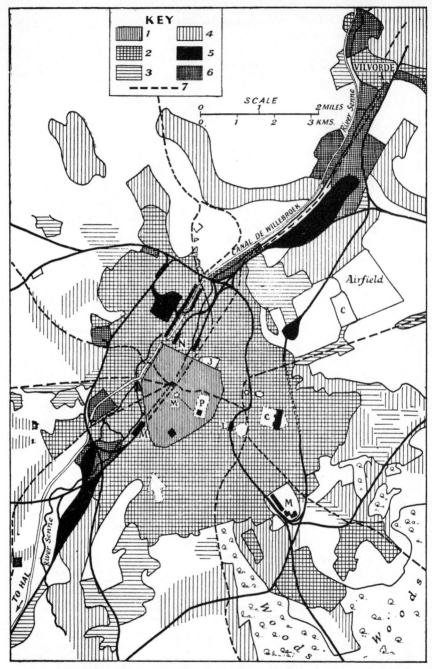

KEY

1
2
3
4
5
6
7

FIG. 36.—The Functional Zones of Brussels. (Scale, 1 : 100,000.)

1. Central or Inner Zone (the old town). 2. Middle Fully Built-up Zone.
3. Middle Partly Built-up Zones. 4. Outer or Sub-urban Zones. 5. Railways
and yards. 6. Industrial Zones. 7. Main roads. M = Grande Place (market-
place). P = Place Royale. J = Botanical Gardens. L = Gare Luxembourg.
M = Gare du Midi. N = Gare du Nord. C = Palais du Cinquantenaire.
M (to the south-east) = Champ de Manœuvres.

the ditch and its wooden palisade. The boulevards to the east in the higher part of the city were soon selected for residences by the wealthy. In the middle of the century a fashionable carriageway, the central *Allée*, was macadamized, and in 1859 it was extended to the outer boulevard between the Louise Gate and the *Allée Verte*. The ditch of the *octroi*, which was stagnant and pestilential, was filled up and converted to boulevards during the 'fifties and 'sixties.

Belgium was the first country on the Continent to establish a railway net. The first station was built in 1835 near the *Allée Verte*, after which it was named ; this was at that time the promenade of the *élite*. In 1841 a new station—the Gare du Nord—was opened at the north end of the town, on marshy ground at the foot of the slopes where the Botanical Gardens were located. At the same time a third station was built on the marshy land on the right of the Senne, facing the quarter of the Vieux-Marché (1840). This was later closed and shifted to the site of the Place Rouppe (1860), and then in 1869 to the site of the present Gare du Midi outside the boulevard to the south of the town. The problem of communication between these stations was solved by making a road on the east bank of the Senne—the Rue Neuve and Rue du Midi (1841)—across the grounds of a convent. This route, formerly occupied by good-class residences, quickly became a commercial thoroughfare with a dense carriage traffic. The Gare de Luxembourg in the Quartier Léopold dates from 1855, and was placed to the east of this residential quarter of the nobility. The stations had an important effect on the growth of the city, for around them were erected commercial buildings and hotels in areas hitherto open ; and around the Gare du Nord and the Gare du Midi whole quarters were soon laid out.

Sanitary measures included the small-scale clearance of slums, the improvement of sanitation in the oldest quarters, the widening and straightening of narrow streets, the building of pavements, and the creation of a covered market (la Madeleine) to relieve the congestion in market squares and on the streets. The building of wider streets attracted better-class houses, but the ousted slum dwellers created a slum elsewhere, since the building of new working-class houses brought no profit. Drinking water was obtained from fountains and wells, but by the middle of the century this was inadequate and a laid-on water supply was built in the 'fifties. In the medieval town, used water was thrown on the street or into the stream, and it was not till the 19th century that underground drainage pipes were introduced. These were laid down in the 'forties, but they were soon inadequate. A modern system of sewage disposal was not possible till after the covering of the Senne, and then great master channels were built in the bed of the river (1870).

New quarters were laid out in the town, and it will be of interest to note some details. The quarter of St. Jean on the east side of the Grande Place was laid out on marshy land on the site of the 12th-century *Hôpital* of St. Jean. This hospital was shifted to the northern edge of the town (1838–43), and the town council took over this old site, which was very extensive, paid compensation to the hospital, and laid out a new quarter with its centre in the Place St. Jean (1846–59). Purchasers of lots had to conform to the regulations of the town council. Other road widenings and rebuilding were effected by the town authorities around the *Vieux-Marché* and in the quarter of the *Grand Béguinage*. The latter, a very characteristic feature of medieval Belgian towns, dated from the 13th century, when it was built on the left bank of the Senne outside the first walls. It was completely surrounded by a wall and ditch.[1] The buildings were demolished in the 'fifties by right of expropriation and a new district laid out with streets radiating from the Place de la Béguinage in front of the church. By order of the town council, houses were limited to two or three storeys. Other smaller quarters and roads were laid out, the land for all these projects being acquired by the town through rights of expropriation, and in several cases by agreements with religious foundations who owned land and buildings. The future plans were drawn up by architects and carried out by the town council, which also stipulated the conditions under which private individuals who had purchased lots might build on them.

(4) Topographic Growth from 1860 to the Present Day

The transformation of the city from 1860 was heralded by three events—the suppression of the *octroi*, the introduction of legislation permitting expropriation by zones in the interests of

---

[1] In much of the modern planning of houses in groups the design of the old religious house foundations (*Godshuisen*) has been followed. These groups of houses, which are found in the old Belgian cities, and number twenty-four in Bruges alone, date from the 12th century and after in the Middle Ages. Each consists of a group of houses in terraces on four sides of a court, which is entered by a large gateway and is thus entirely secluded and quiet.

public use, and Haussmann's achievements in Paris, which affected town planning ideas throughout western Europe. Hitherto, expropriation of property for improvements and sanitation had been effected on the basis of the Napoleonic law of 1810 and a second law of 1835. The main problem was the high cost of buying the land and of carrying on the public utility services, while the owners of the land along new street cuts were subsequently able to fill their pockets from the increased value of the improved sites. In 1858 the first law permitting expropriation by zones, as opposed to individual properties, was introduced, and this was fully established by a second law in 1867. By these laws, the added values of an improved site went to the concern responsible for the improvements, and not to private individuals who happened to hold land and property on it.

Other circumstances precipitated the transformation and improvement of the city, notably the periodical floods of the Senne and the ensuing epidemics of cholera. The river was the main sewage outlet of the town. On its marshy low-lying land building took place in the 19th century, and the lack of sanitation was the main cause of the serious cholera epidemics. The vaulting of the Senne, making it entirely an underground channel in the town, and the building of wide thoroughfares over it, was begun in 1867 and finished in 1872. Two wide thoroughfares now led from the Gare du Nord to the Gare du Midi. This project completely transformed the *basse ville*. More than 1,000 slum buildings and many old mills, tanneries, dye works and breweries along the river were demolished. In their place hotels and large commercial buildings were erected. The city council gave awards to architects for the best building designs : among the competitors was Auguste Rodin. Associated with these two arteries was the rebuilding of the *quartier de la Bourse*, which became the commercial centre of the city and the chief focus of traffic. Here also are the central markets.

A further change was effected in the north-west of the town by the construction of the canal basin in the Senne valley (see Q on Fig. 35). In the 16th century, the Canal de Willebroeck connected the town with the river Rupel and so to Antwerp, and reached the centre of the city by several basins. In the 18th century this *quartier des Bassins* became one of the city's most elegant and frequented districts (the *Allée Verte*). But it lost this character with the opening of new boulevards. After a long period, the project for a ship canal came into effect, the cost of construction being shared between the city and the central government. The construction of the larger basins of Jonction and Vergote outside the boulevards made the old interior ones out of date ; they were filled up (1907–11), and the quarter rebuilt with wide streets and large modern apartment blocks so as to form to-day one of the best residential quarters in the old city. A large new goods depot, called *Tour et Taxis*, was built. Around it were grouped many large concerns and the *Entrepôt* (Custom House), which was shifted from the old basin quarters inside the town.

Changes were also made in the *haute ville*. A whole slum quarter on the north side of the Parc was demolished by a private society, and the present lay-out of streets with good-class residences erected. Their names tell of the date of their origin—the Place de la Liberté, the focal square, and the Place des Barricades, between the Rue Royale and the Boulevard. The majority of the working people were turned out, but they could not find accommodation elsewhere and were left homeless, the ever-recurring problem of 19th-century slum-clearance. They had to find shelter in other working-class quarters, which were already ripe for demolition. On the new sites sumptuous hotels, large commercial buildings, and good-class residences were built. The society, after the completion of its work, went into liquidation in 1885 and the land was bought by the city administration.

A second district to be developed was that along the Rue de la Montagne de la Cour and its continuation the Rue de la Madeleine, which runs steeply down the hill of Coudenberg from the *haute ville* (the present Place Royale) to the *basse ville*. In 1851 the Montagne de la Cour was described as the principal artery of the city, the centre of its commerce, the seat of its luxury shops, and the principal rendezvous *du monde élégant*. This was due not only to its being the old main east–west route through Brussels, but also to its leading to the Court district at the top of the hill. As the main artery of traffic between Germany and Flanders, this through route was always too narrow and steep for the traffic using it. The very fact that it contained the most valuable sites in the city, apart from the difficulties of widening it or building a new parallel road, made the undertaking costly and financially perilous. Old outworn properties lay on the narrow streets which branched from the steep streets of the Montagne de la Cour. The demolition of these took place in the late 'nineties, including one side of the Montagne de la Cour, which was laid out for the Exhibition of 1910 in a great terraced square with fountains and statues overlooking the town.

For many years, during and after the 1914–18 war, the rebuilding of this district and the adjoining districts to north and south at the foot of the hill slopes was held up. This was because no decision could be reached on the suggestion to build a railway through the town to link north and south tracks and to establish a central station, a scheme which had been talked about for many years. The town expropriated property and began demolition, so that during and after the 1914–18 war the centre of the town appeared as a war-damaged ruin. Finally, a fine road was built in 1929—the Rue du Cardinal Mercier—and other road widenings were also effected. The building of blocks of apartments to replace the dwellings which had been destroyed was also begun. The new street widenings of the Rues de Coudenberg and Mercier have given an alternative route to the Rue de la Montagne de la Cour with a much smaller gradient. As a direct consequence of these changes, large new commercial buildings have been erected next to the Palais des Beaux Arts. The old *Steenweg* of the Rue de la Montagne de la Cour has thus been completely side-tracked and has lost much of its former importance. The Rue Lombard has been widened and the buildings adjacent to it demolished so as to afford an alternative route south of the Grande Place between the upper town and the central boulevard. This demolition is in progress. The new Palais de Justice was erected in the south-east of the city at the top of the hill between 1860 and 1883. This was connected with the Palace by the wide Rue de la Régence, with several other road widenings running from it.

Thus, from 1860 the following changes were effected : the boulevards were built over the Senne, now buried underground ; the new quarter appeared north of the Parc ; a new Palais de Justice was erected at the top of the hill overlooking the town, and linked to the lower town, the Palace and the outer boulevards by new street cuts ; the old congested quarters between the hill of Coudenberg and the Grande Place have been demolished ; the narrow and steep Rue de la Montagne de la Cour and the narrow streets branching from it have disappeared ; and this narrow congested main thoroughfare, though in the middle of the last century the most fashionable shopping thoroughfare in the city, has been replaced by wider and less steep roads (including Coudenberg) which now take all the main traffic of the city from east to west. Finally, the old basins in the north-west of the town have become a good residential quarter with tree-lined streets, and new basins have been erected to the north-west, outside the town.

(5) DEVELOPMENT OF THE EASTERN QUARTERS

Before the middle of the century, Brussels had annexed new districts outside the walls to the east—namely, Léopold, Louise, and the North-east. A private society laid out the fashionable Quartier Léopold east of the city beyond the boulevard, adjacent to the Parc and the Court and administrative quarters. In 1837 the main Boulevard de Régent was lined with fashionable residences fronted with carriage-gates and gardens. The new Léopold quarter, laid out on a chessboard plan, was annexed to Brussels in 1853. The district was bounded to the east by a deep valley (later followed by the railway) in which there was a large private estate. This was converted to a zoological garden, then acquired by the city in 1860 and changed into the public park (Parc Léopold) (Fig. 35). Since then, scientific institutions have been built there. Beyond the valley, on the plateau, a large military training ground—*plaine de manœuvres*—was established for the garrison troops, and was converted into a park in 1875. It then passed from the city to the State and was enlarged, and is now known as the Parc du Cinquantenaire (after the National Exhibition celebrating the first fifty years of Belgian independence). To-day it houses various museums and institutions.

The district to the north-east lies between the Avenues Louvain and Loi on the outskirts of the inner town. The city directed this enterprise in the 'seventies, and the plan demanded levelling and terracing, as well as the supply of public utility services. The private owners agreed to defray the expenses of the enterprise by annuities proportional to the value of the land.

The Quartier Louise was laid out by a group of individuals who agreed to build a quarter on the territory of Saint Gilles to the south-east of the city beyond the Boulevard de Waterloo, at the same time that the Quartier Léopold took shape. The boulevard was built up during the first half of the century, and in 1840 the Porte Louise was opened. The main object of the development of this suburb was to connect the city with the fine woods behind the Abbaye de la Cambre across a belt of hills and ravines. The two proprietors of these lands submitted to the city authorities in 1847 a plan for an avenue for the aristocracy in place of the *Allée Verte* in the north of the town. The commune of Ixelles opposed the scheme, and in 1864 the city annexed the Bois de la Cambre, the Avenue Louise and a strip of land on either side of the latter. The success of this avenue as a coach drive and promenade for the *élite* led to land speculation. Sumptuous hotels and residences appeared on the avenue and the streets branching from it. The Quartier Solbosch is a continuation of the Quartier Louise on the east side of the Bois de Cambre. After 1905 it was the site of the International Exhibition, and after 1918 it was used for the new University, formerly housed in the demolished area in the heart of the city. A luxurious residential quarter has been laid out along two main avenues, and this is now the wealthiest and best-constructed residential district in Brussels.

These outer residential districts all lay to the east of the city on the higher land adjacent to the Court quarters. Expansion continued along the two principal axes of the *Rue de la Loi* and the *Rue des Nations*, which have become main arteries of traffic, and from the centre outwards commercial premises have become ever more important.

(6) Development of the Inner Suburbs since 1795

The ramparts, and, after their destruction, the ditch used for the *octroi*, prevented the expansion of the built-up areas. Exit to the surrounding country was possible by seven gates only, each dating from the 14th century. Several other gates were added in the first half of the 19th century. The beginning of extra-mural expansion was naturally to be found outside the gates along the main roads from them, and the surrounding villages were separated from the town by fields and meadows. This was the state of affairs until the abolition of the *octroi* in 1860 and the filling in of the ditch. But the *octroi* barrier served as a real " centrifugal agent " by encouraging building in the suburbs, where, as opposed to the city of Brussels, many goods were tax-free, and taxes on property were also smaller. Other contributing factors were the cheapness of land for building, the location of the stations outside the rampart, and the establishment of factories. The significance of these factors in urban growth varied from one district to another. (See Fig. 34 for the location of the districts.)

It will be noted that the outer areas form to-day a belt of fully built-up land with an average width from the old town boundaries of about 1 to 1½ miles, analogous to the Middle Zone of Paris, which will be described later.   Beyond this zone on all sides there are extensive sub-urban areas.   The chief exclusively industrial areas lie along the Canal de Willebroeck and northwards to Vilvorde and, in much less degree, the Senne to the south.   Here too are the main goods and marshalling yards, and the chief gas works and power plants.   In this outer belt are also the main parks of the environs of Brussels, its airfield (north-east), its chief cemeteries, military training grounds and barracks (south-east), many brick-works (east), sports fields, and racecourse, and its best residential areas.   These are all urban uses that demand, for one reason or another, extensive areas on isolated locations in open country, on cheap land.   Most remarkable is the broad adjustment of the uses to the relief of the land, the industry being confined mainly to the north–south axis of the Senne plain, and the best residences, parks and public buildings being located on the higher and more accidented country or the hillier land to the east.   The whole zone is the equivalent of the Outer Zone described in Paris.   It includes Anderlecht, Molenbeek, Laeken, St.-Josse-ten-Noode, Schaerbeek, Ixelles, St. Gilles, Forest, Uccle.

A main problem of Brussels during the 19th century was that of its territorial limits and the difficulties it had to meet in financing the enterprises it was called on to undertake.   The *Cuve* was abolished in 1810 and Brussels became simply the area inside the rampart.   Residential and industrial development soon spread beyond these limits and the outlying areas were connected with the city ;   the business of building and lay-out was often directed by the city authorities or the *Administration des Hospices* who held land and property on both sides of the ramparts. Moreover, the municipality objected that a large part of the city was taken up by government buildings, since it was a capital city, and that these were exempt from municipal taxes, whereas they should logically assist in the financing of city enterprises.   In the 'nineties, and again in more recent years, it was pointed out by the Mayor that all wished Brussels to be a worthy capital, but that it had only 180,000 inhabitants, whereas around it there were districts housing 300,000 inhabitants who shared in its life and amenities, but escaped its taxes.   A plan was put forward for the modern city, for the extension of its limits, and for the revision of the system of taxation.   The same plea for compensation was put forward to assist the purchase and clearance of property and rebuilding for the central railway junction and the new station, a scheme that has never matured.   The Léopold quarter was added in 1853, Avenue Louise and Bois de la Cambre in 1864. Agitations for the annexation of the railway stations which all lay outside the city boundaries in the 'sixties and 'seventies came to nought, owing to the opposition of the communes. The Parc du Cinquantenaire to the east was bought by the city, though the commune in which it was situated, which became an important residential district, was outside the city limits. Small additions were made in 1897, and in 1921 Laeken, Haren, and Neder-over-Heembeek were incorporated, as well as the district of the maritime basins in the north-west. In 1842 the city had an area of about 2 sq. miles, and, after the annexations, about 11 sq. miles. This area, elongated from north to south, by no means covers all the built-up area of the Brussels community, and excludes nearly all the outlying suburbs to the east, west and south.

(7) Distribution and Movements of Population

From 1526 to 1800 the number of buildings practically doubled, reaching about 14,000 at the latter date. The whole of the urban agglomeration of Brussels, that is, both the city and its contiguous urban and semi-urban areas, had a total of 35,000 buildings in 1846 (the date of the first official buildings census) and 137,500 in 1920—a fourfold increase.

In the decade 1846–56, the inner suburbs [1] increased by a quarter, the same rate as the city itself. One main reason for this, which caused much concern to the city people, was that the suburbs were free of the *octroi*, the duty charged on building materials entering the city ramparts, so that building costs in the suburbs were much lower than in the city. The growth was much faster in the next decade (1850–60) but in the 1860–80 period the number of buildings in the city scarcely increased, while those in the suburbs increased by 70 per cent. This was a period of great transformation, involving much demolition and rebuilding. By 1900 the buildings in the city numbered 21,600 and in the suburbs there were 47,800. Then down to 1910 there was another great increase of building in the inner suburbs, by 30 per cent., rising to a total of 63,000 buildings. In general, the city

---

[1] Middle Zone : Laeken, Anderlecht, Etterbeek, Ixelles, Molenbeek, St. Gilles, St. Josse, [Schaerbeek. These, with the exception of Etterbeek, make up the ancient *Cuve*.

Outer Zone, between the inner suburbs and the city boundary : Anderghem, Forest, Jette-St.-Pierre, Koekelberg, Uccle, Watermael, Boitsfort, Woluwe-St.-Lambert.

shows a rapid increase of buildings from 1846 to 1866, an almost stationary period from 1866 to 1890, then a steep rise to 1900, and no change after 1900, and a small but decided drop after 1910.

The greatest decrease down to 1920 was in the inner suburbs, just outside the old ramparts, but since 1900 this belt has been " saturated ". The decade 1920–30 shows a much larger proportional increase in the outer zone. As for the areas outside the ancient city of Brussels, the south and north districts show the greatest urban development, accounting for two-thirds of the increase of buildings in the whole area outside the old nucleus, while the eastern districts accounted for over a quarter.

These trends may be expressed alternatively on the basis of population figures since 1880. In the first table opposite, the city is distinguished from all the outer areas. It will be apparent that the decrease of Brussels as a whole began in the 1900–10 decade, although its increase from 1880 to 1900 was far below that of the agglomeration as a whole. The second table shows the population for each of the adjacent communes since 1880.

To sum up, before the development of rapid transport permitted the wide separation of work and residence, the nobility and upper *bourgeoisie* lived at the top of the Coudenberg hill in the *haute ville*. At the end of the 18th century, this was extended by the opening of the Place Royale and the Parc, and later gave rise to the quarters of Léopold and Louise, east of, and adjacent to them, outside the *octroi* ramparts. The whole of the eastward expansion has been favoured by the wealthier people for fashionable residence, for two main reasons—the attraction of the royal residence, that has been sited on the hill since the beginnings of the town, and of the pleasant country on the high plateau that extends eastwards from the Court quarter. In the last forty years, with the advent of the electric tram, and then the motor-car, the residential area has expanded in all directions, but while the older, poorer-class quarters are on the flat plain near the factories, the more select residential districts are generally situated on hills, as at Forest, Uccle, St. Gilles, Laeken. Single-family residences for the black-coated worker and the factory worker have spread in all directions. To the east, the built-up area has reached the Forest of Soignes, and to the west the second line of hills on the left bank of the Senne. But the most remarkable expansion has been to the north and south, on the plain of the Senne and on the higher land next to it. The area north from Brussels along the floor of the Senne valley, alongside the Ship Canal, as far north as Vilvorde has become the main industrial area, with a great concentration of railway tracks.

GROWTH OF BRUSSELS, 1880–1930

(from *Recensement général, 1937*, Vol. I, p. 151, Brussels, 1934)

			1880–90	1890–1900	1900–10	1910–20	1920–30
City	.	.	. 11·9	6·6	0·2	− 7·3	− 1·3
Suburbs	.	.	. 24·3	29·1	38·8	11·0	13·8
Total	.	.	. 19·0	10·1	21·2	5·6	9·9

GROWTH OF POPULATION IN BRUSSELS AND THE ADJACENT COMMUNES

(From *Recensement général*, Vol. I, p. 153, Brussels, 1937)

				1880	1900	1930	1938* (Estimated)
Brussels	.	.	.	183·3	218·6	200·4†	191·7
Inner Suburbs :							
Anderlecht	.	.	.	22·8	47·9	80	88·0
Etterbeek	.	.	.	11·7	20·8	45·3	49·2
Ixelles	.	.	.	36·3	58·6	83·9	80·3
Molenbeek-St.-Jean	.		.	41·7	58·4	64·8	62·6
Saint Gilles	.		.	33·1	51·8	64·1	61·3
St.-Josse-ten-Noode	.		.	28·0	32·1	30·9	28·1
Schaerbeek	.	.	.	40·8	63·5	118·7	123·5
Outer Suburbs ·							
Anderghem	.	.	.	2·4	4·7	14·0	18·0
Forest	.	.	.	4·2	9·5	39·6	45·7
Jette	.	.	.	4·7	10·0	22·2	27·7
Koekelberg	.	.	.	4·9	10·6	13·9	14·8
Uccle	.	.	.	10·7	18·0	43·3	52·8
Watermael-Boitsfort	.		.	3·6	6·5	16·1	18·5
Woluwe-St.-Lambert	.		.	1·6	3·5	18·2	24·7
Woluwe-St.-Pierre	.		.	1·6	2·9	13·5	16·0
Brussels Agglomeration (approx.)				431·4	617·4	868·9	902·9

* Estimates from *Le Moniteur Belge*, Brussels, 13 April, 1939.
† Addition of Haren, Laeken and Neder-over-Heembeek, incorporated in 1921.

All this expansion has been effected by individual landowners and by private societies, and, above all, by the *Administration des Hospices*, which, as a union of the religious foundations of the city, held a great deal of land both within and outside the city. Again and again the city authorities had to make deals with it in order to undertake changes in the city, while the *Administration des Hospices* opened up its own lands, especially on the west side, for industrial development and working-class houses. The stations lay on land which belonged to the *Hospices*. The latter also undertook the building and paving of roads and drainage schemes.
In conclusion, it will be observed that there have been certain

elements of permanence in the face of the changing city. We note the concentration of business and of civic buildings around the market-place and along the Senne, and of royalty and State buildings and of the rich residential areas on the higher land to the east. The *haute ville* was selected at the end of the 18th century for the State government buildings. On the other hand, the city administrative buildings are all situated in the centre of the *basse ville*. Here, too, commerce is concentrated. The Bourse has been built near the market-place. Near by is the *Halles*, the public market, and around it in the city there are other market-places. There have also been marked changes of occupance in other areas, especially in the centre of the city. Thus, the quarter in the centre on the slopes of the Coudenberg Hill, on either side of the Rue de la Montagne de la Cour, was originally a residential quarter for the *grande noblesse* ; later it was occupied by the *bourgeoisie* ; then it became a kind of Latin quarter ; and, finally, the city's banking quarter. From the beginnings, however, the distinction between the business city on the plain and the residential city on the hill has always persisted.

CHAPTER 9

AMSTERDAM, ROTTERDAM AND THE HAGUE: POPULATION DISTRIBUTION AND TRENDS

The changes in the expansion and structure of the modern city are obviously associated with a certain pattern of density and movements of population and with certain demographic traits and trends, both for the city as a whole and for its component parts. The broad characteristics of the distribution and movements of population can easily be obtained from the figures for the major census units into which every city is divided. But the results are crude, since these areas are large and usually heterogeneous. What is required is a much more detailed analysis of demographic, social and economic data on the basis of much smaller unit areas, and it is only for relatively few continental cities that such investigations have been made. Fortunately the conditions and processes of urban development are common to all cities, so that sample studies suffice to indicate their nature. We select three cities in Holland, Amsterdam, Rotterdam, and The Hague, since, together with the other towns of the Netherlands, they have been the subject of special investigation.

(1) AMSTERDAM

(a) Site and Development

The population of Amsterdam rose from 220,000 in 1800—when it was one of the largest cities of Europe—to 408,000 in 1850, 510,000 in 1900, 713,000 in 1915, and 793,000 in 1939. There are many smaller towns in its orbit, forming part of what may be called Greater Amsterdam. The total population of this whole area is certainly not far short of the million mark. Though not the capital of the State, Amsterdam ranks as one of the greatest seats of commerce and culture in the world.

The stages in the topographic expansion of Amsterdam are clearly defined by its semi-circular belt of canals and by the disparities in the street plan between the various concentric belts (Fig. 37). Amsterdam had tardy beginnings. In the early 13th century a dyke was built by the Counts of Holland on the south

161

side of the bay of the Ij across the mouth of a little stream called the Amstel. This sea-dyke was designed to prevent the invasion of the water southward from the Zuyder Zee, which had been converted from a medieval lake to an arm of the sea. In order

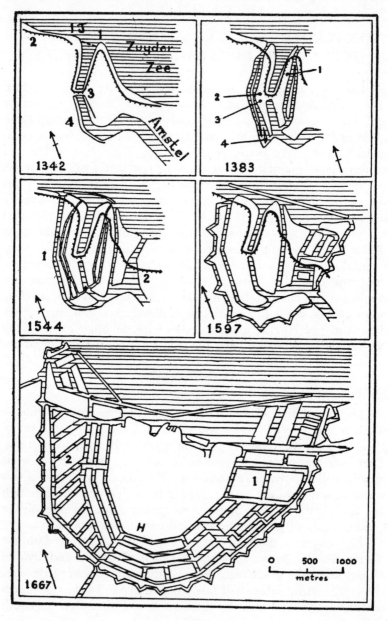

to negotiate the outlet of the river Amstel a *dam* or barrage was built with sluices across it to permit the evacuation of the water from the interior at low tide. Thus the barrage or dam across the Amstel, and the sea-dyke on the south side of the Ij estuary, formed the nucleus of the small new settlement. This had its beginning on the east side of the channel (Oudezijde) but soon spread to the west side (Nieuwezijde) where the old Town Hall was situated on the dam. This is the prototype of numerous towns and villages in Holland. The first defensive ditches were built in 1342, the Nieuwezijde Voorburgwal and the Oudezijde Voorburgwal, one dug on either side of, and parallel to, the Amstel. (The two western moats and part of the Amstel were not filled up until the latter part of the 19th century.) The ditches were connected by sluices with the Amstel and the Ij. The area was about 900 metres in length and 450 metres in width, and covered 250 hectares. In 1383 a second line of ditches was built about 50 metres from, and parallel to, the first, the two Voorburgwallen. These four ditches converged to the south of the town, with their exits to the north at sluice gates across the sea-dyke. Houses were alined on these canals and the river, and were built on timber piles 13 metres long.

Further extension came in 1442, when new ditches were dug to east and west, while a new quarter was annexed to the south of the town. In the large areas so annexed, ample space was available for monasteries, and for the first time the town was fortified (1481–8), with towers commanding the entrances to it. On the alluvial soil of Wallion island, which was bounded by the canals, industries, especially shipyards, were already established.

In 1593 the town was surrounded by bastioned fortifications, and a double barrage was built in the Ij to protect the merchant

FIG. 37.—The Growth of Amsterdam (redrawn from Hazewinkel, " Le Développe-ment d'Amsterdam ", *Annales de Géographie*, Vol. XXXV, 1926, p. 325).

1342 :—1. Presumed site of first dyke. 2. Sea-dyke. 3. Dam. 4. Kalver-straat.

1383 :—Addition of two dykes about 50 metres beyond the first. 1. Old Church. 2. New Church. 3. Town Hall. 4. Beguinage.

1544 :—In 1442 new ditches cut to east and west and addition of district to the south. Town fortified for first time with towers along the canal. 1. Singel. 2. Zwanenburgwal, Oudeschans, and Montelbaantoren.

1597 :—Extension along the Ij to form a semi-circle and surrounded by bastioned fortifications. Extensions on east, housing Jewish refugees (Portuguese, Germans, Poles).

1667 :—Great extension in 1610. Bastions of 1593 destroyed and replaced by the Heerengracht (H) with two others, Kaizersgracht and Prinsengracht. 1. Plant-age (Park). 2. Jordaan. The line of fortifications lay on the Singelgracht, the outermost of the canals.

fleet. Then in 1610 the most grandiose extension took place, probably unrivalled by that of any other historic town in Europe. The area was increased to four times its extent in 1593, reaching 725 hectares with a radius of 1,800 metres. The bastions completed in 1593 were demolished and the Heerengracht canal was dug in their place, with two canals (Kaizersgracht and Prinsengracht) running parallel to the first. Beyond lay the new walls on the Singelgracht. A large area was reserved in the west for a working-class quarter, the Jordaan, but elsewhere the canals were lined by the homes of the wealthy merchants. It was also during the 17th century that many public buildings appeared, and the new Town Hall was built on the Dam, on a basis of 13,000 piles. In 1667 the whole belt was built-up with the exception of the north-east, where a park, the Plantage, was laid out, which by the middle of the 19th century was already covered with buildings.

The municipal authority decided on the position of the three canals, but the planning of the new areas between them and the walls was left to private initiative. Consequently the large area in the west—the main unbuilt-on area to be embraced by the new walls, later known as the Jordaan and Leyden quarters— had its streets and houses laid out in the direction of the existing paths and ditches, and crossed the canals obliquely, so that there was no conformity in street plan between this district and that alongside the three canals. This quarter, however, was spaciously laid out with workers' houses and factories, such as tanneries, woollen and velvet mills, and dye works. The fortifications and the three canals finally formed a vast crescent around the old town. This formed the master plan of the town and took over a hundred years to complete, though the western section was finished by 1650. This section extended south to the Leidsche-gracht and was connected to the existing east wall by a temporary one. This southern section of the town was thus only half enclosed within the fortress. The fortifications were not continued till 1663, and then as far as the Amstel, so that the city was then enclosed by 27 bastions.

When good-class houses were needed in the 18th century the eastern section was undertaken, beginning with the three canals running from the Amstel. It was suggested that one of these might be made into a broad avenue like Voorhout at The Hague, but this was not done till seventy years later when the north-east section was laid out. This north-east section was reserved by the municipal authorities for gardens and parks ; some was sold for high-class buildings, and the remaining open space was used for the Zoological Gardens, Botanical Gardens, and the Park Gardens. The whole section had a grid plan. This became the fashionable residential quarter, although the district has deteriorated and the best residential quarters are to be found farther out in the drained Watergraffsmeer to the south and especially along the banks of the Amstel and Vecht.

A twofold development is to be noted in this extension. The lay-out and the sale of the property throughout the crescent was controlled by the municipal authorities. The congested working-class industrial quarters lie in the west, and high-class residential area and parks in the east. There has been a gradual change of the latter district with the expansion of the town and of the shops, and with the shift of fashionable residences farther afield to the city outskirts.

The population of Amsterdam in 1600 was estimated at 50,000, though it was probably higher, for another estimate gives 100,000 ten years later. In 1663 it was 200,000, and in 1795, the date of the first official census, it reached 217,000. The early 19th century was a period of stagnation. The North Holland Canal was built (1818–25) in order to short-circuit the shallow outlet of the Ij to the Zuyder Zee. During the forty years following 1825 there was building and land drainage without any preconceived plan. After 1865 public attention again turned to the planning of further extensions. This period was marked by the advent of the railway, the building of the North Sea Canal (1876) and the demolition of the fortifications. Two schemes of extension were prepared, including the provision of parks and the siting of a railway station in the southern extension so as to preserve the fine waterfront. The next fifty years witnessed the emergence of another built-up belt around the city, which has been developed with little organic relationship to the old town. The new station was in fact built on the Ij, and the site of the fortifications, instead of being preserved as an open belt as in other continental cities, was sold for building. The annexation of Nieuwe Amstel in 1896 gave an opportunity for further extension, and this was followed by the Amsterdam Plan of 1921.

Much housing development took place on the outskirts in the inter-war period, though this was haphazard and largely concentrated on the highways by private speculators. The population during the 19th century was fairly stable until the last quarter, when it doubled, and then increased by a further 50 per cent. from 1900 to 1920. Housing development in this period in Amsterdam as throughout Holland was conditioned by the Dutch Housing Act of 1901. This law required every town of 10,000 inhabitants and over to draw up a scheme governing its future expansion and to revise its plan every ten years. Co-operative building societies were financed by the State, and the city often acquired land for its housing settlements. The municipal authorities built whole districts.

The first plans for Amsterdam dealt with portions of the city—the Indische Buurt, the north bank of the river Ij, and, most famous of all, the Amsterdam South scheme that was prepared by the architect, Beilage. These sectors soon formed a belt surrounding the old town. But the city spread beyond its boundaries, and, after prolonged delay, a great annexation of area was made in 1921, and the piecemeal schemes of its component parts were merged into a single scheme for the whole of Amsterdam. This was drawn up in 1926 by the Director of Public Works. A special department was established to deal with research and the preparation of a general plan, and it started work in 1929. This plan was finally drawn up in 1933 and accepted by the City Council.

(a) *The Distribution and Movements of Population*

With this general view of the development of the city as a background, we may now examine in some detail the distribution and movements of its population.

DISTRIBUTION OF POPULATION IN AMSTERDAM BY DISTRICTS
(from Leyden)

	1859	1889	1909	1920	1930
Old Town . .	234,000	310,000	268,000	256,000	183,000
New Town .	5,000	94,000	293,000	388,000	459,000
Suburbs. . .	(6,500)	(14,000)	(23,000)	33,500	113,000
Total . .	245,500	418,000	584,000	677,500	745,000

The table above gives the population data for three groups of districts, the old historic town, the new town, that developed mainly in the 19th century, and the new suburbs. These may be referred to as the inner, middle and outer zones of the urban complex.

The limits of the old town were fixed in the 17th century by the fortifications—walls and bastions—of 1663, which were destroyed in the 19th century and are to-day marked by the Singelgracht. This nucleus had an area of 800 hectares (2,000 acres), though with the reclamation of part of the Ij and the building of the harbour this was increased to its present figure of 861 hectares (2,150 acres). It was not until the middle of the 19th century that the city outgrew these limits. The population of the old town in 1859 was nearly a quarter of a million, and reached its maximum (310,000) in 1889. In 1859 virtually all the population was in the old town, but after that the proportion fell rapidly so that in 1889 76 per cent., in 1909 47 per cent., in 1920 38 per cent. and in 1930 24 per cent. of the inhabitants lived in the old town. The first extensions took place in 1865 outside the Utrecht Gate, and at the same time the Vondelpark was laid out to the south-east. But it was not until 1879 that the systematic lay-out of streets on the surrounding polders began, and in 1881 the Ceintururbaan received its name as the outer limit of the first new quarters. The growth of a " city core ", however, had already begun. The northern half of the canal called the Dam was drained in 1840, to make way for the Commercial Exchange. The southern part was drained in 1882. In 1867 the Spuisstraat was laid out on the site of a drained canal, similarly the Spui in 1882, and the Voorburgwal in 1884. Around these relatively wide thoroughfares in the heart of the old town clustered the new city buildings—newspaper firms, banks, warehouses and offices. The city itself had 25,000 persons in 1920 (15,000 in 1930), but the aggregate population of the old town was the same. Between 1889 and 1920 the population in the other parts of the town had almost maintained its level, the decrease for the whole being about 55,000. In 1920 the old town was overcrowded and in the following decade there was a decrease of 73,000.

The greatest changes in the extent and structure of Amsterdam and in the distribution of its population have taken place since 1921 (Fig. 38). The peak of 310,000 in the old town in 1889 fell to 183,000 in 1930, and all districts show a large decrease in the 1920–30 period. But this decrease was not limited to the old town. In the new town outside it the total population increased, but this was confined mainly to the district between

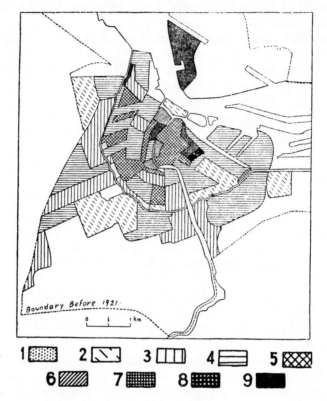

FIG. 38.—Decrease of Population in Amsterdam, 1920–30 (from Leyden).

Percentage decrease :—1. 0·1–1·0. 2. 1–10. 3. 10–20. 4. 20–30. 5. 30–40.
6. 40–50. 7. 50–60. 8. 60–80. 9. Over 80.

Amstel and Nieuwe Vaart and secondarily to the district north
of the Ij. *In all the other districts of the new town there is a marked
decrease of population.*

No less than 102 of the 169 town districts record a decrease of
population from 1920 to 1930, representing a total of 137,138 persons,
i.e. 20 per cent. of the total population in 1920, whereas the total
population of the whole city increased by only 80,000. There is
appearing an entirely new picture of the distribution of population in
the total area of the great city (Leyden).

In 1921 Greater Amsterdam was created by the addition of
outlying communes, between Haarlemare and the Zuyder Zee,
and north of the Ij in the Waterland, so that the area was increased

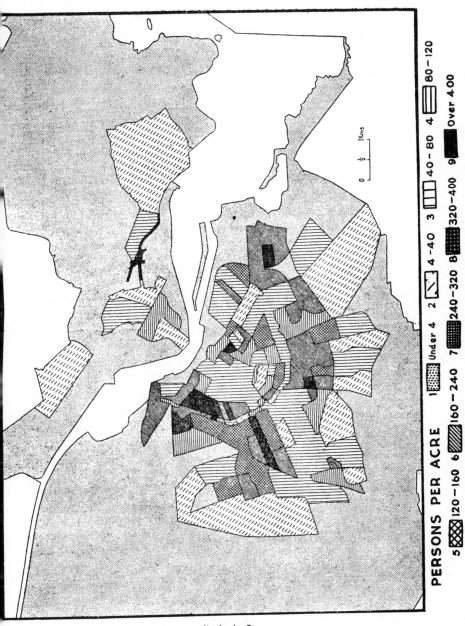

PERSONS PER ACRE

1 Under 4 2 4-40 3 4-40 4 80-120
5 120-160 6 160-240 7 240-320 8 320-400 9 Over 400

0 ½ 1Kms

FIG. 39.—The Density of Population in Amsterdam for 1930 (from Leyden).

to 17,455 hectares (about 7 square miles). The built-up area was thus free to expand, thanks also to the mobile and rapid transport afforded by the motor-bus, and to a planned policy of building development. Cheap but good houses have been built on the outskirts, slums cleared in the old town, and movement outwards encouraged. Thus in the island of Uilenburg in the east of the old town, near the harbour, population was reduced from 3,000 to 400 through the clearance of the slums by the municipal authority. The decrease of population in the inner residential areas that were built at the end of the 19th century until the 1914–18 war is mainly due to the shift of families from the congested tenements, out to the suburbs built since 1918, where they could enjoy better equipped flats at no greater rents.

The concentration of population in the old town down to the end of the 19th century resulted in appallingly high densities of population (Fig. 39). In 1889 the highest densities were reached in Jordaan in the west and in the Jewish quarter immediately east of the city centre in the Uilenburg island. In these districts the average density was over 600 persons per hectare (about 240 per acre) and in many districts it was over 1,000 persons per hectare (about 400 per acre). This was reduced by 1930, and to-day no part has over 1,000 per hectare. Jordaan is still the most densely peopled district in Amsterdam, but the general picture reveals much lower densities in the old town than in 1889. In the " city " in the western half of the old town, 100–200 persons per hectare (40–80 per acre) are the lowest densities. High densities of 300–600 per hectare occur in the tenement districts of the " new town " immediately outside the Segelgracht (the limit of the old town), with, in isolated districts, 400–800 per hectare. The outer built-up districts have 10–100 persons per hectare. The maximum densities in the old town were reached in 1889. Decrease began in the centre of the old town in the 'fifties and spread throughout the western half in the next two decades. In the 1920–30 period the decrease of population in the old town as a whole was greater than in the preceding seventy years. The decline also affected parts of the new town.[1]

[1] Taken from F. Leyden, " Die Entwölkerung der Innenstadt in den Grösseren Städten von Holland ", in *Tijdschrift voor Economische Geographie*, in five parts, 1935–6, Rotterdam, 15 April 1935. Density figures are given in hectares. One hectare is equal to 2·5 acres.

(2) ROTTERDAM

(a) Site and Development

Rotterdam, situated on the north bank of the Nieuwe Maas at the mouth of the small river Rotte, had the same problems of site to contend with as Amsterdam, and had its tardy origins in the middle of the 13th century. It attained town status about 1300 and undertook the building of its first fortifications in 1359. The configuration of the town in 1839 and 1935 is shown in Fig. 40. It began alongside the Rotte and then concentrated along the river front, progressively expanding southwards by the reclamation of land from the alluvium of the river floor for the construction of canals and buildings, until it attained a triangular shape.

Rotterdam, before its destruction in 1940, exhibited in marked degree the high mobility of population associated with a rapid increase in numbers, and the rapid growth of a modern city core on the site of the old buildings of a medieval town.

Rotterdam has grown with remarkable rapidity from about 100,000 persons in the 'fifties of last century to over 600,000 in 1939. It has a natural site unfavourable for a large city. It has grown above all as a great transit port, in which bulk foods are transferred from sea-going cargo ships to barges that ply up and down the Rhine. It has also acquired industries in association with the port. The old town lies on the north side of a branch of the Rhine, while the port, covering a large area, bigger than that of the city itself, lies opposite the old town, with the main modern port downstream (west) of Rotterdam on both banks of the river. Our concern here is with the city (Plate 14).

The triangle of the old town, as defined in the 17th century, is the delta of the Rotte, with its highest point only 6 metres (21 feet) above the surrounding polders and only just over 2 metres (7 feet) above the mean sea level. The old town was imprisoned within its fortifications, and the surrounding lands provided it with vegetables, meat, milk, and fruit. The increase of population in the middle of the 12th century led to ever-increasing congestion on its one square kilometre of area. There was a dearth of good drinking water and the canals had become open sewers. Densities reached over 800 and even over 1,000 per hectare (400 per acre) at the peak period of congestion in 1859.

The first incentive to reduce the congestion was due to a commission appointed in the 'fifties to examine and make sug-

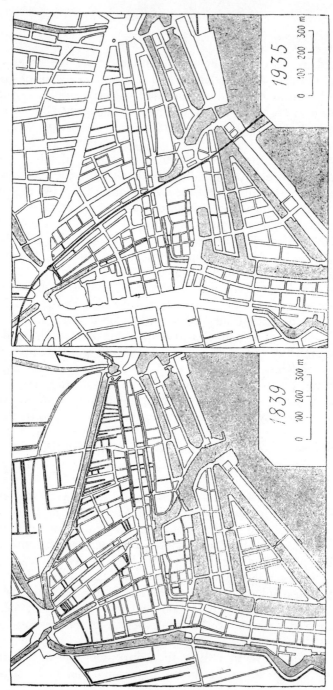

FIG. 40.—The Street plan of Rotterdam in 1839 and 1935 (from Leyden).
(Scale, approx. 1 : 18,000.)

gestions for the improvement of living conditions.   This commission recommended the draining of the stagnant canals in the old town and considered the extension of the town area, to a new canal belt from Singel to a point near the Old Dyke of Kraalingen and the Blommersdijk.   These recommendations were carried out, and permitted the extension of the port and the addition of the district on the south bank of the river immediately facing Rotterdam.   This was the first time that recommendations were made for the improvement of health and housing conditions in a city centre on the basis of population densities by districts within it.   But the maximum densities were not yet reached. The increase of population continued in the eastern part of the triangle.   By 1900 the very high density of the old town had already been relieved except in the north-eastern sector.   In the 'nineties the city was greatly expanded and the population shifted outwards to new built-up areas.   In 1859 several districts had over 1,000 persons per hectare.   By 1879 there was a considerable reduction in the western half, and this started a general decrease of population in the old town.   In 1900 the greatest density in any one district was just under 800 persons per hectare (say 320 per acre).   In 1849 the old town contained 73 per cent. of the total population, in 1879 45 per cent., in 1899 19 per cent., and in 1930 only 4 per cent.

POPULATION FIGURES FOR THE CHIEF DISTRICTS OF ROTTERDAM
(from Leyden)

	1849	1859	1869	1879	1889	1899	1920*	1930
I. Rotterdam proper :								
Old Town .	65,300	69,000	69,500	67,400	63,500	58,900	(43,500)	21,300
Rubroek .	9,100	12,900	19,600	38,700	51,900	69,400	(79,300)	72,800
Blommersdijk	4,500	7,800	9,500	16,300	31,100	60,300	(89,000)	67,500
Cool-Polder	10,100	15,500	18,100	27,900	34,600	35,600	(32,300)	27,300
II. Kraalingen .	3,700	4,600	7,100	11,300	16,700	24,000	(47,900)	40,400
III. Delfshaven .	3,200	4,200	7,900	11,400	17,100	31,700	(109,700)	150,000
IV. Feyenoord .	—	—	—	1,360	8,100	28,800	(34,300)	26,600
Charlois and Katendrecht	3,700	4,300	5,800	7,800	9,700	12,800	(51,500)	143,000

* Estimates.

In the 'sixties and after, the improvements suggested by the commission were made : in the 'seventies, the drainage and filling in of the Binnenrotte and the opening of the Dordrecht railway ; in the 'nineties, the extension of the town to include Delfshaven,

Kraalingen, Charlois and Katendrecht.   Most remarkable of the recent changes in the old town are the opening of the new Town Hall on the Cool Singel, which has shifted the focus of city life right out of the congested quarters of the old town, and the cutting through the latter of a wide thoroughfare.

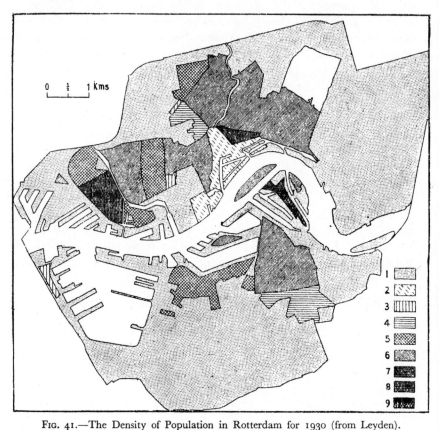

FIG. 41.—The Density of Population in Rotterdam for 1930 (from Leyden).

Persons per acre :—1. Under 4. 2. 4-40. 3. 40-80. 4. 80-120. 5. 120-160. 6. 160-240. 7. 240-320. 8. 320-400. 9. Over 400.

(b) Distribution and Movements of Population

The density of population in 1930 is shown on Fig. 41.

Detailed statistics by districts within the old town are not available after 1910.   Figures for the 1920–33 period have been worked out by Leyden from the voting registers, which are available street by street for small districts, and the changes in the number of voters (men and women) between these two dates.

(Fig. 42). A decrease of 82 per cent. is recorded in the neigh-bourhood of the Town Hall and the displacement of old houses by offices and buildings is evidenced by large decreases of two-thirds in the Kipstraat–Botersloot–Singel triangle, and 50 per cent. between the Binnenrotte and Oppert and Meent.

The most remarkable feature of this latest period (since 1920), distinguishing it from earlier periods, is a considerable decrease in the middle zone districts *outside* the old town—a decrease in

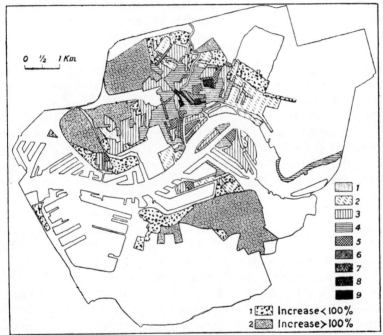

FIG. 42.—The Changes of Population in Rotterdam, 1920–33 (from Leyden).

Percentage decrease :—1. = 0·1–1.   2. = 1–10.   3. = 10–20.   4. = 20–30.
5. = 30–40.   6. = 40–50.   7. = 50–60.   8. = 60–80.   9. = more than 80 per cent.
Percentage increase :—1 = less than 100 per cent.   2. = more than 100 per cent.

some districts of a quarter to one-third. Of the 224 voting districts in 1920, 178 record decreases, 81,000 persons in the aggregate, or 16 per cent. of the total population.

Large increases, however, were recorded in the outer districts. These have been due mainly, as in other Dutch cities, to the planning of whole districts with cheap new tenement dwellings erected by municipal authorities. These districts have attracted families from the middle zone as well as from the centre. Thus, Vreewijk on the south side of the river had 4,000 inhabitants in

1920, and 17,000 in 1933. Blijdorp and Bergpolder had virtually no inhabitants in 1920, but housed 10,000 in 1930.

The great majority of the additional people in these outer districts are drawn from Rotterdam. These new districts are occupiéd by people of low income, who find the rent of their former dwelling too high. Only in this way can the movement out of the western districts be explained, since these consist mainly of relatively new blocks of multi-storeyed flats. The residents in these new outer districts are not " settled in ". On the contrary, a high proportion shift quickly and there are many removals after a short period of those who seek cheaper and better houses in a more desirable neighbourhood. Thus, the new district of Bergpolder at the end of 1934, scarcely one and a half years after the construction of the first houses, had already changed many of its tenants. Of 2,552 dwellings, in October 1934 no less than 380 had second, and 37 third, tenants, and there had been no less than 464 removals ! Of the removed families, only one-third remained in the district, a sixth left Rotterdam (for a neighbouring sub-urban district), but the most remarkable feature is that one-half of the families removed to the older parts of the city in the middle zone.

In Rotterdam on the average there were 50,000 removals annually. Without exaggeration, we can say that a third of the total population is involved in this " nomadic " movement. This mobility, however, in the outer districts is greatest in the tenement districts where there is attachment neither to dwelling nor to neighbourhood. But in Vreewijk to the south, on the other hand, where single-family terrace-houses have been built with two to three storeys and gardens, there is greater stability as compared with the massive blocks of four-, five- and six-storey tenements in the north of the city, as at Blijdorp, Bergpolder, Spangen, and (to the south) Charlois. Leyden concludes that life in blocks of flats, even given modern labour-saving conveniences, is not congenial to the Dutch, who prefer their traditional single-family houses. Detailed investigations of this kind in other cities would give interesting material on the flat v. house problem.

To the north the city boundary coincides with the circular railway, which sets a limit to expansion, although it has not as yet been reached. Trams and buses already run north to Hillegersberg, Overschie and Schiedam. Schiebroek lies on the express electric line from Scheveningen and The Hague to the Hofplein. These outlying districts are growing quickly. Thus

Hillegersberg between 1920 and 1935 grew from 5,000 to 21,000, Schiebroek from 750 to 6,000, and Overschie from 5,000 to 9,000.

It will be clear that a large proportion of the workers in Rotterdam, especially those working in the city, live on the outskirts of the city or beyond its borders. As soon as a family can afford to, it leaves the city, and the well-to-do live outside the unhealthy, flat, and monotonous surroundings of the city proper. But it is remarkable that nearly all the inter-war housing in the outer zone is for working-class persons, not for the wealthier families. The latter live well outside Rotterdam. There are better-class residences in Kraalingen, Delfshaven and along the outer Singel, and on the left bank of the Meuse (Hillevliet), but these lie along one main thoroughfare, forming a façade, immediately behind which are rows of dreary single-family houses of the lower-paid workers. Large numbers of commuters also live in The Hague. Schiedam, another residential town, has about 60,000 inhabitants. It has no trace of a business core, and the population is evenly distributed over its built-up area. Its growth is associated with Rotterdam and the Merwehafen (1923), and the great majority of its new residents work in Rotterdam. Blocks of modern flats occur here as well as more secluded quarters with single-family houses.

The tendency for people to move out of the city to live in more salubrious spots on its outskirts is very marked in Rotterdam. There are few select residential quarters in Rotterdam, and these, moreover, do not form compact districts. They are houses along main boulevards and immediately behind them are monotonous terrace houses. Such boulevards occur east of the Kraalingen, along the Singel, and on the left bank of the Meuse at Hillevliet.

These demographic features have marked effects on the social make-up of the city, as is evidenced, for example, by the distribution of votes at the elections. Thus, in 1933, the location of the better-class districts noted above was reflected in the distribution of Liberal votes, which was fairly even. But in the inner town, where small shopkeepers make up a high proportion of the residents, the Catholic Party was important—for the shopkeepers in Holland, as is well known, are mainly Catholics. In the harbour areas, the lower-paid workers' areas, and in the unstable outer tenement areas, the Social Democrats were dominant. On the other hand, the old village of Charlois, south of the Meuse, had a large Protestant element that voted for the Anti-Revolutionary Party.

(3) THE HAGUE

(a) Site and Development

The Hague was selected by the Counts of Holland as a hunting lodge, situated in woodland on the eastern side of the coastal dunes. They built a castle here in the 13th century which became their permanent residence. The city became the political and cultural capital of the Netherlands, and its building shows the influence of the French architects of the Baroque period. Industry is of little importance, yet the population has continued to increase from 42,000 in 1796 and 66,500 in 1850 to 437,000 in 1930 and 487,000 in 1937. It is the richest city in the Netherlands and is provided with large hotels, fine shops, and restaurants. Its nucleus is the old Court quarter with the Vijver lake in its centre, and the Binnenhof, the original castle of the Counts of Holland, on its southern side, and the Plaats and Butien Hof at its western end. To the west lies the nucleus of the town, centred on the Groote Kerk, between the Vijver to the east and the Royal Palace to the north. This old town was bounded by a ditch (Singel) in the period 1613-19, which enclosed a roughly rectangular area (Fig. 43). Beyond this area are the stations to the south-east, the gas works to the south-west, the Wilhelms Park to the north, and the Bosch (Wood) to the east, all of these having been added to the town in the middle of the 19th century. Extensive woods link the city with Scheveningen, the old village and the new coastal resort on the coast to the north-west.

The old town has been greatly modified by street cuts, and the sub-urban area has extended widely to the surrounding polder and dune areas. The densities of population by small districts for 1930 are shown on Fig. 43. In 1859 the low density in the old town corresponded with the government and court quarter (Vijver) and the high-class residential district along the Prinsengracht. In sharp contrast was the overpopulated sector of the Volksbuurten south of the Prinsengracht. On an area of 3·5 hectares there were 3,920 inhabitants, comparing with the worst slums in Amsterdam and Rotterdam. In the north-west there were also densities of 700 and over per hectare ; a part of these slums still remains. The old town to-day has a clearly defined central business district at the main road crossways centred on the town hall and church bordered by the Vijver and the Royal Palace. The contrast between the Court quarter (Hofstad) and the burgesses' quarter (Volksbuurten) still holds good. The old town on an area of 206·5 hectares had 71,000–75,000 inhabitants in 1899. A decrease had begun in 1900, but sharp depopulation began after World War I, this being relatively late as compared with other large cities. In 1930 the old town had 50,000 inhabitants out of a total population of 437,675 for the whole city.

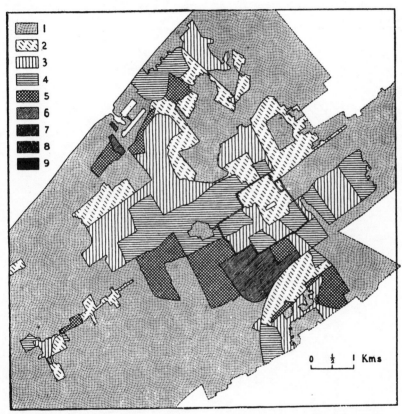

FIG. 43.—The Density of Population in The Hague for 1930 (from Leyden). Persons per acre :—1. Under 4. 2. 4–40. 3. 40–80. 4. 80–120. 5. 120–160. 6. 160–240. 7. 240–320. 8. 320–400. 9. Over 400. The old town as of 1859 is situated in the centre enclosed by a heavy line ; it is district I on Fig. 44. The City area impinges on the North Sea Coast in the north-west.

(b) Growth and Distribution of Population

It will be noted from Fig. 43 that the density pattern is different from that of other cities in that there is not a clearly defined densely populated zone surrounding the old town. The densely peopled quarters lie to the south and the south-west of the old town, and the lowest densities are in its north-east sector and in the adjoining districts north of it. The changes in population from 1919 to 1933 show interesting trends (Fig. 44). The remarkable expansion of the new peripheral settlements since 1919 is outstanding, while the old town inside the 17th-century Singel has decreased in population, especially in areas affected by clearance and new street cuts. Over 800 dwellings were

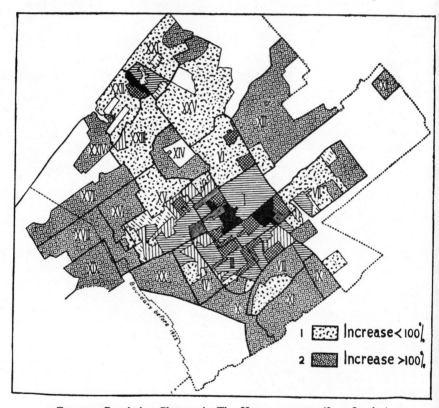

FIG. 44.—Population Changes in The Hague, 1919-33 (from Leyden).

Percentage decrease :—The scale of shading is the same as for Rotterdam on Fig. 42, p. 175. Percentage increase :—1. Increases of under 100 per cent. 2. Increases of over 100 per cent. The numeral I is the old town centre.

demolished between 1919 and 1933, and this large decrease is mainly due to the more attractive residences built on the city outskirts. In other words, the outward shift is due in the main simply to choice, to a voluntary shift to better houses in the country which has become quite a fashion, and not to any compulsive forces initiated in the centre, such as commercial development or slum clearance. In 1841 nine-tenths of the population lived inside the Singel, whereas in 1919 15 per cent. and in 1933 only 7 per cent. lived inside this old centre. The outward expansion after 1840 was caused by three events :—the opening of the railway to Voorschoten in 1841, the opening of the station for Gouda in 1870, and the building of the first gas works in 1875. The Wilhelms Park was also opened in the middle of the century. In 1880 probably only a quarter of the population lived outside the old town. In the 1919–33 period, when the total increased by 95,000, the population decreased in 94 inner districts by 64,000, but in the 86 outer districts increased from 16,000 to 170,000, a remarkable growth, as forty of these districts had no buildings in 1919 and had 80,000 inhabitants in 1933. This mass movement from the city centre has, in this case, been due to the attraction of the outskirts rather than to compulsion by business development and slum clearance. In proportion to the total size of the city, this shift of population from all the central districts to the periphery is phenomenal.

Scheveningen deserves special mention. It is the select bathing place of The Hague, and is in fact contiguous to it. Adjacent to it is the old village, which has been remarkably little affected by changes in its population structure. The native inhabitants stay put, and there has been little movement either in or out. Thus, the outward shift of people from the centre of The Hague spreads over wide areas to a remarkable extent and without any correlation with a decreasing birthrate or the growth of a city centre. This is clearly a remarkable social transformation, even more marked than in either Amsterdam or Rotterdam. Its bases are largely psychological. The ever-shifting movement, writes Leyden, has no decisive focus of dispersal and no definite objective. The areas left become empty and derelict and present the city with a serious future planning problem. Here is the problem of the flight from the city and the blight of the centre going on in one of the most exclusive of capital cities.

(4) CONCLUSIONS

The general conclusions to be drawn from a demographic study of the eight chief cities of the provinces of North and South Holland, of which Amsterdam, Rotterdam and The Hague are the chief, are as follows.

1. The 17th-century core, the old town bounded by canals, in each of the eight cities has decreased in population. This trend

began before the 1914–18 war, but developed greatly in the 1918–38 period. There is a remarkable similarity in the overall densities of the old towns. In the table below it is clear that the density on the whole was much the same in 1830 as in 1930, though in the case of the three big cities there was an appreciable decrease. Rotterdam in particular records a decrease of its density, in the central districts by a third, in this period.

POPULATION OF SELECTED DUTCH TOWNS (from Leyden)

	Area (hectares)	Maximum Population in 19th Century (thousands)	Population 1930 (thousands)	Density of Population per hectare	
				(1830)	(1930)
Amsterdam . .	861	310	202	253	212
Rotterdam . .	100	70	65	650	210
's Gravenhage .	207	75	50	250	162
Haarlem . . .	153	45	20	133	167
Leiden . . .	192	44	34·5	175	150
Dordrecht . .	85	21	17	200	180
Delft	96	25	15	155	190
Schiedam . . .	40	12	10	250	250

2. There has been a steady reduction in the percentage of the total population living in the old towns, so that while virtually all the population was inside the enclosing canals in 1830, to-day only a small fraction live there.

3. The de-population of the old town is a general feature, but it is not an invariable indicator of the growth of business and administration and slum clearance. Such is not the case apparently in Delft and Schiedam, and in Haarlem and Leiden only in a limited measure, and the same applies to Dordrecht and The Hague. Even when the growth of business in the centre does take place it is only a partial, direct explanation for the amount of movement of population from the centre outwards.[1] Just as important, if not more so, are the sanitary measures and street cuts undertaken by the city authorities. Voluntary movement, however, is the primary cause, and is due largely to the attractiveness of a new house or apartment in a new building on the outskirts of the city a little closer to nature, coupled with the dire shortage of houses in the old towns in the years immediately

[1] See R. Eberstadt, " Städtebau und Wohnungswesen in Holland ", *Neue Studien über Städtebau und Wohnungswesen*, Band III, pp. 394 et seq.

following the 1914–18 war. Cheap, frequent, and rapid transport is the other contributing factor.

4. The movement of population indicates that there is a lack of attachment to home or neighbourhood. A habit of moving from one house to another develops. This psychological feature is especially marked in the new and monotonous, characterless multi-storeyed apartment blocks. That type of dwelling does not foster any attraction for hearth, home or neighbourhood. Leyden states that in extreme cases people move rather than do the spring cleaning. This aspect of our present urban society, in effect a sort of " modern nomadism ", is one that deserves very thorough attention from social psychologists ; it is tied up with many of the problems of neurosis and the family, and its study would probably help a great deal to solve the question of the single-family house v. the flat in urban planning. Data of annual removals in Amsterdam and Rotterdam reveal exactly the same trends as at The Hague. The housing shortage after 1918 resulted in a great drop in removals for several years, followed by a peak period of removals in the late 'twenties. These features of the distribution and shifts of population in the great urban complex, closely examined in the case of these Dutch towns, are not peculiar to them. They are inherently characteristic of the whole process of urban growth.

CHAPTER 10

VIENNA AND PRAGUE

(1) VIENNA : CAPITAL OF AUSTRIA

(a) Site and Topographic Development

The site of Vienna lies at the point where the Danube enters a lowland enclosed between the Wienerwald, that tapers out north-eastwards from the eastern Alps to impinge on the river and embrace the modern city, and the parallel line of the Leithagebirge and the Little Carpathians, the gap between which is commanded by the town of Bratislava. This triangular lowland stretches south from the Danube and tapers towards Neunkirchen over a distance of about forty miles, and north from the Danube beyond the wide gravel plains of the March-feld to the fertile lowland of the March valley. At the site of the city two great natural routeways intersect. One of these extends from east to west, along the Danube valley from southern Germany to south-eastern Europe, and the other runs from north to south, through the Moravian Gate between the Sudetes and the Beskides, southwards across the Danube, and thence around the eastern Alps or across their low passes—of which the Semmering is the most important—to the head of the Adriatic and the Mediterranean.

The Roman *castell* was an outpost of the Imperial frontier on the Danube. The medieval town had its beginnings with the eastern advance of German settlement down the river. The new town was founded in 1107 as a German bulwark against the nomads of the Danubian steppes. During the Crusades, trade developed along the Danube, through the Moravian Gate with Poland, and with Italy across the Semmering Pass. The convergence here of Alps, Carpathians and the Bohemian Plateau focused the natural routes so that Vienna ultimately became the geographical centre of the Austro-Hungarian Empire. This great city with nearly two million inhabitants has been confined to the strait-jacket of a small new State since the dismemberment of the Dual Monarchy after World War I.

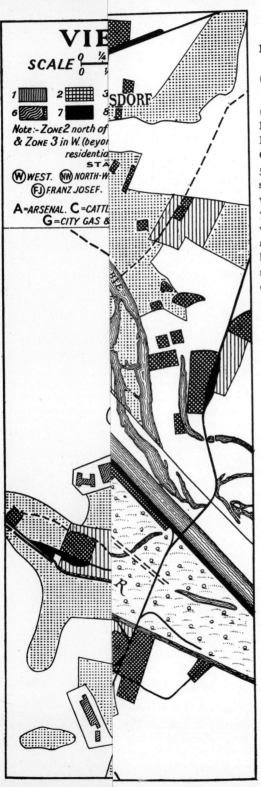

FIG. 45.—The Functional Zones of Vienna. (Scale, approx. 1 : 75,000.)

1. Central or Inner Zone (old town). 2. Middle Fully Built-up Zone. 3. Middle Partly Built-up Zone. 4. Outer or Sub-urban Zone. 5. Industrial Zones, with separate indication of brickworks. 6. Public buildings. 7. Railways, yards and wharves (city railways that are underground are shown by dashed lines). 8. Main roads. 9. Parks. 10. Site of old walls are not shown (see Fig. 46).

The growth of the city is shown on Fig. 46. A Roman *castell* or fort was situated on a raised terrace on the south side of the Danube (to-day the Donau Kanal) between the river and the valley of the Wien tributary to the south. Its immediate natural defences were two small streams that have long since disappeared although the course of that to the north can be traced in the Tiefer Graben. The Hoher Markt lies at or near the crossing of the two main Roman roads, the one running parallel to the Danube, roughly marked by the Wipplinger Strasse-Lichtensteg, and the other from north to south, marked by the Tuchlauben and Marc Aurel Strasse. Another road branched from the first to the west of the settlement, ran to the south of it through the extra-mural settlement and joined up again with it to the east of the camp. This is marked to-day by the Herren Gasse and its continuation in the Rennweg. This area south of the camp and between it and the Herren Weg became the nucleus of the growing medieval town. Here appeared the St. Stephan church in 1157 (first mentioned in 881) and the Neuer Markt (new market) a hundred years later, on the new north–south axis, the Kärnterstrasse, a route that served the Italian trade across the eastern Alps to the head of the Adriatic. The city flourished during the Crusades in the first half of the 13th century and received staple rights and full town status, being described as a *civitas* in 1221. The settlement was walled, and on its southern edge, on raised ground, lay the castle of the Babenbergs, who took up residence here and founded the nucleus of the great Hofburg of later times. To the east the defences reached the steep edge of the Wien valley, and to the north the steep edge of the terrace looked down on the narrow plain of the Danube known as the Salzgries where anchored the ships that plied on the river. The course of this wall is followed by the Basteistrasse and the Seilerstrasse. A bridge was built over the river in 1435–40.

The wall stood for centuries. The suburbs outside it were destroyed during the Turkish raids of 1529. Thereafter the defences were greatly strengthened in accordance with the demands of the new siege warfare, and a wide area outside it, a *glacis*, was preserved from building. This remained unchanged until the beginning of the 18th century (1704–38) when the *Linienwall* was constructed as an outer defence to embrace the growing suburbs. These extended along the radiating thoroughfares and already spread to the west to the lower slopes of the

Wienerwald.   More recent extension has taken place up the valleys of the Wienerwald between the wooded hills. The Danube was regulated in the 'seventies and the river shifted north-

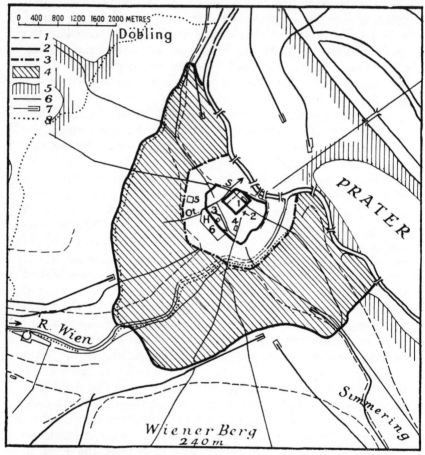

Fig. 46.—The Growth of Vienna (after Braun). (Scale, 1 : 80,000.)

1. Steep edges of terraces (*Hangränder*). 2. Walls of Roman *castell* and medieval town. 3. Fortifications of 1683 and *glacis*, to-day the Ring. 4. Town inside the *Linienwall* of 1704. 5. Limits of outer urban area. 6. Main roads. 7. Railways. 8. Inner and Outer Circular Railway, partly underground (*Gürtelbahn*).
   (1) Hoher Markt. (2) St. Stephan. (3) Castle of the Babenbergs. (4) Neuer Markt. (5) Town Hall (*Rathaus*). (6) Hofburg. S = Salzgries. Ot. = Ottakringer Bach (stream).

wards, and the Prater gardens were laid out on the meadows. Finally, the fortifications were demolished in 1857 and on their site were erected the great public buildings and open spaces of the Ring.

The period of the Turkish wars (1529–1683) was one of decline and stagnation. Renaissance architecture is thus poorly represented in the buildings, and though there are some buildings from the late Gothic period, the great age of the city's prosperity is reflected in the grandeur and number of its Baroque edifices. As the capital of Austria, it grew in splendour and added to its trade with the decline of the German cities.

The Hapsburgs took up residence here in the 18th century, when the city became the capital of the Hungarian, Bohemian and Austrian lands. The Hofburg was their residence in the centre. As in other cities of this age, country palaces were built at Schönbrunn and Favoriten. Royalty was followed by nobility. The medieval houses of the old town core, with their steep gables, were replaced by the town mansions and palaces of the nobility. The Baroque architecture of these structures was markedly influenced by Italian contacts.

The changes of the 19th century led to a further transformation. The growth of industry, commerce and administration brought their corresponding changes. Railways entered radially with their stations as dead ends situated on the *Gürtelstrasse* on the site of the outer fortifications and the *Gürtelstrasse* itself was followed by a circular railway. The regulation of the Danube in the 'seventies and the construction of bridges allowed the incorporation of the Marchfeld and the extension to it of industrial establishments during the last fifty years.

The administrative districts of Vienna are shown on Fig. 47. The district marked with the number 1 is roughly coextensive with the old town (*Altstadt*), which, at its maximum size in the Middle Ages, had about 60,000 inhabitants. Till 1863 there were thirty-four suburbs (*Vorstädte*) outside the *glacis* and in that year they were united to form the seven *Vorstadtbezirken* (numbered 3 to 9). Beyond this belt, however, settlements quickly grew that were still further removed (*Vororte*). These partly grew from, and partly absorbed, old vintners' villages, expanding first up the narrow valleys to the west and then spreading to the hills between them. Although in 1440 there were already four wooden bridges across the Danube, the town did not spread north of the river, and it was late before the *Auengrund* in the floodplain was settled. Here were the hunting grounds in the woods, which are now traversed by the Praterstrasse and the Jewish quarter. These formed the Leopoldstadt (district 2), which suffered from frequent floods until the river was regulated. Not till the 19th century did an industrial settlement grow up here at Floridsdorf. This suburb had only 50,000 inhabitants at the time of its union with Vienna in 1905, and to this day, growth on the far side of the Danube has been slow. The main extension has been to the west and south, towards the hills of the Wienerwald. Here there were a series of town extensions, in 1891, 1905, and 1908, so that

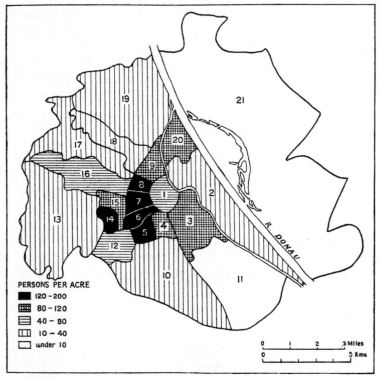

FIG. 47.—The Density of Population in Vienna for 1930. (Scale, 1 : 200,000.) Numbers refer to the administrative districts as listed in the Table on p. 189.

now the city covers 278 sq. km. as against 178 sq. km. in 1904 and only 55·4 sq. km. in 1890, when Vienna was a really great European city. It had 175,000 inhabitants in 1750, and about half a million in 1850. It reached a little over a million in 1880, two millions in 1910, and 1,866,000 in 1923, while in 1934 the total was 1,874,000.

(b) *The Functional Zones* (Plate 18)

In the general build of the whole city, and in large measure reflecting the stages in its historic growth, certain clearly defined zones may be recognized. Each of these has certain common characteristics in respect of the character and density of building, the type of dominant land-uses, and the demographic, social and economic conditions of its population. Certain of these facts are shown in the table below.

VIENNA : POPULATION AND BUILT-UP AREA BY DISTRICTS

District Numbers Built-up Area (Hectares) (1937)	Total Area (Hectares)	Built-up Area : % of total Area	Population (1934)	Density of Population per hectare of :		
				Built-up Area	Total Area	
1. 139	288	48*	40,000	288	139	INNER CITY
2. 243	2,325	10·5	150,000	617	64·5	LEOPOLDSTADT
3. 259	617	42	142,000	548	230	LANDSTRASSE
4. 97	183	53	53,000	546	290	WIEDEN
5. 113	201	56·2	88,000	779	437	MARGARETHEN
6. 90	146	61·6	50,000	556	342	MARIAHILF
7. 108	160	61	59,000	546	369	NEUBAU
8. 67	109	61·5	44,000	657	404	JOSEFSTADT
9. 154	295	52	83,000	539	281	ALSERGRUND
10. 278	2,163	12·9	158,000	568	73	FAVORITEN
11. 234	2,215	10·6	52,000	222	23·5	SIMMERING
12. 188	783	24	109,000	580	139	MEIDLING
13. 397	2,425	16·4	141,000	355	58	HIETZING
14. 91	168	54	69,000	758	411	RUDOLFSHEIM
15. 61	188	32·4	54,000	885	287	FÜNFHAUS
16. 191	854	22·4	150,000	785	176	OTTAKRING
17. 122	999	12·2	84,000	688	84	HERNALS
18. 141	940	16·8	82,000	582	98	WÄHRING
19. 169	2,156	7·8	59,000	349	27	DÖBLING
20. 145	477	30·4	98,000	677	205	BRIGITTENAU
21. 464	10,214	4·5	108,000	233	10·6	FLORIDSDORF
Vienna 3,751	27,806	13·5	1,873,000	500	67	

* This low figure is due to the inclusion of the Ring in the Inner City, and obscures the congestion of the old town.

Vienna falls into several broadly concentric zones, which developed as half-circles on the western side of the Danube, and are grouped around the *Altstadt*, the site of the medieval town.

Around this nucleus is the Ring. Beyond it lies what Hugo Hassinger, a German geographer who has made very thorough studies of the city, called the *Grosstädtischer Vorstadtgürtel*. This *gürtel* or zone was built-up mainly in the 19th century ; it is just as compactly built up as the old town and has very high densities of population. These two together form what Hassinger has called the *Grossstadtkern*, that is, the compact built-up area, with few open spaces, fairly uniform multi-storeyed tenements, and a great intermixture of residence, industry and commerce. Beyond lies the *Grossstädtischer Weichbild*. This is an old German term used by Hassinger to denote the less clearly defined penumbra of urban settlement that is intermixed with rural uses on the outskirts of the compact urban area. It includes old seats of settlement that have been chosen for residence by those who can afford to and care to travel to the city centre ; planned quarters, or estates as we should call them, laid out for residence ; and industrial quarters. This outermost area reaches as far as the houses of families whose wage-earners work in the city and travel daily to and from it. Hassinger found that this limit, which he described as the natural, as opposed to the political, limit of the city, roughly corresponded with a journey-time of one hour in each direction from home to city workplace.[1]

The functional zones of Vienna are shown on Fig. 45 (p. 184). The old town, the medieval core, is clearly defined by the Ring. This is the *Altstadt*. Its buildings are multi-storeyed ; many of them are congested tenements or business premises, and there is a large number of historic buildings and monuments, especially churches. This is District 1, and has a total residential population of 40,000. It is very densely built-up, the low figure (48 per cent.) for the district shown in the table above being due to the inclusion of much open land in the Ring.

The Ring lies on the site of the old fortifications that were demolished in 1857. It is a wide belt of boulevards lined with public buildings, which have been erected since 1860. Here are the Hofburg, the Parliament House, the Town Hall, museums and exhibition buildings, and the Opera House. There are also large open spaces, commercial buildings and cafés.

Around this nucleus there is a clearly defined, closely built-up, zone, described above as the *Grossstädtischer Vorstadtgürtel*, which

---

[1] H. Hassinger, " Beiträge zur Siedlungs- und Verkehrsgeographie von Wien ", in *Mitt der K. K. Geog. Ges. in Wien*, Band 53, 1910, pp. 5–94. Two maps on scale of 1/200,000.

was mainly built during the latter half of last century and is bounded to the west by the Gürtelbahn. It consists predominantly of fully built-up tenement blocks with five or six storeys, with dwelling units including not more than one or two rooms. Beyond this zone comes a second to the west and south of the Gürtel in which the building, though still of the same residential type, is more open. Streets are wider, building blocks are smaller and not so closely built-up, and there are more open spaces in the blocks and public squares. This area was built-up mainly in the late 19th century and most of the building between the two World Wars was in this zone. This recent building is in the form of great blocks of flats, such as the Karl Marx Hof with 1,400 dwelling units.

The outlying sub-urban areas are especially extensive, as we have noted, to the north and north-west of the city, and spread in finger-like extensions up the valleys of the Wienerwald. Beyond the city, but within the new boundary of Greater Vienna, are three extensions of the urban land—the westward extension along the valley of the river Wien has about 12,000 people, the second to the south-west through Liesing to Mödling has 20,000 inhabitants, and the third southwards along the Danube to Klosterneuburg has 20,000 inhabitants.

There are numerous small factories and workshops in the heart of Vienna, as is the case in every great city, especially since so many of the city's industries are concerned with the production of luxury goods and clothing produced in small establishments. The principal industrial areas, however, in which most of the land is devoted exclusively to industrial uses, as shown in Fig. 45, lie to the south-east. These include the gas and electricity works, the arsenal and the slaughter-houses ; the Wien valley south-west of the city, which has a variety of light industries ; an area between the Danube canal and the river, with a great variety of small plants intermixed with densely built residential tenements ; and an area of more recent industrial development in Floridsdorf on the north side of the river. It will be noticed that heavy industry plays but a small part in the life of the city and, in consequence, in its build or physical structure. The heavier industries with large plants are situated on the outskirts to the north and south-east.

Transport is effected by the river Danube and by rail. Nearly three-quarters of a million tons of goods entered the city by water in 1932 as compared with less than a quarter of a million tons of " exports ". Railways, on the other hand, accounted for an incoming goods traffic of 6,367,000 tons in 1930 (4,534,000 tons in 1932) as compared with 1,738,000 tons outward (1,599,000 in 1933). This is the usual structure of traffic to and from a great city, imports including large quantities of bulky goods—food, raw materials for industry, and building materials—and exports being, for the most part, manufactured goods and whole-sale goods for consumption elsewhere, in much smaller quantities. The harbour, that handles the river-borne traffic, has its wharves and warehouses on the west side of the river in the city, but the Winterhafen, the chief modern harbour, with granaries and oil storage depots, lies below the city on the south side of the river.

The principal railway yards lie between the canal and the river and on the southern outskirts. The Stadtbahn or city railway runs partly over viaducts. It includes the Wiental and Donau Kanal line and the Gürtel line. The State railways include the Suburban line, the Verbindungsbahn and the Donau Uferbahn. There are six principal stations. Vienna is badly served by radial railways, and passenger movement is effected by tramcar. Further, the main stations lie in a circle around the compact built-up area of the city.

The industries of Vienna are dominantly luxury industries, and heavy industries have grown elsewhere outside the city. Thus the silk industry, which was important in the first half of the 19th century, has gone, and the clothing industries are now dominant. Engineering is represented by the arsenal, and there are constructional engineering plants ; but outstanding (as in Berlin) are the electro-technical industries. Commerce and administration occupy a large part of the population.

(c) Distribution and Movements of Population

The growth and distribution of population is shown on Fig. 47. While the inner districts (1, 4, 5, 6, 7, 8) show decreases of population through the development of a city core, the belt around them has maintained a slow increase ; but on the peri-phery there is an increase that reaches beyond the city boundaries. Villa quarters lie to the west and north-west, and workers' quarters to the south and east. The centre of the city has shifted westwards, and it was shown in 1910 that the urban area then extended 16 km. from the Stephansplatz, whereas the periphery lay only 10 km. distant to the east and south-east. This asym-metry of growth is shown by the slow growth of District 11

(Simmering). To the west and south, villa quarters extend along the railways to Vöslau and Rekawinkel as far as 35 km. The scenic attraction of the Wienerwald is undoubtedly the main cause for this asymmetrical growth of the city.

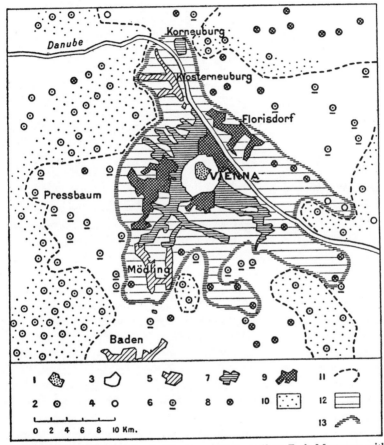

FIG. 48.—Changes of Population in Vienna and Environs (from E. de Martonne, with kind permission of the author and Armand Colin). (Scale, 1 : 550,000.)

Decreasing population :—1. In Vienna. 2. In the villages. Stable population :— 3. In Vienna. 4. In the villages. Increasing population since 1890 :—5. In Vienna and neighbouring towns. 6. In villages. Continuous increase of population :—7. In Vienna and neighbouring towns. 8. In villages. 9. Increases of population up to 400 per cent. from 1870 to 1910. 10. Areas of depopulation. 11. Limit of the areas of depopulation. 12. Areas with constant increase of population. 13. Limit of the areas with constant increase of population.

Interesting features of the movements of population in Vienna are shown in Fig. 48.[1] The centre has been diminishing since

[1] Adapted from de Martonne, *Europe Centrale, Géographie Universelle*, Vol. II, p. 492.

1890. A zone around it, the tenement zone, has shown no appreciable change. The outer zones of the built-up area show a steady increase. Districts to the west of the compact urban area between the old town centre and the Danube, and in Floridsdorf on the north bank, recorded increases up to 400 per cent. between 1870 and 1910. Then, the rural–urban fringe around the city records a steady increase since 1890. This fringe zone reaches from Korneuburg to Mödling and includes a narrow belt along the north side of the Danube with Floridsdorf in the centre. Beyond this there is a rural zone to the north-east, west, and south-west, in which the villages are increasing or have steady populations. Still farther out there are wide areas of depopulation in both countryside and villages. These population trends, thus accurately mapped, reveal the decreasing effects of urban influence as one recedes from the city core.

(d) The Planning of Vienna

Like all continental cities, Vienna has a most serious housing problem, and has sought to solve it, during both the 19th and in the present century, by the construction of great tenements with a very small allocation of space per family. In 1917, a year which illustrates the conditions after the great building phase of the 19th century, out of 554,500 dwelling units, three-quarters consisted of a living-room and a small room (*Kabinett*) in three-to four-storey tenements, that were almost entirely built-up with almost no open central courtyards. It is estimated that there were 612,000 dwelling units just before the recent war. Between 1919 and 1934, 64,000 dwelling units were erected by the municipal authorities, housing 180,000 people, or one-tenth of the population. Half of these units were in multi-storeyed flats (up to six storeys) with open courts. The remainder (8,000) were single-family houses built on the outskirts of the city. Modern blocks of flats, such as the Karl Marx Hof (with 1,400 units) and the Washington Hof (with 1,000 units) are built around open courts and have communal services. Before 1919 the old tenements throughout the compact built-up area around the town nucleus were very congested, with open courts making up less than 15 per cent. of the area of the block, and three-quarters of the dwelling units had fewer than two rooms.

As has been the case in other continental cities, though the civic authorities controlled the expansion, lay-out and uses of their expanding areas, no attention was paid to housing conditions. A step forward was taken in the 'nineties. A building plan (*Bauzonenplan*) for Vienna, for districts 1 to 20, was drawn up in 1893 (see table on p. 189). This limited buildings in the inner town (district 1) to five storeys and to four in the surrounding districts (2 to 9), and to four storeys in the compact built-up areas of the remaining districts. The outermost zone was to have buildings of no more than three storeys. In 1907 the plan for the newly added Floridsdorf district beyond the Danube (21) was extended with allowances for the development of industry. In 1905 Bürgermeister Karl Lueger approved the preservation of a *Wald- und Wiesengürtel*—a green belt. In 1921 provision was made for a *Kleingarten- und Siedlungszone*—a zone of small holdings.

In the years before the 1914–18 war the traffic problem received attention. The Stadtbahn was built to take local traffic away from long-distance routes in the Wienerwald district to the west. Plans for an underground system were brought to a stop in 1914. The political separation of Vienna from Lower Austria and the separation of the Stadtbahn (electrified and unified with tramways, which go beyond the city boundaries), have hampered the development of sub-urban traffic, though this has been eased in recent years by the advent of the motor-bus. These traffic difficulties are particularly important since the city is very densely populated. Vienna is greatly in need of allotment gardens (*Schrebergärten*). Between 1916 and 1922, 40,000 such allotments were made, covering 2,500 acres. To-day, small houses and gardens extend well beyond the city limits, where they have appeared without any semblance of an orderly plan. For all these reasons, a regional plan embracing the city and its environs is a pressing need so as to relate building in the surrounding communes to the needs of the city, and to make adequate provision for building extensions, open spaces, and communications within a co-ordinated framework.

(2) Prague : Capital of Czechoslovakia

(a) Site and Development (Fig. 49)

The city of Prague is situated in the heart of the diamond-shaped plateau of Bohemia at an outstanding focus of main routeways. It lies astride the river Vltava, which is deeply cut into the surrounding plateau. The valley sides are high and steep, and tributary valleys, trending east–west, are short and deep, though the surrounding plateau is open and undulating.

The end of the narrow east–west ridge on the left bank of the river became the site of the cathedral and the fortress of the Hradčany, These buildings overlook the Vltava where there was an early ford (Prah) at a shallowing of the river, and beyond, on the right bank of the river inside its convex bend, the medieval town grew up on flatter land. Two great spurs of plateau country jut out eastwards towards the river—the one holds the Hradčany and the other is the Petrin hill, the site of the Stadium. Between the two is a narrow steep-sided depression. North of the Hradčany the land drops to a great flat, low-lying area that reaches to the Vltava. On the eastern bank is the flat land of the medieval town site. One can clearly see from the magnificent viewpoint of the miniature Eiffel Tower on the Petrin that the land rises steeply to the surrounding plateau and its isolated, wooded hills. South of the old town towards the Vyšehrad steep streets lead immediately from the north–south highway near to the river to the secluded residential sectors. Parks and public buildings lie on the outlying hills of the plateau immediately east of the Wilson Station. Ideal for the growth of a medieval town, for reasons of both defence and trade, this site presents difficulties for the planned expansion of the buildings and communications of a large modern city.

Prague had two early medieval strongholds, which formed its first nuclei of settlement, situated on high land on either bank of the deeply incised river valley. The Hradčany lies at the end of a narrow east–west ridge on the high concave bend of the river, and the Vyšehrad to the south on the right bank of the river on a hill rising some 50 metres above it. A bishopric was established in the 10th century and both cathedral and castle with all the dependent buildings were located within one walled settlement on the top of the ridge. At the southern foot of the Hradčany and on the lower flatter land clustered small parasitic *faubourgs* in the 10th century.

The great town-building era in Bohemia began with the reign of Ottokar II. In 1257 he established the Kleinseite or Malá Strana as a German settlement on the south side of the Hradčany between the hills and the river, and gave it town law on the pattern of Magdeburg law. The chief urban settlement grew on the opposite bank of the river, across which a bridge was built in 1153. An extension of the *Altstadt* to the east was called the Gallusviertel. Ottokar II endowed the *Altstadt* or *Stare Mesto* with town law on the pattern of Nuremberg. A hundred years later, Charles V (1346–78) established the University in the old town and surrounded the Kleinseite with a wall. A great extension to the old town was also made between the *Vorstadt* to the east and the small village along the river between it and the Vyšehrad. This whole town was walled in 1347. It included the rectangular *Rossmarktk*, the *Viehmarkt* (K), and the triangular *Heumarkth* (H), and was a carefully planned settlement. It did not extend much beyond these limits for over 500 years. In the middle of the 19th century the walls enclosed the whole of the Hradčany together with the Malá Strana, and ran along the top of the plateau spur of the Petrin that encloses the Malá Strana to the south-west. On the right bank, in the Stare Mesto proper, the wall extended south to reach the Vyšehrad hill and followed the northern side of a deeply cut valley that reached the Vltava on the north side of the Vyšehrad castle. South of the *Rossmarkt* there was a further extension of the built-up area with another long rectangular market that was used as a cattle market (*Viehmarkt*). Between it and the castle was open hilly land. The walls formed a continuous belt on the eastern side of the town from the valley in the south to the Vltava in the north. The terminus of the railway had already appeared in the north and it actually penetrated to the inner side of the wall. There was also a new lay-out of wide streets, though as yet with almost no building, to the south-east in the district now known as Vršovice. Within this framework and beyond the line of the walls, which were not demolished until 1878, the rapid growth of the city took place, to attain a total population in recent years of nearly one million inhabitants.

This modern growth has been very remarkable. The railway and the small coalfield of Kladno, some 25 km. west of the city, occasioned the growth of modern industry. In fifty years the population of the quarters outside the old walls increased from 25,000 to 250,000. In 1878 the population of the town inside the walls was 300,000, and in 1910 it reached 400,000. In the 20th century growth has been accelerated. New factories have appeared to the south and east towards the head of the tributary valleys. Vysocany along the Rokytka valley is a continuation of Liben. At Holešovice to the north are the wharves of the new river port. Behind the Hradčany, the district of Dejvice-Bubeneč has grown up as a mass of enormous working-class apartment blocks and wide avenues lie on the hillier roads in the west where are the best residential quarters.

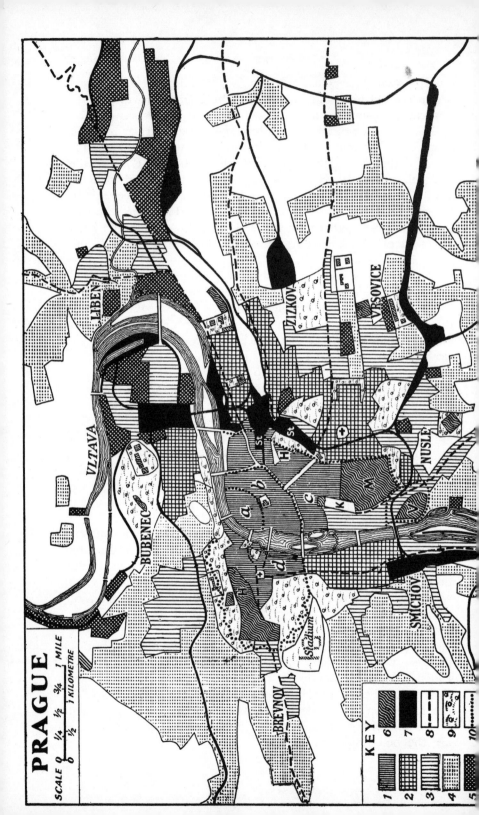

The most remarkable feature of the industrial development is the addition of large engineering plants closely associated with the coalfield of Kladno. The great plants include Ringhofer (wagons), Českomuravska Kolben (locomotives and motor-cars), Breitfeld and Danek at Karlin (refineries, distilleries, steam turbines). Two large plants producing electrical apparatus are also located here. In addition to these heavy industries there are the traditional industries, among which the chief are the making of textiles and glass. The manufacture of clothing, boots and shoes and gloves is also important. These last are carried on by many small concerns in small workshops and factories in the built-up area of the city and are therefore not nearly so evident in its build. But the chief group after engineering is the food industries, including milling, breweries, the refining of sugar and the making of chocolate. Almost all the daily bread of Prague is supplied from one great plant. The chief group of grain elevators is at Holešovice.

(b) The Functional Zones

The build of the city is shown on Fig. 49. The urban areas fall into four groups : the central city area on the east bank of the river; the castle-cathedral complex (the Hradčany) together with the small town of Malá Strana associated with it, on the west bank; the surrounding closely built-up areas, with mixed residential and industrial uses and large quarters devoted to public buildings; and the outer zone of scattered residential and industrial areas on the periphery. The main industrial areas are clustered east and west of the big river bend to the north of the city.

These zones may be described in more detail as follows. The districts referred to are the administrative districts given in the table on p. 203 and shown on Fig. 50 on p. 202. The old town (German *Altstadt* or Czech *Stare Mesto*) together with Josefov (the site of the old Ghetto) lies on the south bank of the river between it and the Na Prikope boulevard, the latter being on the line of the first town wall. This is to-day the chief retail

FIG. 49.—The Functional Zones of Prague. (Scale, approx. 1 : 75,000.) 1. Central or Inner Zone (old town). 2. Middle Fully Built-up Zone. 3. Middle Partly Built-up Zone. 4. Outer or Sub-urban Zone. 5. Industrial Zones. 6. Public buildings. 7. Railways and yards. 8. Main roads. 9. Parks. 10. Site of medieval walls. Sections of the old town are :—(a) the oldest nucleus, later the Ghetto of Josefov ; (b) the extension of the old town ; (c) the new town (mid 14th century) ; (d) Malá Strana. H = Hradčany. V = Vyšehrad. K = Karlovo Namesti. H = Havlickovo Namesti (on east side of old town). M = Medical quarter. St. = Masaryk and Wilson Stations. Vaclavské Namesti is shown between K and H. These were (in German) the *Rossmarkt*, *Viehmarkt* and *Heumarkt* respectively.

and commercial area. It is a congested district with multi-storeyed buildings and mixed types of land use and its architecture includes medieval and Baroque buildings and many modern flats. These last have been built especially since 1900 on the sites of the slums in the Ghetto in the Josefov. The Josefov, so named from the Emperor Joseph, who abolished the Ghetto in which the Jews were confined, bears no evidence of its former Jewish character except for the minute, historic synagogue, built in Gothic style, and the small Jewish cemetery, in which layer upon layer of graves have accumulated, so that its present area is crammed with old tombstones. There is here a complete transformation from the historic character of the Ghetto to a modern apartment section. This area to-day has, of course, a regular street pattern. The plan of the old town is marked by its irregular, narrow, winding streets with its centre in the old market-place (*Stare Mesto Namesti*), overlooked by the old Town Hall, and rows of Baroque-fronted buildings. German Gothic is characteristic of the architecture of its older buildings. This is particularly true of the Tyn Church next to the market-place, which seems to have been an early " immunity ", outside which the first market settlement grew. The Tyn is a completely closed-in built-up area, grouped around this church.

The new town (*Nove Mesto*) is the large area that lies between the old town and the walls of the 19th century. It has its chief thoroughfares in the Na Prikope and the Vaclavské Namesti (German *Rossmarkt*). The latter is nearly half a mile long, and is dominated by the great National Museum at its south-eastern end. This street is to-day the Champs Élysées of Prague. The district is clearly limited by steeply rising land beyond the Wilson and Masaryk stations and by parks and public buildings on hillier land to the south. Buildings are more uniform than in the old town, and date, for the most part, from the 18th and 19th centuries.

The Hradčany consists of the walled castle-cathedral nucleus and the so-called Hradčany town on its western side, both lying on a narrow ridge. To the north lie steep slopes down to a narrow valley beyond which are open parks and gardens with the modern buildings of the Ministry of Justice. The great, high phalanx of buildings of the Hradčany, topped by the spire of the Gothic cathedral, is the outstanding feature of the build of Prague. The stages of its continuous occupance are reflected in the phases of its architectural growth. The greater part of the palace buildings are built in the Baroque style of the 17th and 18th centuries, but Gothic foundations are present and the secluded inner courts have still to be excavated for evidences of early medieval and earlier settlement. To the south, again at the foot of steep slopes, is the town of Malá Strana, which is completely engirdled, except to the south along the river, by steeply rising slopes to north and west, the latter rising to the edge of the plateau known as the Petrin. The nucleus of the Malá Strana is the market-place or Ring known as the Malá Stranské Namesti, around which are clustered many important historic buildings and Baroque palaces of the nobility, many of which are now occupied by foreign embassies or government departments.

Fully built-up areas lie round the historic city so far described. The buildings are predominantly tenements built entirely since about 1850 and before 1900. Overall population densities vary from 60 to 100 per acre, but in some districts they are much higher, especially nearer to the old town where there is greater congestion, and a considerable intermixture of industrial premises.

There has been much extension of the residential areas since 1918. A main feature of the building of all Prague is the domin-ance of the tenement or modern apartment block. Large areas of this type lie in the Holešovice, Bubny, and Bubeneč districts inside the great river bend. The great open space of President Beneš is the centre of multi-storeyed blocks of modern flats, set in the midst of wild grass-covered land, with rough verges, and unpaved street walks. Even in the best residential districts, like those in the hills of Břevnov, west of the Hradčany, detached houses in gardens containing two to four flats are dominant. The side streets are often unpaved without gutter drainage and often overgrown with grass.

Industrial areas include, in the first place, many small factories and workshops in the middle zone just noted, which is thus in large part a zone of mixed residential and industrial uses such as is common to the structure of all western cities. The chief modern industrial plants, extensive in lay-out, isolated from resi-dential areas, but close to the main lines of communication, lie on the periphery of the city, especially to the east and west of the great river bend and alongside the railways to the north-east.

Special attention is drawn to the location of the public build-ings. Apart from the Hradčany and the Vyšehrad, we note two districts. First, on the Petrin hill there are two vast stadiums placed in the midst of woods and gardens. Approached by a

cable railway, this is a main recreative centre for Prague's tenement dwellers. Second, there is the extensive medical quarter
on the raised land to the south of the city centre, centred on the
old Viehmarkt (Karlovo Namesti), which also contains the
Municipal Theatre and Law Courts. Separate public buildings
occupy outstanding architectonic positions in the lay-out of the
city ; this is especially true, for instance, of the position of
the National Museum, that dominates the Vaclavské Namesti.
The great Social Insurance building, lying on a hill beyond the
Wilson Station, is a striking feature of the modern city's profile.

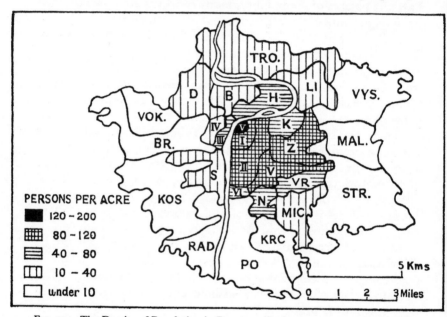

Fig. 50.—The Density of Population in Prague. (Scale, approx. 1 : 200,000.) The
letters refer to the administrative districts as listed in the table on p. 203.

A great memorial also lies on a second hill to the north of the
latter. Within a few yards of the busy radial thoroughfares
seclusion is to be found on these hills at the end of short, steep
streets.

A note, however brief, should be given on the system of
communications. The street tram is the only means of public
transport. There are no buses in the city. Bus services, serving the far-flung suburbs, connect with the termini of the tram
routes. The trams, with up to three coaches, pull steadily up the
long steep slopes from the tram centre, and where the tram routes

end, there end the cubical blocks of buildings of the urban dwellers, and at once one sets foot in allotment, farmland or village. The tram line is the life-blood of the greatly extended urban area and the services run continuously right through the night.

(c) Distribution of Population

The main facts of the distribution of population are shown in the table below and in Fig. 50. It is unfortunate that these data cover only the main administrative districts. The areas of greatest density with over 80 persons per acre for the total

POPULATION DISTRIBUTION IN PRAGUE (from Moscheles)

	Percentage of Area covered by Buildings	Percentage of Area with Buildings, Streets and Parks	Density of Population per Hectare (Acre)	Percentage of Workers to all gainfully employed
Centre :				
Stare Mesto . . .	43·5	63·5	213 (85)	37·2
Nove Mesto . . .	44·2	70·8	215 (85)	33·1
Malá Strana . .	36·1	58·9	170 (70)	36·3
Hradčany . . .	20·3	37·9	56 (22)	37·5
Josefov	52·8	84·9	385 (154)	13·0
Vyšehrad . . .	14·7	36·7	117 (41)	48·4
Karlin	33·3	57·6	149 (60)	36·0
Vinohrady . . .	27·1	61·6	258 (103)	28·6
Middle Tenement Belt :				
Dejvice	6·3	14·4	41 (16)	37·7
Bubeneč	10·6	24·3	73 (30)	28·3
Holešovice . . .	19·6	46·6	103 (40)	40·2
Smichov	14·2	37·5	88 (35)	41·7
Liben	14	28·6	60 (24)	56·8
Zizkov	17·3	37·5	219 (87)	48·8
Nusle	15·4	30	142 (57)	49
Vršovice	15·9	37·1	143 (57)	45
Peripheral Belt :				
Břevnov	5	10·9	28 (11)	49·8
Podoli	3·5	8·3	14 (5·5)	52·3
Strasnice	3·0	9·7	13 (5·2)	55·4
Vokovice	2·9	7·8	7 (3)	62·8
Kosire	2·5	6·9	17 (7)	59·8
Radlice	2·8	10·8	10 (4)	67·9
Krč	3·4	8·0	20 (8)	64
Michle	4·1	13·4	37 (15)	64
Malesice	2·3	7·5	10 (4)	70·5
Vysocany . . .	3·9	12·4	20 (8)	69·2
Troja-Bohnice . .	2·9	6·8	65 (26)	58·8

area of each district are in the city and the neighbouring inner tenement areas to the east of it (Vinohrady and Zizkov) beyond the Wilson Station and railway yards. Nusle, Vršovice and Karlin, which continue this tenement belt, have densities approximating to 60 persons per acre. Areas with densities of 40 to 80 persons per acre border this central area to the south, to the north (the latter in the big river bend), and to the west across the river in the Malá Strana.

In a recent study of Prague by J. Moscheles, some interesting correlations were made between the demographic, social and economic conditions in these twenty districts of the whole city. These districts are listed above and are arranged in three belts, centre, transition or middle, and peripheral belts.[1] They are large districts, with often considerable variations within each, but the broad features they exhibit may be taken as typical of the general socio-economic structure of the great European city. Interesting comparisons may be made with the similar data for Vienna tabulated on p. 189. The main facts to be emphasized are the decrease in the proportion of the built-up land outwards from the old town centre, where it reaches over 60 per cent. in four districts ; and the close correlation between the densities of population and the percentage of each district that is built-up, densities in centre districts reaching well over eighty persons per acre of total area. The density of population per acre of the land actually covered by buildings ranges from 200 to 380 persons in the central zone, 110 to 500 in the intermediate zone, and 90 to 360 in the peripheral zone.

Several further features of the general socio-economic structure may be noted. The proportion of children to the resident population increases outwards from the centre to the periphery, irrespective of social and economic conditions. The average age of the adult population also decreases outwards from the centre. There is also a general decrease in the ratio of domestic servants to each hundred homes from centre to periphery and this is evidently closely related to the age of the population and social and economic status. The percentage of workmen among the employed population is another indicator of socio-economic structure. This reaches 50 to 70 per cent. in the peripheral districts but averages about one-third in the central districts.

These broad demographic characteristics and correlations

[1] J. Moscheles, " Demographic, Social and Economic Regions of Greater Prague " *Geographical Review*, Vol. XXVII, 1937.

have been suggested in other city studies, and they are generally characteristic of the ecological structure of any city. Indeed, the correlations that can be made for social groups for the country as a whole appear in the city by districts in so far as these social groups are geographically segregated. And this is a universal phenomenon of city growth. The city is a cross-section of the State and has district segregations of its main socio-economic groupings, with one or more of these groupings outstanding according to the predominant function of the city as a whole. It is quite clear that such data are needed in much greater detail to permit more elaborate investigation of the social structure of cities, and the processes of social differentiation and of urban growth.

CHAPTER 11

BUDAPEST AND WARSAW

(1) BUDAPEST (Fig. 51)

Budapest has about one and a half million inhabitants, a sixth of the total population of Hungary. It is the geographical heart of the State and virtually monopolizes its industry and commerce as well as being its political and cultural capital. Like Prague, it has a hill fortress on the left bank of the Danube, the site of the ancient Buda, while the modern town of Pest lies on the plain on the east bank of the river. Pest has grown from a settlement of comparatively recent origin similar to the overgrown rural villages of the Alföld, whereas Buda was comparable to the fortress settlements of the German lands. The royal palace in Buda was erected in 1247, and down to 1526 it was the capital of the kings of Hungary. From that year the Turks held the citadel of Buda for 150 years. Pest was derelict, and shortly after the expulsion of the Turks in 1686 it had (1710) less than 1,000 inhabitants. Maria Theresa established a University at Buda in 1777, but it was transferred to Pest in 1784. After 1867 Pest developed rapidly at the expense of Buda. Development has therefore been essentially modern. The population reached 107,000 in 1841 and 300,000 in 1870. The city has attracted a heterogeneous population, and it was not till 1880 that the Hungarian element became dominant. Greater Budapest includes a circle of communes whose population has risen from 12,000 in 1830 to 415,000 in 1930. Even beyond this circle increases of population are recorded since the end of the 19th century through the extension of railways and tramways to the

FIG. 51.—The Functional Zones of Budapest. (Scale 1 : 75,000.)

1. Central or Inner Zone. 2. Middle Fully Built-up Zone. 3. Middle Partly Built-up Zone. 4. Outer or Sub-urban Zone. 5. Industrial Zones. 6. Barracks and Public buildings. 7. Railways and yards. 8. Main roads. 9. Parks, cemeteries, and open spaces.

Note :—1. Inner boulevard (Karoly Korut). 2. Middle Boulevard (Nagy Korut). H = Parliament. B = Belvaros district. L = Lipotvaros district. The Var, a separately walled hilltop nucleus, contains the cathedral and palace. For Anavassy Ut substitute Andrassy Ut.

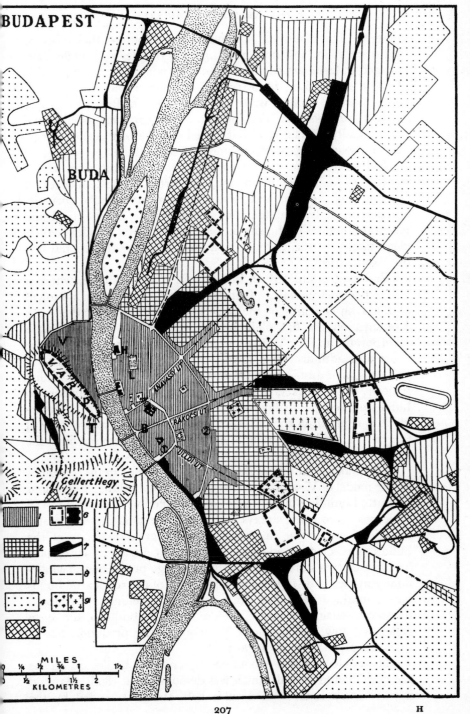

BUDAPEST

BUDA

VÁR

Gellert Hegy

ANDRÁSSY UT

RÁKÓCZI UT

ÜLLÖI UT

1
2
3
4
5
6
7
8
9

MILES
0 ¼ ½ ¾ 1 1½

KILOMETRES
0 ½ 1 1½ 2

H

villages. These outlying communes have doubled their population since 1880, and now have 250,000 people, and while those engaged in farming have decreased by 5 per cent., the proportion of those engaged in industry and commerce has increased by three-quarters. Thus, while the population of Budapest proper is about one million, that of the whole complex socially and economically associated with it, based on the range of the increase of population, numbers one and a half millions.

Industry in the city embraces all the engineering, three-quarters of the textile production, and virtually all the specialized commerce of the Hungarian State. River-borne traffic normally reaches about two million tons per annum. The political and cultural functions of the city as a national capital also leave their clear marks on the city's occupational structure, functional lay-out, and aspect.

Budapest is situated on both banks of the Danube, which is 300 to 650 metres wide. It includes the formerly separate towns of Buda on the hills of the west bank, and Pest together with Kobanya on the flat plain on the east bank. The two were incorporated to form a single municipality in 1872. Buda is the court and administrative town ; Pest is the modern city, with the seats of industry and commerce, housing the overwhelming majority of the workers of the whole complex. Pest is modern in build and regular in lay-out. Its spider-web pattern of boulevards is centred on the old town nucleus, and a long frontage of fine public buildings, palatial hotels, and club-houses lines the river front.

The plan for the city of Budapest was designed in the 'seventies on the model of Vienna. At first the laxity of building regulations permitted building blocks to be entirely filled with multi-storeyed buildings up to seven storeys high. These regulations were later modified, and in the last fifty years the great majority of the buildings, erected outside what is now the central city core, have had one or two storeys, and include a large proportion of single-family houses. In 1930 over 50 per cent. of the residential buildings contained less than four separate dwellings. Budapest, therefore, outside its centre, which is closely built-up, has been called a " low buildings city ", owing to the predominance of single-family houses with gardens.

The nucleus of Pest is bounded by an inner boulevard on the site of the old town wall which was demolished in 1808. Around it there is an inner semi-circular belt, that is bounded by the middle and the main boulevard. Beyond this there is another semi-circular belt which includes large areas of open space and is bounded by an outer boulevard (Hungarian *Korut*). These semi-circular boulevards are crossed by several main radial boulevards (Hungarian *Ut*). Finally, the outermost areas contain the chief industrial districts, new residential areas, and large stretches of open land. The built-up area, then, may be considered under the headings of centre, middle and outer zones as adopted for the other cities considered in previous chapters.

The present business core is the nucleus of the city as it existed in 1880. It is now fully built-up, and its buildings reach an average height of seven storeys. Frequently blocks are almost completely built-up, the small central courts having minimum dimensions of 9 metres square.

Buda is clustered between the river and the hill that trends north-west–south-west. This hill, known as the Vár (or citadel), is the historical nucleus of the city, and in it, enclosed by walls, are the cathedral and palace, several public buildings and government offices, and many old palatial residences of the nobility. Buda is an old town with narrow winding streets and rows of small houses interspersed with public buildings and aristocratic mansions. The town is encircled by wooded hills on which are luxurious country residences.

The city nucleus is congested with narrow winding streets and has a number of public buildings, notably the Town Hall and University, and commercial and business edifices. The chief financial district with Exchange and banks and business houses lies immediately south of the Houses of Parliament in the district leading to the Suspension Bridge. The large fan-shaped area between the West Station (in the north), the Ulloi Ut and the East Station and the middle boulevard is traversed by the Andrassy Ut and Rakoczi Ut. It contains multi-storeyed buildings with modern buildings on the main boulevards. The latter are the chief shopping thoroughfares. Andrassy Ut is lined with museums, theatres, public buildings, shops, and restaurants. Rakoczi Ut is the most important general business and shopping boulevard of a popular kind. It is lined with shops, cafés and theatres, and leads to the East Station. The middle boulevard has some large public buildings and theatres. The points where it crosses the radial boulevards are important traffic nodes and main centres of the life of the city. The intersection of the Rakoczi Ut is dominated by the National Theatre.

There are marked areas of functional segregation in and around the city core. This has in its northern half the ultra-exclusive shopping district. The southern half is the exclusive residential district of the nobility. Here also are the University, and, just outside the boulevard, the National Museum. Houses of the nobility lie outside the boulevard around the museum. This Belvaros district is thus the most exclusive residential and shopping centre of Budapest. It is its West End. A large belt to the south-east of the city that lies between the two boulevards and east of Belvaros is a dilapidated slum and vice area. It stretches from the inner boulevard almost as far as the East Station.

Beyond the central zone, the compact fully built-up middle zone forms a second concentric belt about three-quarters of a mile wide. It includes several large open spaces and parks—notably the Varosliget or town park which covers 240 acres at the end of the Andrassy Ut ; the great cemetery to the east ; and several large open spaces to the south-east. It is mainly multi-storeyed in build and includes high-class villa quarters along the Andrassy Ut. The sectors around the stations which penetrate into the belt are mainly working-class areas. The south-eastern district on both sides of the Ulloi Ut includes the main hospitals and several barracks. The greater part of this belt is a slum and has extremely high population densities.

The outer belt lies beyond the latter concentric belt and contains much open and " sub-urban " built-up land, but there are three main areas which are fairly closely built with factories.

It will be noted that all the main factories lie outside the compact built-up area, a fact due to the relatively recent development of industry in the city. The district to the north-east between the river and the railway includes the main railway yards which run north-east from the West Station. Near the East Station and the goods yards are factories, working-class housing districts, barracks and open spaces. To the south and south-east, along the river, lies an almost exclusively industrial area. Railway sidings, grain elevators and warehouses push right to the centre of the city, and farther south the belt is continued by gas works, slaughter-houses and many large factories. A new port area also lies on an island in the river to the south of the city.

The density of population clearly shows this general pattern of land-use distribution. In 1940 the total population was

1,116,000, and that of the adjacent communes 470,000, giving a total of 1,586,000. The population of Buda and O-Buda is about one-quarter of the total population of the city of Budapest. The central city of Pest within the middle boulevard had a density in 1930 of 150 persons per acre of total area. The zone outside this middle boulevard is the area with the greatest proportion of the population and the highest densities. Over large areas this is predominantly a slum belt with a density of 200 to 300 persons per acre of total area.

Figures for the 121 census tracts of Budapest reveal that the central districts have a declining population, the Vár falling to 4,000 in 1935, the financial centre (Lipatváros) to 2,700, and the district adjoining the western railway station to 22,000. Budapest thus reveals features common to the growth of the historic cities of central Europe and to the modern growth of the West European city.

(2) WARSAW (Fig. 52)

Warsaw is situated on a high terrace of glacial deposits some 30 metres above the Vistula flood plain which is about 12 kms. wide, while the river itself, with a maximum width of some 800 metres, is only about 400 metres wide at the city site. Until the river was embanked from the 18th century onwards, the plain was liable to extensive flooding, but at the foot of the site of the castle on the northern edge of the terrace it followed a fixed course. Opposite the terrace on the right (east) bank was slightly raised ground, only about 5 metres above the river, which was free of flooding, whereas to north and south of it lay marsh. This flood-free sector was the initial east–west boat crossing. The first bridge was built at the end of the 16th century by Sigismund Augustus at the foot of the royal palace, but it lasted only for about thirty years ; others followed, but none survived the floods for long. In 1775 a pontoon bridge was built, but fixed bridges were not erected until the 19th century. Warsaw is not a bridge-town any more than Budapest or Vienna.

The high terrace, with a clearly defined steep edge facing eastwards over the river plain, runs from north to south, abutting on the river at the northern end, where the castle and medieval town are situated. It was at this crossing that the great trans-continental routes met, as early as the Bronze Age, the one north–south along the Vistula, from Italy to the amber-yielding district of Samland on the south Baltic shores (a route also used by

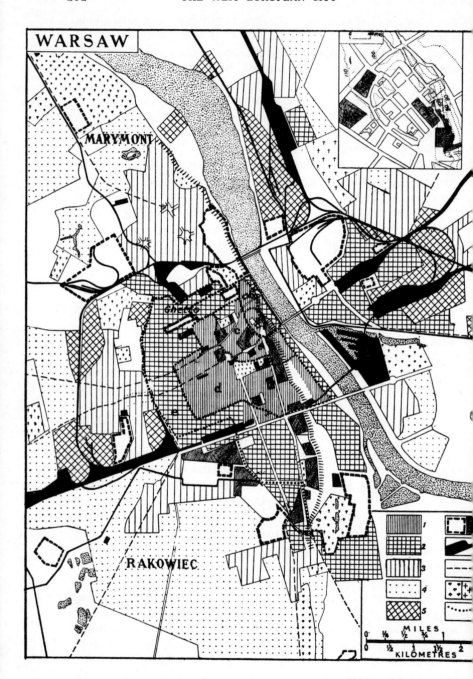

WARSAW

MARYMONT

Ghetto

RAKOWIEC

1
2
3
4
5

MILES
0 ¼ ½ ¾ 1
0 ½ 1 1½ 2
KILOMETRES

the Romans), and the other from the Black Sea and through the Ukraine via Odessa and Kiev to Danzig and Stettin. With the union of the Polish dukedom with Lithuania in the 16th century, Warsaw was clearly destined to become a great capital. The city flourished during the next two hundred years as a royal capital, and its build is markedly stamped by the Baroque architecture of this era. Then came devastation during the Napoleonic wars. Russians, Prussians, and French occupied the city in turn. It was completely destroyed by Suvorov in 1794 and had no more than 65,000 people in 1797 and 81,000 in 1816. It became an administrative capital of Tsarist Russia, the capital of Congress Poland, and its royal palace was the seat of the Governor of the Tsar when in residence. The city lost much of its cultural importance, but its industries grew and above all it became a great military base, being fortified by the Russians with a semicircle of fifteen forts on the west bank, with a citadel on its northern side and extensive barracks. It re-emerged, however, as an industrial city in the 19th century, especially after the advent of the railway, serving the great Russian market to which it had freedom of access. (The first railway, from Warsaw to Vienna, was opened in 1848.) It had grown in importance during the 18th century, in spite of the fact that this was in general a period of decline for Polish towns. This growth was due to its importance as a capital. The kings founded a mint, an arms factory, a pottery industry, and many banks were started to participate in the great process of the colonization of the Ukraine. The population in 1787 was about 100,000. Renewed prosperity came in the first decades of the 19th century. The Warsaw Chamber of Commerce was founded in 1817, the Bank of Poland in 1828, and there were also two great annual fairs. In 1829 the city had 140,000 inhabitants and was the queen of Polish cities. The total population reached 845,000 in 1913 as compared with 223,000 in 1864. With the advent of the railway heavy engineering industries came to Warsaw, favoured by protective tariffs.

FIG. 52.—The Functional Zones of Warsaw. (Scale : 1 : 75,000.)
1. Central or Inner Zone (the old town). 2. Middle Fully Built-up Zone. 3. Middle Partly Built-up Zone. 4. Outer or Sub-urban Zone. 5. Industrial Zones. 6. Barracks and Public buildings. 7. Railways and yards. 8. Main roads. 9. Parks, cemeteries and public spaces. 10. Site of old walls. Hachures show the sharp break of slope on the terrace edge on the west bank of the river. Sections of the historic town shown are :—(a) the old town (Stare Miasto) ; (b) its northerly extension (Nowe Miasto) ; (c) extensions from the 15th to the 17th century ; (d) extensions in the 18th century ; (e) extensions in the 19th century. Inset plan of the Stare Miasto with contours at 10-metre intervals.

Its varied manufactures *de luxe*, like the *articles de Paris*, were now supplemented by heavy, large-scale industry. The old town lay on the western terrace, and the Baroque and modern town grew around it. On the opposite bank, on flat, low-lying land, lay the settlement of Praga, for long a small market trading with the land to the east, but emerging during the late 19th century as a seat of heavy industries and railways and housing the working people. Since 1919 growth has continued, and the distinction in function between the city on the west bank and the industrial–commercial sector on the east bank is maintained, the two being interconnected by two railways and three vehicular bridges. The complex has spread outwards from its congested 19th-century quarters, to a wide sub-urban fringe, while Praga has extensive railway yards, a river harbour and barracks.

In 1925 the population reached almost one million, and reached 1,289,000 in January, 1939. One-fourth of this total were Jews, and the bulk of the rest Poles. Ethnically this is Warsaw's most striking characteristic, distinguishing it, and other Polish towns, from the cities of western Europe. Industry occupied just under a quarter of its population. The engineering industries had steadily become more important, although textile manufactures were the principal group. The Frenchman, Girard, has left his name to the town of Zyrardow, where at the beginning of the 19th century he established a large linen cloth factory. The making of clothing, carried on particularly by the Jews in the heart of the old city, is important, and there is a large output of cheap cloths for the national market. Chemical industries have made their appearance alongside the gas works in the western part of the city and in the port of Praga. Brick-making is important on the outskirts, as in all cities, but had a great fillip with the renewed building activity in the inter-war period. Commerce, together with transport, occupied just under a fifth of the population, and among these occupations that of the small Jewish merchant is conspicuous. Thus, industry and commerce together occupy less than a half of the people. An unusually high proportion is engaged in public service (14 per cent.) and in domestic service (25 per cent.). The first marks the function of the city as a State capital. The second indicates the presence of a large proportion of people in the upper social brackets.

In the inter-war period much was done to enable Warsaw to function as an effective capital and urban community. Quite apart from the necessity for rehousing the mass of its population, which was here particularly urgent, there was the need for improving the navigation of the Vistula and for providing adequate rapid transport facilities to the suburbs outside the congested urban core, by both rail and road. If these provisions were adequate, it has been said that Warsaw might become one of the greatest capitals in Europe. To-day (1946), it is in ruins ; and its construction must begin anew.

Fig. 52 reveals the structure of the city as it was in 1939. Let us first note the old town or Stare Miasto. The 13th-century settlement had its beginnings in four nuclei. The castle, sited on the edge of the terrace (on the site of the military hospital) was originally the hunting lodge of the Dukes of Masovia. Below it, at the foot of the terrace, Solec, a village engaged in the salt trade, was often inundated by the floods of the changing course of the river. Rybitwy, sited to the north below the castle alongside the river, was an old fishing village. Finally, on the plateau, the village of Warszawa lay on the site of the Stare Miasto. In 1289 a new ducal castle was built on the site of the present royal palace and the route from the village of Warszawa to the castle was lined with houses and shops. The foundation of the town took place between 1262 and 1294, and in 1338 it was walled.

The Stare Miasto lay on the north side of the stronghold that commanded the ford crossing. It overlooked a ravine on its south side, and was bordered by another on the north side, which is now marked by the Mostowa street. The castle, originally built of timber, was later rebuilt in stone and finally became the ornate royal palace. The Stare Miasto had a regular ground plan and an oval shape like the German *Kolonialstadt*, and it centred on a square market-place (Polish, *Rynek*) (inset, Fig. 52). A stone wall bounded the town where it overlooked the river, but on its other sides it was protected by a double wall with three towers. The line of these fortifications is evident in the lie of the street called the Podwale. The market-place is surrounded by narrow-fronted patrician and burgesses' houses with four or five storeys, dating from the middle of the 16th century. On the place was the old Town Hall, demolished in 1819. Between the market-place and the castle the parish church of St. John was erected in 1250, and this later became the cathedral with the foundation of the archbishopric in 1817. It was a Late Gothic structure, built of brick in place of the original timber edifice, though it was much modified by later façades (1836–40).

The collection of different craft guilds in quarters of the old town was reflected in the concentration of Jewish craftsmen in certain streets. These are narrow, and the buildings are often two-storeyed with cellars. Walls and towers were demolished in the early 19th century, and many of the older buildings, both private and public, have disappeared, so that the old town is not nearly so well preserved as, for example, Cracow and Poznán. The settlement was of German origin, for it was in 1207 that the Duke of Masovia invited Germans to settle here next to the hitherto unimportant castle. The *Stadtvogt* and the *Schöffer* were German, the town law was German, and the transactions of the town were carried on in Low German. The great Augsburg commercial firm of Fugger had a branch in the town, and the Fugger Haus remained on the market-place.

The further growth of the settlement took place to the north of the Stare Miasto. This is the new town or Nowe Miasto, which dates from the 14th century, and seems to have grown gradually, rather than through a deliberate foundation. It also received German town law in the early 15th century, although it was entirely peopled by Poles. It lay on the slopes of the terrace and ran down to the river front, and was bounded in turn to the north by a short valley (Drna) that reached the Vistula at the foot of the present citadel. It was primarily a fishing and trading settlement.

Further extension took place to the west and south, on high and dry and level land, after 1595, when Warsaw became the seat of the kings, who attracted courts, Parliament and nobility in their train. A Swedish map of 1655 shows only the Stare Miasto and the Nowe Miasto, the former built of stone, the latter mainly of wood. Nowe Miasto had neither wall nor ditch until, with the suburbs, the whole settlement was enclosed by a wall in the time of John Casimir (1648–69). The nobility, who were attracted to the Court and the Diet, sought to avoid the restrictions of the town, and built their mansions in open and pleasanter surroundings in large open spaces outside the city walls. Here they were allocated land that fell within their jurisdiction and in which the lay-out of streets, " squares " and the building of houses was their responsibility. Such territories were called *Jurydyka*. Thus, the Leszczynski nobles had Leszno and the Zamoyski nobles had Ordynacka. Further, the district to the south of the old town was divided into long narrow strips at right angles to the north–south river and the terrace-edge, and these were cut up into building lots, so that there were no through north–south streets. Here, too, the nobles built palatial residences like the country mansions which they had often forsaken. Sometimes the noble laid out his territory around a square. Thus, Marshal Bielinski laid out his *jurydyka* with its centre in a *Rynek* (*Ring*), with roads at right angles to it. He also had built the north–south avenue known after him as the Marszalkowska, which was subsequently extended southwards to form a main avenue in the city. This mode of growth in the nobles' quarters resulted in piecemeal extension, without any regard to the whole and with no organic connection with the old town. Attempts were made in the middle of the 18th century to co-ordinate the growth of the city. A wall and ditch were built around it, lighting was introduced, and the streets given fixed names ; a struggle took place against the power of the nobles, and the union of the Nowe and Stare Miasto was advocated. Unity was eventually effected in 1791. Planning was begun on a radial pattern and the Marszalkowska was extended southwards. But then came calamity, for, after the insurrection of 1830 against Russian rule, many fine mansions of the nobility to the north of the town were destroyed in 1831 to make way for the vast new citadel and barracks that were erected to quell the town. From then on building was forbidden to the north of the city in the *glacis* beyond the citadel and to the north of Pràga, so that growth in this direction was impossible during the 19th century. In consequence the old nucleus, instead of being at the heart of the complex, lies on its northern edge.

Thus, an extensive area of palaces and smaller residences for the nobles and their attendants grew up along the whole length of the terrace edge, partly to the north of the Nowe Miasto, but mainly in a long belt south of the old town and the castle, which commanded magnificent views across the river. There was open space and pleasant surroundings for the nobles' mansions, free from the dirt and congestion of the town and the restrictions on building and living imposed by the town council. This is called the Krakowski Przedmiescie or the Cracow suburb. Extension also took place along the western and south-western sides of the old town and of the palace. On the slopes of the terrace lay parks and gardens. The expansion took place during the 17th century and is clearly shown in Merian's map at the end of that century. The town was enclosed by a ditch and bastions on the line of the present Nalewki-Przejazd. The southerly continuation of the palaces, mansions and gardens was along the Nowy Swiat ("new world") and its continuation, the Aleja Ujazdowska, to form the most exclusive residential district, where were situated the homes of the Polish nobility with gardens and parks behind them, and in which military hospitals and barracks were built later in the Russian period.

The extensions of the 19th century, that housed the masses of people who flocked in to carry on its expanding industrial and commercial activities, were made to the west and south-west of the old town, and also on the right bank of the river in Praga. Expansion also went on westwards from the long strip of land occupied by the nobles' quarter. A regular plan emerged with monotonous arrays of brick-built multi-storeyed tenements of the worst type which absorbed villages as it expanded. There are two main intersecting axes in this grid lay-out, the Marszalkowska road, 3 km. long from north-west to south-east, and the Aleja Jerozolimska, which runs from east-north-east to west-south-west and intersects the former in the centre. The latter road axis runs alongside the main railway tracks and leads to the Ponia-towski Bridge, and thence to Praga on the opposite side of the river. At the intersection of these two main roads is the main railway station. The bridge leads from the edge of the terrace and is built over the lower town at a height of 12 to 20 metres above ground ; it was opened in 1914. The Marszalkowska street is the main shopping and business thoroughfare of the city ; it runs parallel to the Nowy Swiat and its continuation. It should also be noted that the long narrow strip of land along the river, between its bank and the foot of the terrace, was closely built up, so that now the magnificent view of the old town from the Praga side has been spoiled. On the damp, low-lying ground, exposed to the floods of the Vistula, tenements, factories, barracks, and small timber houses are congested. This is the lower town. Wharves played no part in the city's early growth, since the river was not regularly navigable and the regularization of its course did not begin until the 18th century. The palace and the old town on the terrace edge impinge almost directly on the river, and the view here is unimpaired. This is a magnificent natural site for æsthetic urban planning that has been greatly abused.

Around the compact 19th-century built-up area, on the flat plateau surface, there is a zone of barracks, large parade and military training grounds, and the great citadel which has domin-ated the town from the north since the 1830s. All this is the work of the Russians. Building was forbidden throughout this fortified encircling zone throughout the period of Russian occupation, and this, in consequence, leaves great gaps in the build of the city that are still very evident.

The built-up area extended greatly during the 1914–18 war from 3,272 hectares to 8,210 hectares. The annexed suburbs in 1916 contained 109,500 inhabitants, a seventh of the total of Warsaw proper. The density of population at that time in the suburbs was 13 per hectare, as compared with 244 in the city. But from 1920 to 1930 the population of the city proper increased by only 4 per cent., whereas that of the suburbs increased by 28 per cent.

Praga on the right bank has grown up as a bridgehead settlement. Before the advent of the railway and of the river bridges it was negligible, and this side of the river bears much the same relation to Warsaw as does Floridsdorf to Vienna. Three great railway complexes form the nucleus of this area and the small port makes a fourth. There is also a vast barracks complex to the north, erected by the Russians in connection with the citadel on the Warsaw side. Around the railways and the port are large factories and, sandwiched between these, with its nucleus encircled by three of them opposite the Kierbedz Bridge (1859–64), is the centre of Praga. This east-bank area just after the 1914–18 war had 80,000 inhabitants, and in 1939 had about 300,000 inhabitants. Great improvement of the lay-out of this quarter has been effected with the opening of parks along the river and large buildings near the new station.

There have been two main periods in the building of the city beyond the old town nucleus. The first was that of John Sobieski (1674–96) and of the Saxon kings, Augustus II (1697–1733) and Stanislas Augustus Poniatowski (1764–95) ; and the second period was that of the Russian rule after 1815. The magnificent Baroque buildings in the area around the palace and the Cracow suburb date from the first period. A continuous series of Baroque palaces and churches makes up this district. Outstanding is the royal palace, which was rebuilt in the middle of the 18th century after being destroyed by the Swedes ; a part of it was also rebuilt after a fire in the 'seventies. The Russian period after 1815 witnessed the modern uncontrolled growth of the city. Public buildings included a number of Eastern Orthodox churches, notably the cathedral, completed in 1912 in a Byzantine form of architecture, surmounted by cupolas. Situated on the Saxon

Place in the midst of Baroque buildings, the cathedral was badly placed æsthetically. It was as hateful to the Poles as the citadel itself. Several Baroque buildings were given dull façades and converted to military uses. The Belvedere castle is one of the few fine Russian buildings. Various administrative buildings were added during the century in the city itself. After 1831 the Russians fortified the left bank with the citadel to quell the city. It was in the 'sixties that a ring of forts was built around the town to incorporate it into a general system of defences along the Vistula. The forts formed a semi-circle about 8 km. from the city centre. They were newly constructed in the 'nineties, but did not prevent the fall of Warsaw to the Germans in 1915.

Warsaw's development as a great city with a specialization of function by building and district, and with the concentration of business in the centre, has been much more tardy than in the Western capitals. The bulk of its commercial transactions were effected in small shops in the Jewish quarter. But the last fifty years nevertheless show a marked change, for, in 1882, only 37 per cent. of the commercial and industrial establishments were separate from the dwellings of their workers, whereas in 1919 the figure was 88 per cent. This is a simple illustration of the great change in economic and social structure, and, consequently, in space structure, that we have repeatedly emphasized. The centre of Warsaw in 1919 had 80 per cent. of the industrial and commercial establishments, Praga 5·6 per cent. and the suburbs only 3·8 per cent. Nearly three-quarters of these occupied only the ground floor of the building. But they had also spread to the second and third storeys of buildings (9·3 per cent. and 2·2 per cent. respectively). These establishments have thus concentrated in the centre, which has a population of 500 per hectare, whereas in the surrounding districts densities reach 1,000 per hectare. These figures reveal the steady transformation of a semi-Oriental into a Western city.

Warsaw epitomizes the development of the Polish town. The characteristic site of many towns in both Poland and Lithuania is, like that of Warsaw, the edge of a high terrace that drops steeply to the river and affords a relatively easy river crossing. The cathedral does not occupy a prominent position in Warsaw. It was essentially established as a royal residence, and the castle was the nucleus of its growth. The ancient cathedrals of Poland are to be found in the west. Cracow is outstanding, for within the walls of its stronghold were both the castle and the cathedral, and outside them the rectilinear plan of the original German settlement was founded in the middle of the 13th century after the Mongol incursion. Kielce also emerged as a bishopric in the 12th century, subordinate to Cracow. Plock is grouped beneath its cathedral, one of Poland's few Romanesque buildings. Wloclawek, farther downstream, dating from the 11th century, is also dominated by its cathedral. The same holds good for Poznán and Breslau, both of which were for centuries Slav towns, clustered adjacent to their cathedrals, but, clearly separate from them, the German *Kolonialstadt* was founded in each case as a planned settlement.

The castle, of course, is a main element in urban growth throughout east–central Europe. The original communal stronghold was a place where people met periodically for barter and for the worship of their heathen gods. The castles of the Middle Ages were often erected on their sites. Such was the case in Lithuania and in the Baltic lands. The former was probably the most backward of all European countries, for it was removed from the cultural influence of, and trade contacts with, the Germans, Poles and Russians. The case of Grodno, Kovno and the rest is typified by Vilna, which had its first permanent castle in 1320 and did not receive town law till 1387. Town development was earlier, in the Baltic lands to the north, through the work of the Hanseatic League in trading across the Baltic overland to central Russia.

The *Stare Miasto* of Warsaw was founded and peopled initially by Germans, and in this sense it is like many of the other towns of Poland. Here, however, the German influence soon disappeared, and it has long been an entirely Polish city. To the east, however, apart from those that were founded by the Poles themselves in the Baroque period, towns grew slowly and were eventually endowed with town law. This is true of Lithuania, as illustrated by Vilna. This matter is discussed further in Chapter 17.

Finally, there are the post-medieval features of growth. The flowering of Baroque art is especially characteristic of Warsaw and to a lesser degree of Vilna. What, however, gives a particular architectural stamp to these towns is the imprint of the long period of Russian occupation throughout the 19th century. This is reflected in the large and often forbidding Russian Orthodox cathedral, which has often been erected in a dominant position in the heart of the city. There are also the administrative buildings in the centre and the great barracks that were erected on the outskirts of the towns. Warsaw is also distinct from the towns of western Europe in its large proportion of Jews, and this trait is generally true of all the towns, large and small, in east–central Europe. The modern growth of Warsaw, rapid and uncontrolled, is equalled in Poland's other industrial centres, notably in Lodz and Upper Silesia.

CHAPTER 12

PARIS

Paris is situated in the centre of the Department of Seine, the whole of which is part of the urban agglomeration of the city. The Department has an area of 480 sq. km. or about 192 sq. miles (almost the same as Chicago), while Paris proper covers only 78 sq. km. or about 31·5 sq. miles (104 sq. km. if the Bois de Boulogne and Bois de Vincennes and the military zone are included). The Department was created in 1795 in order to embrace both Paris and its potential sub-urban zone, and it is surrounded on all sides by the Department of Seine-et-Oise. The extent of the built-up area is shown on Fig. 54. The population of the Department of Seine was nearly five millions in 1936, with a density of 10,300 persons to the square kilometre or about 4,100 per square mile. Of this total, Paris had 2,830,000.

(1) SITE (Fig. 53)

The major feature in the physical relief of Paris and the areas around it is the river Seine, with its three great meanders. Paris itself is situated in a sweeping northerly bend of the river, and the nucleus of the city lies on an island (*Île de la Cité*) in the middle of the river. From this island, which was early used as a river crossing, the land rises steadily to the south whereas low sandy bluffs lie on the north bank. The old course of the river was to the north along the foot of Montmartre ; this area was marshy until the Middle Ages and was not drained till the 12th century, before which roads north from Paris had to cross it by bridges. It is no wonder, therefore, that the first Roman settlement spread on the hilly south bank, but that the medieval town spread more rapidly on the flat land on the north bank, once this was drained and made suitable for building. The land downstream inside the other two long meanders is flat, sandy, gravelly, and has been invaded only by the modern expansion of the urban area with its nuclei in historic towns and villages on the river banks. The Île de la Cité and the Île St. Louis are the only two remaining islands of the river. The banks of the Seine are liable to extensive floods—the last of which occurred in 1910—and to prevent these,

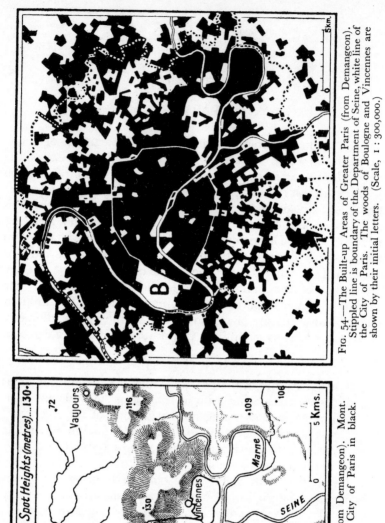

Fig. 53.—The Site of Greater Paris (from Demangeon). Mont. = Montmartre. Boundary of the City of Paris in black. (Scale, 1 : 300,000.)

Fig. 54.—The Built-up Areas of Greater Paris (from Demangeon). Stippled line is boundary of the Department of Seine, white line of the City of Paris. The woods of Boulogne and Vincennes are shown by their initial letters. (Scale, 1 : 300,000.)

and to increase the river's depth and current so as to improve and maintain its navigability, it is lined with stone-built quays.

The exact position of the nucleus of the medieval town was fixed by the route from Orleans to the north at the point where it crosses the Seine, below the confluence of the Marne, in order to avoid crossing several rivers. Here the Seine valley is flat, broad, and marshy, and even to this day liable to floods. But two facts determined the precise course of this route : first, the steep hill of Ste. Geneviève about 50 metres above the river level, and second, that, below this hill, the river, broken by distributaries and islands, contained but one island that afforded a relatively easy crossing to the sandy bluffs, free from flood, on the north bank. The site of ancient Paris was thus an island bridgehead.

The relief of the surrounding land over which the medieval city spread has two outstanding features—the flat, marshy plain, traversed by the great meanders of the wide river Seine ; and the isolated, steep-sided hills, rising from this plain to the north and south of the river. The hills of Ste. Geneviève and the Butte aux Cailles, separated by the valley of the Bièvre, lie to the south of the river, and pass southwards, beyond Montparnasse, to a plateau. Montmartre and Passy lie to the north of the river. Belleville and Ménilmontant to the north-east are the westernmost members of a small line of hills, separated from Montmartre by a low pass or col, which is followed by the canal St. Martin and the chief railways. These hills to the north and the plateau to the south lie on the periphery of Paris, and until the 19th century were covered with fields, orchards and vineyards. The old town lay on the plain at the foot of these hills on the north side of the river, and from the island spread up the slopes of Ste. Geneviève to the south. It is along the flat land, especially up and down the Seine, that the modern city has expanded.

This island bridgehead commanded important routes—overland routes to the north and south, and the river route up and down stream. In the Gallo-Roman period a routeway ran from Orleans along the present site of the Rue St. Jacques across the island of the *Cité*, and then along the Rue St. Martin to St. Denis. When Flanders became the great seat of industry and commerce in the Middle Ages, the great land routes from the Mediterranean first crossed France east of Paris through the Champagne, the seat of the great fairs of Troyes and Provins. But gradually the main route for traffic was attracted through

Paris by the growth of the fairs of St. Denis, which were favoured by the French kings. The development of the road traffic and the utilization of the fine waterway of the Seine waited till Paris was ready to seize its opportunity. This came when it was selected as the capital of the Capetian kings in A.D. 987. It was this event and not the existence of natural routeways that made Paris.

(2) Topographic Formation

The stages in the topographic formation of Paris as marked by its successive lines of fortifications are shown on Fig. 55.

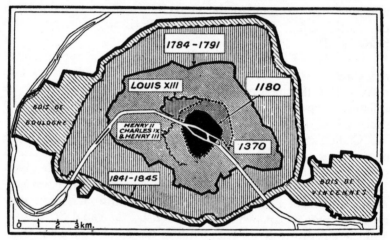

Fig. 55.—The Growth of Paris (from Demangeon). The map shows the dates at which the various fortifications of Paris were constructed. Present limits of the city are shown by the heavy black line. (Scale, 1 : 200,000.)

Under the Roman Empire, a Roman settlement spread widely on the south side of the river on the slopes of Ste. Geneviève. This settlement was completely destroyed by the Teutonic invasions at the end of the third century A.D. As in many other Roman towns, the settlement contracted to a small defensible site, namely, the island in the river, and around it a rampart was constructed. Its name of Lutetia was changed in the 5th century to Paris, after the Parisii, whose ancient capital it was. For centuries the place was confined to the *Île de la Cité* huddled inside the walls of the *castrum* and clustered around the cathedral in the eastern half of the island, while the original site of the palace of the Capetian kings lay in its western half (on the site of the Palais de Justice). A small nucleus of settlement lay on the north and south sides of the island to protect each bridge, each under the command of a châtelet. During the reign of Clovis the basilicas of St. Peter and St. Paul, St. Benoît and St. Severin made their appearance. In the meadows and fields around there grew up two religious houses, both founded in the 7th century, which subsequently played an important part in the city's life. The abbey of St. Germain-des-Près lay to the south, and it established many surrounding villages during the 9th century. The abbey of St. Denis lay to the north, and was a great centre of pilgrimage and fairs.

As the seat of the House of Capet, Paris quickly became the undisputed capital of the kingdom of France. By the 12th century it had taken its permanent medieval shape, which consisted of three parts. The *Île de la Cité* contained the administrative nucleus, with the royal palace and Court, the cathedral and bishop's palace. The building of Notre-Dame was begun in the 13th century, and the church buildings that preceded it were moved to the south bank. Here in 1253 the theological college was founded and the University was grouped around it. On the right (north) bank lay the merchants' quarter, the *Ville*, clustered on the water front. This was the real nucleus of the urban life, and the merchants, who were banded in an association to control the navigation of the river, founded the great fair of Lendit near St. Denis in the 12th century. The chief port lay on the present site of the Place du Châtelet near the Hôtel de Ville and at the junction of routes. On the left (south) bank on the slopes of the hill of Ste. Geneviève was the cultural focus of the city's life, and the seat of the University. In those days this meant a community of colleges, schools, monasteries and churches, and the living quarters of numerous students and of those who catered to their spiritual and worldly needs. By 1210 these three quarters were enclosed by the first wall.

The most remarkable feature of the expansion of Paris in the ensuing centuries was its asymmetry, for the main growth, actuated by both commerce and the Court, was on the flat marshy land on the north side of the river with its nucleus in the town (*ville*) proper. The river front was the main seat of the city's activities ; the *marchands de l'eau* fed Paris, and in the middle of the 13th century their chief became the head of the municipality. Along the river front, and clustered behind it, were the quarters of the craftsmen and artisans who used the river for water, power and transport. Here, too, were segregated financiers—Jews and

Lombards. The kings contributed to this growth, for Charles V shifted the royal residence to the north bank, and built palaces, which attracted the aristocracy, as well as domestics, shopkeepers and artisans. Shifting their residence from time to time between east and west, Louis XIV and Louis XV finally settled in the district of St. Honoré in the west, and a Court district emerged around the Palais Royal. Thus Paris expanded steadily, and most markedly, towards the west. Successive walls had to be built. The fortifications of 1180–1210 by Philip Augustus had 70 towers and 13 gates. These were extended first under Charles V (1370), then under Louis XIII on the site of the great boulevards. The next line of walls was built between 1784 and 1791, and embraced the north and south banks, and included for the first time hilly districts to the north and south. This *Mur des Fermiers-Généraux* served primarily as a fiscal limit for the collection of *octroi* (cf. the *Zollmauer* in Berlin, Ch. 13). Finally, from 1841 to 1845, when the population of the city reached the million mark, the *octroi* fortifications were transformed to boulevards and " places " (Étoile, Ternes, Clichy, Combat, Trône, Italie, Denfert, Maine). Eleven surrounding communes were added and regrouped into eight *arrondissements*. At the same time, new walls were built to include all or most of the hilly ridges to the north, and spread west towards the great bend of the Seine. These new fortifications consisted of fortified walls and a series of forts, and building was prohibited for a distance of 200 metres beyond them. The total population of the city inside the walls in 1861 was nearly one and three-quarter millions.

In the modern period, since about 1850, the city has not expanded concentrically, but by long tentacular extensions towards new outlying nuclei (Fig. 54). The main characteristic of growth in the modern period has been the remarkable increase of industry, first by expansion inside the walls, especially in the eastern and south-eastern sections, and then, since 1900, by extension in a continuous belt outside the city walls in a wide industrial–residential fringe. Canals were built in the 'twenties in the north of the city, on which materials for heavy industries could be carried. Here, too, were opened the railway stations of Est, Nord and St. Lazare near the outer boulevards, the tracks using the gaps to the east and west of the hill of Montmartre. The built-up area grew along roads and railways ; factories and working-class quarters clustered on the plains along the river and canals, especially to the west and north, still mainly on the north side of the river. After the First World War the 19th-century fortifications, which had become an anachronism in modern warfare and a hindrance to urban growth, were demolished. Most remarkable is the extension of the agglomeration along the great plains of the Seine in its big bend below the city. This area is easily reached by rail from the station of St. Lazare across the low col between the hills of Montmartre and Passy. It has become a great urban area, with 450,000 people, including both industrial and working-class quarters, and good residential quarters. To the north, extension has taken place in the broad flat col between Montmartre and Belleville. Here, too, alongside the canals of St. Denis and de l'Ourq and the main railways, which lead to the north and east of France, great industrial quarters have grown on the plain of St. Denis, which houses 175,000 people. To the east the urban belt falls into industrial quarters on the plain and residential quarters on the hills, but beyond, at the confluence of the Seine and Marne, the urban area spreads again, and contains 300,000 inhabitants. To the south, the urban land is discontinuous and scattered, for the southern plateau, with its deep, picturesque wooded valleys, pushes right up to the confines of Paris. Apart from small industrial quarters along the river bank and others near the old fortifications, this is mainly a great residential fringe, and is gradually expanding towards St. Cloud and Versailles.[1]

The great increase of industry beyond the boundaries of the city has been reflected in a very large increase of population. Increases were greatest in the industrial areas to the north-east (Pantin and St. Denis) and north-west, inside the meander of the Seine, and in the south. In the centre of the city, on the other hand, the shift of people to the outskirts, slum clearance, and the displacement of houses by commercial and administrative buildings, are reflected in a steady decrease of population over an expanding area. These features are clearly brought out on Figs. 56 to 59. It is particularly interesting to note that the central area with the decreasing population is roughly bounded by the old *octroi* walls, while between these and the city boundary there have been increases of over 25 per cent., and, in considerable sectors to the east and south-west, of over 65 per cent. The latter areas in particular are largely industrial, and developed in the last decades of the 19th century.

[1] The built-up areas of Paris for 1900 and 1930 are shown in *L'Architecture d'aujourd'hui*, June 1937, p. 36.

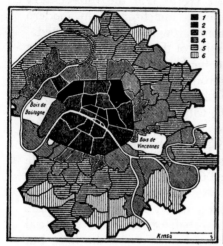

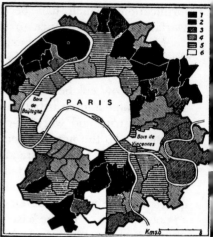

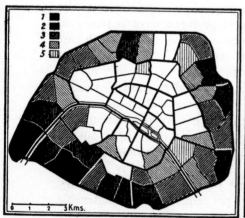

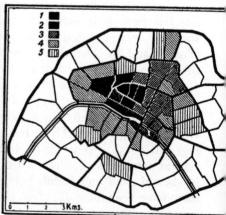

Fig. 56.—The Density of Population in Paris and the Department of Seine in 1931 (from Demangeon, *Paris, la Ville et sa Banlieue*). (Scale, 1 : 450,000.)

Persons per hectare :—1. Over 500. 2. 200–500.   3. 80–200.   4. 40–80. 5. 10–40. 6. Under 10.

Fig. 57.—The Growth of Population in the Department of Seine (Greater Paris), 1876–1931 (from Demangeon). (Scale, 1 : 450,000.)

Percentage :—1. Over   1000. 2. 800–900.   3. 540–720.   4. 330–460. 5. 120–290. 6. Less than 100.

Fig. 58.—The Increase of Population in Paris, 1896–1931 (from Demangeon). (Scale, 1 : 200,000.)

Percentage :—1. Over 150. 2. 65–120. 3. 24–56. 4. 6–16. 5. Under 6.

Fig. 59.—The Decrease of Population in Paris, 1896–1931 (from Demangeon). (Scale, 1 : 200,000.)

Percentage :—1. Over 50.   2. 35–50.   3. 15–27.   4. 5–15.   5. Under 5.

(3) Outer Sub-urban Zone

This zone lies beyond the old walls of the city and consists of an alternation of open and built-up areas. The latter contain great industrial complexes, with recently built-up workers' residential quarters near to them, and sub-urban residential areas. Most notable are the large open spaces of the woods of Boulogne and Vincennes which lie to the west and east. Closely built-up areas stretch to the north-west and south-east along the flat land of the Seine bend and the bends of the Marne down to its confluence with the Seine. There is a great intermixture of built-up areas and open spaces to the north and the south, with fully built-up zones just outside the city limits and open areas out farther in the country. Though building has been proceeding very rapidly, the northern quarters are mainly industrial and the southern mainly residential.

The Paris agglomeration extends over the whole of the Department of Seine, using its land for residence, for factories, for week-end recreation, for growing vegetables and flowers, and for discharging sewage. It is of interest to note that outside the Department there is a great circle of forests—except to the north-east—which make an effective barrier to the expansion of urban land uses. These are St. Germain to the west, continued north-east in Montmorency and Chantilly; Bondy d'Armainvilliers and Senart to the east; and the wooded sandy ridges around Versailles running north-west to south-east through Sèvres and Meudon.

But the whole of this agglomeration, though a unit, does not have a single government. Outside the city of Paris there are 80 communes in the Department, and the urban area stretches beyond the limits of the latter to the west (beyond the Seine), and to the north-east—its chief axis of industrial development lying along the Seine and the canal to the north-east. Many of the communes are not able to care for all the communal needs of their inhabitants and are obliged to co-operate with their neighbours. Over six million people live within 35 km. of Notre-Dame, and the region has been recently organized for the preparation of a long-term plan for Paris and its contiguous urban areas.

(4) Urban Circulations

The railway terminals of Paris were built in the 'forties on the outskirts of the city, but they now lie in its heart and are inconveniently situated. They have been rebuilt and extended and their approaches widened, but their traffic has far outgrown their facilities. The stations are connected by 143 km. of underground railways collectively known as the Métropolitain, the construction of which began in 1900. An underground inner circle (*petite ceinture*) is used mainly for local passenger traffic, as well as by through coaches from the Channel ports. An outer circle (*grande ceinture*), lying well beyond the suburban limits of the city, is used mainly by freight traffic. Radial underground routes reach the various gates of Paris and are being extended to the suburbs. Marshalling yards lie mainly on the outer circle and the goods yards are near the passenger terminals. The latter lie inside the inner circle to the north and south of the Seine. The new plan for Paris provides for a ring road (*rocade*) on the outskirts passing through the chief stretches of forest.

The Seine as a navigable waterway is almost continuously lined with quays. It can take barges up to 1,000 tons, whereas the canals take barges up to 300 tons. Paris receives by the Seine its wheat, wine, wood and building materials. The goods traffic of the port passed from 2·8 million tons in 1872 to 10 million tons in 1900 and to 15 million tons in 1933. The port falls into three main sectors—the Seine in its crossing of Paris, the canals and basins, and the Seine on the outskirts of Paris. The Paris Seine has little traffic in the centre where the public buildings are situated. To the north-east are the great basins of the Villette quarter. These communicate with the Seine by the canal St. Martin, and with the north by the canal St. Denis, and between Villette and St. Denis is the most highly industrialized quarter of Paris. A number of great river ports lie on ·the outskirts of the city, receiving bulky commodities, notably coal, for the big industrial plants—gas works, electricity plants, metallurgical plants—a belt extending continuously upstream and downstream to Argenteuil. The functions of the port as a whole are concerned almost exclusively with supplying the urban agglomeration itself, not its hinterland. In good years, traffic amounts to about 15 million tons, about a half of the total traffic carried by water and rail. Imports of bulky products make up 70 per cent. of the total traffic. Upstream, on the right bank above the canal St. Martin, there are wine, coal, timber, wood pulp, petrol and grain quays. Downstream, there are important coal wharves at Javel.

(5) Distribution of Population

The changes in the growth of population in Paris from 1861 onwards are clearly shown when the *arrondissements* are arranged in three groups, a central zone (I to IV), a middle zone (V to X), and an outer zone (XI to XX) (Figs. 58 and 59). Since 1861 the central zone (north of the river) has shown a steady decrease of its total population. The middle zone, in which are situated the Nord and St. Lazare Stations, increased slowly till 1891, then remained stationary till 1911, and has since decreased. Its boundaries are marked on the outside by the outer boulevards, the Place de la République and the Place de la Bastille to the east, and the Jardin des Plantes, the Luxembourg and Champ de Mars to the south. The outer zone, which reaches out to the administrative limit of the *ville*, has shown a steady increase since 1861, slowing down after 1911 and reaching a total of about 2,000,000 in 1931.[1]

Paris is one of the most densely populated and overcrowded cities in the world, a fact due in no small measure to the lack of an adequate system of long-distance sub-urban lines. In 1936 the city had 33,300 persons living on every square kilometre (the woods of Vincennes and Boulogne excluded) or over 80,000 per square mile. This is a remarkably high density, greater than that of any other capital city. Forty per cent. of the area in 1930 was under buildings, 21·7 per cent. under streets, and 22·6 per cent. under yards and gardens. Public spaces occupied 3·1 per cent. of the area. In many districts there were 500 or more persons out of every thousand who lived in dwellings with more than one person per room. The incidence of disease and mortality is closely allied to the overcrowding in rooms and to the density of the built-up area. Thus, for example, in the quarter of the Champs-Élysées the death rate is 9·4 per 1,000, in l'Opéra 11·5, in Passy 11·8, all these being relatively good-class residential districts, where there is no overcrowding, sanitary conditions are good, and open spaces adequate. On the other hand, the death-rate is 22·7 per 1,000 in Gobelins, 22·8 in Ménilmontant, 27·1 in Buttes-Chaumont, all these being very congested working-class tenement districts. The infant mortality rate is twice as high in *arrondissements* XX and XI as in VI (Champ de Mars) and XVI. Tuberculosis is the cause of six times as many deaths in *arrondissement* XX as in *arrondissement* VIII, between which there are the same salient contrasts in density of

[1] R. Crozier, *La Gare du Nord*, 1941, p. 243.

built-up land, and density of population per room.[1] There is indeed a very high incidence of tuberculosis in the city as a whole as compared with other large cities, and there are wide variations from one quarter to another. The incidence of this disease in the city varies in inverse proportion to the amount of open space.[2]

(6) THE LIMITS OF GREATER PARIS

Where does Paris, as a settlement area, end ? A recent study of the influence of the Gare du Nord on the growth of northern Paris has attempted to answer this question. The results are shown on Fig. 60. Several criteria are mapped as indicative of the limits of certain paramount traits or controls of urban influence. The density of population is one of these. A density of 100 persons per square kilometre (250 per square mile) marks the extreme limit of the close settlement area over against the surrounding rural areas where densities are well under this figure. Nearer to the city, densities of 500 per square kilometre (1,250 per square mile) afford another significant limit of the closely settled fringe of the city complex. This latter area corresponds closely with the area served by the city transport facilities and with the areas in which more than a tenth of the workers are employed in the city. The limits of the *banlieue* may thus be considered from the point of view of distance, time, density of population, and the rate of population increase, and, finally, function, including residence, industry and week-end recreation. Since growth is, in general, radial and concentric, the shape of the whole area is roughly circular, and three main zones may be recognized. The main city nucleus lies within a radius of 5 km. of Notre-Dame, corresponding with the limits of the *ville* and containing a population of 2·8 millions. Then outside the city boundary there is a zone between 5 and 15 km. from the centre. This may be referred to as the sub-urban zone, and contains 2·5 million people. Its boundary corresponds with the limits of the city transport facilities. Finally, the outer or peripheral zone, the *banlieue*, extends between a radius of 15 and 30 km. from the centre. The 30-km. circle corresponds roughly with the limit of the density per commune of 100 per square kilometre, while the limit of area of daily travel of workers to the city lies along the 20–25 km. circle. It may be reckoned that the daily journeys of workers

[1] See G. P. George, *Géographie économique et social de la France*, 1938, p. 103.
[2] *L'Architecture d'aujourd'hui*, Paris, June, 1937, p. 26. See also H. Sellier, *La Crise du logement*, Vol. I, Paris, 1921, with maps of the incidence of room crowding and tuberculosis by districts.

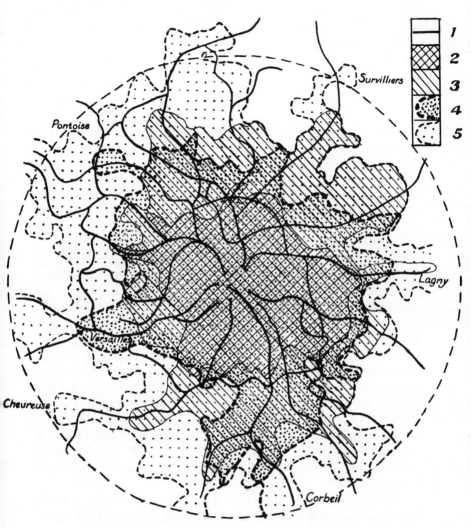

Fig. 60.—The Limits of Greater Paris (redrawn from Crozier).
The outer dashed circle has a radius of 30 km. from Notre-Dame. 1. Railways. 2. Zone served by city transport services. 3. Zone in which daily movements of professional people into Paris exceeds 10 per cent. of the total population in each district. 4. Zone in which the density of population exceeds 500 persons per sq. km. 5. Zone in which the density of population exceeds 100 persons per sq. km.

to Paris reach 25 km. in one hour by bus and 35 to 40 km. by rail. In fact, to the west of Paris 95 per cent. of the season-ticket holders live within 25 km. of the city centre.[1]

[1] Crozier, *op. cit.*, p. 253.

CHAPTER 13

BERLIN

Berlin is particularly interesting as a city since it is (or was !) about the same size as Paris, although its growth has been more recent and rapid. Like Paris, it has been the subject of special studies upon which this chapter is based. We shall emphasize the geographical differentiations within the built-up area and the limits of the urban complex.

(1) SITE AND TOPOGRAPHIC EXPANSION (Fig. 61)

Berlin and its tributary environs lie in the heart of the Prussian province of Brandenburg in the northern lowland of Germany. This great agglomeration is bounded by clearly defined major physical features—the Elbe valley to the west ; the Oder valley below Frankfurt to the east ; the valley linking the Elbe and Oder to the north, which is followed by the Rhin and Ruppin canals west of Oranienburg and by the Finow and Berlin-Stettin canals east of Oranienburg ; and the valley trench marked by the towns of Brandenburg—Baruth—Lubben—Kottbus—Forst— Güben to the south. To the north of this rectangle lies the undulating country of Priegnitz and Uckermark which merges northwards into the lake-strewn wooded plateau of Mecklenburg, and to the south lies the Fläming Heide—sandy uplands which are dry, partly wooded and heath-covered, and partly open cultivated land.

Three depressions cross this area from east to west, namely those on its northern and southern borders, and the Havel–Spree depression, in the centre of which Berlin is situated. These are intercrossed by several smaller depressions along valley floors from north to south. The chief of these are (1) the Upper Havel —Havel See—Nuthe depression (Oranienburg—Spandau—Pots- dam) in the west and (2) the Dahme depression and the lakes in a line north-east from it in the east. All these floors are below about 40 metres in height ; they have many streams and lakes, with some bog and marsh. Though some of the area to-day is drained and used for meadow and market-gardening, the exten- sive areas of sandy soils on the Havel to the west of the city, and the Dahme–Spree to the east, are thickly forested. The borders of the lakes are usually marshy, while drained water-meadows predominate in the plains.

These depressions (shown in black on Fig. 61) separate slightly higher undulating land above 40 metres in height, reaching maximum heights of 100 to 150 metres in Müggelberge (115 m.) east of Köpenik, in the hills immediately south of Potsdam, and in the Prötzeler Forst, 20 miles north-east of Berlin. These higher platforms are practically isolated by the plains around

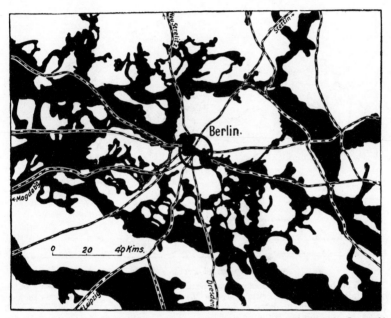

Fig. 61.—The Location and Site of Greater Berlin (from the *Seydlitz'sche Geographie von Deutschland*, 1925). In black are low-lying areas, unshaded are raised glacial platforms. Main railways from Berlin are shown.

them, to which they frequently drop for long distances by steep slopes. They fall into two distinct types of country. Open, hedgeless, arable land (rye being the main crop) is generally characteristic, but there are also considerable stretches of pine forest on sandy soils. The main areas of open cultivated land lie north and south of Berlin, and are known as the Barnim and Teltow plateaux respectively.

Greater Berlin was formed in 1920 by the combination of the *Altstadt* of Berlin or Old Berlin with ninety-three surrounding

Gemeinde or parishes. It has an area of about 880 sq. km. (352 square miles) and had a population in 1920 of 3·8 millions, and in the 'thirties of 4½ millions (roughly the same as Greater Paris). The river Spree crosses the city from west-north-west to east-south-east. The Havel, joining the Spree at right angles at Spandau, and the Dahme at Köpenik, form its approximate east and west borders, and both these areas are marked by belts of lakes. Midway in its course between Köpenik and Spandau the

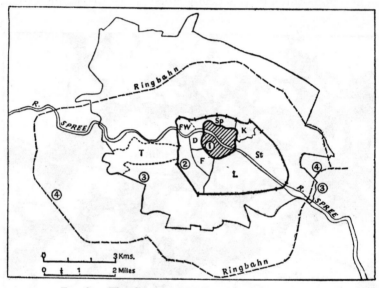

FIG. 62.—The Growth of Berlin.   (Scale, 1 : 150,000.)

1. The first wall.   2. Second wall until 1738 (*Zollmauer*).   3. Boundary of old Berlin after 1738.   4. Circular railway (*Ringbahn*).   The hatched nucleus includes Berlin, Kölln, and the later additions of Friedrichswerder (1662) and Neu-Kölln (1690) to the south-west and south-east.   The Dorotheenstadt (D) was added in 1674, and Friedrichstadt (F) in 1691.   The area of the *Weichbild* of Alt-Berlin, that was formed in 1738, included Friedrichwilhelmstadt (FW), Spandauer Viertel (Sp.), Strahlauer Viertel (St.), Königsviertel (K), and Luisenstadt (L).   T = Tiergarten.

Spree branches, and on the enclosed island was sited the original medieval town of Kölln. Berlin was located on the north bank of the river. These two together, with an area of about 175 acres, were endowed with town laws in 1240 and 1237 respectively, and formed the *Altstadt* of Berlin. Fortifications with bastions in the French style were built in the 17th century and enclosed both Berlin and Kölln as well as Friedrichswerder, which was founded in 1662. The addition of the Dorotheenstadt and the Friedrichstadt as Court districts by the kings of Prussia was

A. ROLLE

B. AARBERG

C. NEUNKIRCH-IM-KLETTGAU

D. BISCHOFSZELL (founded tenth century)

E. LIESTAL (town law 1288)

F. FREIBURG (founded 1178)

I. SWISS TOWNS

2. BASEL View towards the north

3. COLOGNE View from SW to NE

The Functional Zones of the Great City (Cologne). Air view of Cologne in a strip running NW from NEUMARKT (left bottom) to the city outskirts. (cf. fig. 19). Note: (left bottom to top), ALTSTADT (zone 1), Ring, NEUSTADT (zone 2), railroads, green belt, inner suburb of EHRENFELD (zone 3); and (right bottom to top), outer suburban area (single family type), and industrial areas alongside railway tracks (zone 5).

5. **FRANKFURT.** The old town, with Cathedral and Römerberg Square

6. BRESLAU. The old town (Altstadt and Neustadt). Sand Island in River Oder (left), Cathedral quarter N. of the Oder. Note: Ring in centre, Neumarkt to left and Ritter Platz near river opposite Sand Island. (South at top of photo.)

8. Industrial areas and old tenements in the Ruhr

10. Single family houses at Neu Tempelhof, Berlin

7. Modern apartment blocks in Berlin

9. Congested tenement blocks in central Breslau

LIVING QUARTERS OF THE GREAT CITY

11. TOULOUSE View towards the north

12. ARLES

13. LÜBECK View towards the north

14. ROTTERDAM View towards the south

15. **BRUGES**

0 |___|___|___|___|___| 500 METRES
0 |___|___|___|___|___| 500 YARDS

6.

LILLE

400 METRES

400 YARDS

BRUSSELS

500 METRES
500 YARDS

18. VIENNA

19. AIGUES MORTES

20. BRAM (NEAR CACASSONNE)

21. FREIBURG-IM-BREISGAU (BADEN)

22. MÜNSTER (WESTPHALIA)

23. KARLSRUHE

26. MIDDELBURG (ZEELAND)

24. FREUDENSTADT

25. ROCKLITZ (SAXONY)

I

2

1. Central German ha
timbered Gable Hou
(Wildungen)

2. Low German bri
Gable House (Alter Mark
Stralsund)

3

4

3. Upper German sto
Gable House. Note lov
pitched roof and Chur
Cupolas. (Bavaria)

4. Low German timbere
Eaves House (Goslar)

5

6

5. Central German sto
Eaves House (Nuremberg)

6. Low German Gab
House with several stor
and narrow frontage (Bresla

27. TOWN HOUSES IN GERMANY (from GEISLER)

Newer Apart-
nt House
agenhaus
eifswald)

Long House
nghaus and
thaus)
eifswald)

1

2

Older Apart-
nt House
agenhaus)
alle)

Tenement
use (*Kasten-*
s) with flat
f (Breslau)

3

4

Mansard
use (Wurz-
rg)

Tenement
use in S.W.
rmany (*Miets-*
s) in rows
ihenhaus)
issingen)

5

6

28. TOWN HOUSES IN GERMANY (from GEISLER)

A. MONTAUBAN. Market-place

B. CAEN

C. CHARLEVILLE. Place Ducale

D. VILLENEUVE-SUR-LO

E. ARRAS

F. BETHUNE. Market-place and belfry

29. TOWN HOUSES IN FRANCE (from DOYON AND HABRECHT)

accompanied by the lay-out of the Tiergarten. These five settlements covered 6¼ sq. km. (2·5 sq. miles) and had 57,000 inhabitants in the first years of the 18th century. In 1737 the *Zollmauer*
or Customs Wall was erected. This was a palisade intended as
a fiscal limit and not as a defence. The area inside it covered
13 sq. km. (5·25 sq. miles). It was demolished and replaced by
roads after 1850, and then tenements were built over large areas
between it and the *Ringbahn*. The older area inside the Customs

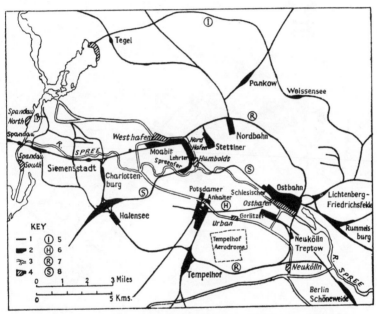

Fig. 63.—The Communications of Berlin. (Scale, 1 : 250,000.)
1. Railways. 2. Goods and marshalling yards. 3. River. 4. River harbour.
5. Industriebahn. 6. Hochbahn. 7. Ringbahn. 8. Stadtbahn.

Wall gradually assumed its present character as the business heart
of the capital.

The pattern of communications in Berlin and its environs
reveals the double characteristic of radial and concentric routes
(Fig. 63). The waterways are in the form of a letter **H** with
the city spreading astride the Spree between the Havel and
Spree–Dahme systems. The railway and road net are predominantly radial, with, however, two marked concentric belts—the
first the *Ringbahn*, the railway that has formed such a fundamental

I

physical barrier in the growth of the city ; and the outer and new autobahn that encircles the whole of the built-up areas with a radius of some 30 km. from east to west and 15 km. from north to south. After about 1900 industry began to shift from the area inside the *Ringbahn* to widely scattered areas beyond it. There has also been an outward shift of population, but this has not been as large as one would anticipate, since a very large proportion of

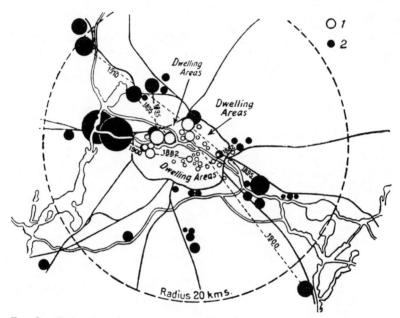

FIG. 64.—Industrial Shifts in Greater Berlin, 1890–1925. The shift of large-scale engineering industries from the centre to the periphery of the city from 1890 to 1925.

1. Location of industries in 1890. 2. Location in 1925 with direction and date of shifts. After Heiligenthal, reproduced from Pfannshmidt, *Standort, Landesplanung, Baupolitik*, 1932.

workers in the outer areas still live in the tenement areas of the inner city.

Some features of these centrifugal trends for the period 1890 to 1925 are shown on Fig. 64. It shows the date, direction and magnitude of movement of the large-scale engineering industries, and the location at that time of the chief dwelling areas of the working population.

(2) The Build of Greater Berlin (1935)

A German geographer [1] has mapped the broad distribution of the major types of urban building in Greater Berlin. The map, redrawn and amended, is shown on Fig. 65. It indicates the broad lines of the structure of the city, and with each type of building lay-out a dominant type of function may be legitimately associated. The map is based on the historical growth of the city in so far as that is reflected in its present build. Important in this respect is the rôle of the town fortifications. This zone, on the outskirts of the city, was normally more open than the central parts, and here were laid out such buildings as factories, hospitals, cemeteries, military establishments, new public buildings, and places of amusement, for which peripheral locations were necessary or desirable. Often a change in the street pattern and in the street name indicates the former function of this zone as a barrier to the extension of the town. Such open zones appear when the fortifications are still in being, but they persist when the city expands beyond them as a distinct belt that is clearly recognizable by its build.

Four types of urban build are mapped (see Fig. 65).

1. Uniform build of " great city type " with buildings of at least four storeys.
2. Varied build of " town type ". This falls into two classes :
    (a) in the city core, there are high buildings intermixed with older and lower buildings of three storeys and less ; and
    (b) on the borders of the urban complex, there is a great intermixture of high and low buildings with factory sites, open settlement (housing estates), open spaces and allotment areas.
3. Main factory areas.
4. Open residential areas on the borders of the city include villas and single-family houses—built mainly since 1918.

The two old fortified zones of the city are marked off on the map by the letters a and b, since these are characterized by distinct traits of land use.

---

[1] Herbert Louis : *Die Geographische Gliederung von Gross Berlin*, 26 pp., 2 maps. Stuttgart, 1936. See also F. Leyden, *Gross-Berlin, Geographie der Weltstadt*, Breslau, 1933. We have not been deterred from presenting this sudy of Berlin, even though much of the city is now laid to the ground. The characters of urban growth are typical of all continental cities and an understanding of the old city will be necessary for the reconstruction of the new.

242 THE WEST EUROPEAN CITY

The Roman numbers on the map refer to the zones. These are as follows :—

I. *The Kurfürstenstadt*

This was the oldest nucleus of the city until the end of the 17th century, when it was fortified with thirteen great bastions. It has narrow and winding streets. Much of it has old dwelling-houses dating from 1600 to 1800, although it has been invaded by the modern buildings of the city since 1860, and most of the area is taken up by shops, offices, workshops and warehouses. The textile industry is important in this quarter, and there are wholesale markets around the Alexanderplatz to the north.

The border of the Kurfürstenstadt, marked (*a*) on the map, lies between I and II and is an old built-up area, such as appears in many large cities, into which the functions of the " city core " have gradually spread. It lies astride the site of the old fortifications. The zone is marked by public buildings, and narrow streets and small places, on the site of the old fortifications and bastions.[1]

II. *The Old Suburbs of Berlin (Vorstädte)*

This zone lies immediately outside the fortification belt of the old town centre, on its north, north-east and east sides. The main streets radiating from the " places " on the site of the fortifications are lined with shops, but the east of this district is a densely populated slum, with an irregular net of narrow streets. These areas were first built-up after the erection of the fortifications at the end of the 17th century. Buildings show a mixture, like the *Kurfürstenstadt*, of storeys, styles, and uses, and there are old town houses of the latter half of the 19th century alongside much older three-storeyed—and even two- and one-storeyed—houses. The belt is 500 to 1,000 metres wide. There are numerous small trades and crafts, dating from the past, and more recent secondhand shops. Associated with these occupations is a large Jewish population. There are also many places of amusement, and outgrowths from beer-gardens that were formerly

[1] Here are the palace, museums, Monbijou palace (1706) in its small park ; to the east is the Exchange (*Börse*) and Alexanderplatz railway station. These are on the *Stadtbahn* which, in 1882, was built on the belt of open land on the site of the fortifications. Here also are Jewish synagogues and cemeteries, hospitals, Kölln Gymnasium, and State buildings, on the sites of which were formerly open spaces, barracks and other buildings.

located on the outskirts of the town. A third of the theatres are in this zone.

Dorotheenstadt and Friedrichstadt. This quarter was built at the end of the 17th century. Dorotheenstadt was built in 1673 with a rectangular grid plan centred on the Unter den Linden. In 1688 the Friedrichstadt was added to the south of it, with wider streets, centred on the Gendarmenmarkt. The two were at first separated by a wall, so that their street nets do not fit together, causing congestion to-day on the main streets. The whole quarter was designed for the residence of Court officials and had two- or three-storey houses, built of stone. The western border abutted on the Tiergarten along the Wilhelmstrasse, which at the end of the 18th century became the residence of the nobility. Wealthy villa quarters appeared in the early 19th century around the Leipzigerplatz, on the south side of the Tiergarten and on the Potsdamstrasse, as well as beyond this centre in the Schöneberg suburb (*Vorstädte*).

To-day the whole of zones I and II form the " city ", which is thus completely changed in build and function. The north-east of the Dorotheenstadt (near to the castle and museum district) is the University quarter, together with the old residential houses ; the north-west, dominated by the Friedrichstrasse station, is the focus of amusements, shops and hotels, and with the completion of the north–south underground railway it will become the central station of Berlin. The financial and business district lies in the old Friedrichstadt. West of the latter along the Wilhelmstrasse are the ministries, embassies and legations.

The areas described above together formed the extent of the town in the middle of the 19th century. Far beyond the built-up area, however, there was the toll wall, erected in 1737 by Frederick William I, to serve as the fiscal and police limit of the town. There was thus much open land between it and the edge of the town : only in the west did the two coincide—Schöneberg and Spandau actually lay beyond it as " suburbs ".

III. Wilhelmian Period (c. 1850–1918) (Grossstadtgürtel)

This was the period of rapid growth in Berlin, its population increasing sixfold from 500,000 in 1860. It is marked by the emergence of the city's present aspect, by both the transformation of the core and the great extensions of the built-up area around it. The latter, a vast zone of dreary blocks of multi-storeyed residential buildings, is the most characteristic feature of modern

Berlin. This is the zone of wide straight streets, lined often with frontages of four- and five-storey houses with (in later years) superficial ornamentation, but with fully built-up blocks and large tenements behind them. Shops are on the ground floors or in the basements, and only on the main thoroughfares do they make a continuous frontage so as to form commercial thoroughfares. These districts have no factories ; these are concentrated along the old wall (*Zollmauer*) and along the Spree, although there are many small establishments lying in the blocks behind the rows of tenements. The whole zone thus lies between the old city and the outer, post-1918, zone of more open building. There are open spaces and large industrial plants, though there is interdigitation of both, and the zone of the open land inside the walls has affected the lay-out and character of land uses.

The zone along the fortifications and on the originally open land between these and the limits of the built-up area is distinct in its land uses. It is marked (*b*) on Fig. 65. Open spaces (parks and cemeteries), public buildings, railways and stations, barracks, hospitals and some factories are its main form-elements.

The densely built-up tenement areas extend beyond the zone of former fortifications to the line of the circular railway known as the *Ringbahn*. These districts form very clearly defined units, separated by belts of public buildings, railways and factories, and have well-known names, such as Moabit, Wedding, and Prenzlauerberg. They are predominantly working-class districts. The western district of Charlottenburg is a better-class residential district with a very large Jewish element. It changes outwards into a zone of flats and single-family houses and villas, with frequent open spaces in Steglitz, Wilmersdorf. An amusement quarter (theatres, cafés, restaurants, and cinemas) grew up after 1900 on the Tauentzienstrasse and Kurfürstendam in this district.

IV. Industrial–Residential Zone

Berlin is a great industrial complex. Over two-thirds of all its industrial establishments lie inside the *Ringbahn*, and almost two-thirds of all its occupied persons work in this inner area. These establishments are small and are housed in small workshops. On the other hand, the fewer establishments outside the *Ringbahn* form vast industrial sites which have been laid out in the last forty years and have given the extensive outer zone its distinctive character. Many of these firms in the outer zone have shifted from the inner town. Industrial plants and residential areas occur as blocks separated by large open areas (allotments, meadows, water and woods), and situated in relation to the railways and navigable waterways. These are : (1) The Spree (the *Stadtbahn*, which passes through the city, is not associated with factory development) ; (2) the *Ringbahn*, finished in 1871 ; (3) an outer ring of several sections to the west and north-west, on the Havel and Tegel lake, an industrial railway running as a belt line from the latter round to the railways at Schöneberg, the Teltow canal to the south, which reaches from the Spree to the Havel in Potsdam. The big industrial complexes lie along and at the junction of the two rings of communication and on the through route of the river Spree, from Spandau to Köpenik.

This zone lies outside the former limits of Berlin and its development has hitherto been subjected to no public control. It contains many villages, which have been completely urbanized and form the nuclei of the present agglomerations. Most of the unbuilt areas are taken up by allotment gardens (*Laubenkolonien*). These are formed normally along the border areas of the village parishes. Large areas are also taken up by parks and cemeteries. Much land lies fallow, and only occasionally does one see a field of rye or potatoes. " The whole area presents the aspect of a very unattractive confusion of half-ready, provisional and partly developed land for purposes of both settlement and rural uses, and the controlling hand of the master planner could effect much improvement " (Louis). The map shows the built-up area as " uneven and mixed ". This differs from that of the core, which is classed under the same heading, in that there are not only high and low buildings, but every other type of building.

V. The Outer Zone

Berlin has spread well beyond the Industrial–Residential Zone since 1919. Villas and rows of single-family houses, many with allotment gardens and orchards, are scattered in the area. But its farthest outposts are the allotment gardens (*Nutzgartensiedlungen*) along the railways, which sell their food in the urban market. Villages are gradually being transformed. Motor-bus and electric railway connect the area with the city. The great expanses of meadows irrigated by sewage water (*Rieselfelder*) provide goods which are marketed in the city. To the north at Heiligensee and Henningsdorf, there is an important industrial and residential area along railway and canal. Grünewald in the west is a well-known high-class residential district of villas in woods. The

Teltow district is an industrial complex. The old towns of
Spandau (with industries) and Potsdam also lie in this outer
girdle.

(3) ADMINISTRATIVE DIVISIONS

The existing twenty administrative divisions inside the city
(with six in Old Berlin) show little relation to the extent of the
geographical divisions as revealed in this study. "Administrative boundaries," writes Louis, "especially in the centre, cut
right across physiognomic and functional boundaries. Each
district includes areas of entirely different character with fundamentally different needs. This is bound to be a source of the
greatest difficulty in any plans for the reconditioning and future
development of the compact urban area."

Administrative divisions occur in bewildering variety.[1]   Each
administration has its own system of division ; the postal districts
are different from the telephone districts ; church areas are
different from those used for justice, the police districts do not
correspond with the tax collectors' districts, and even the existing administrative divisions (*Gemarkungsgrenze*) overlap with railway, postal, water-supply, chamber of commerce and other
districts. After the formation of Greater Berlin in 1921, the
twenty-two historic divisions of the old city (*Alt-Berlin*) were
abolished and twenty new administrative districts were organized.
These were partly based on the historic divisions with six in Alt-
Berlin, while the remainder of the outer area was divided into
fourteen outer districts through the grouping of the historical
Gemeinde, of which there were seventy. These districts take no
account of such obvious features as railway belts and rivers as
natural community boundaries. Certain natural community
boundaries that might be used in the formation of administrative
units are mentioned by Leyden. The *Ringbahn* is a clearly defined
and real community boundary, within which the West should be
distinguished from the remainder of the Inner City. These are
also divided by a line from the Tempelhof marshalling yard,
along the Anhalter Bahnhof to the Brandenburg Tor to the Spree
and thence to the Bahnhof Pulitzstrasse.[2] The district of Moabit
would probably form a separate unit. The eastern sector—the

---

[1] F. Leyden, *Gross-Berlin, Geographie der Weltstadt*, pp. 171, 179–81.

[2] The west and south-west was socially distinct from the east and north. The
west was the residence of the conservative and more wealthy element, as was evidenced
by the high proportion of National Socialists and *Deutsche Volkspartei* and *Staatspartei*
in the elections of 1932 and 1930 ; whereas all the eastern districts were predominantly
Social-Democratic and Communist.

city core—is clearly divided into two parts by the Spree and the Stadtbahn, with the city proper entirely in the southern sector. Around these two (or four) central districts outside the *Ringbahn*, Spandau and Köpenik stand out as the natural historic nuclei of districts. For the remaining area, the Dahme, Spree and Havel and the Teltow canal are natural physical divides. Existing town halls that are often the nuclei of " city " growth might be arranged as the geographical centres of new districts—such are the town halls of Köpenik, Lichtenberg, Pankow, Wittenau, Spandau, Steglitz, Mariendorf, Treptow.

(4) The Distribution of Population

Berlin illustrates excellently the centrifugal trend in the development of modern industry and the movements of population in the great city. The outstanding fact is the effectiveness of the *Zollmauer* (Customs Wall) and then of the *Ringbahn* as barriers. Urban development was confined until the last decades to the oval area inside the *Ringbahn*, while during the last fifty years there has been a great shift of old industry from the *Altstadt* to the open spaces along road and waterway outside the *Ringbahn*. The decline of population began in the heart of the city and then spread outwards to the limits of the *Ringbahn*, while beyond it there has been a large increase, with growing tempo, since the last decades of the 19th century.

Out of a total population of 4,332,000 in 1939 about two and a quarter millions lived inside the *Ringbahn* on an area of about 35 square miles with an approximate overall density of 100 persons to the acre (Fig. 66). The non-residential districts, covered predominantly by railways and public buildings, had densities well below this average. Further, the central business district had densities of only 10 to 40 persons per acre of total area and the " mixed zone " bordering it of 40 to 80 persons per acre. It follows, therefore, that the remaining tenement districts must have had densities much above the average of 100 to the acre. These large areas had, in fact, overall densities of 150 to 300 persons per acre ; in many smaller districts densities were well above the higher figure. The south-western sector, on the other hand—Charlottenburg and Tempelhof—is a middle-class residential area, and had lower densities of 30 to 60 persons to the acre. Outside the *Ringbahn*, built-up areas are scattered and separated from each other by large open spaces, so that overall densities by large administrative districts are much lower. These traits are characteristic of all the major continental cities and, also, of American cities, although the densities in American are lower than in European cities.

The decrease of population in the centre began in the 'sixties,[1] and this steady decrease spread gradually to the surrounding districts, so that it ultimately embraced the whole of Old Berlin. The year 1890 was the turning-point in the distribution of population, occasioned mainly by the development of rapid urban transport and by the fact that the inner areas were often fully occupied. The outer districts of Old Berlin, which had shown large increases after 1870, reached their peak in 1890 and henceforth declined like the more central districts. In the period 1890 to 1910 the decline increased and the trend spread. Berlin and Neukölln decreased by over 50 per cent., Friedrichswerder 47 per cent., Kölln 45 per cent., Friedrichstadt 39 per cent., and Dorotheenstadt 29 per cent., while decreases are recorded in other districts inside the Customs Wall, such as Königsviertel by 6 per cent. In districts just outside the Customs Wall the increase stopped during the 1900–10 decade. By 1910 the growth of population in Old Berlin as a whole ceased, and then it reached its maximum of just over two millions.

(5) THE LIMITS OF BERLIN

The administrative limits of Greater Berlin were formed in 1921 by the annexation to Old Berlin of the surrounding communes that lay, for the most part, beyond the *Ringbahn*, which, in general, may be regarded as the limit of Old Berlin and of the present compact built-up area. The whole of Greater Berlin to its farthest boundaries lies within about 40 km. radius of the city centre and all parts are accessible to the central business district (either Wittenbergplatz or Alexanderplatz) in one hour by train. It is, in effect, a single labour market. But it is made up of diversity of settlements that had little relation with Berlin before 1921. The limits of this Greater Berlin area include the old towns of Spandau, Potsdam and Köpenik, which have been incorporated into the economic and social sphere of Greater Berlin. The built-up area lies within a radius of 20 km. of the city centre along the various radial routeways. The districts to the north (Barnim) and south (Teltow) are higher platforms of open cultivated land that have been very little affected by industry. The districts to the east and west are wooded low-

[1] F. Leyden, *op. cit.*, pp. 84–103.

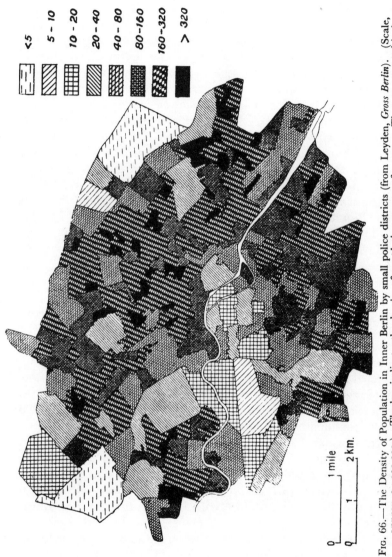

FIG. 66.—The Density of Population in Inner Berlin by small police districts (from Leyden, *Gross Berlin*). (Scale, approx. 1 : 100,000.) The key indicates the density of population per acre for 1925. The area covered is the town of Berlin (Alt-Berlin) prior to the extension in 1921. Compare with the map of the functional zones of Greater Berlin (Fig. 65).

lands, traversed by the lakes and streams of the Spree and Dahme to the east and the Havel and Tegel lakes to the west. Outlying industrial areas that lie within the Berlin labour market are Oberhavel (Oranienburg and Henningsdorf) to the north-west, Potsdam—Nowawes—Teltow to the south-west, the Upper Spree and Dahme (Wildau) to the south-east. Slightly farther afield on the geographical border of the Berlin labour market (about 50 km. distant) are Eberswalde—Finow to the north-east on the Stettin canal, Brandenburg, and Luckenwalde. This outlying belt is within a journey-time of one and a half to two hours of central Berlin. Its industry is relatively unimportant and it serves mainly as an agricultural and outer recreational zone with outlying satellite towns (*Trabantenstädte*). This 50 km. radius is fairly clearly defined by the low-lying west–east valley trough to the north which is followed by the Finow and Berlin–Stettin canals ; and to the south by the similar trough that runs from Brandenburg south-east through Luckenwalde and Baruth.[1]

The six large districts known as the *Landkreise* around Greater Berlin all show increases of population since 1925 as against decreases in the surrounding districts of Brandenburg. The communes along the main lines of communication within a radius of 20 to 30 km. of the city centre nearly all show an increase from 1925 to 1939, whereas in the rural areas of Brandenburg farther afield decreases are general.

The initial distribution and relative importance of the towns of Brandenburg in the early 19th century have been fundamentally affected by the tremendous growth of Berlin—from about 200,000 in 1822 to over five million inhabitants just before 1939. An indication, crude though it may be, is given of the extent of Berlin's influence by the area of high density of population in the North German Plain. This area lies between Stettin, Frankfurt, and Brandenburg, and is bordered to the south by the thinly peopled, sandy uplands of the Fläming Heath and the wooded lake area between the Dahme and Spree, beyond which belt, to the south, lies the Lusatian textile area and the brown coalfield. Along the Elbe, in the Lower Havel area, beyond the marsh land between Werder and Brandenburg, there is a separate axis of high density stretching from Wittenberg to Hamburg, which also owes its economic development in part to its close relation with the Berlin area.

[1] M. Pfannschmidt, *Die Industriesiedlung in Berlin und in der Mark Brandenburg*, Akademie für Landesforschung und Reichsplannung, Berlin, 1937.

PART TWO

CHAPTER 14

THE NATURE OF THE URBAN HABITAT : FUNCTION AND FORM

(1) FUNCTION

The urban habitat arises through the combination, in a fixed settlement, of a variety of special functions that are needed in the service of a civilized society. Many of these functions may be, and are, carried on separately in settlements that are not urban. But when such functions combine, the settlement so formed assumes an urban character. Such settlements vary in character and status, and in consequence various names are used to characterize them at different periods. A *town*, however, has the minimum number of such traits and has a functional status, and in consequence a mode of grouping of its buildings, that distinguish it from the rural village. The particular urban functions require particular building structures or form-elements. These are grouped areally (i.e. topographically) in the space-structure of the urban habitat in such a manner as to serve a mode of living that is distinct from that of the rural community. The urban functions will first be considered, with special reference to their location in the urban complex, and the character of the structures associated with them. This subject will be introduced by means of an historical definition of the terms, town and city.

The term *civitas* originally meant the district of organization of a sedentary community in western Europe under the Roman Empire. The name was subsequently transferred under the Merovingian and Carolingian Empires to the centre of such a district in which a new Christian bishopric was sited. In France this nucleus was known as the *cité*, a term derived directly from *civitas*, and the name is retained to this day to designate the original ecclesiastical nucleus around which in the Middle Ages the nascent economic community grew. The term *civitas* was for long used indiscriminately for the variety of settlements that through their special functions and aspect were distinct from the surrounding villages, but it finally acquired a quite specific meaning in the middle of the 12th century. It referred to a compact settlement that enjoyed a special law, that was walled, and that was usually a market and a seat of industry and commerce. *Civitas* was the name in universal use for this settlement-form, whether it was a large agglomeration like Paris or Bruges, or a small country town no bigger than the villages around it. It was distinct in its aspect and its function and its law. Thus, *civitas* became the exact equivalent of the French *ville* and the German *Stadt* and the English *town*. *Cité* or city—there is no corresponding equivalent in German—referred to the initial ecclesiastical nucleus. It is retained in this sense in the towns of France and, with a similar origin, it is still popularly applied in England to cathedral towns. This is partly a historical and partly a popular usage. Although until the middle of the 19th century the word " town " had this precise meaning, it did not cover all urban settlements. There were many that did not have all the attributes of the legal town as defined above. Some were unwalled settlements that had a more elementary law and usually, though not always, a market. Their character, development, and frequency, varied from one region to another. Moreover, though in some regions all the small country towns were *civitates*, in others the majority were smaller centres. These latter are called *Flecken* in German, *bourgs* in French, and, in general, *market towns* in English. But there was, and still is, no real difference in essential functions between the urban settlement in the country with 1,000 inhabitants and the urban agglomeration with several millions.

In the modern era the growth of urban population has been proportional to the size of the historic town, although many grew disproportionately. Many appeared as entirely new settlements, as seats of specialized activities. In our era, as in the past, it is again the centralized services—functions situated in fixed places so as conveniently to serve the surrounding country and towns— that account above all for the special character of a " town " or " city ". Thus in the modern urban habitat, which has spread far beyond its historic boundaries, this characteristic is reflected in the emergence of a central core which is the dominant focus of the rhythms of urban life. Around this nucleus are arranged the specialized functional districts of the compact urban area.

These two manifestations, the central business core and the areal segregation of particular functions, appear in their most elementary forms in the smallest urban settlement to-day, which is very little changed as a habitat from its historic form. But as the size of the agglomeration increases, so these attributes, of necessity, become more marked. These two features become fully established when the population of the urban settlement passes about 50,000 and, most definitely so, when it reaches 100,000. Such figures are, however, only very approximate guides. There is then a marked separation of the area of centralized services from the surrounding areas of work and residence. The urban folk and the folk of the environs talk quite indiscriminately of going to " town " or to the " city " when they intend going to the central " core " on business or pleasure. In extreme cases in our modern age, specialized urban structures may occur as small groups in the countryside—rows of miners' cottages, or the group of seaside houses, groups of country houses of domestic craftsmen, or as rows of blackcoated workers' homes on the outskirts of a town. Thus, town and city are merely aspects of the same thing, and the small country town with some 1,000 inhabitants has all the same elementary functions, with their corresponding structures, that the large town or city possesses in the higher or highest degree. This centrality of an urban settlement and its leadership are capable of measurement. In such terms degrees of town or city character can be defined, but the general definition we have given here is adequate to our purpose. It follows that while we are primarily concerned with the city that enjoys a high measure of leadership over surrounding towns, yet the same attributes characterize, in varying degrees, all urban settlements from the small country town to the agglomeration with several million inhabitants. The same attributes and problems appear, though they differ enormously in scale. Thus, in this sense, town and city mean essentially the same thing, and the terms are used interchangeably in these pages.

The city, in the widest sense, as it appears throughout all ages and in all lands, as the symbol and carrier of civilization, has certain fundamental characteristics. The first and the most important of these is that it is an institutional centre, the seat of the institutions of the society it represents. It is a seat of religion, of culture and social contact, and of political and administrative organization. Secondly, it is a seat of production, agricultural and industrial, the latter being normally the more important, though in the Middle Ages in western Europe, and particularly in other parts of the earth to-day, the agricultural factor is by no means negligible. Thirdly, it is a seat of commerce and transport. Fourthly, the city is a pleasurable seat of residence for the rulers, the wealthy and the retired (German, *Rentner*, French, *Rentier*), where they can enjoy all the amenities of civilized life that the institutions of their society have to offer. Fifthly, it is the living place of the people who work in it. In all these respects the city serves the area around it as a centre of affairs, although it also serves the whole of society or the State as a specialized seat of production, or as a political capital or as a great cultural or pilgrimage centre. These functions combine in varying ways in different ages and lands to give special character to the city, and they in turn, as in its smaller urban counterparts, are clearly reflected in the character and lay-out of its institutions, houses and streets.

Let us examine each of the groups of functions of the city, in a little more detail with particular reference to conditions in western and central Europe.

(a) *The Social Functions and their Location*

(i) *Cultural Functions.* The social functions are cultural, political and administrative, and recreational. The *cité* of antiquity was a religious and political association, and religious rites have played an important part in the origins and functions of the city of antiquity and in the ceremonies of its inauguration. The site of a new city was selected by the ancients through the inspiration of the gods. In Greece the oracle of Delphi was consulted. The foundation ceremony began with a ritual sacrifice. New towns fêted their birthdays. The ancient city was held to be eternal. City life was impregnated by religious thought and ritual. A difference in gods was a greater barrier than frontiers between neighbouring cities and often prevented the formation of States. Numerous towns in all ages have grown up on sites of religious significance—a hill, a spring, the tomb of a saint, the site of an apparition, a place of burial. Of particular importance in the formation of the early medieval cities is the religious edifice around which the nascent urban centre crystallized. The medieval city in western and central Europe owed its origins in many cases, in the Dark Ages and the early Middle Ages, to the establishment of a cathedral inside the walls of the Roman *castrum*. Others owed their sites to holy places, and their growth to the visits of pilgrims. The dead were brought to such places to be buried, and cemeteries often surround such cities. Thebes, indeed, was a city primarily concerned with the burial of the dead. Greek and Roman cities had their *rues des tombeaux*. In every medieval town the dead were buried for centuries in the cemeteries attached to the town church. Owing to lack of space and for health reasons these cemeteries were eventually disused and new ones opened on the outskirts of the city. The modern cemetery is relegated to the urban fringe.

The religious building played a particularly important part in the formation of the medieval town. The cathedral community was the nucleus of many cities, especially in France, where it lies in the heart of the city. In Germany, though also in the centre, it was often cut off from the town by a wall, to form an ecclesiastical stronghold. In Britain, where the religious building appeared at a later date, the cathedral, with monastery and cloister, sought a secluded site within the small town nucleus. It was sheltered from, but near to, the centre, and formed a separate " precinct ".

The organization of medieval society was in large measure centred on the parish church. The original church of the town nucleus is often called in Germany the *Markt Kirche* or *Stadt Kirche*. A parish church became the focus of the new community as the town expanded. It served as a centre for its social needs— worship, pageantry, teaching and art. In the medieval town the church and the monasteries were also the greatest landowners ; they ministered to the needs of the poor, built houses for them, and in certain towns, as in Belgium where they owned much of the land, played a specially important part in furthering the growth of the urban area.

(ii) *Political Functions.* The city of antiquity, Greek and Roman, was a geographical association of families and tribes bound together through the medium of a common political and religious organization. Such was the Roman *civitas* in Gaul, upon which the ecclesiastical diocese was later based. The equivalent district in pagan Germany was the *gau*. The settlement was the focus of this organization. The term *civitas* or *cité* was later transferred from the area and applied to its central settlement. In the early Middle Ages the kings established fortified camps (*burgs*), controlled by their secular representatives. These served as seats of defence and refuge, as well as seats of administration for the surrounding territory (*comté, Grafschaft*). France in the early Middle Ages and Germany after 1200 were peppered with castle residences of individual nobles, adjacent to which towns frequently grew up. Kings and dukes often controlled the walls around the town and had a castle along them, manned by their representative and a group of warrior knights. The castle afforded protection to the small town beneath its walls when invaders swept by. In some areas, as for instance in northern England, small villages paid their dues to the lord, and in return in times of danger from Scottish raiders his castle became their place of refuge.

Kings and emperors also established their courts in cities, which became, during the Middle Ages, the capitals of States. Despite the changing political pattern of Europe some of these have remained capitals for centuries—Paris, Brussels, Berlin, London. Others—Toulouse and Nancy in France—died early as political capitals with the growth of the nation State. Each of the German States had its capital, with the Court of the king, the political institutions and the full paraphernalia of a capital city. These ranged from such pre-eminent instances as Munich, Stuttgart, Dresden and Hanover, to the diminutive Court city of Dessau, the capital of Anhalt, and the capitals of the small States of Thuringia, such as Gotha and Weimar.

The medieval City-State was a special form of political unit which grew from the city focus. Through its representative bodies, the town council and guilds, the city was an independent political body. Its liberties were confined within its wall, and the laws of town and of country were distinct, and separated two worlds. The city endeavoured to extend its control to the territory surrounding it in order to command the neighbouring towns and villages and to draw from them the food necessary for its existence. It thus pursued an independent " foreign " policy acquiring, through conflict with neighbouring territorial lords, complete political control of its rural environs. Its political function, however, was due to the encroachment of the city upon its environs, rather than to the countryside calling into being a political centre, or to a town being endowed by the State with such functions for a defined district. Basel is a good example of this kind of development.

There is still another aspect of the question. So far we have considered the specialized political function of the capital, the head and centre of a State. But cities other than capitals have political functions. Every State has been divided into provinces of various orders in which centrally situated places carry out administrative functions allotted to them by the State. The ancient divisions in Britain are the counties, in France the provinces, which were superseded by the departments in 1789, and in Germany the small States, that were superseded by new divisions about 1800. During the 19th century a new and more elaborate administrative territorial organization gave to selected towns certain administrative functions as centres in a new hierarchy of administrative districts. These functions are housed in institutions that require appropriate locations in the urban complex.

Cultural or intellectual activity falls clearly into this category of functions. In the Middle Ages, as learning broke away from its strict confinement to the Church, the university came into being as a community of students. The medieval university of Paris grew up in this way on the hill of Ste. Geneviève. A number of cities acquired their own universities, and with the advancement of learning specialized university towns emerged on the Continent. These were particularly numerous in Germany, a fact undoubtedly to be associated with the political disintegration of that country into independent sovereign States. With the spread of formal education at all grades to all levels of the community, the school and the university take a prominent part in the structure of the city as a seat of learning. The modern secondary school serves the town and its district, while the large city falls into sectors served by schools that are (or should be) easily accessible to all parts of the community. Schools, hospitals, scientific and art institutions, the great majority of them built in the last two hundred years, together with cultural activities, play a vital part in the life of both the city and in the build and differentiation of its parts.

(iii) *Administrative (Municipal) Functions.* This set of functions is so named to distinguish the administrative functions of the city proper from the political functions carried out as part of the machinery of the State. After the Middle Ages, through the centralization of affairs in the State, the city authorities surrendered many of their own functions and powers. To-day, municipal activities are again spreading to many branches of city life—the control of transport, water, gas and electricity, co-operative shops, factories, public buildings, places of recreation, and housing for the poorer classes. Under this head, however, we refer particularly to those municipal activities that are housed in special buildings which demand special places in the city structure ; the chief of these is the Town Hall or Civic Centre.

(iv) *Recreational Functions.* The function of leisure in the life of the individual and the rôle of the urban community in providing facilities for the spending of leisure time has in the past been neglected. In our own age it is clearly an essential need for healthy living—both mentally and physically—in great urban agglomerations. The classic instance of the rôle of recreation in city life is found in the Greek city, which was provided with theatres and sports arenas in close connection with the religious cult. Rome had its circus and amphitheatres. All these recreational needs called into being great public buildings in the Greek and Roman city. In the Middle Ages recreation found no such outlet. It was found at the great fairs, and in the plays and pageants of the Church and the guilds.

Facilities for recreation, however, are an outstanding deficiency in the modern city owing to the specialization of the urban way of life, to the ever-increasing amount of time at the daily disposal of the worker, and to the resultant need for seasonal holidays and relaxation. In the city environment leisure begins at home, but this elementary need was entirely ignored by the speculative builders and the municipal authorities of the 19th century. The great majority of dwellings in cities have not even the most elementary human comforts—adequate room space with heating, adequate access to air and sunlight, or adequate playground space for children and adults. The English industrial town lacks wide boulevards where one can stroll in pleasant surroundings. While the continental city has its municipal or State-controlled theatre, there is nothing of the kind in the English provincial city. Museums, art galleries, public baths, recreation parks and the like are deficient in many cities.

Commercialized recreation, as distinct from municipally provided facilities, is available in plenty. In the modern city this takes two special forms. There are the theatre, the café and restaurant, which tend always to be associated with shops and offices in the centre of the city and at conveniently situated sub-centres around it. Accessibility is a prime need in the location of such places of amusement. A special word must be said in this connection on the most obvious manifestations of modern commercialized amusement—the football ground, the " dogs " stadium, the cricket ground, the sports stadium, and the exhibition ground. These facilities have occupied a conspicuous place in the development of continental cities during the last twenty years, especially in Germany, where the great assembly arena was made a fetish by the Nazis. To-day there is the specialized recreational town which provides amusement and relaxation for workers, conveniently situated in relation to the great industrial agglomerations.

(b) Production

(i) *Agriculture*. In western and central Europe agriculture was carried on within the walls of the medieval town, but it gradually decreased as a significant occupation with the growth of commerce and industry. In the medieval town, owing to the slowness of transport, production for the townsfolk by the townsfolk was necessary. It was also a means of protection if the city were besieged and cut off from contact with the sources of supply outside its walls. Medieval Paris had large areas of field and pasture belonging to the bishop, abbeys and nobles. There were vineyards on the slopes of Ste. Geneviève. Pastures were fertilized by the city sewage ; names remain indicating the former location of such meadows—St. Germain-des-Prés, Notre-Dame-des-Champs. There were mills along the Seine ; cultivators and vintners lived side by side with craftsmen and traders. Gradually this land was occupied by buildings as the city expanded and farm land receded outwards beyond the walls. Moreover, what farming is carried out to-day in the environs has changed in character. There is no cereal farming, no open meadows and little stock-raising. Their place is taken by the most intensive market-gardening, especially fruit and vegetable production.[1]

The great army of landless town-dwellers need (and want) some garden space, not merely to grow flowers, as in England, but to grow vegetables. The allotment garden is a very conspicuous feature of the continental city, most of all in Germany, where cities are often engirdled by extensive areas of this kind (*Schrebergärten, Laubenkolonien*). This movement started in the 'seventies of last century to offset the artificial conditions which life in congested tenements involved.

(ii) *Industry*. Industry has played the main part in the growth of modern urbanism in western and central Europe. Existing

---

[1] While the relegation of farming to the city outskirts in the form of market-gardening is typical of the large city of western and central Europe, and agriculture is no longer an " urban " occupation, conditions are different in Russia, Hungary and Rumania, as well as farther afield in Russian Turkestan, the Middle East, north Africa, and even in the Mediterranean lands. In these countries the so-called urban settlements are often, in fact, large, overgrown villages. On the other hand, in Britain and the United States, even rural village settlements have an urban character.

cities have offered to industrial concerns the personnel, capital and markets of a going concern, and have attracted rural labour from the environs. The growth of a landless working-class, often constituting the majority of the population, has brought to the city problems of industrial depression, unemployment and the slum. The ancient and medieval city was a centre of crafts and small workshops, segregated in districts or streets. This segregation was due to various causes. The grouping of crafts was often a family affair, or was due to the control of a guild, with its own patron saints, festivals and administration. Water attracted some industries to the river front, such as flour milling, saw milling, tanning, dyeing and fulling. Segregation made easier the supervision of the guild members, the care of their interests and the imposition of their laws. Street names often clearly indicate the nature of this segregation.

The advent of the factory has radically altered the aspect and function of both city and town. The workshop driven by running water began to be established at the end of the 18th century alongside streams, either in the open country or in the town. In the latter case the factory was inevitably placed as near as possible to the houses alongside the river. With the advent of the steam engine the new factory was necessarily placed alongside the railway or the river on flat land as near to the city as possible, and workers' houses were built as close to it as could be managed. Large new industrial plants were also established in new areas, away from existing cities. These in turn became the nucleus of growing urban centres, as in the Ruhr and Silesia. Since the 'eighties the advent of electricity has brought new industries and made possible the establishment of factories away from rail and water, while the " heavy " industries, such as engineering and chemicals, are still closely tied in their location to both the railway and the river.

(iii) *Commerce*. Commerce in the medieval city assumed a twofold form—retail trade, which was carried on in the open market and to a lesser degree in shops, and was frequently associated with the craftsman who sold his wares direct to the consumer ; and wholesale trade, which supplied the townspeople with their food and special requirements, notably wines, spices, salt, etc., much of which came from overseas through the hands of merchants. Wholesale trade, carried on by the merchants, who moved across country along determined routes under royal protection, marked the beginning of urban life in the Middle

Ages. Merchants settled and planted their warehouses at good nodal points, at the junction of land and river routes. Some of these centres, that enjoyed in these early stages the protection of a stronghold, became the first medieval towns. With the growth of such centres craftsmen were attracted from the surrounding countryside and catered to the needs of those who lived in the stronghold—clerics, courtiers, knights. Ultimately these settlements became independent self-governing communities. The life of such a community centred on the market-place and the route on which were concentrated the daily business of buying and selling. Here were the guild houses, the town hall, the public weighing machines, and, in Germany, the statue of Roland—as at Riga and Bremen—the symbol of the peace of the city (*Stadtfried*). This city reaches its fullest expression in Flanders and northern Italy.

The merchants practically controlled the councils of their cities and became a patrician class, rivalling the aristocracy or the nobility and controlling the government, which took the form of an oligarchy. The wealth of the merchant patricians is reflected in the grandeur of their guild houses, and the munificence of their public benefactions which helped in the construction of public buildings and churches in the later Middle Ages. It was the narrow-minded, selfish rivalries of these very merchant oligarchs and their conflicts with the people, and in particular with the crafts' guilds, together with the irksome restrictions imposed on handicrafts by the guilds, that contributed largely to the decline of town life in the 17th and 18th centuries. Moreover, in this period the absolute monarchs, pursuing their mercantilist policies of economic self-sufficiency, encouraged the growth of old and new industries outside the towns where freedom from the restrictions of the guilds could be obtained.

Fairs were probably the most important institutions of wholesale commerce in the days when transport was slow and costly, and seasonal assemblies were the best means of buying and selling wares. Many of these fairs were held in cities, as at Lyons, Antwerp, Bruges and Leipzig. The fairs of Champagne, on the route from the Mediterranean to Flanders, were especially important in the 13th century. The merchants virtually took possession of the towns during the period of the fair, inhabiting certain quarters of the city and camping outside its walls, as at Beaucaire and Nizhni Novgorod. In this way new industries were introduced into some towns—for example, the silk industry at

Lyons or the treatment of furs at Leipzig. The extensive buildings for exhibitions, fairs and the like are very important elements in the modern space-structure of continental cities.

Commerce, past and present, is most intimately tied up with the routeway, be it a land or water route. Nearly all the great cities a hundred years ago were on rivers and were river ports situated at river crossings, that is, they were bridgehead towns. To-day, the great urban agglomerations are all " ports ", whether considered as sea-ports or inland rail-ports. Meanwhile many of the small river ports of a hundred years ago have lost their functions or have declined greatly in relative importance through the growth of their more favourably placed neighbours. Every great city is an outstanding focus of radiating railways and, what is especially important in these days, of roads. The provision of vital supplies is essential to life in the city. Railways, goods yards, marshalling yards, warehouses, and engine, tram and bus depots are all essential items in the urban space-structure which must be interrelated with each other and with the rest of the city in the interests of speed and efficiency in collection, distribution, and transit.

Modern retail trade in commodities is effected through the medium of shops, department stores, and markets. The business side of commerce and finance gives rise to a world of occupations and businesses on its own, and the majority of these are concentrated in the big cities. The business of the fair is now handled by the Exchange, where the goods do not even appear except by sample, where transactions are effected in crops before they are even planted, and where finance becomes a business in itself. Commodity Exchanges are normally situated in the ports through which the goods are imported, thus, coffee and cotton at Le Havre, cotton at Bremen and Liverpool ; or in the cities which are the headquarters of an industrial region dealing in a particular group of commodities, such as wool at Roubaix–Tourcoing in northern France, or at Bradford, or the Cotton Exchange at Manchester. But these are financial markets. The goods do not necessarily pass through them and are usually sold by sample. There has always been the closest relation between commerce in goods and finance or banking. Finance is the hall-mark of a great city. The bank is the medium for putting surplus capital into circulation. The greatest financial centres in western Europe are London, Paris and Amsterdam, but every great city is, in varying measure, a seat of independent banking, catering to the general and peculiar needs of the city and its surrounding industrial and rural areas. These commercial functions embrace those highly centralized services that are of necessity concentrated in the heart of what we call to-day " the city," the " commercial stronghold ", as Summerson has described it in London. They are of the essence of modern city character, which depends on leadership in business and finance.

(c) Residence : Town Planning and Municipal Organization

Residence is not a specialized urban function in the sense of being the occupation of a part of the community. A place to live in is a primary need of every urban dweller. Attention to the amenities of the town as a fit place to live in is, to-day, one of the chief concerns of government at all levels.

The question of the structure and lay-out of houses and streets is, in effect, the question of the lay-out of the urban habitat as a whole, and this will have to be considered later. Suffice it here to note that the medieval town was small and living conditions primitive. There was no provision for a common drainage system ; there was no communal water-supply ; streets were unpaved ; there was no street lighting. Towns were, however, on the whole spacious, though streets in the old towns were, as they still are, narrow and winding. Most houses had their gardens with space for keeping pigs and hens. In the small planned towns of eastern Germany and southern France living conditions from this point of view were probably better than in the older towns, and towns in the Renaissance and Baroque period, laid out as Court cities, were certainly an improvement in lay-out upon their predecessors. It was not until the phenomenal growth of population in the later 19th century that the appalling housing conditions of the workers gave rise to an ever-increasing though belated concern with the problem of improving the lay-out and housing conditions of the existing town (*aménagement*) and providing for its planned future extension (*plan d'extension*).

The town in the early Middle Ages grew gradually under the ægis of high authority, the lord or bishop, around whose domicile and stronghold the economic community clustered. In the later Middle Ages the towns were planned, again at the instance of a high authority, but many of them, like the older cities, eventually became independent communities and were in varying measure responsible for their buildings and living conditions. Æsthetic and practical urbanism (*embellissement*) grew during the 17th and

18th centuries, but waned and almost disappeared during the great growth of the 19th century just when it was most needed. " Town-planning " dates from the last decades of the 19th century, and " regional town-planning " appeared in the inter-war period. Both have been permissive in character and have failed to stem appreciably the trends of natural, uncontrolled development. With the increasing complexity of urban life and activities the rôle of municipal government has become ever wider and planning increasingly essential.

Traffic, through long ages, was limited to the slow movement of pedestrians and wheeled wagons. Railway in the mid 19th century, tramway, motor-car and motor-bus in the last fifty years, have revolutionized urban life. Cheap and rapid transport permits of the divorce of one's shop, factory, or office from one's place of residence, be it a city slum or a suburb twenty miles from the place of work in the city centre. The density and rhythm of urban circulation now raise tremendous problems that figure most prominently in planning schemes. The " black-out " has demonstrated the importance of artificial light at night-time for urban dwellers. Glass windows were not used until the 16th century, nor was the oil reflecting lamp for street lighting until the latter half of the 18th. The first gas-lights illuminated the streets of the European capitals in the 1820s and 1830s, and the use of electricity dates from the 'seventies. Gas works and, more recently, electricity plants require locations on the urban periphery rather than in the congested centres, where many of them (especially the older gas works) are located. Fresh air is a primary need of the individual, but this fact was completely ignored in the urban growth of the 19th century. Better houses and more open space are other primary needs which the planner must now satisfy. Recreation is another need in which public authority has a part to play, and the theatre, museum, art gallery, sports stadium, and exhibition ground are all features of municipal activity on the Continent.

Protection of the community from enemy attack has always been a prime concern of the city government in periods of danger. All medieval towns were walled after the 12th century except in areas with a strong central government where there was no fear of attack from outside. In the 17th and 18th centuries, however, the wall fell into disuse and stronger fortifications were erected around selected fortress cities on State frontiers to resist the onslaught of artillery. With the growth and congestion of the city, protection against its inherent dangers became a necessity and a main responsibility of the municipal authority. Protection was needed above all from fire, famine and disease. The municipal authority has had to take over the control of markets, the cleansing of streets, the provision of water, gas and electricity supply, sewage disposal, and protection against fire by building regulations and organized fire services, against disease and against flood. Vast systems of underground pipes and tunnels and of overhead wires have been constructed in every urban habitat during the last hundred years. In various ways and with varying efficacy the municipal authorities have controlled, through their by-laws, the rights of the individual builder and have also controlled in varying measure the development of large tracts of city land. There is every indication that, because of the inadequacy of permissive control—planning is hardly the correct term—the private owner or builder is going to be even more strictly controlled in the public interest, so that positive planning will be enforced. The importance of all these activities of communal organization varies from age to age, and the degree to which the needs and welfare of the urban dweller are met depends on the powers and efficiency of the governing authority. In the past, cities have been fed with human material from the countryside. This source is now drying up, and if cities are to survive on their present scale, they must be converted into healthy and happy environments.

(2) Urban Morphology

The urban habitat is a complex of public buildings, houses, open spaces and places, and streets, which, differing in structure and function, differ also in the ways in which they are combined in space to form the whole urban complex. The city, when viewed from this morphological standpoint, is the expression of the activities and purposes of its inhabitants, and of the configuration of the land on which it is sited. Moreover, the character of its structures depends not merely upon the purpose for which they are needed or the materials of which they are built. Architectural features of the separate forms in the build of the city, no less than their architectonic relationships to each other, depend upon cultural contacts, traditions, and current concepts of æsthetic and practical urbanism. The city is not merely a palimpsest of the civilization it represents ; it is also a culture form. Thus, functional and cultural character, viewed in the light of their historical development, are reflected in the changing character of the habitat in which the community lives. Thus, cities, together with their smaller counterparts, towns and townlets, form geographical groups that reflect common trends of development.

The way in which every town acquires its particular morphological character is determined by two processes which C. Jullian many years ago called the *élément de formation* and the *élément de progression*. This distinction applies pre-eminently to the function of the settlement. The nucleus of the town, the site selected for a certain purpose that involved the erection of certain permanent structures, is the *élément de formation*. The settlement's growth in function and in size entails an increase in the number and variety of its public buildings and houses, and this normally means an extension of the built-up area. This is the *élément de progression*. The erection of walls around the medieval town caused congestion and upward growth in its buildings and an ever-increasing density of inhabitants per building until the removal of the walls permitted the extension of the built-up area. This extension, which proceeds in many ways, is determined, in varying degrees and ways, by the gradual juxtaposition of individual houses, or by some system adjusted in varying degree to the relief of the site and to the buildings and routes already there. Such growth goes on, of course, as long as the town is an active centre. It may indeed at some stage of its history grow very rapidly, as did Marseilles, for example, during the 18th century, when, like other French ports, it went through a phase of great commercial activity. On the other hand, the town may have a very unstable basis. It may be an artificial creation, which, having served the purpose for which it was intended, vegetates, declines in population, contracts in area, and it may disappear, to be a mere ruin to-day. This has happened to many cities of antiquity. Several grandiose cities were laid out as royal capitals in Iraq, one of which, Samara, lasted for no more than forty years. In Europe, since the Middle Ages, there have been few such changes. Towns have had their ups and downs, but they have usually been able to adjust themselves to new social and economic conditions and to take on a new lease of life after a period of decline. The functions of many have completely changed. But once a town has been established, it normally stays put ; seldom has a town been shifted from one site to another site, although many, especially after the ravages of fire, have been completely rebuilt on a new street plan. Moreover, small country towns, many of which were founded as medieval fortresses, even though they have never been active towns, still exist to-day, with the same lay-out and size. Western Europe knows few of the vicissitudes of eastern and northern Europe, where towns have been completely devastated only to be rebuilt on the same site. The history of the west European city is continuous from its formation in the Middle Ages ; but in Hungary, the Balkans and Russia, towns have been destroyed or burned again and again only to rise once more on the old site. The war-time destruction of cities and small towns in western Europe is a major tragedy in its history. But it is certain that these cities will revive on the same sites, with plans, however, that can not yet be foreseen. Here is an immediate challenge to the imagination and good sense of the physical and social planner.

Function is the driving force of town life. The functions of the town, each of which must find appropriate places in its spatial structure, are religious, political, commercial, industrial and residential. The needs of rulers and populace must also be catered for—defence against human enemies, against fire, famine and disease ; facilities for the provision of food, water, sewage disposal, and, especially in the lands north of the Alps, heating and lighting ; and, finally, recreation, in the form of theatre, arena, public squares and stadiums. The importance of each of these primary functions in the origin and development of the town varies from age to age, and, in consequence, the structure and composition of the functional elements may vary also. In origin the town in all ages seems to have been a seat of religious worship or the seat of a king, or often the two combined. This was true of the towns of ancient Egypt and Mesopotamia, of the Hittites, Etruscans, Greeks, and Romans. The medieval town in Europe had a similar origin, but the town in western Europe, when it emerged as a corporate entity, was essentially an organized group of burgesses engaged in industry and commerce, whereas in Russia it remained until recent times essentially a seat of administration and religious life. The two functions, religio-political and economic, appeared in one and the same town, that began as a secular and ecclesiastical seat and became an economic centre responsible for its own defence. The lords needed their castles and the towns needed their walls ; often the lord favoured a town and maintained its walls because it served the need of defending and organizing his territory. In the Baroque era, however, the political motive again became of importance in the foundation of capitals and fortresses.   In the modern era the economic motive has been dominant.

(a) Natural v. Planned Growth

The whole process of the topographic growth of the urban habitat, the most complex of all human works on the earth's surface, is at every stage the result of deliberate choice either by the individual householder or by high authority.   There are two diametrically opposed tendencies here, which it is not always easy to distinguish.   On the one hand, houses may be built one by one by individuals without reference to each other, or to any sort of preconceived plan, without any general and single control by a high authority.   The plan will then emerge as the result of *natural*, that is, *unplanned growth*, and may then be referred to as a *natural form*.   On the other hand, a town may be planned from the outset as to site, limits, street pattern, and the location of its chief public buildings and open spaces, with its houses and public buildings adjusted in varying ways to the initial lay-out. Such a plan is the result of preconceived ideas and may be called a *planned form*.   The two types of pattern are frequently inter-mingled in one town, for the nature of the growth may vary at different stages in its development.   Moreover, planned units, whether groups of houses or a lay-out of streets and blocks with enclosed building lots, may be juxtaposed without any unifying design.   Many cities have grown in this way like a beehive ; as in the case of Ur, oldest of all cities.   This was the normal mode of growth of the European city, and is characteristic of the modern real estate development of the American city.   But the distinction between the two modes of growth is a valid one.

There is a further consideration.   Every human settlement has a site on which its whole paraphernalia of settlement must be laid out.   In every great era of civilization, each with its own conceptions of urban life, the elements of the urban habitat have been composed in relation to each other and to the site in different ways.   While many towns are closely adjusted to the relief of the site, in others a preconceived plan has literally been imposed on the site.   The site varies in importance in the plan and build of the town.   Pronounced features of relief become part of the town and cannot be divorced from it.   In other cases, as on flat land, relief has often exercised no pronounced directive influence, so that, as far as plan and build are concerned, it is of little significance. The design or whim of the builder has had free play, although even here local adjustments may be found to small irregularities of terrain which have long since disappeared, such as a stretch of marsh or a drained river-bed or a covered stream, while the lay-out of streets, threaded by water channels, was often adjusted to the slope of the land. The raised site has always been favoured for the placement of temple, church, royal castle or palace, and when the site is flat, a mound is often built and fortified to dominate the town next to it and the country around it. This was true, for instance, of the towns of Babylonia, and of the early Christian bishoprics in the interior of Germany beyond the Rhine, in Poland, Bohemia and Scandinavia. In east central Europe in particular, the ruler was the champion of Christianity, and this is symbolized by the frequent combination of castle and cathedral within the same wall on a hilltop site. There are many possible ways of urban growth on one site. Towns on the same kind of sites that are as identical as Nature permits, may have similar features in detail, but often differ profoundly in respect of their morphology, according to the circumstances of their origin, their functions, and whether they are natural or planned forms. A hilltop or marsh-girt site may have a town with an irregular congested plan grouped around a cathedral, or a plan closely adjusted to the walls that surround the hill slopes, or a rectilinear plan with a large square central market, or a set of curved streets closely adjusted to the relief of the hill slope and in turn to the lie of the walls.

It is clear, then, that the morphology of the town—its plan and build—is the product of two sets of conditions, first, the site, and second, the mode of topographic growth on the site, both by natural adaptation to it, and by the imposition of some pre-conceived system of urban lay-out. These may be called natural and cultural determinants. Let us first consider the facts of physical site to which the plan may, in its detail or broad outline, be adjusted. These positive site determinants are the steep slopes of the hill, the incised river meander, the projecting sea-promontory, the river bank and the sea-front. Since they are main elements in the plan, they may be referred to as *natural dominants*, to use Gantner's term. The hilltop and the incised meander of the high promontory were favourite sites in antiquity because of their association with religious sanctity and because of the natural protection that they offered to towns located there. Such was the rôle of the Acropolis at Athens, the most famous example. The need for defence occasioned the choice of similar sites for the *oppidum* of the Gallic tribes and the *Volksburg* of the early Germans, as for Iron Age man throughout north-western Europe. Then again, in the Middle Ages such sites were favoured by castle and fortress town and were particularly frequent in the Mediterranean lands. The Roman towns north of the Alps frequently lay on the gently sloping bank of a river where important routeways converged on a ford, ferry, or bridge. Towns so placed could function effectively as seats of district administration and maintain direct connection with the outside world, and with Rome in particular, by road. River-front and road play main parts in the growth of the plan in such towns, since these are the arteries of trade and intercourse. Roads run at right angles to the river-front, descending to the bridge, others are parallel to the river-front, and the two sets together may form an approximate grid plan, either by natural or planned growth. The road is the main avenue of contact with the outside world, and the gates in the medieval town are its main point of contact with that world. The river is of profound importance in various ways —as a barrier on whose banks towns grew up as fortified outposts or at convenient crossing points for ferry, ford and bridge ; as a highway in itself, so that on its bank the merchants planted their wharves and warehouses ; as a source of water for the mill, for drinking and washing ; and as a sewer for the disposal of urban refuse. Thus, street and buildings are closely articulated in relation to the main radial routes and to the main river, and, in particular, to the river crossing.

This leads us to consider the second category of determinants, which appear in the plan as the *cultural dominants*. These are the outstanding and dominant urban structures. Chief of these, as just noted, is the road, whether processional avenue or commercial thoroughfare. The latter is one of the most characteristic features of the west European town. It is the life-line of the economic community, and contact with it is sought by market-place, commercial buildings and houses. But the market-place or the public square or large public edifice or monument may also affect the plan. The route, as a main axis, and the market-place, as a focal point for radiating roads, are thus the chief factors in conditioning the formation of the urban plan, whether by natural or planned growth. The public edifice in particular, the most characteristic of urban structures, has been of striking importance in urban growth and must receive special emphasis. The great religious edifices—temple, tomb, church, and public monument —have exercised a profound effect on the towns or parts of towns that grew around them. In ancient Egypt and Mesopotamia and in Greece, the public edifice was the nucleus of a rectangular lay-out that was determined in part by the lay-out of the streets, in part by the juxtaposition of rectangular buildings. Study of the medieval plan in western Europe reveals that buildings are often clustered around the earliest church, usually a cathedral immunity, or a castle, or even an open space or a spring. In some the houses form a continuous circle of buildings around a nucleus, thus affording protection from outside and a place of refuge within. Further growth around it may take the form of concentric belts of houses and streets. The edifice, however, needs contact with the settlement and with the outside world, so that we should expect to find routes radiating from it. This mode of development is very characteristic of the first Christian sees which defended the parasitic built-up clusters around them, and it is also found in many villages and small towns. The same kind of grouping, of course, may be the result of deliberate æsthetic and practical planning, and was a main feature of Baroque lay-out.

Lastly, the fortification is a most important item and determinant of the town plan. In certain epochs of history the urban community has not needed any defence. Such was the case in the heyday of the Roman Empire ; such has been the case in the last three hundred years of urban settlement in the western world. But in the past, in general, the wall was essential to defend the urban community, except in areas where strong unified political control (as in the two epochs noted above) made such defences unnecessary. In some cases the lay-out of the whole plan, when founded as a unit, was adjusted to the shape of the walls and the location of the gates. This is conspicuously true of the *castrum* in Roman times ; it is also the case with many small founded towns in western Europe. In other cases, the wall was thrown around an existing settlement, far beyond the limits of its built-up area, and it has had little effect on the town plan. Adjustments are apparent when building reaches to the wall. The boulevard follows the line of the demolished wall. In many cases the town of gradual growth was walled in stages, when it was deemed necessary to give protection to outlying settlements (*faubourgs*). The houses and streets then grew up to the wall and the lie of streets and the arrangement of blocks show close

K

adjustment to the wall, even when this has disappeared. Street lines occupy the site of walls that have long since been demolished, or of canals that have been filled in, as is often testified by their names.

(b) The Basic Systems of Urban Ground Plan

The second main determinant of the urban plan arises from the application of a conception of lay-out to the design of a part or the whole of the plan. Such conceptions may be either tentative, or rigidly applied as the embodiment of accepted usage. Moreover, this may not merely be a matter of a particular kind of street lay-out. It may, as in the Middle Ages, involve the planning of the town as an entity, so that towns appear again and again with the same essential features, often imposed on different kinds of sites. In other words, such a planned town is itself a culture form. Here we are concerned with the general systems of street lay-out, and these occur under conditions of both natural and planned growth. Three basic systems of street ground plan characterize, in varying degree, each of the great periods of urban growth.

(i) *The Irregular System.* Irregular plans have a maze of streets, haphazard in both width and direction, with houses irregularly disposed in relation to each other, and with no main through routes or dominant focal points, such as a church, castle or market-place. The house is the unit of settlement, and extension of the lay-out has been subject in no way to the control of a high authority. Early students of settlement drew attention, for instance, to the irregularity of the town plans in western, as opposed to the rectangular town plans in eastern, Germany, and postulated village origins for the former. In fact, there are few towns which have grown up from the completely irregular clustered village, and many apparently irregular forms are the products of gradual topographic growth. Their plans and historical development reveal that they belong to the second system noted below. It should be observed, however, that on the Continent, as elsewhere, there is often a close relation in form between rural and urban settlements in the same countryside. This relation is due, not to the gradual topographic and functional transformation of a village, but rather to the adoption of the same principles of lay-out for the town as for the village, modified to suit the needs of an urban community.

Villages which became towns by the addition of a wall and

the endowment of legal town status are relatively few in number in Germany and appear mainly in the 14th century, notably in the Rhineland. Such gradual constitutional and topographical origins were more common in Britain, France, the Low Countries and western Germany. These towns are the result of *natural* growth. But never does one find that utter irregularity of plan which this definition connotes. This planless clustering of build-ings is reflected in an irregular jumble of houses, with streets varying in width and direction, and " living streets " branching off from main streets and ending in *culs-de-sac* like a maze, as a wanderer in such a city, even with a map, will soon discover. This kind of plan is found typically in the Moorish towns of Spain, which, after the expulsion of the Moors, were opened up by means of large open squares and the cutting of new roads in the west European tradition. It is also characteristic, with almost no modern alterations, of the Mohammedan lands in North Africa and the Middle East. The type is especially associated also with the oasis towns of North Africa and Central Asia, such as Ferghana and Samarkand. It occurs again in the " indigenous " towns of Hungary and Rumania, and was characteristic throughout the Balkans in the towns of the Turkish period. In the last fifty years the westernization of these countries has been marked by the completely new lay-out or transformation of these cities on modern Western lines by the addition of planned thoroughfares and open spaces. The contrast between Turkish and modern Sofia is as marked as that between a North African oasis town and a planned 19th-century town in central Europe.[1] The growth and plan of these towns of the semi-arid lands, with their nomadic inhabitants settling down late to sedentary occupations, calls for investigation. They developed as clustered settlements of peasant farmers, without any organized middle class, or any ideas of planning by high authority. They were, and are, large rural communities sheltering the peasants who held lands in the surrounding countryside, rather than trading communities serving that countryside.

(ii) *The Radial-Concentric System.* The two essential features of this system, either of which may be found separately, are the radial arrangement of the main streets and the concentric forma-tion around a central nucleus. This nucleus is often a compact,

<hr/>

[1] H. Wilhelmy, " Hochbulgarien, II. Sofia ", *Schriften des Geographischen Instituts der Universität Kiel,* edited by O. Schmieder, H. Wenzel, and H. Wilhelmy, Band V, Heft 3, Kiel, 1936.

and completely closed, oval-shaped settlement. On the Continent it occurs both as the nucleus of a fully developed radial-concentric plan and as a separate small settlement. A main need of the early medieval settlement was defence, and the fortification, in the form of earthworks or walls or the grouping of buildings around an open space or church, was the main determinant of this nuclear settlement form in the Middle Ages. Like the simple route axis noted below, it is one of the basic forms of all settlement morphology. The type is evident to-day in numerous small settlements of late medieval origin in southern France and elsewhere, and is characteristic of the nucleus of many historic cities.[1]

The fully developed radial-concentric plan is widely distributed as a natural form among medieval towns. It is especially characteristic of the towns of Flanders and of the small unwalled market towns of the English countryside and of northern France and north-western Germany. The natural tendency was for these towns to grow up like a spider-web around a fortified stronghold or *burg*—an old imperial castle or cathedral—or a market-place. More correctly, in the former cases, the settlement grew around the market-place, which was located normally *outside* the old *burg*. Here were clustered the homes and warehouses of the merchants and craftsmen who catered for the needs of the clerics and nobles in the *burg*. This type is best illustrated in some of the largest of the medieval towns in Flanders, such as Ghent, Bruges, Mons and Courtrai. With expansion during and after the Middle Ages, and again later in the 19th century with the construction of boulevards, this radial-concentric plan gradually developed in many towns through " natural " and " planned " extension from the medieval core.

The radial-concentric plan was used in remote antiquity and was adopted side by side with the grid plan. It is frequent among the ancient cities of the Hittites in Asia Minor in the second millennium before Christ. Zendjerli, dating from about 1300 B.C. had in its centre an acropolis defended by an oval-shaped wall, and this was again enclosed by a *double* fortification that is exactly circular with a diameter of 720 metres and cut by three gates. Exactly the same system appears in Kadesh in the plain of Homs and in Carchemish. The latter, one of the ancient capitals of the Hittites, occupied a limestone plateau on the right bank of a river and began as a fortress erected in 2000 B.C., and as the city grew around it, it was surrounded by a polygonal (almost circular) wall with three gates. At a later stage a third enclosure was built with a double wall that was almost rectangular in

---

[1] See in particular Lavedan, *L'Histoire de L'Urbanisme*, 1926, pp. 250–80 and 322–30.

shape. We find exactly the same plan in the Round City, founded in
A.D. 762 by the Abbasid Caliph Mansur on the west bank of the Tigris
a little to the north of Baghdad. It was completely circular, with
three lines of walls, two close together as an outer fortification, and
the third some distance inside that contained the government buildings
and the royal precinct. The diameter of the city was 3,000 yards ;
it was surrounded by moat and dyke and had four gates. This
" fantastic mushroom city " was abandoned soon after (836) and the
new town grew across the river at Baghdad. The resemblance between
all these town plans is remarkable. But it is even more remarkable
that this system was not used in ancient Egypt nor in ancient Greece.[1]

It is a remarkable fact that this type, which is a natural mode
of growth, though very common in the Middle Ages, was nowhere
adopted as a planned form until the Renaissance and Baroque
period (1500–1800). In the new towns and town extensions of
this period the main roads were made to radiate from a central
open place, so as more easily to man the walls from the centre in
new fortress towns, or, in the case of Court towns, to radiate from,
lead to, and be commanded by, a royal residence, as at Versailles
and its imitations by German kings, such as Karlsruhe. This
theme is developed more fully in a later chapter.

This lay-out has developed in many modern cities, both as a
natural and a planned growth, as the ideal solution for traffic
problems, both in the building of towns *de novo*, and in the adaptation of old plans to modern needs. It is worth repeating that
neither the irregular street pattern nor the chess-board pattern is
well suited to the planning of modern traffic arteries. The
rectangular lay-out of the American city is a serious hindrance to
traffic and is offset partly by radial railways and radial avenues,
which perforce must cross the rectangular pattern of streets and
blocks. Some of these radial thoroughfares, it is interesting to
note, are older than the modern grid plan, and date from the
earlier tracks that followed this natural course from the first
centres of settlement. As a planned form the radial-concentric
lay-out is well illustrated by Pest, the modern section of Budapest
on the right bank of the river Danube.

(iii) *The Rectangular or Grid System.* The rectangular or grid
system of enclosed rectangular blocks is characteristic of all ages
of town planning. It appeared in the earliest civilizations of
north-west India, Egypt and Babylonia.[2]

---

[1] See Seton Lloyd, *Ruined Cities of Iraq*, Oxford, 3rd edition, 1945.
[2] See Seton Lloyd, *op. cit.* Mohenjo-Daro in India, dating from the 3rd millennium
B.C. and showing " an organic city in which all parts were designed to function within
the whole ", is certainly the oldest example known.

The Greek city of antiquity was dominated by its great public monuments and the places of public assembly—the Acropolis and the Agora or market-place, its temples and its processional avenues. In the oldest towns these public monuments were grouped on a hilltop, at the foot of which clustered the city proper, while between them, on the hill slope, was placed the open-air theatre. Such was the typical case of Athens. In these early Greek towns the public monuments were carefully planned on the hilltop as individual units and in their relations to each other, but the town at its foot was an irregular, congested, unplanned cluster. There are few remains of these earliest Greek cities. The best are at Thera and Pergamon.[1]

In the founded and planned colonial towns in Italy, Sicily and North Africa, the town was placed on a well-defended natural site, such as a rocky peninsula, and all the public monuments were enclosed by the city walls in the framework of a grid plan of streets, though often both monuments and houses stood back from the street frontage. In the history of the Greek city, the regular planned town does not appear until the 5th century. From then on Greek colonial towns were laid out on definite principles. The amorphous lay-out of Miletus is not unlike the plans of many towns in south Russia and in the recently settled areas of the New World. The later Greek colonial town gradually emerged as an architectonic unity by the introduction of two main, wide thoroughfares crossing at right angles (though not necessarily intersecting in the centre of the town), with the market-place at the intersection ; and by the construction of a wall adjusted to the terrain. An example of such a town is Selinus (Selinunte) in Sicily.

The earliest Roman towns, the *civitates*, appeared in a period of security from invasion and represented the florescence of Roman civilization. In Gaul the *civitas* was placed at the foot of the hill on which had been located the preceding Gallic *oppidum* or stronghold, on slightly raised ground between the *oppidum* and the crossing of a main river, for the Roman settlement sought the highway, as the Gallic stronghold avoided it. The towns were not walled and spread without hindrance. Their wide roads radiated from the river crossing, and along the roads were to be found the public monuments and the forum.

An entirely new arrangement developed with the beginning of the Germanic invasions. The extensive urban area was

[1] P. Lavedan, *Histoire de l' Urbanisme Antiquité, Moyen Âge*, Paris, 1926, Chapter IV.

abandoned and a new settlement erected at the river crossing within the confines of a rectangular walled enclosure. This was called a *castrum*, and served primarily for purposes of shelter and defence. It was designed on the plan of the Roman camp as used in conquered territories for holding down subject peoples. The *castrum* was a further development of the Greek colonial town plan by the introduction of two new features. The walls were given a rigid rectangular shape, and two intersecting axes, the *cardo* and *decumanus*, cut the walls in their centres and intersected in the centre of the enclosure, which was thus divided into four equal parts, with the *forum* or market-place in the centre. This was the ideal form, but many variations were prompted by both historical and terrain conditions. The *castrum* was a planned rectilinear form ; like the Greek colonial city, it was also a stereotyped culture form, and was established by the Romans throughout the lands they controlled.

The grid plan is also characteristic of the towns that were founded north of the Alps from the later Middle Ages onwards. Given the rectangular house lot as a building unit and the street as the axis of expansion, there develop, by natural growth, two rows of buildings facing on to a main through route. This, like the oval-shaped nucleus mentioned above, is the second fundamental nuclear form in the origin, growth and topographic formation of the medieval town. From such a single route axis, lateral and linear growth are the normal modes of expansion, so that there emerges an approximately rectangular pattern of streets and blocks. This is the natural mode of growth with the house on a rectangular plot, just as radial extension is the natural mode of growth from the standpoint of the route from a centre. The rectangular house lot is difficult to adjust to such a radial street pattern. The same kind of linear growth takes place along a canal which, when repeated in the form of parallel canals and streets, gives a form that is characteristic of the Dutch towns. This rectangular pattern is characteristic of all the medieval planned towns and has been typical of every period of city life and city founding in Europe and in the New World, for the simple reason that it is the easiest method of lay-out, both on the drawing board or the map and on the ground, as a preconceived plan.

Through several hundred years we can trace the development of ideas and practice in town building in the Middle Ages. It started in the natural growth of the earliest towns from their pre-urban strongholds and culminated in the lay-out of whole towns, grouped around a market-place and enclosed by a wall, in which the whole plan is determined by accepted principles that are repeated again and again in sections of towns or in entirely new founded towns, that were laid out *ab initio* and *in toto*. The grid lay-out continued to be used in the planning of towns (or additions to the medieval towns) in the following Renaissance and Baroque periods, together with the radial plan, that was experimented with particularly in the lay-out of new fortress towns. The grid system was more commonly adopted, although it differed from that of the medieval town in that the palatial residence of the king or lord and the ornamental squares, rather than the market-place and church of the common people, were its central features, and in that much greater consideration was given to æsthetic considerations.

In the great eras and areas of modern urban growth, the grid plan has been generally adopted as an amorphous lay-out without unity, proportion, or limits in population or extent, all of which are essential for the growth of community life and for the efficient functioning of traffic within it. This amorphous growth is characteristic of the so-called towns in the steppes of south Russia and the middle and lower Danube plains that were settled during the 18th and 19th centuries. It has also been characteristic of the tremendous urban developments in the United States and throughout the lands of Western civilization. The grid pattern of streets, with rows of building structures regularly disposed in regular lots, is the product of individual enterprise building on the cheapest basis for private gain. The radial-concentric system is often applied in combination with the rectilinear in urban plans. Its advantages over the former are evidenced by the frequency of its adoption in modern planning, particularly of main traffic thoroughfares. But the essential point to be made here is that this modern grid plan is simply a mode of lay-out. It was not associated with a concept of the nature of a town as a social and economic unit, as the medieval town was, and it lacked the control of high authority. In consequence, the modern urban agglomeration lacks both the social and architectonic unity that characterized the historic city. The elucidation of such concepts and principles is the grand purpose of modern social survey and city planning.

CHAPTER 15

THE GROWTH OF THE HISTORIC CITY

(1) The Growth and Spread of the Medieval Town
(c. A.D. 1000–1500)

Europe, as a whole, has experienced four great periods of urban growth, and each gave rise to a special type of city that reflected its civilization. Greek civilization began in the Ægean lands, and there its earliest city-states were located, while the Greek colonial city was founded on the coast lands of the Mediterranean, especially in southern Italy. Roman civilization spread the city idea not only throughout the Mediterranean, but also, for the first time, to the mainland of Europe north of the Alps, throughout Gaul as far as the Rhine, throughout southern Europe as far as the Danube, and across the English Channel to the lowland zone of Britain. Then followed the Dark Ages, when urban life and traditions north of the Alps all but disappeared for over five hundred years (c. A.D. 500–1000). The next great phase of urban growth commenced with the turn of the millennium. From A.D. 1000 to 1400 there occurred in western and central Europe on the one hand, and in central Russia on the other, a great expansion of the human habitat and a marked growth of population. The concept of the town developed anew in Gaul and in the Rhineland. By 1400 the whole of western and central Europe was covered with towns and villages. The sphere of western settlement reached north to latitude 60° to the edge of the coniferous forest and the winter frozen seas, and to the east, in the great borderland of central Europe, it merged into the forested lands of the Slavs and the semi-arid steppes of the Magyars and Tatars. The overwhelming majority of the settlements of to-day, throughout the whole of western, central and southern Europe, were in existence at the end of the Middle Ages. Thereafter, from about 1500 to 1800, relatively few new towns came into being. The main areas of town building in this period were Poland, Scandinavia, and above all the steppes of southern Russia and the middle and lower Danube lands. In western and central Europe this period was one of relative stability, the most marked growth being in the capital and Court cities and in the ports.

The second great phase of urban growth took place during the 19th century.   The Industrial Revolution had its beginnings in England and in the adjacent countries of the continental mainland in the last decades of the previous century.   In the middle of the 19th century began the modern phase of coal and iron, the railway, and the steam-driven factory.   The great increase of urban population after 1850 reached its peak in western Europe about 1900.   By then there were already signs that the rate of increase was slowing down.   In the first half of the 20th century there has been a marked decline in the birth-rate in all the countries of western and central Europe, as opposed to the Slav and Magyar lands to the east.

These two latest phases have been named the paleotechnic and neotechnic eras by Patrick Geddes, and he referred to the long preceding era, from about the turn of the millennium to the end of the 18th century, as the eotechnic era.   This broad classification characterizes the main phases in the development of Western civilization and is based on what Lewis Mumford has called the technics of civilization.[1]   The eotechnic era, characterized in terms of power and its dominant materials, is based on a water and wood complex.   It is the era of handicrafts.   The paleotechnic era began with the industrial revolution and is a coal and iron complex.   It is the era of the steam engine.   The neotechnic era is an electricity and alloy complex, and began in the last decades of the 19th century.   It is the era of the dynamo, the electric railway, light and power.   Here we shall deal with the spread and growth of the historic city down to the onset of the modern growth of urban populations in the 19th century. The latter period will be discussed in a later chapter.

With the end of the Roman Empire urban life declined and almost disappeared.   This was the case even in the bishops' centres that were huddled within the walls of the Roman *castra* in Gaul and on the Rhine, and on the sites of preceding Germanic settlements in western Germany beyond the Rhine, east as far as the Elbe–Saale rivers.   The end of the millennium was marked by great changes heralding the beginning of a new phase of urban growth.   The countryside was covered with new fortresses, especially at its more vulnerable route centres, while the existing Roman walls were repaired or extended as a protection from the attacks of Northmen, Huns and Saracens.   Long-distance trade was also revived, and the merchant came into being.   He

---

[1] Lewis Mumford, *Technics and Civilization*, 1934, p. 110.

travelled in companies across the continent, seeking depots and protection under the aegis of the stronghold whose lords and clerics he supplied with luxuries. Finally, the great era of forest clearance brought about the spread of farming, and, with it, the growth of crafts and of local trade. Thus there came into being a new type of settlement, that consisted of a stronghold of Emperor, lord, or bishop, and with a mercantile community outside it. The latter, already enjoying special privileges, became the nucleus of the nascent urban community, that was engaged in trade and crafts, and sought independence from overlords by demanding the privileges of self-government. The mercantile settlements appeared first in the 10th and early 11th centuries, on the rivers of northern France and Flanders and on the great west–east routeway in Germany from Cologne to Magdeburg. Gradually during the 12th century these settlements obtained rights of self-government. By 1150 the term *civitas*, after a long period during which varied meanings had been attached to it, was used to designate the medieval town. According to the historians the medieval town had three essential and universal characteristics— its population was primarily engaged in industry and trade ; it had a distinct legal constitution ; and it was a centre of administration and a fortress.[1]

These early towns were few in number and were situated at the outstanding nodal points, where overland natural routeways and navigable rivers converged. They were particularly numerous in northern France and Flanders, and they had a fairly even distribution in southern France. In the German lands there were two main axes of these towns, along the Rhine, and along the northern border of the central uplands from Cologne to Magdeburg. Two other lines of eastward penetration followed by towns were the Main valley (Würzburg and Bamberg), and the Danube lowland, where Vienna appeared as the most easterly outpost in 1107.

The overwhelming majority of the towns, however, came into being during the period from about 1200 to 1400. Though often

[1] H. Pirenne, *Les Villes du moyen âge*, 1927, p. 153. This definition is true for those fully fledged towns which unquestionably enjoyed this stature. But there were hundreds of small towns at the end of the Middle Ages, covering most of the lands, in which these essential traits of the *civitas* did not always occur in combination. Since the historian is primarily interested in the development of institutions he is concerned mainly with the early and chief towns. But the geographer is concerned with *all* towns and other urban and rural settlements of an area. The traits of the medieval town within the meaning of the above definition varied from area to area in their historical development so that generalizations obscure the realities.

to-day much smaller in size than their predecessors, they cover and serve directly most of the countryside. These towns drew their law, as a rule, from the pattern of the law of one of the older " parent " cities. They came into being in many ways— as a parasitic settlement around a church or a castle, as a deliberate foundation *de novo*, as a market settlement with elementary rights of self-government, or, much more rarely, as a village that gradually acquired one or more of the privileges of a town. Down to 1200 town life had not reached beyond the Elbe and the Saale, but with the eastward spread of German colonization and trade the overwhelming majority of the towns of eastern Germany, central Europe and the Baltic shores came into being as deliberate foundations. They derived their law from the chief cities in the west, above all from Lübeck and Magdeburg. Even the towns of indigenous growth in Russia based their law on the German pattern. The smaller towns of western Europe were the result of a slower and more complicated development. Although towns with distinctive rectilinear patterns were founded in all regions, it was in southern France that they were most conspicuous. Here Montauban, founded in 1144, was the prototype of hundreds of *Bastides* that were built by both French and English during the Hundred Years War.

From the middle of the 12th century the overwhelming majority of towns were established on the models of the earlier towns by the grant of *charters*. These charters contained privileges of exemption from feudal dues and rights of self-government. The liberties were at first of an elementary kind, but were often followed by advanced liberties of full self-government. The charters were based upon the law of existing old towns, and throughout western and central Europe the law of certain of these old towns served as a standard for new foundations. There was a spread of crafts in the countryside, free from the restrictions of the guilds, and this tended to increase the activities of the towns as local seats for their organization.

The towns of France and England were not usually created *de novo* by deliberate foundation. They acquired rights of self-government gradually, and privileges were often extended to existing communities, many of which were villages, or at any rate semi-rural in character. More than half the towns of France had their origin in a village, a castle or an abbey, and grew to be *bourgs* (the French equivalent of a small town or townlet), some of which attained full town status in the Middle Ages.

Their origins mostly date back to the early Middle Ages (900–1200), when France bristled with abbeys and feudal castles, and full town status was acquired during the 13th century.

In France, Louis VI (1108–37) founded the small town of Lorris in the upper Loire valley and its charter became a pattern for many others. The king's charter assured to every settler a house and a lot at a fixed rent, and if he remained there for a year and a day, he was henceforth a free man. The settler was also released from feudal restrictions such as tallage, military service, and forced labour. He could not be brought to trial outside the town and was tried in it by a fixed legal procedure. Fines and punishments were limited. This charter was adopted by later kings and barons in numerous small settlements in northern France. The bastides were similarly founded in southern France and many of them derived their charters on the pattern of the most famous of them all, Montauban, that was founded in 1144.

In England, such privileges were granted by charter in the same period. The Normans brought in special laws that were derived from a place called Breteuil. These were granted to a number of new places that were established along the Welsh frontier and were even carried into Ireland, although many of the places never developed as towns and show little trace of a systematic lay-out of house lots. About the same time Henry I (1100–35) founded several towns, among which were Verneuil in Normandy and Newcastle in England. The king had a castle overlooking the Tyne and granted a group of liberties so as to attract settlers to it. Immigrant peasants were to enjoy freedom after a residence of one year and a day, and these men, known as burgesses, were to be free of servile feudal obligations, with the right of buying and selling land in the town. Within the town they had special privileges, including a monopoly on the right to trade. They were also to enjoy their own legal privileges. These liberties were extended to many other places in northern England and Scotland.

Town life in England developed slowly in the English lowland. Here developed the English kingdom and its relative security accounts for the rarity of the strong castle as the seat of crystallization of a town. Very different were the circumstances and character of urban development in the " frontier " lands of Scotland, Wales and Ireland. The English entered here as conquerors and imposed their civilization upon the native cultures.

Law and order had to be maintained among recalcitrant tribes. The Roman *castrum* was established in the nearer border zones of the English Lowland to the north and east. After the Norman conquest many castles were established in the " marchlands ", as elsewhere in the frontier zones of western and central Europe. The Scottish rulers developed an independent pattern of urban life in which the wall and the castle were important elements as means of defence from turbulent neighbours. The conquest of Wales by the English led to the foundation of many small new " towns " adjacent to castles as foreign islands among the Welsh folk. The same story is, in part, true in Ireland and Scotland, except that here the foundation of towns continued in the 17th and 18th centuries. These are themes that call for further investigation.

The development of small towns in Germany was more tardy than in France and England, and high authority played a more imporant part in their origins. The first new towns were established during the 12th century. Freiburg-im-Breisgau was established as a market settlement (*forum*), and was settled by *mercatores* in 1120. It served as a model for many others in south Germany, while Lübeck, originally founded in 1158, served as a model for the Hanseatic towns. In the early Middle Ages Imperial power was strong in Germany ; the powers of the dukes, bishops and local lords were very limited, and they were not allowed to erect any independent fortifications. Not until after 1200, with the decline of the Imperial power, did feudal anarchy run amok in Germany. Then the land was split up into rags and tatters, and castles and fortress towns were established all over the countryside by the local lords, as castles had been established in France at an earlier date. Between 1200 and 1400, towns appeared in hundreds, serving as centres of local market trade and long-distance trade, and answering to the need for defence and administration of the territories of their petty lords.

To the east of the Elbe and Saale lay the great borderlands between the Baltic and the Black Seas in which Western merges into Eastern Europe. This zone includes the east Baltic provinces, Poland and Lithuania, north of the great swirl of the Carpathians, and the lands of the Danube basin to the south of the latter. Here isolated and backward peoples in the forest and marsh of the north, the Ukraine steppe and the Danube lands, were affected tardily by culture contacts from both western and Byzantine cultures. These peoples were the Finns, Esths, Letts, Lithuanians and Poles to the north of the Carpathians, and the Magyars, Rumanians and Slavs to the south. Western influences, with which we are directly concerned, were those of Roman Catholicism, trade contacts and the western, Germanic, idea of the town as a self-governing community of traders and craftsmen. The eastern influences took the form of the Eastern Orthodox faith, that was accepted by the Russian States through Kiev from Constantinople. Here, too, there prevailed the overlordship of rulers with their seats in their " towns ", in which clustered castles, nobles' residences and churches. There was little economic activity and no independent concept of town government by an homogeneous economic class except in so far as, in the later Middle Ages, German traders who had settled there were granted self-government on the pattern of the German town law. Poland and Hungary accepted western Catholicism about A.D. 1000. In the Danube plains, which were controlled by the Turks from about 1526 to 1683, town development was retarded until the late eighteenth century. Cultural infiltration was effected from the west throughout this zone during the Middle Ages, primarily by the Germans in the centre and by the Swedes in the extreme north, in Finland.

In all these lands there is the same sequence of urban growth. Christianity was spread by the establishment of bishoprics in Poland, Bohemia, Hungary and the north-west of the Balkans, in the 11th century. Defence and territorial organization by native rulers gave the first impetus to the establishment of fixed centres of settlement, and in some of these the bishoprics were situated. Regular long-distance and local market trade developed later, and the spread of the town as a self-governing entity with German law came at varying dates after the lapse of about two hundred and fifty years.

Poland and Bohemia in the early Middle Ages (9-11th centuries) had many periodical markets, places of pagan worship, and communal strongholds, scattered over the countryside. Some of these were selected as seats of permanent settlement with the introduction of Christianity and the establishment of permanent trading centres around cathedral, church and castle. This penetration was effected from the west. But town life in the sense of self-governing economic communities did not appear till the middle of the 13th century, especially after the last great incursions of the Mongols. Then towns, large and small, were founded in the western provinces. In this period of the mid 13th century the foundation of Poznán, Breslau, Warsaw, Cracow and many others took place. Particularly deep was the German penetration along the foreland of the Carpathians, where Lwów (Lemberg) was established as the most remote German town, and into the Carpathians (the Zips area) and Transylvania (the Siebenbürgen area), where the towns maintain their remarkably distinctive Germanic character, in historic architecture and culture traits, to this day.

Brief reference should be made to the spread and growth of the town in the lands around the Baltic Sea, in both Scandinavia and the east Baltic lands. Here urban life developed tardily and the concept of the town as an economic and self-governing community was derived in the 13th century from the German lands. Bishoprics were first established in Denmark in the middle of the 10th century, and attention was then directed to the pagan lands across the waters. Sees appeared at Lund on the southern tip of the peninsula, and at Trondheim, Bergen, Stavanger, and Oslo, in the early 11th century, with a later establishment inland at Hamar. The Goths in the present provinces of West and East Gothland early accepted Christianity, and bishoprics were established at Skara and Linköping. But the Svears in the region of Mälardalen clung hard to paganism, and Christianity did not effectively spread there until late in the 12th century, when bishoprics appear at (Gamla) Uppsala, Strångnås and Västerås. In the east Baltic lands there was no Christian penetration until after A.D. 1200.

Trade, like settlement, had its beginnings on the shores of these northern lands, where ports collected the furs and skins of the forested hinterland and engaged in fishing the herrings of the coasts of south-western Norway and southern Sweden.[1] The first seats of urban settlement in Denmark before A.D. 1000 avoided the coasts, seeking the interior of peninsula and islands. Most of the later towns lay on the coasts, at bridgeheads at the heads of the bays, especially on the eastern coast of Jutland, where they were sheltered and lay on the main north–south routes. They also enjoyed the protection of castles against the Wendish pirates of the day. Copenhagen itself enters history in 1013, its castle, built in 1165, being founded by Valdemar the Great as part of this system of coastal defences.

The principal medieval towns of Norway lay on the south-

---

[1] On early routeways and their relation to urban development see Leighley, *The Towns of Mälardalen.*

western coast : Trondheim, Bergen, Stavanger. Their trade was mainly in fish and their contacts were almost entirely southwards along the coast to the German mainland. Urban growth was much more tardy in the lowlands around the Oslo bay at the head of the Kattegat. Oslo, though it existed as a settlement in the 11th century, did not develop significantly until the 15th, and this seems to have been true of other towns, such as Tönsberg and Porsgrund. Their growth was associated, above all, with the export of timber to the shipbuilding yards of the towns on the European mainland.

Sweden during the Middle Ages looked eastwards to the Baltic. We have considered in Chapter 2 the early growth of the towns of the Mälardalen region, the heart of the Swedish State. Their early development was associated, above all, with the establishment of bishoprics and the growth of trade. Before 1200 these towns were economically insignificant. Those of central and southern Sweden owed their growth in the 13th and 14th centuries not only to the establishment of churches and monasteries, but also to the development of trade and industry. Of particular importance was the development of metallurgy in the Bergslagen, the district lying north-west of Lake Mälar, which in the later Middle Ages attracted many German mining settlers. The province of Schonen in the extreme south-west of the peninsula belonged to Denmark throughout the Middle Ages, and was early brought into the sphere of Christian culture, with its ancient capital at Lund. This place became a bishopric in 1048, an archbishopric in 1104, and was made by Canute the Great into the capital of his eastern Empire. Many castles and fortified towns were founded in this territory to preserve the lands for the Danish crown, and ports developed on the southern coast after 1200 to exploit the herring fisheries.

This brief survey of northern Europe brings into the picture only those centres that appeared as outstanding seats of culture and trade in the early Middle Ages and after. In fact the great majority of the small towns of Scandinavia south of latitude 60° appeared later in the 14th and 15th centuries. They grew up as seats of local market trade, as centres for the felling of timber, mining and fishing, especially on the south-western coasts of Sweden (which until the 17th century were Danish territories hotly contested by Sweden), and as fortress towns.

The east Baltic lands were occupied by backward pagan peoples—Finns, Esths, Letts, Lithuanians and Prussians. Here was a field for militant missionary endeavour, that was exploited by the Teutonic Order. These lands, however, were remote from Germany and Scandinavia, and were barren lands of marsh and forest. But, more important, they controlled the routeways from the Baltic shores eastwards to Russia and the Black Sea. These two factors, the spread of Christianity and of trade, controlled the development of these provinces in the Middle Ages. The earliest towns, which (with the exception of Helsinki) became the chief towns of to-day, are all situated on the coast ; not one appears, even in its incipient origins, before 1200, and not one was well established before the middle of the 13th century.

Medieval Livonia corresponded with the modern States of Esthonia and Latvia. It derived its name from the fact that it fell to the Livonian Order from Visby at the beginning of the 13th century. Occupation by the Order began with the foundation of Riga, which became thenceforth its greatest commercial centre. The coastal towns of Riga and Reval commanded the routes eastwards to Russia, via the Gulf of Finland, the river Neva and Lake Ladoga, and via the Duna valley to Polotsk and Vitebsk respectively, while Dorpat controlled the routes from Reval and Riga to Pskov and Novgorod. These three Hanseatic cities dominated the remaining urban centres, which were relatively small and quite unimportant. Narva could not rival Reval. Pernau lay aside from the main routes, and Mitau could not rival Riga. All these were German towns.[1]

Town life in Finland was strictly limited to the coastal fringe, that was touched at Åbo by the sailing route from Visby and Stockholm and lay in constant contact with Reval. Throughout the Middle Ages the life of Finland was dominated by Sweden, whose influence had its point of penetration and organization in Åbo in the south-western corner of the fringe. But Åbo did not appear as a fully fledged town until about 1300, and Viborg, the smaller fortress town in the south-eastern corner, not until the 14th century. These two towns belonged to the net of Hanseatic trade and culture. Low German was their *lingua franca*, as

---

[1] " The Livonian towns were not Hansa factories like those in Novgorod itself, in Bruges, London or Bergen. They were settlements of Germans, having the same commercial culture as the north German towns themselves, and having also their own interests independent of Lübeck. They had as well their own political relations to watch over—with the Order, with the bishops, with authorities in Sweden and Finland and in Russian territory. They had their conflicts of interest among themselves. Lacking continuous land connection with the territory on which the north German towns were established, they became Livonian towns first and Hanseatic towns only secondarily." Leighley, *The Towns of Medieval Livonia*, p. 243.

throughout the Hanseatic realm from Bruges to Novgorod, and the Swedish authorities in these Finnish towns were in constant contact with the town council in Reval. There were only five other medieval towns on this Finnish littoral ; these appeared during the latter half of the 14th century and were of very little significance.

(2) The Size of the Medieval Town

The emergence of the new mercantile community in the 10th century and the shift of people—merchants, craftsmen, cultivators, nobles, and clerics—from the countryside to the towns to enjoy their manifold privileges, was one of the great revolutionary changes in the economic and social history of Europe. Here we have emphasized the beginnings. During the 13th and 14th centuries urban life experienced its florescence. Great commercial and industrial emporia grew. Numerous small towns served as local seats of trade, industry and defence. In the later Middle Ages long-distance trade grew in the northern lands, under the direction of the Hanseatic League, and in the Mediterranean lands under that of the Italian city-states, especially Venice. The transcontinental trade routes grew in importance, both from the Mediterranean shores across France, and across the Alpine passes through Germany along the Rhine valley and the Hessian corridor, to the cities of Flanders and the Hanseatic ports of north Germany respectively. East–west routes were also important for trade from western Europe to the Slav lands and the east, through such great emporia as Cracow, Breslau, Vienna, and Belgrade. It was under such circumstances that the large cities of western and central Europe developed, their size being proportional to the importance of the trade on the routes that centred on them.

Decline did not set in until the 15th century, for a variety of complicated causes that we cannot fully discuss here. Suffice it to note that the shift of trade from the land routes to the ocean, the blocking of routes across south-eastern Europe and Asia by the Turkish conquests, and, finally, the decline in the efficiency of government in the cities themselves, all contributed to their economic sterility and decline. The foundation of villages and towns and the growth of population waned during the 14th century,[1] and for the next three centuries there set in a period of

[1] For a discussion of urban economy and demography in the late Middle Ages, see H. Pirenne, *Economic and Social History of Medieval Europe*, 1937, Chapters VI and VII : also H. Bechtel, *Wirtschaftsstil des Deutschen Spätmittelalters*, 1930.

relative stability in social and economic life, although there were violent short-period fluctuations. Gustav Schmoller has written of the medieval German Reich :

One can almost say that the picture of the open country and oi the towns, at least in its main features, was not changed from 1350 to 1750. There was not much more forest clearance, the number of villages decreased rather than increased and their population grew scarcely at all, and very few new towns appeared. Almost all the towns declined rather than increased in the period from 1250 to 1800.[1]

As regards the size of the medieval towns it has been calculated that at the end of the Middle Ages the population of the Holy Roman Empire was about 12 millions, of whom some 10 to 15 per cent. lived in towns. There were not far short of 3,000 towns in the Reich, and 12 to 15 of these had over 10,000 inhabitants. Six, according to Sanders,[2] exceeded 20,000, and only Cologne and Lübeck had more than 30,000 inhabitants. From 15 to 20 had between 2,000 and 10,000 inhabitants, and about 150 had from 1,000 to 2,000 inhabitants. The remainder, some 2,800, had between 100 and 1,000 inhabitants, and 2,500 had less than 500 inhabitants.[3] Thus, again in the words of Schmoller, " One can perhaps say that the increase from A.D. 500 to 1340 of two or three fold to 12 millions was a greater achievement than the increase from 15 millions to 64 millions from 1700 to 1900." [4]

Stagnation set in towards the end of the Middle Ages, especially after the ravages of the Black Death in 1348, from which it took centuries to recover. Added to this, there was the incredible number of deaths in Germany resulting from the Thirty Years War, so that the towns often had fewer inhabitants in the 18th century than 300 years earlier. Almost all German towns increased till the 13th–14th century ; then came a rapid decrease, often caused by the oppression of a territorial lord, and then in the 16th century there was another period of growth.

[1] G. Schmoller, *Deutsches Städtewesen in älterer Zeit*, p. 39. See also K. Frenzel, " Die Deutsche Stadt im Mittelalter als Lebensraum ", in *Stadtlandschaften der Erde*, edited by S. Passarge, Hamburg, 1930, pp. 15–28.

[2] P. Sanders, *Geschichte des deutschen Städtewesens, Bonner Staatswissenchaftliche Untersuchungen*, Heft 6, 1922.

[3] H. Bechtel, *Wirtschaftsstil des Deutschen Spätmittelalters : Der Ausdruck der Lebensform in Wirtschaft, Gesellschaft und Kunst von 1350 bis zum 1500*, Munich and Leipzig, 1930, p. 31 *et seq.* At the end of the Middle Ages Cologne had about 30,000–35,000 inhabitants ; Strasbourg, Nuremberg and Ulm about 20,000 each ; Augsburg and Hamburg about 18,000, Basel 9,000, Leipzig, 4,000, and Dresden 3,000. Lübeck reached 22,000 in 1400, while Frankfurt and Zurich had about 10,000 inhabitants. See B. Heil, *Die Deutschen Städte und Bürger im Mittelalter, Aus Natur und Geisteswelt*, No. 43, Berlin, 1921. Also H. Pirenne, *op. cit.*, pp. 172–3.

[4] Schmoller, *op. cit.*, p. 59.

This is clearly revealed in the population curves of such cities as Cologne, Soest, Worms, Basel and Mainz.[1] In Holland, no town, even at the end of the Middle Ages, exceeded 10,000 inhabitants. Rotterdam and Amsterdam were still small settlements, and the latter did not grow appreciably till the 18th century, but then rapidly. In Belgium, the giants among its many industrial and commercial centres were Ghent and Bruges, which probably had about 50,000 inhabitants.[2]

(3) THE RENAISSANCE AND BAROQUE PERIOD (c. 1500–1800)

The network of towns of to-day was virtually completed by the end of the Middle Ages in western and central Europe, though gaps remained to be filled in, especially in northern Europe. The next 300 years was a period of relative stability, in which only a few new towns were founded and the proportion of urban and rural population remained fairly constant. These general features, however, should not obscure the fact that there were important changes in urban activities which are reflected in the size and structure of the town.

During the 16th, 17th and 18th centuries there occurred important changes in the character and distribution of industry which were not without effect on the location and growth of towns. Industry in the Middle Ages was almost exclusively concentrated in the towns and controlled by their guilds. Every town had a variety of handicrafts, which, because of the lack of transport facilities, catered primarily for the folk in the surrounding countryside. The large cities alone were seats of specialized industry. Western Europe was traversed in the later Middle Ages by numerous routes which were great arteries of commerce and on which towns were located where materials were collected from, and goods distributed to, distant markets. Already, however, certain minerals and sand (for glass making) were worked where these materials were obtained, far from the towns, in remote upland districts which would otherwise have been shunned by settlers who sought to live from the soil. Glass making, metal working (gold, silver, copper and tin) and porcelain making were especially important in the uplands of Germany. All these required charcoal as fuel and running water, in addition to their

---

[1] Article by K. Frenzel, *op. cit.*
[2] Pirenne, *Histoire de Belgique*, Vol. I, 1929, p. 285. 80,000 is the figure given by Demangeon for the 14th century, with 40,000 for Ypres in 1257, reduced to 6,000 in 1486. See A. Demangeon, *Belgique—Pays-Bas—Luxembourg, Géographie Universelle*, Tome II, 1927, pp. 101–2.

particular raw materials. This brought about a considerable dispersion of industry. This trend affected also the textile industries. Everywhere freedom from the restrictions imposed by the guilds was sought. This was especially true of Flanders "where peasant handicrafts were pursued everywhere" so that "the whole of Flanders was one vast workshop".[1] There was a similar widespread distribution of textile working in the villages of Picardy in the early 19th century. The same was true of East Anglia, the Cotswolds and West Yorkshire in England. This general development was found also in the German States. In Prussia, the heyday of mining in the uplands came in the 15th and 16th centuries and the Erzgebirge, the high uplands of Saxony, is the only area in western Europe where a considerable number of new towns were founded in this period. The subsequent decline of metal working released a large labour supply that could not possibly eke out an existence from the impoverished soil of small holdings at high altitudes. The kings of Prussia encouraged the development of the textile industries in these areas as a domestic occupation, and this was organized by merchants (*Verleger*) from town centres. Much the same development took place in the States of southern Germany behind the shelter of their tariff walls. Thus, there was a widespread distribution of rural industry in France, the Low Countries, England and the German lands at the opening of the 19th century, and this added to the importance of the town as a commercial centre.

This period was one of active urban development in the northern lands of Europe as compared to the German lands. This was the era of Sweden's greatness—the *Storhetstid*—when Finland, and, for a time, the territories of the old Livonian Order, were a part of the Swedish kingdom. The new era was opened by Gustav I early in the 16th century. Gustav desired to make Sweden independent politically and economically. He sought, as did the kings of Poland and Hungary at the same time, to transfer the control of trade from the Germans to his own people, and to develop commerce and new manufactures. Iron-making was greatly encouraged, the making of wrought bar-iron as well as of finished products. Textile industries were also encouraged and developed in many towns in central Sweden. The traditional method of distributing goods to a widely scattered population through the medium of the wandering pedlar was strictly forbidden by royal edict and trade was to be rigidly confined to

---

[1] A. Demangeon, *op. cit.*, p. 132.

the towns. New towns were chartered at the seats of the new mining area in the Bergslagen and farther north, and their activities often cut into the trade of existing towns. The properties of the Church were confiscated by the Crown, and land formerly occupied by the monasteries eventually fell into the public ownership of the towns and favoured the development of the towns. The decline in importance of the herring fisheries caused the decline of many small fishing ports. The increasing demand for timber, however, and the growth in size and number of sailing ships— in Sweden as well as in Germany and the Low Countries—led to the exploitation of the Swedish and Finnish forests near to the coast where the timber could be delivered to the ports, in which the saw-mills were located. The need for defence of the frontiers of the State, especially against Russia to the east and Denmark to the south, was a primary consideration in the foundation of fortress towns as both military and naval bases.

Thus many towns appear in this period in northern Europe, especially in the lands controlled by Sweden, in the 17th century. They appeared either as new towns, or as new foundations following on the great devastations wrought by fires, the great scourge of the northern towns, which were, and still are, built almost entirely of timber. Mining towns appear well to the north in the hitherto untouched Norrland. New towns appear, too, on the coasts of the Bothnian Sea north of latitude 60°. Indeed, most of those towns on the shores of the Baltic north of Stockholm and Finnish Åbo and Trondheim were founded in the 17th century or later, either as mining centres, or as posts for the assembly and preliminary treatment of ores and timbers, whereas on the Norwegian coast they emerged later as fishing settlements in the 19th century. In southern Sweden, the foundation of Göteborg in 1618 as Sweden's window on the west was the prelude to the conquest of the Danish territories to the south between 1645 and 1660. The port of Stockholm was frozen each year for four or five months, and was too remote to serve as a naval base for the protection of the Baltic entrances, so Charles XI founded Karlskrona in 1685. Stockholm, the capital, was considerably extended at the same period, as were other European capitals, by additions to the medieval town. Many smaller provincial towns were founded at this time, either as new industrial centres or on the ashes of others that had been ravaged by fire. Most of this planning was the work of military engineers. On the other hand, many towns in Scania were decadent during this period, owing to the incessant wars between Denmark and Sweden, and the decline of the herring fisheries which robbed many small ports of their chief means of existence.

New towns were also founded in Norway. As an example we may quote Oslo. The first saw-mills at Oslo are mentioned in the 15th century, and at this time the ports in the bay began to develop. In 1618 the town was burned to the ground and Christian IV built a new city, which he called Christiania, near to the site of the old one, which was clustered around the fortified rock of the Akershus (see p. 440). Its growth was slow until after 1850, even though it became the capital of Norway in 1815 and has remained the capital ever since. In 1700 it had 5,000 inhabitants, in 1815 13,500, but even then it was far exceeded by Bergen.

Finland at this time belonged to Sweden both politically and culturally, and it also experienced a period of prosperity in which many new towns were founded by royal decree and favour. Above all, the port of Helsinki (Helsingfors) was founded on the Gulf of Finland midway between Åbo and Viborg. Its central position, farthest from Swedish and Russian influence, and its favourable location on the Gulf, where it had access to the sea all the year round, favoured its growth in the 19th century as the national and political capital of Finland. Other towns were founded by Gustavus Vasa, Gustavus Adolphus, Charles IX and, later in the 17th century, by Per Braha, the famous head of the Generalship of Finland, who was responsible for the foundation of Helsinki and a dozen other towns. Particularly significant was the group founded during the first years of the 17th century on the coast north of Åbo ; the best known is Uleåborg, founded in 1605. Between 1500 and 1800 twenty-three new towns came into being, two of which disappeared, so that at the opening of the 19th century there were twenty-eight towns, seven of them dating from the medieval period. In 1805 Åbo had 11,000 inhabitants, Helsinki only 4,000, Viborg 3,000 and Uleåborg 3,000.

In Poland, the first phase of town development, through the immigration of German settlers at the invitation of the Polish rulers before 1300, was continued by further foundations in the 14th and especially in the 17th and 18th centuries. Numerous small towns were established, in between the existing principal towns which lav it the chief nodal points, with their origins in most cases dating back to the early Middle Ages. The Polish rulers founded these country towns partly to settle new land and partly to foster new industries. In the western provinces, the textile industry and iron working were encouraged. Many German craftsmen, including large numbers of Protestants, were invited to settle. This migration continued into the 19th century, when growth was still further fostered in the western provinces by the infiltration of Germans into such new towns as Lodz and Czestochowa.

Many estimates have been made of the size and growth of the individual European cities during this period prior to the first census returns about 1800. The fact is that while there were no fundamental changes in the social and economic structure of society, the size of towns was affected not only by their ability to function as seats of industry and commerce for distant markets, but also by their operation as centres for the commercial organization of regional industries. It was also necessary for the town to draw its food supplies from its immediate environs. In Germany, the town was often politically separated from its surrounding area, as was the case, for example, with Cologne, an independent city surrounded by the territory of the bishopric of Cologne. Then again, the continuous growth of a city meant that it had to be supplied with immigrants, for the death rate was abnormally high. Disease and epidemics, as well as famine, often swept the cities like a scourge and reduced their populations. Only immigration could fill the gap. Finally, the guilds and the organization of the town council often fell into the hands of an unscrupulous oligarchy. This is no place to attempt an appraisal of these changes. But it is clear that while many of the chief cities barely maintained themselves, or even declined, others showed a steady but slight increase, while still others developed as active centres of trade and industry.

Among the ports, there was a shift of trade from Bruges, the great emporium in the 13th century, to Antwerp in the 14th century, when the Merchant Adventurers transferred their headquarters thither. This was followed by the shift of the headquarters of the Hanseatic League in the 16th century. The 16th century was the peak of Antwerp's prosperity as a centre of trade in woollen goods brought from England for distribution on the Continent. Bruges, with 29,000 inhabitants in 1584, was already a shadow of its former self, a *ville morte*, whereas Antwerp in 1560 had reached the 100,000 mark and was one of the largest cities in Europe.[1] The emergence of Holland as a new State, controlling the mouth of the Scheldt, spelt the ruin of Antwerp's trade, and it stagnated until the channel was internationalized by Napoleon in 1793, when the modern development of the city began. In 1750 it had 45,000 inhabitants. The decline of Antwerp was followed by the rise of Amsterdam and Hamburg. Hamburg was a relatively small port in the Middle Ages, having in 1400 about 10,000 inhabitants, but in the 17th and 18th centuries it became the leading Hanseatic port and the greatest city in Germany, when it took Antwerp's place in European trade. The Hamburg Bank was established in 1619 and the first Chamber of Commerce in 1665. Severe losses were suffered during the continental blockade of the Napoleonic wars, but during the 19th century growth was rapid. Amsterdam was still a small town in 1300, but by 1400 it was the chief commercial centre of Holland and handled the trade with Scandinavia and the coastal trade from Hamburg to Flanders. The coastal trade had hitherto been handled by Utrecht, which lay on the river Vecht, and could not be reached by the larger sea-going vessels that were being used for the sea-going trade. Amsterdam also grew with the decline of Antwerp in the 17th century, and acquired a new lease of life with the formation of the independent kingdom of the Netherlands in 1815. In 1800 it had 200,000 inhabitants and was one of the greatest cities in Europe.

The principal ports of France—Rouen, Nantes, Bordeaux, and Marseilles—made similar advances during the 17th and 18th centuries and profited especially from the trade with the New World and the East. Marseilles had 75,000 inhabitants in 1700 and over 100,000 at the end of the century. New ports were established by Richelieu and Colbert at Le Havre, Dunkirk, Brest, Lorient, La Rochelle, and Sète.[2]

The growth of the chief inland cities of France may be illustrated by several examples. A slow increase is general during the 17th and 18th centuries. Limoges had 14,000 inhabitants in 1698 and 22,000 in the latter half of the 18th century. Clermont-Ferrand had about 17,000 inhabitants in 1700, 20,000 in the mid 18th century, and 24,500 in 1791. Grenoble had 10,000 in 1600, 20,000 in 1700, and 29,000 in 1801.[3]

---

[1] A. Demangeon, *Belgique—Pays-Bas—Luxembourg*, Tome II, *Géographie Universelle*, 1927, p. 117.

[2] See below, Chapter 18, p. 430.

[3] These figures are taken from the studies of Perrier, Arbos and Blanchard, all of which are listed in the bibliography.

The case of Frankfurt may be taken as an example of the vicissitudes of the German city in this period.[1] Its great prosperity in the 16th century was due above all to the large influx of Walloon and Fleming religious refugees and to the commercial activities of the Jews, in virtue of which it became the greatest seat of banking and finance in Europe. In 1387 its population was 10,000, in 1440 it reached 8,000 as compared with 20,000 for Nuremberg at the same date ; it had 13,000 in 1578 and 17,000–18,000 in 1590. In 1600 it ranked as one of the chief cities of Europe. It did not reach the size of Cologne (37,000) or Strasbourg and Nuremberg (25,000), but was in the same group as Lübeck, Brunswick, Ulm, and Augsburg. During the 17th and 18th centuries, disease and famine, and the emigration of some of its religious refugees to the newly founded town of Hanau nearby, caused violent fluctuations in its fortunes. Gley's estimates are as follows : 1640, 18,000 ; 1700, 29,000 ; 1725, 30,000 (with 3,000 Jews) ; 1800, 35,000 (4,000 Jews). During the Thirty Years War there were huge losses through disease and famine, the deaths during the period 1635–40 amounting to no less than 15,000. In spite of this, there was a slow but general increase in numbers from 18,000 in 1590 to 35,000 in 1800.

(4) The Distribution of Towns in 1830

Fig. 67 shows the distribution of towns in 1830.[2] This distribution was the same as it had been for at least five centuries. Towns were evenly spread over the face of the land and served primarily as centres of industry, commerce and administration for their surrounding territories. The large cities were commercial centres with a great variety of industries catering for markets beyond the limits of the local market district. They were located always on the outstanding avenues of commerce— on the coasts in good harbours (a good tenth of all cities), and on navigable rivers, especially where these were crossed by important overland routes. With few exceptions the chief cities of to-day were the chief historic cities, and they were among the first towns to develop in the early Middle Ages. The numerous smaller towns, with under 20,000 people, appeared in the later Middle Ages (after 1200) and had less natural nodality. They were

---

[1] Estimates are taken from W. Gley, *Grundriss und Wachstum der Stadt Frankfurt-am-Main.*

[2] A. Welte, " Die Verstädterung Mittel- und Westeuropas im 1830–1930 ", *Geopolitik*, 1936, pp. 217–26 and pp. 351–8. Similar maps appear in H. Haufe, *Die Bevölkerung Europas*, showing towns with over 5,000 inhabitants.

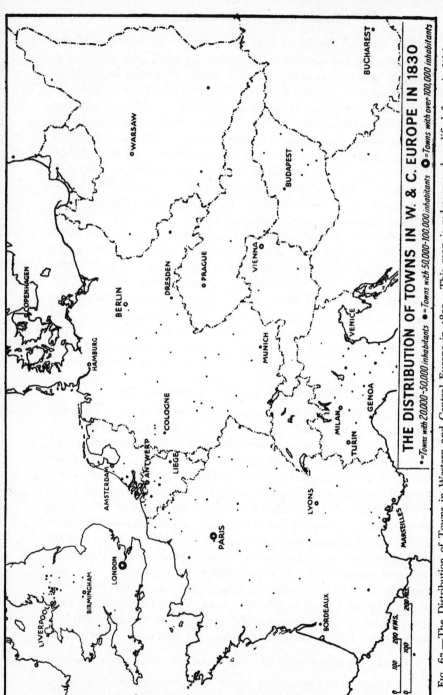

FIG. 67.—The Distribution of Towns in Western and Central Europe in 1830. This map is redrawn and modified from A. Welte, article in *Geopolitik*, 1936. Note :—London and Paris have over 500,000.

situated at the convergence of local routes and often on sites with natural defences—hilltops, spurs, river meanders—without adequate connection with the surrounding countryside for purposes of trade. Finally, the even spacing of many small towns on main routes obviously reflected their importance as stage or thoroughfare resting places (German, *Rastorte*) on the great overland routes. This is particularly true, for instance, of the small towns of Hesse, which grew on the skein of routes that ran from north to south between the Rhine Massif and the Thuringian highlands. It is also true of the remarkably evenly spaced towns along the routes of Thuringia, and of those along the routes of Franconia that in the later Middle Ages radiated from Nuremberg like the spokes of a wheel.

The even distribution of towns was especially characteristic of France. In Germany, on the other hand, the distribution was more uneven. This was due partly to physical and partly to historical causes. The political disintegration of Germany in the later Middle Ages led to the creation of many towns, far more than the countryside required as service centres. In the 17th and 18th centuries " Court cities " such as Mannheim, Karlsruhe, Kassel, Ansbach and Bayreuth, were established in considerable numbers. Ancient cities were located on the Rhine from source to mouth. Another series lay along the great west–east thoroughfares that linked Bruges, Cologne, Hanover, Brunswick, Magdeburg, Halle, Leipzig, Breslau, Cracow and Lwow. In southern Germany, along the network of highways that emerged in the later Middle Ages, each city shown on the map was an outstanding node of routes. Between these main routeways, however, there were relatively few large cities ; they are also markedly absent in the northern lowland of heath and marsh.

In three areas, however, there was a marked concentration of towns, and this is very pronounced if the smaller towns with 5,000 to 20,000 inhabitants are considered. These areas were northern Italy with southern France as an appendage to it, the Low Countries and central England. Northern Italy and Flanders were the earliest seats of urban medieval development and included some of the greatest medieval cities. Southern France was deeply impregnated with Roman civilization, and urban life revived early with the renewal of industry and commerce in the Middle Ages. The towns of central England were essentially the creation of the new Industrial Revolution that as yet had not touched the Continent.

There was a marked clustering of towns with 5,000 to 20,000 inhabitants in south-western Germany, in Württemberg, Baden and Bavaria, and in the northern foreland zone on the border of the central uplands of Germany. Many of these were medieval towns that grew to be small industrial and commercial centres during the industrial development of the mercantilist era. The great majority of towns appeared in the later Middle Ages, but these had under 5,000 inhabitants. Most of these later towns did not enjoy the importance of the earlier towns as route centres. In fact, they lie at local route junctions and were established to serve a local hinterland or to develop local mines. In addition, since many of them were founded primarily as fortresses or were sited next to castles, they were invariably placed on well-protected sites, such as a hilltop, a river meander or a spur, and were for that reason cut off from easy contact with the country around. Many small towns established at this time have failed to function as real centres of urban activity, for this and other reasons, and are to-day nothing more than villages. This is characteristic of many of the towns of southern Germany in Württemberg, where they have been described as " speculative failures " from the point of view of their medieval founders. There are many others, as for example the hilltop *bastide* settlements, in southern France.

A further point to be made here is that while on the Continent over wide areas, especially in Germany, *all* urban settlements were walled towns, the small unwalled market town was dominant in other areas, either by growth from village origins or, much more usually, by the deliberate act of foundation of a new market settlement or the concession to a village of the right to hold a market. Areas served almost entirely by such market settlements are Bavaria south of the Danube, much of north-western Germany, northern France, and the lowland zone of England. Indeed, England is pre-eminently the country of this type of settlement, which the Englishman takes for granted, but which is, in fact, a very distinctive settlement form.

CHAPTER 16

THE MEDIEVAL TOWN (*c.* A.D. 1000–1500)

(1) THE FORMATION OF THE MEDIEVAL TOWN

In the growth of the west European city, as illustrated in our studies in Part I of this book, there have been three main phases of development, the Medieval, from about 1000 to 1500 ; the Renaissance and the Baroque, which, when combined, extend from about 1500 to the turn of the 19th century ; and the Modern. Each of these phases is evident in all towns that have had a continuous growth from their medieval origins. Above all, the rapid growth of the modern era has transformed the city of the past and caused it to extend well beyond the historic nucleus. We shall first consider briefly the general character of urban growth in each of these phases so as to understand the city as it stands to-day. There are two aspects of this morphological approach to the study of the urban habitat, plan and build. Though these, in fact, are inseparably interrelated, we shall deal in this chapter with the plan, and in the next with the build.

(a) *Site* ✓

Every medieval settlement rose from small beginnings, and consisted therefore, in the first place, of a mere dozen or more hutments that were, throughout the whole of western Europe, built of timber and were without doubt like those of the country folk. These beginnings, from the topographic point of view, appeared directly the place became a permanent settlement. Such a settlement had to crystallize at a particular spot, and it undoubtedly grew on a routeway, where it was in touch with the surrounding and outside world. Its nucleus of crystallization may be a site that had already been used by men for temporary assembly : for trade, religious worship, defence and refuge or government. But topographically the first fixed settlement clustered around a permanent monument, such as a stronghold, a castle, a church or cathedral, or, when community life had evolved, on a routeway or around a market-place, built at the convergence of two or more routeways. In some such way a cluster of permanent buildings emerged out of a temporary seat of settlement. The larger such a settlement grew, the more the houses and public buildings it would require and the more complicated would be the circumstances and process of its topographic expansion. While it is often difficult to detect the form of the nuclear settlement in a big town, the numerous villages and small towns in the countryside, some of them of early, others of later, medieval origin, reveal more clearly what the initial settlements of the big towns were probably like.

The house is the unit of settlement, and the urban settlement is primarily a compact group of contiguous units so arranged as to facilitate the activities of the occupants in their relations with each other. This means that the houses, if not contiguous, are close to each other, and spaces called streets are needed for pedestrian and vehicular traffic, as well as places for public concourse and communal institutions. It also follows that at certain periods and in certain areas, under varying conditions, protection from the outside world is needed. This last need was met in the earliest settlements by their attachment, like parasites, to an existing stronghold, although these settlements eventually were surrounded by their own walls. The new towns, that were founded in the later Middle Ages, were almost invariably surrounded by a wall, so that each was, in effect, a fortress in itself.

Starting from these basic assumptions, there are three possible ways in which these units may be articulated in relation to each other and to the site on which they are built. They may be utterly irregular, each house being erected as an independent unit, the streets emerging from pre-existing trackways, which are adjusted to the terrain along the lines of least resistance. Or the units may be arranged in regular series alongside an existing or designed axis, be it a " street " or a " canal " or a " river ". Theoretically, further growth from such an axis may proceed lengthwise at each end of the axis. But since compactness is a primary need of such a settlement, lateral growth will be the normal mode of growth. Narrow alleys or slightly wider living streets will run approximately at right angles to the main axis to form what may be called a rib pattern. A second main thoroughfare may run parallel to the main axis and a few transverse streets interconnect the two to form a parallel pattern. If shaped to the walls or the slopes of a hill site, an elliptical street pattern may develop. Indeed, a transverse axis may intersect the main axis approximately at right angles to form two intersecting rib patterns. In this way an approximate grid arrangement is obtained, with a rectilinear pattern of streets of varying width and spaced at varying intervals. This, however, should not be confused with the grid plan. This is a pattern of equally spaced streets, each of equal width, with houses facing on each street, and with a central block reserved for the market-place. Thus, by the natural growth of house units along existing trackways, there develop plans that may be described as rib, parallel street, elliptical, intersecting rib plans, and grid plans as shown on Fig. 68. All these plans develop from a single route axis. Examples from German towns are shown on Figs. 70 and 71.

There is a third possible arrangement of house units in relation to the streets. The houses may be grouped around a nucleus—an open space, an institution such as a cathedral, church, abbey, castle, or public monument (Fig. 69). Houses and streets encircle this central dominant. There is also a tendency for the streets, and houses alongside them, to radiate outwards from such a central dominant. In this way two trends are apparent in such growth, concentric and radial. Hence the term radial-concentric. This is a frequent result of natural growth among medieval towns. It was not adopted as a planned lay-out in Europe until the 16th century, and then only occasionally in the establishment of a few fortress towns. It became a permanent feature of planning in the Baroque era as the crescent and as the star-shaped focal point in large cities. A rectangular net in combination with the crescent or diagonal are main features of modern urban lay-outs.

The growth of such settlement patterns may be either natural, gradual, unplanned growth; or planned, controlled growth, and both these modes may appear at different dates or within the same pattern. The irregular plan is never adopted as a controlled plan. The rectangular system appears as both a natural and a planned growth; the latter being the dominant system of planning in all the great eras of town development. The radial-concentric system was a natural and frequent form of growth in the Middle Ages, but was not adopted as a planned form in western Europe until the 16th century. The development of these planning ideas may be studied chronologically in the same town or from one town to another. Moreover, in the great planning eras, and not least in the Middle Ages, planning ideas became more or less fixed as stereotyped culture forms, and the same ideas in detailed planning practice or in the foundation of complete town plans were repeated again and again in the same areas. In this way we are able to discern not merely recurring systems of urban

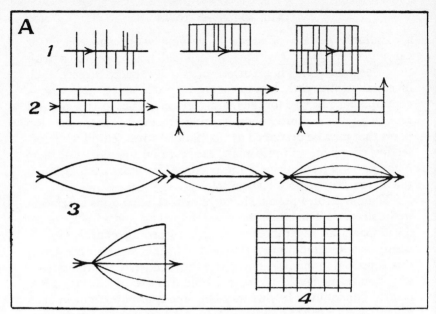

A. Medieval Urban Street Patterns developed on a Route Axis. 1. Rib patterns. 2. Parallel street patterns. 3. Spindle or Elliptical patterns. 4. Grid patterns.

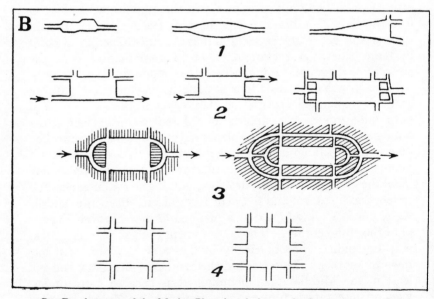

B. Development of the Market-Place in relation to the Route Axis. 1. Street markets. 2. Rectangular or Long Markets (*Längsmärkte*) between two parallel axes. 3. Rectangular or Long Markets in a Spindle pattern. 4. The Square Market-Place in a Grid pattern.

Fig. 68.—The Plan of the Medieval Town, showing the relation of the Street Plan and Market-Place.

plan, but also families of towns which in plan and build have the same basic features, representing not merely the needs of the type of community they served, but also the ideas and traditions of the planners who designed them.

The formation of the urban plan, however, is not merely the

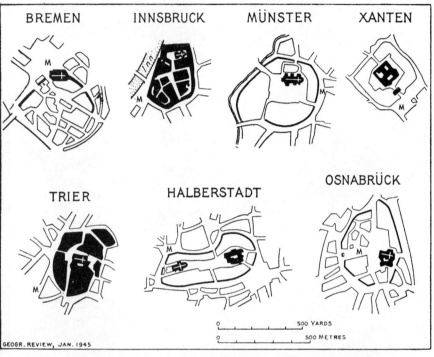

FIG. 69.—Early Medieval Towns in the German Lands, showing the relation of the Stronghold Nucleus and the Market-Place. (Scale, 1 : 20,000.)

Each of these towns began at an outstanding nodal point (usually a river crossing of a land route). The nucleus of settlement is a fortified ecclesiastical stronghold, outside which the first market settlement was founded, and from which later extension was determined by historical and terrain factors. The stronghold is shown in black, either solid block to show the nucleus, or as a heavy line to indicate the wall that enclosed the nucleus.

(*By kind permission of the American Geographical Society.*)

result of a process of juxtaposition of houses on a street system, whether by natural or planned growth, although this indeed is the lowest form of urban " planning " and has characterized much of the growth of the last hundred and fifty years. The composition of the urban plan is also determined by the configuration of the site, and above all by the origin, the functions and the shape

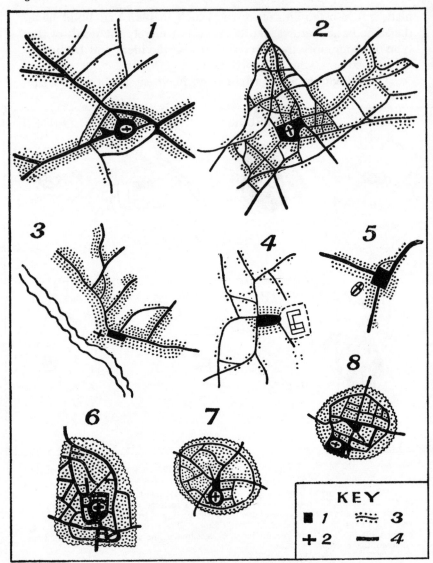

FIG. 70.—Radial Plans in the German Towns.

The small country town (*Flecken*) grew gradually, house by house, like the irregular clustered village. Often, indeed, it grew from such a village and exhibits the same variety of natural forms. There are many examples in the heathlands of north Germany. But church and castle are more important as nuclei of growth. A church as centre with an open space around it and enclosed by an oval-shaped street is often the nucleus of irregular radial growth (e.g. Fig. 1, St. Tönits near Krefeld). Most unplanned country towns do not have a planned market-place; the market is held on a street or on the church place, as in Fig. 1. In Fig. 2 (Meldorf in Dithmarschen), the market-place is enlarged with a rectangular shape and is the of the nucleus of the settlement, and further by the ideas of planning, both practical and æsthetic, which prevailed at the time it came into being and at the various stages of its growth—in other words, by the functions and organization of the community. The plan of the medieval town was closely adjusted to the site. In the history of urbanism, this is one of its most distinctive features. Particularly was this the case when a settlement evolved slowly. It invariably lay on land free from flooding or above marsh level, for the great majority of towns lay on the banks of rivers. Walls were adjusted to the relief, and were sometimes built along the edges of the steep slopes of a hill or promontory, sometimes enclosed land that was slightly raised above marsh or flood level, and sometimes they were confined to one easy exit from a promontory formed by a deeply entrenched meander (Poitiers). Streets were adjusted to the relief, and were articulated along the most gradual slopes (along the contours) so as to ensure the greatest ease of building and movement. But the plan of the medieval town—that is, the articulation of its streets, and the siting of its public buildings and monuments—was also adjusted to the direction and position of its main routes, its main central market-place, or its initial nucleus—cathedral, abbey or stronghold. Growth from such a nucleus may have proceeded by gradual development from house to house along existing track-ways, or by planned extension along streets that, at any rate in part at the centre, were laid down in advance with the blocks

---

centre of an irregular net of streets. As a development from the simple street market the plan of Kettwig on the Ruhr (Fig. 3) shows a planned market-place adjacent to a main route, with the growth of the street net on the ground away from the river floor. Figs. 4 and 5 are simple planned country towns, the first (Ebersberg near Munich) being very characteristic of the small town in old Bavaria. Buildings face the market-place and extension from it, as shown in this example, is unusual. The adjacent building is an initial nucleus, a monastery. Fig. 5 shows a planned rectangular market (Hartenstein in Erzgebirge) that is frequent, and peculiar (according to Martiny) in north-eastern Germany. It is a frequent form, however, in Belgium, as Deventer's maps show, and is clearly an urban " prototype " in that country. Fig. 6, Dambach in Alsace, shows a rare type that evolves like a *Haufendorf*, with an irregular plan, without any focus. The type is limited to western Germany and is found especially in the Rhinelands. Many other larger towns, like Soest, with plans at first glance like this, have in fact grown radially from a nucleus. Irregular radial growth from a nucleus is found mainly in the same area as the west German *Haufendorf*, especially in Westphalia (Halberstadt, Höxter, Münster, and Soest). Fig. 7 (Haltern) shows an irregular radial plan of unplanned growth, and it stands in contrast to the more regular radial plan of Fig. 8 (Iserlohn). In each, the market-place is at the centre of the chief road junction. Haltern grew from one of the oldest church centres of the Münsterland and the church is the focus of its plan and the market-place is adjacent to it. This is the prototype of the growth around the cathedral stronghold (Münster). Fig. 8 (Iserlohn) shows a type in which fairly regularly rectilinear growth has taken place from the main route axes.

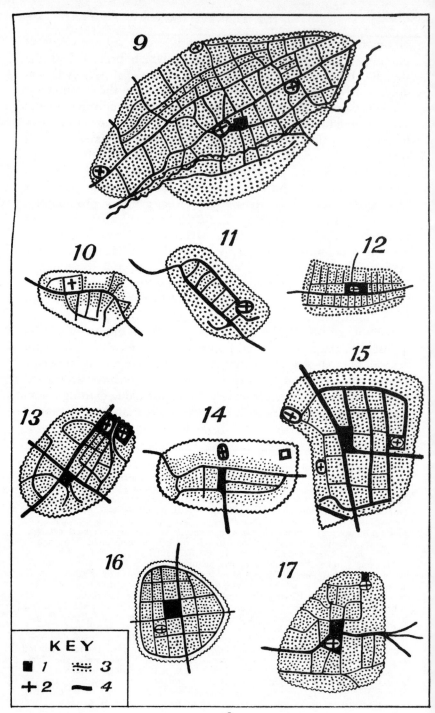

subdivided into building lots. In every case, the main routes, however, formed the skeleton of the plan and these, often of ancient date, once fixed by a river crossing or by a particular adjustment to local terrain—following a ridge of higher land or avoiding a marsh—became axes of growth for the expanding town. Such adjustments are especially clear in the small town. The planned town began as a settlement with elementary urban privileges, but if it was an active centre or one in which the founder took a particular interest, it soon acquired full town status. The planned settlement may have been confined to a market and one or two streets or blocks, and growth from this nucleus proceeded more gradually. In many cases it did not grow at all, and the amorphous plan we see to-day is evidence of an enterprise that misfired. In the case of settlements that were laid out in their entirety, as in the towns of eastern Germany, the whole street plan and the enclosing wall were demarcated at the outset. In these cases the nucleus in which the first buildings were erected lay around the market-place, and growth took place outwards towards the walls.

The kind of site selected for the establishment of an urban settlement, or on which such a settlement gradually evolved, has depended throughout history on the primary functions of the settlement. From this point of view, these functions may be

---

FIG. 71.—Axial and Grid Plans in the German Towns.

Fig. 10 shows the simplest type, that lies along a through main route with side streets, to form a rib plan (Kienzhein near Kaisersberg). This normal mode of growth, house by house, along existing trackways from such a route axis, gives rise to parallel streets and interconnecting streets, as at Goslar (Fig. 9). Regularity of direction and spacing of streets in such a plan indicate controlled growth. Figs. 11 and 12 show such planned forms—11, a street market town (Mühldorf on the Inn) and 12, a rib plan with rectangular market and rib pattern (Heidelberg). Fig. 11 is characteristic of both country markets and towns in Bavaria, but appears elsewhere. The intersection of two rib plans (usually lacking a market-place) is found in Fig. 13 (Isny) and this is peculiar to south-western Germany. The parallel street plan (*Längsanlage*) has wide, main, parallel streets, narrow interconnecting streets at right-angles to these, and buildings front on the parallel axes. The market-place may lie parallel, and adjacent to, the main axis (*Längsmarkt*, as at Leipzig, Fig. 15) or is elongated at right-angles to the main axis (*Quermarkt*, as at Stadthagen, Fig. 14). A kind of approximate grid plan may emerge by normal growth from the parallel street plan. It may also be planned as an entity, as at Koslin (Fig. 16), which is the "normal type" (*Kolonialstadt*) in the eastern colonized lands. This plan shows a combination of rectangular blocks and intersecting streets of equal width and a central rectangular market-place. Attempts at the lay-out of a grid plan may be tentative and modified through adjustment to existing form-elements and to terrain walls, etc. Thus, at Naumburg (Fig. 17), the plan is adjusted to a through main route from east to west and the cathedral stronghold, that lies to the north.

Key to Figs. 70 and 71— : 1. market-place. 2. church. 3. houses and streets. 4. main routes.

regarded as politico-cultural and economic. The religious institution or the stronghold seeks the prominent hill site or the raised hill or promontory surrounded by sea, river or marsh, which dominates the surrounding countryside and has natural defences. The economic community needs contact with the main routes and space in which its habitat may expand, and develops best on sites that are on lower-lying, flatter land, at places where overland routeways converge. The bridgehead or a navigable waterway on gently sloping ground is a particularly favoured urban site in western Europe. These two primary functions, politico-cultural and economic, are eventually combined in one settlement in a hilltop and a valley-side settlement respectively. In the older Greek city, the Acropolis lies on the hilltop and the town on its lower slopes. In the Greek colonial city, the site is a promontory. The combination is represented in western Europe by the cathedral or secular stronghold—or both—situated on a hill or raised ground, and the urban community that lies at its feet on the lower ground in contact with the routeways. Thus, in France and Belgium, we have the *Haute-Ville* and *Basse-Ville*, in Germany, *Bergstadt* and *Talstadt*, or *Oberstadt* and *Unterstadt*. In the later Middle Ages it is represented by the feudal castle situated on an isolated site with good natural defences and the small town under the shelter of its walls. The fully grown, independent urban community, instead of being dependent on the stronghold, took care of its own defence and erected and maintained its own walls ; in smaller towns this was often the task of the lord or his local representative. In the modern era, since the 16th century, with the exception of those places that are situated at important strategic situations, the surrounding wall is no longer necessary and military protection is the duty of the State. Even in the Middle Ages the existence of a strong State control or of geographical isolation likewise made it unnecessary to build walls round urban settlements, and often the walls early fell into decay. This was the case in England, and on the Continent there are areas, such as Bavaria and the Tyrol, in which urban settlements were granted the elementary privileges of self-government but were not walled ; in other words, they remained unwalled market settlements.

(b) Plan

We may now enquire as to the nature of the first nucleus, the *element of fixation*, of the medieval town. Here we are concerned with four possibilities—a politico-cultural or pre-urban nucleus, a market settlement, a village, or a new planned town.

(i) *Pre-Urban Nucleus : The Stronghold.* The first nucleus of settlement in many medieval towns was not an economic but a politico-cultural settlement, that emerged as a fixed settlement after a long period of periodical occupation at times of communal assembly of tribal groups for purposes of trade, religion, or the administration of justice. The early medieval town clustered in its beginning around a secular or an ecclesiastical stronghold. This was also true of many towns in eastern Germany and east central Europe, where a phase of conquest preceded the settlement of craftsmen and traders. The cathedral and its precinct, often inside the Gallo-Roman walls, remains to this day as the *cité*, but in many other cases, when the town became a self-governing community, the territory of the old secular stronghold passed to its ownership, and the old buildings and walls were demolished and the land subdivided among the burgesses. In many towns the existence of this pre-urban nucleus is evident from the irregularity of the blocks and the shape of the whole, and sometimes by the survival of a part of the old stronghold (e.g. Ghent, Bruges). This nucleus is the morphological equivalent of the small enclosed settlements which occur in southern France and in parts of western Germany as illustrated on Fig. 69. It appears as a distinct oval-shaped nucleus in the urban complex that grew around it.

Such a nucleus was the point of topographic origin of the earliest medieval towns in Gaul, the Rhineland and western Germany, and to their development we shall return in the next chapter. Suffice it to indicate here that in these towns, as is well illustrated by those between the Loire and the Rhine, there were four stages of topographic development. Settlement began with the pre-urban nucleus. Then, the mercantile settlement clustered around it and became the dynamic factor in the origin and growth of the truly urban community, with its focus in the market-place. The first wall surrounded this settlement, and the later phases in its expansion were reflected in the construction of walls to embrace outlying suburbs and parishes.

(ii) *Market Settlement.* The great majority of the medieval towns had their topographic and constitutional origins in a market settlement, that had elementary privileges of self-government. These settlements were similar in character to the small market towns that appear in the countryside to-day and had their origins at the same time. We have already drawn attention to the fact that the city as a king among towns is the head of a hierarchy of settlements which are urban in character and are in various degrees its smaller counterparts. This applies to both function and form. There is a marked distinction in form as well as in function and status between the village and the town and the settlement intermediate between these two. This last is by far the commonest type of urban settlement in England. Here the so-called *market town* has been for centuries an unwalled urban settlement, with its focus in a market-place that lies in the centre of the settlement, adjacent to the parish church, or, occasionally in England (more frequently in Wales and Scotland), immediately outside the gate of the medieval castle. Such market settlements vary considerably from one area to another according to the general character of urban life in the area and its historical development. The really remarkable thing, however, which cannot be too strongly emphasized, is that these settlements have still essentially the same features of function, lay-out and size, as they had in the Middle Ages when they had their origin. The name given to this type of intermediate rural-urban settlement on the Continent is *bourg* in France and *Flecken* or *Marktstadt* in Germany. A large proportion of its people are engaged in trade and crafts, business and the professions, but it may also contain a fair number of farm workers and farmhouses. Historically, it has a lower legal status than the town. Such settlements were originally endowed with elementary privileges of self-government in the Middle Ages. This was the normal beginning of a founded town, to which full town law was later granted, together with the right to build a wall. The grant of town law was often followed by the extension of the built-up area to house new settlers. Morphologically, the market settlement is distinct from the town in that it is unwalled and that it normally has a central market-place, though this is not always the case, as in the vine-growing areas of the Rhine valley, for instance, where such semi-urban large villages enjoy this intermediate status. Such settlements are by no means of uniform distribution. They are especially characteristic of England, northern France, and the Low Countries. They are relatively rare in Germany, where almost all the original market settlements became towns in the legal and topographical sense. The market settlement became characteristic in only three areas in Germany, in the Northern Lowlands, the Bavarian plateau and the Alps. This fact is to be ascribed, in part, to the scanty population in the German areas that required very small service centres, and in part to the existence of a single strong political control, so that the construction of walls around the market settlements, that involved much labour and expense, was neither necessary nor desirable.

The market towns reached their medieval status in various ways. Some were the result of natural growth from a village nucleus, with streets radiating irregularly from a central place located outside the church or outside the gate of a castle. Some had planned quadrangular markets ; the majority had a street or widened street market, though here again there are regional variations. The castle settlement was invariably in the first place parasitic on the castle, according to the usual relationship of feudal economy, and the market settlement was established next to it as a distinct entity.

Planned market settlements also occur. The market-place might be a planned nucleus around which the settlement grew along two or more radiating streets. The street market, as a planned form, is especially characteristic of Bavaria and Styria, whereas the rectangular market, with several radiating streets, is the characteristic form in north-western Germany, the Low Countries and England. Some German towns grew from such settlements (*Flecken*) by the reception of town law and the building of a wall around them, as in north-west Germany. But more usually the grant of town law in Germany was accompanied by an extension of the existing settlement.

(iii) *Village.* A third possible mode of town development is for a village to be given town liberties and enclosed by a wall. Quite apart from the constitutional complexities of this question, it is clear that on the Continent such a development was rare, particularly in the German lands. A rural community was often gradually transformed by engaging in trade and crafts, by a lord taking up residence in it, or by the extension to it of some particular privileges, and it might eventually acquire town law. This seems to have often been the case in France and England. But this was a gradual process. It was rare indeed for a truly rural village (that is, a community of farmers) suddenly to be endowed by a lord with full town liberties and to be enclosed forthwith by a wall. It was much more usual for a new settlement to be dove-tailed on to the existing village and for the whole settlement to be walled. Indeed, in Germany, and also in France, the town was often established on *terra nova* and the farmers of the adjacent villages were attracted to it as settlers, so that the villages as settlements completely disappeared (*Wustungsdörfer*) although the farmers often continued to till their lands after they were acquired by the town.   There are, however, frequent instances of a village being granted the elementary privileges of market law, whereby it became a market town with a market-place as described in the previous paragraphs.

There seem to be two chief ways in which the plans of rural and urban settlement are interrelated.   First, through the gradual growth of the village to a market town, and then its ultimate endowment with full town law.   This intermediate stage is the market settlement (*Flecken*).   Secondly, the plan of the villages in an area may have been deliberately adapted and modified by the planners for the lay-out of the new towns.   Thus, Martiny explains the forms of many towns in eastern Germany by the adaptation of the *Angerdorf* in the lay-out of the market-place in the colonial towns, for both villages and towns, often in the same district, were laid out and their settlers recruited by one and the same person, who was called a *Locator*.   This adaptation seems to have been effected by broadening the *Anger*, and by constructing buildings along its centre with two flanking streets, which met at either extremity of the place at the two gates (Fig, 68 B).   Thus, from the morphological point of view it will be evident that there is in fact no clear-cut distinction between the plans of village, market settlement and town in the same area, since they are all associated with similar conditions of land settlement.   The principal differences arise from contrasts in function which leave their imprint upon the character of the whole settlement.

Given the nucleus of settlement, the process of growth is one of expansion from it.   Expansion took place in various ways. Many towns emerged by steady natural growth or piecemeal " planning " from a single nucleus, others by the coalescence of several units that were founded or grew up at different periods and under different circumstances.   In the early towns north of the Alps, monastery, church, Roman camp, and riverside merchants' colony were gradually welded into one community.   The medium of the coalescence, however, was the nascent urban community of merchants and craftsmen, and its focus was a market-place on one or more routes.   This was the active, growing element, and the smaller dying and stagnant elements were swallowed up by the extension of houses and streets.   In all towns, growth took place at different stages, and the plan of each stage is often quite distinct from the others.   In the larger towns, the phases of extension were marked by the successive fortifications. Each section usually formed a separate parish with its own church, and each was ultimately embraced by an extension of the town wall, but retained its individuality as a parish with its life centred on its church as a dominant community centre.

There was segregation of activities and people, though necessarily on a small scale, owing to the small size of the town, and to the need for home and workshop to be near to each other or even in the same building with master and apprentices living under a single roof. There was segregation of the guilds in particular streets, as is evidenced to this day by the survival of street names and of certain localized industries, such as leather dressing and fulling along the riverside. Merchants' buildings clustered around the market-place. Indeed, in the case of the founded towns, as at Lübeck, the merchants' lots were the first to be marked out on the market-place, and these same merchants controlled the government as a privileged class. Monasteries and hospices, on the other hand, appeared on the outskirts of the town, by the roadside, but usually within the walls. Many settlements were established adjacent to each other, each with its own wall and its own legal constitution. Several nuclei of settlement were common in the early medieval towns of France, and they long remained separate. In Germany, it was the custom to establish such settlements adjacent to each other, especially in north-eastern Germany. Each section of the whole settlement, be it parish, *Vorstadt*, *Faubourg*, or separate town, was a small social unit, with its centre in the church or market-place or both. The population of any such unit rarely exceeded 10,000 and in the great majority of cases was well under 2,500. All social classes were represented in the community which was a microcosm of medieval society.

(c) Street and Block

The structure of the medieval urban habitat, with which in this chapter we are primarily concerned, mirrored medieval ideas and institutions, and these were dominated by the church and the market-place. Parish and diocese became the " fundamental political divisions of society " ; the central cathedral and the more neighbourly parish churches were principal forces in the daily life of the townsfolk. The guild was a second medium of corporate life, and it was in many ways a religious fraternity. Craft guild, merchants' guild, and municipality were centred in the market-place—except that craft guilds were clustered on streets where workshops and masters and journeymen could be more effectively organized. The market-place and the church, both in a central position, were the centre of town life, fulfilling the functions of Agora, Acropolis and Amphitheatre in one. Here was the stage on which were enacted the daily drama of buying and selling, religious pageant, tournament, and procession. Life in the town was protected, militarily, economically and legally. The wall separated the townsman from the outside world. Church and guilds cared for the social needs of the people. The town was not normally a congested unhealthy environment, as is so often supposed. Houses had their gardens. Alms-houses, hospitals, monasteries and churches cared for social and religious needs. Coulton reckons that there was one parish church for every 100 families—a very important fact to be borne in mind when discussing the idea of the " neighbourhood unit ". " This decentralization of the essential social functions of the city not merely prevented overcrowding and needless circulation : it kept the whole town in scale." [1]

The building lot is the cell of the town, and is closely related to the street pattern. In the early towns of natural growth irregularity of street plan is reflected in the irregularity of block and in the orientation of the houses in relation both to the street and to the adjacent houses. There is often a curved belt of lots surrounding the old cultural dominant, and an irregular arrangement of building lots reveals the site of the old stronghold that has long been replaced by houses. In all the axial and grid plans, on the other hand, the rectangular lot and block are characteristic, and the blocks attain increasing symmetry of composition with the development of the grid plan. The rib patterns have narrow side streets and elongated blocks running back from the main street and a few side streets on which the houses have their frontages. In the parallel and elliptical plans the narrow cross streets are few, and the blocks are consequently elongated back from the main thoroughfare on to which the houses front. In the rib plan the blocks have housing frontage on one or two sides only. In the fully developed grid the block is evenly subdivided and there are house frontages on all four sides. Related to this building arrangement are the main thoroughfares which are normally about 6 to 8 metres wide, the living streets (*Wohnstrassen*) 2 to 3 metres wide, and narrow alleys that cut through the blocks. With the market-place as the generating centre of the

[1] Lewis Mumford, *Culture of Cities*, p. 55.

plan, the blocks are continued to the edge of the walls, which themselves may be of the same rectangular shape as the market-place, or the blocks and streets are truncated by walls oval in shape. More frequently the block composition is a compromise, and there appears a belt of long curved blocks with irregular streets adjacent to, and adapted to the lie of, the walls. The entire developmental history of the town plan is a struggle between these two plans, straight and curved, angular and round, in order to get a convenient division of blocks and suitably-shaped building lots.

The arrangement of the living streets thus affects the whole build and aspect of the town, since houses have their frontages on these streets and the arrangement of lots thus depends on the street pattern. This question of the house as an element in the build of the town will be discussed in the next section.

(2) THE MEDIEVAL HOUSE

The study of the house in relation to its urban milieu may be approached from a threefold angle, the influence of historical events on the house, the relation of population to the house, and the structure of the house itself.

The fortunes of the town, restricted within its walls, affect the character and development of its houses. In Rouen for example, as studied by Quenedy, there were three phases of prosperity, the 13th century, the second half of the 15th and first half of the 16th centuries, and the 18th century. Each was a period of active building. The disappearance from the town of agriculture, which was an imporant occupation in the 13th century, as commerce and industry grew, caused changes in house structure and in-creased congestion of building space in the centre. The first streets appeared when the settlement was primarily agricultural. The houses were irregularly disposed in relation to each other and the streets were narrow and winding, so that as urban life increased they were ill-adapted to the new needs. Similarly they lacked market-places and public squares. Streets had to be widened, house frontages straightened, and building regulations introduced so as to prevent buildings encroaching on the public thoroughfare on the ground level, and to prevent the building-over of the street above, since this prevented the movement of traffic and kept out the light. Building encroachments on the public thoroughfare were forbidden throughout France by royal decree by edicts dated 1496 and 1607. In Rouen they were prohibited by the town council in 1520. Proximity of buildings and the need for the upkeep of streets early led to the development of public services. At Rouen there are examples of forced duties in the 13th century. Buildings erected in gardens behind the main buildings in the 16th to the 18th centuries often led to rights of way. Public services which received attention were the maintenance of streets, paving (at the expense of the inhabitants), clearance of street refuse, lighting of the streets, first cared for by the inhabitants and later by the town council, provision of water, sewage disposal, the regulation of markets, and the localization of crafts in particular streets.

The study of population raises the fundamental question of the relation between the number of inhabitants and the building. The number of households (*feux*) rather than the number of inhabitants is the figure given in early historical records, and it is this figure that is of special importance in studying the historic town. The dwelling unit had a fairly standardized minimum number of rooms—a work room, a general living-room (these two often combined), a kitchen, a store room and several bedrooms. Though varying as between rich families and poor, this arrangement was proportional to the number of households rather than to that of the inhabitants of a town. The medieval house seems to have been in general a single-family house, so that the number of households in general was the same as the number of houses.

The density of households (or houses) is an important aspect of town life. It is expressed by the number of households per unit of area. Areas can be calculated from town plans to which accessible statistics apply, such as parishes, streets or quarters, and the densities then calculated. At Rouen, Caudebec, Troyes, Annecy, Hyères and Colmar, the density oscillated around 50 households per hectare in the later Middle Ages down to the middle of the 17th century, then rose in the 18th century when it reached a maximum of 70 to 90 households per hectare. Conditions were thus fairly uniform in these varied towns in all parts of France, and densities were fairly constant, following the same general progression to the 18th century.

The population of the suburbs or *faubourgs* long remained very small in comparison with the central walled town. At Rouen in the 13th century it was 9 per cent. of the whole and was the same in 1700 ; then it rose gradually to about 14 per cent. in 1762 and 48 per cent. in 1821. At Troyes it was 12 per cent. in 1500 and

19 per cent. in 1774. Fear of attack in times of civil war and the attraction of the privileges of living in the town accounted for this. It was after the end of the 18th century that building expanded beyond the town walls and spread to the suburbs. But the wall was not always a rigid barrier as is generally supposed. At Rouen, for example, the first wall, that dated from the third century, soon had settlements outside it. A second wall was built in the 12th century and then destroyed at the beginning of the 13th for the purpose of enclosing outlying suburbs. These suburbs had existed for a long time, as indicated by the number of parishes in the 12th century which lay outside the first wall. But the apparent uniformity of population density for the town as a whole is misleading, as is indicated by figures, when available, for districts within it. Building did not always spread uniformly to the town walls and produce a uniform density and a uniform degree of congestion, as we are often led to believe. Three zones with separate densities have been determined for the 13th century in Rouen, and of these one had a markedly high density, reaching 66 households to the hectare, as compared with an adjacent zone with only 23 households per hectare. In 1707 the densities in the same two zones were 117 and 30 respectively.

It is often stated that the walls were the chief reasons for the growing congestion of the medieval town. This explanation is too simple, for there were other contributory factors in the city itself. Several other factors help to explain the density of households in the historic city. The walls certainly prevented expansion, but houses were not evenly distributed within them. Religious orders on the outskirts and public buildings in the centre took up a large area of the town after the 15th century. At Rouen between 1589 and 1658 ten religious communities were established. Two other factors were the growth of population (by natural increase and immigration) and the development of commerce. The development of commerce in the centre of the town seems to have been the main factor which accounted for the high densities no less than in the modern city, for it is precisely in the zones of highest density, in the special cases studied by Quenedy, that the greatest concentration of craftsmen and traders is evident.

Finally, the increase in the number of storeys of the town house that took place after the end of the Middle Ages was not simply due to congestion of space. It resulted largely from a change in social habits which was marked by the dedication of rooms to special purposes and the allocation of one room to one person instead of the communal living that had prevailed in the Middle Ages. Add to this the increased demands for workshops, warehouses and shops, and we have the main reasons for the construction of buildings with three, four and five storeys in Rouen and other towns throughout western Europe in the 17th and 18th centuries.

The structure of the house will now be considered, with special reference to France and Germany. Two general points may be emphasized here. The house has a rectangular base with four outside walls and a roof. The increasing size of the building and the increasing complexity of its interior structure called for expansion in either width or depth or both, the last giving rise in the 17th and 18th centuries to a cubical detached building (*la maison à l'angle*). The medieval house was usually built in depth with a narrow gable-end facing the street, and with a frontage of one or two windows. With a greater frontage than this, however, the house was built in width, with the gable-end at right angles to the street front and the eaves parallel to it. Alternatively, the house might be built on a square base. Thus, in the house-building of the Baroque period the so-called eaves-house, with the eaves running parallel to the street frontage, or the mansard roof on a square structure, became the rule. A second main feature was the persistence of the contrast in roof type between northern and southern France. This latter point may be expanded (Fig. 83, p. 358).

The traditional building of the Midi has a gently sloping roof and a portico, both of which can be traced back to the buildings of the Roman villa and town. The traditional building of the Nord has a steep roof, the style evidently being derived from that introduced by the Benedictine monks in the 11th and 12th centuries, as is shown by the remains of their monastic buildings, especially of their old barns (*granges*). The flat roof is particularly adapted to the curved or hollow tile or the *tuile romaine*. Its northern limit approximates to that of the dialect of southern France known as the *langue d'oc* which has close Latin affinities, and its area to that which until the end of the *ancien régime* employed the Roman written law (*droit écrit*). These coincident distributions reflect the close association of this method of building with Roman civilization. This derivation is revealed by the remarkable similarity between extant old houses in the Midi and ancient reproductions of villas of the Roman days. The northern limit of the flat roof is a cultural and not a climatic one. It is found, for example, in the wet areas of the Vendée and the Basque country, and it occurs in the buildings of Lorraine, where it probably spread northwards along the Roman highways and was retained owing to the relative isolation of the district from the Gothic area of the Paris lowland and from the German lands to the east in the Rhineland. In northern France, the steep gable with a thatched roof was widely adopted| in the Middle Ages, although it is now usually covered with flat tiles (*tuile plate*) as in the Île de France, Normandy, Burgundy, Champagne ; or with slate, as in the Loire lands, Brittany, Cotentin and Caux. The mansard roof, introduced in the 17th century by a French architect of that name, is also covered with flat tiles or slates, and is found especially in the northern half of the country, where it gives special character to some of the small towns of Burgundy and to others in the east that were rebuilt during this period after destruction in war.[1]

The building materials of the walls, the main structural part of the house, differ from region to region, in town and country alike. Thus the main area of brick building in Flanders scarcely crosses the northern frontier of France. The chief French brick-building region is in the middle Garonne lowland, where the cities of Toulouse and Albi are the outstanding representatives. Dressed stone, on the other hand, especially limestone, appears as the main building material in Angoulême, with extensions to Périgord and the Agennais, parts of Touraine, the Barrois, parts of Lorraine, the Île de France, the Soissonnais and parts of Provence. The use of this material is primarily determined by the existence of good building stone in the locality. The half-timbered structure (*pans de bois*) with lath and plaster is character-istic of areas where timber was immediately available and was

---

[1] Roofing material falls into several classes, as follows : The curved or hollow tiles are the more ancient, and were those originally used by the Romans ; hence their name, Roman tiles. To-day there are two types. The *tuiles romaines* or *tuiles canals* use the same tile for the *imbrices* and the *tegulæ* ; these are the tiles used in the Midi and Lorraine. The *pannes du Nord* or *tuiles en S* were developed by the Flemings in the early Middle Ages, and were used in Picardy and along the shores of the North Sea as far as the Scandinavian lands. These tiles are flat and are better fitted than the Roman tiles as a cover for steep roofs ; hence their general coincidence with the steep-roofed house in the Nord. Such roofs are to-day made of slate, as in Anjou, Brittany, the Ardennes, the north and west of the Auvergne, parts of the Alps, Bigorre, and slate is used generally as the roofing material of public buildings, castles and old houses in the Nord. Lavas are used in the Auvergne, Alps, Burgundy, Manche and Anjou. Flat tiles, replicas of the slate slabs, are found in Burgundy, Île de France, Normandy, Nièvre, Dordogne, Champagne, and Loiret.

See Doyon and Habrecht, *L'Architecture rurale et bourgeoise en France*, p. 186. See the illustrations in Doyon and Habrecht, Plate VIII, No. 1, Plate IX, No. 2, Plate IX, No. 3, and the plans of houses on p. 68, Fig. 43, and p. 70, Fig. 45.

more accessible and suitable for this type of building. Thus, it was the traditional style in much of the Nord in the Middle Ages, and is found to this day in the older buildings of Rouen, Lisieux, Bayeux and Verneuil in Normandy, at Beauvais, in the towns of Picardy such as Abbeville, in Troyes, in Champagne east of Reims, in the Argonne, and in Brittany at Rennes, Morlaix and St. Brieuc. This half-timbered style also extended farther to the south, at Angers and Bergerac, and in the Landes and in the Basque country, where it is predominant. Such buildings are relatively infrequent in the Massif Central and Burgundy, where Mâcon contains the most southerly representatives.

Domestic buildings in Germany in the earlier Middle Ages were made entirely of timber, for which reason the towns were frequently ravaged by fire ; even the town defences were for a long period built of timber, as is evident from the engravings of Danish towns, for instance, at the end of the Middle Ages and after. In western Europe, walls began to be built of stone in the 12th and 13th centuries. In south and south-west Germany, however, stone seems to have been more common as a building material. In Freiburg-im-Breisgau, for example, houses were early built with the ground floor and gable walls of stone and the first and second floors of timber. Brick was the main building material in the eastern colonized lands, but elsewhere the main structure was always in half-timber (*Fachwerk*) as in northern France.[1]

The danger of fire caused the municipal governments at an early date to prescribe building in stone, though this developed very slowly in districts that used timber. And in all the smaller towns half-timbered work continued to be used almost exclusively, especially in northern and central Germany. Buildings at street corners in particular were ordered to be built of stone in order to prevent the spread of fires. Stone building, however, developed slowly, and at first was used mainly for the large houses of the nobility and the wealthy. The building material in northern Germany was baked brick and in the south hewn stone. The former began to be used by the Dutch colonists in the 12th and spread into central and southern Germany in the 14th century.

Roofs were originally made entirely of straw or wooden shingles, and it was not until the end of the Middle Ages and the Renaissance that tile or slate roofs became the rule by municipal

---

[1] O. Lauffer, *Das Deutsche Haus in Dorf und Stadt*, 1919, and A. Grisebach, *Die Alte Deutsche Stadt in Ihrer Stammesgebiet*, 1930.

decree. Of particular importance for the prevention of fire was the erection of party-walls. In areas where the gable house dominated, the houses were built separate from each other with an entry between them that offered some protection against the spread of fire, and here decrees for the erection of *gemeinsame Mauern* or party-walls were rare. In south Germany, on the other hand, where houses usually had their eaves parallel to the street, house was built against house and the erection of party-walls was early decreed. Records date back to the 14th and became common in the 16th century, even in the regions where gable houses were common. The erection of party-walls did not become general, however, until the 19th century.

The average height of the house in south Germany in the earlier Middle Ages was two storeys. The *Sachsenspiegel* (1215 to 1235) allowed three storeys, one below ground level, so that higher building did not come about until the end of the 13th century. In north Germany two storeys were built above the hall or *Diele* (which counted as two storeys in the south German structure) and building was not higher till the 14th century. In the 16th century buildings reached five storeys. The upper storeys were then built to overhang those below them in order to acquire more building room. This narrowed the streets to such an extent that decrees had to be issued to regulate the practice ; in some towns the number of overhanging storeys was limited to one or two, in others they were even forbidden. Naturally, when stone was used, for structural reasons, no overhang was possible. Like the overhangs, arcades restricted the street width and impeded traffic. The maintenance of a minimum width in the streets of the medieval town to permit their use by traffic was known as *Stangenrecht* and is recorded at a very early date.

In this section attention has been drawn to the general character and trends of the development of domestic architecture in the Middle Ages. As the town house did not acquire definite form until the 16th century and after, it will be studied further in a later chapter.

(3) THE MARKET-PLACE

The growth of the trading community in the 10th and 11th centuries involved a permanent settlement with houses and appurtenances for trade and communal living. With the growth of the settlement, the market became the focus of the new community, for the weekly sale of retail produce, and for the display of the craftsman's wares to the merchant, and as a place around which trade and intercourse could concentrate. Here too clustered the principal buildings of the town, as well as its church. In settlements of feudal origin the market was held and controlled by the lord or abbot or bishop, and the market-place lay directly before the gate of the castle, church, abbey or monastery. " In towns of Roman origin, at the meeting-place of the old and the new settlement, in towns born of an abbey or castle, at the gate of the abbey or the castle. This is a law which is verified in all countries," writes P. Lavedan.[1]

The mercantile settlement grew up in the first place along a main highway near to a river frontage or approaching a river crossing. In the older towns of unplanned growth the market trade soon demanded more space than was available on a narrow highway, and neighbouring streets and small places were adapted for special purposes. The evolution of the form of the market as a planned entity is to be sought in the founded market settlements which came into being in the 12th century. Here the founder had to provide facilities for weekly trade on the market-place and for the easy movement of traffic through the three or four gates of the town wall to its central market, as well as some kind of provision for the by-passing of through traffic from one gate to another. Further, the land had to be subdivided into building lots of equal size and similar shape. Such measures would meet with difficulties in a large existing village, and so the settlements were usually laid out near to an earlier nucleus of some kind but upon a site that was not built over (*aus wilder Wurzel*). The planned settlement did not emerge in its final form suddenly, but developed as the result of a long process of planning and experiment lasting two or three hundred years. In the towns of the German lands, as well as in the founded towns of southern France in particular, we find these ideas in practice. The problem was to give architectonic unity to a compact urban

---

[1] P. Lavedan, *Histoire de l' Urbanisme, Moyen Âge*, pp. 449 and 450. " In the towns which grew out of the old *castella*, whether they became bishops' cities, like Regensburg, Cologne, Strasbourg, Basel, Constance, or merely the seat of a monastery or court palace, the market is usually outside the walls, in a position well placed for trade." Rietschel, *Markt und Stadt*, pp. 36–7. In Chateau-Thierry the town lies on the right bank of the Marne near the castle which lies on a hill, the *marché* is at the foot of the castle at the principal entrance to it. At Fontainebleau, castle and town are adjacent ; the main route passes through the town alongside the castle and at its entrance the street widens (*Grande Rue*) and here are the *marchés de blé, vin, charbon*. The market-place lies immediately outside the abbey gate at St. Denis. The reader can probably provide many other examples.

area, which was divided into street blocks, with its centre in a market-place and the church, and its limits in the fortifications.

Three market forms constantly recur, the long wide street thoroughfare, the triangular market, usually situated at the convergence of two main highways, and the rectangular market. The irregular form, however, is not always the result of accident. It sometimes shows, for instance, a very nice adjustment to the shape of the town, and, indeed, to the configuration of the site. This is the case in the planned town of Montauban (p. 352) and in the unplanned town of Bazas, both in south-western France. A further distinction between the natural and the planned form lies in the size of the market. In the older town there is a lack of open space and trade overflows into adjacent streets and places, always keeping near the centre, and often clinging to the main route. On the other hand, in the new towns, the market-place is laid out as the first and essential feature of the new settlement, with a size judged adequate to serve the future population. Sometimes, of course, a too optimistic *Locator* overestimated the possibilities of a place and the market-place remains far too large for the settlement. But this is rare, and the sizes of the market and of the town enclosed by the walls are usually well proportioned. In the new town the market-place is secularized ; in the older settlement the market-church is in the middle of the place, whereas in the newer town it lies in a block specially reserved for it to one side of the market-place. The position of the church in the centre with the market-place before it is very characteristic of the small market town. In the older town, the demand for space for weekly markets and especially for large fairs was such that spaces were laid out beyond the gates of the town. This is a very characteristic feature of the towns of northern France, where one often finds a very large rectangular space, remaining to this day, outside the old town and named Marché à Chevaux or Marché aux Moutons or Marché des Bœufs. Chartres and Angers are good examples (pp. 344–6). The specialization and shift of market-places is well illustrated by Limoges (pp. 121–3).

(4) THE CULTURAL DOMINANTS

(a) *Ecclesiastical Buildings.* The rôle of the monument or edifice in the formation of the town has already been indirectly noticed. Chief among these structures were the symbols of the First and Second Estates, castle and church, while the Third

Estate was represented by the public buildings of the town community. In the Gallo-Roman towns the cathedral, placed within
the *civitas*, was the chief centre of human activity in the Dark
Ages. It was sited in a quadrant of the *castrum* and invariably
lay up against or astride the Roman walls ; often indeed the
material of the walls had been used for building the cathedral.
It became the centre of activities for several hundred years, until
the development of the trading community beyond the walls of
the *cité*. The cathedral then became the centre of these early
medieval towns, and streets and houses were built around it.
This relationship was in marked contrast to the English cathedral
city, where the cathedral was introduced at a much later date
and was associated with monasticism. Moreover, in England,
the original bishop's sees were often first situated in the country
and were shifted later into the towns. As a result the cathedral
had its monastery and its cloister, and it sought seclusion within
a walled enclosure. In Germany, the first cathedrals were
situated on raised ground at route centres, and because of the
raids of the 10th and 11th centuries the bishops encircled them
by walls within which they had rights of immunity or asylum
(*Domfreiheit*). This walled nucleus appears in many towns in
north-western Germany and the medieval economic community
grew round it (Fig. 69, p. 305). Farther east, the cathedral was
also an outpost in a wilderness of paganism, and it frequently
occupies a dominating position on a hill, or a high spur overlooking a river. This is characteristic of the bishoprics along the
Elbe and the Saale (e.g. Meissen), and is also found in the towns
of Sweden. In east central Europe, castle and cathedral are
combined within one wall on a high and well-defended site. This
is typical, symbolizing the process of invasion and control, in the
towns established by the Teutonic Order in the Baltic provinces,
as at Riga (Fig. 108, p. 406). In central Europe the most outstanding example is the Hradcany at Prague (Ch. 10). In all
these cases, castle or cathedral, or the two together, form an
entirely distinct complex, which, as a pre-urban stronghold,
formed the nucleus around which the town has grown.

The chief ecclesiastical buildings of the town apart from the
cathedral were the parish churches and the monasteries. In the
first place, the parish church usually had a cemetery adjacent
to it, but for hygienic reasons this was early shifted outwards to
the outskirts of the town, and often the open space that remained
was eventually filled up by buildings that reached right up to the

walls of the church. The old monastic Orders, such as the Benedictines, built their monasteries at first on the outskirts of the town near the gates, but eventually, as the town expanded, the monasteries were surrounded by buildings. The younger Orders, which began to become active after about 1250, such as the Franciscans and Dominicans, sought a place in the town, though the town fathers were loth to accept them and in some cases only did so on the recommendation of the Pope himself.

(b) *The Castle.* The castle was essentially the defended residence of the territorial lord, together with the buildings for the garrison and dependants. Many were placed in the older communal strongholds, but the majority were erected on new sites with good natural defences. The evolution of the castle in western Europe began in the 9th century, but it was not common until after the 10th century. It developed first in northern France, where it was adopted by the Northmen in Normandy, and transferred to England by them. It also spread eastwards through Lorraine into Germany. By the year 1000 the horizon of every province of France was fretted with castles. The age of castle building in Germany, however, was retarded by some two hundred years, for until the end of the 11th century the German castles were royal property and were usually in the towns, as at Frankfurt and Regensburg. Individual castle building came at a much later date. Until about 1200 most of the so-called castles were in fact fortified manor houses. Even the kings did not have real castles, for they lived in low-roofed wooden structures called a *Palatium* or *Pfalz* (German), while the castle proper was left to the garrison in the strongholds and towns.

The reason for the early spread of the castle in France and its tardy appearance in Germany is related to differences of feudal evolution. After the fall of the Carolingians, France collapsed into chaos, whereas in Germany the great tribal duchies, based upon the old tribal units, maintained their independence for some time. While in France in the early Middle Ages a swarm of petty sovereignties came into being, Germany had but a few large units. Out of this feudal chaos, there emerged in France a strong centralized state. In Germany the procedure was reversed, for political disintegration came with the fall of the Hohenstaufen line after about 1200, when the west German lands split into a contending swarm of petty sovereignties. The real castle age in Germany did not begin until after 1200. Castle construction was begun by Henry IV in Thuringia and Saxony, and by 1300 Germany was as thickly studded with castles as France.

(c) *Public Buildings.* When the early towns became self-governing communities, independent of lord or bishop, public buildings were erected in which to carry on the activities of the town—those of government, public assembly and commerce. Special reference may be made to the German town. The chief building was the town hall (*Rathaus*). The first of these appeared during the 12th century, and they became numerous in the 13th. The earliest and most typical buildings had two storeys, the ground floor being normally a large hall used for setting out goods, for public assemblies, for the law courts, and the like, while the first floor contained a large hall and several rooms, and had an outside staircase. They are built in Gothic style, the building material being stone in the west and brick in the north and east. The cellar or *Ratskeller* was later used for the storage of beers and wines, the sale of which was often monopolized by the city authorities, and the cellar was also used as a storehouse as well as a place of convivial assembly. Important also was the merchants' hall (*Kaufhaus*) and guild house. The former normally had two storeys, and its structure was similar to the *Rathaus*. Indeed many towns had but the one building, and it is impossible to say which of the two uses came first ; a good example is the Kaufhaus at Freiburg-im-Breisgau. The Kaufhaus was often used for a specific purpose and reflects the main industrial activity of the town. Thus the cloth hall (*Gewandhaus*) was widespread. A salt house is still found in some towns where salt was a product of the neighbourhood and the town held a monopoly of it. Dyers' woad was produced on a considerable scale in parts of Thuringia, where halls in the towns were devoted to its sale, as well as in Görlitz, where the woad was distributed to the cloth makers in Silesia. There is also a corn hall in most towns. In certain towns there was a shoe house, a bread house, a butcher's house, or, as at Frankfurt-am-Main, a linen house. Most of these buildings date from the 14th and 15th centuries.

(d) *Wall.* For centuries the Roman walls fell into decay, and their materials were even used for building. It was not until the 10th century that they began to be strengthened and extended. Ditch and mound were the earliest fortifications around the first towns, timber palisades being constructed along the latter with wooden towers at the gate entrances where the roads entered the town. These wooden defences were early, but gradually, replaced by stone, first at the tower gates and then along the intervening sectors of the walls. The wall was usually a single thick wall and had a wooden balcony (German, *Wehrgang*) running around its inside for the use of the defenders. These fortifications were constantly modified and improved from the 12th to the 14th century, but thereafter changes were trifling and there were no substantial alterations (in spite of the treatise of Albrecht Dürer, published in 1527), until the 17th century, when the new ideas of fortification were introduced by Vauban as a defence against gunpowder and artillery.

But the changes introduced during the Middle Ages were important. The single circuit of stone or brick with towers was gradually altered. This happened in the 14th century, no doubt as a result of the introduction of new ideas brought by the Crusaders from the Near East. Square, circular or semi-circular towers were built out from the walls so that besiegers could be attacked in the flank. Further, an outside line of palisades or a second wall lay outside the main wall but inside the ditch, and the sheltered belt between (German, *Zwinger*) could be used for the assembly of the besieged for unexpected sorties beyond the fortifications upon the enemy attackers. This system was retained throughout the 14th and 15th centuries, and since later changes in the 17th century and after were confined to a few towns of strategic importance, the great majority of existing town fortifications belong to this type. It is interesting that the townsmen were so slow to react to the new methods of warfare that came into being with the introduction of powder and cannon in the 14th century, even though there were theorists enough among the Italians, and Dürer himself contributed to such theories. The reason was undoubtedly that the new methods of warfare and the concentration of power in the hands of strong rulers of large States reduced the importance of the individual town, quite apart from the tremendous labour of design and construction involved in the new system of defence as perfected by the French engineer, Vauban.

(5) ASPECT OF THE TOWN : TOWN PROFILE

The relative importance and the position and architectonic relationships of the three Estates, church, nobility and burgesses, in the plan of the town is clearly reflected in many of the profiles which are available in the atlases of the 17th and 18th centuries. The same essential features are still clear in the same towns of to-day. The town, confined by its walls, is dominated by the towers and spires of its churches and monasteries, and the turrets of its castles and walls. Dominating the bishop's city are the spires of the cathedral and the group of ecclesiastical buildings around it. The church on raised land often completely dominates the smaller towns, such as Wetzlar and Limburg in western Germany, or the small towns of central Sweden, to take two groups of extreme examples. The castle and the associated small walled town on a hilltop, bounded by steep slopes and with a road leading from its gate down to a bridgehead, or with the town situated at its feet strung out along the road, are characteristic profiles of small towns. Among the burgesses' towns of the Low Countries, the old abbey that was the first nucleus of settlement stands out above the town, but lies to one side of its geographical centre, where the market-place and its municipal buildings are situated. Here, conspicuous above all, is the lofty tower of the belfry.

The historical character of the town in the past is clearly reflected in its aspect of to-day. This is especially clear when the historic walls have been cleared away and replaced by a wide belt of gardens or woodland, or when the old town is surrounded, as in Holland, by moats and embattlements. These features are most clearly represented to-day in the smaller towns, that have been least affected by the impact of industry and commerce, where new structures have displaced the old. In the larger city, the growth of multi-storeyed buildings in the old centre causes it to appear as a block of buildings of uneven height and varied structure, rising stolidly above the general level of the sea of buildings around it. The historic buildings, however, still remain its symbols.

In the 12th and 13th centuries there was a marked increase in the rate of growth of the towns. The Crusades introduced new ideas of building and defence. The monastic movement flourished. This was, too, the great day of the craft and merchant guilds in the towns, and was also the era that immediately preceded the feudal chaos and strife to which much of western Germany fell victim after the fall of the Hohenstaufen dynasty in the middle of the 13th century. Another factor contributed to the expansion of the town. The townsfolk needed common pasture for their flocks that fed them. It often happened that an adjacent rural parish (*Landgemeinde*) was absorbed for this reason by the town so as to give it the necessary amount of pasture

(*Allmende*). In such cases the peasants shifted their homes into the town and became fully privileged townsmen. Gradually, building extended beyond the existing town walls, and it had to be extended. Throughout the Middle Ages the single-family house was the rule so that growth was lateral rather than vertical, and this meant outward expansion. Upward growth did not begin till the 16th century. Fields and gardens outside the town gates were cultivated by townspeople, and here too were peasant holdings, often clustered around a monastery. Especially was this the case with the Cistercians, who marketed their goods in the town, while the later mendicant Orders often had perforce to settle outside it. These outlying suburbs were eventually enclosed by a new wall and incorporated into the town. Entirely new towns were also founded adjacent to existing towns.

The territorial growth of the medieval town and the construction of walls around it ceased in the early 15th century. It is difficult to generalize as to how far the trend to vertical growth was due to an increase in population and how far to the change in social habits, which more living-rooms per house required. Since the population of most towns remained stable during this period, it would seem that the second factor was the more important, but this is a subject that requires closer investigation, as we have suggested in a previous section. It also seems that further walled extensions were not embarked upon because the town could not face the great undertaking of erecting new fortifications consistent with the new demands of warfare, or of providing the man-power to defend them. Moreover the latest walls often included much cultivated land which was needed to feed the flocks in case of siege. Indeed, in the later Middle Ages it became common for towns, instead of building new walls, to erect all kinds of temporary defence works outside the old walls, such as ditches, mounds, fences and hedges to hamper an attacker (*Landwehren*), a practice that was adopted on a much larger scale in the following centuries, and especially in the 19th. In many towns decline set in during the 14th and 15th centuries owing to the many restrictions imposed by the guilds on production and buying and selling. Only the chief towns, that lay at crossways of important routes and were seats of long-distance commerce, seem to have continued to thrive, and even these were badly hit, as were all the towns of the German lands, by the ravages of the Thirty Years' War.

In spite of the appalling sanitary conditions of the medieval town, it survived, even though death-rates were high and the population had to be maintained by immigration. A main redeeming feature, contrary to popular belief, was the large amount of open space within it that provided it with natural lungs. There was plenty of open space behind the rows of houses on the street front, and open space engirdled the built-up area often well within the town walls. The medieval town, as we have emphasized, had in its early days a very considerable agricultural element, and this continued to be important in the later Middle Ages, although it was completely dwarfed by the spread of building and the growth of crafts and commerce in the larger towns. The medieval town had gardens, orchards, and vineyards, such as covered the slopes of the hill of Ste. Geneviève in Paris in the early Middle Ages. In Poitiers each house had its orchard, and in the 13th century vineyards covered two-thirds of the town area. In 15th-century Nancy there were arable fields. Livestock were kept by most townsmen, especially pigs and poultry, although these generally had to fend for themselves on the refuse of the street. The amount of this open space decreased during the Middle Ages in the towns that continued to grow, but right down to the 17th and 18th centuries the town was in general well ventilated. In the later Middle Ages, however, while the area of rural land often decreased, much space was taken up by the large enclosures of the monasteries and these helped to maintain the semi-rural aspect of the outskirts of the historic town.

CHAPTER 17

TYPES OF HISTORIC TOWN IN WESTERN EUROPE

We have discussed in the previous chapters the formation and build of the historic town in general. It will be apparent that towns differ markedly in their morphology according to the conditions of their development, the nature of their dominant activities, the degree of their natural and planned growth, and the conditions of site with which they had to contend. Families of towns may thus be recognized, not only as types, but also as regional groups. Moreover, it is evident that towns in western Europe as a whole show marked contrasts to those of the adjacent major cultural areas of the Continent. Finally, it will be clear that the morphological approach cannot be based on fragmentary comparisons, for cities which differ widely in essential character have similarities in the detail of their aspects. To describe widely differing cities as " canal cities " because they are threaded by canals gives in itself a very shallow basis of comparison. The approach must be genetic ; in other words it must seek homologies of form in the light of historical development and function.[1] In this chapter we shall attempt to outline the regional variations of the historic town, without attempting the impossible task of submitting a comprehensive classification. This, then, is essentially a typological study, and is illustrated by annotated plans to show types of urban habitat and trends of urban topographic formation.

(1) FRANCE

The historic town in France shows remarkable continuity of development from its origins to the early Middle Ages. Over a hundred places are recorded in the Carolingian and Merovingian

---

[1] In this morphological study of settlement forms we are constantly reminded of the beginnings of physical geography. The famous German physiographer, Oscar Peschel, began his studies by the recognition of what he called " homologies of form ", that is, similarities in the shape and configuration of the earth's surface features. Some of these homologies proved entirely fortuitous, and were as little use as if a historian were to classify kings by the shape of their noses or by their stature. Some homologies, however, as, for example, the remarkable indentations of fiord coasts, led to real understanding of the physiographic development of this type of coastal feature. The geographical study of settlement proceeds on exactly the same basis, conditioned throughout by a genetic (that is, historical) approach.

periods as being *civitates* (Fig. 72). The majority of these were seats of cathedrals and were sited within the Roman *castra*. These in turn were situated in or near the hilltop *oppida* of the Gauls. Each was thus a focus of roads that were invariably the same as the preceding Roman roads. The early Middle Ages was the feudal era *per excellence* in France, when kings, counts, lords and

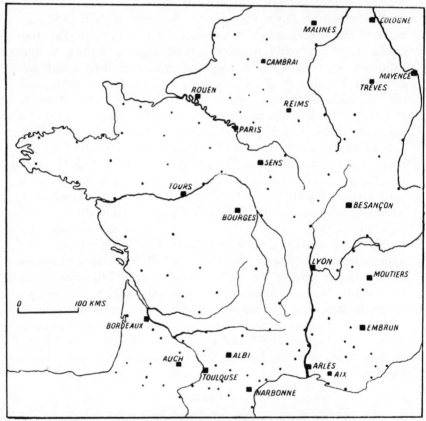

FIG. 72.—Archiepiscopal and Episcopal Sees in Merovingian Gaul about A.D. 700 (after Mirot, *Manuel de Geographie Historique de la France*; see also East, *An Historical Géography of Europe*, 1947, p. 114). Squares with names are Archbishoprics and Circles are Bishoprics.

clerics clustered in these strongholds, all of which were walled during this period. Then, too, there emerged the new community of merchants and craftsmen, to whom rights of self-government were granted. Thus, there emerged the *ville*, centred on its markets, which were the real focus of medieval urban growth, as opposed to the stronghold, which often became known as the *cité*, and was centred on its cathedral. Few changes took place in this urban structure until the classical era of the 17th and 18th centuries, in the days of the Intendants, when new ideas of æsthetic and practical planning were put into practice. Then followed the Revolution that brought about a new politico-geographical organization, and the end of the old era and the onset of the new. These events changed the structure and aspect of the town, causing many historic buildings to be converted to new uses and new ones to be erected for new administrative and cultural purposes. During the second half of the 19th century, the advent of the railway caused changes in the small French town, which were manifest in larger cities—the spread of factory and residential districts and changes in the historic core. These trends have been examined in Chapter 7.

Our concern here is with this historic core, and the processes by which it was changed in the Middle Ages. In all the older cities and towns these primary motive forces had their clear expression in the form-elements of the towns and the manner in which the town grew to shape. These form-elements are the church, the castle and the market-place, while fourthly, the self-governing community needed facilities for trade and provision for defence. In this light we may interpret the historic towns of France.

The topographic formation of the early medieval town west of the Rhine was the product of a long and complicated historical development. The town was thus pre-eminently a natural growth, that was not guided by an overall plan. It grew up piecemeal, so that the habitat was adjusted in detail to the needs of the community and to the configuration of the site. The main features of these earliest towns are the pre-urban nucleus, the mercantile settlement, then the growth of the latter into the self-governing urban community with its centre in the market-place, followed by the construction of an encircling wall, with later extensions beyond the wall as the town grew in size.

These same general features are repeated in the small towns, which are much more numerous, serve the greater part of the land, and morphologically are just as important as the large city. Moreover, as we shall see, there is a close morphological relationship between all settlements, urban and rural, which form as it were a habitat complex that varies from one area to another. As regards the small towns, even though they often have only a few thousand inhabitants, we can often trace the same mode of

M

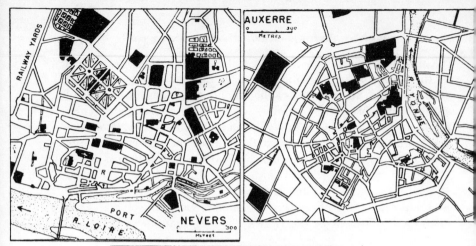

NEVERS

AUXERRE

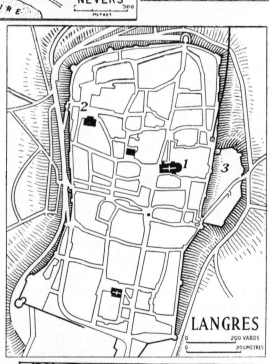

LANGRES

0   200 YARDS
0   200 METRES

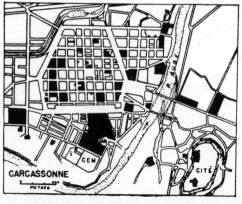

CARCASSONNE

development as in the older towns, though the nature of the stronghold may differ. In some cases, the new towns, whether formed by the bestowal of privileges on an existing settlement, or by the foundation of a new one, were closely associated with a preceding nucleus of settlement. In the growth of the small town we find the same features of natural expansion as in the large towns, and also the same juxtaposition of two or more legally and topographically separate settlements. Examples of the development and plan of such smaller towns are Aurillac and Bar-le-Duc (with four hill nuclei and a valley settlement). They are situated in constricted valleys, bounded by steep hill slopes (Fig. 10, p. 48, and Fig. 78, p. 348).

With these preliminary remarks we may now proceed to a comparative study of the urban settlements of France.[1]

After the fall of the Roman Empire the Gallo-Roman towns in northern Gaul underwent changes which are generally common to them all and clearly reflect historical developments in their function and growth. The trend is clearly reflected in the specific instances of Toulouse and Bordeaux (Chapter 7). Other

[1] See the latest comprehensive study, with plans, of F. L. Ganshof, *Étude sur le développement des villes entre Loire et Rhin au Moyen Âge*, Paris–Brussels, 1943.

FIG. 73.—Types of Historic Town in France.

Auxerre is grouped around its cathedral, on the western bank of the Yonne river. This small oval-shaped area marks the nucleus of the town (on the south side its limit is indicated by the street name Sous les Murs). This is the *cité*. On its western side and along the main north–south route (Rue de Paris) is the centre of the *ville* with market-place and Hôtel de Ville. Beyond this lie compact built-up areas with public buildings that reach as far as the boulevards, built on the site of the medieval walls. Beyond lie the *Faubourgs* with vineyards and isolated public buildings (cf. Chartres).

Nevers has an oval-shaped nucleus that encloses the cathedral, ducal palace and Hôtel de Ville (*cité*). This has been partly opened up by the clearance of the Place de la République. This nucleus lies on the slopes of a hill that dominates the confluence of the Nièvre and the Loire. Old-established pottery works and iron foundries lay along the swift-running water of the Nièvre. More recent wharves lie along the canalised Loire. The railway tracks lie to the north-west of the town. Extensions of the 17th and 18th centuries lie around the nucleus. Entry to the old town is marked by flights of steps up the steep streets of hills and slopes. Note the public squares just outside the old gates.

Carcassonne illustrates the features that typify the towns of the Midi. The oldest settlement, the *cité*, was a fortress on a hilltop, defended by walls and a castle and containing a very irregular street plan ; here too were the homes of lesser nobility. The *ville basse* lies on lower land on the opposite bank of the Aude river with a rectilinear plan and a central square market-place, characteristic of the founded *bastides*.

Langres lies on a flat plateau that is bounded by steep slopes. Note the adjustment of the medieval walls and the street pattern to the edges of the plateau, and the north–south road axis, with the market-place and cathedral placed centrally to the town on this route. 1. Cathedral. 2. Hôtel de Ville. 3. Faubourg sous Murs.

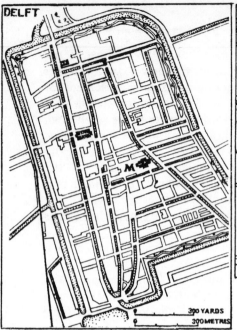

DELFT

300 YARDS
300 METRES

TRÈVES
METRES 300

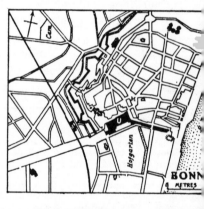

Hofgarten

BONN
METRES

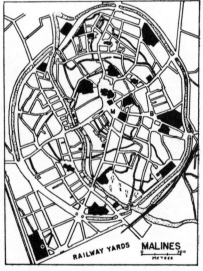

RAILWAY YARDS   MALINES
METRES

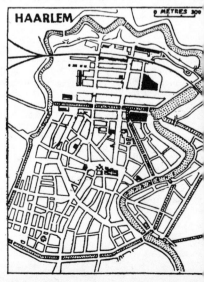

HAARLEM   METRES 300

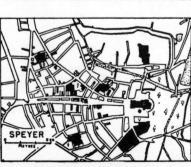

SPEYER
METRES

examples are Orleans and Rouen (Fig. 75). During the Merovingian and Carolingian periods the cathedral and its associated buildings lay within, and usually alongside, the walls of the *castra*. Some of these walls dated from the Germanic invasions at the end of the third century, or new walls had been built or the old ones repaired during the 10th century, owing to the insecurity brought about by the inroads of invaders.

The plan of the *cité*, which was formerly rectangular, based on the plan of the *castrum* of the Roman colonial camp, has been disturbed and often wellnigh obliterated through the centuries. Such changes have occurred in three ways (Figs. 76 and 77). First, the rectangular form of the walls, the four gates, and the control exercised by the river frontage and the bridgehead, resulted in the reappearance of the right-angled street crossing, although

---

Fig. 74.—Types of Historic Town in the Rhineland and Low Countries.

Speyer is an old bishop's town sited on the western bank of the Rhine. It is noteworthy here for the partial radial-concentric arrangement of the street pattern centred on the cathedral as the architectonic dominant of the plan.

Malines is characteristic of the towns of Belgium and eastern Holland and north-western Germany that have a radial-concentric pattern grouped around a church and market-place. The original nucleus lies on the east bank of the river Dyle. Between it and the outer limits of the town (that are so clearly defined in this plan dated 1890) there is a more regular (later medieval) lay-out with churches serving the different sectors. Special market-places lie in the margin of the old nucleus (e.g. Marché de Betail, B). Note the regular extension to the south-west with streets radiating from the site of the gate to the railway station. Boulevards and water surround the town.

Haarlem and Delft are characteristic of the towns of the old province of Holland, in the zone immediately behind the coastal dunes. Haarlem has a nucleus with radial streets centred on a large church and market-place ; this nucleus is bounded by an old filled-in channel (Oude Gracht). More regularly laid quarters lie to the north and south and the whole is surrounded by canalised fortifications (Singel Gracht), to-day occupied by open spaces (Plein) and parks. The markets lie on the wharves of the river on the east side of the town. Note the similar alinement of streets and canals.

Bonn is situated on the west bank of the Rhine and sited on a terrace just north of the site of an ancient Roman *castrum*. The settlement grew around the cathedral (St. Cassius Stift) and was known as the *civitas Verona*. This is centred on the Münster Platz. Outside it grew the market settlement around the present Marktplatz (market-place). This expanded to the river front and the whole settlement was walled in 1243. It became a residence of the Elector Clement Augustus in the 18th century when the castle residence and gardens were laid out. The University occupies the latter. The town has spread beyond the fortifications since 1880. Building was allowed on the site of the fortifications at the end of the century and Bonn thus lacks the wide boulevards that are characteristic of other cities.

Trier (Trèves) occupies a sector of the whole area of its predecessor, the Roman city on the east bank of the Moselle. Its built-up area even lies well within its rectangular walls as built in the 13th century. The nucleus is formed by the cathedral that is bordered on the west by the main north–south road on which lies the triangular market-place (the road that follows the curved border of the old defended cathedral nucleus is here called Graben Str.). The main roads run south from the market-place, roughly in the direction of the old Roman road, and south-west to the bridge across the river. Note the radial arrangement of streets from the horse market in the north-west. Plan dated 1878.

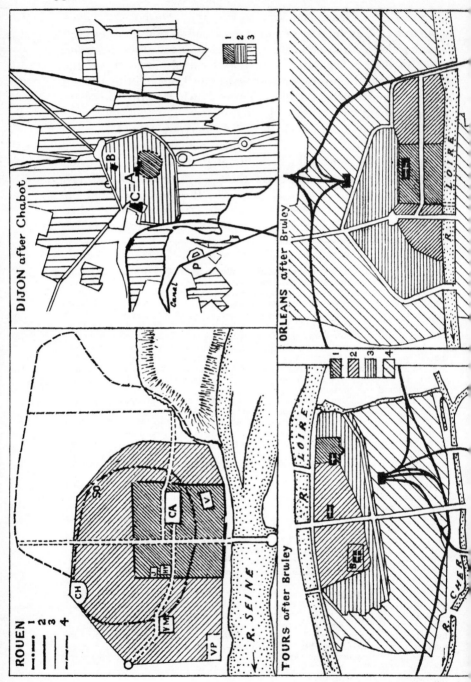

DIJON after Chabot

ORLEANS after Bruley

ROUEN

TOURS after Bruley

R. SEINE

R. LOIRE

R. CHER

this is not necessarily the direct lineal descendant of the *cardo* and *decumanus*. Secondly, in some cases the walls are oval in shape, and this results in a curved alinement of the streets, as at Senlis and Châlon-sur-Saône. Thirdly, the new monuments function not only as foci of community life, but also as *points d'appui* in the defence of the settlement. They therefore occupy eccentric positions. Thus the cathedral is usually built on or near the walls, and, in varying degree, the new grouping of houses and streets is focused upon it, as at Dijon and Nantes.[1] This applies to other public buildings, notably to the castle of the comte or of the châtelain, his representative. These buildings are often on the site of an earlier Roman public edifice, the cathedral, for instance, being on the site of a Roman temple.[2] Lastly, beyond the walls of the *cité* there grew up new settlements (*vici*)—abbeys and monasteries and churches—which sheltered the tombs of saints, such as St. Sernin at Toulouse, St. Germain-des-Près and Ste. Geneviève at Paris, with demesnial settlements clustered around them. Here too, in the 10th and 11th centuries, there emerged the trading colony (*portus*) with its own market (*forum*) and occasionally its own church (*ecclesia mercatorum*), and some-times at an early date it had a wall (*negotiatorum claustrum*). The castle residence of the count was placed in his capital city, often in the centre of the town (where it was frequently taken over by the Palais de Justice at a later date) or in a corner, in the walls, so as to protect the town from attack from without, as at Angers and Paris, where the castle protects the up-river route.

Markets and fairs became of great importance in the north. By about 1100 the northern countryside was dotted with castles, monasteries and churches, many of which first became the seats of parasitic serf communities and later of country market towns

[1] Lavedan, *Histoire de l'Urbanisme*, p. 234.
[2] See C. Jullian, *La Gaule Indépendante* (1920), Vol. VIII, pp. 230, 236, 314.

Fig. 75.—The Growth of Four French Cities.

Rouen (scale, 1 : 25,000). 1. Gallo-Roman settlement. 2. Walled Roman settlement. 3. 2nd wall. 4. 3rd and 4th walls. VP = Vieux Palais. Ch = Château de Philippe Auguste. SO = Abbaye de St. Omer. J = Palais de Justice. HV = Hôtel de Ville. V = Vieille Tour (Château des Ducs). CA = Cathedral. VM = Vieux-Marché.

Tours and Orleans (scale, 1 : 50,000). 1. Gallo-Roman settlement. 2. 14th- and 15th-century extensions. 3. 16th-century extensions. 4. Present urban area. B = 10th-century Bourg St. Martin in Tours. Dashed line shows site of the old bridge in Orleans.

Dijon (scale, 1 : 50,000). 1. Castrum. 2. Town at the end of the 17th century. 3. Present urban area. A = Palais des Ducs. B = Prefecture. C = Cathedral St. Benigne. P = Port.

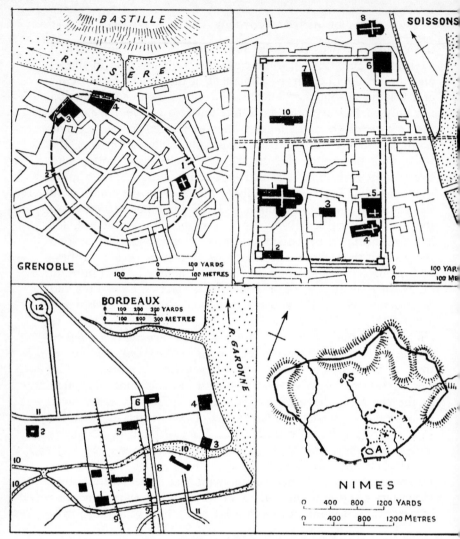

Fig. 76.—The Roman origins of Four French Cities.

Grenoble (scale, 1 : 10,000). Dashed line shows the site of the Roman wall with two of the gates (1 and 2). 3. Hôtel de Ville. 4. Palais de Justice. 5. Cathedral.

Soissons (scale, 1 : 7,500). Rectangular Roman wall. 1. Cathedral. 2. Bishop's palace on site of Roman temple. 3. Hôtel Dieu. 4. Notre Dame. 5. St. Pierre. 6. Tour des Comtes (Château Gaillard). 7. Palais de Justice. 8. St. Léger. 9. Roman road to Amiens. 10. College.

Bordeaux (scale, 1 : 20,000). Rectangular wall astride the Dévèze stream. 1. Ancient temple and site of the cathedral St. André. 2. Basilica of St. Martin. 3. Ancient temple, site of St. Pierre church. 4. Modern Bourse. 5. Temple of Mercury. 6. Forum. 7. Piliers de Tortelli. 8. Cardo maximus (Rue Ste. Catherine). 9. Aqueducts. 10. River Dévèze. 11. Old roads. 12. Amphitheatre.

Nimes (scale, 1 : 50,000). Irregular outer Roman wall and an inner medieval wall (with a dashed line) based on the Roman amphitheatre. Dotted lines show the main streets in the medieval town. S = spring, the nucleus of the Roman settlement. A = the amphitheatre (Arènes), and the cross shows the cathedral in the centre of the medieval town.

(All maps adapted from Blanchet.)

with elementary, or in some cases, full rights of self-government. Whether on the site of a Roman settlement or not, the cathedral and the market-place next to it became the dominant features of the life and build of the episcopal cities of the Nord (Chartres, Fig. 77*a*). Eastwards, towards the Rhine, the great market-place surrounded by the townsmen's parish church, the guild halls and the belfry symbolized the type of new self-governing community of burgesses that emerged in the early Middle Ages, free from the restricting influence of the Church. North of Paris, in Picardy and Flanders, such communities had to wrestle with the power of the bishop, whose cathedral dominated the town, as at Cambrai, Tournai and Soissons. But the new towns in Flanders, and some of the towns of northern France, were essentially towns of merchants and craftsmen, who controlled their affairs with little interference from the courts and none from the episcopal authorities, except in a few cities of this character like Liége and Maastricht.

In southern France urban development took on a somewhat different stamp from that of the north. Roman civilization had penetrated deeply, especially in the south-east with its chief centres in the Roman towns of Nîmes, Arles, Orange and Avignon. Here the Roman municipal tradition survived, and Roman law was accepted as the basis of justice, as opposed to the customary or feudal law that emerged in northern France. The development of the French city in the Midi is thus usually reflected in the dominant position occupied by the cathedral. On the other hand, there are very few medieval town halls in these towns to-day ; they were normally rebuilt during the succeeding centuries. This is a marked contrast to the essentially burgesses' city of Flanders and Picardy, where the town hall and the guild halls are among the finest examples of late medieval Gothic architecture in Europe and are still to be found in the heart of the historic town.

The chief towns of the Midi had a somewhat different topographic development from those of the north. In Provence and Languedoc *castra* were not built to protect the people of these great Roman cities. In the 10th and 11th centuries protection was afforded by building an entirely new fortification or by using the ruins of a large Roman public building for this purpose and incorporating it into the medieval walls of the new settlement, as in the case of the amphitheatre at Nimes and Arles. Separate nuclei of settlement also seem to have retained their independence

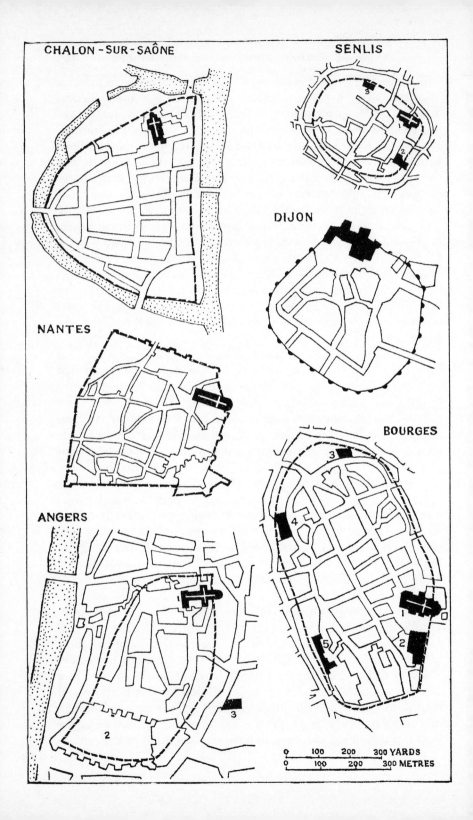

CHALON-SUR-SAÔNE

SENLIS

DIJON

NANTES

ANGERS

BOURGES

| 0 | 100 | 200 | 300 YARDS |
| 0 | 100 | 200 | 300 METRES |

and separateness for a longer period than in the north. The result is a much more irregular plan than is found in the episcopal cities of northern France. Moreover, churches were established on new sites and were surrounded by entirely new fortifications during the early Middle Ages ; these towns form a distinct group which is referred to below.

Thus, the Gallo-Roman towns had in the early Middle Ages several separate nuclei of settlement, although for ten centuries, writes Vercauteren of the towns of northern Gaul, the settlement had lain huddled inside its Roman walls to which no changes had been made. These nuclei were the *cité*, which was clustered around the cathedral and often lay within the Roman *castrum* ; the *bourg*, which was growing around the new merchants' colony ; the *vicus*, which was the manorial unit clustered around the abbey or monastery ; and the *château*, which was occasionally found as the seat of a territorial lord with a manorial settlement also attached to it as a *vicus*. Finally, these nuclei were eventually unified within one wall, although each leaves its impress on the medieval and modern plan. The walls were built in the first place by the bishops, but at later stages, when the nascent urban settlement had attained complete independence, the townsmen built the walls. In some cases, as the settlement grew, several successive walls were built to embrace new *faubourgs* lying outside them. Thus the episcopal city on the site of a Roman *castrum* took shape. Toulouse, Bordeaux, Rouen, and, on the biggest scale of all, Paris, are examples of such urban evolution.

There is a very distinctive group of episcopal cities of early medieval origin, contemporary with the Gallo-Roman cities, but distinct from the latter in that they were not associated with an existing Roman *castrum* and began as new medieval religious seats. A cathedral or abbey or monastery became, in the same way as the *castrum*, the nucleus of their subsequent urban growth.

Fig. 77.—Roman walls in early medieval towns in France. (Scale, 1 : 10,000.)

In each case the medieval town developed inside the walls of the Roman *castrum* with the street pattern adjusted to the walls and to the new cultural dominants.

Note the interrelation of site, wall, street pattern and public buildings. Senlis :—1. Notre Dame. 2. St. Frambourg. 3. Château (site of Roman prætorium). Nantes :—Cathedral against the wall. Dijon :—Stronghold (Palais des Ducs) against the wall, both public buildings being foci of the street pattern. Angers :—Commanding the Loir river. 1. Cathedral against north-east corner of the wall. 2. Castle in south-west corner, commanding the river approach. 3. Église Toussaint. Bourges :—On raised land bordered by marsh. 1. Cathedral. 2. Archbishop's palace. 3. Old Hôtel de Ville. 4. Hôtel Jacques Cœur (1443–50). 5. Prefecture.

(Nantes and Dijon from Lavedan, the rest from Blanchet.)

Chartres is an outstanding example (Fig. 77a).   A large number of smaller towns also fall into this category (see Fig. 78).   The essential feature of the morphology is the walled, oval-shaped

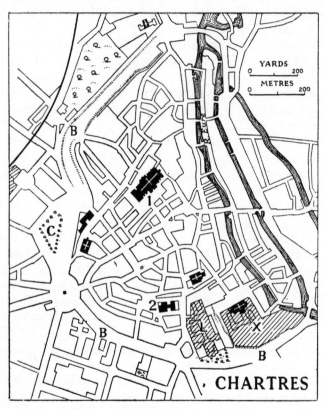

FIG. 77a.—Chartres.   (Scale, 1 : 15,000.)
1. Cathedral.   2. Hôtel de Ville.   B = Boulevards.   X = Barracks.   L = Lycée.
C = Marché aux Chevaux (Horse Market).

Chartres grew under the ægis of its cathedral.   Situated on rising ground on the west bank of the Eure river, it was an early centre of Gallic worship, and this site was selected for the foundation of the cathedral, that is dedicated to the Virgin.   Continuity of tradition in the siting of the religious edifices is reflected in the tradition that the cathedral was established above a grotto where the Druids celebrated the worship of a " maiden who should bear a child ".   The building of the present cathedral took place in the early 12th century, and it is one of the finest specimens of Gothic architecture.   The Counts of Chartres were also powerful in the city in the feudal era.   It is the market centre of the grain lands of Beauce to the east of it and after the Revolution, it became the capital of a Department.

nucleus, made up of blocks, sometimes with long circular blocks surrounding it, and centred on the public monument, be it church, cathedral, abbey or monastery.   Extension from this nucleus depended on the site and historical conditions, but the enclosed oval nucleus in the centre around the initial settlement is the most marked feature.   It is found very characteristically in Limoges. Other examples of the same mode of growth are Beaune (Fig. 78), Brive, and Mende, St. Afrique, Marjevols in the Causses region (Fig. 79).   The type is particularly frequent among the towns of the south of France, where religious institutions, particularly early cathedrals, were established in the first centuries of the Christian era on entirely new sites not defended by Roman walls.   This mode of growth from a defended oval-shaped nucleus appears also as a distinct type in Germany.

A third type of medieval settlement was the so-called castle town.   Many of these emerged as small manorial settlements parasitic on the castle, to which, once the concept of town government had evolved in the older cities, elementary rights of self-government were granted.   The feudal castle, erected as an individual residence and strongpoint by the territorial lord, emerged during the 10th century in France at the same time as the larger communal stronghold.   It was from this early structure that the Norman castle and the subsequent design of the medieval castle emerged.   Such castles were constructed over much of France in the early Middle Ages (from 900 to 1100), and the lords granted rights of elementary self-government to their communities on the pattern of those developed in these earlier towns. The castle consisted of the *donjon*, the residence of the seigneur, the *motte*, the quarters of the soldiers, and the *basse-cour*.   The last was embraced by outer defences—palisade, ditch or wall— and held the quarters of those dependent upon the seigneur and his soldiery : it was also a place of refuge for the folk of the surrounding district and their stock.   When danger was prolonged refugees stayed there.   Groups of merchants and artisans joined the peasants, and a *bourg neuf* or *bourg franc* was often annexed to the *basse-cour*.   One or several churches were built and a market was opened.   The human hive grew.   All that remained was to enclose these nuclei of settlement in a single wall and to make the contiguous *bourgs* the *quartiers* of one *ville*.   Such were the beginnings of Chateauroux (952), Niort (10th century), and Alençon (11th century).[1]

In northern France parasitic settlements, relying, as indicated above, on the castle for refuge and protection, often grew up within the castle walls in the *basse-cour*.   In the later development

[1] Flach, *Origines des lieux habités en France*, 1894, Vol. II, p. 302.

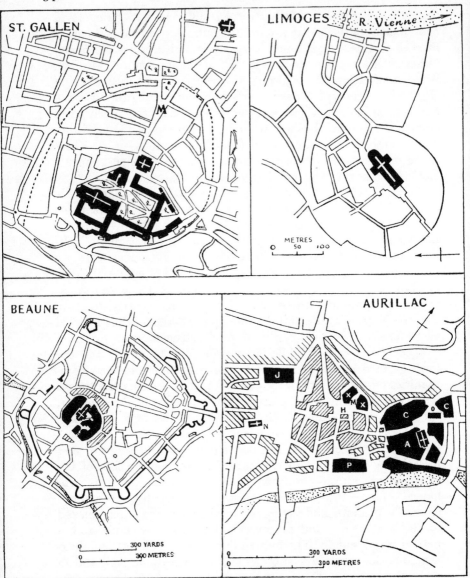

Fig. 78.—Early medieval towns with an ecclesiastical nucleus.

St. Gallen (1 : 10,000) in the Aargau of Switzerland has its nucleus in the Bene-
dictine monastery with rectangular lay-out of buildings, founded in the 8th century
by the Irish monk, St. Gall. The *Altstadt* did not become an Imperial city until
1415. The *Stiftskirche* dates from 674. The dashed line shows the site of the medieval
wall, corresponding with elongated blocks and an encircling wide street. Note the
long widened street market leading to the monastery nucleus with roads branching
from it.

Aurillac (1 : 10,000) lies on the north bank of a deeply cut valley. A is the abbey the small market settlement with elementary rights of self-government was established outside the castle walls and was often finally enclosed by walls that joined it up with those of the castle. In the later development of the castle fortifications, towns were founded or grew up within the circle of its system of defences, by which the town was virtually an outer ward of the castle. This characterizes the Edwardian castle of North Wales, and those of the Teutonic Order in East Prussia and medieval Livonia. The same relationship is found in many towns in France. Thus, at Coucy the castle is situated upon a high well-defended hill site, flanked on three sides by steep slopes and on the fourth by a moat. Adjacent to it is the *place d'armes* (the bailey), a large open space surrounded by stables and barracks for the garrison of the castle. This is bounded by a wall through which a gate leads to the town, the third unit, that is bounded by steep slopes and a wall. The castle was thus a third and last defence in case of attack. Many other towns are cited by Viollet-le-Duc as having a similar site and lay-out, such as Guise, Château-Thierry, Châtillon-sur-Seine, Falaise, Meulan, Dieppe, Saumur, Bourbon and Montfort.

The plans of these towns, however, vary greatly because of both the circumstances of their historical development and the relation which castle and town bear to the site, which was normally marked by good natural defences. Thus there are many cases in which castle and town lie together on a hilltop or on a promontory. In others the town lies adjacent to the castle with the castle alone on the hilltop and the town below it on the slopes or at the foot of the hill or river meander, sometimes with the castle sited on a promontory and the town below on the banks of a river, with its plan adjusted to the lie of the land, to the river-banks and to the main route that pass through it. In yet other cases both castle and town lie on a plain, so that the site did not affect the plan, and cultural factors were decisive in topographic growth. It is very rare, however, for a town to have grown up concentrically around a castle nucleus on a plain site.

and in black the abbot's town, with the old College (C) and the site of St. Clement's church (O). The old town is the shaded area to the west, and beyond it the newer areas near the station (off the map). Note in the old town the Hôtel de Ville (H) (formerly the site of the parish church), the market-place (M) and the old Hospice (X). Open space, formerly for fairs, in newer part, has the Palais de Justice (J) and the church of Notre Dame aux Neiges (N). P is the Prefecture.

Limoges (1 : 7,500) shows the *cité*, as described on p. 120 (based on a 17th-century plan), consisting of the cathedral and an enclosure of elongated blocks (cf. the plans of the southern bastide in France, Fig. 82, p. 356).

Beaune (1 : 18,000) shows concentric growth around an ecclesiastical nucleus with the market-place (1) outside it, and radial growth from it.

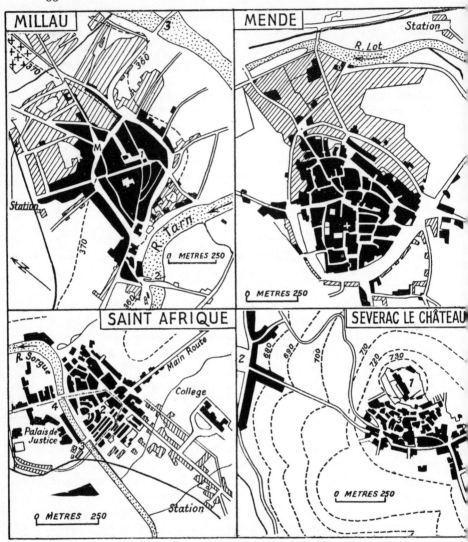

FIG. 79.—Four small towns of the Grands Causses in France (from Marrés, *Les Grands Causses*, 1936.

Mende. (Scale, 1 : 20,000). In black, the built-up areas in 1789. Hatched, later extensions.

Mende, the ancient capital of the *pays* of Gévaudan, is situated in the broad flat valley of the river Lot at the contact of the granite plateau country of the Gévaudan and the limestone country of the Grands Causses. It lies on a terrace between the river and the scarped edge of the limestone plateau of the Causses, at the foot of which springs and streams issue from a river in the town. St. Privat took refuge in the limestone caves, and in the 10th century the site became a centre of pilgrimage and was occupied by a bishop's see in 998. In the early 12th century it was the spiritual centre of Gévaudan. Towards the end of the century the place was walled by

Many towns were founded in the later Middle Ages in the south, and have a more or less rigidly planned lay-out, obviously determined by definite planning principles, whose development can be traced from town to town through the Middle Ages. Here, we may add, the distinction between the lay-out of town and village is often as impossible to define as is the essential character of either. These are the *villes créées* as opposed to the *villes spontanées*. The beginnings of planned settlement followed five centuries of invasion and devastation during the *Völkerwanderung*. In the 10th and early 11th centuries settlements called *sauvetés* were

---

Aldebert III of Toulouse. The wall was heart-shaped, and is now replaced by boulevards. The old town is dominated by the cathedral that towers in its centre. Séverac le Château. (Scale, 1 : 20,000.) 1. Castle. 2. Station. 3. Place de la Fontaine.

Séverac-le-Château is clustered around a strong castle, the head of a medieval barony, on the top of an isolated limestone hill that commands extensive views and an important routeway. The *bourg* lies on the steep slopes of the hill at the foot of which a spring rises in the town (Place de la Fontaine). Never a town of any importance, some growth has been occasioned by the advent of the railway to the west of the *bourg*.

Saint Afrique (from Marrés). (Scale, 1 : 15,000.) 1. Church nucleus and original market-place on its south side. 2. Place aux Herbes. 3. Old bridge. 4. New bridge. In black, built-up areas in 1862. Hatched, later extensions. Dot-dash line, the boulevards (*Aires*) on site of the 18th-century fortifications.

St. Afrique, situated where the river Sorgue opens out at the confluence of three valleys, commands the routeway from the Albi to the south-west to the Rhône plain. It began in obscurity as the refuge of a Christian saint (St. Afrique) in the 6th century and the town was granted liberties in 1257 by the count of Toulouse. The original nucleus, commanding the bridge-head, enclosed both the church and the first market-place with horse-shoe-shaped blocks. The ditch surrounding this nucleus is now replaced by boulevards.

Millau. (Scale, 1 : 20,000.) Black, built-up areas in 1862. Hatched, later extensions. 1. Place de l'Hôtel de Ville. 2. Old bridge (12th century). 3. New bridge (13th century). M = Market-place.

Millau is situated in a fertile lowland on the north bank of the river Tarn on slightly raised ground away from the river flood plain. It early commanded a route on the site of a Roman road from Bas Languedoc to Gévaudan and the Auvergne, and developed particularly as a thoroughfare and outfitting centre. The Roman road crossed the river by a ford and formed the east–west axis of the town. Bridges were built below (1156) and above (1282) the ford and narrower curving streets at right-angles to the first run from north to south, joining the bridges to the market-place at the intersection of the roads in the heart of the town. It thus began as a ford town and developed as a bridge-head town. In 1778 the place had 5,000 people; then commenced the growth of the glove-making industry, and the population reached 17,000 in 1896 (the first railway appeared in 1874). The lay-out and extent of the town were substantially the same as in the Middle Ages, except that boulevards had taken the place of the walls and extensions had taken place beyond. The old town has narrow and crooked streets, and, closely built-up with multi-storeyed houses, it has the aspect of a " faubourg napolitaine ". The market-place has its arcades, like the towns of Aquitaine. " Dans cette ville règne une animation qui lui confère un caractère méridional. Ses avenues ont l'affluence et la gaieté des *Cours* des villes provençales." These aspects of the town, coupled with its surroundings of limestone hills, and vine- and orchard-covered slopes, reminds one forcibly of the towns of the Mediterranean lands.

established under the auspices of the Church. While these were rural in function, they did show some attempt at design. The rectangular lot was used, and there was usually an amorphous grouping of blocks in which the rib pattern is traceable. The end of this preliminary period and the beginning of the main town-building era was marked by the creation in 1144 of one of

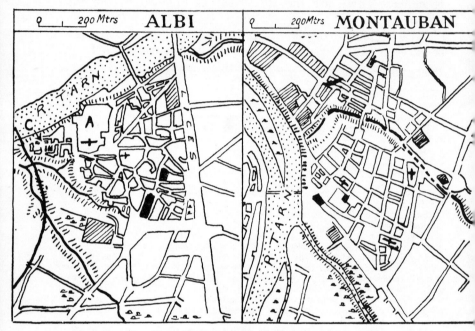

Fig. 80.—Two Town Types in Southern France. Albi and Montauban.
(Scale, 1 : 15,000.)

Albi lies on a bluff overlooking the river Tarn. Beginning with the oppidum in the west (C), the bishop's seat was established to the east as a fortified cathedral (A), with commanding views up and down the river. The town is clustered on the east side of the cathedral nucleus, while the Lices is a wide thoroughfare planned in the 18th century. Note the irregular, congested plan in relation to cathedral and bridge. This is very characteristic of the towns of the Midi.

Montauban lies on a similar site on the Tarn, but was founded in 1144 and has a regular lay-out, with a central quadrangular market-place, that is closely adjusted to the terrain (drawn from Baedeker plans).

the most remarkable towns in France, Montauban (see Fig. 80). Founded by the Count of Toulouse, it was sited on a high peninsula of old terrace gravels. Its fortifications are adjusted to the lie of the land, and give to the plan a trapezoid shape. This is in turn reflected in the direction of the streets and the shape of the central market. The rectangular block is skilfully fitted into this scheme, and it is known that rectangular lots of equal size were employed in the original survey. Owing to its harmonious design and skilful adaptation of this town to its site it has been described by Brinckmann as " the first manifestation of Gothic urbanism ". It stands in complete contrast to its near neighbour, Albi, which, though on a similar site, has an entirely different morphology, since it grew gradually as a fortified cathedral (Fig. 80).

From 1150 until 1350 there followed a period of active town building. In the fourteen departments of south-west France, bounded by the Dordogne to the north, the Central Massif to the east, and the Pyrenees to the south, about half the towns were founded during this period. *Bastides* (a Provençal word meaning a fortress) were founded as sources of revenue, but principally as fortified centres whither settlers were attracted, and their loyalty assured, by the granting of liberal charters. The Counts of Toulouse founded a number of such fortress towns in the 12th century, of which Montauban is the most conspicuous example. In 1152 England obtained control of the provinces of Guienne and Gascony, and after the Albigensian Wars (1229) the King of France obtained indirect control of Toulouse, which, with the death of Alphonse of Poitiers in 1271, passed directly to the Crown. Alphonse established many new towns in his new possessions as a means of swelling his revenues, quelling the nobility and protecting his frontiers. The same motives actuated the founding of many towns during the long struggle between England and France. Henry III and Edward I early created a cordon of *bastides*. The chief disputed zone lay between the Garonne and the Dordogne ; the latter river, indeed, was long regarded as the frontier between the two powers. Here the majority of the towns were founded between 1250 and 1350. These settlements drew mainly upon the local population. The name of the *bastide* suggests the novelty of the experiment (Villeneuve), the liberties promised to the colonists (Villefranche), its security (Sauveterre), a feature of the site (Beaumont, Montjoie), the name of its founder (Libourne, named after Roger of Leybourne), a famous town whose name appealed to the founder (Cordes, Cologne, Barcelona). These settlements caused in considerable measure, a regrouping of the population, particularly, according to Deffontaines, in these areas where hitherto there were few nucleated settlements, or where there was much uncultivated land. But far too many *bastides* were founded. Many were failures, as is clearly evident

PUYMIROL

GRENADE-SUR-ADOUR

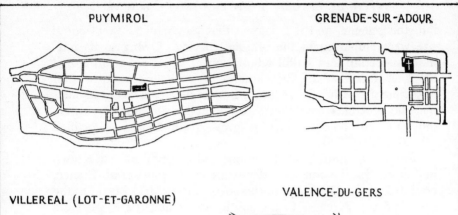

VILLEREAL (LOT-ET-GARONNE)

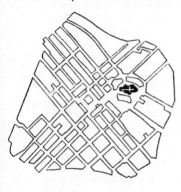

VALENCE-DU-GERS

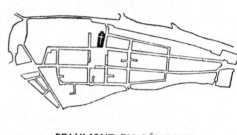

BEAUMONT-EN-PÉRIGORD

MONPAZIER

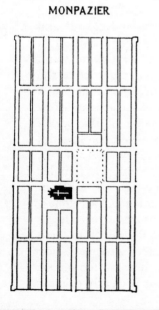

CORDES (TARN)

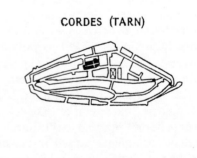

1:10,000

| 0 | 100 | 200 | 300 | 400 | 500 YARDS |

| 0 | 100 | 200 | 300 | 400 | 500 METRES |

from their uncompleted plans, and others have since declined to the status of rural villages. A variety of plans of *bastides* is shown on Fig. 81.

Lavedan recognizes four main groups of plans among the *bastides* : (*a*) those with no clear generating axis and a crude, irregular block composition ; (*b*) those which consist of an irregular grouping of rectangular blocks, focused on a nucleus such as church, place, or a group of small blocks, a type that is comparable with the radial-concentric system ; (*c*) those with a route as a generating axis ; (*d*) regular grid plans. The axial plans are all elongated and consist of a regular composition of blocks along an existing highway. The blocks are arranged in two or more series. Further, the rectangular market is adjacent to the main route and transverse axes are not well developed. Plans developed on two, three, four or five axes are variants of this group. In addition there are included plans on two intersecting axes, and finally a spindle pattern (*fuseaux de route*). The last, which is a rare type in southern France (but common as a highly developed form in eastern Germany, as we shall see later), is formed through the adaptation of the plan to the wall and the site.

The grid plans all have a regular composition of rectangular blocks, a series of axes intersecting at right angles (that is, there is no single generating axis) and a central block is reserved for the market-place. These plans vary greatly in their composition, and although the right angle is rigidly applied, the plan of Monpazier, which is perhaps the best known to English readers, is an outstanding exception in the regularity of all its features in combination. A number of these plans show a general adaptation of the pattern to the relief of the site.

Finally, attention must be drawn in particular to the first two types (*a*) and (*b*) above (Fig. 82). The incomplete forms are usually the early attempts at planning villages by ecclesiastical

---

FIG. 81.—Bastide Towns in Southern France with Rectilinear Plans
(redrawn from Lavedan). (Scale, 1 : 10,000.)

These plans show the varying kinds of composition of the rectangular blocks in relation to the streets, especially the main route axis, the market-place and church, and the terrain of the site.

Note the highly developed parallel street plan at Puymirol, the irregular grouping of blocks at Grenade, the combination of these two motifs at Valence, the grouping of blocks, as a planned motif, around the church at Villereal, and the eccentric position of the church at Beaumont in its parallel street plan.

Monpazier and Cordes are two extreme examples. Monpazier is rigidly planned inside a rectangular wall with a focal market-place and an enclosure reserved for the church adjacent to the latter. Cordes is a typical hilltop site, such as occurs often in south France, and the whole plan is adjusted to the steep hill slopes. The hill rises by 100 metres above the lowland. There are three walls, each oval in shape, adjusted to the hill contours, and the earliest surrounds the flat summit of the hill, which has a main east–west axis (6–8 metres wide). The church lay along the first, and earliest, wall and was fortified, as at Albi, Montpellier, and Narbonne. The market-place lies in the centre of the summit. It dates from the 14th century and is arcaded in Italian style. Parallel streets along the contours lie along and between the walls.

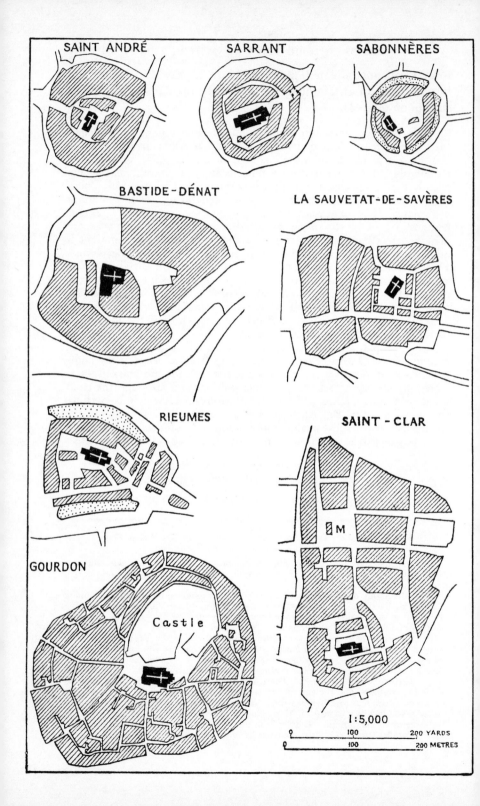

SAINT ANDRÉ   SARRANT   SABONNÈRES

BASTIDE-DÉNAT   LA SAUVETAT-DE-SAVÈRES

RIEUMES   SAINT - CLAR

M

GOURDON

Castle

1:5,000

100   200 YARDS

100   200 METRES

authorities and were known as *sauvetés*. Of special importance, however, is the type that consists of a circular grouping around a central element, be it church or open space. This grouping was undoubtedly due to the imperative need for defence in this country during the centuries of war that ravaged it, notably the Albigensian wars and then the long wars between the English and the French. The plan is precisely similar in character to the earliest cathedral strongholds that emerged in medieval times. Homologues are found not only in bigger cities like Limoges, Beaune and Münster, but also in many smaller places that were established in the later Middle Ages (see below for western Germany).

There are marked contrasts in the nature of the smaller urban settlements between the Nord and the Midi. The Nord is the domain of the small market town, which served both as a seat of handicrafts and as a market for the surrounding countryside, and, as in England and the Low Countries and north-western Germany, a great many of these are unwalled. They are usually centred on a market-place on one main route or at a focus of routes with houses spreading along the routes. Some of these grew gradually from village origins, while others, like the principal towns, were the result of a deliberate foundation adjacent to an existing settlement, castle, monastery, or abbey. As an example of the town with village origins, it has been shown that the town of St. Peter Port was gradually transformed in the constitutional as well as in the topographic sense.[1] The second type is illustrated by Étampes, where at the end of the 11th century there were two settlements, the *castrum* and the *vicus*, while in the early 12th century a market settlement was established with its centre in the church of St. Gilles between the two older settlements on the main road from Paris to Orleans.[2]

[1] J. H. Le Patourel, " The Early History of St. Peter Port ", in *Trans. de la Société Guernaise*, 1934, pp. 171–208.
[2] M. Prou, " Une Ville Marché du XIIᵉ siècle : Étampes ", *Mélanges offerts à H. Pirenne*, 1926, pp. 379–89.

FIG. 82.—Bastide Towns in Southern France with Radial-Concentric Plans.

These are examples of a mode of grouping that is very common among the small *bastides* of southern France. The outstanding feature is the grouping of elongated blocks around the central church, or enclosure, as a means of protection. Exactly the same grouping occurs in the nucleus of many larger towns throughout western Europe. An example in southern France is Saint-Clar with an enclosed nucleus around the Church, adjacent to which is a planned rectilinear lay-out with central rectangular market. Gourdon is an example of irregular concentric growth around a castle and church, which morphologically is the same as the smaller *bastides*, since its growth was due to similar needs. All these plans show the essential nuclear features of the radial-concentric pattern (from Lavedan).

By way of contrast, in the Midi, the compact, congested town is much more characteristic (see Fig. 79). It is neither rural nor urban, but occupies an intermediate rôle, serving as the habitat of peasants, who hold land in the surrounding country-

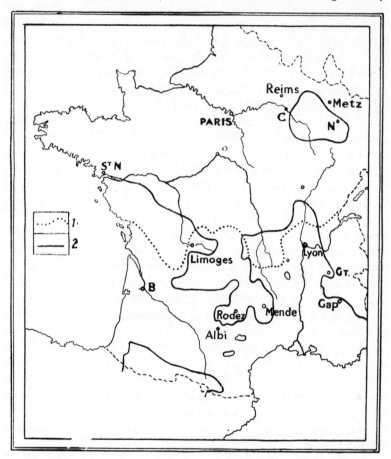

FIG. 83.—The Distribution of House-roof Types in France (redrawn from Brunhes, Vol. II, pp. 122 and 441).

1. Boundary between areas using the *droit écrit* in the Midi (south) and the *droit coutumier* in the Nord (north). 2. Boundary between houses with steep roofs and flat tiles or slates in the north and gently sloping roofs with hollow tiles in the south.

side, as well as of craftsmen and traders. In many cases such a settlement emerged by selection from the clustered villages that characterized the countryside of the Midi. Moreoover, such settlements invariably occupied naturally defended sites as opposed to the market settlements of the Nord which were invariably situated at local nodal points of routes. The compact hilltop *bourg*, both village and small semi-urban settlement, is to-day characteristic of the southern Alps south of the Isère basin.[1] In the middle Rhône basin it occurs frequently, and downstream it becomes more characteristic until in Languedoc and Provence it is the dominant settlement type.[2]

In Aquitaine, according to Deffontaines, two-thirds of the towns—including the *bastides*, that give to this region a quite distinctive character, have hilltop sites.[3] These contrasts are also associated with types of rural settlement. The three-field system and the irregular clustered village were characteristic of northern, and the two-field system with individual buildings in hedged fields and compact hilltop villages were characteristic of southern France.[4] Morphologically, the small urban habitat in the Nord has its prototype in the rural settlement, for the small town began as such a settlement, and was transformed in size and function in proportion to the measure of its urban activities.

Further contrasts between north and south are reflected in architecture. Northern France is the domain of Gothic, whereas the basis of the architecture of the Midi is Romanesque with Gothic as an intruder—although the churches of the *bastides* were usually built in the 15th and 16th centuries in the Flamboyant style and stand in marked contrast to the Romanesque churches in the country villages. Further, the Midi has buildings with flat, tiled roofs, as is shown on the map prepared by Deffontaines and Brunhes (Fig. 83). The northern boundary of the flattish roof runs from the mouth of the Loire to latitude 46° and thence from Mâcon on the Rhône, and south across the Alps to Nice. To the north the steep roof of slate, tile, thatch, or wood is dominant. This contrast bears no direct relation to rainfall, as is sometimes rather superficially assumed. " En vérité, les deux genres de toits français caractérisent les deux Frances septentrionale et meridionale."[5]

2. THE LOW COUNTRIES

(a) *Flanders*. The origins and topographic formation of the towns of Flanders have been carefully studied by historians,

---

[1] R. Blanchard, *Les Alpes Françaises*, 1934, p. 77.
[2] D. Faucher, *Plaines et Bassins du Rhône Moyen*, 1927.
[3] Deffontaines, *L'Homme et ses Travaux dans la Moyenne Garonne*, 1934.
[4] See A. Demangeon, on types of village settlement in France, *Annales de Géographie*, Vol. XLVIII, 1939.
[5] Brunhes and Deffontaines, *Géographie Humaine de la France*, Vol. I, p. 439, map on p. 441. See pp. 317–23.

especially by Prof. H. Pirenne. An excellent atlas of town plans is also available in Deventer's atlas of the 16th century.[1] Jacques Deventer was commissioned by the Emperor Philip II to survey the towns of the Netherlands. He began the work in 1545 and it was not far short of completion when he died in 1575. According to a contemporary authority, the Spanish Netherlands had 320 towns *closes et murées*, and about 230 *villes ouvertes*. The Deventer atlas of Belgium contains plans of about a hundred towns. Of these 22 were unwalled, that is, *villes ouvertes*, and 14 had a ditch (*fosse*) with gates. The 16th century witnessed the emergence of new methods of defence with the advent of gunpowder and the new system of fortifications. The old walls of certain towns had bastions added to them, while about 16 towns were established under Charles V as new towns or were fortified with large citadels. The remainder of the towns had medieval walls that remained unchanged except by the ravages of time. By modernizing the fortifications Charles V strengthened the southern frontiers of the *Pays-Bas* against France. Later these areas passed to France and were again strengthened by Louis XIV so as to serve for defence in reverse. The medieval walls of most of these towns were destroyed during the 17th century or fell into decay unless they were strengthened. Towns which fell to France have often preserved their walls to this day. Many town walls were cleared away by law during the 19th century.

The Flanders plain and the Meuse valley were the first areas in north-western Europe in which genuinely urban activities appeared with the turn of the millennium. During the 9th and 10th centuries new *burgs* or strongholds were established by the counts of Flanders as fortresses for the secular administration of the surrounding districts and as places of refuge. Abbeys, monasteries and churches were also established, and in northern Gaul bishoprics appeared. During the 10th and 11th centuries small merchants' colonies grew up adjacent to those of the strongholds that enjoyed the best situations with regard to the existing natural routeways. This new type of settlement was the *portus*. The merchants were joined by craftsmen who immigrated from the surrounding countryside—particularly as cloth workers in the Scheldt valley and metal (iron and copper) workers in the Meuse valley. Gradually these communities acquired rights of self-

[1] Ch. Ruelens, *Atlas des villes de la Belgique au XVIᵉ siècle, 100 plans du géographe Jacques de Deventer, 1885–1895*, and edited since 1912 by Em. Duverleaux, J. van den Gheyn and others. See Ch. Ruelens' article in *Bull. soc. royale belge de Géog.*, Vol. VIII, 1884, also the review by H. Haack in *Petermanns Mitteilungen*, 1913, LIX, p. 93.

government and the guilds were responsible for the building of walls, roads, houses, public buildings and market-places. In these cases the growth of the urban community was unhindered by the stronger local interests of a commercial organization or the ecclesiastical rights of abbot or bishop. Usually, at an early date, the guilds constructed fortifications around the settlement for protection and as a limit to the field of its jurisdictional powers and the special peace to which it was entitled. Market-place and church formed the nucleus of the settlement, and around the former grouped the guild halls, town hall, cloth halls, belfry and in a secluded position, the church. From this centre growth took place radially along the streets, individual sectors being planned by the municipal authorities with a fairly rectangular lay-out between them. The more thriving cities were enclosed by two or more successive walls, so as to give the whole plan a radial-concentric pattern. The original *burg*, the initial nucleus of crystallization and the seat of feudal authority, was absorbed by the town, its buildings sometimes demolished, and the land ceded to, and subdivided by, the burgesses. Its oval form, even when the castle has disappeared, is recognizable in the modern plan, by the shape of its irregular group of building blocks. All these towns became essentially craftsmen-merchant communities with full self-government, and this is clearly recognizable in their plan and build to this day. In only two cases were there bishops' cities, in which, though the development was similar, it was more tardy, owing to the opposition of the vested interests of the bishops. These towns were Liége and Utrecht.

The general traits in the development of these towns are reflected in their topographic formation (see Bruges, Fig. 84). The first stronghold commanded a river crossing or was situated on prominent ground. The trading colony or *portus* was located alongside the river front. The town then began to develop as a seat of crafts and commerce, situated at a crossing of important highways with its focus in a market-place. When the townsmen attained their independence they erected their own public buildings on and around the market-place. The surrounding settlement that clustered around monasteries and smaller parish churches was embraced by the walls or ditches that were built by the townsmen in one or two successive phases. In some cases the old stronghold entirely disappeared, the land being acquired by the townsmen and subdivided for building, and all that remains to-day is the street name. In others, as is well illustrated at

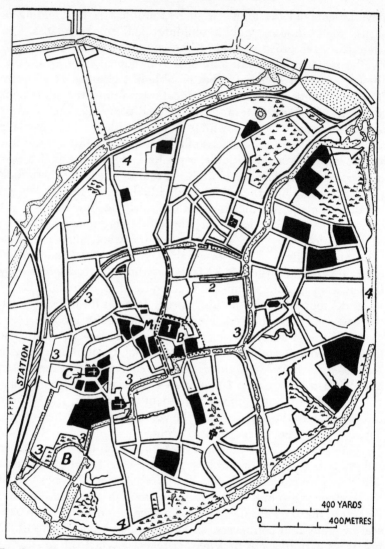

FIG. 84.—The Growth of Bruges. Based on Baedeker plan for 1885 with additional
data from Ganshof. (Scale, 1 : 20,000.)

Streams and canals are stippled. Public buildings are in black. B = Beguinage.
C = Cathedral. M = Grande Place (market-place). B = Place du Bourg.
Extension of the medieval town : 1. The burg enclosed by a dotted line. 2. First
canal, built as a forward defence of the burg about 1089. 3. The first town wall,
possibly built before 1089, certainly before 1127. 4. The second town wall,
1297–1370.

Bruges has origins and a medieval plan that excellently typify the growth of the
Flemish town. A *bourg* (German, *burg*) (*curtes comites*) or stronghold was built here
by the counts of Flanders in the 9th century on the west bank of the river Reie. This
was enclosed by a moat in 865. There was also a second, and indeed an earlier,

Mons, the castle was situated on a low but prominent hill, but soon it ceased to be the focus of the life of the town, which shifted to the market-place at the convergence of routes near to the castle nucleus but quite distinct from it. The latter was a dead element that was either absorbed or completely surrounded by the rapidly expanding built-up land. The parish church was an important local gathering-point in these towns, and usually one church situated on or near the central market was the chief church of the town. A little farther south, such Gallo-Roman towns as Tournai and Cambrai illustrate the medieval town that underwent the same kind of early growth as those of Flanders. However, these were dominated by their great cathedrals, where the grant of rights of self-government was retarded and opposed by the bishops, whereas the secular rulers of Flanders encouraged the grant of such rights.

Brussels has already been noticed as an example of this kind of growth. Louvain, with a similar site and situation on the

nucleus of settlement, in the cathedral of St. Sauveur and the adjacent church of Notre Dame, which lay about 400 to 500 metres west of the burg. Both these settlements lay on slightly raised sandy ground that was completely surrounded by low-lying marsh. This primitive topography is evident in the street names. The site of the burg is evident from the shape of the blocks south of the Grande Place between it and the Reie and by the Place du Bourg and the Rue du Vieux Bourg. The sandy land on which the churches were built is evidenced by the Rue du Sablon, and the marshes by such names as Rue du Marécage, and the process of reclamation and lay-out of new streets by both the more regular lay-out around the nucleus and by such names as Rue Terre Neuve. Count Baudouin in A.D. 915 built fortifications and gates around the burg and the churches along the canal of the Quai du Miroir to the Rue Nord du Sablon. A rural *vicus* housed serfs around the churches. Outside the burg there appears a *forum*, with merchants and craftsmen as its settlers, and a chapel, St. Christophe, was founded *juxta forum* near the present Grande Place in A.D. 961. The self-governing urban community (*Keuve*) was bounded to the north by a canal that still exists in the town, running from the Pont des Carmes west to the site of the railway station. This bounds the compact, fully built, and the oldest, part of the town. It was about this time, with the growth of industry and of commerce by the river with the sea, that the Grande Place became the focus of its life and during the 13th century the Hôtel de Ville, the belfry, cloth halls, and Halles were erected. At the end of the 13th century the new canals and fortifications, with eight gates, were built, so that the area of the town was enlarged sixfold and remained until the end of the 18th century. This period was marked by the rapid growth of the town, that was fast becoming a great port. About 12,000 people lived here in the early 11th century and the maximum population at the height of the Middle Ages was not greater than 80,000. The striking feature of the town, as evidenced by its present plan, is the marked contrast between the core and the large area around it between the two belts of fortifications. There are still large open spaces in this belt. In it there are many churches, monasteries and the large Beguinage to the south-west, and several market-places. Moreover the streets are more regular and bear evidence of their reclamation from the marsh and their lay-out in separate sectors. The medieval town spread to the north-east downstream in the direction of the Zwyn, but with the decline of the port this trend ceased. To-day, there is a clear orientation of the building towards the station that lies in the south-west corner of the old town near the cathedral nucleus. Newer public buildings lie on the outer margins of the town, but all lie inside the walls.

river Dyle, has the same features.   More typical, however, are
the chief medieval Flemish towns—Ghent, Bruges (Fig. 84 and
Plate 15), and Ypres (Fig. 85).   St. Quentin and Douai in
northern France belong to the same group (Figs. 85, 86).

The towns of Flanders form a distinct morphological group.
Within the Flemish-speaking area there are almost a hundred
medieval towns, almost a third of them unwalled.[1]   These are

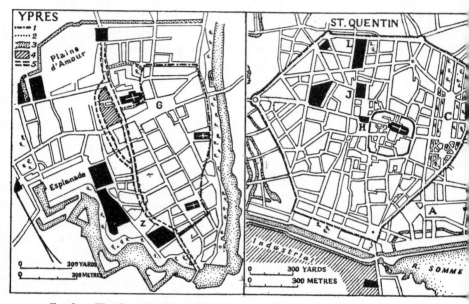

FIG. 85.—The Growth of Ypres (scale, 1 : 20,000), and St. Quentin (scale, 1 : 22,000).

Ypres.   1. The first wall, 1127.   2. Extension of the wall, begun in 1214.   3.
Water.   4. Site of the original *castrum*.   5. Old course of the river.   G = Grande
Place (market-place).   Z = Zaalhof.

St. Quentin, showing first nucleus of settlement grouped around the cathedral,
with the market-place outside it, the medieval wall embracing the whole of the settlement that consists of roads radiating from the market-place.   Post-medieval more
regular extensions lie on the border inside the walls.   H = Hôtel de Ville.
J = Palais de Justice.   L = Lycée.   C = Gardens.   A = Arsenal.

characterized by the dominance of the focal market-place,
situated at the intersection of radial main routes, often with the
site of the remnants of the initial burg adjacent to the place—
the stronghold that formed the nucleus of crystallization of the
early medieval town.   A remarkable feature of numerous small
towns, as shown in the Deventer Atlas, is the frequency with which

[1] F. Leyden, " Die Städte des Flämischen Landes ", *Forsch. zur Deutschen Landes-
und Volkskunde*, Heft 2, 1924, pp. 127–83.

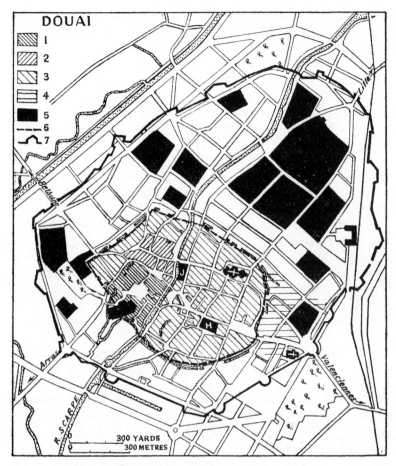

FIG. 86.—The Growth of Douai. (Scale, 1 : 18,000.)

1. Castrum. 2. Duaculum. 3. Duacum in the 10th century. 4. Extension in the 12th century. 5. Public buildings. 6. 10th-century fortifications. 7. The walls in the 14th century, strengthened by bastions in the 17th century. See G. Espinas, *La Vie Urbaine de Douai au Moyen Age*, Paris, 1913, 4 vols., reviewed by F. Clouzot, with map, in *La Géographie*, Vol. 30, 1914, pp. 30–4.

Douai lies in a marshy area, and, though its name dates from Gallo-Roman times, it remained a rural *villa* for centuries. It enjoyed a strategic situation at the junction of the provinces of Flanders, Artois, and Hainault, and a *castrum* stronghold was founded here at the end of the 9th century. Two settlements clustered around this nucleus in the 10th century, one, Duaculum, a rural settlement parasitic on the stronghold, and Duacum, the merchants' colony. Here, too, there grew a market or *forum* which became the centre of Duacum. This settlement lay at the confluence of roads on the navigable river Scarpe. Textile workers clustered in the settlement. A wall embraced the three nuclei, Castrum, Duaculum, and Duacum, in the 10th century. This settlement then extended in the 11th century east beyond the *forum* and north along the Scarpe in the 12th century. The whole settlement was embraced by a final medieval wall in the 14th century, and this was in turn embraced by the bastioned fortifications in the 17th century.

there occurs the combination of a central market-place, irregular in shape and obviously enlarged by the clearance of some buildings ; the winding streets that radiate from the place ; the encircling wall that usually lies well beyond the built-up area, with open spaces lying between it and the town, and with houses alined along the radial streets ; the frequent accompaniment of the wall by a ditch ; and the occurrence of a small moated castle on the line of the walls, which was usually held by the *châtelain*, the count's representative, or was occasionally a lord's residence. Belfry and church lie on or near the market-place. This sort of market settlement is quite clearly the prototype of the settlements in which the major towns had their beginnings outside the pre-urban stronghold.

The size of the settlement within the earliest and the late medieval walls gives an indication of its formation and growth in the Middle Ages. Within its late medieval walls Brussels had an area of 416 hectares, Louvain 395, Bruges 362, Antwerp 352, Ghent 298, Malines 160, Courtrai 144, Tirlemont 128, Dunkirk 128, Lier 120, and Ypres 112, whereas the area of the oldest nucleus within the first walls amounted to 101 hectares at Bruges, 88 at Ghent, 61 at Brussels and Louvain, 53 at Antwerp, and twenty other towns had areas of 25 to 8 hectares. It is likely that the largest of these, Ghent and Bruges, had about 80,000 inhabitants.

These Flemish towns were little affected by the Baroque building of the 17th and 18th centuries, with, of course, the exception of Brussels, the capital. The type is characterized above all by the great belfry, that served as a rallying point for the burgesses and as a landmark in a flat countryside. The church steeple too was lofty and also served as a landmark. The belfry occasionally occurs in northern France, as at Tournai and takes the form of a tower attached to a castle at Mons, Soissons and St. Quentin. It is not found, however, in the towns east of the Scheldt. The belfry is a separate building on the market-place, with a height of 91 metres at Ghent, 100 at Bruges, 70 at Ypres and 90 at Dunkirk. The town church also reaches such heights, as for example that at Bruges, which is 122 metres high, and the original spires of the two churches at Malines, which reached heights of 140 metres and 175 metres. Everywhere these lofty spires, rising up from the market-place, dominate the town. The Flemish town itself is characterized by its network of narrow, winding streets, centred locally on parish churches, and by the dominance of two-storey buildings with two narrow frontages. The irregular core which formed the initial *burg*, the focusing of winding main streets on the market-place, the more regular rectangular lay-out of the areas between the first and second walls, with open spaces (often markets),[1] *Béguinages* (houses for the aged grouped around a quiet enclosure), and the monasteries—all these are characteristic of the build of the Flemish town.

(*b*) *Holland*. The development of the town in Holland came relatively late as compared with Flanders and the Sambre-Meuse trough, for, apart from Leiden and Utrecht, there were no Roman settlements in the area and medieval origins were tardy. A few towns had developed during the 12th, but the majority appeared during the 13th century. It would seem probable that Utrecht, Nijmegen, Leeuwarden, Gröningen, and Leiden were already towns by about 1200, but the majority received their charters in the 13th century. Amsterdam and Rotterdam did not reach this status until the early 14th century. The chief of these towns grew up on the coasts as ports, concerned particularly with the herring fisheries. Others grew up along the navigable waterways. These waterways in the Middle Ages were the Waal, the Lek and the main outlets of the Rhine which, at that time, were to the north, by the old Rhine past Leiden, and northward past Utrecht by the Vecht. The Yssel was also a navigable waterway to the north. Most of these towns were seats of trade, and many of them were members of the Hanseatic League, and many were centres of cloth-making and brewing.

While some towns declined as ports with the silting of their harbours, like Middelburg in Zeeland, others continued to function as active centres, like Leeuwarden. Others declined with the shift of the Rhine waters and the increased size of ships in the 14th century, as did Utrecht and Zutphen. Others were able to participate in the great development of the overseas trade of the Netherlands in the 17th century. A general decline followed in the later 18th century, though in modern times many of these small towns have acquired new industries. Finally, all these towns, apart from their specialized functions as ports or industrial centres, have always served as market centres for the surrounding area, and thither are still brought on market days dairy produce, especially cheese, and cattle. The medieval

---

[1] Huhnermarkt, Rindermarkt, Kornmarkt, Garnmarkt, Freitagsmarkt, etc. See Leyden, *op. cit.*, p. 152.

N

Dutch town was essentially a self-governing community of merchants and craftsmen, engaged in fishing and water-borne trade and in marketing the products of its immediate countryside.

The prototype of the Flemish town is the irregular net of streets grouped around a market-place.   That of the Dutch town is even more remarkable.   One finds in the Atlases of Deventer and Blaeu the recurrence of the same grouping in the smallest towns and the villages.   This consists of two series of buildings facing either side of a canal.   In the larger settlements two or more canals each with two series of houses lie parallel to each other, with a *dam* across one of the canals in the middle of the town.   Examples are Amsterdam (Fig. 37, p. 162), Rotterdam (Fig. 40, p. 172) and Delft and Haarlem (Fig. 74).

The build of the Dutch town clearly reflects its past, especially in those numerous small unspoiled towns, quiet and unfrequented except on market days, which typify the Dutch countryside. Canals thread through the towns.   In riverside towns the canal is split by the *dam*, the head of navigation, in the town centre, through which are the sluice gates draining the polder land behind.   The *dam* is the central feature.   The houses follow the canals with their narrow frontages and gable-ends facing on to the water.   The market-place is the central feature of all the towns, and there too are the town hall, the town church and other public buildings.   The whole town is normally surrounded by a vast moat (*Singel*).   Some of them still have fortifications dating from the Middle Ages or from the 16th and 17th centuries.[1]

(3) The West German Lands

The beginnings of urban development in the German lands are to be sought in the bishoprics that were established on the sites of the Roman *castra* on the Rhine and the Danube, and in the episcopal and imperial castle seats established in the Carolingian era in western Germany, adjacent to earlier German hilltop *oppida*.   The chief of these early German seats lay along the great routeway along the northern border of the central uplands from Cologne eastwards to Magdeburg.   At the end of the eleventh century there were about a hundred of such settlements, with embryonic urban character, at the chief nodal points, at the intersection of river and overland routes in the Rhineland and along

---

[1] The towns of Holland have been mapped by Deventer.   *Nederlandsche Steden in de 16e Eeuw*, Platte Gronden by Jacob van Deventer, Martinus Nijhoff, The Hague, edited by R. Fruin, Algemeen Rijksarchivaris, 1916–23.

the northern border of the central uplands from Aachen to Magdeburg. There was also a third group along and south of the Danube, between it and the foot of the Alps, reaching east to Vienna, founded in 1107. Each of these towns, like the early medieval towns in France, began with a stronghold or *burg* around which, *in suburbio*, clustered the nascent urban settlement. The burg was a fortified nucleus and the seat of ecclesiastical and secular administration, though the earliest walls sometimes included some settlement, and, as in the Carolingian centres of France, a weekly market was held in the precincts of the cathedral. Most of these early centres were bishoprics and monasteries ; a few were secular strongholds, either imperial residences or communal strongholds such as were established widely at this time in western Europe, as for instance in Flanders.

The new urban settlement normally grew up outside the stronghold as a mercantile community, and consisted of a few buildings strung along a routeway (Fig. 69). With the growth of population, through the settlement of merchants and craftsmen from the surrounding countryside, the built-up area spread from the route and found its new nucleus in the market-place, exactly as in the early towns west of the Rhine. With further growth the limits of the town were fixed by successive lines of fortifications, or separate settlements were founded. The stronghold nucleus still stands out in these towns, sited on the highest land, with its limits traceable on the plan by the line of streets which have replaced the earliest fortifications. Topographic growth from this nucleus varies according to the site, conditions, and circumstances of historical development. Each of these places has a bridge point, and the frontage at right angles to it conditioned the main frame of the ground plan. They grew without a preconceived plan, and often have an irregularity of lay-out akin to that of the clustered village. While in Flanders the townsfolk rapidly acquired undisputed control of their town, in the episcopal centres the bishops retarded the transfer of authority to the townsfolk. This was the cause of bitter disputes and pitched battles between burgesses and clerics.

In the Rhine and Danube lands the bishoprics were established without exception in or near Roman settlements. At Strasbourg (Fig. 33), Regensburg (Fig. 87), Cologne (Fig. 18) and Worms, the bishop's settlement lay huddled within the surviving Roman walls, and outside it appeared the new mercantile settlement as a *nova urbs* at Strasbourg, the Rheinvorstadt at

Cologne, or a *pagus mercatorum* at Regensburg.   In other cases the fortified cathedral immunity or imperial residence emerged as an entirely new walled unit, the traces of the Roman *castrum* being so small as to leave no trace in the modern town-plan, and the market-place grew up as the focus of the settlement at some distance from the stronghold.   Such cases are Constance, Basel and Passau which grew from bishops' sees, St. Gallen (Fig. 78) which grew from a monastery (with which may be noted a clearly defined rectangular lay-out of its component monastery build-

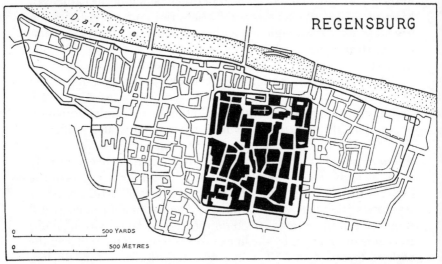

Fig. 87.—The Growth of Medieval Regensburg.   (Scale, 1 : 18,000.)   The cathedral immunity and the palaces of the bishop and emperor (*pagus clericorum*) were inside the rectangular Roman *castrum*.   The mercantile settlement (*pagus mercatorum*), which became the town and was walled in A.D. 920, lies west of the *castrum* and along the river front.   Later extensions to east and west were walled between 1230 and 1320 (after Gradmann).   Compare with Strasbourg, Fig. 33, p. 137.

ings) ; and Frankfurt, Aachen (Fig. 88), Coblenz (Fig. 97), Ulm, and Bingen, which grew from imperial residences.

In inner Germany, beyond the Rhine and the Danube, the effective beginnings of urban settlement are to be found in the fortified strongholds with their roots in either the Saxon (German) *oppida*, hilltop fortified refuges akin to the earlier *oppida* of Gaul, or in the Frankish *curtis*, a small rectangular enclosure used as a resting and outfitting point on a main route during the Carolingian era.   There were two modes of expansion from such a nucleus. West of the Weser, as in the Rhine lands, the built-up area extended radially from the stronghold and the main route was widened to form a street market on which the townsmen's church (Marktkirche) was built. Examples are Münster (Fig. 93), Osnabrück (Fig. 94), and Soest (Fig. 89). East of the Weser, on the border of the central uplands in the open belt of country that formed a great routeway from the Weser crossings to Magdeburg, and where, on the border of the Harz, the first capitals of the Saxons were located, a different type of development took place.

Fig. 88.—The Growth of Aachen (after Aubin and Niessen).
(Scale, approx. 1 : 22,500.)

1. Nucleus of the Carolingian palace (*Pfalz*), church, and baths, around which clustered the first urban settlement (*bürgerliche Siedlung*). 2. Areas walled by Frederick Barbarossa. 3. Areas walled in the 14th century.

Here expansion often took the form of several separate foundations to which the market was shifted from the original street market. Examples of this kind of combined settlement form, consisting of several distinct towns, often separated from each other by walls and each carrying the full paraphernalia of a town, are Hildesheim (a cathedral immunity), Brunswick (with seven separate settlements), Quedlinburg and Lüneburg, each of which began as a secular stronghold (Figs. 92, 95, 96, 98).

Fig. 89.—Soest (scale, 1 : 20,000) grew on the east–west route at salt springs and ponds as a Frankish *curtis*, followed by the churches of St. Peter and St. Patroklus. This was the walled nucleus, and, though the first markets were held inside it, the first market settlement grew outside it on the northern side (M). Note the rectangular shape of the nucleus, probably reflecting the shape of the original Frankish *curtis*; the radial streets running to the nine gates in the walls; and the general irregularity of the plan.

Water stippled, railways black.   M = Market-place.

Fig. 90.—Paderborn (after Peschges).

(Scale, 1 : 20,000.)

1. First wall, around the cathedral (*Domburg*), adjacent to the springs. 2. Extension in the 19th century. 3. Third wall. M = Market-place.

FIG. 91.—Halberstadt.
(Scale, 1 : 20,000.)
1. Cathedral (Dom).
2. Liebfrauen Kirche.
3. Martini Kirche.
4. Rathaus. Fr. = Fronhof.
H = Holzmarkt (timber).
F = Fischmarkt. B = Breite
Weg (main route). The
immunity was fortified in
1020 and is situated on
raised ground. The market
settlement grew on the main
route south of the cathedral
stronghold. Market rights,
989, *Marktkirche* or market
church (*ecclesia forensis in
civitate*), dated 1186 ; whole
settlement embraced by one
wall in early 13th century.

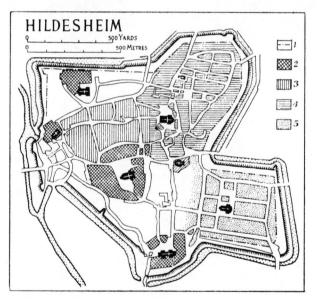

FIG. 92.—Hildesheim (after Hamm). (Scale, 1 : 20,000.)

1. Wall around the whole settlement built in the late 13th century. 2. An early bishop's seat on rising ground east of a river crossing on the main east–west route. Rights of market, mint, and tolls granted to the bishops and held in the immunity, walled about A.D. 1000. 3. Mercantile settlement outside the burg on the main route, a long narrow street market (*Altermarkt*). Monastery to south (cross hatched) was linked to the immunity by the Burg Strasse. 4. A new town was founded during the 12th century and here were Rathaus and guild-houses, the town joining the Hansas in 1200. 5. A new town founded in the early 13th century (*nova civitas orientalis*) with a rectangular plan.

These features are characteristic of the early medieval towns, which include the majority of the cities that have over 100,000 inhabitants to-day.   But if we consider all the towns—and this means in fact four out of every five of the towns of to-day—we find big variations in their morphology from one area to another.   The findings of numerous individual and comparative studies may be summarized as follows.

Although both the plans and functions of the urban settlements

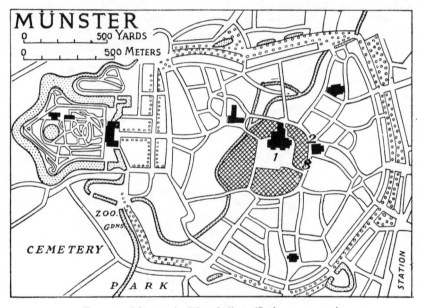

FIG. 93.—Münster in Westphalia. (Scale, 1 : 20,000.)

1. The site of the bishop's immunity is slightly raised ground enclosed by the river Aa.   It was first the site of a Frankish *curtis*, and this was succeeded by the bishop's immunity that was enclosed by rectangular defences like the *curtis*, and then extended and enclosed by the oval wall ; this is the *Domburg*, with a central quadrangular place next the cathedral.   2. A street market was held on the main route on the south side of the burg, and was enlarged to a market-place with adjacent town church (Lamberti Kirche) in 12th century.   Radial extension of streets from this oval nucleus and settlement walled in late 12th century.   The walls were strengthened in the 17th century and the bishops erected a citadel west of the city that was later converted to a palace.

varied regionally, the great majority were the results of deliberate foundation with features in their lay-out that are often repetitive, and bear evidence not only of common origin and function but also of the adoption of the same planning ideas by professional town planners.   In the Rhine lands in particular, it would seem that a considerable number of towns appeared through the gradual transference of town rights to existing villages.   These, however, are a small minority. In north-western Germany, on the heath and low moorland where settlement was thin, and where, as in the Münster archbishopric, the influence of the Church was strong, it

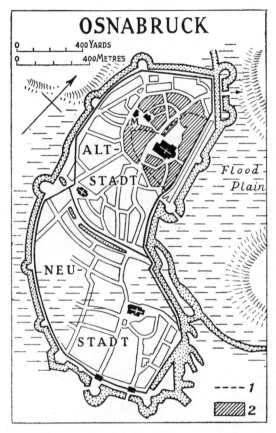

FIG. 94.—Osnabrück. (Scale, 1 : 20,000.)

Situated at a constriction between hills on the west terrace of the Haase river on a main north–south route, the cathedral was established here as an immunity about A.D. 800. This immunity area is crossed by the main route, west of which lay the market-place. Market rights were granted in 882 and renewed in 1002. St. Johannes church is recorded in 1011 and the market church in 1177. 1. Limit of the cathedral immunity. 2. The earliest settlement around the cathedral immunity, later extended to the Altstadt. Neustadt developed to the south and the two enclosed by one wall in 1306 (after Niemeier and Dörries). Marsh in dashed lines, steep slopes in hachures.

would seem that the towns grew up gradually from market centres with a focal market-place and adjacent church. The towns are walled, but small unwalled market settlements are in a majority, and they are characterized by the dominance of a main

FIG. 95.—Lüneburg. (Scale, 1 : 20,000.)

K = Kalkberg, limestone hill on which the Hermann Billungs built their first stronghold at whose feet lay the salt springs that gave the site importance. Here appeared the first monastery and market. 1. St. Michaelis church, and market held on a street (Auf der Altstadt). Between the hill settlement and the river lay the main north–south road, and here were founded the second market settlement, Am Sande (2) and the third (3), the present market, and Rathaus, *nova forum*, in 1371. The castle was destroyed in 1371. Note the radial-concentric plan of the nucleus on the slopes of the burg, and the elongated rectangular markets of the two town foundations.

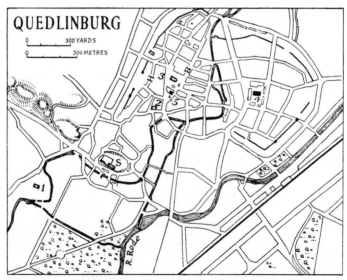

FIG. 96.—Quedlinburg. (Scale, 1 : 20,000.)

1. St. Wiperti church. 2. St. Blasii church. 3. Benedikti church. 4. St. Nikolai church. 5. Rathaus (town hall). S. Schlossberg (castle hill). B. Main street of *Altstadt*. There were four nuclei of settlement in A.D. 1100—St. Wiperti church (on site of *Volksburg*), with a *curtis*, Schlossberg, castle and church on a hill established by Henry I, street market on the north border of the castle hill west of the St. Blasii church. Market shifted to the Altstadt (St. Benedict church) in 11th century. Neustadt (St. Nicholas church) founded in 12th century.

street. In the area east of the Weser the great majority of the towns lie in the belt of open arable country on the northern edge of the uplands, where, at the convergence of the west–east highway with north–south routes, many market settlements were added to the earlier mercantile settlements in the period 1150–1250. Some of these began as Saxon communal strongholds or

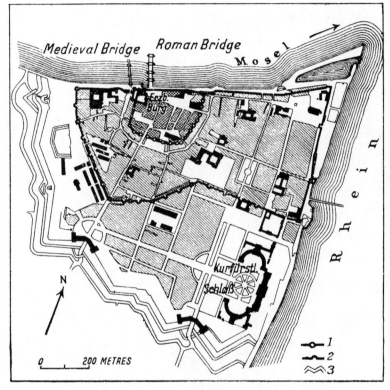

FIG. 97.—Coblenz (from Aubin and Niessen). (Scale, approx. 1 : 15,000.)
 1. Roman wall. 2. Medieval wall (13th century). 3. 18th-century fortifications. Note the archbishop's castle near the Moselle bridge, and the palace of the *Kurfurst* of Trier (Clemensstadt), erected in 1780 facing the Rhine.

imperial castles, a fact evident from the frequency of the suffix *burg*. Almost all these settlements speedily obtained town law, whereas the new foundations were often attached to existing towns so as to form what have been called " combined forms ". In all these towns, outside the irregular plan of the earliest nucleus, a single route forms the axis of the town plan with a focal marketplace. A wide street market with no side streets, a street market

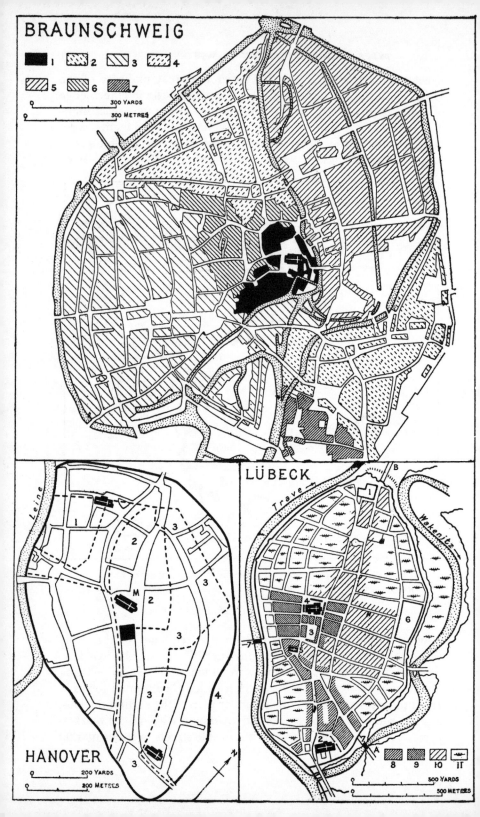

BRAUNSCHWEIG

1 2 3 4
5 6 7

300 YARDS
300 METRES

LÜBECK

Trave

Wakenitz

B

1

4

3

5

M

6

7

2

A

8 9 10 11

500 YARDS
500 METRES

HANOVER

Leine

1

2

M

2

3

3

3

3

3

3

4

N

200 YARDS
200 METRES

with several parallel streets to it, and planned rectangular markets in the centre of such a parallel street plan, are the basic motifs of these towns. An excellent example is Brunswick (Fig. 98).

Farther south, in the Rhine Massif, compact towns with irregular plans lie in the Rhine gorge and are difficult to distinguish in historic development or present aspect and function from the vintners' villages adjacent to them. None of the towns on this great axis of medieval trade has signs of planned extensions, and none, in the historical sense, was a deliberate foundation. They grew gradually from privileges acquired from their lords, culminating in the granting of town law and the right to build their own wall. They are all essentially vintners' villages. The fact that they have never functioned as market centres for the countryside is evident in the absence or small size of their market-places, which served only as places of local assembly and trade. On the other hand there are route plans of both natural (Neuss and Xanten) and planned growth (Goch and Calcar), on the route northwards in the Rhine plain (Figs. 99–100). In striking contrast are the towns of the Rhine plateau, almost all of which appeared in the later Middle Ages as seats of administration attached to a pre-existing settlement, usually a castle such as Nideggen (Fig. 99). Special note may be made of the old church centres of Wetzlar and Limburg, both of which have a clearly defined oval-shaped nucleus on a hill site overlooking a river. A similar type of later settlement is to be found in towns, as at Kempen, with an oval-shaped nucleus centred on a church, the market-place outside the nucleus, and streets radiating to the town walls that are oval in shape and concentric with the central nucleus (Fig. 100). This type is common on both the plateau and

---

FIG. 98.—Medieval Towns of Northern Germany.

Braunschweig (Brunswick) (scale, 1 : 11,000). The town grew from seven separate settlements on the swampy plain of the river Oker. 1. Dankwarderode, a burg established in the 10th century. 2. Altewiek, a village that became a town in 1200. 3. Mercantile settlement that began as a street settlement on the main east–west route with a market and church (*ecclesia forensis*) and formed the nucleus of the founded Altstadt in 1107 on the main route from Frankfurt to Lübeck. 4. The Neustadt and 5. The Hagen were both founded at the end of the 12th century. 6. Sack became a town in the 13th century. 7. The St. Aegidien monastery and market. The five towns were walled separately and the whole group of seven settlements was not merged into one unit (*Stadtgemeinde*) until 1697.

Hanover (scale, 1 : 11,000) :—1. *curia* (small secular stronghold). 2. Market settlement. 3. Extensions. 4. Walls (after Leonhardt).

Lübeck (scale, 1 : 20,000) :—AB = main route (*via regia*). 1. Castle. 2. Cathedral. 3. Market. 4. Marien Kirche (town church). 5. Petri Kirche. 6. Johannes monastery. 7. First bridges. 8. Original settlement, 1143–57. 9. First market settlement, 1158. 10. Built-up area in 1225. 11. Marsh (after Lenz and Rörig). (*By kind permission of the American Geographical Society.*)

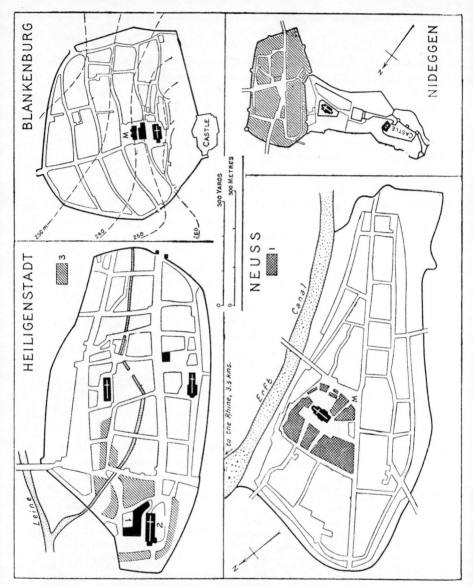

FIG. 99.—The Small Medieval Town in Northern Germany. (Scale, 1 : 10,000.)

Heiligenstadt (Thuringia) :—1. Frankish *curtis*. 2. Lord's church. 3. Demesnial village settlement (Fronhof). Note the street market motif with rib plan, and the irregular nucleus of the demesnial settlement. There is evidence here of the twinning of two founded street settlements on either side of the stream.

Blankenburg is a planned castle town, established in the northern Harz in the late 12th century as a mining centre adjacent to the hilltop castle ; note the location of castle, church, and market (with town hall), and the parallel street plan.

Neuss, on the west bank of the Rhine opposite Düsseldorf, has its nucleus in the cathedral immunity that grew on the site of the Roman *castrum* between the Roman road and the Rhine (I) ; just outside this nucleus is the market-place (M) ; the town

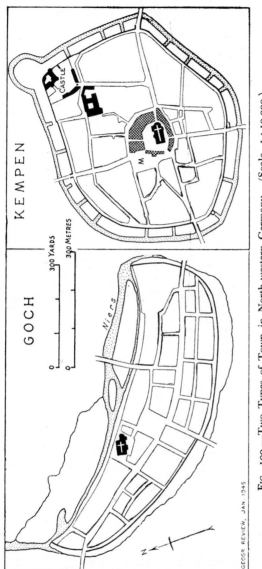

GOCH | KEMPEN

300 YARDS
300 METRES

GEOGR. REVIEW, JAN. 1945

Fig. 100.—Two Types of Town in North-western Germany. (Scale, 1 : 10,000.)

Goch is elongated along a route axis, like Neuss, but has the characteristics of a planned form. It was founded in the marshy valley of the Niers in 1341 and was walled in 1366.

Kempen illustrates a type of north-western Germany. It has an oval-shaped nucleus with a church in its centre, with the market-place just outside the nucleus, and streets radiating to the outer town walls, which are concentric with the nucleus. This type is common on the plain and in the Rhine Plateau. It is closely related to the Westphalian towns and has its counterpart in the well-known plans of Münster, Aachen, and Soest. The enclosed nucleus appears as a single and complete grouping in small settlements such as those of southern France (Fig. 82, p. 356). This form was undoubtedly adopted as a means of defence and is a basic mode of grouping of buildings in the urban habitat, standing in complete contrast to the linear grouping along a route axis, as illustrated by Goch (from Renard, Aubin, and Niessen).

extended along the route axis and was walled about 1200. Note the combination of oval-shaped stronghold nucleus, adjacent main axis with rib plan, and market-place outside the nucleus adjacent to the route axis.

Nideggen is an example of a castle town in the Eifel plateau. The castle (*Burg*) was built at the end of a high spur above the river in 1177, the parasitic settlement or *Burgflecken*, with the Lord's church (*Stiftskirche*), was walled in the 13th century ; a market settlement was founded in the 14th century at the neck of the spur on the main route, and the three units were later enclosed in one wall.

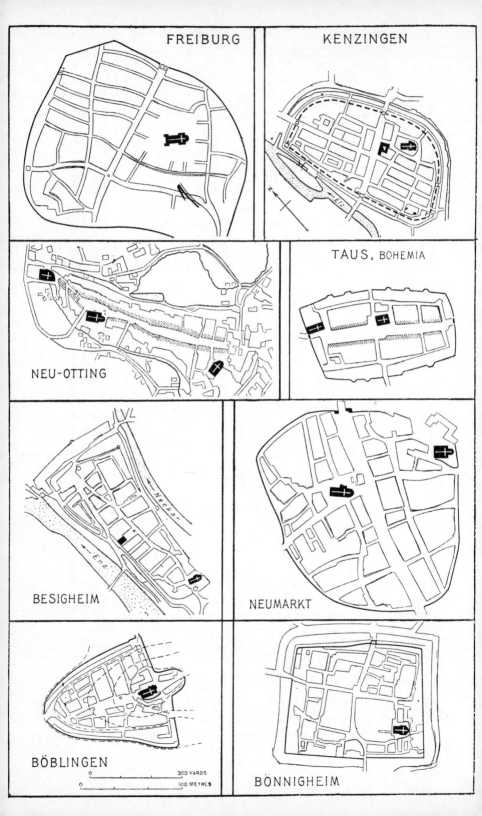

FREIBURG

KENZINGEN

TAUS, BOHEMIA

NEU-OTTING

BESIGHEIM

Neckar

Enz

NEUMARKT

BÖBLINGEN

BÖNNIGHEIM

300 YARDS
0
300 METRES

the plain, and is probably associated with the need for defence. Morphologically it is associated with the fortified stronghold already noted in the important towns of western Europe and in later small towns and villages in southern France.

In Hesse in the later Middle Ages a skein of routes ran between the Rhine Massif and the Thuringian Highland, and the majority of the towns are oriented along a through main route ; many are adjacent to a castle, and all are surrounded by walls.

In south Germany the towns have quite distinctive forms (Fig. 101). The plan is usually dominated by one through route which runs from gate to gate and is generally widened to form a street market, or a rectangular market lies adjacent to it. Irregularly radial plans are rare, the classic example of the radial-concentric plan at Nördlingen being an exception in south Germany. Very small towns with a thousand or so inhabitants, with all the external aspect of a town, are common, and reflect the days of territorial competition and excessive zeal for town founding in the later Middle Ages. The simple street plan, as an unwalled market settlement, is characteristic of the Bavarian plateau between the Alps and the Danube and of Switzerland, where it occurs on a variety of sites as a stereotyped planned form. It was laid out in the 13th century and carried as a definite settlement form to the large colonized area of the eastern Alps. Other recurring types are rib, parallel and ladder street plans. A crossways of two rib patterns (never a grid) with a rectangular enclosure is frequent in the south-west (Württemberg, Baden, and Alsace). It was certainly associated with the adoption of similar ideas of planning and descended from the plan of the initial town foundation in the south-west at Freiburg-im-Breisgau (Fig. 101). The

FIG. 101.—Types of Medieval Town in Southern Germany. (Scale, 1 : 10,000.)

Freiburg-im-Breisgau is built on a route axis, with the main street serving as the market and with the side streets branching from this axis. The church is in a separate enclosure away from the main route (after Hamm).

Kenzingen was founded a century later than Freiburg, also by the Zähringen dukes, and reveals the same ideas of lay-out, with two routes intersecting at right-angles, one serving as a through street market, while the church, as at Freiburg, is separated from the main roads (after Hamm).

The remaining six plans are drawn from southern Germany. They are all small towns founded in the later Middle Ages. Neu-Ötting is characteristic of the small planned and unwalled market settlement on the Bavarian plateau, while Taus is an example of the same basic features as laid out in the towns of the Böhmer Wald. Besigheim, Böblingen, and Bönnigheim are characteristic of the small towns of the Neckar basin in Württemberg, and show the predominance of the street market *motif* and the choice of hilltop and river meander sites. Bönnigheim has a rectangular walled enclosure, that is frequently found in the south-west of Germany. Neumarkt is a characteristic walled street-market town in Franconia.

(*By kind permission of the American Geographical Society.*)

majority of the towns in southern Germany were fortress towns and the unwalled market is rare except on the Bavarian plateau. Castle towns are characteristic of the wooded uplands, in particular where they command valley routes.

(4) THE EAST GERMAN LANDS

The wave of German colonization that spread eastwards beyond the Elbe and the Saale and into the eastern Alps and beyond, began in the first years of the 13th century, after various abortive starts in the 12th. It reached its peak about 1300, and died out during the 14th century. By the end of this period the spearhead of German settlement had reached its limits, and German trade and traders had penetrated into Russia, where German town law was widely accepted. This was a systematic, planned settlement of both countryside and town. Both villages and towns were laid out and settled by people from western Germany. The *Locator*, who was responsible for opening settlements and inviting settlers, drew his ideas from the western homeland and from the plans that were found in the existing Slav settlements in the new land—either by modification of settlements already occupied or by the deliberate imitation of them in new settlements. The most widespread village settlement, for example, that was used as a planned form by the German settlers was the *Angerdorf*. Moreover, even with definite planning ideas, the particular lay-out was usually adjusted to the lie of the land and the direction of the main routes, but towards the end of the period even stereotyped plans were imposed on the topography of the terrain. In the north-eastern lands a great variety of planned forms emerged which have been thoroughly studied. In a first zone east of the Elbe–Saale, stretching from Holstein to Bohemia, settlement took place between 1150 and 1250. The first stage of military conquest and Christian conversion is reflected in the appearance of an oval nucleus (often now subdivided and recognizable by the shape of the building blocks and street names) which was the original stronghold—morphologically akin to the more ancient strongholds in the west. Many such towns, with a roughly planned market settlement attached to such a nucleus, are found in the Altmark. A variety of irregular plans are also found in the middle Elbe basin where the process of settlement was long and complicated. Plans akin to the *Rundling* (a central market and an irregular cluster of blocks inside an oval wall, as at Jena) occur here, as well as in Thuringia and Saxony.

The main zone of German colonization in the 13th century lay to the east. It is here that we find the development of thoroughly planned forms, including the double street, parallel street and meridional plans, and, above all, the central market plan with a rectangular street net of streets of equal width and a group of equal-sized blocks. These types have already been noticed as to their general features in Chapter 16 (Fig. 68, p. 304), and Fig. 102 contains a selection from hundreds of town plans, all of which have essentially the same features. A special variant occurs in East Prussia, where the Teutonic Knights established fortress towns attached to a castle with a rectangular wall, and a church often alongside it. These are peculiar features among the *Kolonialstädte* of eastern Germany, that probably had Oriental origins brought to Europe through the Crusades.

In the south-eastern lands the old street market, as developed in old Bavaria, was carried as the dominant plan of urban settlement. Most of these were very small and were unwalled markets, as in the Tyrol and Styria.

Special mention must be made of the distinctive towns that developed on the coasts of the Baltic Sea as the great ports of the later Middle Ages. The mother of these cities was Lübeck, which gave birth to a town law and a plan that, with modifications, was adopted throughout these northern coast lands. Its plan is shown on Fig. 98. Situated on a peninsula between the river Trave and its tributary the Wakenitz, the site rises gently to a height of 30 to 50 feet, along which a main route ran from north to south. The first German settlement, founded by Adolf II of Holstein in 1143, lay at the southern end of the peninsula where the cathedral was later built ; the castle lay at the northern end. Henry the Lion founded the second settlement in 1158, giving the responsibility for its lay-out and organization to a number of merchants. This initial settlement was placed in the middle of the peninsula with a rectangular market-place between two north–south streets to one side of the main road already mentioned. Lots with dimensions of 25 feet by 100 feet, with the narrow front facing the market, were divided equally among the members of the consortium. A rectangular space on the north side of the market was reserved for the church. To the west, four streets were laid out with long, narrow blocks, each with two sets of lots with the narrow ends fronting on to the streets. Extension of the built-up area grew from this initial lay-out with adaptations to the terrain, and followed an

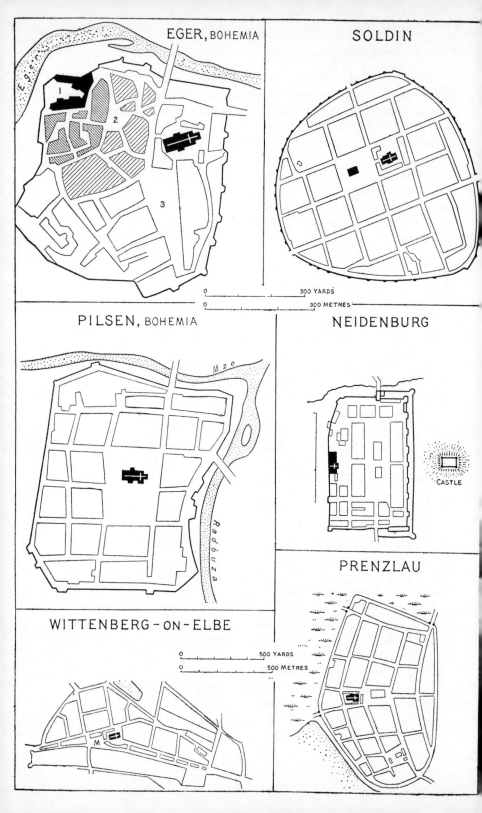

EGER, BOHEMIA

SOLDIN

1

2

3

PILSEN, BOHEMIA

Mze

Radbuza

NEIDENBURG

CASTLE

300 YARDS

300 METRES

PRENZLAU

WITTENBERG - ON - ELBE

M

500 YARDS

500 METRES

approximate grid plan that was, however, closely adjusted to the site.

Lübeck stands in marked contrast to the town of Freiburg, which, as the earliest of the foundations of the Zähringen in south-western Germany, was undoubtedly the model for the town plans of the south-west. Lübeck became the model for those of eastern Germany, and more especially for the coastal towns. Freiburg had one main axis, widened in the centre to serve as a market, with streets broadening from it in a rib pattern and with an adjacent space reserved for the church. The houses were built lengthwise with their gables parallel to the street on lots measuring 50 by 100 feet, the result being a striking contrast, in both plan and build, between the towns of northern and of southern Germany. Lübeck was the parent of the port cities that were founded on the Baltic shores, and its early plan had a profound influence on the development of the lay-out of the *Kolonialstadt* in eastern Germany. The law of Lübeck, as well as its lay-out and architectural styles, was transferred to these new cities, in whose origin and development Lübeck merchants played an important rôle.

These Baltic merchant cities emerged during the 13th century, stretching as far as Reval and Riga. They were modelled in constitution and build on the parent city of Lübeck, the head of the Hanseatic League, and mother of them all. Because of their association with that league and their maritime activities, they

---

FIG. 102.—Planned Towns in the East German Lands. (Scales, 1 : 10,000, except Wittenberg and Prenzlau, 1 : 20,000.)

These plans, repeated in hundreds of small towns in the east German lands, show the characteristic features of the small, country town. Eger (Bohemia) :—1. The imperial castle was built in 1180 on the site of an old Czech stronghold overlooking the river Eger, and a settlement clustered around it (*Burgflecken*), and to this was added the first market settlement (2). A planned market settlement with an elongated market-place was added in the 13th century (3), and the whole settlement embraced by a common wall. Note the remarkable similarity of these planning motifs to the old town of Prague. These features are found in many towns in the east German lands and in east central Europe, where a founded settlement was added to a pre-existing nucleus that was either an ecclesiastical or secular stronghold. Soldin and Pilsen and Prenzlau are good examples of the grid plan with a focal rectangular market-place, with a walled enclosure adjusted to the terrain of the site. The rectangular-shaped wall is adopted as a deliberate plan in the towns of the Teutonic Order, as illustrated by Neidenburg in East Prussia. These towns are usually associated with a castle and the church often lies alongside the wall, not in the centre of the town. Wittenberg on the Elbe has a plan characteristic in the east German lands, especially in Silesia. It has two parallel streets in spindle form with an intervening market-place and church. It may be referred to as the double-street plan and is morphologically related to the *Angerdorf*.

(By kind permission of the American Geographical Society.)

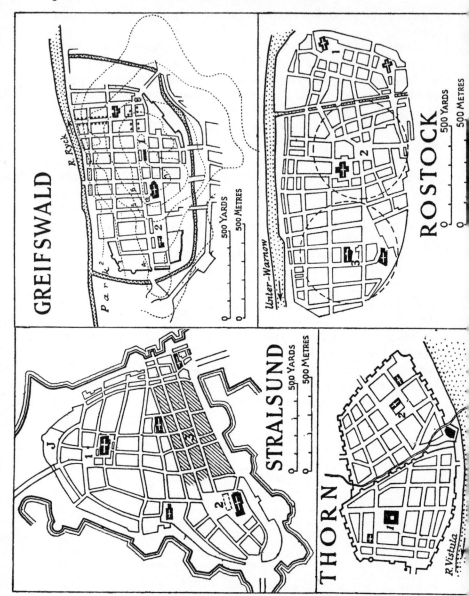

Fig. 103.—Four Medieval Hanseatic Ports in Northern Germany.

Stralsund (scale, 1 : 20,000).   1. First settlement on island site in 1234 around the Altermarkt (Altstadt), on the highest point of the island (10 metres).   2. Neustadt founded in 1240 around the St. Marien Kirche.   3. Extension, with regular plan, of the Frankenvorstadt.   Whole settlement surrounded by one wall and ditch in 1272–8. Outer reclaimed land and fortifications date from the Swedish period of occupation in the 17th century.   Reclamation for modern harbour facilities in 1862–72.

all bear the stamp of similar medieval origins, growth and functions. The towns were placed on dry land sites, girt by marsh and water, adjacent to navigable water-fronts. Although the German settlement was sometimes preceded by a Slav settlement, its site was new, and the Slav settlement completely disappeared and left little trace on the new town. In some cases growth was so rapid that new towns were grafted on to the old in rapid succession. At Rostock, Wismar, Griefswald, Stralsund, Danzig, Elbing, and Königsberg the conditions of development and function were the same (Fig. 103). In each a regular planned lay-out is apparent, centred on the market-place, and a series of parallel streets link up the main route and the market with the water-front. Market, guild houses and public halls are the foci of each of these settlements, with the church in a reserved space to one side of the busy nucleus. These are pre-eminently burgesses' and merchants' cities, and the castle, if there is one, is small and peripheral to the town. The main defence was afforded by the walls, built and maintained by the town council.

In the design of all these planned towns the aim of the planner was clearly conditioned by the needs of the community, as we may learn from the numerous towns of eastern Germany. The planner had to consider such needs as ease of access for each house to the central market-place, around which were always grouped the town hall, church, and guild halls. He also had to consider the problem of through-traffic from gate to gate and the accommodation on separate streets of through and local traffic from house to house, from house to market and house to gate, from gate direct to market, and from gate to gate, along streets with a width sufficient to avoid congestion. The centre of affairs was the market-place. In the early medieval town market-places were small and often improvised in the streets before the church or castle. When the urban community became independent and self-governing, the town council frequently laid out more spacious

---

Thorn (scale, 1 : 20,000). 1. Altstadt. 2. Neustadt. Subsequently surrounded by bastioned fortifications.

Rostock (scale, 1 : 20,000). Founded on the left bank of the Warnow on a plateau some 12 metres high surrounded by marshes. The first settlement was founded in 1218 around St. Petri and St. Nikolai churches, bounded by the steep slopes down to the water's edge and by a depression in the plateau to the west. This is the Altstadt (1). The Mittelstadt to the west of it (2), followed in 1232 with a more regular grid, centred on the market-place and St. Marien church. The Neustadt (3) was added with an exact grid and focal market in 1252.

Greifswald (scale, 1 : 20,000). Similar site, as shown by contours (1m. interval). At its east end was a Slav village (see dots on streets). Contains two settlements, each with a grid plan and central market-place.

squares that formed the focus of the town.   The fact that market-places in the towns of western Europe have forms that are repeated again and again, such as the long street market, the triangular market, and the square market, is a clear indication that these were laid out with intent and were not simply fortuitous " natural " growths.   Further, the medieval town planner, especially on the Continent, had to think in terms of defence.   The wall became a fixed feature of the continental town in the course of the 12th century, and its circumference and shape and the number of its gates were important as factors in the lay-out of the town.   There was a real need for settlements to have some kind of defence works amid the general insecurity that prevailed during the invasions of the Northmen and the Huns, and during the feudal conflicts which followed in the Middle Ages.   The wall was no longer needed as a means of defence in the later Middle Ages, though it took years to build.   It was, however, a fixed part of the idea of a town, and was needed to demarcate it from its rural surroundings, a fact of real significance, especially for reasons of economy and administration.

Certain features common to the planned " Colonial " towns of the east German lands may be emphasized.   There was a harmony in the size and proportions of their parts.   Since the majority had under a thousand inhabitants, the circumference of the walls was small, the market-place was always central, and usually the same size as the building blocks around it.   The distance from the market-place to the wall was seldom more than four times the dimensions of the market-place, so that every townsman was within a few minutes of the centre of the town.   The medieval town was emphatically not congested ; it became so with later growth in the 17th century and after, because of the barrier imposed by the walls.   Most houses had their gardens, and the householders had their livestock and rights of pasture on the common outside the town walls.

(5) East Central Europe

Poland had its nucleus in the middle basin of the Vistula, between the Oder to the west and the Bug to the east, beyond which lay the vast Pripet marshes.   To the north lay a wide zone of wooded and marshy hill country that stretches north-east to the Valdai Hills and merges into the plains on the Baltic shores.   To the south lay a wide, open zone at the foot of the Carpathians that opens out widely to the east in the Ukraine.

The Polish kings, and notably Boleslaw Chrobry (992–1025), established large strongholds, two of which were Gneizno (Gnesen) and Poznán (Posen), and from these the country was organized in districts similar to the *Kastallanei* or *Burgbezirke* in the east German lands. Strongholds were also organized by the nobility and the warrior knights. Here too were seats of pagan worship. A gradual growth around church or castle, on sites that commanded the main overland and river routes, was common to the earliest Polish towns, such as Warsaw, Lublin, Plock, Kielce, and Czestochowa. It is true that the concept of the town as a self-governing community of burgesses was introduced from Germany in the 13th century, but centres of social and economic life, comparable with the nuclei of the earliest German towns, existed at the beginning of the 11th century. Danzig, Gneizno, Poznán, Glogowa, Breslau, Cracow, Plock, Sandomierz, and Giecz are described by contemporary authorities either as *civitas* or *urbs*. Gneizno, Cracow, Poznán, Breslau, and Plock were bishoprics at this time, and are consistently referred to as *civitates*. Other centres enjoyed special status though they were not bishops' sees.

German influence penetrated early into these lands as Christianity spread through monastic Orders, mainly the Cistercians, and missionaries. In 1237 the capital of Masovia, Plock, was provided with an additional German settlement at the instigation of the Polish Duke Konrad. At the same time Kulm (Chelmno) was founded. In 1253 the German town of Posen (Poznán) was founded opposite the stronghold across the river in which the cathedral and the bishop's quarters had been established early in the 11th century. Seventeen villages were founded simultaneously around the town. Breslau was established about the same period under precisely similar circumstances, after the Mongol destruction of the town, adjacent to the old bishopric that lay across the river on an island (pp. 90–2). In both cases the cathedral quarter has since stood aloof from the main town and its life. In 1257 Cracow was founded, likewise after the Mongol destruction, adjacent to the Polish castle, the Wavel, and the town was given Magdeburg law. The salt-mining town of Wieliczka, in the foothills of the Carpathians, was founded in 1290. German settlers first appeared in Warsaw in the early 14th century when the German town was established, as at Cracow, under the ægis of the new castle residence of the Dukes of Masovia. These were the first and the chief German towns. Altogether over 80 towns and markets were established during the 13th and 14th centuries. German settlement extended beyond the eastern limits of Poland to Kovno, Grodno, and Vilna. Trade connections extended into Russia to the towns that were founded by the Varangian (Scandinavian) traders on the routeways from the Baltic to the Black Sea shores. German merchants are recorded in Kiev in the 12th century shortly before the incursions of the Mongols along the same routeway. In the 13th century German settlements appeared in the towns of Kulm (1237) and Lemberg (Lwow) (1270) ; both were granted Magdeburg law in 1352.

While the towns of Poland [1] often had their origin in stronghold, seat of assembly and administration, or of heathen worship, where also periodical markets were held, town life in the full sense was introduced by the German traders and missionaries. Thus it had its beginnings in the west in the early 11th century, when the earliest bishoprics were founded. The period of town foundations adjacent to these bishoprics began in the middle of the 13th century, and the process spread steadily eastwards, so that by the end of the 15th century the majority of the principal Polish towns of to-day were in being as self-governing German communities. It is not surprising, therefore, that the rectilinear plan of the German *Kolonialstadt* is dominant among them. It was in use in the 13th-14th centuries. In modified Baroque form it was used in the many other towns that were established in the 17th and 18th centuries by the Poles themselves.

These later Baroque foundations, however, have quite distinctive features. They have a very extensive lay-out with wide streets and an enormous central market-place, and in consequence the houses are widely scattered, with much open space between them. This extensive lay-out is due to the fact that these small country towns were, and are, mainly of an agrarian character, and the town proper, clustered around the market-place, is only a fraction of the total area. The market-place at Lomza, for example, measures 200 by 200 metres, and that at Przasnysch 100 by 100 metres. The medieval town, on the other hand, had a small administrative area marked by its wall within which the lay-out was compact and well proportioned. Moreover, while in the medieval town the streets approached the market-place at right angles at its corners, in these later towns there were sometimes broad boulevards leading from the middle of the sides of

[1] K. Hager, " Die Pölnischen Städte, Grundlagen und Ergebnisse ihrer Städtebaulichen Entwicklung ", *Stuttgarter Geog. Studien*, Heft 43, 1930.

the market-place, a feature common to the planning principles of this era (e.g., Tomaszow, Czestochowa, Kielce). The circular and polygonal places of this period, however, are rare. Places in Lodz and Warsaw alone date from this period. The railways built by the Russians are usually far outside the towns, and there is often no direct access from one to the other. Building lots in the town centres usually measure 100 metres in depth and 30 metres in width and reach from street to street. Streets are almost always straight and 8 to 12 metres wide, though in more modern quarters they have a width of 20 to 30 metres. Avenues 40 metres wide, lined with trees, are common. Pavement accounts for at least one-seventh of the width of the street. Houses are usually built with their eaves parallel to the street, although both eaves and gable houses are found mixed in the small towns, depending, it would seem, on the shape and size of the blocks. A clustering of small buildings at the side of and behind the main house, which almost invariably has but one storey and fills up all the building lot, is characteristic of the Polish town. The front of the house is usually used for business, the large family being housed in the additional buildings at the back and side. The dominant house type resembles that of the country farmstead. It has the rectangular, elongated plan with a single storey and a gable or hip roof ; the door is in the centre of the long frontage with rooms at either side (Fig. 104).

The small country town is to-day built almost entirely of wood. The central market-place is surrounded by higher buildings, the town hall and the fire station; it is the social rendezvous of the town. Religion makes a sharp impress on the aspect of the town. Churches, monasteries, seminaries, together with the Orthodox churches with their conspicuous cupolas and the Jewish synagogue, rise above the mass of its squat buildings. On the borders of the built-up area, but inside the town limits, cluster small peasant houses of two rooms comparable to the Russian *isba*. The small town house has one storey and is built of timber, and has a shingle roof. On the Rynek, or market-place, the buildings normally have two storeys, with narrower frontages (10 to 15 metres) and a greater depth. Lots usually reach back from the main street to the back street. Buildings are often grouped around a yard. Elsewhere they are like the German towns in which the houses have only one street frontage. Jews were a prominent element, and gave the town a special character.

There were 636 towns in pre-1939 Poland, and when classified

1. Unit House.

2. Jewish influence on the build of the Polish town house.

3. Unit House with one storey and a street frontage.

4. Unit House with a street frontage, and tenements built back from it to form a court.

5. Unit House with two storeys and a street frontage.

6. A tenement block in Warsaw and Lodz.

Fig. 104.—Polish Town Houses (from K. Hager, *Die Polnischen Städte*).

according to the character of the materials of the walls and roofs of their buildings the following regions may be recognized.[1]

(1) *Western Poland.* Town buildings of fireproof materials with stone or brick walls and a roof of tile or corrugated iron.

(2) *Central Poland* is transitional between 1 and 3.

(3) *Eastern Poland.* Timber buildings are predominant, and roofs are of shingle or boards, occasionally of thatch.

(4) *Podolia.* Buildings are made of brick or clay with roofs of tile or thatch. The building material here depends on local building material.

(5) *Carpathians.* Buildings are of timber with wood roofs. This is a predominantly forested area.

Apart from areas 4 and 5, where the building materials depend on the environment, the rest show a contrast between the use of refractory materials in the west and the more primitive building methods practised in the east.

" The incombustible building materials penetrate the industrial centres from densely to thinly peopled areas. The expansion penetrates by two zones, one to the north to Vilna, the other to the south to Volhynia and Podolia. These are the two ways by which Polish culture always penetrated eastwards."

The boundary of the western area runs roughly through Lodz and Cracow, and that between the centre and east runs north–south roughly through Bialystok and Lwow. Region 4 lies south-east of Lwow.

The immigration of Germans into new towns was eagerly encouraged by the Kings of Bohemia and the Margraves of Moravia [2] (Fig. 105). Some towns grew up adjacent to a stronghold, a village, an older market-place ; these were then endowed with town law, and new German colonists settled them as townsmen (Eger, Fig. 102). Farther to the east, entirely new towns were founded on new sites or *aus Wilder Wurzel*, with plans like those of the German homeland. Magdeburg law was widely adopted, though the law of Brünn (Brno) was adopted in Moravia. The law of Prague was derived from that of Eger (Cheb), and this in turn from that of Nuremberg. The law of Vienna or Iglau (Jihlava) was used in other towns. The mining towns of the Zips (Spiš) region in modern Slovakia were also founded by German miners and the law of these is closely akin to that of Freiburg in Saxony, the headquarters of the mining country in the Erzgebirge whence most of the colonists came. As might be expected, there is a close relation between the plan and architecture of these medieval towns and those in Germany from whence the migrants

---

[1] L. Stanislaw, " Les Types physiognomiques des villes en Pologne ", *Comptes-Rendus du iv Congres des Géographes et des Ethnographes Slaves*, Sofia, 1936, 1938, pp. 172–9.

[2] Kötschke and Ebert, *op. cit.*, pp. 60–6.

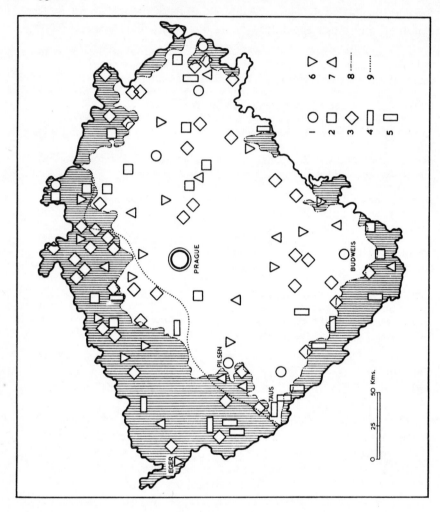

FIG. 105.—The Distribution of Medieval Town Plans in Bohemia (after Hoenig).

1. The east German central square—market plan (*Zentralanlage*). 2. Variants of 1. 3. Modified grid plan. 4. The south German long-market plan (*Längsanlage*). 5. Variants of 4. 6. Irregular block plan. 7. Totally irregular plan. 8. German-Czech linguistic boundary (prewar). 9. Southern limit of half-timbered house construction (*Fachwerkbau*).

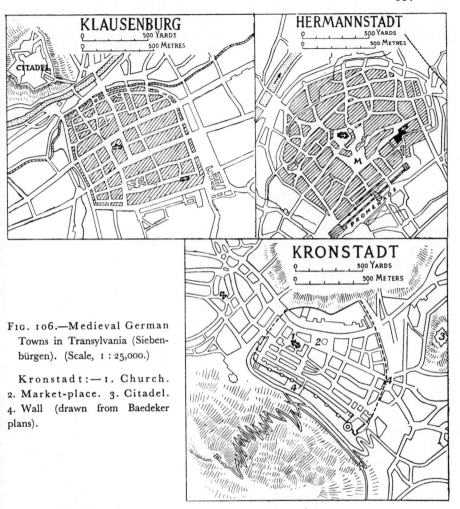

Fig. 106.—Medieval German Towns in Transylvania (Siebenbürgen). (Scale, 1 : 25,000.)

Kronstadt:—1. Church. 2. Market-place. 3. Citadel. 4. Wall (drawn from Baedeker plans).

came. The grid plan with a central square market-place is dominant in the northern and eastern parts of Bohemia as in Pilzen (Fig. 102), while the elongated market (*Längsmarkt*), that is so characteristic of southern Germany and of the founded towns of Austria, appears also on the wooded western fringe of Bohemia, as illustrated by Taus (Domazlice) (see Fig. 101).[1]

Hungary began to receive German settlers in the middle of the 12th century. The uplands of Transylvania, inside the curve of the Transylvanian Alps, were the first area of German

[1] A. Hoenig, *Deutscher Städtebau in Böhmen*, Prague and Berlin, 1921.

town settlement. Men from Flanders and Saxony were recorded at the end of the century, and the Teutonic Knights were called in to settle around Kronstadt (Brasov) to check Rumanian incursions westward through the Carpathian passes, though in 1225 the Order abandoned the area for its main scene of conquest in old Prussia. The rights of the German settlers were declared in a document of 1224 issued by the King of Hungary. Settlement took the form of both villages and towns, the latter functioning as fortresses, market and mining centres. Hermannstadt (Sibiu) and Kronstadt, Klausenburg and Schassburg (see Fig. 106) were the principal towns. This area of German settlement became a separate and independent political unit (*universitas Saxonum*).

The Slovakian Ore Mountains in the western Carpathians were also a scene of early German settlement. German Saxons were already there by about 1200, and the first mining centres to grow were Schemnitz (Banska Stiavnica) and Kremnitz (Kremnica). The Zips (Spiš) area was the chief field of German settlement south of the Tatra. Settlement here began at the end of the 12th century as in the Siebenbürgen. In 1271 privileges were granted to the whole of the German mining community, of which Leutschau (Levoca) and Kesmark (Kezmarok) (Fig. 107) were the important centres.[1]

(6) NORTHERN EUROPE : THE EAST BALTIC LANDS

We have dealt in an earlier chapter with the spread and character of urbanism in Scandinavia, with particular reference to the central region around Stockholm. We may therefore turn here immediately to the lands on the eastern shores of the Baltic. These lands, occupied by the inter-war states of Finland, Esthonia, Latvia, and Lithuania, have had varied relations with east and west, with Sweden and the German lands, and more recently, during the whole of the 19th century, with Russia. This fact is reflected in the origin, medieval character, and modern growth of their urban settlements. Finland derived its culture and town life in the main from Sweden, the territory of medieval Livonia (Esthonia and Latvia) from the German Teutonic Order during the 13th and 14th centuries. Lithuania, on the other hand, isolated by the stretches of forested land between the valley of the Niemen and the coastlands of East Prussia, was in constant conflict with, but never submitted to, the Teutonic Order.

---

[1] Kötzschke and Ebert, *op. cit.*, pp. 94–9.

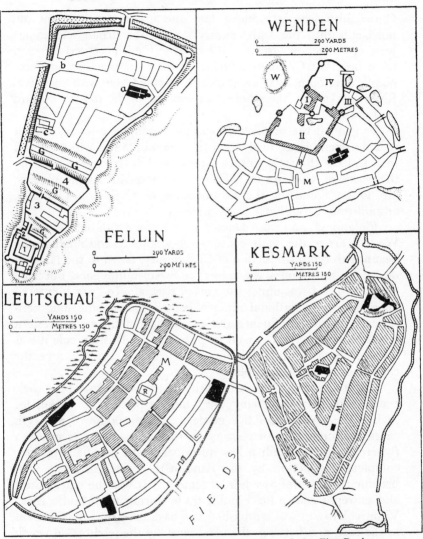

FIG. 107.—Medieval German Towns in Livonia and the Zips Region.

Fellin and Wenden (scale, 1 : 10,000) are both district castle towns of the Teutonic Order in the Baltic Province of Livonia (*Stadt und Ordens Komturei*).

Fellin :—1. *Konvent* of the Order, 1224. 2. 1st *Vorburg*. 3. 2nd *Vorburg*. 4. 3rd *Vorburg*. G = Ditches. *a* = Parish church of the town. *b* = Hay market. *c* = Franciscan monastery and church.

Wenden :—W is an old encampment (*Wallburg*). I. *Konvent* of the Order. II. 1st *Vorburg*. III. 2nd *Vorburg*. IV. 3rd *Vorburg*. M = Market-place. R = Town hall.

Leutschau (Levoca) and Kesmark (Kosice) (scale, 1 : 7,500) are examples of medieval German towns founded in the mining area of the Zips in modern Slovakia (from Schurer, *Deutsche Archiven f. Landes u. Volksforschung*, Vol. 2). Both are after plans of the end of the 18th century.

Christianity was introduced late and urban development did not begin until the 15th century. Here the urban settlements were of indigenous growth ; the chief of them accepted German town law, but German influence in their architecture and economic development is insignificant as compared with medieval Livonia. In fact, the whole area was one of the most backward in Europe.

In general the medieval towns as they appear to-day bear a striking resemblance to those of the German lands, while beyond their walls lie the 19th-century extensions that were erected during the period of Russian rule. Other evidences of Russian influence are to be found in the introduction of Orthodox churches, administrative buildings and barracks.

Finland has had close contacts in its history with both East and West.[1] From the 12th century when the Swedish expansion began with the introduction of Christianity, down to the Napoleonic wars, the country was subject to Swedish influence, but from 1809 to 1917 it was under the ægis of Russia. In 1917 it entered on its career of national independence. During the long centuries of Swedish influence the capital lay in the south-western sector of its inhabited coastal strip, but under Russian rule it was transferred to Helsinki (Helsingfors), which in turn became the capital of the new republic.

Christianity was introduced by the Swedes in 1154, their centre of penetration being the " market-place " of Turku, for such is the meaning of this name. In the middle of the 13th century church and fortress lay on the banks of the river Aura (where they were built a few miles below the original site after complete destruction by the Russians). This settlement then became the pivot of Swedish settlement. It was the chief transit and entrepôt centre for Finnish trade during the Middle Ages. Viipuri (Viborg) was established as a bastion against the Russians to the east, and between the two towns lay the territory in which the nascent Finnish nationality emerged in more modern times. Hanseatic trade concentrated in these two cities, but with the creation of the Grand Duchy of Finland in 1536 a closer liaison with Stockholm grew up. Hanseatic influence declined, and was finally ousted. The trade of Turku declined, that of Viipuri increased, and Helsinki was created at the mouth of the small river Helsinge, on a deeply indented coast girt by islands, as a

[1] W. R. Mead, " Turku and Helsinki : Capital Cities of Finland ", *Scottish Geographical Magazine*, Vol. 59, 1943, pp. 18–24.

new port to capture some of the trade of the flourishing Hanseatic port of Tallinn (Reval) across the Gulf of Finland.

In the Finnish towns fortresses and churches are built of the native building stone, granite, but the overwhelming majority of the buildings in every town, even in the capital, are built of timber. Fires have repeatedly devastated the towns, to such a degree that they have been razed to the ground and new towns laid out, sometimes on the old site (without a trace of the former plan), sometimes on an adjacent site that lay nearer to the coast where the settlement could enjoy adequate port facilities. In Ostrobothonia, for example, the uplift of the coastline caused the harbours to silt up and the coastline to retreat and so the new towns were shifted seawards, and small outports constructed. For these reasons there are few medieval structures remaining. The two small towns of Borgå and Raumo, in which the buildings are still clustered around cathedral and monastery respectively, give a good idea of what the medieval town looked like. Borgå has its street lines adjusted to the relief of a highly accidented site. The majority of the towns, however, have some kind of rigid grid plan laid out since the Middle Ages, and, since they lie on rivers, the grid is adjusted to the river bank and a pre-existing main through route, or to both.

Helsinki was founded in 1550 by Gustavus Vasa of Sweden at the mouth of a small river north-west of the present city. During the 17th century the Swedish Governors-General fostered economic development and established new urban settlements both on the south coast and on the coast north of Åbo, exactly as in Sweden. This florescence was epitomized in the foundation of the University of Turku in 1640. Helsinki was reconstructed in 1639 and entirely re-planned, and a new site was selected on the peninsula, and the old port gradually disappeared. The reverses suffered by the Swedes in the 18th century caused this commercial settlement to become a forti-fied frontier base protected from the sea by the famous fortress of Sveaborg (1749). Russian pressure during the 18th century gradually pushed the Swedish boundary westwards till at last the whole country was acquired by the Slav power. Thus, the commercial port of Hel-sinki was made into a fortified frontier base by the Swedes, and eventually Turku was the last foothold and stronghold of the Swedes in the country before they finally quitted it. Under the Russians the capital was shifted to Helsinki in 1812, which then had about 10,000 inhabitants and was the second most populous city in the Dukedom, enjoying a central location as a political capital as well as seaward contact with the outer world. Here, too, emerged the new embryo Finnish nationality. Turku was completely destroyed by fire in 1827, and this meant the definite leadership of Helsinki, just as an earlier fire at Turku had stimulated the original foundation of Helsinki in 1545. The university was also transferred from Turku to Helsinki 1827.

Modern Helsinki has grown up on a much dissected and low-lying peninsula. The town was completely destroyed by fire in 1808 and rebuilt thereafter. A regular grid plan is imposed on the undulating granite country of the peninsula. Granite is the predominant building stone, but timber houses of a century ago are still found in the city intermingled with stone ones. Deep water surrounds the shores of the narrow, bottle-necked peninsula and it has at least six principal natural harbours. Its waters are non-tidal and sheltered. But the peninsula is so small as to restrict growth, which has taken place by the development of outlying suburbs. Only in recent years has urban growth taken place beyond the bottle-neck that links the peninsula with the mainland.

Turku has a rectangular plan which was adopted in the mid 19th century in the reconstruction that followed its destruction by a big fire. Its site is entirely different from that of Helsinki. It is on low land in the broad lower valley of the river Aura and, unlike Helsinki, it lies on the mainland with no restriction to its expansion, though it is protected on the coast by islands and is approached by narrow channels between these and the coast. Moreover, a shallow coastal sea has tended to silt up the channels. The timbered buildings of the old town clustered around the cathedral, sited on raised land at the east end of the present town. Founded about 1200, and raised to the status of a cathedral in 1300, this was the cultural focus of the land. After the ravages of war and fire the town was laid out on a grid plan in 1827.

The favourable seaward location of both cities has been decisive in their modern growth, for both are accessible to sea-going ships all the year round through ice-free channels. This is coupled with the fact that they lie in the fertile closely settled strip of Finland which they primarily serve, and they are able to act as foreign outlets for the products of the deep interior. To-day while Turku has some 70,000 inhabitants, Helsinki reaches the remarkable figure (for such a small country) of nearly 300,000. These figures compare with 30,000 and 60,000 respectively for 1890 and reveal the great growth of Helsinki in the last fifty years. This growth has been due, in large measure, to its importance as port and seat of industry, especially since the advent of electrical energy (a matter of fundamental importance in the development of Finland, since the country is lacking in other sources of power). Turku has continued to be the cultural centre of the country and the centre of the Swedish-speaking Finns, while Helsinki is the capital of Finnish nationalism.

Esthonia has a quarter of its population living in urban centres, of which Reval (Tallinn, 147,000), and Dorpat (Tartu, 70,000) are the chief, followed by ten others. Narva (the largest of these) has 27,000 and the smallest has 1,000 inhabitants. In Latvia a third of the population live in urban centres, the higher proportion being due to the large size of Riga, the capital (385,000), followed by Libau and Dünaburg (57,000 and 100,000 inhabitants) and 35 other towns with populations ranging from 50,000 to 1,000. Lithuania has 26 towns, ranging from Kovno (Kaunas) with just over 100,000 inhabitants, down to the smallest with 2,000 inhabitants, while still smaller urban settlements (urban villages and market settlements) are particularly characteristic of this State. If these urban villages be included, the urban settlements are spaced at intervals of 10 to 15 km., but if they are excluded, the interval is 20 to 30 km. Many of the towns have an irregular village-like character, but in others the rectangular central market-place occurs as elsewhere in western Russia.[1]

The towns of medieval Livonia were essentially fortress towns that grew up around castles associated with the Teutonic Order or with vassals of the bishops. The purpose of these castles was to keep the native peoples in order, and only the frontier castles were built with the intention of keeping out foreign invaders. The towns that were associated with them were in general very small, and were concerned primarily with local market trade. They were unable to maintain their own costly fortifications and were " organically articulated with the castles and definitely subordinate to them ".[2] In other words, their sites were dictated less by commercial needs than by the military needs of the castle. After the Middle Ages, when the defence of towns became the concern of the State, only a few towns with strategic situations were fortified, and so most of the towns of Livonia, as elsewhere in Europe, ceased to have any military significance after the end of the 16th century.

An interesting point concerns the siting of these castles. As in the rest of the glaciated lowlands of the great North European Lowland, the country does not lend itself to the selection of good, naturally defended hill sites, which were a primary requirement of medieval castles. Two kinds of site presented possibilities, first, the spurs that formed the intersection of steep-walled valleys entrenched in glacial deposits, and second, outcrops of the horizontal limestone deposits that form plateau or spur outliers along the northern coast against the bay of Finland. The former occur in the middle courses of the rivers, whereas their upper and lower courses are flat and marshy and here ditches had to serve as

---

[1] M. Haltenberger, *Die Baltischen Länder, Enzyklopädie der Erdkunde*, Leipzig, 1929, p. 62.

[2] Leighley, *The Towns of Medieval Livonia*, p. 258.

defences. There were many native strongholds when the Livonian Order arrived, and some had permanent settlements adjacent to them, called by contemporaries *castrum* or *burg* and *suburbium* or *hachelwerc* respectively. The Livonian castles were probably sited on or near such early strongholds, the great majority of which, however, simply fell into disuse.

The classification of the towns of medieval Livonia submitted by Leighly, is not unlike that used by Lavedan in his treatment of the castle towns of France. He recognizes five groups and " the order in which they are presented leads from less to more regularity in their plans ".

(1) Towns built on smooth ground without regard to defence : these are the settlements in whose origin and development commerce was a prime factor. They are sited on smooth land in direct contact with road, river and sea. These towns included Riga and old Pernau.

(2) Combinations of acropolis and commercial town. Examples are Reval, Wenden, Hapsal, Lemsoe, Dorpat, and Wesenberg.

(3) Combinations of castle and town on interfluve spurs. Examples are Kokenhusen, Wolmar, Fellin.

(4) Combinations of castle and town on sites of indifferent relief. Examples are Mitau, Weissenstein, Narva.

(5) Combinations of castle and town on smooth land beside streams. Examples are Windau, Pernau.

The towns of Livonia have few buildings left to recall their medieval character. Reval has a number of medieval burgesses' houses which are well preserved, because of the fact that through its eclipse by St. Petersburg it was left to vegetate in the 19th century, whereas in Riga industrial and commercial development have caused the replacement of most of the old buildings by modern structures. The older buildings of Reval, like those of Visby, are of limestone, whereas those of Riga, as in Lübeck and its lesser sisters, are built of brick. The medieval building styles were brought in by the Germans from the towns of north Germany and the coasts of southern Scandinavia. The traditional house had its gable turned to the street with a narrow street frontage. The following is a passage quoted by Leighley regarding the manner of building of burgesses' houses in Riga in the 18th century.

The oldest houses in Riga were built in the following manner. The first high storey, with high windows, had thick walls above which rose a gable like a church gable, with pilasters in the Gothic style and with many windows. This manner of construction had its basis in the contemporary mode of life. Everyone kept his wares in the vestibule (*Vorhaus*), where hemp and flax were stored.   The upper part of the house was provided with several storage lofts one above the other, and the few dwelling-rooms were placed in the rear, next to the courtyard.   When the high and wide vestibules were empty of merchandise, they were decorated with large paintings, stags' heads, etc., and used as halls for festivities.   In a rear corner of this vestibule lay the kitchen, as one still finds it in our houses, that have not been completely remodelled.[1]

With the introduction of Renaissance ideas in the 16th century and after, these gable houses were provided with a façade on the street, capped by a pediment or by a false roof line that had a gentler slope than the real roof.   This is found in the houses around the market-places of Stralsund and Rostock.   In one form or another the gable house was built in Livonia until the end of the 17th century, though it was often plastered with Baroque detail.

During the 18th and 19th centuries eastern European influences became paramount.

Monumental effects were gained by means of the classicism affected by leading social circles in Russia.   On a humbler plane the traditional building material of the country, wood, asserted itself, and with wood came the undistinguished forms of the East-European small town.   A little of the Hanseatic spirit remains in the 18th-century buildings about the old market-place in Pernau, but in Fellin's market-place and in Mitau's the triumph of East-Europeanism is complete.[2]

Riga and Reval dominated these towns and we may select them for more detailed consideration.

Riga (Fig. 108) lies about 15 km. from the mouth of the Duna river on the bay of Riga on both sides of the river, which has a width of about 800 metres.   On the left bank of the river stretches a low-lying, marshy plain.   Riga lies at a narrowing of the river where it could be crossed by means of islands.   The town was founded by Albert von Apeldern, the third (German) bishop of Livland, in 1201. It was located alongside the Rigebach, a small river joining the Duna, enclosing the town on its eastern and southern sides.   The planned nucleus had its main streets parallel to the river front and other streets branch regularly from it.   The town expanded westwards and south-wards to cover the whole area to the Duna.   In the mid 16th century the whole town was strongly fortified.   It was not until the final demolition of the walls in 1860 that the town could freely expand, as it has since done, to both sides of the river.   The ditch and walls around the nucleus were changed into the town canal.

Quite separate from this old town, although it controlled the initial development of the town, lies the Ordensburg to the north-west of it. It has its own defence works outside the town walls, a fact that suggests the frequent conflicts between the Order, the townsmen, and the

---

[1] Quoted by Leighley, *op. cit.*, p. 288.   [2] Leighley, *op. cit.*, pp. 290–1.

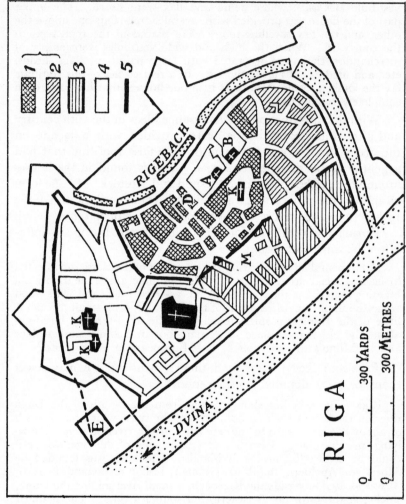

RIGA

0   300 YARDS

0   300 METRES

FIG. 108.—The Growth of Riga
(from *Handwörterbuch des Grenz
und Ausland-deutschtums*, Vol. II).
(Scale, 1 : 10,000.)

1. Oldest town, founded 1202.
2. Extension and, with the 1, the
first walled town (1210). 3. Extensions till the mid 13th century.
4. Extensions till about 1300.
5. Town walls, with original fortifications around the oldest town
nucleus. Main wall dates from
end of the 13th century, and the
ring of fortifications around it from
the 16th century. E is the second
castle of the Teutonic Order
(1330). A is the first castle of the
Livonian Order (*Schwertbrüder*).
B is the bishop's palace. D is the
probable site of the first cathedral.
The first market-place lay on the
west side of this nucleus, then on
the planned rectangular place,
marked M. The sale of goods
shifted in the 16th century to the
Duna quay. On the market-place
are the town hall, weighing-house,
and guild-houses. K shows
churches and C the cathedral and
chapter-house (1211).

bishops of Riga.   In the old town, St. Mary's cathedral was the seat
of the archbishopric of Livonia and Prussia.   The townsmen's church,
St. Peter, lies adjacent to the cathedral.   Originally built of timber,
it was rebuilt in the Gothic style in the 15th century, though it has
been rebuilt several times since, and its modern Renaissance tower
(1743–6) is an exemplary work of timber architecture.   The third
outstanding building is the St. Jacobi church.   The majority of the
old houses in the old town date from the 16th and 17th centuries.

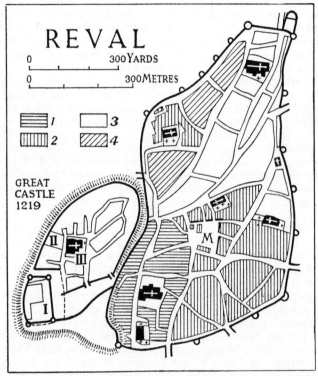

Fig. 109.—The Growth of Reval (from *Handwörterbuch*, Vol. II).   (Scale, 1 : 10,000.)
The hilltop site contains the castle of the Order (I), the bishop's palace (II), and
the cathedral (III), the whole enclosed by a wall.   The town is surrounded by a
wall, and is separate from the castle.   1. The nucleus, 1230–48.   2. Extensions,
1248–65.   3. 1265–1310.   4. 1310–30.   M is the market-place and town hall.

During the latter part of the 18th and 19th centuries settlement and
industry have spread to the suburbs around the old town on both
banks of the Duna.   In 1913, out of 472,000 inhabitants, 78,000 were
Germans, 187,000 Letts, 100,000 Russians, 36,000 Poles, and 21,000
Jews.   Between the wars the Letts appeared as competitors with the
Germans in the professions, although the latter were still dominant.
Population in the 'thirties was about 400,000.

Reval (Fig. 109), in contrast to Riga, lies on a steep cliffed coast.
The lower town lies on a terrace on the Reval bay, while on the edge

of the limestone plateau, 80 metres higher, is the upper town, clustered around the cathedral.   The site was used by the Esths both as a seat of assembly and as a stronghold.   In the early 13th century (1219) Albert of Riga, with the aid of Denmark, quelled a rebellion of the Esths, who were assisted by the Russians.   He captured their stronghold in Reval Bay, and speedily erected a new fortress in its place. Beneath this a town was established in 1228 which in 1248 received the town law of Lübeck from the Danish king.   Shortly after, the conflict between Albert of Riga and the Kings of Denmark caused the latter to withdraw, and the hill fortress became a castle of the Order. German settlers were drawn to the town from Visby.   This territory again became Danish in 1238, and a representative of the Danish king held sway in the fortress.   But the town remained German and became a member of the Hanseatic League in 1285.

The cathedral, which caps the hills, dates from 1233.   Adjacent to it, in the 19th century, the Russian-Orthodox cathedral was built.   At the south-western end of the hill, overlooking the old town, is the castle of the Order.   Clustered around these buildings are the palaces of the nobility.   The lower town, separated from the upper town by steep slopes and flights of steps, falls into three sectors.   The oldest, dating from 1230 to 1248, lies around the Rittersstrasse and the Nicolai church ; then comes an extension (1248–65) grouped around the large central market ; and finally the northerly extension (1265–1310) along the Breite and the Langestrasse.   The whole was surrounded by a wall, a good part of which remains.

The town expanded under the Russians, but did not reach the size of Riga.   It was particularly an importing port for the industrial area of Moscow, and it was also developed as a fortress and naval base. Since 1919 it has been the capital of Esthonia and had about 130,000 inhabitants in 1930.

Dorpat (Tartu) is first recorded in 1030, when Jaroslav I captured the stronghold of that name in a compaign against the Esths.   This seat of heathen worship and defence of the Esths was replaced by a permanent fortress, Jurjew.   In 1224 it fell to the Germans and became a bishop's see, with a bishop's castle residence on the right bank of the Embach river.   A castle of the Order was also built next to this. Below this nucleus down to the river grew the medieval town, which, with the cathedral–castle complex, was walled.   The modern town has spread on both sides of the river.   Its medieval pre-eminence was recognized by the establishment of the University by the Swedish Gustavus Adolphus in 1632, but shortly after it was closed down and was refounded by Alexander I in 1802.   The buildings lie partly on the cathedral hill and partly on its slopes in the lower town.   It had 70,000 inhabitants in 1930.

Lithuania was able to resist the Teutonic Order, and its urban settlements were of slow indigenous growth.   It emerged as a State in the 13th century, and soon extended its territory as far as the Black Sea, uniting with Poland in 1386.   Down to the 15th century the country was isolated from Prussia to the west by the great forested *Wildernis* lying west and south of the river Niemen. The country was inhospitable, and thinly peopled. Christianity was not introduced until the 14th century, and did not spread effectively till the 15th and 16th centuries. The smaller urban settlements were not defended ; the people sought refuge in times of danger in the surrounding woods. The main strongholds lay on the site of the later towns and were the seats of native organization, of government, royal residence and pagan worship. Some of the towns have grown out of smaller market settlements, and the houses are still built almost exclusively of timber. In all these respects, the urban life of Lithuania has always been more closely associated with the Russian than the western (Gothic) sphere. Urban development and morphology are epitomized in the capital cities, Vilna and Kovno (Figs. 124 and 125, p. 478).

Vilna (Wilno) lies at the bend of the broad, deep valley of the Viliya, which is the north-easterly continuation of a main north-east–south-west valley route. This is an historic highway that linked Warsaw with the medieval Russian towns of Nizhni Novgorod and Moscow. The Viliya and its left-bank tributary the Vileika cut through the morainic hills and form a hilly countryside, covered with meadows and woods, in the shape of an amphitheatre which faces southwards and in which the city is sited. This narrowing also attracted the main route from north-west to south-east along the belt of morainic hills at an easy crossing of the otherwise wide and marshy floor of the valley. This route ran from the Baltic shores to Minsk on the northern side of the Pripet marshes and thence to Kiev. Vilna thus lies on a well-favoured site at the convergence of two historic routeways.

The town has its nucleus on a low hill that was formerly engirdled by the Vileika stream, but has been drained, at its confluence with the Viliya. A Lithuanian ruler erected an altar to the god of his people in 1272 on this old residual hill between the two rivers. Then about 1320 near this site another Lithuanian ruler built the first castle. Around this castle hill lies the old town, congested and irregular in plan, overlooked by many churches and monasteries whose towers rise to heights of some 100 ft. At the foot of the hill lay the royal castle of the Polish kings, where a park and a villa for the Russian commandant were located later. Of the Polish castle only a part of the chapel remains. Near it is the Roman Catholic cathedral of St. Stanislaus, built at the end of the 14th century and rebuilt at the beginning of the 18th in the classical style. Town law was granted in 1387, based on that of Magdeburg. The small market town with its squat wooden buildings clustered around the Lithuanian royal stronghold, then became a town with an enclosing wall, with burgesses' and patricians' houses built of stone, and many churches and monasteries. German, Polish, and Italian architects and masons took part in the building. In many respects the later Gothic art of the old town is reminiscent of the German towns.

The line of the medieval wall is evident in the elliptical shape of the old town next to the castle hill. The main street runs from a remaining gate to the south to the castle hill and to the Viliya river and on it lies the old market-place. Roads radiate irregularly from this market-place, and these in turn are interconnected by narrow streets of irregular width. The town includes the very densely built-up area of the Ghetto. Vilna is the result of gradual growth around its castle with its nucleus in the market-place. It stands in marked contrast to the founded towns that predominate farther west and in the Baltic lands. The quaint congested houses and narrow winding streets of the old town, closely adapted to the site, with its Baroque and Renaissance buildings, includes also the more modern Russian administrative buildings on the Napoleon Place and around the cathedral place.

In marked contrast to the nucleus are the outer suburbs built under Russian rule. These have a grid lay-out based on the main radial routes. The whole of the terrace, lying 20–30 metres above the Wilja, on which the old town is situated, has been built on, and building has even spread to the hills that enclose the terrace. A star-like growth is thus very marked.

Vilna was a Russian provincial capital in the 19th century, and buildings for administrative and military purposes have left their heavy stamp on the city. The University was founded in 1579 and formed a distinct quarter in the old town, but it was closed down after the Polish rising of 1831. Many Russian monuments to famous personages were erected. The population of Vilna was about 175,000 in 1909, of whom 96,000 were Poles, 65,000 Jews, 9,000 Russians (officials and their families), 2,000 Lithuanians and 2,000 Germans. The total figure reached 200,000 in 1914, and this was its approximate size in the 'fifties.

Kovno (Kaunas) (200,000), the between-the-wars capital of Lithuania, lies at the junction of the Viliya with the Niemen, and commands the north–south route that follows the latter river, being also situated in historic times at a break-of-bulk point on the river. The place is first recorded in 1000 as a pagan stronghold. But its growth, like that of the State of Lithuania, was tardy and its rise to importance began with the Teutonic Order. The town evidently began as a stronghold situated on a low river terrace at the river confluence, and around it clustered a market settlement *in suburbio*. In 1362 the Master of the Order destroyed the Lithuanian stronghold here. It changed hands several times during this troublous period, and finally fell to the Lithuanians in 1398. The Catholic cathedral was founded in 1387, and is the oldest foundation in Lithuania. The town was then granted Magdeburg law in 1418, and during the 15th century, with the cessation of the conflict with the Teutonic Order and the free flow of trade, it flourished, but was soon eclipsed by Vilna. In 1800 it had only 4,000 inhabitants as compared with 21,000 in Vilna.[1] The old town, which was fortified towards the end of the 15th century, is located

---

[1] H. Mortensen, *Litauen Grundzüge einer Landeskunde*, Osteuropa Institut in Breslau, 1926, p. 292.

on the north bank of the river in the confluence. Extension on a rectilinear plan took place to the east under the Russians in the 19th century to cover a large area on the river terrace and framed by the steep wooded scarp of the surrounding plateau (70-80 metres).

(7) General Considerations

We have now briefly reviewed, with selected examples, the development, functions, and plan of the historic towns of western and central Europe, and it is now appropriate to ask in what respects the urban development of this great unit is distinct from that of the rest of the continent. This is tantamount to delimiting this area as a distinct culture sphere, since the town is the fullest expression of civilization and as such bears close relationship to the character of rural settlement also. The area includes all western and central Europe, to the limits of Germanic settlement on the east and south, and south to the Pyrenees, though south-eastern France has close affinities with the Mediterranean sphere. To the north it includes southern Scandinavia, where until the 19th century both rural and urban settlement was limited to about latitude 60°.[1]

The whole of this area may be referred to in the broadest sense as the Medieval Gothic Culture Sphere. It is shown on Fig. 110. The Gothic type of architecture developed in northern France, where it left its most glorious legacy in the cathedrals, and extended thence northwards to Britain and eastwards to Germany. In southern France it spread but sporadically, and appears in only a few cathedrals, as at Bordeaux. In southern France, Romanesque architecture is dominant in the country churches and also in the cathedrals of the older cities, as at Perigueux, where there is a marked Byzantine influence in its cupola structures. In the Low Countries the Gothic art was modified so as to be applied to the secular architecture of guild halls, municipal buildings and domestic buildings, in a new material, brick. In the German Rhine lands the earlier churches are Romanesque in style, as at Mainz and Bonn and the older churches of Cologne, to mention but a few. The same is true of the earlier towns of inner Germany. But in the Rhine lands Gothic art, as adopted for instance in the cathedral of Cologne, is much changed, indeed degenerate, as compared with that of northern France. A new Gothic expression was found in Germany. The contrast is well marked in the development of the narrow-fronted " gable house " in the north, as it is found also in the Low

[1] To-day, settlements north of this limit are small specialized centres engaged in fishing, mining or the timber trade. There are no market centres as in western and central Europe.

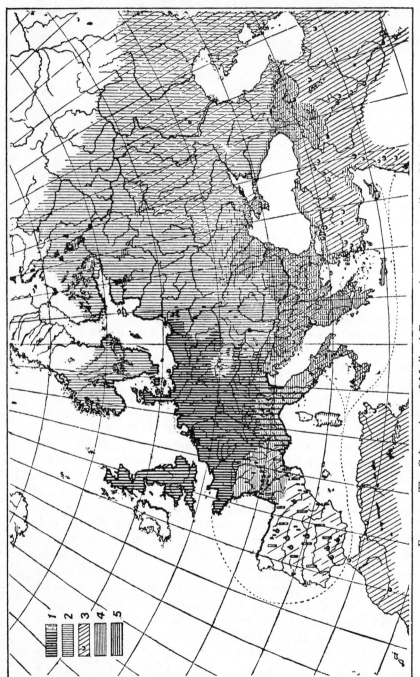

Fig. 110.—The Culture Areas of Medieval Europe, about A.D. 1500 (from Gluck).

1. Gothic.   2. East and North European (timber and wood work).   3. Islamic.   4. Romanesque.   5. Byzantine.

Countries, and the long-fronted " eaves house " of south Germany. In the lands of eastern colonization the primary concern was always with secular buildings and defence works for self-governing communities. Here an entirely new style of Gothic building was evolved, using brick as its medium. This style was carried to the limits of German architecture, and the development of town life associated with it, as well as village settlements and field systems, stand in marked contrast with the lands to the east. In a wide and vaguely defined zone from the Baltic to the Adriatic the change is still strikingly apparent to the observer. Town development in the Slav and Magyar lands has been slow ; German law was generally accepted in the Middle Ages, and German merchants, and later the Jews, formed the only middle-class trading element in its nascent and heterogeneous settlements around church or castle. The Russian town, even as late as the 17th century, consisted of an irregular agglomeration of houses around a stronghold which was enclosed by a palisade or wall and contained the administrative buildings and the churches (*gorod*). Moreover, buildings were almost entirely of timber. This applies to the Polish lands also except in the southernmost parts. Further, while town origins in central Russia between Kiev and the head of the Gulf of Finland date back to the merchant settlements established by the Varangian Northmen on the north–south routes from the Gulf of Finland to the Black Sea, Christianity was introduced from the south by the Byzantine Church through Kiev. Town development, however, in the wide zone of east–central Europe—between the Russian and the German spheres—made a tardy appearance in these most isolated and backward of European regions. In the west, Poland accepted Catholicism, and its first episcopal sees were established at Poznán, Gniezno, Breslau, and Cracow. It is to be noted that each of these bishoprics became the seat of a German community based on a planned market settlement with a central market plan.

In this intermediate zone, which was controlled by Lithuania and Poland, urban development came last, except on the great routeway along the northern border of the Carpathians from Cracow through Lwów to Kiev. Urban life began at the old centres of Poznán, Gniezno, Breslau, and Cracow after the Mongol invasions in the middle of the 13th century. The development of medieval culture and town life reached Lithuania last. Here Vilna and Grodno had their nuclei in strongholds on bluffs overlooking river crossings.   On each of these sites, there was an early communal stronghold, and here too in the 14th century were the ducal castles of Lithuanian princes and their pagan temples, replaced later, on the acceptance of Christianity, by the cathedral. In each case the town grew up under the ægis of the castle—cathedral complex, irregular in form, and included a variety of peoples—Ruthenians, Lithuanians and Jews, and German merchants.   But the development of both towns was tardy, and they did not receive town law until the late 14th century.

In Poland the towns grew up in the late 13th, 14th and 15th centuries, especially around castles and bishops' sees on high sites commanding river crossings.   The Germans carried their Gothic art with them beyond the limits of their homelands, and built burgesses' houses and town halls and churches in Gothic style.   The brick building of the German Gothic secular and church architecture stands to-day in marked contrast to the building in timber of church, castle and house alike.   Wood was likewise the medium for art in general in the Slav lands of Poland and throughout eastern Europe.

In south-eastern Europe there appears a third culture sphere marked by distinct urban and rural settlement forms, which reflect both its historical development and ethnic character.   The steppe of the middle Danube lowland were settled relatively late.   Medieval German settlement reached its western border on the eastern fringe of the eastern Alps, and both German and Magyar communal strongholds were established in the border region of the Burgenland.   An outstanding instance was Bratislava (Pressburg).   Here the subsequent urban settlement was of German origin clustered beneath a castle, as at Graz.   But in the steppe proper we find to-day the irregular labyrinthine agglomeration of the Alföld, a plan that appears in village and town alike. Houses are mostly flimsy, squat, peasant homes.   There is no clearly marked orientation of streets to a central market ;   the narrow crooked living streets end in culs-de-sac.   This is the genuinely irregular plan of which we have spoken in Chapter 14. The type is found in village and so-called town alike, and there is no fundamental distinction in build or plan between them except for the changes introduced by modern growth in the centre. Bucarest itself is a striking illustration of the type.

This kind of agglomeration, essentially rural in origin and not based on any clear conception of urban living as it was in western Europe, is not peculiar to the Magyar folk of the Alföld.   The same type is found throughout central Asia in the towns of Turkestan, in the Near East, and in North Africa. It is also found in Spain as a heritage of the Moorish occupation. " An irregular entanglement of streets, houses and blocks characterize these towns." [1] After eight centuries of Moorish domination came the golden age of an indigenous Spanish architecture which spread from the north southwards. The great era of Spanish urban architecture, from the 14th to the 17th centuries, was marked by the construction of cathedrals and castles and the building of open spaces (*Plaza*), encircled by arcades and balconies, in the midst of the old towns. In these ways the old Moorish towns were transformed, but their plan and their domestic architecture—typified by the flat roof and the enclosed building centred on a *patio* with no openings to the public street—are still the basic features of the town throughout most of Spain. They are similar to those of the Alföld towns, though in an entirely different physical and cultural environment.

Finally, consideration of Spain leads to a comment on the Mediterranean Culture Sphere of southern Europe. Since Italy lies in the same sphere of Western Christianity as western and central Europe, there are naturally striking likenesses in the development and forms of their towns. But there are certain contrasts between the medieval Gothic and the Romanesque or Mediterranean culture spheres that are fundamental. Above all, there is the tendency for people to live in large compact settlements, village and town alike, so that there is no clear-cut contrast between the rural and the urban community. Both village and small town are basically rural communities whose people work in the fields around the settlement. Further, while the small urban settlement in north-western Europe is essentially almost always a focus of industry and commerce, in the small Mediterranean city this function is of less relative importance. Another striking contrast lies in the much greater importance in Italy of the non-productive resident group in the development of towns, which economically may be described as a consumers' group —*reinen Consumenten* or *Rentner* in Sombart's sense. In western and central Europe, the original stronghold settlements of bishops and lords and their dependants were essentially consumer groups, and it was for this reason that in the early Middle Ages they attracted parasitic settlements of peasants and craftsmen as well

---

[1] Jessen, " Spanische Stadtlandschaften ", *Stadtlandschaften der Erde*, ed. S. Passarge. Hamburg, 1930.

as merchants with their precious wares. But in the developing medieval town the feudal nobility had no place ; the noblemen preferred life in their country castles, and were not wanted by the townsfolk and the wealthy patrician classes. It was not until the 17th and 18th centuries that the nobility began to seek residences in the towns. On the other hand, it would seem that this element has played a much more important part in the growth and structure and character of the historic city in the Mediterranean lands. The land-holding nobility lived in the towns, and made a significant contribution to their growth. This was also true throughout the Orient. From the earliest times, a type of town developed in which the land-owning class has been a dominant element. This is clearly seen in an extract from an 18th-century traveller's record on Tuscany. He said that the name *città* was given only to those places where bishops and the high nobility live. Places called *terra*, *borgo* or *castello* are occupied by burgesses, some of whom rank as lesser nobility who dare not reside in the cities. These nobles, in both kinds of places, do not cultivate their estates themselves, but leave them to the care of farmers, who live on the land and share the returns with the owner. If a number of craftsmen and other workers also live in such a place, it is called a *villaggio*. What in Germany is called a village does not exist in Tuscany. This element has always played an important rôle in the Mediterranean city.[1] Finally, the town is compact within its walls, and other features are the narrow and crooked streets, the irregularity of plan, and the multi-storeyed character of its buildings, which are normally of stone.[2] Public buildings of the city, patricians' and nobles' residences, appear in the great Italian republics. In the cities of Italy, as north of the Alps in France, the cathedral lies in the centre of, and dominates, the town.

This brief sketch shows, therefore, that not only is western and central Europe a distinct cultural unit with respect to its town development and morphology, but also that towns within it can be classified according to function and plan. In both these respects the towns vary regionally according to the circumstances of their physical environment and historical development.

[1] Quoted from Jagemann, *Reisebeschreibung von Toskana*, by Hans Bobek in " Über Einige Funktionelle Stadttypen und ihre Beziehungen zum Lande ", in *Comptes-Rendus du Congrès International de Géographie*, Amsterdam, 1938, Tome II, *Travaux de la Section III a, Géographie Humaine*, pp. 88–102.

[2] These features of the Mediterranean town, as opposed to the market settlement of the central European type, are discussed for the Balkan peninsula by Cjviic, *La Péninsule Balkanique*.

CHAPTER 18

THE RENAISSANCE AND BAROQUE TOWN
(*c.* A.D. 1500–1800)

(1) SOCIAL CHARACTER OF THE PERIOD AND ITS EFFECT ON URBAN PLANNING

From the 15th to the 18th century a new complex of culture traits took shape in Europe, and these found physical expression in both the plan and the architecture of the newly founded town or the new section attached to an existing town. This new complex arose from the growth of mercantilist capitalism and a centralized " enlightened " despotism within the framework of the State. In the medieval era feudal lords, bishops, and kings had exercised personal supervision through their local representatives. Kings and emperors kept control through the movement of their residence and court from one place to another. The increasing complexity of government and the centralization of authority brought about the emergence of the capital city, which, at the same time, became a cultural capital, stamped in, and stamping, the national image. Here were the royal courts around which gathered the nobility, whose residences had hitherto been on the country estates. This is the era of capital cities. These grew rapidly to large proportions in the large nation-States, and developed in large numbers in the small court cities of the German Reich. The size of the capital cities in 1815 is a reflection of this development. The same feature is characteristic, in lesser degree only, of the provincial capital, where the nobility built their town residences and enjoyed the social amenities of cultured life. This was very true of the provincial capitals of France, where the *Parlements* were held and the nobility assembled ; of the county towns of England ; of the many small German provincial capitals like Münster, where great mansions of this period, with court, gardens and wrought-iron railings and large gates, lie in secluded streets. Thus, " the age of free cities with their widely diffused culture and their relatively democratic modes of association, gave way to the age of absolute cities ; a few centres that grew inordinately, leaving other towns either to accept stagnation or to stultify themselves in hopeless gestures of imitation." [1]

[1] Lewis Mumford, *The Culture of Cities*, p. 82.

Military considerations became dominant in the foundation of new towns. The advent of gunpowder necessitated complicated, massive, and costly defences in place of the simple masonry wall. While the old walls could easily be knocked down and rebuilt to enclose a new " suburb ", these 16th- and 17th-century walls girded the town with a ring of steel and caused new building to concentrate inside it. The old towns so converted, and especially the capitals, became congested, and the competition for space forced up land values, so that the bulk of the population lived in slum conditions cheek by jowl with the luxurious living quarters of the courts and aristocracy.

The change in the art of war and the increased power in the hands of the State rulers, with their standing armies, brought changes also in the design of new towns and the aspect of old ones. In the Middle Ages, the enclosing wall was an essential feature of the town, both to protect it from without and to demarcate it clearly from its rural environs. But, in the age of unified territorial control under strong monarchs, the town wall had no place. There are many records of the neglected and decadent condition of the walls during the 17th and 18th centuries. Attention was now directed by the ruler to the protection of his territories. New fortifications were given to old towns at strategic points on the frontiers, or new fortress towns, carefully designed to serve this purpose, were erected in suitable strategic situations. The design of the new town was conditioned by the need for organizing and defending it as a fortress. In the old town there were army barracks, which became as characteristic of the Baroque as the monastery had been of the medieval town. There were also the parade ground—*champ de mars*—triumphal avenues, and arsenals. It is well to recall, as an example, that in 1740 soldiers or their dependants constituted one-fifth of the population of Berlin. Strasbourg and Lille both became fortress cities with large garrisons.

It was also an age of abstractions, and this fact is reflected in the application of the elaborate geometrical plan to the theory and practice of city planning. The growth of wheeled traffic, the demands of military considerations, the wish to create the maximum effect of " order and power ", all fostered the planning of spacious, straight avenues, in marked distinction to the relatively narrow, winding, medieval thoroughfares. There is also uniformity of building and design in quarters as well as in squares and avenues, designed always, and only, for the aristocracy. The diversity of build which reflected the social diversity of the medieval town has gone. The military parade also had its counterpart in the shopping parade. The market-place for the people no longer figured in the Baroque city. The new type of shop had windows, the display market was replacing the open market, and the function of the middleman grew. The demands of the aristocracy resulted not merely in the fashion parade, but in the specialized type of exclusive spa and watering-place, such as Bath, Margate, Brighton, Ostend, and Karlsbad. The Church no longer played such a dominant part in the lives of all classes of the town community. Thus, writes Mumford, " city building in the normal sense was an embodiment of the prevalent drama and theme that shaped itself in the court : it was, in effect, a collective embellishment of the life and gestures of the palace ".[1] The theatre (with the separation of classes according to the ability to pay), the art gallery and the concert hall, the landscape park (e.g. Regent's Park in London), the pleasure garden, the museum and the zoological and botanical garden, all developed during this period. All these new amenities were designed for the wealthy and the aristocracy : the mass of the poor, the great majority in numbers, were ignored. The separation of house from the workplace also began for the wealthy, who had their own wheeled vehicles or had their homes near to the city. Changes in social life also took place, so that houses began to be subdivided into rooms, as individual bedrooms and for special purposes—a marked change from the simple communal living of the Middle Ages, which contributed quite as much to vertical growth as did the limitations to lateral expansion that were set by the town walls. Almost all building dating from this period, the 16th to the 18th century, was for the wealthy. This is evident in the size of the houses—three or four storeys with basement, with ornate overdecorated exteriors ; domestic space had now become specialized and rooms were private.

All the ostentation in building and planning was accompanied by the steady deterioration of the old quarters where lived the mass of the people whom it became customary to regard as a " servile proletariat ". Appalling sanitation, overcrowding and pestilence were now accepted as the due order of things until the 19th century when the social conscience awoke.

Town growth and town planning reflect these social trends. Straight and wide avenues, the rectangular and radial plans are

[1] Mumford, *op. cit.*, p. 108.

characteristic. The prototype of the "asterisk" variety of avenue plan, Mumford suggests, is the royal hunting-lodge in the park. It appears at Versailles and Karlsruhe and was often imitated. The same plan, however, was adopted for military reasons in the "starlike" system of fortification in the fortress city, bounded by the polygon of its enclosing bastioned walls. The rectangular system, however, was almost always used in the new Baroque towns—in France, the German states, Scandinavia, and the Baltic lands. The planners devoted themselves above all to setting off the public buildings as symbols of grandeur and power. But some are of real architectural value when they form small self-contained units in the city, such as the Place Vendôme in Paris (1708) and the 18th-century squares of London (Bloomsbury), Dublin and Edinburgh.

The number of new towns that came into being in these three hundred years, together with those that were either transformed through the addition of new fortifications or extended by the building of court or aristocratic quarters, was small in comparison with the total number of the medieval towns. What was of more general significance was the gradual transformation of the aspect of the town through the development of domestic architecture. Stylized types of building replaced the ramshackle medieval houses, squat, and built of wattle and daub with thatched roofs, that were so often ravaged by fire. The old houses in the towns of to-day date almost entirely from the period after 1500. Whether built of half-timber or stone, whether with gable ends fronting on the road or with gables parallel to it (the former especially characteristic of northern Germany and of the North Sea and Baltic towns, the latter of south Germany), or the mansard type of house that was built in the Baroque period for the aristocracy, these are the building types which dominated the Baroque town, and even the medieval town, where the plan of the streets is much older than the houses alongside them. In this period also many new public buildings were erected— churches, palaces, mansions and other structures, that bear the imprint of the Baroque architecture.

(2) RENAISSANCE PERIOD : THE THEORISTS

The contributions of the Renaissance theorists to the question of the town plan are significant in the history of urbanism (Fig. 111). During this century many treatises on architecture appeared in which the problem of planning the town as a fortress received particular consideration. Leone Battista Alberti wrote a ten-volume work on architecture (1452–60) and Pietro Cataneo an eight-volume one (1554–67). In each of these there was a design for an ideal town, in which the lord's citadel was placed outside the town so as to be ready for defence against the attacker from outside, as well as against attack from within the city itself. Antonio Averulino Filarete in 1460–4 described the plan of an ideal town, Sforzinda, which had a radial lay-out with a central square on which were grouped the church, town hall, and other public buildings. The walls were polygonal in shape with sixteen sides, shaped like a star. Theatre and hospital were given an eccentric position. Francesco di Giorgio Martini, in a work that appeared between 1480 and 1500, designed an ideal plan for a fortress town with a radial-concentric lay-out, in which the central place was shaped, together with the blocks, like the outer octagonal walls (Fig. 111*b*). Girolamo Maggi in 1564 designed a fortress town with radial streets and a central market (Fig. 111*d*). Erard in 1600 published an ideal plan which foreshadowed that of Karlsruhe by a hundred years, in which the castle residence is the focus of a series of radiating streets.

Other designs followed those of the Italian theorists. A plan by Jacques Perret, a French architect, appeared in 1601 ; it had a perfect circular shape with radial streets, a ring road just inside the walls, and a castle on the border of the town walls. An independent work first published in 1589, and again in 1608 was that of Daniel Specklin, a German (*Architektur von Festungen*). He planned his town with radial streets and octagonal walls. The streets and blocks were parallel to the walls and grouped on a central place ; space was reserved for the castle residence next to the place (Fig. 111*c*). Cattinara in Italy was built on this plan, as was Nice, founded almost at the same time (about 1680). As applied to Nice, the plan formed a quarter of a circle with six bastions and a tree-filled space occupying the rest of the enclosure, with the castle in the far corner situated on a rocky eminence

---

Fig. 111.—Planned Towns of the Renaissance Theorists (after Lavedan).

a. Filarete's ideal town, mid 15th century. *b.* Giorgio Martini's ideal, mid 15th century. *c.* Specklin's ideal fortress town, 1589. *d.* G. Maggi's ideal fortress town, 1564. *e.* Scamozzi's ideal town, 1615. *f.* Albrecht Dürer's ideal town, 1527. *g.* Schuckhardt's final plan of Freudenstadt, Germany, founded 1599. *h.* Henrichemont, France, the present plan, founded in 1608. *i.* Vitry-le-François, founded 1545 (scale, 1 : 20,000). *j.* Perret's plan of an ideal fortress town, that was adopted by Sully in founding Henrichemont. *k.* Mariembourg, a fortress town founded in 1552 by Henry II of France. (Scales, 1 : 10,000). *l.* Philippeville, a fortress town founded in 1552 by the Prince of Orange. (Scale, 1 : 10,000). [*See Figs. overleaf.*

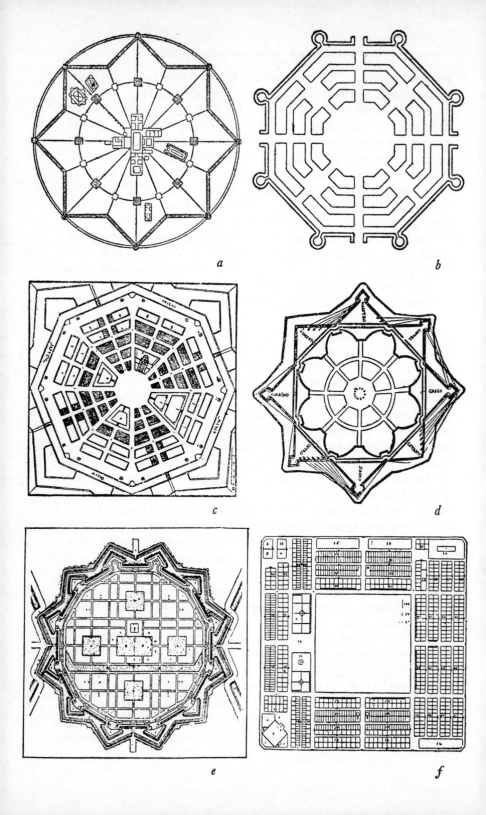

a

b

c

d

e

f

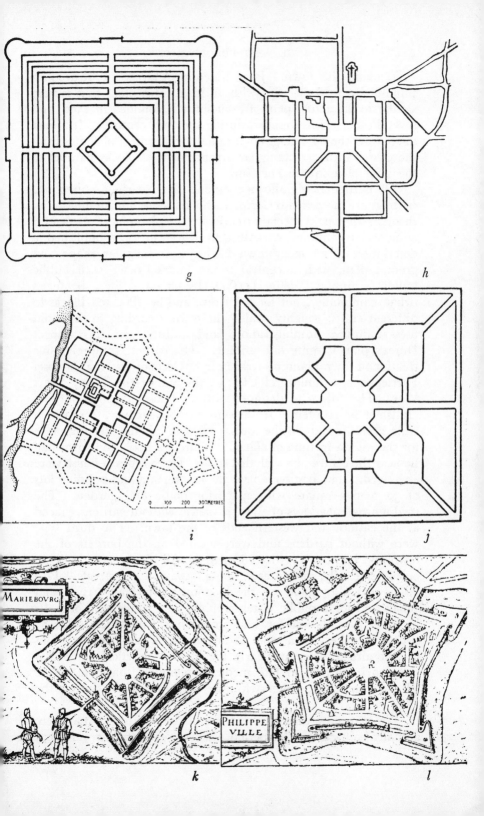

g

h

i

j

MARIEBOVRG

k

PHILIPPE VILLE

l

overlooking the town. Jean Valentin Andreae of Strasbourg published a work in 1619 with an ideal town plan, that is very similar to the actual plan of Freudenstadt, founded in 1599, and several other towns founded during the 17th century. It aimed at securing the advantages of a radial arrangement of routes from the centre with a rectangular arrangement of blocks parallel to the sides of a square enclosure.

Of particular significance among these early architectural writings are those of two German scholars, since, unlike the Italian theorists, they paid special attention to the planning of a town for a balanced community. Albrecht Dürer in 1527 published a description of an ideal town having a rectangular shape and ground plan, with a central square market-place with public buildings around it (Fig. 111f). His plan was for a balanced urban community, not for a fortress, and he allocated blocks to different crafts, roughly zoning the town according to the main uses—industry, administration, and culture. In this respect Dürer's plan is quite outstanding. The earliest comprehensive treatise on town planning written by a German was that of Josef Fürttenbach, a builder of Ulm, at the end of the Thirty Years War. The town he designed was to house a community of craftsmen and traders. In the centre is the armoury, from which wide streets radiate to the walls. Next to it is the meeting place for the militia in time of alarm. Church, school, and town hall lie near the centre in a secluded spot. Three types of house were envisaged. The best were near the centre, and had building lots of 32 metres square with space for house and garden. The medium types had lots of 16 to 32 metres without gardens, placed at the eastern and western ends of the town. The third type were without gardens and were located on the borders of the town and had lots 17·5 by 26 metres. All blocks were built up on one side only, so that each house lot lay on two streets. Provision was also made for the location of navigable river and canals and for a public water supply. The segregation of crafts by streets was allowed for, and provision was made for traffic by stipulating the width and arrangement of the streets. This treatise already sets out clearly the kind of practical considerations, so important in late medieval planning, that came to be felt as primary, together with the æsthetic aspect, during the 18th century.

We may now turn to the plans of the few towns that were actually built during this period. Three requirements were kept in mind by the builders, and these received varying degrees of consideration ; first, the position of the castle, whether that of a peace-loving lord or of a suspicious tyrant ; second, in the case of a fortress town, the accessibility of the walls to troops from a central *place d'armes* ; and third, the need for a focal place around which could be sited the public buildings of the community.

Several small towns were founded in the 16th century in France, and in them we find predominant the idea of the rectangular plan. Even though the radial-concentric plan was adopted in theory by the architects who designed towns as

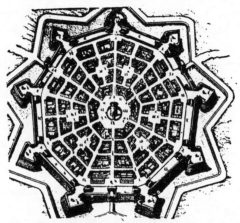

Fig. 112.—Palma Nova in Italy, after Braun and Hohenberg, founded in 1593 (from Lavedan). (Scale, *c.* 1 : 15,000.)

fortresses, the rectangular system was in fact used in the first fortress towns that were planned. In the middle of the century France's eastern frontier was attacked and towns were devastated and rebuilt. Fortress towns were established. The chief of these was Vitry-le-François (Fig. 111*i*), where the rectangular plan shows two new features, the division of each block into two equal rectangular sectors, and the large central place which received the main street axes in the centre of each of its sides. In both these respects it is clearly distinct from the medieval grid plan. Other fortresses to be established on this eastern frontier were Hesdin, Villefranche-sur-Meuse, Philippeville (Fig. 111*l*) and Mariembourg (Fig. 111*k*), Rocroi and Charleroi. In all of these we find the radial-concentric system applied. The rectangular system, on the other hand, was used in the lay-out of Valetta in Malta and in Zamość, a town in Poland south-east of Lublin, planned by an Italian engineer. The triumphant application of the radial-concentric plan to the fortress town is first found in Palma Nova in Italy in 1593 (Fig. 112), and in Coeworden and Willemstadt in Holland in 1597 and 1583 respectively. The radial-concentric system as a design for the fortress town was later renounced by military engineers, and Vauban in particular used the rectangular system in the few fortress towns that he founded. From this same period date the beginnings of Le Havre.

Towns established as seats for religious refugees included Freudenstadt, Pfalzburg, and Henrichemont, founded in 1608 (Fig. 111*h*). But the chief work of urbanism at the end of the 16th century was the creation of Nancy and Charleville. The building of Nancy (Fig. 113) involved the creation of a new town, dovetailed on to the medieval town. It was laid out in 1588 and planned by an Italian. Charleville on the Meuse (Fig. 114) was laid out between 1608 and 1620 by a noble, after whom it was named ; it differs from the other towns of the 16th century in the attention given to the æsthetic aspect, though it is very similar in plan to Freudenstadt, mentioned below.

Town planning in Germany was little affected by the Italian Renaissance ideas. The right-angled system of the medieval town continued to be applied in modified forms. We may mention the suburb of Stuttgart established at the beginning of the 16th century ; Neu Hanau, attached to old Hanau, at the end of the century, with a central market-place in its rectangular plan and a polygonal fortification ; Mannheim, initially founded in 1606 with a rectangular plan and a circular wall ; and the abortive proposal for the reconstruction of Magdeburg in 1631, which would have provided for three roads parallel to the river front and two at right angles to it. The most famous and important instance of town planning of this period is undoubtedly Freudenstadt, which was founded in 1599 in the Black Forest. (Fig. 111*g* and Plate 24).

Freudenstadt was intended as a domicile for refugees, Protestant miners from Carinthia and the Steiermark, as Neu Hanau was intended for Protestant refugees from the Netherlands. It was designed by a German architect, named Schuckhardt, who had been trained in Italy, at the instigation of the Duke. The original design adopted a grid plan with a central square market-place, with the central place smaller and the building blocks larger than in the actual town. The architect placed the chief public buildings—church, town hall, school, and the ducal residence—one in each of the four corners of the place. The Duke, however, decided differently, and the town was planned

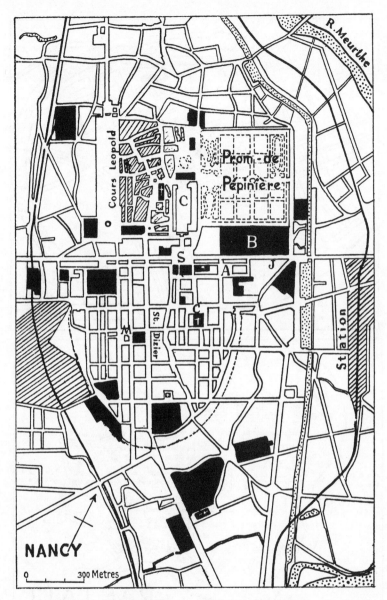

FIG. 113.—Nancy. (Scale, 1 : 20,000.)

The historic town falls into three parts :—the medieval town (hatched) ; the town founded as a " court " residence at the end of the 16th century, with its axis on the Rue St. Dizier and its focus in the market-place (M) ; and the Baroque town of the dukes of Lorraine (18th century), between and east of the first two. Water in stipple, railway yards in hatching, public buildings in black. C = Place de la Carrière, with Palais du Gouvernement at its northern end. S = Place Stanislas. A = Place d'Alliance. B = Barracks. C = Cathedral. J = Botanical Gardens. M = Market-square.

427

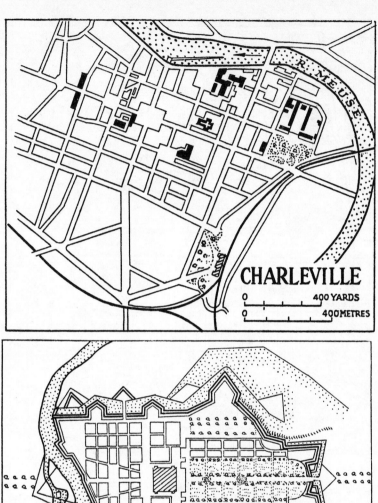

FIG. 114.—Two Baroque Towns.

Charleville, on the Meuse, in France, founded 1608. (Scale, 1 : 15,000.)

Rastatt in Baden, founded 1700. Note the similarity of the lay-out to that of Versailles. Situated in a meander of the Murg river, the castle lay at the confluence of two roads. The plan dates from 1700 and was designed by an Italian architect.

with a much larger central market-place, with the large castle residence, rectangular in plan, situated in the centre of the place and dominating the town.

(3) Baroque Planning

While Italians took the lead in the theoretical planning of the 16th century, the French town planners led Europe in the 17th and 18th centuries, guided by definitely progressive ideas of æsthetic

FIG. 115.—Brest (after Musset). (Scale, 1 : 20,000.)

1. Wall of 1341. 2. Fortification of 1595. 3. Vauban Fortifications, 1683 (destroyed section showed by dashed line). 4. Fortifications of 1840. Naval establishments border the banks of the Penfeld and cover all the northern sector of the town.

and practical urbanism.   The Italians regarded their town as a military fortress.   The French saw it in the light of contemporary social needs and æsthetic ideas.   Thus, planning in France took three forms—the creation of new towns, the beautification or " embellishment " (embellissement) of the existing towns of medieval character, both large and small, and the extension of existing towns.   Thus, new ports were established to meet the demands of

France's overseas trade, at Le Havre, Brest, Rochefort, Lorient and Sète; and Marseilles was greatly expanded (Fig. 115). Vauban erected and refortified about 150 towns on the eastern frontiers of France.[1] Residential and court towns make a third

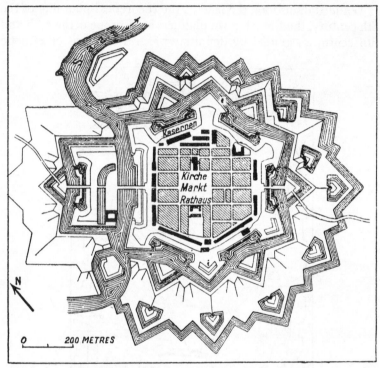

FIG. 116.—Saarlouis (from Aubin and Niessen). (Scale, approx. 1 : 15,000.)

Founded by Louis XIV as one of a series of fortresses on the eastern frontier of France. The central rectangular market-place contained the headquarters of the Commandant (now the town hall). Note also the large area of the fortifications in comparison with the area of the town.

group. Outstanding, of course, are Versailles and Nancy. Karlsruhe and Mannheim are the chief of many such towns founded in Germany. The replanning of existing towns was

[1] The following are listed by Lavedan; the list is not complete : Dunkirk, Bergues, St.-Omer, Condé, Valenciennes, Cambrai, Lille, Bethune, Douai, Arras, Peronne, Maubeuge, Landrecies, Philippeville, Mariembourg, Avesne, Roerdi, Givet, Mezières, Sedan, Verdun, Thionville, Metz, Montmédy, Luxembourg, Longwy, Biches, Phalsbourg (Pfalzburg), Marsal, Toul, Sarrlouis, Le Rhin, Strasbourg, Vieux Brisach, Huningue, Belfort, Landau, Besançon, Joux, Fort-de-l'Écluse, Grenoble, Briancon, Fenestrel, Menedauphin, Pignerol, Casal, Entravaux, Antibes, Toulon, Colliouves, Perpignan, Montlouis, Bayonne, Hendaye, St. Jean-Pied-de-Port, Brest, Rochefort, Cherbourg. See A. Menabrea, in *Urbanisme*, 1934, quoted by Lavedan, *Histoire de l'Urbanisme, Renaissance et Temps Modernes*, p. 224.

taken up vigorously and with foresight and imagination by the provincial governors, the Intendants, who paid attention to street alinements, wide street cuts, the prevention of floods, provision of water, erection of new public buildings, and the lay-out of avenues, places, statues, and triumphal arches. Parallel changes were taking place in Germany, Scandinavia, and Poland, and the marked influence of French ideas is evident in the frequency with which French architects were called in by royalty to plan their towns. The Dutch, too, who had special skill in dealing with drainage problems, as at Amsterdam, were also active town planners of international repute.

(a) *The Work of the French Intendants*

We may instance the work of Tourny, a great Intendant of the 18th century. Tourny, posted first at Limoges and then at Bordeaux, was responsible for the cleaning up and beautification of many medieval towns in the Limousin and in Guienne, the regions that came within his purview as Intendant. He persuaded municipal authorities to spend lavishly of their slender finances, and private landowners to yield their properties, often without compensation, for the common good, and he enlisted the services of brilliant architects, such as Gabriel, and sculptors, such as Fracin, to undertake the task of reconstruction. He inspired such changes in many towns of the south-west—at Limoges, Brive, Libourne, Villeneuve-sur-Lot, Périgueux, Agen, and, above all, at Bordeaux.[1]

What was the condition of these towns in the early 18th century? The fortifications that engirdled and confined the towns were outdated, useless and neglected. Walls were even used for the quarrying of building stone, and it was of little avail for a city council to spend great sums of money on structures that were useless. At Bordeaux (pp. 127–9), the land along the *glacis* of the Château-Trompette was a derelict quarter with old walls, old houses, interspersed with rubbish dumps and filth that *n'attiraient que la soldatesque, les dévergondes, les malfaiteurs, et les filles de joie*. The same derelict condition was evident on the site of the Square Gambetta. Tourny himself wrote that it was impossible for traffic to make its way from one gate to the other, and that gates through the walls were so narrow as to be wellnigh impassable. In the town, roads were crooked, there was no street aline-

---

[1] M. L'Heritier, " L'Urbanisme au XVIIIe Siècle. Les idées du Marquis de Tourny ", *La Vie Urbaine*, Vol. 3, 1921, pp. 47–63.

ment of frontages, and garrets and balconies blocked the streets,. prevented their free aeration, and kept out the light.   There was no paving, and the monuments and public buildings were buried in this confusion of building.   Circulation and hygiene suffered under such conditions.   The town, however, was growing and *faubourgs* were appearing outside the town walls in an entirely haphazard manner.   How could the city administration improve this situation ?

Feeble attempts at beautification were made by many city authorities.   In Bordeaux, for example, a site was required for a Place Royale, in order to serve as a fitting setting for a statue of Louis *le Bien-Aimé*, an aspiration of all the big provincial cities at this time.   Designed by the father of Gabriel, who was an architect rather than a planner, the new place, the Place Royale, now known as the Place de la Bourse, was placed outside the town next to the port, and aside from the main traffic thoroughfares.   It is a Place de la Concorde without a Champs-Élysées and a Rue de Rivoli.   It is a grand architectural work, but made no contribution to the solution of Bordeaux's problem of urban circulation. Such piecemeal work was not that of Tourny.

Tourny saw the city as a whole, and planned each item in relation to it, with regard to both æsthetic and economic needs. He was particularly concerned with circulation or traffic needs and the routeways to and through the city, a fact that was undoubtedly due to the attention he had to pay at Limoges to the construction of country roads linking town with town.   He regarded a town as a *carrefour*, and always thought of roads and spaces in terms of the main through routes which traversed the town.   Thus, in the old, congested town, he widened, straightened and paved the through roads, such as the Rue St. Catherine at Bordeaux, and opened up existing " places ", as at Limoges, where he shifted the butchers' stalls from the Place des Bancs, where they caused congestion, to the outskirts of the town (p. 122).   On the outskirts, where much land was held by monastic institutions, he persuaded the monks that their debts could be paid by selling to the authorities some of their land.   Here he built through roads and allocated property for building.   At Bordeaux Tourny also sought to control the plans of architects and masons for building new properties in the city, his primary concern being to ensure *une largeur commode et une droite ligne* on the thoroughfares.

But Tourny's biggest contribution was the opening of a circular belt around the old town, between it and its suburbs.

Here again his main concern was to relieve the congestion in the old centre by affording a wide circular route to by-pass it. Ditches were filled and an outer road was built outside the walls. He considered that routes from town to country should concentrate on the gates, at which radial roads should converge. This applied to both new roads from the outside and cuts or existing roads in the inside, large open spaces being reserved on both sides of the gate. He also intended to improve navigation on the river and the bridges that carried the roads across it. Some of these plans were carried out by his successors, and others have gone astray. Thus, at Bordeaux, he planned three gates for the southern side ; one of these was not built, and in consequence there is great congestion at the other two. The land along the boulevard was divided into equal lots and the houses built were of exactly the same general design, so that there appeared a continuous façade along it. Moreover, he sought to combine the city with the *faubourgs* by providing points of contact between them. This was the function of the large open places at the gates, which were designed to encourage building along the circular boulevard whose impressive façade faced outwards to the *faubourgs*. Finally, he regarded the public garden as a common meeting ground binding the two, and the *Jardin Royal* was laid out, which, together with the roads radiating from it, became the centre of a distinct quarter.

Tourny did not merely concern himself with roads and circulation ; he also tried to improve the hygienic conditions. He noted that at Bordeaux there were no " promenades ", and his *Jardin Royal* was to serve such a purpose, for he thought of it as a popular rendezvous, and, thinking of the business man, he envisaged it as *une seconde Bourse, une Bourse du soir*. He called in Gabriel to lay out the garden, but kept a careful watch over its progress. This was the only public garden he built, although he had plans for one at Périgueux, but other towns received their " allées ". The boulevard was a grandiose conception, laid out with lines of magnificent lime and elm trees. His wide " allées " were built on the boulevard at the best points—near an open place, at a gate, at a particularly interesting viewpoint, or near a populous *faubourg*. The best examples are the Gravier at Agen, the Allées at Libourne and Périgueux, and, above all, the famous Allées of Bordeaux, not as they are to-day, but as they originally were, much wider and with lines of massive trees, for they are now reduced in width and bereft of trees. These Allées ran from the

Place de la Bourse and around the *glacis* of the Château-Trompette to the Pavé des Chartrons. He wished to demolish the
Château, but not being able to manage this, he was at least able
to give it an aureole of trees which he described as his " Tulieries ".

Tourny often repeated that he intended to make Bordeaux one
of the finest cities in Europe, and he enlisted the services of architects and sculptors. Such urban beauty he saw in alinements,
order, and symmetry. His attention in this respect was given
above all to the façade and its architectural units, and the siting
of monuments he considered only in relation to the whole. Gothic
monuments received little sympathy if they did not conform with
these requirements. A castle that impeded traffic or a gate that
caused congestion must be demolished. But he respected and
restored churches, especially when they were in the countryside,
because they served to guide the traveller on the road. His main
interest, however, was in the creation of public buildings, like
the Bourse at Bordeaux. Gates were also important in his
plans, since they were so important in directing traffic flows.
Beginning with the small gate at Limoges, the Marquis ended by
erecting veritable *Arcs de Triomphe* at Bordeaux. The Porte
d'Aquitaine and the Porte de Bourgogne are examples. The
construction of these great monumental gateways was probably
his greatest contribution to urbanism.

This brief account of the work of one great figure in town
planning of 18th-century France serves a double purpose. It
illustrates in some detail what was going on all over France and
in other countries of western and central Europe at this time.
It also illustrates that in his planning of the great provincial cities
Tourny selected Paris, the capital, as a model, and that the
provincial city was planned to follow the pattern of the national
capital.

The architectonic grouping of places developed in the middle
of the 18th century and was in particular an achievement of
French town-planning architecture. This idea is usually traced
to the design of the gardens at Versailles towards the end of the
17th century. This type of grouping, however, appears in the
Place Royale of Reims (1758), built at the request of Louis XV,
and the two most outstanding examples are at Copenhagen and
Nancy. The Amalienborg–Frederikskirke group in Copenhagen
was clearly derived from the French school. At Nancy (Fig. 113),
the Duke of Lorraine occasioned the building of royal residences
between the old town and the newer town founded in 1587 by

an Italian architect. The *Place de la Carrière* had already been built in this district in the early 18th century, and the new buildings and places were grouped around it. The whole group is called the *Place Royale* and includes, in strict rectangular arrangement, the *Place de la Carrière, Place Stanislas, Palais du Gouvernement*, with the *Hemicycle* (a triumphal arch to the memory of Louis XV), and the large park called *La Pepinière* on the site of the old town walls. The work took over ten years to complete. In Paris, the Place de la Concorde dates from 1753 to 1763, the Place de l'Odéon from 1780, the Rue de Rivoli from 1800. Substantial street cuts were made in Tours (Rue Nationale) and Orléans (Rue Royale). These led to bridges across the rivers.

The *Place Royale* occupied a prominent place in French urban planning of the 18th century. It is marked by its geometrical design, its aloofness from traffic, by its being practically entirely enclosed by buildings, and by the æsthetic proportions of these buildings. It glorified the greatness of the monarchy and often served as a site for royal statues to the memory of the monarchs. Paris had four of them—Place Dauphiné, dating from the early 17th century, Place des Vosges (formerly Place Royale), also dating from the early 17th century and the first great model of its kind, Place des Victoires and Place Vendôme (Figs. 117 and 118). The last two date from the reign of Louis XIV and they are the work of J. H. Mansard, the builder of Versailles. Similar structures appeared in a number of the provincial capitals—Dijon, Caen, Rennes, and Montpellier (the Peyrou). A number of other " places " were dedicated to Louis XV. Among these are the Place de la Concorde, and others in Rennes, Bordeaux (Place de la Bourse), and Nantes. At Bordeaux the Place de la Bourse is an elongated rectangle 100 by 120 metres. Outside France such a square was built in Brussels at the end of the 18th century, where it was associated with the lay-out of the new town around the court. Another example is the Amalienborg in Copenhagen.

(b) Town Planning in Germany

The Baroque city in Germany clearly shows the work of the dominant authority in its life and government, as in the French cities. Capital cities, such as Dresden, Munich, and Hanover, and, on a lesser scale, Weimar, Erlangen, and Baden-Baden, have palaces and gardens and other specimens of Baroque art and architecture that are of outstanding merit. Equally characteristic was the building carried out in the cities where the great

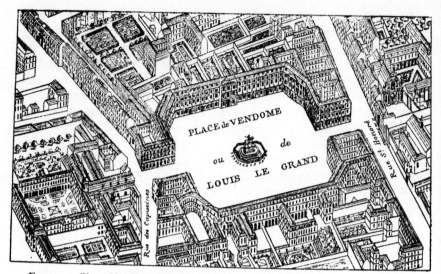

Fig. 117.—Place Vendôme, Paris, designed by Mansard, 1708. From the Turgot
Plan of Paris (1734–9).

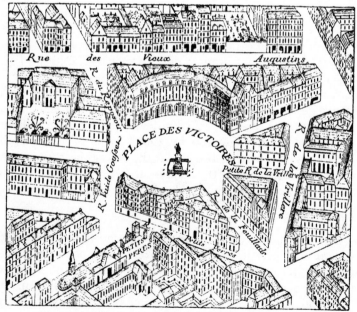

Fig. 118.—Place des Victoires, Paris, designed by Mansard, 1685. From the Turgot
Plan of Paris (1734–9).

Prince-Bishops 'ived. They built for themselves sumptuous new houses, and sometimes massive fortifications, while in such ecclesiastical centres many new churches gave these towns a very distinct character. At Münster the bishops built a great palatial residence on the western outskirts of the town (Fig. 93). This was also the case at Bamberg and Würzburg. Other examples of bishops' cities are Salzburg, Passau and Mainz. This Baroque building and planning is particularly characteristic of the Roman Catholic states in the south of Germany. The two classic instances of Baroque planning are Mannheim and Karlsruhe.

Mannheim was originally laid out in 1607 by the Kurfurst Frederick IV of the Palatinate as a strong fortress on the flat land at the confluence of the Rhine and the Neckar. Next to the castle residence—the Friedrichsburg—was the town which was designed to receive non-German Protestant refugees. It had a grid plan with a central market-place on the medieval pattern. This first settlement was destroyed by Tilly in 1622. A second town grew up with the same plan in 1648 and new immigrant settlers were invited—Dutch, Walloons, and Huguenots from France ; its population reached 12,000 within a few years. In 1689 the town was again razed to the ground at the orders of Louis XIV, and after the Treaty of Ryswick it was rebuilt (1720) for a third time. This new town embraced a larger area owing to the smaller dimensions of the royal residence, but it retained the same rectilinear plan, with more rigidly laid out blocks, several of which were reserved as open spaces. Castle and town now formed part of a single plan, surrounded by bastioned fortifications, whereas in the earlier town the fortress had been almost as large as the town and the town had entirely separate, though contiguous, fortifications. This shows clearly the development in ideas of planning from the Renaissance to the Baroque era.

Karlsruhe (Plate 23) was also a royal residential town, built for the Margrave of Baden in 1715. Here the radial system is applied as at Versailles, in complete contrast to Mannheim. A circle with radial routes and the castle residence at its centre is the basis of the plan. Only one quarter of the circle of roads is built up on the southern side, the remainder being taken up by woods and parkland. Not only is the castle the centre, but the side buildings are constructed along the radial axes which have their common limit in an arc of the circle called the Ringstrasse. The idea was copied from that of the lay-out of Versailles, with its three radial roads focused on the Place d'Armes before the royal palace. Of 32 radial axes only nine were used as streets, the remaining 23 running through the great forest that was originally sought out by the Margrave for his shooting lodge. A great open space before the castle was used as a parade ground. The Langestrasse, that cuts across the radial streets, was an old highway and served as the main highway of the new town. There are two arc-like streets, the Aussere and Innere Zirkel, while the radial streets had a central axis at the end of which was the market-place and the Lutheran church. As the town grew the church was removed and several places were established. At first all houses were of one storey ; the only two-storeyed houses lay on the Innere Zirkel where the nobility lived, and public buildings were erected around the square before the palace. The plan of Karlsruhe was copied elsewhere by German rulers. The first of these was Neustrelitz in Mecklenburg (1726) and it was built by Adolphus-Frederick III as a court residence. Karlsruhe in Silesia was founded in 1743 with the palace in its centre. Ludwigslust, 100 miles north-west of Berlin, was begun in 1765 by the Dukes of Mecklenburg-Schwerin ; its salient feature is the great avenue that leads to the castle.

Many smaller towns were founded in the German states during this century as refuges for Protestants. Among these were Neuwied (1653), Karlshafen-a.-d.-Weser (1699), Ludwigsburg near Stuttgart (1709), the extensions of Berlin, known as Dorotheenstadt (1673) and Friedrichsstadt (1688), Potsdam, the new residence of Frederick the Great, Erlangen (1686, extended 1706) for French Huguenots, Rastatt (1689), Magdeburg, rebuilt in 1731, and the extensions of Dresden, Bonn, Kassel (1685), Düsseldorf (1798), Koblenz, Tübingen and Trier, and Saarbrücken and other places. In almost all these cases variants of the right-angle system are used. Exceptions are Rastatt, which was a miniature copy of Versailles, and the Friedrichsstadt extension of Berlin that was added to the Dorotheenstadt extension with its rectangular system. A radial pattern is found in the plan of Neustrelitz and Karlsruhe in Silesia.

(c) Town Planning in Northern and Central Europe

The erection and reconstruction of towns were actively carried on during this period in the countries of northern and central Europe. We have already discussed in Chapter 17 the character of this development and the features of the many small towns that appeared in this period in the Baltic lands and Poland. We may now turn to the Scandinavian countries where Baroque planning was very active. Examples of new towns are shown on Fig. 121. In Denmark and Norway planning is associated with the reign of Christian IV (1588–1648). The activities of this monarch spread widely, for his realm included Norway, Denmark, part of Schleswig-Holstein and Scania, the southernmost province of modern Sweden. At the time of his accession there were 81 towns in Denmark, 10 in Norway and 9 in Schleswig-Holstein. He rebuilt many towns and founded others, aided in

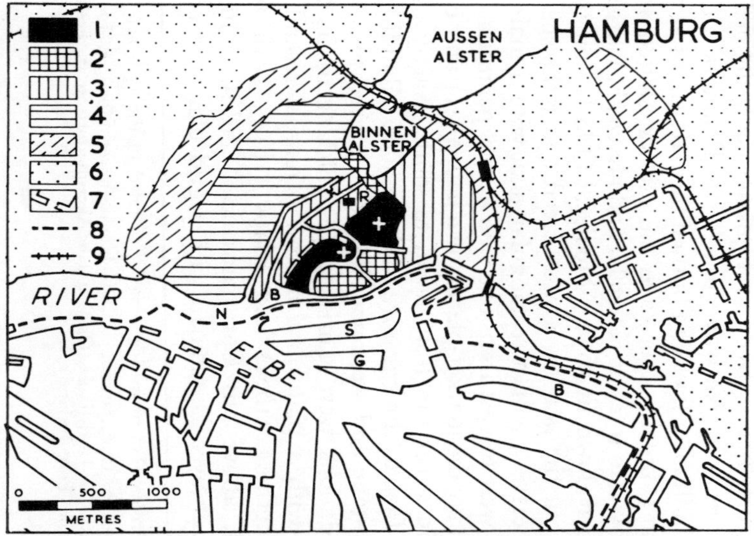

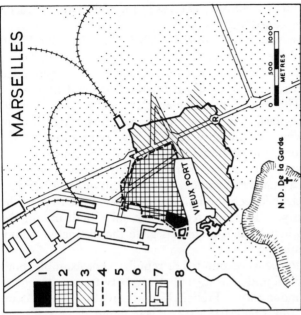

FIG. 120.—Marseilles (scale, 1 : 50,000) (adapted from G. Rambert, *Marseille*, 1934)

1. Original early medieval stronghold on St. Laurent hill. 2. Medieval Town. 3. Built-up area circa 1800. 4. Medieval Wall (and original coast line). 5. 18th-century fortifications. 6. Extensions since *c.* 1800. 7. Port Area developed in 19th century. 8. Main Boulevards. A and R are places at gates through the 18th-century walls and J is Joliette, the first reclaimed harbour.

FIG. 119.—Hamburg (scale, 1 : 50,000) (adapted from G. Braun, *Deutschland*)

1. Town in 1200 with sites of St. Petri and St. Nikolai churches. 2. Extensions by 1250. 3. Town in 1550 (R = Town Hall). 4. Extensions 1650–1830. 5. Site of Fortifications in 17th century. 6. Extensions since 1850. 7. Port Area including old port area (B = Inner Harbours, N = Nieder Hafen, S = Sandtor Hafen, G = Grasbrookhafen, B = Baaken Hafen) and (in dashed line) the Free Port developed since the 1880's.

particular by Dutch architects, whereas in the 18th century French architects were called in.

Copenhagen was transformed by Christian. He established the Arsenal and the Exchange on the island of Slotshomen, which was the seat of the castle and the heart of the city. He founded the port of Christianshaven in 1617 as an independent twin of the capital. This had a rectangular plan, with a central rectangular market-place, and a maritime canal cut through it as in the Dutch towns. In the city itself he was responsible for the places of Nytorv and Bammeltorv (old and new market) and raised a new wall, that more than doubled the area of the city. The Nyboder, a quarter of workers' houses built on long building lots with gardens between the houses, was laid out in 1631 to the north of the city. This quarter was not fully built-up till the 18th century when French architects gave the distinctive stamp to the Amalienborg.

Provincial towns were founded or rebuilt. For example, Soro in Denmark was founded as a small University town adjacent to a Cistercian monastery. Frederickssund (1648) was a commercial town and Fredericia (1650) was founded as a fortress with a rectangular net of streets in a quarter circle defined by its fortified bastions. In Norway (united to Denmark in 1523) towns were rebuilt after fires had burned them down, as at Bergen and Marstrand ; but in other cases the site was shifted and the population moved to it, as at Kongelv, and above all, Christiania, that was burned down in 1675. Medieval Oslo lay on the bay of Bjorviken, but the new town was placed under the shadow of the Akershus fortress, with a rectangular plan with a main street running from west to east from one side of the peninsula to the other and on it lay the market-place, town hall (1641) and church. A second main street ran from north to south, exactly perpendicular to the first, to the entrance to the citadel. Buildings had to be built of stone and were not allowed to exceed two storeys.

New foundations were Christianopel (Blekingen) in Scania (about 1600) with a plan on a narrow peninsula resembling a bastide ; Kongsberg (1624) and Roros (1644), both mining centres ; and, above all, Christianssand. Christianssand was planned in 1641 by a Dutchman with a grid plan that covered

FIG. 121.—Baroque Towns in Scandinavia, founded in the 17th century.
1. Christianopel. 2. Christianstad. 3. Glückstadt (lower Elbe). 4. Jonköping. 5. Göteborg in 1620. 6. Christiania (Oslo) and the Akershus fortress. 7. Frederickssund. 8. Fredericia (East Jutland).

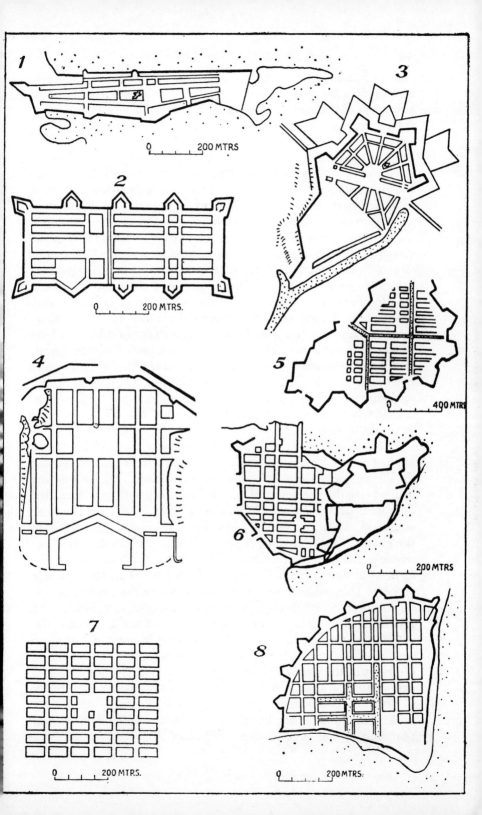

two and a half times the ground area of Christiania and was surrounded by water on three sides. Southern Sweden was primarily of military significance, for Denmark hoped to preserve it from invasion by Sweden. Christianopel (1599), situated on a long, narrow peninsula, has an elliptical or spindle plan like that of the bastide of Cordes in France. Erected as a fortress, to-day it is a dead town. Christianstad (1614) in Scania has a plan that is reminiscent of Monpazier, except that the town is divided into two parts by a canal. Moreover, it had a triple function as a garrison, a farming community (space was reserved for 60 farms in the town) and a commercial centre. In Schleswig, the towns of Bredsted and Glückstadt were founded. Glückstadt, situated at the mouth of the Elbe in Germany, was designed by a French engineer. This is the only one of these towns to have a radial-concentric plan. In all the others, most of which were planned by Dutch architects, the grid plan is strictly applied.

Towns in Sweden were founded by successive rulers. Many others were rebuilt. Gustavus Adolphus founded sixteen towns, including Göteborg. His daughter Christine founded Helsingfors in Sweden in 1639. At the end of the century, in 1680 Carlskrona was founded. Many other smaller towns, ravaged by fire, were completely rebuilt in the 17th and 18th centuries. A good example is Jonköping.

Göteborg was founded in 1630 and was planned by Dutch engineers as a Venice of the North. It lies on an accidented site on the banks of Gota Elf, which was canalized and became the central axis of the town plan. Its northern half was threaded by canals, though some of them have been filled up during the course of the 19th century. At the right-angled confluence of the chief canal lay the market-place (Gustav Adolfstorget). The whole settlement was embraced by strong fortifications in the form of a semi-circle based on the Gota Elf. This last example serves to re-emphasize the great importance of the work of Dutch engineers in Scandinavia in this period and the part they played in introducing and maintaining the ideas of the grid plan, the canal, and the central square market-place in the build of these new towns. In all these plans, with the single exception of Glückstadt, the rectilinear system is used in both Scandinavia and east–central Europe. The radial-concentric plan was a rarity in planning practice for a town as a whole, although this design, under French influence, became characteristic of the monumental planning in the historic cities of France.

(4) Extensions of Ports

The growth of old ports as well as the establishment of new ones is characteristic of this period as a reflection of the growth of overseas trade and of naval activities. In 1815 Hamburg and Marseilles were among the great European cities, each with over 100,000 inhabitants, but their rapidly expanding sea-trade had still to be accommodated essentially within the framework of their historic boundaries. The great port extensions did not take place until the last decades of the century. (See Figs. 119 and 120.)

Hamburg is situated on the north bank of the lower Elbe. The first settlement lay on a peninsula of raised sandy " geest " that reached from the north-east between the Alster to the north, and the Elbe to the south. The Alster was dammed to form a lake and power was obtained from running water. The earliest bishop's settlement clustered around the Cathedral (demolished in the early 19th century) and the St. Petri Church on the east–west route that ran along the edge of the " geest ". (It was never a river crossing, and the Elbe was not bridged until the late 19th century.) The merchants' settlement was founded in 1189 to the south of this on a low island in the Alster marsh on the Nikolai channel, and centred on the St. Nikolai Church. Further growth took place to the east around the St. Catherinen and Jacobi churches in the 13th century. In the early 13th century all these settlements were merged and surrounded by one wall and the town hall (and later the Exchange) were built, adjacent to the Alster. A new wall was not built until the mid-16th century, though it followed the same course as the medieval fortification. It was outside this wall that the great extensions of the town took place in the next three hundred years. A new wall was built in the early 17th century under the direction of Dutch engineers and the area of the town was doubled. The course of these fortifications gave to the town an approximately oval shape, bisected by the Alster with the old town to the east and the new town to the west on the dry geest. In 1820 these fortifications were demolished and their place taken by boulevards and later (to the east) by railway tracks.

In 1816 the first steamships entered the Elbe and the growth of trade demanded ever greater harbour facilities. Ships entered the canals of the Alster and the Nicolai canal along which were located unbroken series of merchants' houses. These buildings, erected on long lots with narrow frontages, were several storeys in height and accommodated offices, warehouses and dwelling quarters. These were the homes of the wealthy patricians, and the majority were of half-timbered construction. The river Bille was diverted westwards in the 13th century to join the waters of the Alster in the Inner Harbour, the main entrance to the town-port. A further extension was made downstream in the 16th century, the Niederhafen, alongside the main stream of the Elbe. These were the harbour facilities until well after 1800. With the growth of demand for more and larger

vessels, the marshland on the south side of the town was first developed
for wharf space in the sixties and, after 1888, when Hamburg became
a free port, the houses of nearly 20,000 people were demolished on
the Brook to make room for the wharves and warehouses of the first
free port.   A canal net was also cut in the marsh to the east of the
town in the middle of the century to accommodate barges and provided industrial sites.   The first docks were cut along the defence
ditch on the south side of the town and then in 1869–72 the Grasbrook
basin was cut in the marsh.   No more space was available for further
extensions next to the town on the north bank.   The city had to turn
to the large area of unsettled marsh on the south bank.   This did not
begin until the late eighties and the vast free-port area was rapidly
developed so as to cover a total area far larger than that of the city
on the north bank.

Marseilles grew around its Old Port, the Lacydon of the Greeks.
This is a natural, rectangular harbour, bordered by steeply rising,
low limestone hills to the north ; by a limestone platform to the
south, that shelves beneath the shallow water of the harbour and
rises to the south to steep hills commanded by Notre Dame de la
Garde ; by two promontories at its western entrance ; and, originally, by the marshy plain of several converging streams, that has been
filled since Greek times and now forms the heart of the modern
city.

The Greco-Roman settlement lay on the northern hills and their
steep southern slope down to the sheltered waterfront.   The medieval
town grew on the same site.   It had its beginnings in the 9th-century
fortress of the Viscounts on the St. Laurent hill.   A settlement grew
to the east of it along an east–west street axis with the Place de Lenche
between them as the chief market place of the town.   These units
were enclosed by one wall about 1300 and the town lay within these
limits until the end of the 17th century, congested with narrow steep
and tortuous streets, some 30 of which run steeply down to the
waterfront.

A great impetus to the growth of the town came with the plans
of Colbert, in the 1660's.   A vast royal arsenal was established at the
south-eastern corner of the harbour.   The city was given the privileges
of a free port with a monopoly of trade with the Levant.   Plans were
put forward for the extension of the town, though not without the
opposition of the city fathers.   New walls were begun in 1670 and
completed in 1694.   These embraced large open areas to the east and
south that were filled by buildings during the 18th century.   A plague
in 1720 killed off half the population of the town.   In later years until
the Revolution the town prospered.   Colbert's plans of expansion
included two boulevards intersecting at right angles, one from north-
north-east to south-south-east interconnecting the wall gates (Aix and
Rome), the other running westwards to the harbour front (Can-
nebière). Further planned extensions with a rectilinear layout and
wide boulevards took place on the flat land well beyond the fortifications to the east, and in the areas between the southern shores of
the harbour and the city wall at the foot of the limestone hills.
Demolition of the walls began in the 1790's and continued after the

Napoleonic wars.   The main station to the north-east was built about mid-century.

The growing sea-trade of the town continued to be carried on in the small area (28 hect.) and shallow water (6 metres) of the old port.   Traffic increased from 800,000 tons in 1827 to 3 million tons in 1847.   There was no space for new wharves, the harbour was rapidly silting, and vessels had to wait three deep to pull alongside the narrow quays.   It took ten years to hew a small harbour out of the solid limestone in the south-western angle of the harbour to a depth of 6 metres.   New docking facilities were essential.   The coast to the north offered the only possibility at the time.   Several capes and bays had to be evened off and a great protective dyke was built parallel to the new shoreline within which projecting moles were to separate a series of basins.   The first of these (Joliette) was opened in 1853, and others followed in rapid succession to the north.   The jetty to-day has a total length of 4,750 metres and future growth is planned at the entrance to the old port.   Meantime, heavy industry has localized on the sheltered shores of lake Berre some 10 miles north of Marseilles beyond the limestone ridge of Nerthe.   This has direct contact with Marseilles for 1,500-ton barges via the Rhone canal and has direct contact with the sea through its outlet at Port le Buc.

CHAPTER 19

THE GROWTH OF MODERN URBANISM

(1) THE STAGES OF MODERN URBAN GROWTH

The second great phase of urban development began in Britain with the Industrial Revolution in the latter half of the 18th century, but it did not seriously affect the Continent until the middle decades of the 19th. The whole phase falls into two stages, the first characterized by the railway and the steam engine, the second by the internal combustion engine and the dynamo, the two stages being divided approximately by the turn of the 20th century. The second stage is also associated, throughout the Western countries of advanced civilization—the United States and Canada and all the countries of western Europe—with a deep-seated biological phenomenon, namely, a falling birth-rate. Among the Slav and Magyar peoples in east-central Europe, however, the birth-rate remains high.

The economic forces of the 19th century resulted in a great concentration of inhabitants in compact urban agglomerations. Factories, offices and houses had to be crammed into the smallest possible area. Power could not be transmitted beyond the shaft-belt, and workers had to walk to their jobs. This period began in Britain in the last decades of the 18th century. It came later to northern France and Belgium, but did not get a real hold in Germany until after the establishment of the Reich in 1871. In northern Europe industry was, and still is, mainly concerned with the handling of raw materials ; since it lacks coal, its industrial development, and, in consequence, the main growth of urban population, have taken place mainly within the last fifty years along with the advance of electricity. Industrial penetration into east–central Europe and Russia was slight until after the foundation of the independent nation-states in that area, and after the Bolshevik Revolution, in the present century. Throughout western and central Europe the characteristic feature of urban development in this stage has been the complete dominance of centripetal forces, which led to the concentration of as many people and activities as possible on the smallest area. This growth, however, was not apparent in all towns. The great majority of the small towns in the countryside lost population to the cities, the degree of attraction the city exercised being proportional to its size. Rural depopulation began in western Europe in the 'fifties, and affected the majority of small towns with less than 10,000 inhabitants. On the other hand, during the 19th century growth was most rapid in towns with over 100,000 inhabitants.

The opening of the present century saw the beginning of another stage of urban development, and this has been accompanied by fundamental changes in demography. These changes have produced long-term problems for society and States that must be taken into account in all plans for post-war building. The rate of population growth decreased, while the development of motor-car and electricity resulted in greatly increased social mobility. In the railway era a great degree of mobility was confined to the railway route. With the advent of the electric tramcar and motor-bus, mobility of both goods and people was greatly increased on all motorable roads. Thus, the choice of a factory site, provided it is not too rigorously tied down to certain sources of bulky raw materials, is now much wider than it was fifty years ago. Similarly there is a much wider range of location for the builders of houses for city, factory and office workers. Lastly, with decreasing families, more married couples, and more elderly people, there has been a steady rise in the standard of living. All people should have the best type of housing that modern science and technique can supply ; and these changes in social structure must be provided for now in the planning of future homes in town and country.

This, then, is an era in which the centrifugal trends in urban growth have grown to greater importance than the centripetal trends. It is the era of sub-urban development and of the shift of industry from city centre to city outskirts—of deconcentration rather than decentralization. The 19th-century cities have often filled up their own administrative areas, and have spread, and must spread further in the future, beyond these limits, to form great areas of brick and mortar which invade contiguous administrative districts. While during the 19th century the force of attraction in human groups was in general proportionate to their mass, the rate of growth of these big cities with their restricted limits has often fallen below the general average for the country in which they are situated. This fact is sometimes more apparent than real, for often the administrative (i.e. census) area of the city is fully built-up and new immigrants, though working within it, are forced (or choose) to live beyond its borders. If we consider urban aggregates that comprise two or more contiguous administrative areas, rather than those that lie within a single administrative boundary, it will be found that the force of attraction of such areas, though varying from one to another, has in the last fifty years been such as to draw an ever-increasing proportion of the population of the country into their orbits.

(2) THE GROWTH OF THE GREAT CITIES

The great urban agglomeration is characteristic of our age. In 1800 there were less than 50 cities in the world with over 100,000 inhabitants. To-day there are about one thousand. In 1930 Europe, excluding Russia and Turkey, had 182 cities with over 100,000 inhabitants accounting for 19 per cent. of the total population. In the late 'fifties there were 286 such cities accounting for nearly 25 per cent. of the total population.

Various attempts have been made to define the extent and population of the major urban agglomerations. The term " conurbation " was used some fifty years ago by Patrick Geddes to describe an agglomeration of towns. C. B. Fawcett defined such areas in Britain on the basis of the continuity of urban land uses. The United States Census has used criteria of social and economic association as the definition of an extended " standard metropolitan area ", but in 1950 it used continuity of urban land uses as the basis of a more restricted definition of an " urbanized area ". Similar definitions have been attempted in other countries but there lacks a comparative basis of world-wide assessment. This has recently been undertaken by the International Urban Research group at the University of California and their data are used here. Their definition is based on that of the standard metropolitan area in the United States Census and adheres to administrative divisions. A metropolitan area is defined as " an area with 100,000 or more inhabitants containing at least one city (or continuous urban area) with 50,000 or more inhabitants and those administrative divisions contiguous to the city (or continuous urban area) which meet with requirements as to metropolitan character.[1] Contiguous areas are defined as administrative units in which over 65 per cent. of the employed persons are in non-agricultural occupations, or, when these data are not available, in which the density of population is at least one-half of the density of the central urban core, or at least twice the

[1] See *The World's Metropolitan Areas*, University of California Press, 1959.

density of the next ring of divisions at a greater distance from the urban core. This definition permits us to review the situation throughout western Europe (excluding the Soviet Union).[1]

TABLE I

EUROPE (EXCLUDING SOVIET UNION) : MILLION CITIES, 1956
(Figures are in thousands)
(*Source :* The World's Metropolitan Areas, International Urban Research, University of California Press, 1959.)

Greater London	10,491	Munich	1,270
Paris	6,736	Cologne	1,244
Essen–Dortmund–Duisburg	5,356	Bucarest	1,236
West Berlin (2,195) East Berlin (2,049) Berlin	4,224	Tyneside	1,136
		Lisbon	1,130
West Midlands	2,576	Turin	1,028
S.E. Lancs.	2,499	Stockholm	1,021
Milan	2,154	Amsterdam	1,017
Hamburg	2,107	Prague	971
Rome	1,959	Rotterdam	936
Katowice–Zabrze–Bytom		Lille–Roubaix–Tourcoing	899
(Upper Silesia)	1,921	Düsseldorf	883
West Yorkshire	1,901	Hanover	868
Glasgow	1,859	Wuppertal–Solingen–	
Vienna	1,865	Remscheid	850
Madrid	1,840	Lodz	844
Budapest	1,783	Antwerp	833
Barcelona	1,455	Lyons	817
Merseyside	1,625	Leipzig	801
Warsaw	1,595		
Naples	1,565		
Frankfurt	1,520		
Athens	1,490		
Brussels	1,372	*Additions**	
Istanbul	1,365	Nuremberg	930
Stuttgart	1,336	South Wales	1,138
Copenhagen	1,293	Sheffield–Rotherham	850
Mannheim–Ludwigshafen–		Nottingham–Derby	850
Heidelberg	1,278	Marseilles–Aix	990

* G. Isenberg, *Die Ballungsgebiete in der Bundesrepublik*, Institut für Raumforschung, Bad Godesberg, 1957. T. W. Freeman, *The Conurbations of Great Britain*, Manchester, 1959.

We may first look at the metropolitan areas with more than one million inhabitants. These are listed above. Greater London has 10·5 million, Paris 6·7 million, the Ruhr 5·3 million and Berlin 4·2 million inhabitants. There are in addition to these

[1] The only objection to it is that it would exclude a cluster of small towns, none of which exceeded 50,000, though the whole may exceed 100,000, e.g. The Borinage (Mons) coal-mining area in Belgium.

four giants, 30 agglomerations with over one million. There are, however, another ten cities with 800,000 to one million inhabitants that certainly qualify for this category. We point out below that at least five other areas can be regarded as million-clusters. Thus, Europe (excluding the Soviet Union) has 50 metropolitan areas with over about one million inhabitants.

(a) Great Britain

The seven major conurbations in Great Britain are Greater London, West Midlands (Birmingham), West Yorkshire (Leeds-Bradford), Tyneside (Newcastle), Clydeside (Glasgow), Merseyside (Liverpool), and South-east Lancashire (Manchester). Far below these are 20 cities with 250,000 to 750,000 people, and another 30 with 100,000 to 250,000 people. Ireland has three major cities (Dublin, Belfast and Cork). In this listing, however, there are three clusters of towns that are close and interdependent, and their built-up areas rapidly merging. These are South Wales (the coal-mining valleys together with the coastal cities), called " Waleston " by Geddes ; the Sheffield-Rotherham-Barnsley areas, called " South Riding " by Geddes ; and the Nottingham-Derby area. Each of these might well qualify to be million agglomerations in exactly the same sense as, say, West Yorkshire. Though the last two probably fall a little short of the million mark, they are added to our list of million cities in Table I.

(b) Germany

It has been calculated that in 1933 there were 58 urban agglomerations in Germany housing 24 million people or 30 per cent. of the total population.[1] In spite of the tragic destruction and depopulation of the cities of Germany during the war, these losses have now been made good, at any rate in Western Germany, and some cities such as Frankfurt, Munich and Stuttgart, are growing at an alarmingly rapid rate. There are within the boundaries of Potsdam—Germany, a total of 51 metropolitan areas with over 100,000 inhabitants. These are listed in Table II. Berlin (West and East combined) had 4·2 million people (as compared with 4·6 million in 1939). Further individual cities that far exceed the rest are Hamburg (2·1 m.), Frankfurt (1·5 m.), Stuttgart (1·3 m.), Mannheim-Ludwigshafen-Heidelberg (1·3 m.), Munich and Cologne (1·2 m.), Düsseldorf (0·9 m.), Hanover

---

[1] K. Olbricht, " Die Entwicklung der deutschen Grossstädte ", *Geographischer Anzeiger*, Vol. XXXV, pp. 247-52.

(0·9 m.), and Wuppertal-Solingen-Remscheid (0·8 m). Leipzig (0·8 m.) and Dresden (0·7 m.) still stand as the chief centres in Eastern Germany. The Ruhr cities (Duisburg, Essen, Dortmund being the largest) together make up a total population of some 5·3 million.

TABLE II

GERMANY—CONURBATIONS, 1955

(Figures are in thousands)

(*Source :* The *World's Metropolitan Areas*, International Urban Research, University of California Press, 1959.)

East Germany

West Berlin ⎱ Berlin ⎰ 2,195 ⎱ East Berlin ⎰ ⎰ 2,049 ⎰		4,244
Leipzig		801
Dresden		741
Halle		536
Karl-Marx-Stadt (Chemnitz)		495
Magdeburg		478
Zwickau		351
Erfurt		249
Rostock		191
Dessau		184
Gera		172
Gürlitz		135
Jena		124

West Germany

Essen–Dortmund–Duisburg (Inner Ruhr)		5,356
West Berlin		2,195
Hamburg		2,107
Frankfurt		1,520
Stuttgart		1,336
Mannheim–Ludwigshafen–Heidelberg		1,278
Munich		1,270
Cologne		1,244
Düsseldorf		883
Hanover		868

Wuppertal–Solingen–Remscheid	850
Nuremberg	698
Krefeld–M. Gladbach–Rheydt	669
Bremen	667
Bonn	531
Karlsruhe	484
Braunschweig	448
Wiesbaden–Mainz	425
Aachen	397
Saarbrücken	374
Kassel	355
Lübeck	319
Darmstadt	304
Augsburg	293
Bielefeld	288
Kiel	257
Münster	249
Osnabrück	242
Hildesheim	200
Koblenz	160
Flensburg	157
Hamm	146
Bremerhaven	131
Pforzheim	131
Freiburg	129
Regensburg	124
Oldenburg	121
Salzgitter	99
Wilhelmshaven	98

(c) *France*

Population figures were calculated for France in the 'thirties on the basis of aggregates of contiguous communes. They have also been officially defined in the Census of 1955.[1] We shall

[1] J. Soulas, " Les Conurbations Françaises ", *Annales de Géographie*, 1939, pp. 466–78, and Institut de la Statistique et des Etudes Economiques, *Villes et Agglomérations Urbaines*, Paris, 1955.

use here, however, in the interests of consistency, the I.U.R. estimates. Thirty metropolitan areas are listed. Paris dominates the situation (6–7 m.), but the Lille, Lyons and Marseilles agglomerations have each close on one million inhabitants. There is a big drop to the next group, beginning at Bordeaux with under 500,000, with a steady decrease in size down to Montpellier with 100,000 people. Since this definition must have one nucleus with over 50,000, it omits several important clusters of lesser towns that in aggregate have around 100,000 inhabitants. These are the iron-mining area of Briey-Thionville with 33 communes in Lorraine (1936, 155,000) ; the Valenciennes district with 22 communes (1936, 147,000), the *Côte d'Azur* from Cannes to Antibes with 7 communes (1936, 102,000), and Dunkirk and suburbs (1936, 95,000).

TABLE III

FRANCE—CONURBATIONS, 1955

(Figures are in thousands)

(*Source :* The World's Metropolitan Areas, International Urban Research, University of California Press, 1959.)

Paris	6,737	Le Havre	201
Lille–Roubaix–Tourcoing	899	Clermont Ferrand	180
Lyons	818	Metz	173
Marseilles	798	Grenoble	170
Bordeaux	460	Rennes	154
St. Étienne	368	Douai	147
Lens–Henin–Liétard	364	Brest	144
Rouen	335	Tours	143
Strasbourg	317	Dijon	140
Toulouse	300	Le Mans	138
Nice	300	Reims	130
Nancy	279	Angers	127
Nantes	275	Orleans	121
Toulon	247	Limoges	113
Mulhouse	202	Montpellier	100

(d) Other West European Countries

Belgium has five large agglomerations with over 100,000 inhabitants. Brussels with its contiguous urban areas, has 1·4 million. Antwerp has 833,000 and Liège 600,000 people. The other two are Ghent and Charleroi, each with just under 500,000. Holland has fourteen 100,000 agglomerations ; Amsterdam, with one million is in the same category as Brussels, and is closely followed by Rotterdam (935,000) and The Hague (766,000). Indeed, these cities, together with Haarlem and several smaller cities form a ring with a diameter of 40 km., housing a total population of 3·5 million people or one-third of the population of the country. Poland has 12 such agglomerations ; Warsaw is in the million class, and Lodz comes second with about 844,000 people. The whole of Upper Silesia has 1·9 million inhabitants. Switzerland has five 100,000 cities, but there is no dominant urban centre in the million category. The largest city is Zurich with 588,000 inhabitants. Austria has five large cities ; Czechoslovakia has five ; Hungary three, and Rumania two. Each of these states has a dominant capital city—Vienna (1·8 m.), Prague (970,000), Budapest (1·8 m.) and Bucarest (1·2 m.).

In northern Europe, Finland is dominated by Helsinki (513,000), and has two other towns with just over 100,000. In the Baltic States there are Tallinn (Reval) (257,000) ; Kaunas (Kovno) (195,000) ; Vilna (Wilno) (200,000) ; and Riga (565,000). In Scandinavia, Copenhagen with 1·3 million people has a fifth of the population of Denmark, while in Sweden, Stockholm has one million inhabitants, followed by Göteborg with 458,000. Oslo in Norway, has now over half a million inhabitants. Thus, in brief, the total number of large urban aggregates in western and central Europe, including Britain, is about 200.

(e) Rate of Growth of Cities

Particular attention should be paid to the rate of growth of the big cities with over 100,000 inhabitants compared with that of the country as a whole. The first general point is that continental towns did not increase much in the first decades of the 19th century. The increase began with the advent of the railway in the 1840's. This was followed by fairly steady increases in the middle decades down to about 1900, with a subsequent slowing-up. But growth curves differ from one city to another, because of the varying size of the administrative unit, and the city's functional development.

The German town, with a few exceptions, reached a maximum of population in the 17th century just before the Thirty Years War. It was still confined within its medieval fortifications. Although during the ensuing centuries many new buildings appeared, the general aspect and extent of the town remained the same till late in the 19th century. Cities which, in the last three centuries, increased both in population and in their built-up area were notably the royal residential cities of the age of absolutism—Berlin, Dresden, Munich, Kassel, Hanover, Stuttgart,

Karlsruhe, Düsseldorf ; the North Sea ports—Hamburg and Bremen ; and the growing industrial centres of Elberfeld-Barmen and Krefeld.

The Machine Age as it affected Germany began in the middle of the 19th century, but it was not till after 1870 that industrialization and the concentration of workers' homes near mines and factories really started. With the development of rapid local transport (electric tramway, 1881) after 1900, concentration in city centres gave way more and more to decentralization. New settlements grew up on the outskirts of the cities both as industrial settlements, grouped around large new factories, and as residential areas, serving as homes for workers in the city centres. Much of this expansion took place beyond the administrative limits of the city, though the new settlements were functionally a part of the city. This led to the expansion of the administrative areas of some of the great cities, as in the case of Cologne. The urban area may be taken as 40 km.—the distance that can be covered in one hour from the city centre by road or local train. This expansion is evidenced by the high density of population, the predominance of non-agricultural activities, and the prevalence of long-distance commuting.

A recent study has been made of these wider urban regions in Western Germany, each with an urbanized core and an associated periphery of rural areas and lesser town centres.[1] These regions are listed below. They house 42·4 per cent. of the population of Western Germany. Note that this list brings Hanover and Nuremberg close to the million mark and these cities are therefore added to Table I.

TABLE IV
MAJOR URBAN REGIONS IN WESTERN GERMANY, 1956
(Figures are in thousands)
(*Source* : Isenberg, *op. cit.*)

	Total Area	Urban Core
Rhine–Ruhr	10,010	6,730
Hamburg	2,240	1,780
Rhine–Main (Frankfurt) . . .	2,170	1,110
Stuttgart	1,640	600
Rhine–Neckar (Ludwigshafen-Mannheim) .	1,450	440
Munich	1,270	970
Hanover	930	530
Nuremberg	930	520
Bremen	720	510

[1] G. Isenberg, *Die Ballungsgebiete in der Bundesrepublik*, Institut für Raumforschung, Bad Godesberg, 1957.

In Germany (1937 area) the total population was 69·3 millions in 1939 as compared with 67·4 millions in 1925. A number of towns (within their administrative limits) lost population in this period, a trend, indeed, that was already apparent in some towns —Dresden, Frankfurt, Wuppertal, Chemnitz, Gelsenkirchen, Bochum, and Plauen—in 1925. Some other cities showed an insignificant increase. The reasons for these changes vary from one town to another, but outward migration from the city to the surrounding suburbs was a chief factor. In the period 1939 to 1955, the nine great urban regions shown on Table IV increased by 23·4 per cent., as compared with 28·0 per cent. for the whole country. From 1950 to 1955 there was a remarkable increase of 13·7 per cent. as compared with 5·5 per cent. for the country.

In the case of France, there was little urban growth before 1841 ; then came a general incréase up to 1870. Some of the smaller cities that were primarily regional or provincial capitals increased slowly, such as Rouen and Toulouse. Others had a rapid growth. These were either ports or industrial cities, such as Bordeaux, Havre, Lille, Lyons, Marseilles, Nancy, St. Étienne. In the 1926–36 decade Marseilles showed a very large increase (40 per cent.) owing to its remarkable development as a port and as an industrial centre. Nice grew by a third and Toulouse by nearly a fifth, Toulon by nearly a third, and Strasbourg by a tenth in this period. The other towns remained stationary. From 1936 to 1950 the urban agglomerations record very small gains, like the country as a whole. While the total population of France increased by 5·6 per cent. from 1946 to 1954, the 100,000 centres increased by only 2·6 per cent.

(3) THE DISTRIBUTION OF CITIES IN 1930

The distribution of towns in 1930 is shown in Fig. 122. The growth of cities in the 19th and 20th centuries has been conditioned by their ability to establish communications by river, as in the past, and by rail, the new means of communication, and latterly, to an important degree, by road, with the outside world as well as with the environs. Cities must be able to collect bulky materials for industry and bulky foodstuffs for the consumption of their inhabitants, and to distribute great quantities of manufactured goods far and wide. Old towns situated at the head of navigation of a river a hundred years or more ago have lost their earlier importance to other towns with better riverside and sea-water facilities. Numerous historic towns that were formerly

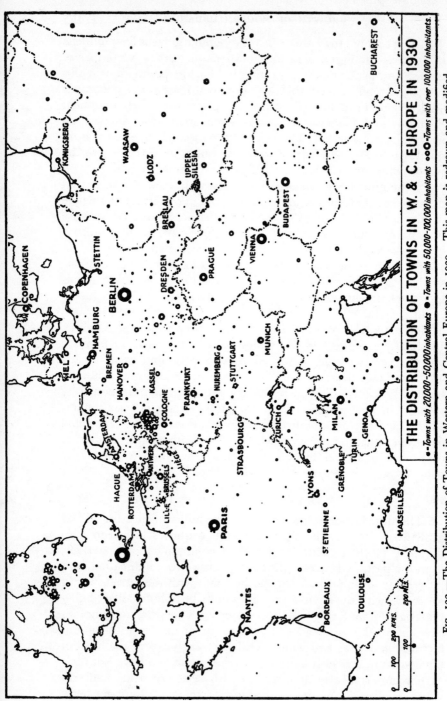

FIG. 122.—The Distribution of Towns in Western and Central Europe in 1930. This map is redrawn and modified from A. Welte, article in *Geopolitik*, 1936.

456

important river ports are to-day negligible. Orleans on the Loire is an excellent instance of a river port formerly of great importance which has been completely eclipsed in this respect by Paris on the Seine and Nantes at the estuary of the Loire. Other cities, such as Bremen, Bordeaux and Antwerp, have deepened and regularized their estuaries, though even they have been obliged to establish outports to accommodate the largest sea-going vessels. Still other cities built entirely new canals capable of taking sea-going vessels ; such are Ghent and Brussels and Manchester. In the case of Amsterdam the seaward connection of the city has been reversed, for its ship canal leads westwards to the North Sea instead of eastwards to the Zuyder Zee, which was formerly crossed by all sea-going vessels using the port. Finally, urban growth has been particularly associated with the coalfields and the industries dependent on them.

The extent of the changes in the distribution and size of towns between 1830 and 1930 is clear from a comparison of Figs. 67 (p. 298) and 122. There is least change in France. In that country, the most notable increase was in the ports, which absorbed a fifth of the aggregate urban increase. The number of medium-sized towns (50,000–100,000) increased from 40 to 102. Some of these were new towns like St. Nazaire (40,000) and Biarritz (20,000), both of which were insignificant places in 1830. Others increased well above the average because of the development of industry, as, for example, St. Étienne (30,000 to 95,000), Le Creusot (1,600 to 32,000) and Nice (19,000 to 184,000). But in general, urban increase in France was moderate, as industry was widely distributed in small towns. There are, however, major concentrations of industry in Paris, Marseilles, Lyons, St. Étienne, Clermont and Rouen. In French and Belgian Flanders the old textile industries developed further by the concentration of factories in old towns or near local coalfields, and the Lille complex is now their dominant focus. This belt extends eastwards through the Belgian coalfield along the Meuse valley and through Dutch Limburg to Aachen in Germany.

In Germany, Austria, Bohemia and Moravia, and the Low Countries taken together, there were very marked changes in distribution. The number of medium-sized cities (50,000–100,000) increased from 40 to 252, and that of great cities (with over 100,000 inhabitants) from 4 to 64. Some individual cities increased 10- to 15-fold, and this is rare in France. While in 1830 Vienna was the greatest city, with 286,000 inhabitants, in

1930 there were 13 cities with over 500,000 inhabitants and 3 with over a million. Berlin itself increased from 220,000 to over four and a quarter millions.[1]

There is also a marked change in the distribution of cities in central Europe. This was caused by the development of industry in the coalfield areas and the advent of cheap and rapid transport by rail. The great concentration of urban population in the industrial areas of the Ruhr, Upper Silesia and the Saar is most remarkable. In 1830 these areas do not even appear on the map. The Ruhr in 1830 had only two places with over 20,000 people, namely the neighbour towns of Elberfeld and Barmen. To-day it has a swarm of cities, small, medium and large.[2] There is also a string of industrial towns stretching west from Cologne and Düsseldorf to the frontier of Aachen and thence further westwards through the Belgian coalfield to northern France.

Some cities grew that were already old-established craft centres, like Nuremberg, Augsburg, and Bielefeld. This was also the case with many towns in the upland areas of Saxony, Silesia, Württemberg and Baden. Others enjoyed the advantage of a good situation as a route centre and acquired new industries, such as Strasbourg, Cologne, Breslau, and smaller centres like Würzburg, Münster, and Erfurt. Still others grew because they were capital cities, such as Munich, Stuttgart, Hanover, Dresden, Prague and, above all, Vienna.

In three areas removed from the coalfields, there appear to-day clusters of towns. These are along the Rhine, on the northern borders of the central uplands of Germany, and on the northern coast. The whole of the Rhineland from Holland to Switzerland had in 1930 38 great cities with over 100,000 inhabitants and 129 medium-sized cities with over 50,000 to 100,000 inhabitants. The towns of the Lower Rhineland together with those of the Low Countries were able to take advantage of the modern conditions of growth. Ghent, Utrecht, Haarlem, and Groningen have become large cities with over 100,000 inhabitants, while Bruges,

---

[1] In Germany (1919 boundaries) there were in 1830 only two large cities with over 100,000—Berlin (220,000) and Hamburg (112,000), whereas in 1930 there were 52 with an aggregate over 2 million inhabitants. In 1830 Cologne had 62,000, Munich 66,000, Breslau 82,000, Leipzig 41,000, Dresden 56,000, Frankfurt 43,000, Stuttgart 31,000. Almost all the other big cities of to-day had under 30,000 in 1830, and many under 20,000.

[2] Essen, with 630,000 in 1930, had 4,750 in 1830 ; Dortmund, with 540,000 in 1930, had 4,450 in 1830 ; Bochum, with 315,000 in 1930, had 2,300 in 1830 ; Duisburg, with 422,000 in 1930, had 6,000 in 1830. Gelsenkirchen and Oberhausen were small villages.

Malines, Louvain, Delft, Leiden, Nijmegen, and Maastricht are historic medium-sized cities with over 50,000 people. Entirely new industrial cities are those in the heathland of eastern Holland —Almelov, Eindhoven, Enschede, and Hengeloo. Brussels, Antwerp, Amsterdam, Rotterdam, and The Hague are the great cities of the Low Countries. The German Rhine, as a great navigable artery, has favoured the modern growth of its historic cities as seats both of commerce and industry. Heavy industry in particular has concentrated on the Rhine at and below Cologne (notably at Düsseldorf and Duisburg), owing to the proximity of the coal of the Ruhr and direct contact by river with the sea.

A second series of towns lies between the Rhine and Upper Silesia along the northern border of the central uplands. This is the chief German axis of west–east communications, and in it, at the convergence of north–south routes from southern Germany along the valley-ways through the central uplands, many towns appeared in the Middle Ages. Here, too, are important industries, both in the towns and in the uplands to the south ; metal working and textiles are especially important in the latter. The mining of coal, ores and salts, and above all of lignite or brown coal, has contributed to the modern growth of industry in this belt. This modern development of industry in the middle Elbe basin has not resulted in any large new mushroom agglomerations, but has fostered the growth of existing small towns. The group of small historic cities, together with commercial and industrial centres, is clearly distinguished in the centre of the belt ; it includes Osnabrück and Bielefeld, Minden, Hildesheim, Brunswick, and Hanover. There is also a great cluster of cities in the middle Elbe basin, within the triangle formed by Magdeburg, Plauen, and Dresden. In this latter area there were in 1930 6 great- and 34 medium-sized cities, with a total of 3,000,000 people, as compared with only 4 towns in 1830, none of which reached the 30,000 mark. Together with northern Bohemia, the middle Elbe basin has 80 medium and 10 large cities.

The ports on the northern coast form a third series. The North Sea ports, especially Hamburg and Bremen, showed marked increases in population. On the other hand, the growth of the Baltic ports was relatively slow. Exceptions are Stettin (27,000 to 270,000), which is a provincial capital and industrial centre and serves as a port for Berlin, with which it is connected by ship canal ; and Kiel, which reached 20,000 in the 'sixties, and then increased rapidly to 100,000 in 1900 when with the opening of the Kiel canal it became a naval base.   Danzig increased from 55,000 to 235,000, though its growth was retarded by its political separation from its hinterland in the Vistula basin, which throughout the 19th century formed the Russian territory of Congress Poland.   Hamburg was already in the 18th century the chief port and the greatest city in Germany.   After hard times during the Napoleonic wars, it reached 112,000 in 1830, then rose to 410,000 in 1880, and reached 1·2 millions in 1930.   Together with Altona and Harburg-Wilhelmsburg it exceeds 1·5 millions. Bremen increased from 35,000 to 325,000.   It has supplementary deep water ports at Bremerhaven (25,000) and Wesermünde (77,000) on the east side of the mouth of the Weser, which together form one complex with about 100,000 inhabitants.

In order to complete the survey, a word may be said about the towns of east–central Europe.   Small towns with under 50,000 inhabitants are widely spaced.   Regional industrialization is rare, and large-scale urban development is much more localized. Warsaw, Prague, Vienna, Budapest, and Bucarest dominate the life of their respective States.   The one great exception, of course, is the big industrial complex on the coalfield of Upper Silesia, which a hundred years ago was a very thinly populated forested area.   In Poland there is a fairly even distribution of cities of small (20,000 to 50,000) and medium (50,000 to 100,000) grades. The historic routeway on the northern border of the Carpathians from Cracow to Lwów is marked by a chain of small cities in Galicia, to which industrial development has made some contribution.   The extensive townless areas associated with the Carpathians in Slovakia and the Alps in Austria (except for Graz, Innsbrück and Linz) present a marked contrast to the cluster of " towns " in Hungary, east of Budapest.   These are large agricultural villages with some handicrafts and commerce, and, apart from the four or five larger centres, are of a very different character from the towns of western Europe.

CHAPTER 20

THE MODERN URBAN PLAN

The phenomenal growth of modern urbanism has resulted in the concentration of population in a relatively few agglomerations. These were normally flourishing historic centres, that were able to grow further by reason of their momentum and the favourable conditions of their location. In a few instances, entirely new agglomerations emerged through the exploitation of local raw materials. Mushroom industrial towns of the latter character on the Continent, however, invariably had their nuclei in a historic town, as did Essen, Duisburg, and Dortmund, in the Ruhr. There are, however, entirely new urban areas between these nuclei in the coal-mining districts on the northern border of the Ruhr and in Silesia. British 19th-century growth, as is well known, often centred on small market-crafts towns, of no historic significance, such as Manchester and Birmingham, and numerous new mining settlements appeared on the coalfields. This entirely new growth is more rare on the Continent, and it is far more usual for the new growth to be concentrated around the large historic cities.

A further point is that the growth did not effectively take hold on the Continent, as we have seen, until the last decades of the century and, in consequence, presents marked contrasts to British urbanism. The development of industry, commerce, administration, and service demanded growth around the historic centres and the transformation of these centres. Such changes have taken place there mainly since 1850, and during the last fifty years at an accelerated pace.

(1) Phases of Growth of the Modern Town

From our preceding analysis of the growth of urban populations, it will be clear that the topographic expansion of the west European town is in general divisible into three historic phases. The first period was marked by the appearance of the town as a compact settlement unit with its focus in church or market and its limits set by the wall. On the Continent the wall was an almost invariable accompaniment of the town, whether large or small.   In England the wall was confined to a few of the larger towns, and soon fell into disuse ; the boroughs of Wales, Scotland, and Ireland were more often walled, and sometimes assumed continental characteristics.[1] The larger towns grew by stages, and the last walls in fortress cities were the bastioned structures that were built in the 16th and 17th centuries after changes in siege warfare had been introduced by gunpowder and artillery. Towns seldom reached these walls, and there was little growth beyond them except outside the gates on the main roads.   After the great devastations of the Black Death in the 14th century the population of most towns remained stationary for several centuries. The changes were mainly of an architectural kind—new public buildings, embellishments of the old, the construction of domestic buildings, and in particular the erection of mansions for city burgesses and landed gentry, both in the town and on its immediate outskirts, both inside and just outside the walls.   Many towns were extended as the seats of the heads of small States in Germany, and such deliberate extensions were usually based on a grid plan and were grouped around the royal residence.   Other towns were established as fortress centres, and still others as mining centres, as in the Erzgebirge : but these were new towns, and, like the medieval towns, they served as the cores of crystallization for the subsequent growth.

The second phase of urban expansion is variously called the Industrial, Modern, or Technical Era.   It is marked by the greatest increases in population the Western world has experienced, and, above all, by the great concentration of people in urban agglomerations.   In this process of growth during the 19th century certain events were of decisive importance.   The first phase of growth was caused by the advent of the steam-engine, and the introduction of steam-driven machinery.   This brought into being the steam-driven factory, which appeared on the Continent at various dates during the first decades of the 19th century, though very slowly and on a small scale as compared with Britain.   The new factories were normally outgrowths from old water-driven factories, and grew up on the same sites.   They were on low flat land, usually near a river, and were almost always in or next to the built-up area, usually within the town walls.   New factories grew out of old ; they expanded, and workers' homes had to be built next to them.   The spread of the

---

[1] See for example the vivid description of Edinburgh in the reign of Queen Anne, in Dr. G. M. Trevelyan's *English Social History*, p. 438.

urban areas on the Continent in this phase was slow, as is evidenced by the relatively slow increase of town populations down to 1850.

This second phase of growth resulted from the advent of the railway, which marked the first real onset of urban growth and expansion on the Continent. Quite apart from the rapid concentration of people in the towns, there was now expansion around them along the railway routes. But this linear expansion was not in fact very marked, since there were only two or three routes it could follow, except in the largest cities. There was, in fact, during this period no rapid local and universal transport within the urban areas. The horse-drawn tram did not appear till about the middle 'sixties and the 'seventies, and even then its rate of progress was not much quicker than walking. Consequently, the new urban areas were necessarily compact, and builders sought to erect houses as close as possible to the existing town and its factories, and with the highest possible density.

During this period on the Continent the walls became a serious barrier to expansion and traffic. They were demolished, and their place was taken by great wide circular boulevards lined with public buildings. These boulevards are not merely streets. They are avenues with vistas of great buildings and social promenades for the people. They provide an invaluable asset to urban life in which the British city is almost entirely lacking. Some great new thoroughfares were cut through the old city of Paris by Haussmann in the 'fifties. The same idea of wide thoroughfares and circular belts inspired the city planners of the last decades of the 19th century, as is evident in the lay-out of Cologne, Vienna, and Budapest, to name but three. Unfortunately no attention whatever was paid to the control of housing, and the private speculator, conforming to the laid-out street plan and the demands of local by-laws, was able to build vast tenements in the building blocks. Thus as many people as possible were housed in congested barrack-like flats.

The next phase begins towards the end of the 19th century, but it is short, and ceases in effect with the outbreak of the First World War. It was marked by several changes which permitted the wider expansion of the urban area, and the imposition of new building regulations which brought about better housing. The electric tramway enabled the city to expand. Regulations forbidding the entire building-up of blocks with tenements, and the spread of better housing ideals, notably the " garden-city " conception, resulted in some better-class housing. But this phase was short, and the built-up areas dating from it are much smaller in extent than those of the first or the third periods.

The third phase is the post-1919 period, which is marked by the addition of the motor-car, the motor-bus, and the surface or underground electric railway to the means of urban transport. It saw the advent of electricity and the growth of numerous new light industries. It is an era of outward movement of persons from the city to new homes in the outskirts, and of industry to more spacious and cheaper factory sites. All these traits had appeared before the war of 1914, but they were combined after 1919 with the tremendous demand for new houses, and brought about the definite " explosion " of the city and its wide geographical expansion, with the resultant " blighting " of the city centres.

It is thus apparent that every large continental city reveals a crust-like growth from its centre in which, in its topographic and architectural formation, four phases can easily be recognized. These are, the medieval within the final walls, the Renaissance and Baroque extensions from about 1500 to after 1800, the 19th-century expansion from 1800 or 1850 to about 1914, and the inter-war period from 1919 to 1939. The lay-out of these continental cities was affected by the clear limits which the walls imposed on the successive phases of expansion of the built-up area and by the belts of open land alongside the fortifications. When the walls were demolished, open sites for the erection of public build-ings and magnificent boulevards were available. Moreover, the existence of such a belt meant that the railway stations had to be built there or just outside, and certainly not in the old town area itself—a fact which helped to relieve congestion in the city centre. Again, with the full advent of the industrial era in the second half of the 19th century, factories had to be located on the outskirts of the city, though some were built on open spaces inside the wall and along river fronts. This development is not so clear-cut in British cities, which have grown, in the majority of cases, not from a clearly defined medieval nucleus but from a very small unwalled " market-crafts " town. Examples of the former type are Newcastle, Bristol, and Southampton, and of the latter the great industrial cities of Birmingham, Manchester, Leeds, and Glasgow. They were small market towns in 1750, with a few thousand inhabitants, but they have grown steadily in numbers. The built-up area of each has no clearly defined unitary plan. It is compact in the centre and spreads outwards along and between the main roads.

The larger the population of the modern urban agglomeration is, the larger is the proportion of the modern urban lay-out around its historic and transformed centre. The lay-out of the whole is clearly recognizable from the plan and from the air. The rectilinear pattern is dominant, with rows of houses or fully or partly built-up building blocks. Two differing patterns are often contiguous, with no real relation to each other, and the areas may have been built at different periods. Main diagonal and concentric streets are found very frequently in the continental town, with local application of radial streets around a focal point, although the intercrossing of diagonal and rectilinear streets raises problems of lay-out for the rectangular ground plan of the building lot. This particular combination is well exemplified in the *Neustadt* of Cologne, although occasional examples can be found throughout the history of the west European town. Order within disorder characterizes large areas, such as the zones of fortification thrown open to private speculators, as in Paris, where a diversity of large multi-storeyed buildings has appeared in the last twenty-five years. In other zones of this kind, however, municipal authorities have had the chance to plan on a uniform pattern, even though the plan did not conform to the general lay-out of the whole town. This zonal extension, subject to municipal planning, is illustrated by the 17th-century growth of Amsterdam, and later by that of Geneva. Geneva was enclosed by its strong fortifications until the middle of the century, and these covered a wide zone of some 200 to 300 metres. This zone was owned by the municipality, and after the demolition of the fortifications building was controlled by municipal regulations, so that to-day it is the best laid-out part of the city.[1] But this zone shows no clear harmonious relationship either with the old town core or with the areas that have subsequently grown up outside it. The same sort of development is clear in the *Neustadt* of Cologne that dates from the 'eighties, although beyond it, the semi-circular zone of the fortifications is still for the most part not built on and forms a magnificent green belt.

Finally, attention may be drawn to the areas of modern suburban growth on the outskirts—an open growth more characteristic of the British than of the continental city. On the Continent

---

[1] Hans Bernouilli, *Die Stadt und ihr Boden*, Zürich, 1946, with two maps of Geneva on pp. 120–1.

rural land is normally excessively subdivided into narrow strips. When such land lies on the city outskirts and scattered strips are sold for building, growth is haphazard. The result is an utterly irregular distribution of single houses, or rows of flats or tenements, in the midst of open land, without any relation whatever to each other or to the roads. In Britain, since fields are larger and more compact, lots have been sold for building mainly along the roads, thus giving rise to the ribbon growth that is so much deplored. Rows of single-family houses are found in the suburban areas of Germany without any attempt at grouping. Rows of separate three-storey dwellings, each housing two to three families, characterize one of the *cités ouvrières* built by the Michelin firm at Clermont-Ferrand. These features are far more typical of our own appalling 20th-century growth. On the Continent since 1918 rows of flats have often been built on rural land oriented in relation to slope and to maximum sunshine and space. There are very few instances of sub-urban lay-outs that bear evidence of a striving after real principles of community living. Hampstead Garden Suburb is an exception.

This expansion of the urban area from the site of its historical nucleus shows both general and detailed adjustments to the underlying terrain. Factory and warehouse in the latter half of the 19th century sought river and railway frontages on flat land as near to the urban area as possible. In the 20th century the large plants have sought peripheral locations where more land was available at lower cost than in the urban area itself. Houses which were built near the factories, were congested in the older 19th-century districts, but were much more open in lay-out in the newer peripheral areas of the 20th. The type of residence varies often with altitude or proximity to a pleasant situation such as a park or a river frontage or a pleasant landscape. It often happens that the cheapest and least desirable houses are situated on the flat land intermixed with, or adjacent to, the factories and other non-residential uses, while the best residences are situated on the higher land. It should always be remembered, however, that such adjustments are often counteracted nearer the urban area by the centrifugal forces of urban growth : these forces are discussed in a later chapter. There is often an adjustment in detail as to type of house along one street, the houses showing an improvement in quality and upkeep as one ascends a street up a hill or as one recedes from a main thoroughfare. Further, the direction and rapidity of growth in the last hundred years have been closely related to the distribution of flat and often damp and marshy land, and higher, better drained areas, with fresh air. In a still more general sense, London and Paris have been able to spread freely from their late 19th-century limits, whereas Amsterdam is surrounded by flat, low-lying polder land that is too scarce and valuable for indiscriminate urban use. Stockholm is surrounded by forested granitic uplands, and is itself divided by stretches of water into many sectors. Other big cities find their growth impeded by the wide rivers on which they are situated, and the main urban areas are then located on one side of the water. When low-lying land lies on the opposite bank from the raised land forming the site of the historic town, a marked distinction arises between the two banks. There are numerous examples of this arrangement. Warsaw is situated on the left bank of the Vistula, while the flat river plain on the east bank (Praga) has grown up more recently as the industrial, railway, and working-class quarter. This is the same at Cologne, Magdeburg and Bordeaux. Vienna is essentially a one-bank city, and its extension to the river plain on the north side of the Danube in Floridsdorf is but recent. The growth of Pest on the east bank of the Danube is likewise recent, but it has become the main city owing chiefly to the greater suitability of its land for urban extension as compared to Buda on the west bank. Among ports, the outstanding instance is Hamburg, where the whole of the modern port complex has been established on the alluvial land on the south side of the lower Elbe between the river and Harburg-Wilhelmsburg (p. 439). The vital need for interconnections between the two sectors of the complex, one preponderantly the place of residence and the other the place of work, gives rise to transport problems in relation to long-distance as well as to regional inter-urban communications. Many other towns have grown up more or less symmetrically on both sides of a river, although there is usually a marked contrast in the development and function of the two sides. This is conspicuously true of Paris and London.

Relief may set severe problems to urban expansion. This is particularly the case where cities lie on hill sites or deeply entrenched river valleys. The modern outer town is quite separate from the inner town. This is true of Poitiers ; an English parallel is Durham. The linkage of the outer areas with the centre raises the question of bridge construction. Every town has features of growth and problems of organization that arise from the permanent features of its site, no matter how much these may be transformed by the drainage of marsh, the levelling of low hills, the control of floods, or the construction of bridges and tunnels. Supplies of drinking water and problems of sewage disposal, building sites and underground workings of all kinds must always contend with the unchangeable conditions of the site and its geological formation.

(2) The Urban Plan in the 19th and 20th Centuries

The bottom dropped out of town planning in the Western world in the early decades of the 19th century.[1] In the modern growth of urbanism, " there have been few builders of towns, but an infinite number of builders of individual houses and streets ".[2]

In the industrial towns of Britain three periods of housing may be recognized. In the first period there was no control whatever over the private builder. Houses were crowded together on a minimum of space next to the factories with no regard to the essential amenities of air, light, and sanitation. From 1840 onwards, a series of Sanitary and Public Health Acts led to slight improvements. The main type of dwelling in this period was the back-to-back house, with only one side exposed to light and air. The houses formed a long double row and backed on to each other under one gable roof, and usually abutted on to the pavement at the front and had courts behind. These houses had no separate water supply ; they had communal closets, and were often built at a density of 60 per acre. This type continued to be built until 1875, when the Public Health Act of that year brought a big change. It perpetuated the old type of street lay-out by permitting the duplication of the house unit. Model by-laws prescribed the size of rooms, the space behind the house and the width of roads. " The by-law period of town planning has surrounded all our business towns with rings and quarters of houses at an average density of 40 to 50 houses per acre and has planned away every feature of natural interest and beauty." The roads were standardized to a width usually of 36 feet, too wide as approaches to the house and too narrow to function as traffic thoroughfares. Long blocks of houses, arranged in a

[1] Patrick Abercrombie, *Town and Country Planning*, Home University Library, 1933. Quotations in this paragraph are drawn from this source, except when otherwise indicated.
[2] T. F. Tout, *Medieval Town Planning*, Manchester University Press, 1934 (originally published in the *Bulletin* of the John Rylands Library, Vol. 4, No. 1, 1917).

double series fronting on to a street on each side, were crossed at regular intervals by narrow cross-roads.   The third period began with the turn of the present century.   Garden villages, such as Saltaire (1852), Port Sunlight and Bournville, were built by some enlightened industrialists for their workers in the latter half of the century.   But the conception of a fully fledged " garden-city " was not developed until 1898 by Ebenezer Howard in his book *Tomorrow*.   This idea, however, degenerated into the universal practice of building houses, each with a garden, at a standard density of 12 to the acre.   These conditions of housing development are reflected in the build of every English town.

On the Continent there was likewise very little public control of building during the latter half of the 19th century, though there was municipal control of the general lay-out.   Thus, Haussmann cleaned up much of inner Paris by opening up wide new roads. The demolition of fortifications in semi-circular belts afforded admirable opportunities for planning, which were often seized, as at Cologne and Vienna.   The lay-out of Budapest at the end of last century was based on that of Vienna, and combined the radial and concentric lay-out of main thoroughfares.   The principle of " zoning expropriation ", first established in Brussels in 1867, provided that if the owners of more than half of a given territory wished for an improvement project they could demand its enforcement.   The Rue Royale in Brussels owes its origin to such facilities.   The same powers of expropriation were introduced in Germany in 1875 for rebuilding streets.   The municipal authorities were also concerned with the siting of great public buildings to a degree unknown in Britain—theatres, opera houses, museums were placed along the great new boulevards as the fortifications were demolished.   But where all this planning and building failed was in the lack of attention given to the building in the blocks enclosed by the streets, whose lay-out, width, and frontages were rigidly controlled.   This building was left to private builders, who, as in England, sought to use the available space as profitably as possible, by erecting vast tenements with small central courtyards, that were often only a few yards square.   The Krupps set an example of better housing by building sections of three-storey flats, with gardens and parks, for their workers in Essen (*Arbeiterkolonien*).

Thus, in Berlin, Paris, Vienna, Copenhagen and all the other continental cities, blocks of flats were built higher and higher and

closer and closer together, one of the most popular designs being constructed six or seven storeys high, with three, four or even five courtyards leading from each other, served by one entrance from the street,
estates being composed of one- or two-roomed dwellings off long, dark,
interior corridors. Buildings often covered 90 per cent. of their sites,
and light, air, and space in such homes became unattainable luxuries
for the mass of the poorer citizens.[1]

The Berlin plan of 1858 allowed for six- and seven-storey
flats to be built with tiny courtyards, back buildings and side
wings, all designed to save expenditure on road costs and land
charges, but resulting in intense urban land speculation and
inflated site values.[2] Under the old building regulations in
Vienna, 85 per cent. of a site area could be built over in tenements
of six, seven, or eight storeys. This resulted in such a lack of air
and light that in the revised building by-laws of 1929 no new
building was allowed which had less than 45° angle of light,
while no more than 50 per cent. of the site could be built over.[3]

The inter-war period from 1918 to 1939 is marked by a
tremendous increase in the building of houses, especially in the
third decade. This building was characterized by the tenement
on the Continent, built on or near the outskirts of the city, and
in Britain by the single-family house with its own garden, built
at a standard density of 12 houses to the acre. But there has
been relatively little advance in planning ideas, which have shown
rather a degeneration of the " garden city idea " to the standard
12 houses to the acre in Britain, without any attempt at community planning. The great blocks of multi-storeyed flats in
Paris are admirably provided with community amenities, but
they are erroneously described as *Cités Jardins*. There was no
real advance in the powers of local authorities to control building
on the basis of established principles of social planning, and this
applies both to private speculators and municipal authorities.
Houses have been built with gardens in this country ; that,
unfortunately, is all. The mere fact that such a great deal has
been said and written about Letchworth, Welwyn, Hampstead,
Wythenshawe, Port Sunlight and Bournville, is an indication of
how exceptional and experimental has been Ebenezer Howard's
garden city idea. The products of these years are the housing
estate in Britain and the multi-storeyed block of flats on the
Continent and in the United States.

[1] Elizabeth Denby, *Europe Rehoused*, London, 1938, p. 26.
[2] *Ibid.*, p. 124.   [3] *Ibid.*, p. 155.

There have been three main fields of development in respect of town planning during the inter-war period. First, the powers of expropriation, as explained in a previous paragraph, have facilitated some clearance of slums, rebuilding, and new road construction inside the built-up area. In Britain, unfortunately, few such powers have yet been bestowed on municipal authorities, and we have only recently reached a solution of the problems of compensation and betterment. Second, general proposals for the use of land within the areas of individual local government authorities, known as " zoning ", are now adopted for most cities. Third, voluntary co-operation of geographically contiguous local authorities has permitted the submission of proposals for such matters as housing, open spaces, communications, and zoning over areas which are larger than the individual local government unit. In brief, laws of expropriation began to appear during the latter half of the 19th century on the Continent. In France, Belgium, and Holland such measures permitted a good deal of slum clearance and internal reconstruction in the city centres, where space was required to an increasing extent for business purposes. The defect of such changes, as observed in Paris, Brussels, Amsterdam and elsewhere, was that the city centres were cleared of old, condemned property, and new roads and boulevards were built and space provided for offices, hotels, and public buildings, but no adequate provision was made for rehousing in cheap and hygienic new homes the folk who had lived in the slums.

Town planning, in its modern sense, began in the first decades of the 20th century and was fairly well established by the outbreak of the First World War. Its defect is that in all town-planning schemes attention is devoted primarily to such questions as broad permissive zoning, roads and open spaces, and not sufficiently to the type of planning that is necessary to meet adequately social needs. Regional planning, in the sense of advisory committees submitting planning proposals, developed *after* the 1914–18 war and followed more or less the same lines in Europe and America. But none of these bodies, except that concerned with the Ruhr in Germany, had legal powers to carry out its proposals. We seem now to be passing into a fourth phase, in which greater powers are being given to such planning authorities. These powers carry with them the recognition that regional authorities intermediate between the local authority and the State are needed to plan the country effectively in the public interest.

CHAPTER 21

THE MODERN URBAN AREA

We have already emphasized that specialization of function of individual building structures has been the key-note of the structural development of the modern urban organism. Such specialization has always been characteristic of the public building —the church, castle, royal residence, municipal building. But, until the early 19th century, even in the greatest cities, virtually all the buildings were dwellings, and the merchant reserved in his home space for storage in the loft or in the cellar or in out-houses, while the craftsman reserved space for his workshop and the shopkeeper had his premises in the ground floor of his house. Even in the case of the mills and tanneries that were sited near the river front, the craftsman lived on the premises or nearby. The functions were gradually specialized in the largest cities in the spreading urban area at the end of the 18th century, and in the majority of cities after the advent of the railway in the middle of the 19th.

Thus, in approaching the study of the urban habitat, we have to recognize that its buildings have four attributes—use or function, age, physical structure (the interior arrangement of rooms and number of storeys), architectural style. We will consider each of these in turn. The reader must bear in mind that our remarks apply, unless otherwise stated, primarily to the continental town.

(1) Use or Function

Every urban survey is confronted by the primary problem of plotting buildings according to their uses. This is rendered difficult by their great range, especially as concerns industries, and by the great diversity of uses that characterize the city centre and its margins. Classifications adopted in such surveys are legion, but a broad classification may be submitted as follows.

Public Buildings.   1. Administrative and Political. (State, District Municipal)
2. Educational.
3. Religious.
4. Social Service.
5. Amusement.
6. Military.

Private Buildings. 1. Dwellings.
                    2. Dwelling and factory.
                    3. Dwelling and shop.
                    4. Industrial.
                    5. Commercial.
                    6. Communications.
                    7. Urban Open Spaces (Cemeteries, Sports fields, Parks).

We require detailed statistics of the land uses of cities on a comparative basis. Few such data are readily available even for single countries, where the statistical basis would be uniform. Some attention has been given to this matter in the United States, and the general features are typical of all cities of Western civilization.

The following figures apply to sixteen cities in the United States as average percentages of the urban land uses.

LAND USES IN SIXTEEN CITIES IN THE UNITED STATES

Total City Area		Total Developed Area	
Single Family	21·8	Single Family	36·1
Two-Family	1·3	Two-Family	2·1
Multiple Dwelling . . .	0·7	Multiple Dwelling . . .	1·1
Commerce	1·4	Commerce	2·4
Light Industry	2·0	Light Industry	3·2
Heavy Industry	1·7	Heavy Industry	2·7
Railroad Property . . .	3·2	Railroad Property . . .	5·5
Streets	20·2	Streets	33·0
Parks	4·0	Parks	6·3
Public and Semi-public . .	4·5	Public and semi-public . .	7·6
Vacant Land	40·0		

One-fifth of the entire area or one-third of the developed area is taken up by streets. The area devoted to commerce, which contains the skyscrapers and other business structures, covers only 2·5 per cent. of the developed area, and that devoted to industry 6·0 per cent. Nearly 40 per cent. of the developed (urban occupied) area is devoted to residential uses. These average figures cannot be taken as typical of any one city, for the functional character of each city is reflected in considerable variations from this norm. Data of this kind are given for German cities on p. 527. We seriously need such comparative data for our British cities.[1]

(2) AGE OF THE BUILDING

Specific criteria for study and cartographic representation of structures are the interior arrangement of the rooms, the number of storeys, the type of roof (a very important fact that affects the

[1] See H. Bartholomew, *Urban Land Uses*, Harvard, 1932 ; also Ely and Wehrwein, *Land Economics*, New York, 1940, p. 450.

whole aspect of a historic town centre), the mode of grouping, and density of buildings per acre.

Here it is important to summarize the main historical phases in the development of architecture, since these phases are reflected not merely in details of style, but also in the structure of the buildings and the mode of their grouping. These phases form a basic framework for the study of all aspects of urban building, and without a good knowledge of the development of urban architecture it is impossible to appreciate the build of the town, large or small, or the regional variations in town build in western Europe. It is not the purpose of this book to deal with the phases in the history of architecture, but the reader should certainly become familiar with one of the standard works. The architect, it should be remembered, is concerned with the creative nature of man as expressed in his buildings. The geographer is concerned with the urban habitat *as a whole,* and, in consequence, with precisely that period that interests the architect least—the industrial era of the 19th century. The main phases of architectural development, with particular reference to the Continent, may be broadly summarized as follows.

(*a*) *Medieval (before 1500) (Gothic).* Very few houses belong to this period. Its only representatives are found in the great public buildings, ecclesiastical and secular—cathedrals, parish churches, monasteries, town halls and guild halls, castles, occasionally the town wall, and a few houses. These last are of great importance as indicating the probable character of some of their contemporaries, while the medieval public buildings were the foci of growth of the medieval urban habitat. With its origins in northern France, Gothic architecture permeated the whole of that area, and spread to Germany eastwards to the limits of German colonization, where it assumed special forms with brick as the building medium, as well as to southern Scandinavia and Britain. This is the Gothic culture area. The pointed arch was used in its public buildings, and the steep gable roof was just as characteristic of its domestic buildings. It did not penetrate deeply into the Romanesque sphere of southern France (Fig. 110, p. 412).

(*b*) *Renaissance (1500–1600).* Italian influences penetrated slowly. Building methods were the same as in the medieval period, and from this era date the finest of the half-timbered town houses of northern France, Germany, and Britain. The new influences affected the details of external style. New buildings

revealed their Gothic affinities by the irregular grouping, battle-
mented turrets and traceried windows.   In Britain foreign influences were derived mainly from Holland, whence were derived
the increasing use of brick in building and such minor features
as the use of the stepped gable.

(c) *The Classical or Baroque* (*1600–1800*).   The architecture of
this period developed the Classical Style of the Renaissance with
the addition of distinct structural and ornamental motifs.   It
used the dome, the rounded arch, the colonnade, and the cross
and the oval.   Baroque first reached its peak in Italy in the
17th century, but its greatest achievements appear in the buildings
of the 18th century in south Germany and Austria, where architects found wealthy patrons in prince, bishop and abbot.   After
the devastations of the Thirty Years War there was a period of
rapid and simple building, but in the 18th century building
became grandiose and architects were lavish with external ornamentation and drew their inspiration from Italian sources.
Many churches and episcopal palaces were built in this period
in the Roman Catholic countries, and their cupolas adorn the
" Baroque cities " of south Germany and Austria.   On the other
hand, the architecture of the Protestant lands of northern Europe
was more restrained.   Very few new churches were built, for
St. Paul's in London and the Dôme des Invalides are magnificent
exceptions.   This was an era of domestic architecture in these
lands, and architects developed the Renaissance designs for town
and country houses of Andrea Palladio of Vicenza.   Secular
building is everywhere characterized by the terrace house, the
individual villa (*Hôtel*) in town or country, and the square in
England.   Buildings are marked by the harmonious composition
of their elements, the adaptation of classical styles, and hori-
zontality, as opposed to the verticality of the Gothic.   Northern
Europe drew its inspiration largely from Holland and France.

The Classic French style of the age of Louis XIV is the style of
absolute monarchy.   The Classic Dutch style of the same decades has
the qualities of the wealthy trading republic.   Both influenced Britain,
the French style chiefly in official, the Dutch more in private and City
architecture.[1]

The crowning British achievements of this period are the works
of Sir Christopher Wren, which included his abortive plan for
the reconstruction of London with the principle of the *rond-point*
borrowed from France.   The mansard roof is widely adopted in

[1] N. Pevsner, *op. cit.*, p. 116.

the housing of this period, and either it or the eaves house became the prevalent building style on the Continent.

(d) *Neo-Gothic and Neo-Classical* (c. *1800–1900*). This was a degenerate period in the history of architecture. It is marked by the revival of Gothic and Classical styles, the former being used for churches and schools, the latter for secular buildings. The Corn Exchange in England is the typical representative of the Neo-classical style, and an example of the Neo-Gothic is the Law Courts in London, built in 1874. The new factories and the hovels and tenements for the working classes were built of brick. This phase affected Britain most, but the Continent only in small degree, where the architectural styles of the Rococo period were continued. The latter half of the 19th century witnessed the rapid growth of urban populations and the extension of brick and mortar. It is known in Germany as the *Gründerzeit*. Cast iron began to be used for the new structures, as a framework of columns and beams for brick buildings. The Crystal Palace, built in 1851, revealed new possibilities, that were quickly realized in such structures as railway stations and bridges, and the framework of new large buildings. The Forth Bridge was erected in 1884–90 and the Manchester Central Station in 1880. The growth of the central business district began, and a great variety of tasteless structures appeared in the centre intermixed with the older buildings. The brick-built tenement and factory were dominant in many of the continental towns during this period.

(e) *The Modern Period* (*1900–39*). The two outstanding features of this era are the use of steel-frame construction and of reinforced concrete (first used in France in the 'nineties) in multi-storeyed building, and the concentration of architectural energies on the " wealth-producing " buildings—banks, offices, shops, factories. The public building received little attention, and the revival of interest in the civic building is one of the main concerns of contemporary architecture and planning. Cubist and functional designs dominate in the building of larger structures, while brick building becomes almost universal for the enormous number of new houses erected in the latter part of the inter-war period. This is the era of the skyscraper in the United States, which has its structural counterparts in western Europe.

Urban geographers have given much attention to this subject on the Continent. Some of their results for particular cities are summarized at the end of this chapter, and the maps of Basel (Fig. 16) and Strasbourg (Fig. 123) illustrate their methods.

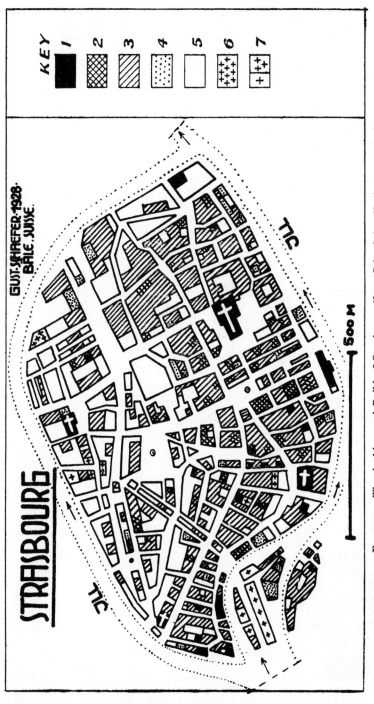

FIG. 123.—The Architectural Build of Strasbourg (from Schaefer). (Scale, 1 : 10,000.) 1. Medieval (Gothic) up to 1500. 2. Renaissance, 16th century. 3. Baroque and Classical, 1600–1800. 4. Neo-Romanesque, Neo-Gothic, Neo-Classical, 1800–50. 5. Modern, since 1850. 6. Technical and Industrial. 7. Churches and Cemeteries. The area corresponds with the districts marked I, II, III and C on Fig. 33, p. 137.

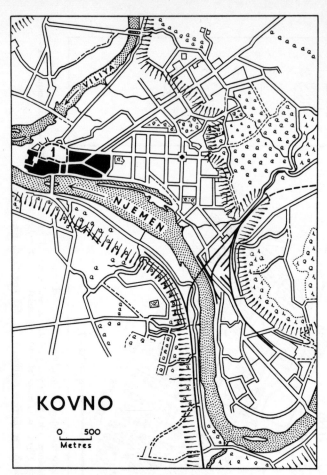

KOVNO

0   500
Metres

FIG. 125.—Kovno (scale, 1 : 75,000) from Baedeker plan (dated 1931).

1. Stronghold of the Teutonic Order ; black, medieval town. Scarp indicates break between low river terraces and the main plateau (70-80 m.).

FIG. 124. — Vilna (scale, c. 1 : 40,000) (from Baedeker plan dated 1902) and Congrès Int. de Géographie, Varsovie, 1934, Excursion B1, pp. 25-34.

Dashed line shows site of walls of the old stronghold with : 1. Cathedral ; 2. Lower Castle ; 3. Upper Castle. Black, the medieval town bordered originally by streams around the stronghold and on west side of the town.

(3) Street, Place and Open Space

This would seem to be the appropriate juncture at which to introduce a brief consideration of streets and open spaces in the modern urban area. Streets cover a substantial part of the urban area—a minimum of 20 to 25 per cent. in the densely built-up central districts. Open spaces are notoriously inadequate in these districts and are irregularly and inadequately distributed throughout the urban complex. The street may be considered from the point of view of direction, width, and use or purpose. The medieval town had narrow streets ; even a planned town like Monpazier with its main wagon streets (*Verkehrstrassen*), 8 metres wide, and its narrow living streets (*Wohnungsstrassen* or *rues d'habitation*) only 2m. 50 wide. In many of the big cities and old port quarters narrow streets, too narrow for single carriage traffic, have a width of about one metre. There is also a strict limit to the gradient of streets. A modern main thoroughfare cannot have gradients of more than about 2 to 3 degrees. Slopes of over 10 degrees demand staircases. It is clear, therefore, why the streets on the hilly sites favoured by small medieval towns run along the contours, and why in the construction of modern highways raised ground has to be cut through to maintain a fairly level surface.

German students usually refer to the two main types of street, which were particularly well defined in the medieval towns, as the commercial route (*Verkehrstrasse*), which was the main traffic thoroughfare, and the living street (*Wohnungsstrasse*), which contained the dwellings of the townsmen and was not used by the wheeled traffic of the town. But in a more general classification other categories must be recognized. There are the wide thoroughfares built in the 17th and 18th centuries for sauntering and as fashionable carriage drives. Such are the *Allées* of Toulouse and Brussels, the *Rambla* of the Catalonian towns, the *Promenades* of other French towns, the *Cours* of Bordeaux, Paris, Marseilles, and Agen, the *Mail* of Chateaudun and Blois, and the Mall of London. There are also the *Boulevards*, built on the sites of the old fortifications, and the long, wide, traffic thoroughfares that were cut during the 19th century in France in particular. Shorter roads were also made to set off large public monuments, such as the *Avenue de l'Opéra* in Paris. Others appeared as through cuts, commonly in the French towns, where the most famous were those cut by Haussmann in Paris. The finest promenades

are the *Champs-Élysées* in Paris, dating from the 17th century, with
a width of 70 metres ; *Unter den Linden* in Berlin, dating from
the 18th century, with a width of 60 metres ; and the *Ring* of
Vienna, built during the mid-19th century, with a width of 57
metres. A minimum width of 12 metres is essential to permit
the passage of two vehicles, with a pavement of about 2 metres
(one metre, or just over one yard, on each side). This is about
the standard width of the streets of the modern built-up areas,
but there are main traffic thoroughfares, as just noted, with much
greater widths. Paris has 60 kilometres of roads with widths
over 20 metres, including, in addition to the Champs-Élysées,
the Grands Boulevards (35 metres), Avenue de l'Opéra (30
metres), Avenue de la Grande Armée (70 metres), Avenue de
Vincennes (83 metres) and the Avenue Foch (120 metres), the
last three being among the most recently planned of the great
Parisian thoroughfares.

The public place is an integral part of the urban plan, from
the standpoint of traffic, trade, and æsthetic planning. The
idea developed particularly during the Baroque era of the
17th and 18th centuries. The life of the medieval town centred
on the market-place, and as its size and trade grew, the authorities
established new markets. These were improvised on streets, or
held on street widenings, or on large, well-laid-out places on the
outskirts of the town, often just outside its gates. The names of
the markets often indicated their purposes and their date. Such
markets, as suggested on p. 325, may be classed as street markets,
triangular markets, and rectangular markets, although this excludes many markets with a great variety of shapes, sizes and
uses. Many have been reduced in size by the encroachment of
buildings since the Middle Ages, or temporary booths have been
replaced by permanent buildings, thus greatly reducing their
original area. The large, open place appeared in the 16th
century and after in the newly planned towns and in the opening
up of the existing medieval towns. It reflected the spirit of the
age. It served as a promenade, and as a military parade area
(*Place d'Armes* or *Paradeplatz*). It was also used to set off the great
public monuments that were erected in this era, notably the
statues of the monarchs. The Place de la Concorde was the
setting for the statue of Louis XV. There were four other *places
royales* in Paris, and *places royales* in such towns as Caen, Bordeaux,
Dijon, Rennes. The Place Stanislas at Nancy, the Place Peyrouin
at Montpellier, the Place Royale in Brussels, the Place Amalien-

borg at Copenhagen, and the Place Gustavus Adolphus at Stockholm, are other examples. Furthermore, the buildings that had invariably surrounded the church in the medieval town, were now cleared away and the church set off by a large square (*Parvis*). The same sort of open space was reserved in front of many new public buildings in the 16th century and after, such as town halls, castles (or palaces as they are now more appropriately called), and the government buildings. Among town-hall places we may note the Rathaus Platz in Vienna, and the places before the town halls of Paris and Brussels. The palaces with places include those of Versailles, Berlin, Darmstadt, Stuttgart and others. Buildings such as the federal palace at Bern with its Bundesplatz and the Palais de Justice at Brussels are examples of government buildings set off by squares. In the 20th century, places have been erected at, or serve primarily as, traffic nodes. The *place de la Gare*, it has been said, serves to-day much the same sort of function as the medieval market-place.[1] In London and Paris it is conspicuous by its absence, but the places at Stuttgart, Frankfurt and Karlsruhe are amongst the largest in the whole town. Such places occupy a particularly large area where stations have been recently re-erected. Deliberate traffic nodes, with radial thoroughfares, with monuments placed in the centre of the place (the monument being secondary to the nodal function), are well illustrated by the Place de la Bastille (Colonne de la Bastille) and the Place de l'Étoile (Arc de Triomphe).

The structure of the place may be considered either as an element in itself or in relation to the routes that centre on it. In the former sense there are three main categories, the rectangular, the circular, and the triangular. The first is the most common, as it has been throughout the ages of city life. It was almost universal among the planned towns of the Middle Ages. The circular place is obviously a carefully designed form, and, like the radial-concentric plan, it does not appear until the 16th century. In the best-known cases the routes radiate from the place like the spokes of a wheel, as in the Place de l'Étoile, Place de la Nation, and Place d'Italie in Paris. The same theme is found in the *Circus* of British 18th-century planning, and in many French and German cities. Semi-circular forms were laid out in relation to a monument with routes radiating from it, as at Karlsruhe. The triangular form, so frequent in the Middle Ages, appears rarely in the succeeding centuries ; this is the form

[1] P. Lavedan, *Géographie des Villes*, p. 101.

adopted for the Place Dauphine in Paris in the 17th century.
Places may be regarded from still another point of view—those
that are open to the highways of commerce, on the route, a
widening of it, or to one side of, but in contact with it ; and those
that are isolated from the main thoroughfare in quiet seclusion.
The two types occur with remarkable clarity in the places of the
Classical era.

Parks include the ornamental gardens and the parks proper,
as well as the wide, tree-lined Promenades in some cities.   The
parks and gardens include private parks that have passed into
public ownership, forests on the borders that have been incorporated in the city, like the Tiergarten in Berlin, and the Bois de
Vincennes and Bois de Boulogne in Paris.   There are also woods
that have been purchased, and open spaces that have been transformed into gardens.   Some parks are the relics of common lands,
ecclesiastical properties, or royal estates.   This was notably the
case in London, where Kensington Gardens, Regent's Park, St.
James's Park and Green Park were formerly attached to royal
residences.   Hyde Park was a royal domain, and became a
fashionable rendezvous in the 17th century.   Hampstead Heath
had its nucleus in a tract of common land acquired by purchase
in the late 19th century.   Playing spaces are notoriously scarce
and inadequate in the large cities ; they are mainly on the
urban outskirts.   Public parks and playing spaces accessible to
the whole of the urban population are quite inadequate.   Many
cities have a great river crossing through the town, but while
some, such as Paris and Budapest, have used this to great æsthetic
and sanitary advantage, others, notoriously London, have ruined
their natural amenities by allowing the uncontrolled erection of
buildings along its double frontage.

(4) Building Heights

The height of buildings depends on historical tradition as well
as on 19th-century building regulations.   The several-storey
building is characteristic of both the rural and urban house in
the Mediterranean lands.   It developed in the houses of the 16th
and 17th centuries and after in the old towns as social customs
gradually changed.   In continental Europe it appeared as the
tenement.   With somewhat obscure medieval origins, probably
associated with the clan system, it is found in the tenements of
Scotland.   On the other hand, the single- or two-storeyed house
is generally characteristic of the smallest homestead and is found

in the small cottage of the English countryside, and in rows in the small English town. Similarly the home of the peasant of south-west France is a small single-storey homestead (*échoppe*). It is well represented in Bordeaux, where it was established by the settlers from the countryside, and stands in marked contrast to the great tenements of Marseilles. The single-storey homestead, built of timber, is the traditional type in the country towns of Scandinavia and Poland.

There was a general tendency for the height of buildings to increase after the end of the Middle Ages, and the historic house has invariably several storeys, with a minimum of three. The extensive areas of flats built in the continental city during the 19th century have normally four to five storeys. A marked change in city structure came about after 1889, when the first skyscraper was built at Chicago. It was New York that took up the idea by building on the solid foundations of granite rocks on the island of Manhattan. Chicago with its soft basis of sands and gravels is second only to New York as a skyscraper city, the engineer constructing his buildings on " floating " concrete rafts. The enormous heights of the skyscrapers in the down-town district is the most remarkable feature of the American city profile. Though their construction began in the 'nineties, the majority of the skyscrapers have been built in the last 25 years. It is a well-known fact that every small town in the States seeks to have at least one skyscraper in its down-town district. The European city has adopted the skyscraper, though no building competes in height with the Empire State Building's height of 380 metres. Thus, in France the highest are found at Villeurbanne in Lyons, with an 18 storey building, and, ironically enough, at the *cité-jardin* of Muette at Drancy on the outskirts of Paris, where there is a structure with five towers and 15 storeys.

In most European cities the municipal authorities have set a limit to upward growth. A Paris law of 1783 fixed the minimum width of streets at 10 metres and the height of houses at 20 metres. The same width was used by Haussmann, who also forbade houses to have more than five storeys. An edict of 1902 established a fixed proportion between the width of the street and the height of the building—namely, for streets with a width of under 12 metres, houses should be 6 metres high ; for streets 12 metres wide, houses 18 metres high ; streets 12 to 20 metres wide, buildings 18 metres high, plus one-quarter of the excess in width above 12 metres, with an absolute maximum height fixed at 20 metres.

This maximum may be exceeded provided that the highest storeys are stepped back, staircase-fashion. In other countries, we find such limitations on upward growth, and heights of building vary between 20 and 25 metres. Thus the limit of building in Brussels is 21 metres, in Berlin 22, London 24, Vienna and Warsaw 25 metres.

(5) STRUCTURE OR FORM

The basic contrasts of structure are in general functional since the buildings are erected for, or converted to, particular uses. We need careful classifications of urban structures as a basis for mapping the city.

(a) *Industrial Buildings*. The classification of industries by product or process presents far greater difficulties than the classification of *factories* as structures. While many attempts have been made to classify by industry, no attempt, to our knowledge, has been made in Britain to classify by structure. The usual method adopted, in urban surveys in particular, is to distinguish between heavy and light industries. The former deal with bulky materials, and require large structures and large ground space, or create obnoxious smells and smoke. These are the industries that are kept clear of residential areas in modern zoning. On the other hand, the light industries are concerned with processes that create no objectionable noise or smell and may therefore be allowed with limitations in zoned residential districts.

But from the point of view of what is, and not what shall be, how are factories, as buildings, to be classified as a means of determining the significant features of their distribution and the causes of their location? Some types of structure are obvious, since the function dictates the build, such as a blast furnace, a coke oven, a heavy chemical works, or a thermal electric plant. But there are numerous industries which cannot be brought into such a classification by product. They must be grouped by size or process, as expressed in the physical structure of the factory. Factors to be considered in such a classification of factories are ground space, number of storeys, building materials, date of establishment, location in relation to rail, water and road, and transport facilities needed by the plant (storage yards, rail depots, wharves, garages, etc.)

Such study is especially important for the so-called mixed zones that lie invariably in the inner areas of the big agglomerations near to the city core, and for certain kinds of industries that are scattered throughout a large part of the urban area, without marked localization.[1]

(*b*) *Public Buildings* are specialized buildings and are usually outstanding in the build of the urban complex. They clearly reflect the historical development of the city, and in this respect impinge on the whole field of ecclesiastical and civil architecture. They can most appropriately be dealt with on the basis of the architectural epoch to which they belong. Some are situated in or near the centre, others, which demand more space, are placed on the outskirts, while others, though originally built on the outskirts, are now enveloped by built-up land and their removal to a better site is long overdue. There are also the smaller establishments concerned with daily service to the whole community. These serve smaller parts of the whole, and are such as schools, local offices of public departments, and churches and chapels.

(*c*) *Commercial Buildings* have many of the same attributes of structure as the factories, especially in mixed areas where workshop and warehouse and office appear on different storeys with shops, offices, cafés, etc., on the lower floors. The following are clear and present no particular problems of mapping or siting : railways and yards, wharves, sheds, warehouses (number of storeys, inner structure, storage capacity, date), multi-storeyed shops, and single-storey shops with one or two or more residences or mixed uses above them, office blocks, and special buildings such as Exchanges. The character of the commercial functions gives special character to the streets, and these may be classified on various bases for cartographic representation.

It was not until the end of the 18th century that special structures began to be erected and that commerce began, so to speak, to leave an " architectural deposit " in the town. Then, too, certain of the commercial functions began to concentrate in the centre of the town, where they were most conveniently accessible to the whole urban area and its environs and to each other. This is clearly illustrated by London, the greatest of all agglomerations.

In the early Georgian period in London, the port was a succession of wharfs. Warehouses were in cellars and outbuildings in the merchants' houses, while their offices were on the ground floor of the latter, and shops were front-rooms with enlarged window openings,

---

[1] Reference should be made to the work entitled *Conurbation*, published by the West Midland Group, 1948, for an important study of industry in Birmingham and the Black Country.

and markets were streets or squares. But in the middle of the 18th century specialized commerce began to leave an "architectural deposit". Dock construction began, especially towards the end of the century, shops and shop-fronts emerged "to full architectural consciousness" in the second half of the century with bowed fronts and classical cornices. Exchanges also appeared. The Royal Exchange was rebuilt after the Great Fire, and it shed some of its varied activities to a separate Corn Exchange in 1749–50, to which a second was added in 1827. In subsequent years such buildings were erected in nearly every English market town in heavy Victorian architecture as symbolic of the age and of the life of the town. The Stock Exchange appeared in 1802. It was then too that the first big banks and insurance buildings were erected. The closed market appeared in the 16th century and after in English towns, like the market at Oxford, and an arcaded market was built over the Fleet river in 1737. But markets in London were mostly blocks of shops and the big markets did not appear till the early 19th century. Thus, Covent Garden began in the open square in the 18th century, but the building was not erected till 1828–30 (the first of its type was built at Liverpool in 1819) and was followed by others. The first railway terminal arrived in 1838 and by 1844 there were six, and by 1877 the main railway net was complete.[1]

(d) *Residential Buildings*. We come finally to the residential structures, the houses. Houses make up at least two-thirds of the total built-up area of the urban complex, and a larger proportion if the old converted houses of the city centre are included. This then is the most important "areal" item of the urban complex, and should receive special consideration. It has been neglected in British studies, presumably, among other reasons, because the old buildings, to say nothing of the sea of 19th-century building, present little of architectural interest to the historian or the architect. But the historic house type in the continental town has a long history behind it. It is evident in very characteristic structures which give a distinct character not only to individual towns, but also to groups of towns in particular regions, like the plan of the town as a whole. This is true even of the big cities that have had their centres most transformed. These remarks are primarily concerned with the town house on the Continent, but the general points apply to British towns as well, though they need to be worked out in their particular detail for individual cities.

The great majority of the houses in the big cities, of course, have been built since about 1850, and in some cities since 1900. But in the smaller cities and towns, that have suffered relatively little change through modern growth—and these make up the great majority of the towns on the Continent—this predominance

[1] John Summerson, *Georgian London*, 1946.

is not so marked. In fact in these cases the majority of the houses may antedate 1850.[1] We may turn now to a more detailed consideration of house types and their development.

(6) THE HOUSE

The first general basis of classification of buildings of all kinds in the modern urban complex is the distinction between close settlement and open settlement. The first term applies to settlement that consists of continuous rows of building on a continuous street pattern, in which the building blocks have buildings on two or more of their four sides. The area is one of continuous urban use. Open settlement applies to areas in which two sides or one side of the block are built up, or the buildings are well spaced from each other and separated by open land ; urban uses are discontinuous. In general, in an area of close settlement, about a third or more is taken up by buildings and streets. In areas of open settlement there is a much larger proportion of open land, even though the structures may be of the same type as those in the areas of close settlement. In Britain, open settlement has become the rule with the expansion of the house with its own garden at a density of 12 units to the acre. On the Continent, in general, the building has been much more markedly confined to the compact urban area, and even outward expansion to the surrounding rural area has generally taken the form of rows of flats rather than single family houses.[2]

[1] Thus, as an example, Göttingen has nearly 50 per cent. of its houses dating from the Rococo period, when it acquired cultural importance and attraction through the building of the University. Einbeck and Northeim, its near neighbours, that are much smaller, show particularly large proportions (about 30 per cent.) from the Baroque Period ; since then there took place much rebuilding after devastations caused by the Thirty Years War, and the same two towns have about the same proportion built during the Classical period, following fires that devastated each town about 1830. About half the houses of Göttingen were erected between 1850 and 1923, and 10 per cent. of the other two towns were built in this modern period, thus reflecting the quicker growth and change in aspect of the larger town. We need more studies of this kind, and when British cities are studied on a standardized basis this aspect of investigation should receive its due place. These data are taken from H. Dörries, *Die Städte im oberen Leinetal : Göttingen, Northeim und Einbeck.*

[2] On this subject, in its applicability to English urban areas, see H. Rees, " The Representation of Housing Patterns on the Fifth and Sixth Editions of the Ordnance Survey One-Inch Map ", *Geography*, September, 1946, pp. 110–16. Three types of housing are officially recognized in Italy according to the vertical and horizontal density of building. 1. Intensive (Closed) Construction, in which a high percentage of the land is built-up, and buildings have at least 4 to 5 storeys, with many rooms, and staircases are used by various tenants on each floor, with communal life due to the juxtaposition of families. 2. Extensive (Open) Construction, in which a low percentage of the land is built-up, buildings have not more than 2 or 3 storeys, and the staircase is not used by many tenants on each floor ; it is more private. 3. Intermediate, with no buildings of 3–4 storeys, isolated and not in blocks, with the mode of construction as in 1. See the article " Casa " in *Enciclopedia Italiana.*

(a) Close Settlement

(i) *Historic House Types.* The medieval house types in the towns of western Europe date almost entirely from the Renaissance period and after. There are very few domestic buildings in any town antedating about 1500. Although inspired by the new ideas of architecture, structures were faithful to the traditional house type until the advent of the modern era of building in the 19th century. Thus, the flimsy medieval structures were gradually replaced during the 16th century and after. It was during the 17th and 18th centuries that Classical ideas caused the development of new structures and styles. An important social change was the new form of family life whereby separate rooms began to be allotted for different purposes, so that more storeys were required than in the smaller medieval houses with communal living-rooms. Warehouses, workshops and public buildings and shops demanded more space, and these economic and social changes, just as the barrier to growth formed by the enclosing walls, caused increasing congestion in the town. The result was the upward growth of its buildings to three, four, and five storeys. The danger of fire caused city governments to prescribe building in stone, although this spread very slowly, and in the small towns the timber-framed building continued to be built until the 19th century. Fire protection also caused the introduction of the party wall and the gradual displacement of the house built in depth with its gable-end facing the street by the house built in length, with its eaves parallel to the street frontage. Similarly, thatched roofs began to be replaced by slate or tile.

There are marked regional variations in the type of urban house, dependent partly on local building materials and regional building styles, and partly on much more obscure traditional building styles that are based on deep-seated cultural relations.

Some general features of the development of the medieval house have already been stated in pp. 317–23. Roof type, the interior arrangement of rooms, and the number of storeys are the chief items in this consideration of building structures. The expansion in the size of the house in the 17th and 18th centuries, to which we have already drawn attention as due to a change in family life and organization, called for a change in domestic architecture. The narrow frontage of the gable house was not suited to a larger structure with more rooms. In consequence, the eaves house, built in length, and the rectangular structure for which a new type of roof was adapted, called the mansard roof, became the accepted building types of the Baroque period, each being accompanied by the decorative themes appropriate to the period. The various roof types, including the variants of the mansard roof, are shown on Fig. 126. House types as developed in France in the Baroque (or Classical) Period are shown on Fig. 127.

In France there is a marked contrast between the town and country houses of the Midi, with flattish roofs and porticoes and balcony, and the steep gabled houses, with larger windows, and often timber-built, in the north of France. The latter, in the Middle Ages, were thatched, and then were gradually roofed with Flemish tiles, rather than with the Roman tiles that for

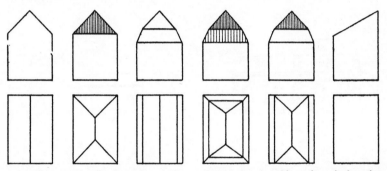

FIG. 126.—Roof Types of the Historic Town House, showing side and vertical sections (from Muller, *Die Alstadt von Breslau*). From left to right :—Saddle roof, Hip roof, Mansard roof, Gambrel (modified Mansard) roof, modified Hip roof, Sloping roof (*Pultdach*).

centuries had been used in the Midi. A recent study by Doyon and Habrecht of house structures in France lays down principles of classification, but makes only incidental reference to regional distributions and types. Several regional features, however, may be emphasized. On the assumption that the rectangle is the basis of its plan, the house is classified by these authors according to the number of its bays in lateral succession and the number of its storeys (see Fig. 127). Certain features of house structure are characteristic of towns in general as opposed to the country residence or farmstead ; others have a significant regional distribution. The unit of classification is the smallest building with the gable facing the street and three or four storeys. A double frontage may have a gable roof facing or at right angles to the street front. Houses may be built from this unit with up to five

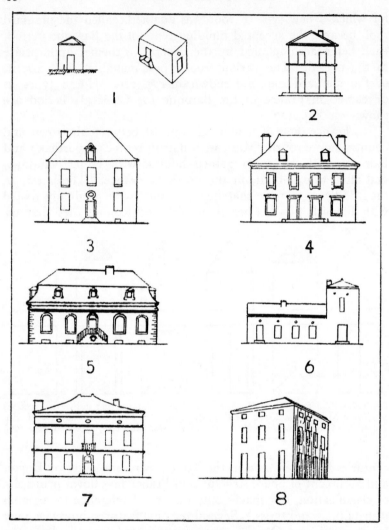

Fɪɢ. 127.—Town Houses in France in the 17th and 18th centuries
(from Doyon and Habrecht).

1. The simple unit house in the north (left) and in the south (right). 2–5. Houses with two, three, four, and five windows in width, with dormer windows, and two or more storeys. 6 and 7. Town houses in southern France, without dormer windows, but with mezzanine floor, and one or more storeys. 8. Individual cubical structure (*maison à l'angle*) with similar frontages on four sides, with mezzanine floor.

bays, with one or two storeys or more, and with lateral or side extensions on two or more sides of a rectangular courtyard. The arrangement of windows and storeys reveals contrasts between the Nord and the Midi. Characteristic of many towns in the

Midi is the house with an upper mezzanine floor, just beneath
the roof, with a row of small windows, rectangular or circular in
shape, a series of large middle storey windows on the middle and
main floor with verandah, and a portico in the ground floor.
These features bear striking resemblance to those of the Italian
and Spanish building styles of the 16th century.   In the Nord,

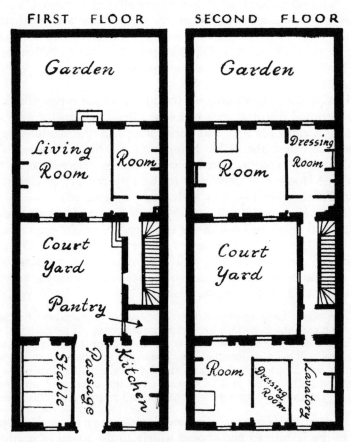

FIG. 128.—The Plan of a 17th-century Town House in France
(from Doyon and Habrecht, p. 69).

these features are very rare ; characteristic here is the dormer
window in a steep roof (see Plate 29).
   The ground plan of the small town house in France is more
or less standardized.   The house of a well-to-do citizen of the
17th century at Tours (Fig. 128) is divided into two parts on either
side of a court, inter-connected by a loggia at the ground floor and

a gallery on the upper floors.   It has a main entrance from the courtyard to the staircase, which was contained in a small tower. This type was widespread in the towns of France in the later Middle Ages, and forms the basic type in the older parts of most towns, though it has been greatly modified by subsequent alterations and additions.   The same kind of arrangement on a larger scale is found in large town houses like that of Jacques Cœur at Bourges.   The addition of more rooms, a stable and gardens is found in the *hôtels* of the 18th century, together with the large interior staircase which is found especially in the town houses of the Midi, where it often takes on unexpectedly large proportions in small houses.

In Germany, there are two traditional house types, which in their regional distribution are closely allied in character with the country farmsteads and had their origins in the Middle Ages. These are called the Gable House and the Eaves House.   The third historic type, as noted above, may be referred to as the Mansard House that developed in the 17th century in Germany as in France (see Fig. 129 and Plates 27 and 28).

The *gable house (Gabelhaus)* is the oldest type of German town house, and developed out of the farmstead in north, central, and southern Germany.   Congestion of space, alinement along a street, the shedding of farm buildings, notably of the barn, and the adaptation of the structure to the needs of craftsman and the merchant, led to the transformation of the initial farm type.

The house form remained the same, as the inhabitants changed their occupations from farming to urban purposes.   The house of the craftsman was originally no different from that of the merchant, and only gradually did differentiation appear.   The *Diele* became workshop or warehouse or office, and finally, in the patrician's house, a reception hall.   Since lack of space within the town wall prevented lateral growth, the houses grew in height and acquired several storeys.

In northern Germany, the Low German town house developed out of the farmstead and spread widely to the towns of northern Germany and the colonized lands to the east.   In central Germany, a distinctive town house emerged from the Frankish farmstead,

---

Fig. 129.—The Town House in Germany (after Geisler).

Historic House Types :—
The Gable House :—1. Low German House.   2. Low German Patrician House. 3. Middle German House.   4. Upper German House.   5. The Eaves House (*Traufhaus*).   6. The Mansard House.
Modern House Types :—
7. Long House (*Langhaus*).   8. *Firsthaus*.   9. Old apartment house (*Etagenhaus*).

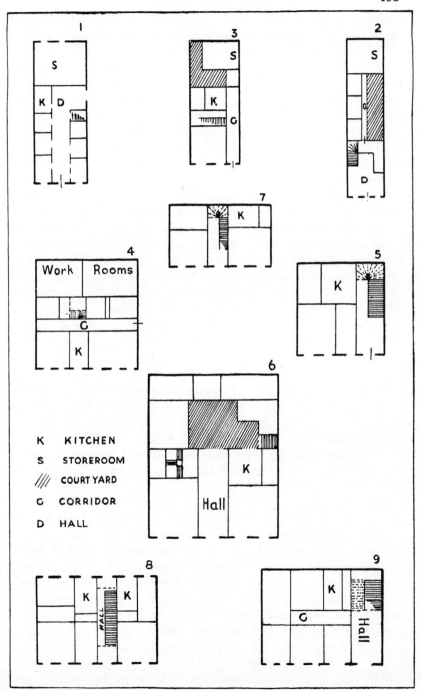

which was also a gable type, and in the south the *Oberdeutsche Bürgerhaus* developed from the south German unit farmstead.

The North or Low German house is half-timbered in north-western Germany, but built of brick in the colonized lands of north-eastern Germany and in the Hanseatic cities of the North Sea and Baltic coasts. Excellent examples are to be found in the small towns of northern Germany, such as Osnabrück, as well as in the great warehouses and patricians' and merchants' houses of such cities as Lübeck, Hamburg, and Danzig. The type is well developed in the patrician house of Danzig, with Renaissance and Baroque decorations, several storeys, a narrow street frontage with sets of three windows and a door in the centre, inside staircase and hall (the original *Diele* of the country farm-stead) with a balcony and two rooms upstairs. The central courtyard or *Hof* is absent in these houses, except in occasional instances where it was introduced from the south. The town house in central and south Germany has its main gate entrance to one side of the gable front opening on to a central courtyard or *Hof*, with the buildings grouped around it. Stone is the building material in the Main valley, but half-timber is the rule in Hesse, Franconia, and Swabia. The well-developed *Hof*, with surround-ing galleries in the later patrician houses of Frankfurt and Augs-burg, shows definite Italian influences during the Renaissance period. The town house in the extreme south appears in the small market towns of Bavaria, with a wide street frontage and a flattish roof and widely spaced, low windows, with an outside balcony and an overhanging shingle roof.

The *eaves house* (or *Traufenhaus*) is so named because its eaves run parallel to the street, and the gable end touches the gable end of the next house, so that the high slope of the roof faces the street. The roof is usually covered with red, flat tiles or slates as in the Rhine Plateau, Thuringian Forest and parts of Hesse, and contains varying numbers and tiers of windows. Variations occur in the handling of the façade, as in the gable house, and there was a north and central German eaves house built of half-timber and stone, and an upper German type built of stone only, so that there is often a close similarity in outward appearance between the two basic types. The eaves house, however, was a later development, and became predominant when town life was fully established, and was more standardized in its structure. In many towns the two types, gable and eaves house, are found side by side, and the latter takes up the same amount of frontage and has the same depth as the former. Such cases occur in Goslar, Hildesheim, Halberstadt, and Brunswick and in the towns of Thuringia and Hesse. These are probably the oldest types of eaves house.

In general, however, the eaves house has a longer street frontage than the gable house, probably through the grouping of the original house lots, so that such houses have a width of six or even more windows, instead of two or three as in the oldest, smaller, types. The emergence of the eaves house, which afforded more space and was easier to expand by the addition of new buildings, was particularly associated with public buildings such as nobles' residences, monasteries, town halls, for which the gable frontage of the burgess' house did not afford sufficiently large space under one roof. The structure was gradually adopted in domestic architecture, but it did not become established until the Renaissance period in the 16th century in south and central Germany in such towns as Frankfurt and Dresden. The main changes introduced in this period were the added attention paid to the façade, and the roof arrangement was better adapted to the construction of party walls for the prevention of the spread of fire. Thus, during the 18th century, the eaves house was gradually imposed on builders by city laws, as, for example, at Frankfurt, where, in 1719, gable-fronting houses were forbidden and all houses had to have their gables parallel to the street. This development appeared more tardily in northern Germany,[1] where Geisler regards it as a structural development from the original gable house.[2] The predominance of the eaves house became general in the building of the 17th and 18th centuries, as we have already noticed in France.

The distribution of the eaves house is not the same as that of the gable house in Germany. The eaves house is virtually absent in the towns of the northern shores and first appears in southern Niedersachsen as one goes south, with examples at Holzminden and Gandersheim. It is also found frequently in the Harz towns. In the Rhineland, the Cologne area has a large proportion of gable houses, built of brick through Dutch influence, but in the Rhine plateau, especially east of the Rhine, the two- or three-storey eaves house is common, Cologne being situated at the junction of the two culture areas. The eaves house is characteristic in the towns of central Germany. Saxony and Brandenburg

---

[1] O. Lauffer, " Das Deutsche Haus in Dorf und Stadt ", *Wissenschaft und Bildung*, No. 152, 1919, pp. 115–16.   [2] W. Geisler, *Die Deutsche Stadt*, p. 522.

are areas in which the eaves house is dominant in the towns.   It is, for instance, found among the oldest houses of Leipzig, although here, and elsewhere in the large cities of the eastern provinces, these old houses have often been replaced by modern business buildings.   In the south, the eaves house appears in Nuremberg and Munich and other towns, though here it frequently has a modified roof that resembles the mansard roof and often has great height and is built of stone.   By these traits it is distinct from the eaves house of the central German towns.

The *Mansard House* is named after the roof type that developed during the Baroque period, and was characteristic of most of the big residences built throughout western Europe at this time.   In the new ideas and practice of town planning, the house was subordinated to the street frontage and the height of buildings and their frontages in each block were kept uniform.   Individual houses had to conform to general regulations or houses were built as single groups with a uniform architectural design.   Population grew and housing catered mainly for the well-to-do class.   New house types evolved, among which two main groups may be recognized, the *Mietshaus* or lodging house, that appeared in the larger agglomerations ; and the residences of the wealthy *bourgeoisie* and of the nobility.   In the former, the better apartments were at the front, the inferior ones at the back and sides of the building.   The number of storeys reached five or more, as at Dresden, but in south-western Germany the number was limited to three.   Building laws were passed in all the chief towns to control the design of the façade.   The arrangement of windows and doors and projecting buildings, bays and towers, that had become the vogue in the later Middle Ages and in the 16th century, was now forbidden in the light of current ideas of æsthetic and practical urban planning.   The central feature of all these new residential buildings was an irregularly shaped courtyard.   But the most distinctive general feature was the mansard roof, which was adopted to allow for the inclusion of more living-rooms in buildings of several storeys.   The regular spacing of windows of uniform design, together with the smooth and regular façade of the main building, are the most attractive features of the design of the Baroque house.

The distribution of the mansard house has some interesting features.   It took firmest roots in the south-west, where the rulers were active founders of new towns that were built-up during this period, as at Karlsruhe, Mannheim, Erlangen, Ludwigsburg and elsewhere. It was generally associated with the planned extensions of this period in many existing towns. This applied also to some of the towns that were destroyed by the French in the Rhineland, as at Heidelberg, although here they are not of particular architectural merit. Landau, Zweibrücken, and Kaiserslautern are good examples, and others are Speyer, Mainz, Strasbourg, Metz, Saarbrücken, and Trier. The Baroque building is strongly developed in Bavaria, as at Straubing, and the influences spread from the capital, Munich, which is one of the most famous seats of Baroque architecture. The bishop's city of Würzburg has many fine Baroque buildings, as have the small residential towns of Thuringia, together with the residential town of Kassel and the bishop's see of Fulda. Dresden, as a capital like Munich, was also an outstanding centre of northern Baroque art and its styles spread into such places as Chemnitz and Zwickau. The towns of Silesia were ruthlessly destroyed during the Thirty Years War, and much of their present building dates from this epoch. On the other hand, mansard houses are fewer in northern Germany, and in the towns of the eastern provinces they rarely form continuous street frontages or even sectors of the town as they do in those we have referred to.

The general regional variations of the architecture of the historic German town may in conclusion be briefly summarized. Timber was the most widespread of building materials in the later Middle Ages. However, brick was dominant in northern Germany, Swabia, and Bavaria and in the lands of the Oder, and stone in the lands of the Main, the upper Rhine, and the Weser. Building styles, however, regardless of building material, differed widely from one region to another according to tradition and culture contacts. Moreover, the functional character of a town left its deep imprint on its outward forms. Thus, the bishop's town had its churches, monasteries, and schools, as at Paderborn ; the capital city had its palaces, public buildings and mansions ; the large trading emporium had its wealthy patricians' and merchants' homes, and rows of warehouses along the river fronts.

The eaves house is characteristic of the old houses of the towns in the upper Rhineland and also of Nuremberg, in spite of the fact that these houses usually have a small street frontage. The same feature is found among the towns of the Harz, where the eaves house is known to have been built in the Middle Ages. It was also the main house type in the original lay-out of Freiburg-im-Breisgau.

The east and the north clung longest to the gable house, and it is dominant to-day.

When one travels from the northern coast of Niedersachsen southwards one reaches south of Hanover the towns with eaves houses in the Harz foreland. These stand apart from the neighbouring towns of Hesse where the gable house is dominant. In Franconia and Swabia gable and eaves houses are intermixed. In Bavaria there is a marked division of the two types, for in the west the gable house is dominant, in the Bavarian Ostmark, south beyond the Brenner, and in Switzerland the eaves house is dominant. In Bohemia and Silesia the gable house again dominates. In brief, Germany reveals in respect to house types alone more variety in its towns than any other land.[1]

The Renaissance brought no essential change in structure or style except for decorative themes that came from Italy. These outside influences were more strongly felt in Franconia and Swabia than in Bavaria. In north Germany, Dutch influence penetrated. The Baroque style, after the Thirty Years War, affected the town or groups of buildings as a whole that were planned by king, lord or ecclesiastic.

In Bavaria, Austria, Bohemia, and Saxony there appear palaces and burgesses' houses with marked Italian influences. In the west, on the other hand, French influences were dominant from the Swiss border northwards to the lower Rhine in the lands west of the river.

In the Classical period, and in the late 18th and early 19th centuries, the influence of Holland was just as important in the north as that of France had been in the west, especially in the northern lands, as exemplified by Friedrich Wilhelm I's Dutch quarter in Potsdam.

The contrast between the Protestant and the Catholic town is evident in their architecture. The Protestant towns of Nuremberg and Ulm stand in marked contrast to the Catholic towns of Würzburg and Munich, although a northern Catholic town like Münster is more strongly affiliated in its architectural styles to those of Protestant Holland.

In the 17th and 18th centuries houses were built in large measure for the wealthy. In London the wealthy merchant lived in a terrace house, whereas the corresponding Parisian house was a detached *hôtel*. The plan of the London house was standardized before the end of the 17th century. " With its entrance on one side, leading straight to the staircase, one large front room and one large back room on each floor, and the service rooms in the

---

[1] A. Grisebach, *Die Alte Deutsche Stadt*, p. 5.

basement, it remained practically unaltered for the largest and the smallest house until the end of the Victorian era." [1] The pattern of the French town *hôtel* was based on the arrangement of a court screened from the street, with service rooms and stables in wings and the *corps de logis* at the back, while the chief rooms overlooked a garden at the back of the house (Fig. 128).

These brief remarks merely serve to indicate some of the contrasts in the types of houses that occurred in the " historic " town down to the beginning of the 19th century, and, indeed, are still found in all the hundreds of small towns that cover the countryside in Europe. These house types are also found in the bigger towns and cities, although many of them have been replaced by modern structures. It should be emphasized, however, that on the Continent the historic houses, even in the large city, frequently remain intact, and have not been displaced by modern structures to nearly the same extent as in England, where few old houses ever existed in the new industrial agglomerations of 19th-century growth.

(ii) *Modern House Types.* The construction of the historical building types came to an end during the first half of the 19th century. Then began the modern phase during which the large cities have witnessed the construction of the majority of their buildings. In the older, compact built-up areas, Geisler recognizes in Germany six types of house, the *Langhaus*, the *Firsthaus*, the *Mietshaus* of south-west Germany, the *Kastenhaus* or tenement block, and the old and new types of apartment house (*Etagenhaus*). These are illustrated in Fig. 129 and Plates 27 and 28 and may be briefly described as follows.

The Long House (*Langhaus*) runs lengthwise along the street with a saddle roof (in which sense it is an eaves house), but it has very little depth and only one interior dividing wall parallel to the street frontage. Moreover it has only one or two storeys. Many of these had their origins in the attractive country house of the wealthy *bourgeois* that lay just outside the town, some of which were absorbed into the expanding town, while others were built in the town alongside the houses of the Baroque-built districts. It also is derived, in its simple design, from the simple country cottage, and rows of such houses were built for labourers. This type was widely adopted in the towns of northern Germany in place of the older timber gable houses when these were burnt down by fire. Structurally it is akin to the simple back-to-back

---

[1] N. Pevsner, *op. cit.*, p. 122.

house or the cottage of Britain, and it is also found in the Low Countries and northern France.

The *Firsthaus* has at least two storeys, a simple saddle roof, and a considerably greater depth than the long house. It is structurally derived from the eaves house and the mansard house. Its division into rooms is such that it can be adapted for at least four family dwellings. There is no hall, as in the mansard house, and there is a central staircase. It became common in the middle of the 19th century and was the predecessor of the tenement (*Mietshaus*). It has the same distribution as the Long House, but is especially common in medium-sized towns. The main area is in the smaller towns of northern Germany.

The tenement or *Mietshaus* of south-west Germany is a development from the mansard house. It is rectangular, with a mansard roof, and has three or four storeys. It is separated from its neighbours by a narrow space, from which there is a side door entrance. It is especially characteristic of the smaller towns of west and south-west Germany, where the growth of population was not so rapid and great as elsewhere in Germany.

The *Kastenhaus* or tenement, unlike the type just noticed, has a flat roof, and became common in north and eastern Germany. It is box-like in structure, there is no limit to its size, and as many families as possible are housed under the one roof. They are, in effect, like barracks of the worst kind. The large tenement is more frequent in the cities of eastern Germany, and of all the industrial districts it appears most extensively, and in its worst forms, in Upper Silesia. Breslau, Hamburg, and Berlin are cities in which the bulk of the people are densely crowded into such tenements. Multi-storeyed brick-built tenements fill up whole blocks with virtually no open enclosure, like a deep central well a few metres square, lacking both space and air (Plate 9).

The older apartment house (*Etagenhaus*), with three or four storeys, was essentially the same in structure as a tenement, but, in order to make it more attractive, its front and roof were disguised with a crude ornamentation façade. Such houses were built especially in the 'seventies and 'eighties and characterized most of the building in the latter half of the 19th century in cities, large and small, without any difference from one part of a town to another, or from one part of the country to another. Magdeburg, Halle, Leipzig, Stettin, Kiel, Königsberg, Breslau are all dominated in their inner areas by this type of building along all the main thoroughfares. It is characteristic of French cities also.

The newer apartment house began to be built after about 1900, when the builder sought to erect better apartment houses with better internal arrangement of rooms, with separate lavatory and bathroom, and a less monotonous appearance from the outside. This improvement in design was further facilitated by the introduction of ferro-concrete into building practice. Rooms became larger, frontages and roofs more tastefully designed, and such apartments catered for the middle class and the well-to-do business and professional classes. These buildings appear in the large and medium-sized cities throughout western Europe where the more prosperous classes were well represented, but rarely in small or purely industrial towns. They were always erected in compact rows, and formed entire streets and usually distinct quarters.

(b) Open Settlement

Since about 1900 building has become more open through the introduction of belated building regulations. Houses and flats have been erected on street fronts with considerable areas of open land around them, while some houses had open spaces attached to them at back and front. The type of building is extremely varied, ranging from the sumptuous villa to workers' housing estates (*Arbeiterkolonien, Cités ouvrières*). Such districts can be just as monotonous as, if less unhealthy than, the older compact districts in the town centre.

Classification of residential buildings must be based on the units of the single-family house and the flat. Single-family houses may be detached, semi-detached or form a group of four or more, or a continuous terrace, all these arrangements being disposed in relation to a street pattern laid out for the purpose. On the other hand, urban houses may also be erected in a countryside along main roads or country lanes as independent units, irregularly distributed and disposed, depending in large measure on the locations of pieces of land available for sale. Select residential areas frequently take this form. The other modern residential unit is the flat. In the last thirty years the aim has been to provide such buildings, as a rule, with fewer storeys and more light, air, and open space. Blocks may be built up on four sides, but there is a large open space in the centre ; flats may be built on one, two or three sides of a block ; or they may be arranged in parallel rows or as a single row on a street front. A variegated pattern may also be adopted. The number of storeys is often limited to two and seldom exceeds four.[1]

While the single-family house, built at a density of twelve to the acre, has been universally adopted in Britain during the inter-war period, the flat has been generally adopted on the Continent. Particular mention should be made, however, of the persistence of the terrace house in Dutch towns, with a density of thirty houses to the acre (including open spaces). These building units are erected in groups to form separate districts, the recognition of which, as to physical, social and economic character, is the purpose of geographical study, as we have indicated by the specific city studies in Part I.

(c) House Types in England

In conclusion, it will be of interest to summarize some of the main building types that occur in England, by way of general comparison with those of the Continent. The following types of housing are recognized in the County of London Plan as typical of London and they are indeed typical of all the English towns :—

(i) Old cottages which formed the pre-19th century villages around London and are now engulfed by the growth of the urban area. Pre-by-law housing of the two-storey terrace type, built mainly during the first half of the 19th century. There are large districts of this type in all parts of London, but especially in the east and immediately south of the river.

(ii) Relatively large houses of three storeys plus basement, built for single-family use 50 to 80 years ago, but now accommodating a number of families. This type is found especially in the north-west and south-west districts and around the original villages in the suburbs.

(iii) Buildings originally used as stable and coach accommodation, attached to large houses and now used as dwellings (known as " mews "). These occur in small groups, especially in central London, and in the inner districts that were high-class residential areas 50 to 80 years ago ; the Belsize Park district is a good example. Such buildings are, of course, relatively unimportant in the provincial cities.

(iv) Isolated or detached villas in the suburbs with large gardens and spacious lay-out.

(v) Two-storey and three-storey houses, built 50 to 60 years ago and extending over very large areas, mainly in the Metropolitan boroughs.

(vi) Tall tenement blocks erected during the last quarter of the 19th and the first quarter of the 20th century.

---

[1] A number of interesting examples of modern flats will be found in Elizabeth Denby, *Europe Rehoused*, to which reference has already been made.

(vii) Spacious and dignified terraces and squares of the 17th and 18th centuries in Bloomsbury and other districts. These are also found in the formerly high-class residential districts in provincial cities, particularly in the Spas of the period, such as Bath (with its Crescents), Harrogate, Cheltenham, Buxton, and in many county towns, as well as in the two capital cities of Dublin and Edinburgh.

Such house types were duplicated in all the provincial cities, and even in the street of the small country town where the managerial, professional, and retired folk resided.

In the big cities that grew up during the 19th century as industrial centres the houses have distinctive features. The main type is the "back-to-back" house. This type was built in a double row under a single roof, one facing the street, the other the paved courtyard, with a net housing density of 60 houses to the acre. In Birmingham these houses contain 100,000 to 150,000 people. In Leeds the back-to-back houses some twenty years ago numbered about 80,000. The oldest and worst, built at the beginning of the 19th century, form long continuous blocks opening directly on to the street on both sides, with densities of 70 to 80 houses per acre, and totalling 34,500. Others are built in groups of eight units and have sanitary conveniences provided in the open spaces between the blocks ; there were 29,000 of this type. The best and latest type numbered 14,000 ; it has an open space of 15 feet between the front of the house and the road.

The so-called " tunnel-back house ", built at a density of 20 to 30 houses to the acre, was the builder's answer to the insistence of the early building by-laws in the latter half of the 19th century on a minimum space on at least two sides of every dwelling. It is built back from the narrow street front to a considerable depth, two adjacent houses being separated from their neighbours by a narrow alley. Each has a parlour with a bay-window, then behind it a living room, scullery, coal-house and W.C., with three bedrooms, behind each other, upstairs. This was the respectable " black-coated worker's " and artisan's house in this period. To-day they are dismal in appearance, dark and insanitary.

The " universal house " is marked by the advent of the garden-house complex into which the Garden City idea degenerated in the first decade of this century and especially in the inter-war period. It is the standardized house built in blocks of four or six or even detached, with two living rooms, a scullery, two or three bedrooms, bathroom, lavatory, coal store and larder. This type ranges widely from the smallest council house to the large detached or semi-detached villa, although the house structure is essentially the same in its interior design and purpose.

It is apparent that there has been a remarkable and unfortunate standardization of housing since 1900 and especially since 1920. This housing is predominantly of the flat type on the Continent and of the single-family type in Britain, but all building is more open than in the past. Many such districts have been planned by municipal authorities over large areas of land which they have acquired. There has, however, been a great deal of haphazard growth through the purchase of land from farmers, on the city outskirts, along the main routeways, thus giving rise to what is generally known in Britain as ribbon development. On the Continent such farm land often consists of very narrow strips, and blocks of flats often soar up from the fields around them and are scattered along the routes or down trackways on strips of land that formerly belonged to the farmer. Acquisition of the land by a single authority, as the medieval and Baroque town has revealed, is essential for orderly urban planning in the interests of æsthetic taste and practical convenience.

(7) GEOGRAPHICAL STUDIES OF THE URBAN BUILD

Particular attention is given in many studies in urban geography to the development and present distribution of house types. These take as criteria the internal structure of the building, the number of storeys, the roof type, and the economic status of the occupants. Such studies are based on whatever data are available or are deemed best for the purpose, such as rentals, rates, or quality of upkeep of the houses. Our special concern here is with the structure of the house as a living space, as the cell of the urban habitat, which in its distribution gives rise to a distinctive kind of district. It is impossible to arrive at general conclusions from such studies, but certain examples may be quoted to illustrate the approach and some of the points we wish to emphasize. The following sample studies exemplify the technique that geographers have grappled with for many years, but that has only recently come within the purview of those engaged in town studies as a basis for planning.

Le Mans,[1] the ancient capital of Maine in western France, has a dominant house type that makes up three-quarters of its 21,600 houses.

---

[1] J. Garnier, " Le Mans ", *La Vie Urbaine*, No. 51, 1939, pp. 135–59.

It has two storeys, a slate roof, a façade of 6 metres with two upper windows and one lower window with a door alongside. Street after street conforms to this type. The same type of single-family house, monotonous in aspect, occurs in Nantes, and in the suburbs of Bordeaux, each with a small backyard and garden and a back kitchen.

Göttingen, Northeim and Einbeck are small towns in central Germany. Dörries mapped the buildings according to the historical periods that characterize the buildings of Niedersachsen in general. These periods he arranges as follows : Medieval (1000 to 1490), Gothic (1490–1530), Early Renaissance (1530–1600), Full Renaissance (1600–50), Baroque (1650–1735), Rococo (1750–1800), Classical (1800–50), " Gründerzeit " (1850–90), Most Recent (since 1890). The Medieval Period has bequeathed no buildings to the modern town owing to the ravages of fire that periodically scourged all towns in the Middle Ages. Churches and town walls date from this period. Limestone and sandstone, from the neighbouring countryside, are the building materials. The Gothic period gives the oldest dwelling-houses. The type is the *Niederdeutsche Bürgerhaus*, which has no resemblance to the farmstead of that region with its eaves parallel to the street front (*Traufenhaus*). They are entirely half-timbered houses with a large hall (*Diele*), though this has largely been built up to form two storeys. Such houses have very little exterior decorative work. The Early Renaissance houses are the same as the Gothic, except that the external decoration is much more prominent. The Renaissance period brings the first new types, and the first building dates from 1600. The intermediate storey of the medieval building overhangs like the upper storey, and the house-front has a horizontal rather than a vertical structure. Otherwise it is like the Gothic building with heavy external decoration. The Baroque period is one of calamity, famine and decline of population following the Thirty Years War. Houses are two-storey timber structures with eaves parallel to the street front. The Rococo period begins in the early 18th century with the building of the University at Göttingen in 1734. By this time the overhang of the upper storey has gone, and there is a smooth frontage of all three storeys. The upper parts of windows and doors are slightly curved, the mansard roof is adopted, broken by a small gable roof facing the street. The type is still a half-timbered, three-storey eaves house in the traditional style. The Classical period has the same features as the preceding periods. Windows are rectangular and spaced at equal intervals, and the doors alone break the regularity of the street frontage of rows of such houses. The latter half of the 19th century (*Gründerzeit*) is marked above all by the disappearance of timber work and the use of brick for houses and sandstone for public buildings. Three-storey houses were built in the outer town, but more were built in the old town. The Modern period, since 1890, is characterized by brick and cement and ferro-concrete as building materials. The mansard roof is in common use. In the inner town the old three-storey houses are replaced by four- to five-storey buildings with plaster fronts (*Putzbauen*), whereas in the outer town partly one- to two-storey single-family houses and partly three- to four-storey multi-family houses appear. The tenement is rare in these towns. It follows that in the outer town areas buildings date exclusively from the last periods, whereas all nine periods are represented in the inner town.[1]

Basel and the towns in a wide area around it have been studied from the same comparative point of view. Basel itself has been carefully mapped on a scale of 1 : 5,000 by a geographer (Fig. 16). Three types of building are recognized, farmhouse, factory, and town house. The town house is mapped according to its structure and style into the following periods—medieval (down to 1500), (single buildings intermingled with buildings of the Renaissance and Baroque periods into the 17th century) ; the Renaissance (16th century) ; Baroque and Classical (end of the 16th, 17th and 18th centuries) ; old styles revived, Neo-gothic, Romanesque, and Classical, in the first half of the 19th century ; and Modern in the second half of the 19th century to the present day. The towns of Lure (Haute Saône, France), Bern, Biel, Solothurn, Rheinfelden, Dijon, Strasbourg, Freiburg-im-Breisgau and Mühlhausen have been mapped in the same way (Fig. 125).[2]

Marseilles has a dominant house type which seems to have evolved from the houses of the medieval town and was adhered to steadily in the houses built up to the end of the 19th century. The old house in the medieval town, of which there are still some representatives, had a narrow frontage with two or three windows, considerably greater depth (often double the frontage), and, as one can still see in the old town of to-day, a number of storeys inverse to the steepness of the slopes, so that on the steepest slopes the houses have only two storeys, whereas on the flat land, especially near the port, they have as many as four. The buildings are arranged in continuous rows and have no back courts. The same type was adopted in the extensions of the late 17th century, with three windows and a wider frontage in proportion to their depth, but differing in no essentials from the old types except in the attention given to a continuous alinement on the street. The building is approached by a small entrance and a long dark corridor leading to a staircase, completely in the dark, at the end. There is no through ventilation and no open court. It is normal for each floor to form one apartment, but one floor may be divided into two apartments, each with three rooms. In the houses of the more well-to-do, the whole building is (or was) tenanted by one family. No really new type, for either rich or poor, was introduced until the 1860s, when the lodging-house (*Maisons casernes*) appeared, but it added neither to the health nor to the beauty of the city. It was built to a height of 20 metres with a wide frontage and varying depth, a *rez-de-chaussée*, an *entresol*, four full storeys and an attic floor, with a very small and inadequate

---

[1] H. Dörries, *Die Städte im oberen Leinetal, Göttingen, Northeim und Einbeck*, 1925, pp. 176–81. Also " Entstehung und Formenbildung der niedersächsischen Stadt " *Forschungen z. deutschen Landes- und Volkskunde*, 1929. See also R. Scheibner, *Das Städtische Bürgerhaus Niedersachsens*, Dresden, 1910 ; H. Ebinghaus, *Das Ackerbürgerhaus der Städte Westfalens und des Wesertales*, Dresden, 1912 ; and O. Lauffer, *Das Deutsche Haus in Dorf und Stadt*, Leipzig, 1919.

[2] Gustav Schäfer, *Kunstgeographische Siedlungs-Landschaften und Städte-Bilder : Studien im Gebiet zwischen Strassburg-Bern-Dijon-Freiburg-i-B.*, 12 maps, Dissertation, Basel, 1928, 89 pp.

court. Each floor is subdivided for separate families. This type was used almost exclusively in the Jolette quarter, and is a cheap boarding-house occupied by transients and seafaring folk from the port. These features, Rambert suggests, are characteristic of the other towns of Provence. Add to this the fact that roofs are gently sloping and building material is entirely of stone, and we realize the striking con-trast they make to the town houses of northern France.[1]

Breslau was refounded in 1241, and from that time date its earliest Gothic buildings—its churches and the town hall. The burgesses' houses of this period were built of timber with thatched or shingle roofs, but in the 14th century brick and half-timber became the rule. After the middle of the 14th century brick was invariably the building material, owing to the devastation caused by fire to timber structures. At the end of the Middle Ages (about 1500) the *Ring* (the central market-place) was surrounded by high buildings of three to five storeys and steep gables, intermixed with lower timber houses. All these buildings have since disappeared.

The Renaissance is not nearly so important as the Gothic in the build of the city. The high spires of the town hall and churches were taken down and replaced by cupolas that still remain. High buildings with up to eleven storeys were erected around the *Ring*, but their narrow frontages did not allow sufficient space for the free adoption of Renaissance styles, so that the build and art are strikingly Gothic in character.

The Baroque was much more important in the *Altstadt*. In the period of the Counter-Reformation many churches and monasteries appeared, notably those of the Jesuits, including the University build-ings. Burgesses' houses, under the influence of this ecclesiastical art, began to be altered by the addition of Baroque façades, portals and doors. When Silesia passed to Prussia, the Baroque era came to an end and the Classical period began in the latter half of the 18th century. This period is most notable for the work of the architect Langhaus (1733–1808) and his son (1771–1869), who built the Palais Hatzfeld, the old Theatre, Bankhaus von Pachaly, and several burgher houses, the Elizabethstrasse (1821) and the old Börse (Exchange) in 1822–24.

The growth of population in the latter half of the 19th century brought congestion. The *Kastenhaus* was universally adopted and the medieval single-family house disappeared. The gable house was dis-placed by the eaves house in the Baroque period, and this steadily changed to the flat roof of the tenement. Gable forms dominate in the older houses and they are often like the Low German patrician house with a large hall (*Diele*) entered directly from the main entrance with two windows on either side of it, and with an inner staircase leading from the hall to the upper storey.

Roof type, number of storeys and building material are important features of the house. The most frequent roof types are the saddle roof (*Satteldach*), *Walmdach*, *Mansardendach* or mansard roof, sloping roof (*Pultdach*), and flat roof (*Flachendach*) (see Fig. 126). The gable

---

[1] G. Rambert, *Marseille : La Formation d'une Grande Cité Moderne*, Marseille, 1934.

frontage was characteristic of the Gothic period, but eaves houses began to be built in the more roomy houses of the Renaissance and the roof type changed to a saddle roof in the eaves house, then to the mansard in the Baroque, then to the sloping roof (*Pultdach*), and finally to the deteriorated flat roof in the tenement. In 1890 over a quarter of the buildings of the old inner town (*Altstadt*) had over four storeys, nearly a third of the whole town ; 45 per cent. had four storeys, just over a quarter of the whole town ; 20 per cent. had three storeys in the inner town and 16·5 per cent. in the whole town. Thus in the inner town four-storeyed houses were dominant, and in the town as a whole, nearly 60 per cent. of the buildings had either four or more storeys. In the *Altstadt* in 1920 13 per cent. had three storeys, 47 per cent. had four storeys, and 40 per cent. had five or more storeys, so that the proportion of five-storey buildings has greatly increased since 1890. Around the inner town there is a broad ring of five and more storeyed buildings. These are tenements. The building material, apart from the brick-work of the old Gothic churches, is overwhelmingly plastered brick. Half-timber work is not unusual in the older houses.[1]

Danzig illustrates the Hansa city of the North Sea shores. The house type remained unchanged until the middle of the 18th century. It is a multi-storeyed building with a steep gable facing the street on a very narrow frontage with two or three windows. This type spread eastwards to the colonial areas. The hall (*Diele*) takes up the whole width of the house. A timbered staircase leads to the living room over the first floor, and the large living room and bedrooms on the upper storeys and the rooms at the back connect with the front by a covered gangway. Later the hall was built in to form an intermediate storey, called the *Hängetage*, with a decorated window overlooking the hall. The back part of the latter in the merchant's house is used as his office.

In the patrician's house there was a balcony at the front, richly ornamented, with a stone staircase leading to its entrance, a fact due to the dangers of flood which caused the living rooms to be raised above the street level. This structure persisted, though its external decorations vary with the periods. From the period of the Teutonic Order there are few remaining houses, and very few also from the 15th century, so that the medieval Gothic leaves little imprint on the town. The patrician houses date mainly from the period of greatest prosperity, from 1580 to 1620, and the influence of Italian and Dutch art is quite clear in building styles. For façade work on brick houses stone was imported from Sweden. Similar adornment characterized the Baroque and Rococo periods.

Because of lack of space and the subdivision of building lots, this house type is common in the heart of the old town. Towards the periphery the houses are intermixed with wider street fronts as first developed in the Italian *Mietshaus*. In the outer districts there was more room for building, land was not so subdivided, and houses with

---

[1] E. Müller, " Die Altstadt von Breslau : Citybildung und Physiognomie : Ein Beitrag zur Stadtgeographie ", *Veröff. d. Schlesischen Gesell. für Erdkunde*, Breslau, 1931.

broad fronts became more characteristic with the passage of time. A new building period begins with the removal of the wall on whose site new tenements (*Mietshäuser*) were built without any architectural connection with the traditional styles. A map of the city on a scale of 1 : 10,000 shows land uses and houses according to the number of storeys (one, two, three, four, and over) and it reveals clearly that four–five-storey buildings dominate the old town. The great warehouse quarter of the *Speicherinsel* has multi-storeyed structures in the Danzig style.[1]

[1] W. Geisler, *Danzig : Ein siedlungsgeographischer Versuch*, Dissertation, Halle-Wittenberg, 1918.

CHAPTER 22

URBAN ZONES AND URBAN LIMITS

The growth of the modern city is characterized by the operation of centripetal forces, which were predominant during the 19th century, and by centrifugal forces that have become more important during the present century. The expansion of the urban area has been marked, especially since about 1880, by specialization of function and by the segregation of related structures in districts or zones. This expansion, whether by accretion or centrifugal spread, and the functional differentiation of districts, centred on the business and cultural core, is the essence of the process of modern urban growth. This has already been examined in general terms in a previous book, *City, Region and Regionalism*, and the main facts are summarized as follows in the light of the detailed specific studies of various aspects of this growth in different cities that have been presented in Part I.

(1) THE PROCESS OF URBAN GROWTH AND FUNCTIONAL DIFFERENTIATION

The general processes that underlie the growth and differentiation of urban agglomerations have already been discussed in *City, Region and Regionalism*, and we here reproduce the introductory paragraphs dealing with that topic.

(i) *Concentration.* This is the tendency for people to cluster in cities as near as possible to each other, to their work, and to the amenities of city life. It is essentially centripetal in character. The " friction of space " has been described [1] as the essence of the process of urban growth and of differential segregation. It is also the prime cause of concentration in cities, since the services demanded can most efficiently be carried out in clustered communities at suitable locations —whether for purposes of industry, commerce or administration—and where the work is, there the workers must live, with daily access to their place of work. The nucleus of this urban growth is the old town, that to-day is normally the hub of the city, from which the built-up area has spread steadily outwards both concentrically and radially, or by the growth of physically separate centres that gradually merge with

---

[1] R. M. Haig and R. C. McCrea, " Major Economic Factors in Metropolitan Growth and Arrangement ", in *Regional Survey of New York and Environs*, Vol. I. New York, 1927, pp. 38–9.

the main urban area. The phenomenon of urban concentration is one of the outstanding features of our modern civilization, and has been frequently studied, so that we need pursue it no further.

(ii) *Centralization* denotes the " distributive pattern of population and institutions in the area of (urban) concentration, and the process whereby the patterns appear ".[1] It refers to " the drawing together of institutions and activities, i.e. the assembling of people to work rather than to reside in a given area ".[2] This process of concentration . . . manifests itself in the emergence of a central business district in the heart of the city and of commercial sub-centres around it, in the concentration of factories in distinct areas, and, in consequence, in the daily rhythm of movement of workers between homes and workplaces. The essential feature, therefore, is the separation of workplace and residence, and the segregation of workplaces into distinct districts according to function. By a process of competition, establishments seek out, and segregate themselves in, that area in which their optimum conditions are to be found and in virtue of which they are normally able to exclude others. . . .

In regard to the segregation of functions in different sectors of the urban area, the most outstanding feature, common to every city, is the law that its business and services concentrate in the centre, the " 100 per cent. locations ", from all parts of the urban area. This central district is very small—often facing on to a market-place or a single street in the case of the small town—but it becomes larger and more compact in larger cities, until not only is there a general concentration of business and services—shops, hotels, offices, restaurants, public buildings, etc.—but the different services are segregated in districts within it. Owing to the great demand for space in this centre, land values are always here the highest in the city, and the great demand for space has a twofold effect on its structure. First, there is the trend of vertical expansion, that is, the construction of multi-storeyed buildings, which reaches its extreme in the skyscraper. Second, there is the trend of horizontal expansion, that is, the expansion of the business area to the adjoining streets and districts. This horizontal expansion usually takes the form of the conversion of residential properties, often quite unsuited for the purpose, to the use of business. Ultimately such properties are destroyed and make way for modern structures which adequately serve the new function, be it a modern hotel, office or civic building. This extension may be caused by private enterprise or by municipal slum clearance. The effect of the existence and lateral expansion of the city centre, with its high land values, is to raise values on the land around it. In consequence, just as the owner of the farm land on the city outskirts " freezes " land until the time is " ripe " for building, so the owner of property in the neighbourhood of the city, in anticipation of selling at a great profit, allows this to deteriorate, though at the same time demanding high rentals. It is for this reason that this dingy-looking zone around the centre is apparent in every large city. The expansion of the centre—

---

[1] Gist and Halbert, *Urban Society*, p. 148.
[2] Queen and Thomas, *The City*, 1939, p. 262.

especially of its high-class shopping and hotel quarter—is normally in the direction of the high-class residential district, as in the shift towards Kensington in London, and northward in Manhattan to Central Park in New York City.

(iii) *Deconcentration*. This term refers to the tendency for people and institutions to shift out from the existing urban area to the open land on its outskirts. It is the result of centrifugal as opposed to centripetal forces, and has developed particularly during the last fifty years, and especially in the inter-war period. It arises from the availability of cheap transport services to the city centre and to all parts of the urban complex, and from the congestion in the central business district, and from the obsolescence of the old, often condemned, living areas clustered around it. This is a most fundamental and remarkable feature in the development of the modern city during the past fifty years.

(iv) *Decentralization* is to be distinguished from deconcentration. The latter implies simply the expansion of the brick and mortar of the urban complex from the centre outwards. Decentralization, on the other hand, implies the shedding of certain of the city's activities— such as industry or commerce and administration (the dispersal of the latter has been particularly important during the recent war)—to a distinct and separate town that itself functions as an independent local and regional centre. This process has been going on for a considerable period both around the big cities and over the wider countryside. Through the development of existing small towns and the establishment of " garden cities and satellites " (in the full sense of these terms) planned decentralization is advocated as an alternative policy for the future reconstruction of urban life, as opposed to excessive concentration in large urban complexes. This policy is now being actively pursued in the planning of Greater London.

(v) *Residential Segregation*. This refers primarily to the concentration of residents into districts, similar to the district concentration of distinct economic uses. It implies, according to the sociologist, " the clustering in space of persons or institutions ". Individuals tend to gravitate not only to areas in which they can compete for a livelihood more efficiently, but to areas populated by other of similar race, interests, culture or economic status.[1] The principle of residential segregation is, in a measure, inherent in building practice, for houses of exactly the same type are built in groups or in large estates, usually nowadays so that they automatically cater for people with the same economic and social level. Thus, areas of residential segregation are normally clearly defined by the type of housing, and the geographical extent of that type may be blocked out as a district. This does not mean, of course, that houses are necessarily tenanted in the way originally intended, for with time they become old-fashioned or dilapidated and their status may completely change preparatory to demolition. It is in this latter special type of segregation that the sociologist in particular is interested.

---

[1] Gist and Halbert, *op. cit.*, p. 175.

(vi) *Invasion and Succession* are terms used to indicate this process of change in buildings, their use and their occupants. It is referred to by American geographers as " sequent occupance ". The process is one of the displacement of one dominant type of land use or population group by another. The history of a housing district in the inner zone of London or of houses near the business district of a town illustrates the process. Floors and single rooms are rented as residences, offices or workshops. The building appears dilapidated and the social and economic status of such a district is changed, usually for the worse. This process is usually most marked—this can certainly be considered as a basic law—on the margins of the city centre and along the great highways radiating from it, and adjacent to undesirable areas such as factory districts and railway yards. In the first cases it has its root causes in the growth of land values in districts of old property. This phenomenon of deterioration, in various stages and degrees, covers a large part of the inner and middle zones of our cities and constitutes one of their greatest problems. The same process operates in areas devoted to business uses : competition segregates utilities of similar economic strength into areas of corresponding land values, and at the same time forces into close proximity those particular forms of service which profit from mutual associations such as financial establishments and automobile display shops. Once a dominant use becomes established within an area, competition is less ruthless between its units, and an invasion of a different use is for a time obstructed.

(vii) *Functional specialization* of individual structures and segregation of similar functional structures are implicit in the above statements of process, but need special emphasis. This tendency characterizes the whole of the modern urban complex. Such functions, according to their particular requirements, seek certain locations in the urban complex—nearness to the centre of its affairs, or nearness to the periphery, or nearness to rail, navigable waterway, or road, or, in the case of residential areas of the better type, to sites of scenic attraction, such as higher land, a river frontage, or nearness to a park or royal court. The main types of use can be simply classified as industrial, commercial public buildings, and residential, and transport.

(2) Urban Zones

It will be well to emphasize at the outset that the tendency for distinct districts to emerge in the urban complex is not peculiar to the modern city or to the large city—a fact which our studies in Part I have revealed. The earliest medieval towns had their separate nuclei and even in the fully developed medieval urban community these quarters were distinct. Such were the *cité* or *Domburg*, with its ecclesiastical function, and the mercantile-crafts quarter, while the castle attracted the residences of the nobility and their retainers. This distinction became even more marked when accentuated by differences in site values, as where trade, crafts and markets were situated on the lower land on the main routes, and the aristocratic quarters and the church sites were placed on the higher land.   This distinction is very clearly marked in the case of Blois, as we have seen in Chapter 3.   In other cases there were several self-governing towns, with markedly different characteristics, that were walled, but dovetailed together.   This was not only true of the more flourishing towns with 10,000 to 20,000 inhabitants in all, such as Brunswick and Hildesheim.   It was found in numerous very small places, of which Bar-le-Duc is a good example, with its four separate walled settlements, each of which had only a few hundred inhabitants (Fig. 10, p. 48). Further, this zonal arrangement in the modern urban settlement is found in the small modern town with under 50,000 inhabitants. Blois again illustrates this point.   Outside the old town, there is a very marked cluster of public buildings in the north-eastern sector and the railway with associated factories and warehouses in the north-western sector.   Blois, be it noted, has only about 25,000 inhabitants.   The same features are illustrated by the other small towns.

Just as in the modern urban complex, so in the medieval town, there was specialization of function by streets and even by districts.   In the early medieval towns the merchants segregated in distinct quarters outside the precints of the cathedral and the secular rulers.   Thus, at Regensburg there was a *pagus regius*, a *pagus clericorum* and a *pagus mercatorum* (Fig. 87, p. 370).   Similarly at Cologne the merchants' quarter lay on the river front outside the Roman wall of the city (Fig. 18, p. 82).   There were similar mercantile settlements in the early Middle Ages in the Rhine cities of Mainz and Worms, where the merchants' class included Frisians and Jews.   In the fully developed medieval town there was segregation of both merchants and craftsmen, a fact that is suggested by the street names of any old town.   At Paris, for example, there is a *Vieille Draperie, Vieille Tisseranderie, la Rue de la Vieille Monnaie* and a host of other examples.   Slaughter-houses and butcheries were always segregated (as in the Shambles of the English town) in the heart of the town, although this was hygienically an unfortunate location, and we often read of the slaughter-house being rebuilt on the outskirts of the town on the orders of the town council.   In 1366 it was recommended in Paris that the river bank away from the congested part of the town would be a better location for the *abattoirs* than the centre, but the butchers' guild was able to resist this move. At Amiens the *halles des bouchers* were burned down in 1391 and shifted to another site. Cemeteries also were moved by the authorities to the outskirts of the town. Similarly the location of tanneries and smiths was carefully regulated, a riverside location for the former being both desirable and necessary.

The segregation of particular ethnic groups is most marked in the case of the Ghetto for the Jews. This feature is, however, apparent in the separation of Slav and German quarters in the founded towns of eastern Germany, while the juxtaposition of distinct ethnic groups is still a characteristic feature of the town in eastern Europe, the Mohammedan lands and in the Far East. Homogeneity was, and still is, a main feature of the west European city, but the Jewish ghetto was the marked exception to the general rule. The idea of the ghetto as a distinct quarter, walled off from the rest of the town, seems to have developed in the eastern Mediterranean in the Byzantine epoch and spread thence to western Europe. But it was in Germany and east–central Europe that it acquired its special characters. In France such distinct quarters did not appear. There were particular streets in which the Jews voluntarily segregated, but there were no laws for enforced segregation as there were in the east.

The idea of the University which developed in the later Middle Ages also resulted in the growth of distinct quarters. In Paris, for example, students and teachers lived in the quarter around the church of Ste. Geneviève, although it was a long time before special buildings were erected for them. Toulouse well shows the distinct quarters of student, trader, and noble. In the south, between the Château-Narbonnais, where the Parlement met, and the cathedral of St. Étienne and the great enclosures of the Augustinian and Carmelite monasteries, was the quarter in which the Parlementaires lived. Farther to the north the *Rue des Changes* and *La Rue de la Bourse* were the heart of the merchants' quarter. Still farther north, around the ancient *Bourg de St. Sernin*, on raised ground as at Ste. Geneviève in Paris, were the schools, the University and many colleges, founded in the later Middle Ages. (The University buildings have since been built in two main parts at opposite ends of the town.) On the other hand, the student body was not always so segregated, for the famous University of Orleans was scattered throughout the city, and its professors held their classes in private houses all over the town.

Let us now turn to the structure of the modern urban complex.

This may be considered in its areal differentiations under five main heads—the land use or functional zones, the distribution of population, its social and economic groups, traffic flows, and the outer limits of the urban area.

In a preceding section we have discussed the phases of topographic formation and expansion of the city in terms of the phases of its historical development. These general features have also been indicated in the cases of particular cities in Part I. It is now pertinent to summarize the main features of the process and character of the growth of the modern city and the functional differentiations within it. These conclusions are based on a series of maps, similar to those presented in the first part of this book. A special comment may be interpolated at this juncture on the method of compilation of these maps. A detailed *land use* map of any city demands field work on the spot. A map or aerial photograph on the largest scale cannot reveal the kinds of use within a building of several storeys in which uses are mixed. If, however, concern is with the physical structure of the city, then all data can be gleaned direct from such a map or from air cover, and, given the organization and trained personnel, the preparation of a series of such maps is practicable. Data to be recorded would be the degree of compactness of the urban areas and the character of the buildings, especially in the centre, and the number of their storeys. All exclusively industrial areas can be at once blocked out from the lay-out of factory buildings, and the central area picked out from the irregular pattern of its streets and the high density of building. The residential areas can also be easily classified on the basis of the pattern and density of the buildings. A standardized scheme of mapping, for instance, on the lines we have adopted, could easily be prepared for English towns. The important facts, however, that can *not* be so accurately gleaned from such sources are the *commercial* uses and the *mixed* uses, where residential units are intermixed (often in the same building) with shops, offices, warehouses, and small factory units. To indicate these data accurately demands field work. The other main categories can be accurately shown, and, especially in the continental city, they are often quite clear-cut owing to the controlling influence on urban expansion exercised by encircling walls and boulevards. The central core of the continental city is usually far more clear-cut on the large-scale plan or on the air photograph than that of the English city. It is primarily on the interpretation of the map on a scale of 1 : 25,000

or 1 : 10,000 when available, as also on air cover (1 : 10,000)
that our maps of the west European city were based, and in some
cases it has been possible to supplement these data by published
maps of land uses. The zones as described in the following
paragraphs are shown in aerial and ground photographs in this
volume, and reference should be made to them.

Broadly speaking, the following concentric zones are characteristic of the build of the modern continental city : the central
fully built-up zone, which is the modern city core and usually
includes in its centre the site of the historic town ; the belt of
boulevards that surrounds the historic town ; the compact and
fully built-up middle zone that was erected mainly during the
19th century ; and the outer partly built-up zone in which urban
and rural uses are mixed, and to which urban uses have penetrated
mainly during this century. These zones are illustrated by a
transverse sector through Cologne that is shown on Plate 4 and
photographs are shown on Plates 7 to 10. A corresponding
general arrangement is apparent in the British city.

(a) *The Central Zone :* This lies on the site of the historic town,
which to-day is easily distinguished on the map by four features :
first, the fact that it is normally bounded by one or more boulevards on the site of the demolished fortifications ; second, that
the area is much more fully built-up than the rest of the city
(70–75 per cent. built-up, excluding streets and places) ; third,
that it has a distinctive ground-plan, with narrow streets and small
market-places, the nature of which, as indicated in a previous
chapter, depends on the conditions of its medieval development ; fourth, that it contains a very large proportion of the
city's historic buildings. Further examination would also reveal
the architectural heterogeneity of its buildings, old and new.
There is also the predominance of non-residential over residential
properties, for it is pre-eminently the " city core " of the whole
modern complex, teeming with life by day, a " dead heart " by
night. It includes some residential properties, some of which are
appallingly congested slums, while others are new apartment
blocks, which, owing to the high cost of the land and of the
buildings, are normally tenanted by the wealthy. This is the
ville of the French and the *Altstadt* of the German city.

The *Boulevard System* deserves special mention, as it is so outstanding a feature of the continental city, though one that is
absent in the British city, and is one of the goals toward which
British planners strive in their new plans for the reconstruction

of their cities. The idea of the boulevard as a circular thoroughfare on the site of destroyed fortifications was first introduced in
Paris by Louis XIV, and was copied in the provincial cities of
France during the 18th century. It was adopted by Napoleon
in Brussels, and it became a universal feature in the growth of
the larger cities in the 19th century. Cologne and Vienna are
two random outstanding examples (Plates 3 and 18). Their
boulevards were built during the latter half of the last century,
and have attracted modern building. Along them there are many
public buildings, good residences, high-class shops, business offices
and theatres. Many of these are municipal or State buildings,
since the demolition and new building were in large measure
controlled by the municipal authorities.

(b) *The Middle Compactly Built-up Zone :* This is a large area
surrounding the core. It was built for the most part during the
latter half of the 19th century. It normally consists of congested
tenements on the Continent and rows of terraced houses in Britain.
The blocks are almost entirely built-up and there are few public
spaces. The zone is sometimes defined in the largest cities by
the line of the latest fortifications, as at Berlin, Paris, and Cologne.
It stands out clearly from the central zone by its more regular
lay-out and the greater width of its streets and main thoroughfares, which often radiate from the gates in the old medieval walls.
A remarkably large proportion of the blocks are built-up. In
general, the older sectors nearer the city centre are the most
congested. The outer areas are a little more open (with squares)
and have a smaller proportion of built-up blocks, since the buildings line only one or two sides of the block and there is ample
open space left in the centre.

These general features are varied, however, by other traits in
the ground plan. Sometimes a river crosses the whole area, and
on it are to be found factories, wharves and warehouses. Further,
the railway stations were built in the mid 19th century as near
as possible to the limits of the town at that time. Thus, although
they were originally situated on the outskirts of the town, they
were soon swallowed up by the extension of the urban area. In
consequence, this inner area is broken up into segments by the
rivers, the railway tracks and stations. This is admirably illustrated in the cases of Paris and Berlin. Each station attracted
building, and in the smaller cities a main street usually joins the
station to the town.

The Middle Zone is by no means exclusively residential. In

standard land use maps, as prepared by city authorities, its inner portions at least are described appropriately as "mixed", indicating a mixture of varied types of land use. It contains relatively few large industrial plants, but it has numerous small warehouses and workshops especially near the city core. In the 19th century the best houses were built here, especially on the higher land or at places overlooking a good view (such as a river), or near a park. Here, too, were situated many public buildings —the first hospitals and clinics and the first University buildings. Very often these buildings are grouped together in the continental city to form quite distinct districts.

(c) *The Outer Partly Built-up (Sub-Urban) Zone.* This is a discontinuous belt surrounding the completely built-up central and middle zones. It has been invaded by urbanism almost entirely since 1900. It includes many old villages and small towns that have been urbanized and transformed to become the nuclei of sprawling urban areas. Its growth has taken place along main routes—rail, road, river, and canal—and in compact blocks, by "frontal" rather than "linear" expansion. But the built-up areas are often separated by large areas of open land—farm or forest or waste land. In this zone are situated the really large industrial plants, some of which cover large areas, bigger than those of the medieval town. Some of these have been established as entirely new concerns ; other are new plants of old concerns that were formerly situated on smaller and inadequate premises in the town. This is the zone that has been referred to as the urban-rural fringe [1] (*banlieue urbaine, Stadtrandzone*) and whose growth is illustrated particularly well in the case of Vienna (Chapter 10). This fringe often bears no relation to the political boundary of the city and extends well beyond it, except in those cases where the city boundary has been so greatly extended as to include all its present, and as far as one can see, its potential settlement area. Such greater extensions have been made in a number of continental cities, so that there is ample scope for regional planning. Such is the case for instance in Amsterdam, Cologne, Berlin, and Vienna. The opposition of local authorities in Britain, whose views receive much more sympathetic consideration, hinders the extension of our great cities over the areas that are needed for planning purposes and in which planning proposals might be enforced by law. It is still necessary for an alternative solution of this urgent problem to be found.

[1] See *City, Region and Regionalism*, pp. 120–3.

The development of this outer zone is not only associated with the expansion of the great industrial plants. Here too are located such establishments as barracks, cemeteries, large power plants, brick works, and some of the obnoxious industries. There is also an expansion of the residential area, mainly in the form of rows of flats or, more occasionally on the Continent, single-family houses. The latter, it may be noted, on the Continent are usually the homes of the wealthy on the best residential sites, and the flats are the homes of the less wealthy—which is often the reverse of the conditions in Britain. Such areas house both city workers and workers in the near-by workplaces, although in the continental city there is a much larger diurnal movement of workers from flats in the compact inner zones to the factories on the outskirts. This is notably so in the case of Berlin. Allotment gardens and sports fields are outstanding features of the periphery of the continental city, where the family is normally housed in a congested tenement apartment. Sewage waste is also used to fertilize the fields for crop production (*Champs d'épandages, Rieselfelder*).

The whole of this outer area may, indeed, very appropriately be called the sub-urban fringe, when this term is used in the sense of an urban area of low density of urban building and urban population, with extensive open spaces, that surrounds the compact urban area as a more or less continuous belt. One of its most remarkable features, in terms of which it may be defined, is that it has an increasing population, and a decreasing proportion of strictly farm workers and their dependent services.

It will be well to repeat here that the tendency to the formation of concentric zones by outward growth from the centre is not a process peculiar to the modern city, though it is most clearly developed there. In the city of the past there has been a similar natural (uncontrolled) tendency to such zoning of use and residence as we have noted above. Moreover, of the two modes of urban expansion, one of which may be called *frontal* expansion, the expansion of whole districts along a broad front, and the other *linear* expansion, the expansion along radial route-ways, the former is the dominant one both in the city of to-day and yesterday. Ribbon building by extension along roads became a special problem in Britain during the inter-war period. Every city tends to assume a circular shape by growth along its radial axes and by the slightly slower filling up of the areas between them through frontal expansion.[1] In Britain, owing to the absence of regulations to prevent it, such ribbon expansion was in general much more widespread than on the Continent, where in general ribbon areas and their outlying sectors were more compact.

The second point we would recall is the principle of the invasion and succession of land uses that is a result of the outward expansion of the built-up area. The periphery of yesterday with its marginal land-uses may become a part of the compact built-up area of to-day. In the continental city the result is often recognizable by its distinct lay-out and land uses, the latter often being successors to the original uses. Clear examples occur in Basel and Berlin. This applies also to residential properties, for the good-class residence near the city centre often changes and usually deteriorates in use, until the buildings are finally demolished and replaced by new structures that more adequately serve the purposes for which they are needed. This trend is very evident in all English towns and is clearly illustrated in the small French towns studied in Chapter 4. The same process, among others, seems also to operate in the sorting out of social groups. Though clearly recognizable in the continental city, whose outward growth has been clearly guided in stages by the barriers of the wall and the encircling railway track, such features are less clearly defined in the British city, where the growth of the urban mass has gone on with little topographic or human guidance.

The growth of Georgian London, that is, London during the whole of the 18th century and the first three decades of the 19th century, has recently been portrayed and illustrates the process discussed in the previous paragraphs.[2] The sub-urban trend was already manifest at this time and the mode of extension well illustrates the normal manner of growth in the English city, that was unrestricted by an engirdling belt of impassable fortifications. In addition to drawing fruits and vegetables and certain industrial products from the countryside, and using it as a place of recreation at the week-ends, residence was spreading there from the city. This sub-urban trend took four forms : the transformation of outlying villages through the addition of luxury houses, either singly or in terraces, as at Hampstead and Highgate ; the building of large and luxurious country villas situated in spacious ornamental grounds ; roadside development ; and estate development. The

[1] This is clearly shown in the maps of the growth of London's built-up area since 1840, prepared by S. E. Rasmussen and reproduced in the *Greater London Plan*, 1944-5, by Sir Patrick Abercrombie.
[2] John Summerson, *Georgian London*, 1947.

last two are of particular importance. Roadside development was long inhibited on the outskirts of London and indeed in all cities in western Europe, by the love of propinquity rather than a desire for a life of isolation in the country, along roads that were too bad to permit quick, comfortable or even safe travel by horseback or carriage. With the improvement of roads at the end of the century traffic increased and " from 1815 onwards stretches of road between London and the nearest villages attracted all sorts of building ".[1] Such building was of a most miscellaneous character and included private houses, built singly or in terraces, nursery gardens, brick-kilns, soap factories and the like. The London to Islington road was a conspicuous example of this development ; another was on the road south from London Bridge, but it became general along all the main arteries that radiated from the city.

Estate development was carried on in the unbuilt wedges between these arterial roads, where cheap land attracted factories, breweries, brick-kilns and, nursery gardens, all with associated cottage properties. In some districts, even more compact areas were built-up with regularly laid-out terrace houses in an attempt to plan groups of streets and squares. Such land was held by wealthy owners and was developed by a builder commissioned for the purpose, or it was bought by private speculators. Very often such a new district bears the name New Town, or the name Town is added to that of the landowner or builder. Such are, in London, Hans Town (Sloane Square, Cadogan Square and Hans Place) built at the end of the 18th century, Somers Town, begun on the land of the first Lord Somers of Evesham in 1786, and Camden Town, begun in 1791 on the land of the Lord Chancellor Camden. Several estates appeared off the roads leading through Islington, though these were part of the general outward spread rather than separately planned districts. Extension of a similar kind was more haphazard in the eastern districts of the parish of Stepney. In general, then, these compactly laid-out estates, which now are mainly areas of deteriorated property in the inner districts of London, were built between the arterial roads, with their ribbon building, adjacent to the existing built-up areas of the city. Land was often held idle in expectation of profitable sales for building.

---

[1] Summerson, *op. cit.*, p. 261.

(3) THE DISTRIBUTION OF POPULATION

The broad features of the distribution of population in the detailed studies in Part I show that the most densely populated sections lie in the Middle Zone where overall densities of over 100 persons per acre are the rule, with even from 200 to 300 over considerable areas, and above 300 to 500 in extreme instances. Such maxima are attained for example in Paris, Berlin, Hamburg, Breslau, Vienna, and Prague. The decline of population in the central zone began in the latter half of the 19th century with the clearance of slums for new buildings and the construction of wider streets for the growth of business and administration. This decrease has continued since 1900 and has spread outwards from the centre to the borders of the middle zone. The whole of the latter, which continued to increase in its outer areas down to 1900, has tended to decrease since then in the large cities. Large increases, on the other hand, are recorded in the outer urban–rural fringe, which, since 1900, has been the main scene of residential and industrial development. Here again, we would remind the reader that the flight from the centre has been due only in small part to the growth of a business core—for it has affected a much wider area. As Leyden has shown in the case of the Dutch cities, it is due to the housing shortage and to the attraction of new and more up-to-date houses or flats on the outskirts of the city, at fairly reasonable rents and in locations accessible to the workplace. It is partly a voluntary movement, which has brought in its train deep-seated social and economic changes and problems (Chapter 9).

Centripetal forces draw centralized occupations and services to the centre, while centrifugal forces cause people and factories to shift from the centre to the periphery. Entirely new industries are located here, such as the electrical and automobile industries in Paris and Berlin. Both these cities are surrounded, outside their political limits (the *ville* of Paris and the *Altstadt* of Berlin), by a wide engirdling belt in which industrial plants are now concentrated. The rubber industry in Clermont-Ferrand ; the large new rubber and chemical plants north of Hanover alongside the Mittelland Canal ; the heavy iron and steel industries on the open flat lands on the east bank of the Rhine opposite Cologne and on the south-eastern outskirts of Düsseldorf; and the industries on the outskirts of such smaller cities as Basel—these are all instances of a general feature that is particularly well shown in the maps of city zones that are presented in Part I of this book.

(4) Social and Economic Structure of the Urban Complex

It is unfortunate that there are no detailed studies of continental cities to compare in any way with the recent studies of the community structure of the American city. Nor, indeed, for that matter, are there any continental studies comparable with the social surveys of British cities. It is thus not possible to make a detailed presentation of the economic and social structure of an individual city before 1939 that can compare with the studies of Chicago, New York, Columbus, Cleveland, or Los Angeles. It is interesting that two general studies on these lines have recently appeared as articles by geographers, one on Prague, the other on Budapest. The conclusions of these studies appear in Chapters 10 and 11, and reveal a general similarity with the principles and characteristics of urban growth that have been elaborated by the Chicago School of Social Sciences. The main facts emerging from all these studies are as follows. Burgess over twenty years ago put forward the hypothesis that there is a tendency towards a concentric growth in the development of cities, a trend that is not only apparent in the broad and obvious zoning of the city, but also in the more detailed movements and succession of land uses and of populations in the urban complex itself. These trends are most clearly marked in the very large complex with over about half a million inhabitants. In smaller cities the urban complex is not large enough for such gradations and movements to become clearly evident. It is obvious that this trend is offset by others, and particularly by the tendency for every urban complex to become arranged into distinct functional districts. Functional specialization is the keynote of the structure of the modern city, and this is dependent on a number of factors. These include not only the site of the city, but also the ethnic characteristics of its inhabitants, land values, the circumstances of its historical development, and its particular process of topographic formation in relation to the physical characters of the terrain. Burgess' theory is obviously one of many factors involved in the process of urban growth and we need careful studies on these lines for individual European cities.

The important feature of the process of concentric growth, however, is not the tendency to the formation of broadly concentric belts of built-up land ; this is sufficiently obvious to the casual observer.   The really significant fact is that social processes and the succession of urban land uses within the built-up urban complex tend to reflect this concentric arrangement around the centre.   Around the central district, that is the area of most rapid social and economic " metabolism ", there emerges a zone of congestion and deterioration, spreading outwards from it.   This zone of deterioration has varied land uses, with obsolescent housing, and is invaded by offices and workshops in properties that often are, or ought to be, condemned.   Its houses are old and dilapidated, and it degenerates into a congested, overpopulated slum.   This phenomenon is known as " blight ".   In such areas socially disorganized groups are to be found, with no social consciousness, and many socially undesirable traits, with a high incidence of vice, night clubs, houses of prostitution ; and among its inhabitants social disorders, such as criminality, juvenile delinquency and the like are particularly prevalent.   The poorest types of people without family connections also tend to segregate in the same areas, living in boarding-houses, " doss " houses and crowded tenements.

While these conditions are basic characteristics of the process of urban growth, we would, however, emphasize a second element, that in its general features also is sufficiently obvious.   There are marked contrasts among human groups in all countries according to social character and economic status.   These differences are mirrored in the structure of the urban complex, in which there is, in consequence, extreme social and economic differentiation by districts.   There are to be found marked contrasts in the density of population, the areas of overcrowding, the infantile mortality, disease rates, the social traits and the economic level of the population, as well as of occupational structure.   The details of this process have been illustrated in several of the studies in Part I of this book.   The general social, economic, and demographic structure of the city is illustrated in the case of Prague. We may also note the study of Budapest, which was evidently inspired by the work of the social scientists in Chicago.   Here it was found that in the radial-concentric arrangement of the town of Pest, on the right bank of the Danube, a wide slum and vice area lies around the city centre.   The same traits have been found in the Merseyside Survey, where such areas of extreme deterioration are described as " black spots ".   These distinct associations of social, economic and demographic phenomena bear only a general and obvious relation to the arrangement of concentric zones around the centre. There is, however, no doubt that the movements of institutions and of families (e.g. as evidenced by " removals " of households) do show some outward shift by stages in larger cities, but this is a matter needing further investigation. The investigation of Dutch cities in Chapter 9 illustrates this process very clearly.

It will be of interest to compare the densities of the built-up areas and of the population in a number of cities for which comparable data are available.[1] Such data are published for all the German cities, several of which have been studied in Part I of this book. The table below gives the statistics in 1935 for twelve of the largest of these cities. The following general features are apparent.

1. The total built-up area ranges from 25 to 55 per cent. of the whole of the administrative area. This clearly depends on the area inside the city boundaries, which varies greatly. With the exception of Hamburg (40) and Dresden (55), both of which have political areas that are smaller than the urban areas of which they form the chief part, the proportions are remarkably constant, ranging from about a quarter to a third.

2. The density of population per acre of building of all kinds ranges from 125 (Hamburg) to 43·5 (Dortmund). The density per acre of the total built-up area ranges from 83 to 28, and would be lowered by a few per cent. were the open spaces included. The cities with the greatest densities are Hamburg, Berlin, Leipzig, Breslau, and Hanover. These are the tenement cities. On the other hand, the " garden city " of Germany, Dresden, has a density of only 51. Those cities, in which a large proportion of the built-up area is under industrial uses, have naturally low densities on this basis. It is not surprising therefore that Dortmund and Essen come low in the list, although this is also due to the frequency of smaller tenements and single-family houses in these cities. Cologne and Frankfurt are " average " cities in this respect. Hanover and Breslau, in particular, indicate the characteristics of the compact, congested complex with a considerable area under railway yards and large industrial lay-outs and a predominance of large tenements (see Chapter 6).

---

[1] *Statistisches Jahrbuch Deutscher Gemeinden*, Jena, 1936.

LAND USE IN THE PRINCIPAL GERMAN CITIES IN 1935.

	Total Area (Acres)	Built-up Area: Houses, Factories, Gardens, Yards: Percentage of Total	Streets, Places, Railways: Percentage of Total	Total Built-up Area: Percentage of Total Area	Open Spaces, Parks, Gardens, Cemeteries	Population 1939 (thousands)	Density of Population per acre — Buildings	Density of Population per acre — Total Built-up Area
Berlin	220,900	19·7	11·5	31	10,400	4,327	97·5	61·5
Hamburg	33,900	26·5	13·6	40	2,400	1,400	125·0	83·0
Altona	23,200	18·0	9·0	27	1,500	245	57·0	38·0
Cologne	62,800	17·0	9·5	26	4,300	770	72·0	46·0
Munich	47,000	21·3	8·5	30	3,100	825	73·5	52·5
Leipzig	33,100	23·0	12·5	35	2,500	720	93·5	60·5
Essen	47,100	24·5	9·2	34	3,200	668	56·5	41·0
Dresden	29,800	41·0	14·0	55	1,500	640	51·0	38·7
Breslau	43,700	15·0	17·0	32	3,000	620	96·0	45·8
Frankfurt	48,800	16·8	8·0	25	1,250	570	67·5	46·0
Dortmund	67,900	18·3	10·2	29	2,400	550	43·5	28·0
Düsseldorf	39,700	19·0	10·0	29	1,500	528	66·0	43·0
Hanover	32,900	15·5	15·0	30	2,600	450	86·7	44·5

Source :—Statistisches Jahrbuch Deutscher Gemeinden, 1936, Jena.

527

S

(5) ADMINISTRATIVE DISTRICTS AND COMMUNITY AREAS

The rapid expansion of the urban area in the 19th century produced areas of tenements or terraced houses in which community life and the formation of conscious social groups could not develop. Indeed, the elementary needs of food, clothing, and shelter were all inadequately provided for. Nevertheless, there are marked contrasts in the physical build and functions of the city by districts, the precise sociological structure of which still awaits detailed investigation. Such district variations are based upon two main factors—first, position with respect to the centre of the city, the chief focus of its inward and outward movements ; and second, functional differentiation that emerges through historical development in relation to the condition of site and to the existence of physical barriers such as river, railway belt, boulevard, open space or industrial belt. Further, on the urban–rural fringe in particular, the old village or town centre has been swallowed in the urban expansion. Such a nucleus, however, often retains its individuality in aspect as well in function, and has emerged as a district commercial, amusement and business sub-centre.

The great city has a framework of administrative divisions which has been handed down from the past, or arbitrarily imposed upon it, to serve a great variety of purposes without any respect to the existing space relations or needs, and without any attempt to co-ordinate the different areas. A map of such *ad hoc* administrative units within the built-up areas of the city reveals a bewildering intercrossing of areas, which have long been a nightmare to the student, a source of meaningless confusion to the individual, and a tragic hindrance to the efficient working of government and administration. All these shortcomings have been made glaringly obvious in Britain by the emergencies raised by war-time conditions and needs.

A note must be inserted here with regard to terminology in such sociological and geographical studies.

Neighbourhood is one of the few terms in general usage among sociologists in the United States with a specific meaning and, in the interests of clarity, it should be reserved to express that concept. A neighbourhood is the smallest social group outside of the family, a group characterized by the feeling of " neighbourliness ", or friendship with one's neighbours. It is an intimate face-to-face group of several hundred people. There are many large areas in town and countryside where the feeling of neighbourhood is dying

out or simply does not exist ; there are others in which it persists, and it is equally important to determine both conditions. The same applies to the urban complex. There is, beyond the neighbourhood, a social-geographical grouping which is based on some kind of association through the medium of common institutions ; it is organized in some degree as a community, but no face-to-face relationship of all its members is involved. This community grouping applies to wider units than the neighbourhood, and, for example in rural areas, the kind of grouping next above the neighbourhood is called the *rural community area*. Such a group has its centre in a thriving local seat of centralized institutions in a relatively large village or small semi-urban centre. The Americans call this the *rurban community*. In the same way, the grouping in the city, above the neighbourhood (which is limited to two or three streets with perhaps 100 to 200 families) is an *urban community area*. Obviously this latter may be of two kinds, either the area in which the people have the same social and economic character (and this depends mainly on the type of housing) or one in which one or more institutions serve a single district. In short, all such wider areas defined in such terms should have some name other than neighbourhood, and the term which is now generally used in the United States is *community area*. It is the community areas of American cities that have been used as a basis for sociological study and for the new population census districts in the city. Let us also use the same two terms, keeping their meaning as distinct as possible.

With these natural functional groupings the existing administrative divisions of the city that exist for purposes of local government and statistics show little relation. There is need for a rearrangement of administrative units and their subdivision into smaller community units, the framework for which is to be found in the existing community structure. The meaning and value of this is revealed, for example, in the social studies of Chicago, where 75 community areas and 500 small census tracts, which are in use for social investigation, have been adopted by the Bureau of Census as the permanent basis for population and demographic records.[1] This now applies to all the large American cities. British and most European cities have only the large and irregularly-shaped unit of the ward or its equivalent to work on. We need many more smaller and more homogeneous units like those of the Chicago community areas in order to understand the city

[1] See *City, Region, and Regionalism*, Chapter 5.

and the whole question of the demographic, social, and economic structure of the population and its processes and trends. We need to know not merely the general trends in the country as a whole, but also the related trends in the various sectors of the city in the greatest possible detail. This knowledge could be acquired through the medium of a census assessed on the basis of small census units, but certainly not through such large antiquated and heterogeneous units as the wards of British and continental cities.[1]

(6) TRAFFIC FLOWS

The goods traffic movements of a great city have been emphasized in the studies of Paris and Berlin. They involve the import of raw materials for industry and building, and of foodstuffs, and the export of manufactures for the international, national, and regional markets. There is thus a vast inward movement of goods in bulk—among which coal, sand, and building stone are usually the bulkiest—and a much smaller outward movement of manufactured goods, smaller in bulk, higher in value, and varied in consignments. The inward flow is handled in the marshalling yards, the goods yards and the river ports ; the outward traffic is handled pre-eminently by the railway and secondarily, in the last thirty years, by road. Further, there is the inward and outward movement of traffic to and from the city core, this being effected through its passenger railway stations and, to a much less degree, through its airports. Thirdly, there is the enormous internal daily movement of goods to and from goods depots, and of passengers to and from their work and to and from the central business district as well as to and from the local sub-commercial centres. Rail, road, and water are the media for these traffic movements.

Let us first glance at the problem of railway transport.[2] The railway is concerned with the transport of both passengers and freight. As regards the former, it must provide (a) for the transport of the sub-urban worker to and from the city and the factory, with marked concentration of traffic at two specific " rush-hour " periods ; and (b) main-line services to other cities, the main stations being either at " dead-ends " or located on

---

[1] It would be a tremendous gain to have such data for the Administrative County of London, for it would be possible to give much clearer definition to the social and economic structure and especially to the more precise definition and mapping of community areas, an attempt that has been made more diagrammatically in the *County of London Plan*.

[2] S. H. Beaver, " The Railways of Great Cities ", *Geography*, June, 1937, pp. 116–20.

routes which pass through the city. From this point of view, the railway plan should consist of a series of routes, radiating from the city, with branches on its outskirts serving the suburbs. Ideally, there should also be transport facilities between the great terminals in large cities—by either surface or, better, underground railway—though this in fact is seldom the case. As regards the second, freight traffic, the main problem is to provide efficiently for the import of vast supplies of food and raw materials for the daily requirements of population and industry. There will also be a great traffic of goods through the city, either for direct transmission, or for storage and redistribution as an entrepôt. It is necessary, therefore, for the city to have (1) sorting facilities where traffic from all directions can be assembled for its destinations, that is, marshalling yards for such entrepôt traffic, and goods yards for distribution within the city ; (2) adequate connection from one radial main line to another ; and (3) intra-city connections and yards, which should as far as possible avoid the compactly built-up areas. Thus, the belt or girdle line (on the outskirts of the city) becomes an almost inevitable feature of the railway pattern. Marshalling yards spring up on the outskirts of the city near to the belt line, while goods stations lie in the vicinity of the terminals in closer touch with the urban areas of the city to and from which goods are distributed and collected.

The normal historical development of the railway net of a city, varying with its size and location, results in routes to or through the city centre—that is, routes built at the time of their construction on open land bordering the town and along which the major industrial and built-up areas have largely gravitated ; terminals built originally at the outskirts of the city and radiating from it ; the final emergence of one or more inter-connecting belt-lines. " The ideal railway plan for a large city thus somewhat resembles a wheel : the city is the hub, the main lines are the spokes, the circumference is the belt line." [1] The symmetry of the railway plan varies, in fact, according to the historical conditions of its development and according to the city's site, historical development and its present size.

London, for example, has 15 well-developed radial routes, inter-terminal connections by the " Inner Circle ", and transverse " tube " lines. Terminal passenger stations south of the Thames, lying nearest to the heart of London, where little land was available at the time of construction, do not have goods stations

---

[1] Beaver, *op. cit.*

adjacent to them.   These latter facilities are available in the low-lying Thames-side area, which was formerly waste land.   The northern terminals were built on the edge of London where more land was available, so that passenger and goods stations are close together.   Outer belt lines are the North London, linking all northern lines to the Docks, the West London and the North & South-West Junction.   The marshalling yards are located where the radial and belt lines meet.   There is no belt line on the south-east.

Paris has its terminals connected by underground railways. There is an inner circle (*petite ceinture*), used mainly for local passenger traffic (as well as by through coaches from the Channel Ports) ; an outer circle (*grande ceinture*) well beyond the sub-urban limit of the city, used mainly by freight traffic.   Marshalling yards lie mainly on the outer circle belt and the goods yards are near the passenger terminals.   The last lie inside the inner circle, to the north and south of the Seine.

Berlin (Fig. 63) has an inner circle (Ringbahn), which limited the expansion of the city area and follows the outskirts of the compact built-up area, and inside which (as in Paris) are located the chief passenger terminals and goods yards north and south of the Spree.   An overhead railway, the Stadtbahn, runs right through the city centre from west to east, and the Hochbahn south of the river links two of the stations on the Ringbahn. Marshalling yards lie on the main radial lines outside the Ring-bahn and right outside the built-up ·areas (Wustermark to the west, Seddin to the south-west) and there are five along the Ringbahn at the junction of the chief radial routes.   An outer belt or industrial railway to the north links the industrial area of Tegel by a circular route with the radial routes running east-wards from the city.   It will be further noted that the chief railway terminals for combined goods and passenger traffic lie inside the Ringbahn (built in 1882) but were built on the outer edge of the built-up area of Berlin in the 1850's.   Freight in transit runs mainly from the Wustermark yards to the yards south-east of the city, traversing the city by the Ringbahn.   There is no outer railway belt to the south of the city, but its place is taken by the Teltow canal, which lies just outside the Ringbahn.

The radial pattern with a circular or semi-circular girdle is found in most of the other great cities, such as Rome, Milan, Budapest, Warsaw, Bucarest, Brussels, and Vienna.   Its improve-ment or creation is a main object of planning proposals, as is· so well illustrated in the case of Amsterdam. Here a belt line is to encircle the south of the city, running to the new port area to the west of it.

A main feature of most of the great cities—outstanding exceptions are Bucarest, Milan, Warsaw, and Birmingham—is that they lie on, or alongside, wide navigable rivers. By these rivers vast quantities of foodstuffs, raw materials and building materials are imported into the city. Each water-front, with its concentration of wharves, railway sidings and industry, is a main life-line of the city. In the cases of London, Berlin, and Paris, the city lies astride the river. Warsaw and Budapest, though they lie astride their rivers, have expanded relatively recently to the opposite bank. Pest is to-day the main portion of the city as opposed to the small capital city of Buda. In the case of Warsaw the main part of the city lies around the capital, and extension to Praga on the flat bank opposite, with its main railway terminals and factories, is recent. Prague is closely analogous to Budapest. In all these cities, as in many others, the river presents a great problem in the growth of the city and its communications, in respect of traffic across it by bridge, ferry, and tunnel, and expansion along it—for the river front offers one of the greatest opportunities in town planning from the æsthetic as well as the economic point of view.

River transport requires wharf and warehouse facilities for loading, unloading, and storage. Such facilities demand space and a central position for effective collection and distribution. Originally such facilities were provided in the city, but in the cases of the big river ports one finds the more spacious modern wharves located on the more open land on the outskirts of the built-up area, but with adequate road and railway connections with it. The demands of road transport in the city may be ideally met by two sets of roads, one set running radially from the centre, the other set forming two or three concentric belts, one around the city centre, the second on the borders of the compact middle zone, and the third through the outer urban–rural fringe, interlinking its main industrial and residential complexes. These facilities are present in the continental city to a marked degree as a result of its normal mode of historic growth, or they can be readily adapted to the existing pattern. In the British city, which has been much more amorphous in its growth, such facilities are put forward as goals, but can only be achieved at very great expense. Compare the actual plan of Paris, Berlin, Frankfurt or Amsterdam with that

of any British city, and with the scheme, in particular, for the
creation of ring roads in the County of London Plan.

(7) THE LIMITS OF THE CITY

The city is the focus of patterns of urban land uses and organizational areas that cut right across the patterns of rural land uses.
It is the most important driving force in creating that symbiosis
of areal relations of which, in principle, the designer of new
administrative units and the planner of new land uses must take
full cognisance.   Regional planning in the town-planning sense
normally deals with the provision of lines of communication to
accommodate traffic flows, utility services, electricity, gas, water
and other piped services, housing and recreational facilities.   It
should also make provision for the growth of community life—
hospitals, libraries, schools, churches, shops, clubs, etc.   In all
these respects the city is the centre of a multiplicity of functions,
differing in character and in the extent of the areas embraced or
served.

These areal space relations of the city with its environs may be
summed up under the following heads.   They are revealed most
clearly in the case of Paris (Fig. 60, p. 235).

(a) *Land Use.*   Urban land uses—structures and spaces for
living, work, recreation, and transport—make up the urban
complex.   This is compact in its central districts, ragged on its
margins, with prolongations along the main routes.   In order to
determine the limit of the urban complex, careful mapping of its
peripheral areas is required, with regard to both the actual extent
(and classification) of built-up areas and urban open spaces, and
the densities and increases of population per unit of the smallest
census areas.

The limits of the areas with a certain minimum density of
population or with a high increase of population as compared to
more distant rural areas, that have lower densities and normally
lower rates of increase (or even a stationary or decreasing population), are among the most significant limits of the urban complex.
A minimum limit of 400 inhabitants per square kilometre (about
1000 per square mile) was found in the case of Paris to be
a significant break against surrounding rural areas (p. 234).
Jefferson suggested years ago 10,000 per square mile as a minimum
density, and the population map of the Ordnance Survey of
Great Britain takes densities of over 400 persons per square mile

as " sub-urban and industrialized rural " and over 6,400 per square mile as " urban."

In a special study of sub-urban trends in the big cities of south and central Germany by M. Reichert, the suburbs (*Vororte*) were first defined by listing for each city those places that were considered as suburbs by the city authorities (irrespective of administrative limits). Out of 20 cities with over 100,000 people, there were 274 suburbs. The criteria of sub-urban character are taken to be the lay-out, occupational structure, economy, and transport facilities to the city centre. Places with densities of over 1,000 persons per square kilometre were called fully urban (*grossstädtisch*) ; high densities are considered to fall between 500 and 1,000 persons per square kilometre.[1] Through the varying combinations of these sub-urban traits in sub-urban places, and especially if such a place has grown from a pre-existing nucleus, certain types of community were recognized. These range from the transformation of a rural village, by the gradual infiltration of urban traits, to the development of entirely new districts and the complete demolition or disappearance of the original village buildings. In other cases, the village buildings remain, though they are transformed in function. The ground plan remains the same, but normally the village buildings disappear in time. Population increases faster than in the city. Density also increases above that of the rural village, in all cases, to over 100 persons per square kilometre (250 per square mile). From the economic point of view, about a half of the suburbs have no industry. The great majority have connections by bus, tram, or train, though many lack the last.

From this study the following sub-urban types are recognized by this author in south Germany, as stages in the transformation of existing settlements on the urban periphery. The *Anfangstyp* still carries dominantly the traits of the initial settlement. In the *Mitteltyp* the original aspect of the settlement reveals changes affected through the urban impact. In the *Endtyp* the sub-urban character is dominant. The beginning of " sub-urbanization " is marked by the increase of population, the construction of some new urban buildings, or the development of market-gardening. In the middle stage the settlement acquires new traits which become far more obvious to the eye in the build and lay-out of

---

[1] It should be noted that the Germans make a distinction between a *Vorstadt*, an outer district outside the old town but a part of its fully built-up urban area, and a *Vorort*, an outer urban area, cut off from the city centre but allied to it socially and economically.

the settlement. In the end stage, the district is completely sub-urbanized, though it does not become a part of the city. In south and west Germany half of the suburbs fall into the third category.

(b) *Movement of Persons*. This involves immigration from the surrounding towns and country, and the recent " reflow " of city workers back to the country or to the city outskirts through the great expansion of the urban area known as the " sub-urban trend ". There is also involved with the latter the daily movement of workers to the factories of the urban area and to the offices of the central business district. Finally, there is the daily, weekly and seasonal movement of persons to the city, seeking the amenities of its shops, theatres, and institutions.

Accessibility, by road and rail, is the primary determinant of these movements, and for this reason the mapping of isochrones—lines of equal time-distance from a city core—has often been undertaken as a method of fixing the potential extent of a city area, given no change in its transport services. Indeed, such maps also serve to indicate those districts which are not adequately served and where extensions of transport services may be made. But it cannot be too strongly emphasized that the urban complex does not expand by the one process of concentric growth from a central core in which all the workers are occupied or even interested in visiting frequently. The accessibility of the centre is certainly a necessary limitation to the radius of residence of the people who work in the city and wish to enjoy its amenities. But the essential feature of the growth of the modern city is that it has outgrown itself by accretion, for its outer areas form quite separate and amorphous complexes that have little connection with the city centre. They have their own places of work, their own shops and often their own public buildings, though the last are often notoriously inadequate. The limits of such a large complex are fixed by accretion and not by accessibility to the centre. Thus, far more important to the residents in the peripheral areas is the accessibility of their local factories and shops. A worker's home may be an hour's journey from the city centre but only ten minutes from his workplace, or he may live an hour's journey out in the country, well removed from his workplace on the urban fringe. Growth takes place by residential expansion from an already overgrown nucleus, and by the growth of outlying sub-centres which are independent units. There are two processes at work here, deconcentration and decentralization. The former implies the expansion of the existing complex, the latter implies the shedding some of its activities to independent or satellite communities that are physically separate from it.

(c) *Public Utility Services.* The areas of supply of gas, water, electricity, and transport often extend beyond the municipal limits to include large contiguous urban and rural areas. The spread of these services to contiguous urban areas, that are in fact a part of the city, socially and economically, is a main cause of the constant cry for the extension of municipal boundaries, in the interests of efficiency, of organization and financial economy.

(d) *Movement of Goods.* This includes the movement of consumers' and producers' goods in and out of the city. These are, in effect, the " imports " and " exports " of the city. The city itself is the terminal for vast quantities of bulky materials required for its own consumption, such as coal, timber, grain, and building materials ; whereas in bulk its exports are small, consisting mainly of the manufactured goods produced in its factories. The degree of concentration of " imports " and " exports " in the city varies with its importance as a communication centre—a port, for example, combining the functions of sea and " inland " port, having much stronger ties with its hinterland. But, in general, the bulk traffic in coal and the raw materials of industry avoids the city core, whose predominance lies in the multitude of smaller goods it handles by collection, storage, and redistribution, in much the same way as an entrepôt port.

Milk and vegetables are among the chief food imports of a city from its rural environs. Other foodstuffs can also be drawn from much wider areas and may indeed be imported from abroad. Goods in the latter category normally pass through the markets and warehouses of the city, or, failing that, their transference is negotiated in the offices of the city. This applies to imported foodstuffs and raw materials and manufactured foods that are consumed in the city and in the country and towns of its tributary area. Banks, offices, multiple shop branches, etc., are located in many towns of the environs as branches of main concerns in the central city.

(e) *Movement of Ideas.* The city is a fount of opinion, reflecting and serving the interests and aspirations of its region. This is the most intangible of all regional functions, and can only be appreciated in terms of the historical development of the city and its region. Its influence may be measured, as to character and weight, by its press, educational institutions—we are now beginning to speak of Regional Universities—learned societies, movements, and its rôle in the political life of the nation.

(f) *Organization.* The city is a centre of commerce, finance, administration and, in varying degree in different centres, of political organization. If a political capital, past or present—as often on the Continent—it invariably combines all these functions. If an economic metropolis (like Manchester or Birmingham) it acquires administrative status and plays an important rôle in the national life, through the devolution of administrative functions from the capital.

The range of influence of an urban complex may then be determined by studying the accessibility of its centre, population curves for all the surrounding urban and rural areas, and changes in the character of their occupational structure. The areas with an increasing population indicate clearly a main urban limit, especially if such areas lie within a larger area in which rural depopulation (largely through immigration to the city itself) is characteristic, so that the reflow outwards from the city can easily be examined. This is the type of study that has been made for Vienna (Fig. 48), and has been illustrated in the case of Stockholm.[1]

(g) *Social and Economic Conditions.* The influence of the city on social and economic conditions is a problem that has been considered in a few American studies, but has not been undertaken with thoroughness for any individual city, except for Kuske's excellent study of Cologne.[2]

It is apparent that the regional relations of the city become increasingly nebulous with increased distance from it, and many of its contacts and services extend over a wide field that does not appear as a compact geographical unit. The influence of the city reflects only a part of a wider social and economic unit whose activities are centralized in and directed from two or more cities. Such is the case of Cologne in its relation to the Ruhr and the rest of north-west Germany. Moreover, the specialized products and services of the city have a far-flung geographical distribution, that is both nation-wide and international.

(h) *Political Limit of the City.* In all the above respects the city's influence extends to its environs, and in more or less degree, and with more or less effectiveness and usefulness, its limits in these various respects may be determined. What is of real practical significance, however, is the *de facto* political limit of the

---

[1] Robert E. Dickinson, *City, Region, and Regionalism*, pp. 137–44.
[2] B. Kuske, *Die Grossstadt Köln als wirtschaftlicher und sozialer Körper*, Cologne, 1928.

city within which it is an organized unit of self-government and over which it has clear-cut controls over the organization of community life and services. The essential point here is that through its rapid modern growth and the extension and intensification of its manifold relations with its surroundings, the city has exploded beyond its political limits to a wider surrounding area that forms an integral part of the city complex as an economic and social unit. This, of course, is a familiar story, but it cannot be too often repeated. It is the reason why cities over the last hundred years have sought again and again to extend their political area to include outlying suburbs of various kinds. This process of political expansion has taken place very markedly on the Continent, where many cities now have large areas that are more than adequate as potential settlement areas and in which, therefore, the city government can work out its own planning problems. Such is the case, for example, in Paris, Amsterdam, Berlin and Cologne. Very often the urban complex includes many small contiguous administrative units, which are in effect *de jure* political units. In the last fifty years centrifugal trends have resulted in the " proletarianization " of the central city which has to maintain the expensive upkeep of its services for the advantage of relatively well-to-do people who live outside its limits and escape its taxes. This has become a first-class crisis in the affairs of many cities, especially of those that in themselves do not offer particular amenities of site for urban living, as, for example, Rotterdam, where this precise problem assumed serious proportions in the 'thirties. Again, residential areas have grown up outside the city boundaries, and the process of rebuilding that is now urgently necessary after the destruction of the city centres and the inner and older housing districts, will necessitate a considerable expansion of the built-up areas on the urban outskirts of smaller towns. The cry for room for " overspills " that is now heard in Britain will also be heard on the Continent as a basic problem of city planning and as one of the main arguments for the extension of city planning to the wider fields of regional and national planning.

From these general considerations, it is clear that the most important overall criterion of the spread of the urban relationships of the city is the limits of its more or less continuous built-up area ; second, the demographic limit, within which the relationships with the city are reflected in the growth of residential houses for urban workers, peripheral factories and their associated houses ; third, the service limit, that cannot be defined in any sense by a line, but only by the relationships of different specific kinds between the urban complex and the households in farmstead, hamlet, and town. The service relationships reveal, however, two main areas, an inner area which, owing to ease of accessibility to the urban complex, is more intimately tied up with it in both daily and weekly connections ; and a still wider area in which relations of this kind with the city are occasional and for special purposes, particularly for those nebulous but fundamentally important cultural and directional relationships in respect of which the city functions as a regional capital.

(8) Planning the Great City

The expansion of the urban area far beyond its administrative limits and the heavy congestion of traffic and the competition of uses in the urban complex demand not only public control over the development of land in each administrative unit, but unified control over all those contiguous administrative units that form a part of one socio-economic complex with a great urban nucleus. A number of the great cities of western Europe now have their plans with the authority of law, and these extend beyond the city to embrace its contiguous areas. Rome, Prague, Paris, Amsterdam, for instance, have their plans. These plans all have certain common features, in that they pay primary attention to communications, land uses and open spaces. It is in the sphere of housing, guided by new concepts of community living, that the County of London Plan has undoubtedly taken the world lead, not merely in theory, but also in practice. We may summarize the provisions of the plans for two continental cities.

(a) The Plan for Greater Amsterdam

The new plan for Amsterdam contains reports on the ground (site), parks, land and water transport, the relation of the plan with that of the separate district beyond the Ij, and the future of the city generally. The plan provides for a maximum population of about one million inhabitants. It aims at a compact centralized urban area, rather than a diffuse settlement area with widely scattered sub-urban communities. It is assumed that the centripetal rather than the centrifugal forces are likely to remain dominant in the life of the city, since it is pre-eminently concentrated around its harbour ; in addition the scarcity and the costliness of the polder land which surrounds the city is not favourable to the production of cheap, single-family houses covering a large area on a low density basis. New, compact residential areas, a new harbour, new industrial districts, parks and highways are planned for. The main features may be summed up as follows :

Communications. The existing roads form a pattern of radial and circular routes. Eleven of them are suggested as trunk roads. A tunnel is suggested for rail and car transport under the Ij, but passenger traffic will be accommodated by the ferry services. The existing canals are to be conditioned for the carriage of heavy traffic and wholesale goods, and for small-scale goods traffic by fast motor boats. A new circular railway line is a main feature of the plan for goods traffic to the western harbour, for transit traffic and for inter-communal and local passenger transport. Provision is made for a new airport near the existing marine base so as to accommodate seaplanes.

Industrial Areas. These are planned in the closest association with transport facilities by water and by land. They are as follows :

Harbour. It was decided in 1913 that the new harbour should be situated on the west side of the city on the North Sea Canal, whereas the existing port was situated to the east, facing the Zuyder Zee, which till 1876 was Amsterdam's only direct contact with the sea. This *volte face* in the orientation of a port is a most decisive element in the future development of Amsterdam and in its whole urban structure.

Industrial Sites. Five categories of sites are allowed for :— for gardening, horticulture and agriculture ; for industries that prefer central locations in the city ; sites which must be away from housing areas ; industries that prefer inland water ; industries that prefer the deep water of the sea.

The port area on the banks of the Ij is reserved as the main industrial area. A smaller industrial area is to be reserved to the south-east of the city.

Housing and Parks. The west and south are reserved as the main areas for future residential development. Parks are provided for between the city and the western residential area, and especially south of the city in the polders, 13 feet below sea level (area 2,125 acres). Ribbon development and the sprawl of suburbs is to be stopped. Multi-storeyed flats and single-family houses are to be intermixed with open streets, parks, and recreation grounds.

A detailed plan for the first sector covers Bosch-en-Lommer in the north-west, near the industrial area. It is to have 35,000 inhabitants, housed in four-storey flats, with gardens and recreation grounds ; old people are to be housed in two-storeyed flats. It is considered that these new settlements in the outer areas of the city will need 75 shops per 1,000 dwellings, increasing to 105 per 1,000 in the inner circle. Community needs are given careful consideration in this residential development.

A main feature in this plan for Amsterdam is that it shows the possibility of the centralized growth of multi-storeyed flats with adequate space for light, parks and recreation, as compared to the widespread kind of " sub-urban " community which the garden-city idea, with a low density of single-family houses with large individual gardens, would create.[1]

(b) The Plan for the Paris Region.

The spread of Paris beyond its administrative limits has taken place without any public control, with all the accompanying defects of uncontrolled conversion of land from rural to urban uses. The plan for the controlled development of the Paris Region is an attempt to direct the future trends of this expansion.

In 1911 a commission for the extension of Paris (*Commission d'Extension de Paris*) was established, and published two reports in two years. In 1919 there were enacted the laws for extending the fortifications of Paris. At the same time the municipal council of Paris and the *Conseil général* of the Seine Department organized a competition for the planning of Greater Paris and created a special department to deal with this problem. The law of 1919 made planning measures the concern of the *commune*, applicable to Paris as a whole, but in its environs a separate plan was necessary for each commune. There were 81 communes in the Department of Seine. A department was established to deal with planning problems of Paris and the communes of the Department of Seine, only eight of which chose to prepare their own plans. In 1928 the problem of planning the Paris Region was first effectively brought before the government by M. Poincaré and at his instigation the Minister of the Interior obtained the formation of a *Comité supérieur de l'aménagement et de l'organisation générale de la Région parisienne.* In 1932 a law was passed prescribing the

---

[1] See the *Architectural Review*, Vol. 83, 1938, pp. 265–76, with maps of proposed areas, historical development, roads and water, and parks.

establishment of a plan for the region, which was to apply to the Department of the Seine, and to the communes of Seine-et-Oise and of Seine-et-Marne situated within a radius of 35 km. of Paris, a total of 656 communes. The total area has approximately 500,000 hectares (1,470,000 acres) and a population of 6·3 millions. On May 14, 1934, the report on the plan for the Paris Region was submitted to the government.

In accordance with its directive, the project is confined to the broad plan of future development, the details being left to the discretion of the 656 communes. The provisions apply to roads, open spaces, protection of sites, land use, building, and public services.

Land Use and Building Regulations. The project delimits in each commune a zone of urbanization, on such an area that each commune can finance within fifteen years the provision of piped services—water, electricity, and sewage—as well as the public services necessary for administrative organization—schools, post-offices, police, refuse disposal, etc. In order to determine these areas of urban development and the zones within them, the 656 communes are divided into four groups, according to their density of population (Paris included). Class A covers the 26 communes in the Seine Department and includes some considerable towns. Their plans are to show zones for multiple and individual houses, and industrial and mixed zones (industry and residential) where occasion arises. Class B includes 49 communes that lie astride the limits of the Departments of Seine and Seine-et-Oise. Class C includes 178 semi-rural communes all of which lie within a circle of 21 km. from the centre of Paris. In the communes in classes B and C there will be no mixed zones, and there will be open zones in which building of houses and factories will depend upon the permission of the *Comité Supérieur*. Class D includes 403 small communes, entirely rural in character, which are being depopulated like most of the French countryside. Their territory is divided into areas for urban development and includes areas that are not zoned.

By this plan the Paris Region will have 88,436 hectares of developed urban land and 430,411 hectares of open land. Building regulations vary according to the four classes of communes and in each commune according to the zone. Thus it will not be legal to build up more than 5 per cent. of the total area of a property in the zones of single-family residences in classes A and B, 30 per cent. in Class C, and in any part of the developed area of

Class D.   Street frontages, heights and width of street frontages are to be strictly regulated.

Open Spaces and Protection of Sites.   New open spaces, an important need for the overcrowded city of Paris, will be provided by the creation of promenades and playing fields, and by spaces for other non-industrial public uses such as airports, garden cities, and cemeteries.   Industrial enterprises are to be controlled in respect of noise, smoke, and smell.   There are also provisions for the protection of the principal sites of the Île de France—the perspective of Marly, the *grands axes* of Versailles, Sceaux and Meudon, and the terraces of St. Germain and of Meudon, in order to preserve their æsthetic amenities.

Public Services.   It is asserted that in the provision of public services, past experience has revealed the need for organization over areas larger than those controlled by the municipal authorities.   The services of water, electricity, sewage, the disposal of domestic refuse, transport, and gas are considered.

Roads.   This subject, in many ways, is the most essential part of the report as a means of facilitating evacuation from the urban area.   Thus, a decree dated 25 July 1935, co-ordinated certain road works with works of national defence and provided for the payment of the cost of their construction by the State.   The main aim of the new road proposals is to permit entry to and exit from Paris of motor-cars.   Auto-routes are the main planned highways. Provisions are made for the widening of existing roads to 24–30 metres (a road width permitting the passage of four to six rows of vehicles with pavements six metres wide) ; zones *non aedificandi* to permit future widening to 40–50 metres ; the creation of by-passes around urban agglomerations ; the improvement of certain crossways.   In addition, five new roads will link up existing roads on the outskirts of Paris.   These will have a width of 60 metres with *zones de servitude* of 40 metres for future expansion.   They will leave the military boulevards and will be interconnected on the outskirts by a great *rocade*, or circular route, around the outskirts of the city, which will pass through the chief stretches of Paris.

The authority for the planning of the Paris Region has full legal powers to carry out its plans.   These plans, however, are elastic, and are now in process of substantial revision, particularly in the light of the new concepts of local community planning.

CHAPTER 23

CONCLUSION

This book has been concerned with the structure of the city and not with city planning, but the knowledge and the expertise needed for such analysis are essential as a basis for sound future planning. This fact is now generally recognized, as is shown by the amount of attention given to such study in Britain and in the United States in recent years. It is, however, the Continent that has been the special concern of this work, and it is here that the business of reconstruction is now particularly urgent.

Coventration. We all know in a general way what this means. Air-Marshal Harris has recently told us.[1] The R.A.F. developed a technique of " area bombing " or " city-gutting " such as the Germans attempted in a very small way on British cities at the beginning of the war. The centre of the British town suffered most, and a like technique was adopted by Bomber Command. Air-Marshal Harris writes in regard to the raids on the Krupp works, that form a massive complex in the heart of Essen—

> But it must be emphasized that in no instance, except in Essen, were we aiming specifically at any one factory during the Battle of the Ruhr ; the destruction of the factories could be regarded as a bonus. The aiming points were usually right in the centre of the town ; the average German city spreads outwards from the old centre, which was naturally more densely built-up than the newer and well-planned suburbs ; it was this densely built-up centre which was most susceptible to area attack with incendiary bombs. The objective of the campaign was to reduce production in the industries of the Ruhr at least as much by the indirect effect of damage to services, housing, and amenities, as by direct damage to the factories or railways themselves.

Official post-mortem statistics on the results of this onslaught are not published, but the figures given by Air-Marshal Harris himself are enough for our present purpose. Seventy German cities were attacked by Bomber Command : in other words, practically all the sixty cities with over 100,000 inhabitants, as well as a number of smaller ones. Twenty-three of the cities which were attacked had more than 60 per cent. of their built-up areas destroyed, and 46 had about half of their built-up areas

[1] Marshal of the R.A.F. Sir Arthur Harris, *Bomber Offensive*, Collins, 1947.

destroyed. Thirty-one had more than 500 acres destroyed. Hamburg and Berlin each had over 6,000 acres destroyed, and Düsseldorf and Cologne just 2,000 acres. Over 700 acres were demolished in the first raids on Lübeck and Rostock. The former was not an important industrial target, but useful as a try-out for the effectiveness of incendiary attack. Between 1,000 and 2,000 acres were devastated in each case in Dresden, Duisburg, Essen, Frankfurt, Hanover, Munich, Nuremberg, Mannheim, and Stuttgart. These figures compare with Coventry's 100 acres, London's 600 and Plymouth's 400. Sixty-one per cent. of the houses in Hamburg and 50 per cent. of those of Düsseldorf were destroyed.

In other words, much of what we have written in these pages is already past history. The cities are in ruins. The people are living a troglodytic existence. What happened to the German cities also happened elsewhere, partly from German attacks, as in the case of the flattening of the centre of Rotterdam and the destruction of Warsaw ; partly from the Russians, as in Vienna and Budapest ; and partly from the western Allies, as in the towns of Normandy. Here, not only the larger towns, such as Caen, Le Havre, and Rouen, have suffered grievously, but many small country towns have been laid level with the ground ; in some, such as Aulnay, not a wall stands. A few larger continental cities remain intact. Paris, where precision bombing was confined to industrial targets on the city outskirts, was fortunate, and so were Brussels and Amsterdam. But in all the countries of western Europe that were involved in the war one of the most urgent problems is the reconstruction of cities, large and small, and the provision of homes. Physical planning is one of the most urgent needs and must be tackled with the least possible delay. It is here that the scientist has a great part to play in working out the principles of social and physical reconstruction as aids to the planner and the architect.

Let us close on a more optimistic note, and look at the building of the city of the future in the light of our European studies.

The town is a community of people, a geographical group, and its buildings and amenities should be designed to make it possible for the members of this group to lead a good life. In the Middle Ages, the great majority of towns were sufficiently small in population and area to be social units in spite of the inadequacies of their lay-out and the appalling conditions of sanitation, which made the town more or less a death-trap and always dependent for its continued existence on a flow of immigrants from the surrounding countryside. Even in the bigger cities—such as the capitals and the metropolitan cities of the Low Countries—there was a natural segregation of trades by streets, a clustering of commerce and social life around the market-place, and a tendency for surrounding districts in larger towns to be segregated round their parish churches.

With the great growth and expansion of the modern city, social needs demand a different solution of the planning problem. This problem must accept the large agglomeration and the interdependence of adjacent cities and towns as basic facts of our civilization. This consideration should be the springboard of modern planning. The problem is to rebuild so that the city amenities, in the fullest sense, are available to all its inhabitants. It is one of evolving a lay-out, of streets, boulevards, open spaces, houses and flats, and industrial and commercial quarters, in such a way as to allow the city as a whole to function and develop as an entity, and to permit the spontaneous development of social groupings around local sub-centres, be they in the urban complex or separate small towns some distance from it. The city core should be the hub in which are concentrated the essential and culminating economic and cultural services which demand a central location. Such a re-orientation and rebuilding must obviously be based on the existing pattern that has grown through unplanned, natural growth.

The reconstruction of the city is a main aspect of this overall programme. Most of the houses in the greater part of the inner areas of the city are, or will be in a few years, derelict and ripe for demolition. Principles must emerge for the reconstruction of these areas. This involves the reconstruction and expansion of the central zone and the erection of new residential buildings around it. Two essential points need to be borne in mind in this connection. The central city core contains the centralized services and the best that civilization has to offer. Many of these services need not be in the centre ; large business and administrative concerns can be decentralized (dispersed), as has been done during the recent war. Many public buildings need not be in the city centre, as for example hospitals and museums. Congestion of building should be relieved as far as possible. Next, the city centre should have buildings worthy of its people and architecturally permanent ; most modern buildings, however, are built for a short life. Traffic facilities should give easy access to the centre and divert as much traffic as possible from the centre by circular or other by-passes. Shopping streets should be reserved for shoppers and barred from vehicular traffic. Such goals are far from the reach of our industrial cities of the north, but cities such as Manchester and Glasgow have it in their power to effect such changes. The post-war reconstruction of continental cities such as Rotterdam, Essen and Stuttgart, reveal ideas in the planning of city centres from which we can learn much.

Next, there is the question of residence. Far more allowance should be made for an outward shift than has so far been done in certain British post-war plans. The back-to-back houses and other old building areas should be replaced by varied types of building unit to fit with the existing and, so far as can be foreseen, future family units. They should have open spaces and adequate provision for neighbourhood development centred, among other things, on the elementary school with the main thoroughfares as social divides (as indeed they often are). This process was supported by the New York Regional Plan and in recent years by the County of London Plan. In the vexed question of house v. flat it is obvious that every house in the central urban areas cannot have a garden, nor is it necessary to think in terms of multi-storeyed flats. There is a great deal that can be done with terraced housing, at a fairly high density, but with all modern conveniences in the house and ample open space and light. Dutch housing demonstrates this. Moreover, two- or three-storey housing would allow for a density that would, in various combinations, meet housing and density needs, and would give adequate provision of light and open spaces. Variety of building and styles should be the keynote to building, from the point of view of æsthetics and practical needs.

It is a platitude that urban living is an artificial mode of life for a human being, since it is almost completely divorced from soil and country. On the Continent, and only in less degree in Britain, the multi-storeyed apartment block, for rich and poor, has dominated, and will, it appears, continue to dominate urban building. Many such blocks have been endowed with communal facilities, such as laundry, crèche, restaurant, and club-room, but the great majority have not. Very often, as in the northern districts of Prague, monstrous blocks of flats, even though well constructed and provided for, lie in the midst of derelict land and undecorated, unfinished roads, whose primary purpose is utility for traffic. A passion and a vital urge for fresh air, open country, and exercise are without a doubt main contributory causes of the spread of Communism in such working-class districts, as well as the remarkable growth of organized sport, like the Sokol movement.

Britain has chosen a different course. This country adheres to the single-family house and garden, but in the post-war years the flat has been generally accepted and many towns now have blocks of flats up to twelve storeys high. The garden city idea originated in England, and, although it ran to seed between the wars, the idea has been taken up as part of the official policy of the Government in its adoption of the idea of the new towns around London and elsewhere. Letchworth and Welwyn have shown what can be done. Further, the idea of neighbourhood grouping has taken hold of planners, and such groupings are not merely to be fostered in cities like London, but also methods of grouping buildings are being devised in which such a spirit of neighbourliness may grow up. The adoption of such ideas in the monstrous arrays of tenements in great continental or American cities is an impossibility. These buildings foster an impersonal attitude. From this point of view the present concepts that lie behind planning proposals augur well.

All these suggestions call for the reconstruction of the great city through planned decentralization and deconcentration, and the reconstruction of the old, ugly, congested areas of the central and middle zones. Planned development does not mean the continuance of past trends, accepting aggregation and " megalopolitanism " as inevitable. It seeks to retain and develop what is best in the life and organization of the great city, and to open it up into smaller units, over a wide area. In this way, planning may cater for the social needs of the individual within each small unit, as in the small town, and in the city as a whole.

This book has been concerned with the structure of the city. We have examined the character and grouping of its elements under the heads of location, site, growth, plan, build, and zonal arrangement of its present physical and demographic structure. It is the combination of these elements, grouped in varying degree according to the exigencies of site, the accident of uncontrolled growth, and the design of a planning authority, guided by ideas of aesthetic and practical planning, that determines the structure of the urban habitat. We have seen that out of the uncontrolled growth of the early Middle Ages there emerged ideas of town planning that were adopted in the later medieval period in the planning of new towns as entities and in the extension of others. The period from 1500 until the onset of the 19th century was characteristically, though not always, marked by the planning of new towns on definitely conceived principles, and by the transformation and extension of old towns to meet the demands of the æsthetic and practical urbanism of the age. The greatest era of growth during the latter half of the century was dominated for the most part by an uncontrolled policy of *laisser faire*, whereby individual speculators were responsible for new building. In many cases on the Continent city governments owned the land and were able to impose a uniform plan and control the uses through building by-laws. Even there, however, the extent of this land is often indicated only by its lay-out, that is, with the old town within it and the 19th-century extensions beyond it. Seldom does one find a unity of design indicative of purposeful development.

The so-called town and regional planning of the last fifty years has been permissive rather than constructive in character. It has not sought to control building in the light of the elementary human needs of air and light and space, or of communal needs in the way of group living and social services. It has paid attention mainly to the " zoning " of land, prescribing building regulations for existing built-up areas—notably excluding industry from certain areas and confining it to others and separating residential from obnoxious non-residential uses—controlling the height of buildings within the built-up areas, and reserving outer unbuilt areas for future uses, residential, industrial and commercial, and communications. Housing conditions have hitherto received little attention from high authority, although the progress of slum clearance in the heart of the continental cities has been more marked than in the case of the industrial British cities. The stupidity of zoning when not guided by scientific principles and overall nation-wide considerations is revealed by the fact that the areas reserved for residential use in the schemes of local government authorities in Britain would have accommodated thirty million people at a density of twelve houses to the acre. The population is, in fact, a little more than fifty millions, and present trends undoubtedly indicate a decline rather than an increase of this figure in the future.

Planning, in other words, must be based on a thorough knowledge of the actual character of urban land uses and the way in which they have come into being ; and secondly on the demographic and economic trends and demands of the urban community. It is precisely this sort of basic understanding that was absent in the planning of the inter-war period in Britain. The prevailing need in all countries is for such factual studies. These are practised now by social scientists and government authorities in Britain, but they need to be further developed by the pure scientist as ends in themselves. Such developments have taken place during the recent war and Britain has now undoubtedly taken a world lead in the business of urban and rural survey and planning. Even so, certain lines of investigation are needed in this country in order fully to understand the urban habitat in which at least four-fifths of our population live. We need thorough studies of individual cities and particularly of groups of small towns in rural areas and of the great conurbations. In recent years such studies have been largely devoted to functional analysis, but we need also comparative study of the forms of the urban habitat and their natural groupings.

Secondly, we need thorough land use surveys of urban areas on the broad lines we have indicated. Even in recent surveys one does not find very often a careful classification and mapping of existing uses on the lines suggested in Chapter 21, although we are aware that such studies are now in hand or complete in certain of our cities. Such a map has been prepared, for instance, for the whole of the West Midland conurbation on a six-inch scale, and it is to be hoped that it will eventually be published on the scale of 1 : 25,000 as a model for all urban areas.[1]

In such surveys there are two possible sources of information, ground work and the interpretation of large-scale air photographs together with good ground plans, each on a scale of 1 : 5,000 or 1 : 10,000. The air photo can be used for the study of structures but its value for the interpretation of urban land uses is limited, especially with regard to commercial uses and the mixed zones in the inner urban areas. Such facts can only be obtained from study on the spot. But air cover of all towns permits at once a standardized classification of structures, computation of the density of building and the mapping of all urban areas in one office and under a single supervision. We need the air cover, we need the staff to carry out such a systematic survey, as a matter of the highest priority.

---

[1] This work, prepared by the West Midland Group, is now published under the title of *Conurbation*. This excellent study and the other publications of this group are examples of the kind of analysis to which we refer in these pages.

Population, social and economic data also need careful analysis, but here again the main difficulty is the unsuitability in Britain of the existing census districts, the wards, for such study. We need something like the census tracts of the United States Census. At any rate for census purposes, districts are needed that are fairly homogeneous from the standpoint of their use, with fairly clearly defined physical limits. Such areas could be quickly demarcated by a group of trained geographers, under single supervision, from air cover and maps. It is true that there are local authorities capable of doing such work, but what is required is the application of the idea on a single standardized basis so that results will be ultimately comparable. There is a need for the establishment of a special Geographical Department in the Registrar General's Office for such research in connection with the Census. It is precisely this kind of rôle that is played by the Geographer of the Census in the United States.

We have already emphasized in various places that these labours demand a standardized system of cartographic representation. A series of maps of all the towns and large cities is needed on a standard basis and on a standard scale, together with short explanatory monographs comparable with those of the Land Utilization Survey for rural areas. We have suggested the types of map that might be produced in such studies in *City, Region and Regionalism*. Such a project can only be carried out by a single authority under a single direction, assisted by local authorities and voluntary workers on a clearly conceived directive.

These are various lines of research that are urgent in this country for the understanding of its urban problems and for the future planning of the urban habitat. The writer's attention has been drawn to this field of study by the preparation of such a series for all our major continental cities, samples of which have been given in this book. Similar methods should be applied in Britain. Lastly, the techniques of such urban survey, which are now very laboriously being worked out by a few enthusiastic workers, with excellent results, are not new developments either of concept or technique. Such studies, as the examples in this book illustrate, have been part of the geographer's technique for fifty years. Unfortunately most of these studies have been undertaken by foreign geographers, hence the reason for the choice of continental cities for this study.

The whole idea of physical or space planning is essentially geographical ; it arouses interest in and demands a knowledge of the *where* and the *why* of items on the earth's surface in terms of their space relationships. There is therefore a strong case and a definite necessity for the allocation of geographical workers to certain government departments. Moreover, the fact that stands out with ever-increasing clarity is the need for the co-operation of the various social sciences in the study of the problems of the structure, the life, the organization and the future of the urban community.

SELECTED BIBLIOGRAPHY

PART ONE

There are numerous geographical studies of continental towns which have appeared as articles and books, and it is impossible to list them all here. These refer particularly to studies of small towns and comparative urban studies. Representative studies are listed in the bibliography to Chapter I, and reference is made in Part I only to those works that have been consulted in preparing this book. In addition to the geographical periodicals, special attention is drawn to *La Vie Urbaine*, a quarterly published for the Institut de l'Urbanisme of the Sorbonne, commencing in 1920 and ceasing publication in 1940. There are numerous first-class studies of towns in its pages.

CHAPTER 1

AHLMANN, H. W. VON, and others, *Stockholms Inre Differentiering*, Meddelande från Geografiska Institutet vid Stockholms Högskola, No. 20, 1934.

ANDREWS, J., "The Settlement Net and the Regional Factor", *Australian Geographer*, Vol. 2, 1935, pp. 33–48.

AUROUSSEAU, M., "Recent Contributions to Urban Geography : A Review ", *Geographical Review*, Vol. XIV, 1924, pp. 444–55.

——, "The Distribution of Population : A Constructive Problem ", *Geographical Review*, Vol. XI, 1921, pp. 563–92.

BLANCHARD, RAOUL, "Une Méthode de Géographie Urbaine ", *Revue de Géographie Alpine*, Grenoble, Vol. XVI, 1928, pp. 193–214, first published in *La Vie Urbaine*, Paris, 1922, pp. 301–19.

BOBEK, H., "Grundgragen der Stadtgeographie ", *Geographische Anzeiger*, Vol. XXVIII, 1927, pp. 213–24.

——, *Innsbruck*, in *Forschungen zur deutschen Landes- und Volkskunde*, Vol. XXV, 1928, 155 pp.

BUSCH-ZANTNER, R. O., "Zur Kenntniss der osmannischen Stadt ", *Geographische Zeitschrift*, Vol. 38, 1932, pp. 1–13.

CHABOT, G., *Les Villes : Aperçu de géographie humaine*, Collection Armand Colin, Paris, 1948.

CLERGET, M., "L'Habitation Indigène au Caire ", *Annales de Géographie*, Vol. 40, 1931, pp. 527–43.

——, *Le Caire : Étude de Géographie Urbaine*, 1934.

DEFFONTAINES, P., "The Origin and Growth of the Brazilian Network of Towns ", *Geographical Review*, Vol. 28, 1938, pp. 379–99.

DICKINSON, ROBERT E., *City, Region and Regionalism*, London, 1947.

——, "The Scope and Status of Urban Geography : An Assessment ", *Journal of Land Economics*, Madison, Vol. 24, 1948, pp. 221–38.

DÖRRIES, H., "Der gegenwärtige Stand der Stadtgeographie ", *Petermanns Mitteilungen*, Ergänzungsheft Nr. 209, 1930, pp. 310–25.

——, "Siedlungs- und Bevölkerungs-geographie (1908–38) ", *Geographisches Jahrbuch*, Vol. 55, 1940, Erster Halbband, Gotha, 1940, pp. 3–380. Exhaustive bibliography for the world and its parts. Europe, pp. 191–380.

FAWCETT, C. B., "British Conurbations in 1921 ", *Sociological Review*, Vol. XIV, 1922, pp. 111–22.

——, "The Distribution of the Urban Population in Great Britain in 1931 ", *Geographical Journal*, Vol. LXXIX, 1932, pp. 100–16.

554

GEDDES, P., *Cities in Evolution*, London, 1915.
GEISLER, W., " Beiträge zur Stadtgeographie ", *Zeitschrift der Gesellschaft für Erdkunde zu Berlin*, 1920, pp. 274–96.
——, " Zur Methodik der Stadtgeographie ", *Petermanns Mitteilungen*, Ergänzungsheft Nr. 214, 1932, pp. 39–47.
GIST, N. P. and HALBERT, L. A., *Urban Soçiety*, New York, 1941, especially Chapters 6 and 7.
GREEN, H. W., " Cultural Areas in the City of Cleveland ", *American Journal of Sociology*, Vol. XXXVIII, 1932, pp. 356–67.
GUTKIND, P. A., *Revolution of Environment*, London, 1946.
HARTSHORNE, R., " The Nature of Geography ", *Annals of the Assoc. of American Geographers*, Vol. 29, 1939, pp. 171–658.
HASSINGER, H., " Über Aufgaben der Städtekunde ", *Petermanns Mitteilungen*, 56 Jahrgang, 2. Halbband, 1910, pp. 289–94.
HETTNER, A., *Die Geographie : Ihre Geschichte, Ihr Wesen und ihre Methoden*, Breslau, 1927.
——, " Die Lage der menschlichen Ansiedlungen ", *Geographische Zeitschrift*, Vol. I, 1895.
——, " Die wirtschaftlichen Typen der Ansiedlungen ", *Geographische Zeitschrift*, Vol. VIII. 1902.
JURGENS, O., " Spanische Städte, Ihre bauliche Entwicklung und Ausgestaltung ", *Abhandlungen aus dem Gebiet der Auslandskunde*, University of Hamburg, Band 23, 1926.
KAPPE, G., *Die Unterweser und ihr Wirtschaftsraum*, Bremen, 1929.
LEFEVRE, A., *Habitat Rural et Habitat Urbain*, Brussels, 1929, 11 pp.
LEHMANN, H., " Das Antlitz der Stadt in Niederländisch-Indien ", *Festschrift Norbert Krebs, Länderkundliche Forschung*, 1937.
LEVAINVILLE, J., *Rouen*, Paris, 1913.
LOUIS, H., *Die Geographische Gliederung von Gross-Berlin*, Stuttgart, 1936, 26 pp. with two maps.
McKENZIE, R. D., " The Ecological Approach to the Study of the Urban Community ", in *The City*, by R. E. Park, E. W. Burgess and R. D. McKenzie, Chicago, 1925, pp. 63–4.
MARTONNE, H. DE, " Buenos Aires ", *Annales de Géographie*, Vol. xliv, 1935, pp. 281–304.
MECKING, L., " Japans Häfen : ihre Beziehungen zur Landesnatur und Wirtschaft ", *Mitteilungen der Geog. Ges. in Hamburg*, Vol. XLII, 1931, pp. 1–592.
——, " Die Seehäfen in der geographischen Forschung ", *Petermans Mitteilungen*, Ergänzungsheft, No. 209, 1930, pp. 326–45.
——, " Die Grosslage der Seehäfen insbesondere das Hinterland ", *Geographische Zeitschrift*, Vol. XXXVII, 1931, pp. 1–17.
MUKERJEE, R., *Man and his Habitation : A Study in Social Ecology*, London, 1940.
PASSARGE, S., *Stadtlandschaften der Erde*, 1930.
RÜHL, A., *Die Nord- und Ostseebäfen im deutschen Aussenhandel*, Berlin, 1920.
SARGENT, A. J., *Seaports and Hinterlands*, London, 1928.
SCHLÜTER, O., " Bemerkungen zur Siedlungsgeographie ", *Geographische Zeitschrift*, Vol. V, 1899.
SCHULZE, J. H., " Die Häfen als Glieder der Kulturlandschaft ", *Festschrift für Prof. G. W. Zahn, Geog. Mitt. Thüringen*, 1931, pp. 37–55.
——, *Die Häfen Englands*, Leipzig, 1930.
SPATE, O. H. K., and TRUEBLOOD, L. W., " Rangoon : A Study in Urban Geography ", *Geographical Review*, Vol. 32, 1942, pp. 56–73.
TREWARTHA, G. T., " Japanese Cities ", *Geographical Review*, Vol. 24, 1934, pp. 404–17.

WHITTLESEY, D., ' Kano : A Sudanese Capital ", *Geographical Review*, Vol. 27, 1937, pp. 177–99.

WILHELMY, H., " Hochbulgarien, II. Sofia, Wandlungen einer Grossstadt zwischen Orient und Okzident ", *Schriften des Geographischen Instituts der Universität Kiel*, Band V, Heft 3, 1936.

WILLIAM-OLSONN, W., " Stockholm : Its Structure and Development ", *Geographical Review*, Vol. XXX, 1940, pp. 420–38.

WRIGHT, J. W., " The Diversity of New York City ", *Geographical Review*, Vol. XXVI, 1936, pp. 620–39.

ZIERER, C. M., " Melbourne : a functional centre ", *Annals of the Association. of American Geographers*, Vol. 31, 1941, pp. 251–88.

CHAPTER 2

LEIGHLEY, J., *The Towns of Mälardalen in Sweden. A Study in Urban Morphology*, University of California Publications in Geography, Vol. 3, No. 1, 1928, pp. 1–134.

CHAPTER 3

AMMANN, H., " Die Schweizerische Kleinstadt in der mittelalterlichen Wirtschaft ", *Festschrift f. W. Merz*, Aarau, 1928, pp. 158–215.

CAROL, H., " Begleittext zur Wirtschaftsgeographischen Karte der Schweiz ", *Geographia Helvetia*, 1.Jahrgang, 1946, Heft 3, pp. 185–245.

FRUH, J., *Geographie der Schweiz*, 4 vols., Vol. 1, Part 3, St. Gallen, 1930–8.

GANTNER, J., *Die Schweize Stadt.*

VOSSELER, F., " Das alte Bürgerhaus der Schweizer Stadt . . .", Comptes-Rendus du Congrès International de Geographie, Amsterdam, 1938, Section IIIa, pp. 222–32.

CHAPTER 4

CROZET, R., " Blois ", *La Vie Urbaine*, No. 21, 1934, pp. 147–73.

——, " Poitiers ", *La Vie Urbaine*, No. 48, 1938, pp. 325–62.

KOPP, J. M., " Laon : sa vie, son evolution, son avenir ", *La Vie Urbaine*, No. 25, 1935, pp. 29–58.

RASCOL, P., " Albi : Étude Géographique ", *Revue Géog. des Pyrénées et du Sud-Ouest*, January 1935, pp. 73–125.

CHAPTER 5

FRÜH, J., *Géographie der Schweiz*, Vol. III, (*Die Einzellandschaften der Schweiz*), pp. 1–11.

HASSINGER, H., " Basel ", *Beiträge zur Oberrheinischen Landeskunde, Fe 22, Deutschen Geographentag*, ed. F. Met, Breslau, 1927.

SCHAEFER, G., *Kunstgeographische Siedlungslandschaften und Städtebilder*, Dissertation, Basel, 1928, 72 pp., 12 maps.

——, *Kunstgeographischer Plan der Stadt Basel*, 1 : 5,000, Basel, 1929.

CHAPTER 6

DRISKE, P., *Der Wirtschaftsorganismus Gross-Breslau : Ein Beitrag zur Wirtschaftsgeographie einer Grossstadt*, Zur Wirtschaftsgeographie des Deutschen Ostens, ed. W. Geisler, Band 12, Breslau, 1936.

GLEY, W., " Grundriss und Wachstum der Stadt Frankfurt-am-Main. Eine Stadtgeographische- und Statistische Untersuchung ", 10 figures. *Festschrift zur Hundertjahrfeier des Vereins für Geographie und Statistik zu Frankfurt-am-Main*, 1936, pp. 55–100.

KNIBBE, H., *Die Grosssiedlung Hannover : Die Wirtschaftliche Verflechtung der politischen Stadt mit dem Vorraum*, Mitt. des Statistischen Amts der Hauptstadt Hannover, Neue Folge, Nr. 9, Hannover, 1934.

Köln, Herausgegeben von der Stadt Köln, Cologne, 1948. A symposium edited by Bruno Kuske.

KUSKE, Bruno, *Die Grossstadt Köln als wirtschaftlicher und sozialer Körper als Beitrag zur allgemeinen Grossstadtforschung*, Cologne, 1928.

MÜLLER, E., *Die Altstadt von Breslau : Citybildung und Physiognomie : Ein Beitrag zur Stadtgeographie*, Veröff. d. Schles. Geog. Ges. f. Erdkunde, Heft 14, Breslau, 1931.

CHAPTER 7

BLANCHARD, R., " Deux Grandes Villes françaises—Lille et Nancy ", *La Géographie*, Vol. XXX, 14–15, pp. 103–22.

Bordeaux : Etude Régionale d'Urbanisme, Special number of the review *Urbanisme*. May–June, 1934, Paris. Articles on " Bordeaux : Une Métropole " by P. Courteault (Professor of History) and " Le Cadre géographique et les paysages de Bordeaux ", by H. Cavaillés (Professor of Geography), with aerial photographs.

BRAUN, G., " Entwicklungsgeschichtlich-physiognomische Planskizze von Strasburg ", *Petermanns Mitteilungen*, 1914 (plan, 1 : 15,000).

FAUCHER, D., *Toulouse : Capitale Régionale*, Bulletin Municipal de la Ville de Toulouse, July, 1935.

JULLIAN, C., *Histoire de Bordeaux depuis les origines jusqu'en 1895*, Bordeaux, 1895.

LHÉRITIER, M., " L'Urbanisme au XVIII Siècle les Idées du Marquis de' Tourny ", *La Vie Urbaine*, Vol. 3, 1921, pp. 47–63 (map of Bordeaux in 18th century).

PERRIER, A., " Limoges, Étude de l'évolution urbaine ", *La Vie Urbaine*, 1935–6, also in *Annales de Géographie*, Vol. XXXIII, 1924, pp. 352–64.

——, " Limoges, Étude de Géographie urbaine ", *Revue Géographique des Pyrénées et du Sud-Ouest*, Tome IX, Fasc. 4, 1938, pp. 317–86.

REWIENSKA, W., " Quelques remarques sur la physiognomie de la ville de Toulouse ", *Revue Géographique Pyrénées et du Sud-Ouest*, Tome VIII, 1937, pp. 73–88, 7 figures.

——, " Études sur la démographie des alentours de Toulouse (3 figs.), *Revue Géographique des Pyrénées et du Sud-Ouest*, Tome VII, Fasc. 4, 1936, pp. 325–39.

SCRIVE-LOYER, " L'Agglomération Lilloise : Étude d'aménagement et d'extension ", *La Vie Urbaine*, Vol. 5, 1923, pp. 415–41.

——, " Les Conditions du développement de l'agglomeration Lilloise ", *Bulletin de la Société Géographique de Lille*, Vol. LXIII, 1912, pp. 143–62, 199–226, and 279–308.

Strasburg, Map and text in *Elsass-Lothringen Atlas*, 1931.

CHAPTER 8

LEDENT, A., " Esquisse d'urbanisation d'une capitale : Bruxelles, son passé, son avenir ", *La Vie Urbaine*, No. 41, 1937, pp. 319–51, No. 42, 1937, pp. 401–24, and No. 43, 1938, pp. 45–66.

VERNIERS, L., " Les Transformations de Bruxelles et l'Urbanisation de sa Banlieue depuis 1795 ", *Annales de la Société Royale d'Archéologie de Bruxelles*, Tome XXXVII, 1934, 142 pp.

CHAPTER 9

HAZEWINKEL, J. F., " Le Développement d'Amsterdam ", *Annales de Géographie*, Vol. 35, 1926, pp. 322–9.

LEYDEN, F., " Die Entvölkerung der Innenstadt in den grösseren Städten Hollands ", three articles in *Tijdschrift voor Economische Geografie*, January, 1934, June 1935, August 1935.

CHAPTER 10

DENBY, ELIZABETH, *Europe Rehoused*, 1938, Chap. 7.

HASSINGER, H., " Beiträge zur Siedlings und Verkehrsgeographie von Wien ", *Mitteilungen der K. K. Geographischen Gessellschaft von Wien*, 1910, pp. 5–88.

——, *Kunsthistorischer Plan des I Bezirks der Stadt Wien*, 1 : 10,000, Vienna, 1913.

——, *Kunsthistorischer Ubersichtsplan von Wien*, 1 : 25,000, Vienna and Leipzig, 1915.

——, *Kunsthistorischer Atlas von Wien, Österreich. Kunsttopographie*, Vol. XV, 19 coloured maps, with town centre on a scale of 1 : 3,960, 1916.

——, *Beiträge zur Stadtgeographie von Wien* ", *Geographische Zeitschrift*, Vol. 39, 1933, pp. 193–207.

KREBS, N., *Die Ostalpen und das Heutige Österreich*, 1928, 2nd volume, pp. 408–17.

LANGBEIN, O., " Grande Vienne ", *Annales de Géographie*, Vol. 48, 1939, pp. 513–7.

MOSCHELES, J., " Demographic, Social and Economic Regions of Greater Prague ", *Geographical Review*, Vol. XXVII, 1937, pp. 414–29.

CHAPTER 11

BAILLY, R., " Une ville qui redevient capitale ; Varsovie ", *La Vie Urbaine*, No. 28, 1935, pp. 231–54 and No. 29, 1935, pp. 373–84.

BEYNON, E. DOANE, " Budapest : An Ecological Study ", *Geographical Review*, XXXIII, 1943, pp. 256–75.

CHAPTER 12

CRONE, G. R., " Site and Growth of Paris ", *Geographical Journal*, Vol. 98 1941, pp. 35–47.

DEBUC, R., " L'Approvisionnement de Paris en lait ", *Annales de Géographie*, Vol. 47, 1938, pp. 257–66.

DEMANGEON, A., " Paris : La Ville et sa Banlieue ", *Monographies Départementales*, Paris, 1934.

——, " The Port of Paris ", *Geographical Review*, Vol. 20, 1920, pp. 277–96.

GALLET, P., " L'Approvisionnement de Paris en Vin, *Annales de Géographie*, Vol. 48, 1939, pp. 359–68.

GALLOIS, L., " Origin and Growth of Paris ", *Geographical Review*, New York. Vol. XIII, 1923, pp. 345–67.

Paris. Articles by various authors on demography and planning in *La Vie Urbaine*, Nos. 1, 2 and 3, 1919, 1920 and 1921.

POËTE, M., " L'Urbanisme Classique : La leçon de Paris ", *La Vie Urbaine*, No. 24, 1934, pp. 331–60.

——, *Paris, son évolution créatrice*, Paris, 1941. Appeared as series of articles in *La Vie Urbaine*, No. 40, 1937, pp. 195–220, No. 41, 1937, pp. 283–318, No. 42, 1937, pp. 359–74, No. 43, 1938, pp. 21–43, No. 44, 1938, pp. 79–109.

SELLIER, H., " Les Évolutions comparées du Logementet de la population dans le Département de la Seine de 1896–1911 ", *La Vie Urbaine*, Nos. 3–4, 1921–22.

CHAPTER 13

HEGEMANN, W., *Das Steinerne Berlin : Geschichte der grössten Mietskasernenstadt in der Welt*, Berlin, 1930.

LEYDEN, F., *Gross-Berlin : Geographie der Weltstadt*, Breslau, 1933.

LOUIS, H., *Die Geographische Gliederung von Gross-Berlin, Länderkundliche Forschungen, Festschrift N. Krebs*, 1936, Stuttgart, pp. 146–71.

PFANNSCHMIDT, M., *Die Industriesiedlung in Berlin und in der Mark Brandenburg*, Stuttgart and Berlin, 1937.

PART TWO

ABERCROMBIE, P., *Town and Country Planning*, Home University Library, London, 1938 and 1943.

AMMANN, H., " Das Städtewesen des Mittelalters." Erläuterungsband zum Elsass-Lothringen Atlas. *Veröff. d. Wissenschaftl. Inst. d. Elsass-Lothringer im Reich an der Univ. Frankfurt*, ed. G. Wolfram and W. Gley, 1931.

——, " Die schweizerische Kleinstadt in der mittelalterlichen Wirtschaft " in *Festschrift, f. W. Merz.*, Aarau, 1928.

AUBIN, H., " Die deutschen Stadtrechtslandschaften des Ostens ". Vom deutschen Osten, Festschr. zu M. Friedrichsen, ed. H. Knothe, *Veroff. d. Schlesischen Ges. f. Erdkde*, Breslau, H. 21, 1934, pp. 27–52.

——, " Zur Erforschung der deutschen Ostbewegung ", *Deutsches Archiv f. Landes u. Volksforschung*, I, 1936, pp. 37–70, pp. 309–31 ; II, 1937, pp. 562–602. (Thorough treatment of the present status and problems of research into the German eastward movement in the Middle Ages.)

BARTHOLOMEW, H., *Urban Land Uses*, Harvard U.P., 1932.

BRINCKMANN, A. E., " Die Geschichtliche Anlage der Deutschen Städte ", *Monatshefte f. Kunstwissenschaft*, 1921, pp. 14–28.

BEAVER, S. H., " The Railways of Great Cities ", *Geography*, Vol. 22, 1937, pp. 116–20.

BECHTEL, H., *Wirtschaftsstil des Deutschen Spätmittelalters : der Ausdruck der Lebensform in Wirtschaft Gesellschaft und Kunst von 1330 bis zum 1500*, 1930.

BELOW, G. VON, " Das ältere deutsche Städtewesen und Bürgertum ", *Monographien zur Weltgeschichte*, 3rd ed. 1925.

——, " Die Entstehung des modernen Kapitalismus und der Hauptstädte ", *Schmollers Jahrbuch*, XLIII, Part I, Munich, 1919.

——, " Territorium und Stadt ", *Historische Bibliothek*, Vol. XI, Munich, 1900.

BERNOUILLI, H., *Die Stadt und ihr Boden*, summary and legends in English, Zurich, 1946.

BLANCHET, A., *Les Enceintes romaines de la Gaule. Étude sur l'origine d'un grand nombre de villes françaises*, Paris, 1907, 356 pp.

BOBEK, H., " Über einige funktionelle Stadttypen und ihre Beziehungen zum Lande ", *Comptes rendus du Congrès international de Géographie*, Amsterdam, 1938, Tome II : Géographie Humaine, Leiden, pp. 88–102.

BRINCKMANN, A. E., *Platz und Monument*, 1908.

——, *Stadtbaukunst, Geschichtliche Querschnitte in neuzeitliche Ziele, Handbuch der Kunstwissenschaft*, Berlin, 1920.

BÜCHER, K., " Die Grossstädte in Gegenwart und Vergangenheit ", in *Die Grossstadt, Jahrbuch der Gehestiftung*, Dresden, 1927.

——, " Burgenland " in *Handwörterbuch des Grenz- und Auslandsdeutschtums*, ed. K. Petersen and O. Scheel, 1933.

BURGESS, E. W., " The Determination of Gradients in the Growth of the City ", *Publications of the American Sociological Society*, xxi, 1927, pp. 178–84.

——, " The Growth of the City ", *Proceedings of the American Sociological Society*, xviii, 1923, pp. 85–9, reprinted in Park, R. E., Burgess, E. W., and McKenzie, R. D., *The City*, Chicago, 1925.

——, " The Determination of Gradients in the Growth of a City ", *Publications of the American Sociological Society*, xxi, 1927, pp. 178–84.

CAROL, H., " Begleittext zu Wirtschaftsgeographischen Karte der Schweiz ", *Geographica Helvetica*, 1.Jahrgang, 1946, Heft 3, pp. 185–245.

CHAMBERS, W. T., " Geographic Areas of Cities ", *Economic Geography*, Vol. vii, 1931, pp. 177–88.

Chicago Land Use Survey, Vol. I, *Residential Chicago*, 1942, directed by the Chicago plan Commission, conducted by the Work Projects Administration, and sponsored by the City of Chicago.

CLARKE, M. V., *The Medieval City State, An Essay on Tyranny and Federation in the Later Middle Ages*, London, 1926.

CLERGET, P., " L'Évolution des Fonctions Urbaines, Étude de Géographie Sociale ", *Bulletin de la Société neuchâteloise de Géographie*, 1936, pp. 40–73.

CLOUZOT, E., " Le Problème de la Formation des Villes ", *La Géographie*, Vol. 20, 1909, pp. 165–76.

COLBY, C. C., " Centrifugal and Centripetal Forces in Urban Geography ", *Annals of the Association of American Geographers*, Vol. xxiii, 1933, pp. 1–20.

CURIE-SEIMBRES, *Essai sur les villes fondées dans le S.-O. de la France du XIII et XIV siècles*, 1880.

Demographic Studies of Areas of Rapid Growth, Milbank Memorial Fund, New York, 1944.

DEZNAI, V., " Essai d'une classification générale des villes ", *La Vie Urbaine*, No. 28, 1935, pp. 255–69 ; No. 29, 1935, pp. 283–323.

——, " Essai d'une Chronologie Urbaine ", *La Vie Urbaine*, No. 19, 1935, pp. 29–52 ; No. 20, 1934, pp. 74–115.

DICKINSON, R. E., *City, Region, and Regionalism*, 1947, Chs. 4 and 5.

——, " The Development and Distribution of the Medieval German Town ", *Geography*, Vol. 27, 1942, pp. 9–21 and pp. 47–53, with bibliography and maps.

——, " The Morphology of the Medieval German Town ", *Geographical Review*, Vol. XXXV, 1945, pp. 74–97.

——, " Le développement et la distribution du plan médiéval en échiquier dans le Sud de la France et l'Est de l'Allemagne ", *La Vie Urbaine*, No. 47, 1938, pp. 271–96.

DOPSCH, A., *Wirtschaftliche und soziale Grundlagen der europäischen Kulturentwicklung*, 2 vols., 2nd ed., Vienna, 1924.

——, *The Economic and Social Foundations of European Civilization*. London, 1937. (Abridged translation.)

——, *Wirtschaftsentwicklung der Karolingerzeit*, 2 vols., 2nd ed., Weimar, 1922.

DÖRRIES, H., " Die Entstehung und Formenbildung der niedersächsischen Stadt ", *Forsch. z. deutsch. Landes- u. Volkskde.*, Vol. XXVII, 1929.

——, *Die Städte im oberen Leinetat : Göttingen, Northeim und Einbeck*, Gottingen, 1925.

DOYON, G. and HABRECHT, R., *L'Architecture rurale et bourgeoise en France : Étude sur le technique d'autrefois et leurs applications à nôtre temps*, Paris, 1942.

ELY, R. T., and WEHRWEIN, G. S., *Land Economics*, New York, 1940.

ESPINAS, G., " Histoire Urbaine : Directions de recherches et resultats ", *Annales d'Histoire Économique et Sociale*, No. 21, 1933, and No. 34, 1935.

FLACH, J., *Origine des lieux habités en France, Enquête sur les conditions de l'habitation en France*, 1894.

FLEURE, H. J., " The Historic City in Western and Central Europe ", *Bulletin of the John Rylands Library*, Vol. 20, No. 2, 1936.

——, " City Morphology of Europe ", *Journal of the Royal Institution of Great Britain*, 1932.

——, " Some Types of Cities in Temperate Europe ", *Geographical Review*, Vol. X, 1920, pp. 357–74.

FRIEDRICH, W., " Die historische Geographie Böhmens bis zum Beginn der deutschen Kolonisation ", *Abh. d. k. k. Geog. Ges.*, Wien, Bd. IX, 1912, 209 pp.

GANSHOF, F. L., *Étude sur le développement des villes entre Loire et Rhin au Moyen Âge*, Brussels, 1943.
GANTNER, J., *Grundformen der Europäischen Stadt: Versuch eines historischen Aufbaues in Genealogien*, Vienna, 1928.
GEISLER, W., *Danzig, ein Siedlungsgeographischer Versuch*, Inaugural Dissertation, Halle-Wittenberg, 1918.
——, *Die Weichsellandschaft von Thorn bis Danzig*, Hamburg, 1922, with coloured map, scale 1 : 10,000.
——, Die Deutsche Stadt, Ein Beitrag zur Morphologie der Kulturlandschaft, *Forschungen z. deutschen Landes u. Volkskunde*, Vol. XXII, 5, 1924.
GERLACH, W., " Die Entstehungszeit der Stadtbefestigung in Deutschland ", *Leipziger Histor. Abh.*, XXXIV, 1913.
GERSTENBERG, K., *Ideen zu einer Kunstgeographie Europas*, Leipzig, 1922, 28 pp.
GIST, N. P., and HALBERT, L. A., *Urban Society*, New York, 1941.
GLASS, D. V., *The Town and a Changing Civilisation*, London, 1935.
GLÜCK, H., " Das kunstgeographische Bild Europas am Ende des Mittelalters und die Grundlagen der Renaissance ", *Monatsheft f. Kunstwissenschaft*, 1921.
GRADMANN, R., " Die städtischen Siedlungen des Königreichs Württemberg." *Forsch. z. dtsch. Landes- u. Volkskde.*, XXI, 1914, 89 pp.
——, *Süddeutschland*, 1931, 2 vols.
GRISEBACH, A., *Die Alte Deutsche Stadt in Ihrer Stammesgebiet*, 1930.
GROTELÜSCHEN, W., " Die Städte am Nordostrande der Eifel ", *Beitr. z. Landeskunde d. Rheinlande, Veröff. Geog. Inst. Univ. Bonn*, 2.Reihe, H.1, 1933. 112 pp.
HAMM, E., *Die Deutsche Stadt im Mittelalter*, 1935.
HAMPE, K., " Der Zug nach dem Osten. Die kolonisatorische Grosstat des deutschen. Volkes im Mittelalter ", *Natur und Geisteswelt*, No. 731, 1921.
HARRIS, Sir A., *Bomber Offensive*, London, 1947.
HAUFE, H., " Die Bevölkerung Europas ", *Neue Deutsche Forschungen, Abt. Volkslehre u. Gesellschaftskunde*, Band 7, Berlin, 1936.
HOENIG, A., *Deutscher Städtebau in Böhmen*, Prague, 1921. 42 plans.
HOLFORD, W. G., and EDEN, W. A., *The Future of Merseyside*, New Merseyside Series, No. 5, University of Liverpool Press, 1937.
HUGHES, T. H., and LAMBORN, A. E. G., *Towns and Town Planning, Ancient and Modern*, London, 1923.
JONES, CARADOG, D. (ed.), *The Social Survey of Merseyside*, 3 vols., Liverpool, 1934.
JULLIAN, C., *Histoire de la Gaule*, 8 Vols., 1920-9.
——, " Le Rôle des Monuments dans la formation topographique des Villes ", *Revue des Cours et Conférences*, 22e Année, No. 8, 1914.
KAINDL, R. F., *Geschichte der Deutschen in den Karpathenländern*, 3 vols. 1907-10.
KLAIBER, CH., *Die Grundrissgestaltung der deutschen Stadt im Mittelalter, unter besonderer Berücksichtigung der Schwäbischen Lande*, Berlin, 1912.
KLETLER, P., " Nordwesteuropas Verkehr, Handel und Gewerbe im frühen Mittelalter ", *Deutsche Kultur., Hist. Reihe*, H.2. 1924.
KOHL, J. G., *Der Verkehr und die Ansiedlungen der Menschen in ihrer Abhängigkeit von der Gestaltung der Erdoberfläche*, 2nd ed., Leipzig, 1850 ; 1st ed., 1841.
KÖTZSCHKE and EBERT, W., *Geschichte der ostdeutschen Kolonisation*, 1937. (Most scholarly study of recent years, with maps and full bibliography.)
KUHN, W., " Die deutschen Siedlungsräume in S.O. Europa ", *Deutsches Archiv. f. Landes- u. Volksforschung*, 1937.
LAUFFER, O., " Das Deutsche Haus in Dorf und Stadt ", *Wissenschaft und Bildung*, No. 152, 1919.
——, *Dorf und Stadt in Niederdeutschland*, Berlin, 1934, 234 pp.

LAVEDAN, P., *Qu'est-ce que l'Urbanisme?* 1926. Introduction to *L'Histoire de l'urbanisme.*

——, *Histoire de l'Urbanisme ; Antiquité—Moyen Âge,* Paris 1926.

——, *Histoire de l'Urbanisme : Renaissance et Temps Modernes,* Paris, 1941.

——, *Géographie des Villes,* Paris, 1936.

LEIGHLEY, J. B., *The Towns of Mälardalen in Sweden : A Study in Urban Morphology,* Univ. of California Publications in Geography, Vol. 3, No. 1, 1928, pp. 1–134.

——, *The Towns of Medieval Livonia,* Univ. of California Publications in Geography, Vol. 6, No. 7, 1939, pp. 235–314.

LEYDEN, FR., " Die Städte des flämischen Landes ", *Forsch. z. deutschen Landes- und Volkskunde,* 1924, 61 pp..

LIEPMANN, K., *The Journey to Work,* Kegan Paul,·London, 1944,

LOT, F., L'Histoire urbaine du Nord de la France de la fin du IIIe à la fin du XIe siècle, *Journal des Savants,* 1935.

MALECZYNSKI, K., " Die ältesten Märkte in Polen und ihr Verhältnis zu den Städten vor der Kolonisierung nach dem deutschen Recht ", *Osteuropa Institute,* Nr. 4, 1930.

MARTINY, R., " Die Grundrissgestaltung der Deutschen Siedlungen ", *Peterm. Mitt., Ergänzungsheft,* Nr. 197, 1928, 75 pp.

MAUNIER, R., *L'Origine et les Fonctions Économiques des Villes : Étude de Morphologie Sociale,* Paris, 1910.

MEIER, P. J., *Niedersächsischer Städteatlas, Die Braunschwiegischen Städte,* Abt. I (1926) and II (1933), Veröff. d. Hist. Kom. f. Niedersachsen.

METZ, F., " Die elsässischen Städte ", *Beitr z. Oberrhein. Landeskunde,* Breslau, 1927, pp. 203–21.

——, " Die Tyroler Stadt ", *Geog. Jahresber. aus Osterreich,* Bd. XVI, 1933, pp. 157–81.

MEURER, FR., *Die Mittelalterliche Stadtgrundries im nördlichen Deutschland in seiner Entwicklung zur Regelmässigkeit,* Berlin, 1914, 98 pp., 56 plans.

MEURIOT, P. M. S., *Des Agglomérations Urbaines dans l'Europe Contemporaine : Essai sur les causes, les conditions et les conséquences de leur développement,* Paris, 1898 (special reference to France).

MUKERJEE, R., *Man and His Habitation ; A Study in Social Ecology,* London, 1940.

MUMFORD, LEWIS, *The Culture of Cities,* London, 1938, with bibliography.

——, *Technics and Civilisation,* London, 1938.

OLBRICHT, K., " Die Entwicklung der deutschen Grosstädte seit dem Mittelalter ", *Geographischer Anzeiger,* 1926, pp. 70–2.

——, " Die Entwicklung der deutschen Städte seit dem Jahre 1910 ", *Geographischer Anzeiger,* 1930, pp. 311–14.

——, " Die Entwicklung der deutschen Grosstädte ", *Geographischer Anzeiger,* 1932, pp. 371–78 (useful maps).

——, " Die Entwicklung der deutschen Städte in den letzten acht Jahren ", *Geographischer Anzeiger,* 1934, pp. 247–52 (useful maps).

PARK, R. E., " Succession : An Ecological Concept ", *American Sociological Review,* April, 1936.

PASSARGE, S. (ed.), *Stadtlandschaften der Erde,* Hamburg, 1930.

PIRENNE, N., *Medieval Cities,* Princeton, N.Y., 1925.

——, *Economic and Social History of Medieval Europe,* 1937.

——, " Northern Towns and their Commerce ", *Cambridge Medieval History,* Vol. 6, pp. 505–27.

POËTE, M., *Introduction à l'Urbanisme,* Paris, 1928.

PROU, M., " Une ville-marché au XIIe siècle. Étampes, Seine-et-Oise ", *Mélanges d'Histoire offerts à H. Pirenne,* Tome 2, Brussels, 1926.

Püschel, A., " Das Anwachsen der deutschen Städte in der Zeit der mittelalterlichen Kolonialbewegung ", *Abh. z. Verkehrs. u. Seegeschichte*, Bd. IV, 1910.

Queen, S. A., and Thomas, L. F., *The City : A Study of Urbanism in the United States*, New York, 1939.

Quenedy, R., " L'Habitation urbaine et son évolution ", *Annales d'Histoire économique et sociale*, Vol. 6, January, 1934, pp. 62–8, and March, 1934, pp. 138–47.

Rauers, F., " Zur Geschichte der alten Handelsstrassen in Deutschland ", *Petermanns Mitt.* Vol. 52, 1906 ; also *Ver. f. Hansische Geschichte*, 1907.

Recknagel, M., " Die Städte und Märkte des bayerischen Donaugebiets ", *Mitt. d. Geog. Ges. München*, Bd. XX, H. 1, 1927.

Reichert, M., " Die Vorortsbildung der Süd- und Mitteldeutschen Grossstädte ", *Stuttgarter Geog. Studien*, Reihe A, Heft 54/55, 1936.

Rietschel, S., *Markt und Stadt in ihrem rechtlichen Verhältnis*, 1897.

——, *Die Civitas auf deutschem Boden*, Leipzig, 1894.

Rörig, F., " Die Gestaltung des Ostseeraumes durch das deutsche Bürgertum ", *Deutsches Archiv f. Landes- u. Volksforschung*, 1938.

Roxby, P. M., " Aspects of the Development of Merseyside ", *Geography*, xiv, 1927, pp. 91–100.

Sander, P., " Geschichte des deutschen Städtewesens ", *Bonner Staatswissenschaftl. Untersuchungen*, H. 6, 1922.

Schaefer, G., *Kungstgeographische Siedlungslandschaften und Städtebilder*, Dissertation, Basel, 1928, pp. 40–50.

——, *Kunstgeographischer Plan der Stadt Basel ;* 1 : 5,000, Basel, 1929.

Schirmer, R., " Die städtischen Siedlungen des Obermaingebiets und des Fichtelgebirges ", *Heimatkundl. Arbeiten. Geog. Inst. Univ. Erlangen*, H. 3, 1930.

Schlüter, O., " Über den Grundriss der Städte ", *Zeit. d. Ges. f. Erdkunde, zu Berlin*, vol. xxxiv, 1899.

——, Articles on (a) " Deutsches Siedlungswesen ", and (b) " Stadt ", *Hoops Reallexikon d. german. Altertumskunde*, Bd. I, 1911, pp. 402–39, and Bd. IV, 1918–19, pp. 240–44.

Schmoller, G., " Deutsches Städtewesen in älterer Zeit ", *Bonner Staatswissenschaftl. Untersuchungen*, H. 5, 1922.

Schönemann, K., " Die Entstehung des Städtewesens in S.O. Europa ", *Veröff, d. Arbeitsgemeinschaft f. sudosteuropäische Forschung an d. Univ. Berlin*, Bd. I, 1937.

Schott, S., *Die grossstädtischen Agglomerationen des Deutschen Reiches, 1787–1910.* Breslau, 1912.

Schrader, E., " Die Städte Hessens ", *Jahresber. d. Frankf. Ver. f. Geog. u. Statistik*, 1922.

Schuchhardt, K., *Die Burg im Wandel der Weltgeschichte*, 1931.

Schumacher, K., *Siedlungs u. Kulturgreschichte der Rheinlande*, 3 vols. 1921–5.

Schwan, Bruno, *Städtebau und Wohrungswesen der Welt*, Berlin, 1935.

Seeger, H. J., " Westfalens Handel und Gewerbe vom 9. bis 14. Jahrhundert ", *Stud. z. Gesch. d. Wirtsch. u. Geisteskultur*, Bd. I, 1926.

Sert, J. L., *Can Our Cities Survive ?* Harvard, 1943.

Sidaritsch, M., " Die steirischen Städte und Märkte ", *Zur Geographie der deutschen Alpen, Festschrift zu R. Sieger.*, 1924.

Siedler, E. J., *Märkischer Städtebau im Mittelalter*, Berlin, 1914 (with numerous plans).

Simon, Sir E., *The Rebuilding of Manchester*, London, 1938.

——, *Rebuilding Britain*, London, 1945.

Sitte, C., *L'Art de Bâtir les Villes*, Paris, 1902 (1st edition in German, Vienna, 1889).

SMITH, W., *The Distribution of Population and the Location of Industry on Merseyside*, University of Liverpool Social Science Dept., Statistics Division, Univ. of Liverpool Press, 1942.

SÖLCH, J., " Die Städte in der vortechnischen Kulturlandschaft Englands ", *Geog. Zeitschr.*, XLIV, 1938, pp. 41–56.

SOMBART, W., " Ursprung und Wesen der Stadt ", Vol. II in *Das Moderne Kapitalismus*, 4 vols., Munich, 1902–7.

——, " Der Begriff Stadt und das Wesen der Stadtbildung ", *Archiv f. Sozialwissenschaft und Sozialpolitik*, Bd. XXV, Berlin, 1907.

SOULAS, J., " Les Conurbation Françaises ", *Annales de Géographie*, 1939, pp. 466–78.

——, " Villes-Marchés et Villes à Industrie de Haute Normandie ", *Annales de Géographie*, Vol. 45, 1936, pp. 399–413.

STEIN, W., " Handels- u. Verkehrsgeschichte der deutschen Kaiserzeit ", *Abh. z. Verkehrs- u. Seegeschichte*, Bd. X, 1922.

——, (*a*) " Deutscher Handel ", and (*b*) " Verkehrswesen ", *Hoops Reallexikon*. Bd. II, 1913–15, pp. 373–410 ; and Bd. IV, 1918–19, pp. 390–99.

STEPHENSON, C., " Borough and Town : A Study of Urban Origins in England ", *Monographs of the Mediaeval Academy of America*, No. 7, 1933.

STUEBBEN, J., *Der Städtebau*, Berlin, 1890.

SUMMERSON, J., *Georgian London*, 1947.

TAYLOR, G., " Environment, Village and City : A Genetic Approach to Urban Geography ", *Annals of the Assn. of Am. Geographers*, xxxii, 1942, pp. 1–67.

TOUT, T. F., *Medieval Town Planning*, Manchester, 1934.

VERCAUTEREN, F., *Étude sur les Civitates de la Belgique Seconde*, *Académie Royale de Belgipue*, Sér. 2, Vol. 33, Brussels, 1934.

VOGEL, W., " Die Ordenskolonisation in den südlichen Küstenländern der Ostsee ", *Verhdl. u. wissenschaftl. Abh. d. 24. Deutschen Geographentages, Danzig, 1931*, 1932.

WALKER, M. L., *Urban Blight and Slums : Economic and Legal Factors in Their Origin, Reclamation and Prevention*, Harvard Planning Studies, xii, 1928.

WEBER, ADNA F., *Growth of Cities in the Nineteenth Century. A Study in Statistics*, 1899.

WEIZSACKER, W., " Eindringen und Verbreitung der deutschen Stadtrechte in Böhmen und Mähren ", *Deutsches Archiv f. Landes- u. Volksforschung*, 1937, pp. 95–109.

WELLER, K., " Die staufische Städtegründung im schwäbischen Württemberg ", *Vierteljahrschr. f. Landesgeschichte, Neue Folge*, Jhrg. XXXVI, H. 3 and 4, 1937.

WELTE, A., " Die Verstädterung Mittel- und Westeuropas, 1830–1930 ", *Zeit. f. Geopolitik*, Vol. 13, 1937, pp. 217–26 and 351–58.

ZEHE, E., " Die Städte des Schwarzwaldes ", *Heimatkundl. Arbeiten Geog. Inst. Univ. Erlangen*, H. 4, 1930, 42 pp.

ZUCKER, P., *Die Entwicklung des Stadtbildes*, Munich, 1929.

Note—Among publications that have appeared during the 'fifties, special reference may be made to the following.

BARRÈRE, P., " Les Quartiers de l'Agglomération bordelaise", *Revue Géog. d. Pyrenées et du SO*, Tome XXVII, 1956, pp. 5–40, 161–94, 268–300.

CHARDONNET, J., *Metropoles Economiques* (Studies of London, Amsterdam, Antwerp, Liège, Frankfurt, Mannheim, Nuremberg, Linz, Barcelona, Genoa, Naples, New York), Cahiers de la Fondation Nationale des Sciences Politiques, Paris, 1959.

CHOMBART DE LAUWE, P. H., *Paris et l'Agglomération parisienne*, 2 vols., Paris, 1952.

COPPOLANI, J., *Toulouse : Etude de Géographie Urbaine*, Toulouse, Privat, 1954.

——, " Agglomérations et Conurbations dans le Midi Aquitain et Languedoc ", *Revue Géog. d. Pyrenées et du SO*, Tome XXVIII, 1957, pp. 337–88.

FREEMAN, T. W., *The Conurbations of Great Britain*, Manchester, 1959.

——, *Geography and Planning*, London, 1957.

GALLION, A. B., *The Urban Pattern : City Planning and Design*, New York, 1953.

GEORGE, P., *La Ville : Le Fait urbain à travers le monde*, Paris, 1952.

HAWLEY, A., *A Theory of Community Structure*, New York, 1950.

" Die Heutige Struktur deutscher Grosstädte", *Die Erde*, 1954, pp. 64–111.

INTERNATIONAL URBAN RESEARCH, *The World's Metropolitan Areas*, Berkeley, 1959.

SCHOLLER, P., " Aufgaben und Probleme der Stadtgeographie ", *Erdkunde*, Band 7, 1953, pp. 161–84. Contains long bibliography.

SCHULTZE, J. H., *Zum Problem der Weltstadt*, Festschrift z. 32 Deutschen Geog. Tag, Berlin, 1959.

Special attention is drawn to many articles that have appeared in *Raumforschung und Raumordnung* (quarterly), Bad Godesberg, and to monographs in the *Forschungen zur deutschen Landeskunde*, Remagen, as well as the standard periodicals for geography and town planning.

INDEX

(Numbers in italics indicate figures in text)

Routledge Social Science Series

Routledge & Kegan Paul   London and Boston

68–74 Carter Lane   London EC4V 5EL
9 Park Street   Boston   Mass 02108

Contents

*Authors wishing to submit manuscripts for any series in
this catalogue should send them to the Social Science Editor,
Routledge & Kegan Paul Ltd, 68–74 Carter Lane,
London EC4V 5EL*

●*Books so marked are available in paperback*
All books are in Metric Demy 8vo format (216 × 138mm approx.)

International Library of Sociology

General Editor John Rex

GENERAL SOCIOLOGY

Barnsley, J. H. The Social Reality of Ethics. *464 pp.*
Belshaw, Cyril. The Conditions of Social Performance. *An Exploratory Theory. 144 pp.*
Brown, Robert. Explanation in Social Science. *208 pp.*
● Rules and Laws in Sociology. *192 pp.*
Bruford, W. H. Chekhov and His Russia. *A Sociological Study. 244 pp.*
Cain, Maureen E. Society and the Policeman's Role. *326 pp.*
Gibson, Quentin. The Logic of Social Enquiry. *240 pp.*
Glucksmann, M. Structuralist Analysis in Contemporary Social Thought. *212 pp.*
Gurvitch, Georges. Sociology of Law. *Preface by Roscoe Pound. 264 pp.*
Hodge, H. A. Wilhelm Dilthey. *An Introduction. 184 pp.*
Homans, George C. Sentiments and Activities. *336 pp.*
Johnson, Harry M. Sociology: *a Systematic Introduction. Foreword by Robert K. Merton. 710 pp.*
Mannheim, Karl. Essays on Sociology and Social Psychology. *Edited by Paul Keckskemeti. With Editorial Note by Adolph Lowe. 344 pp.*
Systematic Sociology: *An Introduction to the Study of Society. Edited by J. S. Erös and Professor W. A. C. Stewart. 220 pp.*
Martindale, Don. The Nature and Types of Sociological Theory. *292 pp.*
●**Maus, Heinz.** A Short History of Sociology. *234 pp.*
Mey, Harald. Field-Theory. *A Study of its Application in the Social Sciences. 352 pp.*
Myrdal, Gunnar. Value in Social Theory: *A Collection of Essays on Methodology. Edited by Paul Streeten. 332 pp.*
Ogburn, William F., and **Nimkoff, Meyer F.** A Handbook of Sociology. *Preface by Karl Mannheim. 656 pp. 46 figures. 35 tables.*
Parsons, Talcott, and **Smelser, Neil J.** Economy and Society: *A Study in the Integration of Economic and Social Theory. 362 pp.*
●**Rex, John.** Key Problems of Sociological Theory. *220 pp.*
Discovering Sociology. *278 pp.*
Sociology and the Demystification of the Modern World. *282 pp.*
●**Rex, John** (Ed.) Approaches to Sociology. *Contributions by Peter Abell, Frank Bechhofer, Basil Bernstein, Ronald Fletcher, David Frisby, Miriam Glucksmann, Peter Lassman, Herminio Martins, John Rex, Roland Robertson, John Westergaard and Jock Young. 302 pp.*
Rigby, A. Alternative Realities. *352 pp.*
Roche, M. Phenomenology, Language and the Social Sciences. *374 pp.*
Sahay, A. Sociological Analysis. *220 pp.*
Urry, John. Reference Groups and the Theory of Revolution. *244 pp.*
Weinberg, E. Development of Sociology in the Soviet Union. *173 pp.*

FOREIGN CLASSICS OF SOCIOLOGY

●**Durkheim, Emile.** Suicide. *A Study in Sociology. Edited and with an Intro-duction by George Simpson. 404 pp.*
Professional Ethics and Civic Morals. *Translated by Cornelia Brookfield. 288 pp.*
●**Gerth, H. H., and Mills, C. Wright.** From Max Weber: *Essays in Sociology. 502 pp.*
●**Tönnies, Ferdinand.** Community and Association. (*Gemeinschaft und Gesellschaft.) Translated and Supplemented by Charles P. Loomis. Foreword by Pitirim A. Sorokin. 334 pp.*

SOCIAL STRUCTURE

Andreski, Stanislav. Military Organization and Society. *Foreword by Professor A. R. Radcliffe-Brown. 226 pp. 1 folder.*
Coontz, Sydney H. Population Theories and the Economic Interpretation. *202 pp.*
Coser, Lewis. The Functions of Social Conflict. *204 pp.*
Dickie-Clark, H. F. Marginal Situation: *A Sociological Study of a Coloured Group. 240 pp. 11 tables.*
Glaser, Barney, and Strauss, Anselm L. Status Passage. *A Formal Theory. 208 pp.*
Glass, D. V. (Ed.) Social Mobility in Britain. *Contributions by J. Berent, T. Bottomore, R. C. Chambers, J. Floud, D. V. Glass, J. R. Hall, H. T. Himmelweit, R. K. Kelsall, F. M. Martin, C. A. Moser, R. Mukherjee, and W. Ziegel. 420 pp.*
Jones, Garth N. Planned Organizational Change: *An Exploratory Study Using an Empirical Approach. 268 pp.*
Kelsall, R. K. Higher Civil Servants in Britain: *From 1870 to the Present Day. 268 pp. 31 tables.*
König, René. The Community. *232 pp. Illustrated.*
●**Lawton, Denis.** Social Class, Language and Education. *192 pp.*
McLeish, John. The Theory of Social Change: *Four Views Considered. 128 pp.*
Marsh, David C. The Changing Social Structure of England and Wales, 1871-1961. *288 pp.*
Mouzelis, Nicos. Organization and Bureaucracy. *An Analysis of Modern Theories. 240 pp.*
Mulkay, M. J. Functionalism, Exchange and Theoretical Strategy. *272 pp.*
Ossowski, Stanislaw. Class Structure in the Social Consciousness. *210 pp.*
Podgórecki, Adam. Law and Society. *About 300 pp.*

SOCIOLOGY AND POLITICS

Acton, T. A. Gypsy Politics and Social Change. *316 pp.*
Hechter, Michael. Internal Colonialism. *The Celtic Fringe in British National Development, 1536–1966. About 350 pp.*
Hertz, Frederick. Nationality in History and Politics: *A Psychology and Sociology of National Sentiment and Nationalism. 432 pp.*

Kornhauser, William. The Politics of Mass Society. *272 pp. 20 tables.*

Laidler, Harry W. History of Socialism. *Social-Economic Movements: An Historical and Comparative Survey of Socialism, Communism, Co-operation, Utopianism; and other Systems of Reform and Reconstruction. 992 pp.*

Lasswell, H. D. Analysis of Political Behaviour. *324 pp.*

Mannheim, Karl. Freedom, Power and Democratic Planning. *Edited by Hans Gerth and Ernest K. Bramstedt. 424 pp.*

Mansur, Fatma. Process of Independence. *Foreword by A. H. Hanson. 208 pp.*

Martin, David A. Pacifism: *an Historical and Sociological Study. 262 pp.*

Myrdal, Gunnar. The Political Element in the Development of Economic Theory. *Translated from the German by Paul Streeten. 282 pp.*

Wootton, Graham. Workers, Unions and the State. *188 pp.*

FOREIGN AFFAIRS: THEIR SOCIAL, POLITICAL AND ECONOMIC FOUNDATIONS

Mayer, J. P. Political Thought in France from the Revolution to the Fifth Republic. *164 pp.*

CRIMINOLOGY

Ancel, Marc. Social Defence: *A Modern Approach to Criminal Problems. Foreword by Leon Radzinowicz. 240 pp.*

Cain, Maureen E. Society and the Policeman's Role. *326 pp.*

Cloward, Richard A., and **Ohlin, Lloyd E.** Delinquency and Opportunity: *A Theory of Delinquent Gangs. 248 pp.*

Downes, David M. The Delinquent Solution. *A Study in Subcultural Theory. 296 pp.*

Dunlop, A. B., and **McCabe, S.** Young Men in Detention Centres. *192 pp.*

Friedlander, Kate. The Psycho-Analytical Approach to Juvenile Delinquency: *Theory, Case Studies, Treatment. 320 pp.*

Glueck, Sheldon, and **Eleanor.** Family Environment and Delinquency. *With the statistical assistance of Rose W. Kneznek. 340 pp.*

Lopez-Rey, Manuel. Crime. *An Analytical Appraisal. 288 pp.*

Mannheim, Hermann. Comparative Criminology: *a Text Book. Two volumes. 442 pp. and 380 pp.*

Morris, Terence. The Criminal Area: *A Study in Social Ecology. Foreword by Hermann Mannheim. 232 pp. 25 tables. 4 maps.*

Rock, Paul. Making People Pay. *338 pp.*

●**Taylor, Ian, Walton, Paul,** and **Young, Jock.** The New Criminology. *For a Social Theory of Deviance. 325 pp.*

SOCIAL PSYCHOLOGY

Bagley, Christopher. The Social Psychology of the Epileptic Child. *320 pp.*

Barbu, Zevedei. Problems of Historical Psychology. *248 pp.*

Blackburn, Julian. Psychology and the Social Pattern. *184 pp.*

●**Brittan, Arthur.** Meanings and Situations. *224 pp.*

Carroll, J. Break-Out from the Crystal Palace. *200 pp.*

●**Fleming, C. M.** Adolescence: Its Social Psychology. *With an Introduction to recent findings from the fields of Anthropology, Physiology, Medicine, Psychometrics and Sociometry. 288 pp.*

● The Social Psychology of Education: *An Introduction and Guide to Its Study. 136 pp.*

Homans, George C. The Human Group. *Foreword by Bernard DeVoto. Introduction by Robert K. Merton. 526 pp.*

● Social Behaviour: *its Elementary Forms. 416 pp.*

●**Klein, Josephine.** The Study of Groups. *226 pp. 31 figures. 5 tables.*

Linton, Ralph. The Cultural Background of Personality. *132 pp.*

●**Mayo, Elton.** The Social Problems of an Industrial Civilization. *With an appendix on the Political Problem. 180 pp.*

Ottaway, A. K. C. Learning Through Group Experience. *176 pp.*

Ridder, J. C. de. The Personality of the Urban African in South Africa. *A Thermatic Apperception Test Study. 196 pp. 12 plates.*

●**Rose, Arnold M.** (Ed.) Human Behaviour and Social Processes: *an Interactionist Approach. Contributions by Arnold M. Rose, Ralph H. Turner, Anselm Strauss, Everett C. Hughes, E. Franklin Frazier, Howard S. Becker, et al. 696 pp.*

Smelser, Neil J. Theory of Collective Behaviour. *448 pp.*

Stephenson, Geoffrey M. The Development of Conscience. *128 pp.*

Young, Kimball. Handbook of Social Psychology. *658 pp. 16 figures. 10 tables.*

SOCIOLOGY OF THE FAMILY

Banks, J. A. Prosperity and Parenthood: *A Study of Family Planning among The Victorian Middle Classes. 262 pp.*

Bell, Colin R. Middle Class Families: *Social and Geographical Mobility. 224 pp.*

Burton, Lindy. Vulnerable Children. *272 pp.*

Gavron, Hannah. The Captive Wife: *Conflicts of Household Mothers. 190 pp.*

George, Victor, and **Wilding, Paul.** Motherless Families. *220 pp.*

Klein, Josephine. Samples from English Cultures.

   1. Three Preliminary Studies and Aspects of Adult Life in England. *447 pp.*

   2. Child-Rearing Practices and Index. *247 pp.*

Klein, Viola. Britain's Married Women Workers. *180 pp.*

The Feminine Character. *History of an Ideology. 244 pp.*

McWhinnie, Alexina M. Adopted Children. *How They Grow Up. 304 pp.*

● **Myrdal, Alva,** and **Klein, Viola.** Women's Two Roles: *Home and Work. 238 pp. 27 tables.*

Parsons, Talcott, and **Bales, Robert F.** Family: Socialization and Interaction Process. *In collaboration with James Olds, Morris Zelditch and Philip E. Slater. 456 pp. 50 figures and tables.*

SOCIAL SERVICES

Bastide, Roger. The Sociology of Mental Disorder. *Translated from the French by Jean McNeil. 260 pp.*

Carlebach, Julius. Caring For Children in Trouble. *266 pp.*

Forder, R. A. (Ed.) Penelope Hall's Social Services of England and Wales. *352 pp.*

George, Victor. Foster Care. *Theory and Practice. 234 pp.*
Social Security: *Beveridge and After. 258 pp.*

George, V., and **Wilding, P.** Motherless Families. *248 pp.*

● **Goetschius, George W.** Working with Community Groups. *256 pp.*

Goetschius, George W., and **Tash, Joan.** Working with Unattached Youth. *416 pp.*

Hall, M. P., and **Howes, I. V.** The Church in Social Work. *A Study of Moral Welfare Work undertaken by the Church of England. 320 pp.*

Heywood, Jean S. Children in Care: *the Development of the Service for the Deprived Child. 264 pp.*

Hoenig, J., and **Hamilton, Marian W.** The De-Segregation of the Mentally Ill. *284 pp.*

Jones, Kathleen. Mental Health and Social Policy, 1845-1959. *264 pp.*

King, Roy D., Raynes, Norma V., and **Tizard, Jack.** Patterns of Residential Care. *356 pp.*

Leigh, John. Young People and Leisure. *256 pp.*

Morris, Mary. Voluntary Work and the Welfare State. *300 pp.*

Morris, Pauline. Put Away: *A Sociological Study of Institutions for the Mentally Retarded. 364 pp.*

Nokes, P. L. The Professional Task in Welfare Practice. *152 pp.*

Timms, Noel. Psychiatric Social Work in Great Britain (1939-1962). *280 pp.*

● Social Casework: *Principles and Practice. 256 pp.*

Young, A. F. Social Services in British Industry. *272 pp.*

Young, A. F., and **Ashton, E. T.** British Social Work in the Nineteenth Century. *288 pp.*

SOCIOLOGY OF EDUCATION

Banks, Olive. Parity and Prestige in English Secondary Education: a Study in Educational Sociology. *272 pp.*

Bentwich, Joseph. Education in Israel. *224 pp. 8 pp. plates.*

● **Blyth, W. A. L.** English Primary Education. *A Sociological Description.*
1. Schools. *232 pp.*
2. Background. *168 pp.*

Collier, K. G. The Social Purposes of Education: *Personal and Social Values in Education. 268 pp.*

Dale, R. R., and **Griffith, S.** Down Stream: *Failure in the Grammar School.* *108 pp.*

Dore, R. P. Education in Tokugawa Japan. *356 pp. 9 pp. plates.*

Evans, K. M. Sociometry and Education. *158 pp.*

● **Ford, Julienne.** Social Class and the Comprehensive School. *192 pp.*

Foster, P. J. Education and Social Change in Ghana. *336 pp. 3 maps.*

Fraser, W. R. Education and Society in Modern France. *150 pp.*

Grace, Gerald R. Role Conflict and the Teacher. *About 200 pp.*

Hans, Nicholas. New Trends in Education in the Eighteenth Century. *278 pp. 19 tables.*

●   Comparative Education: *A Study of Educational Factors and Traditions.* *360 pp.*

Hargreaves, David. Interpersonal Relations and Education. *432 pp.*

●   Social Relations in a Secondary School. *240 pp.*

Holmes, Brian. Problems in Education. *A Comparative Approach. 336 pp.*

King, Ronald. Values and Involvement in a Grammar School. *164 pp.*

  School Organization and Pupil Involvement. *A Study of Secondary Schools.*

● **Mannheim, Karl,** and **Stewart, W. A. C.** An Introduction to the Sociology of Education. *206 pp.*

Morris, Raymond N. The Sixth Form and College Entrance. *231 pp.*

● **Musgrove, F.** Youth and the Social Order. *176 pp.*

● **Ottaway, A. K. C.** Education and Society: An Introduction to the Sociology of Education. *With an Introduction by W. O. Lester Smith. 212 pp.*

Peers, Robert. Adult Education: *A Comparative Study. 398 pp.*

Pritchard, D. G. Education and the Handicapped: *1760 to 1960. 258 pp.*

Richardson, Helen. Adolescent Girls in Approved Schools. *308 pp.*

Stratta, Erica. The Education of Borstal Boys. *A Study of their Educational Experiences prior to, and during, Borstal Training. 256 pp.*

Taylor, P. H., Reid, W. A., and **Holley, B. J.** The English Sixth Form. *A Case Study in Curriculum Research. 200 pp.*

SOCIOLOGY OF CULTURE

Eppel, E. M., and **M.** Adolescents and Morality: *A Study of some Moral Values and Dilemmas of Working Adolescents in the Context of a changing Climate of Opinion. Foreword by W. J. H. Sprott. 268 pp. 39 tables.*

● **Fromm, Erich.** The Fear of Freedom. *286 pp.*

●   The Sane Society. *400 pp.*

Mannheim, Karl. Essays on the Sociology of Culture. *Edited by Ernst Mannheim in co-operation with Paul Kecskemeti. Editorial Note by Adolph Lowe. 280 pp.*

Weber, Alfred. Farewell to European History: *or The Conquest of Nihilism. Translated from the German by R. F. C. Hull. 224 pp.*

SOCIOLOGY OF RELIGION

Argyle, Michael and **Beit-Hallahmi, Benjamin.** The Social Psychology of Religion. *About 256 pp.*
Nelson, G. K. Spiritualism and Society. *313 pp.*
Stark, Werner. The Sociology of Religion. *A Study of Christendom.*
  Volume I. *Established Religion. 248 pp.*
  Volume II. *Sectarian Religion. 368 pp.*
  Volume III. *The Universal Church. 464 pp.*
  Volume IV. *Types of Religious Man. 352 pp.*
  Volume V. *Types of Religious Culture. 464 pp.*
Turner, B. S. Weber and Islam. *216 pp.*
Watt, W. Montgomery. Islam and the Integration of Society. *320 pp.*

SOCIOLOGY OF ART AND LITERATURE

Jarvie, Ian C. Towards a Sociology of the Cinema. *A Comparative Essay on the Structure and Functioning of a Major Entertainment Industry. 405 pp.*
Rust, Frances S. Dance in Society. *An Analysis of the Relationships between the Social Dance and Society in England from the Middle Ages to the Present Day. 256 pp. 8 pp. of plates.*
Schücking, L. L. The Sociology of Literary Taste. *112 pp.*
Wolff, Janet. Hermeneutic Philosophy and the Sociology of Art. *About 200 pp.*

SOCIOLOGY OF KNOWLEDGE

Diesing, P. Patterns of Discovery in the Social Sciences. *262 pp.*
● **Douglas, J. D.** (Ed.) Understanding Everyday Life. *370 pp.*
● **Hamilton, P.** Knowledge and Social Structure. *174 pp.*
Jarvie, I. C. Concepts and Society. *232 pp.*
Mannheim, Karl. Essays on the Sociology of Knowledge. *Edited by Paul Kecskemeti. Editorial Note by Adolph Lowe. 353 pp.*
Remmling, Gunter W. (Ed.) Towards the Sociology of Knowledge. *Origin and Development of a Sociological Thought Style. 463 pp.*
Stark, Werner. The Sociology of Knowledge: *An Essay in Aid of a Deeper Understanding of the History of Ideas. 384 pp.*

URBAN SOCIOLOGY

Ashworth, William. The Genesis of Modern British Town Planning: *A Study in Economic and Social History of the Nineteenth and Twentieth Centuries. 288 pp.*
Cullingworth, J. B. Housing Needs and Planning Policy: *A Restatement of the Problems of Housing Need and 'Overspill' in England and Wales. 232 pp. 44 tables. 8 maps.*

Dickinson, Robert E. City and Region: *A Geographical Interpretation* *608 pp. 125 figures.*
The West European City: *A Geographical Interpretation. 600 pp. 129 maps. 29 plates.*
● The City Region in Western Europe. *320 pp. Maps.*
Humphreys, Alexander J. New Dubliners: *Urbanization and the Irish Family. Foreword by George C. Homans. 304 pp.*
Jackson, Brian. Working Class Community: *Some General Notions raised by a Series of Studies in Northern England. 192 pp.*
Jennings, Hilda. Societies in the Making: *a Study of Development and Re-development within a County Borough. Foreword by D. A. Clark. 286 pp.*
●**Mann, P. H.** An Approach to Urban Sociology. *240 pp.*
Morris, R. N., and **Mogey, J.** The Sociology of Housing. *Studies at Berinsfield. 232 pp. 4 pp. plates.*
Rosser, C., and **Harris, C.** The Family and Social Change. *A Study of Family and Kinship in a South Wales Town. 352 pp. 8 maps.*

RURAL SOCIOLOGY

Chambers, R. J. H. Settlement Schemes in Tropical Africa: *A Selective Study. 268 pp.*
Haswell, M. R. The Economics of Development in Village India. *120 pp.*
Littlejohn, James. Westrigg: *the Sociology of a Cheviot Parish. 172 pp. 5 figures.*
Mayer, Adrian C. Peasants in the Pacific. *A Study of Fiji Indian Rural Society. 248 pp. 20 plates.*
Williams, W. M. The Sociology of an English Village: *Gosforth. 272 pp. 12 figures. 13 tables.*

SOCIOLOGY OF INDUSTRY AND DISTRIBUTION

Anderson, Nels. Work and Leisure. *280 pp.*
●**Blau, Peter M.,** and **Scott, W. Richard.** Formal Organizations: *a Comparative approach. Introduction and Additional Bibliography by J. H. Smith. 326 pp.*
Eldridge, J. E. T. Industrial Disputes. *Essays in the Sociology of Industrial Relations. 288 pp.*
Hetzler, Stanley. Applied Measures for Promoting Technological Growth. *352 pp.*
Technological Growth and Social Change. *Achieving Modernization. 269 pp.*
Hollowell, Peter G. The Lorry Driver. *272 pp.*
Jefferys, Margot, *with the assistance of Winifred Moss.* Mobility in the Labour Market: *Employment Changes in Battersea and Dagenham. Preface by Barbara Wootton. 186 pp. 51 tables.*

Millerson, Geoffrey. The Qualifying Associations: *a Study in Professionalization. 320 pp.*

Smelser, Neil J. Social Change in the Industrial Revolution: *An Application of Theory to the Lancashire Cotton Industry, 1770-1840. 468 pp. 12 figures. 14 tables.*

Williams, Gertrude. Recruitment to Skilled Trades. *240 pp.*

Young, A. F. Industrial Injuries Insurance: *an Examination of British Policy. 192 pp.*

DOCUMENTARY

Schlesinger, Rudolf (Ed.) Changing Attitudes in Soviet Russia.
2. The Nationalities Problem and Soviet Administration. *Selected Readings on the Development of Soviet Nationalities Policies. Introduced by the editor. Translated by W. W. Gottlieb. 324 pp.*

ANTHROPOLOGY

Ammar, Hamed. Growing up in an Egyptian Village: *Silwa, Province of Aswan. 336 pp.*

Brandel-Syrier, Mia. Reeftown Elite. *A Study of Social Mobility in a Modern African Community on the Reef. 376 pp.*

Crook, David, and **Isabel.** Revolution in a Chinese Village: *Ten Mile Inn. 230 pp. 8 plates. 1 map.*

Dickie-Clark, H. F. The Marginal Situation. *A Sociological Study of a Coloured Group. 236 pp.*

Dube, S. C. Indian Village. *Foreword by Morris Edward Opler. 276 pp. 4 plates.*

India's Changing Villages: *Human Factors in Community Development. 260 pp. 8 plates. 1 map.*

Firth, Raymond. Malay Fishermen. *Their Peasant Economy. 420 pp. 17 pp. plates.*

Firth, R., Hubert, J., and **Forge, A.** Families and their Relatives. *Kinship in a Middle-Class Sector of London: An Anthropological Study. 456 pp.*

Gulliver, P. H. Social Control in an African Society: a Study of the Arusha, Agricultural Masai of Northern Tanganyika. *320 pp. 8 plates. 10 figures.*

Family Herds. *288 pp.*

Ishwaran, K. Shivapur. *A South Indian Village. 216 pp.*

Tradition and Economy in Village India: *An Interactionist Approach. Foreword by Conrad Arensburg. 176 pp.*

Jarvie, Ian C. The Revolution in Anthropology. *268 pp.*

Jarvie, Ian C., and **Agassi, Joseph.** Hong Kong. *A Society in Transition. 396 pp. Illustrated with plates and maps.*

Little, Kenneth L. Mende of Sierra Leone. *308 pp. and folder.*

Negroes in Britain. *With a New Introduction and Contemporary Study by Leonard Bloom. 320 pp.*

11

Lowie, Robert H. Social Organization. *494 pp.*

Mayer, Adrian,C. Caste and Kinship in Central India: *A Village and its Region. 328 pp. 16 plates. 15 figures. 16 tables.*
Peasants in the Pacific. *A Study of Fiji Indian Rural Society. 248 pp.*

Smith, Raymond T. The Negro Family in British Guiana: *Family Structure and Social Status in the Villages. With a Foreword by Meyer Fortes. 314 pp. 8 plates. 1 figure. 4 maps.*

SOCIOLOGY AND PHILOSOPHY

Barnsley, John H. The Social Reality of Ethics. *A Comparative Analysis of Moral Codes. 448 pp.*

Diesing, Paul. Patterns of Discovery in the Social Sciences. *362 pp.*

●**Douglas, Jack D.** (Ed.) Understanding Everyday Life. *Toward the Reconstruction of Sociological Knowledge. Contributions by Alan F. Blum. Aaron W. Cicourel, Norman K. Denzin, Jack D. Douglas, John Heeren, Peter McHugh, Peter K. Manning, Melvin Power, Matthew Speier, Roy Turner, D. Lawrence Wieder, Thomas P. Wilson and Don H. Zimmerman. 370 pp.*

Jarvie, Ian C. Concepts and Society. *216 pp.*

Pelz, Werner. The Scope of Understanding in Sociology. *Towards a more radical reorientation in the social humanistic sciences. 283 pp.*

Roche, Maurice. Phenomenology, Language and the Social Sciences. *371 pp.*

Sahay, Arun. Sociological Analysis. *212 pp.*

Sklair, Leslie. The Sociology of Progress. *320 pp.*

International Library of Anthropology

General Editor Adam Kuper

Brown, Paula. The Chimbu. *A Study of Change in the New Guinea Highlands. 151 pp.*

Lloyd, P. C. Power and Independence. *Urban Africans' Perception of Social Inequality. 264 pp.*

Pettigrew, Joyce. Robber Noblemen. *A Study of the Political System of the Sikh Jats. 284 pp.*

Van Den Berghe, Pierre L. Power and Privilege at an African University. *278 pp.*

International Library of Social Policy

General Editor Kathleen Jones

Bayley, M. Mental Handicap and Community Care. *426 pp.*

Butler, J. R. Family Doctors and Public Policy. *208 pp.*

Holman, Robert. Trading in Children. *A Study of Private Fostering. 355 pp.*

Jones, Kathleen. History of the Mental Health Service. *428 pp.*
Thomas, J. E. The English Prison Officer since 1850: *A Study in Conflict.*
258 pp.
Woodward, J. To Do the Sick No Harm. *A Study of the British Voluntary Hospital System to 1875. About 220 pp.*

International Library of Welfare and Philosophy

General Editors Noel Timms and David Watson

● **Plant, Raymond.** Community and Ideology. *104 pp.*

Primary Socialization, Language and Education

General Editor Basil Bernstein

Bernstein, Basil. Class, Codes and Control. *2 volumes.*
1. *Theoretical Studies Towards a Sociology of Language. 254 pp.*
2. *Applied Studies Towards a Sociology of Language. About 400 pp.*
Brandis, W., and **Bernstein, B.** Selection and Control. *176 pp.*
Brandis, Walter, and **Henderson, Dorothy.** Social Class, Language and
Communication. *288 pp.*
Cook-Gumperz, Jenny. Social Control and Socialization. *A Study of Class
Differences in the Language of Maternal Control. 290 pp.*
● **Gahagan, D. M.,** and **G. A.** Talk Reform. *Exploration in Language for Infant
School Children. 160 pp.*
Robinson, W. P., and **Rackstraw, Susan D. A.** A Question of Answers.
2 volumes. 192 pp. and 180 pp.
Turner, Geoffrey J., and **Mohan, Bernard A.** A Linguistic Description and
Computer Programme for Children's Speech. *208 pp.*

Reports of the Institute of Community Studies

Cartwright, Ann. Human Relations and Hospital Care. *272 pp.*
● Parents and Family Planning Services. *306 pp.*
Patients and their Doctors. *A Study of General Practice. 304 pp.*
● **Jackson, Brian.** Streaming: *an Education System in Miniature. 168 pp.*
Jackson, Brian, and **Marsden, Dennis.** Education and the Working Class:
*Some General Themes raised by a Study of 88 Working-class Children
in a Northern Industrial City. 268 pp. 2 folders.*
Marris, Peter. The Experience of Higher Education. *232 pp. 27 tables.*
Loss and Change. *192 pp.*

Marris, Peter, and **Rein, Martin.** Dilemmas of Social Reform. *Poverty and Community Action in the United States. 256 pp.*

Marris, Peter, and **Somerset, Anthony.** African Businessmen. *A Study of Entrepreneurship and Development in Kenya. 256 pp.*

Mills, Richard. Young Outsiders: *a Study in Alternative Communities. 216 pp.*

Runciman, W. G. Relative Deprivation and Social Justice. *A Study of Attitudes to Social Inequality in Twentieth-Century England. 352 pp.*

Willmott, Peter. Adolescent Boys in East London. *230 pp.*

Willmott, Peter, and **Young, Michael.** Family and Class in a London Suburb. *202 pp. 47 tables.*

Young, Michael. Innovation and Research in Education. *192 pp.*

●**Young, Michael,** and **McGeeney, Patrick.** Learning Begins at Home. *A Study of a Junior School and its Parents. 128 pp.*

Young, Michael, and **Willmott, Peter.** Family and Kinship in East London. *Foreword by Richard M. Titmuss. 252 pp. 39 tables.*

The Symmetrical Family. *410 pp.*

Reports of the Institute for Social Studies in Medical Care

Cartwright, Ann, Hockey, Lisbeth, and **Anderson, John L.** Life Before Death. *310 pp.*

Dunnell, Karen, and **Cartwright, Ann.** Medicine Takers, Prescribers and Hoarders. *190 pp.*

Medicine, Illness and Society

General Editor W. M. Williams

Robinson, David. The Process of Becoming Ill. *142 pp.*

Stacey, Margaret, *et al.* Hospitals, Children and Their Families. *The Report of a Pilot Study. 202 pp.*

Monographs in Social Theory

General Editor Arthur Brittan

●**Barnes, B.** Scientific Knowledge and Sociological Theory. *About 200 pp.*

Bauman, Zygmunt. Culture as Praxis. *204 pp.*

● **Dixon, Keith.** Sociological Theory. *Pretence and Possibility. 142 pp.*

●**Smith, Anthony D.** The Concept of Social Change. *A Critique of the Functionalist Theory of Social Change. 208 pp.*

Routledge Social Science Journals

The British Journal of Sociology. *Edited by Terence P. Morris. Vol. 1, No. 1, March 1950 and Quarterly. Roy. 8vo. Back numbers available. An international journal with articles on all aspects of sociology.*

Economy and Society. *Vol. 1, No. 1. February 1972 and Quarterly. Metric Roy. 8vo. A journal for all social scientists covering sociology, philosophy, anthropology, economics and history. Back numbers available.*

Year Book of Social Policy in Britain, The. *Edited by Kathleen Jones. 1971. Published annually.*

Printed in Great Britain by Unwin Brothers Limited
The Gresham Press Old Woking Surrey
A member of the Staples Printing Group